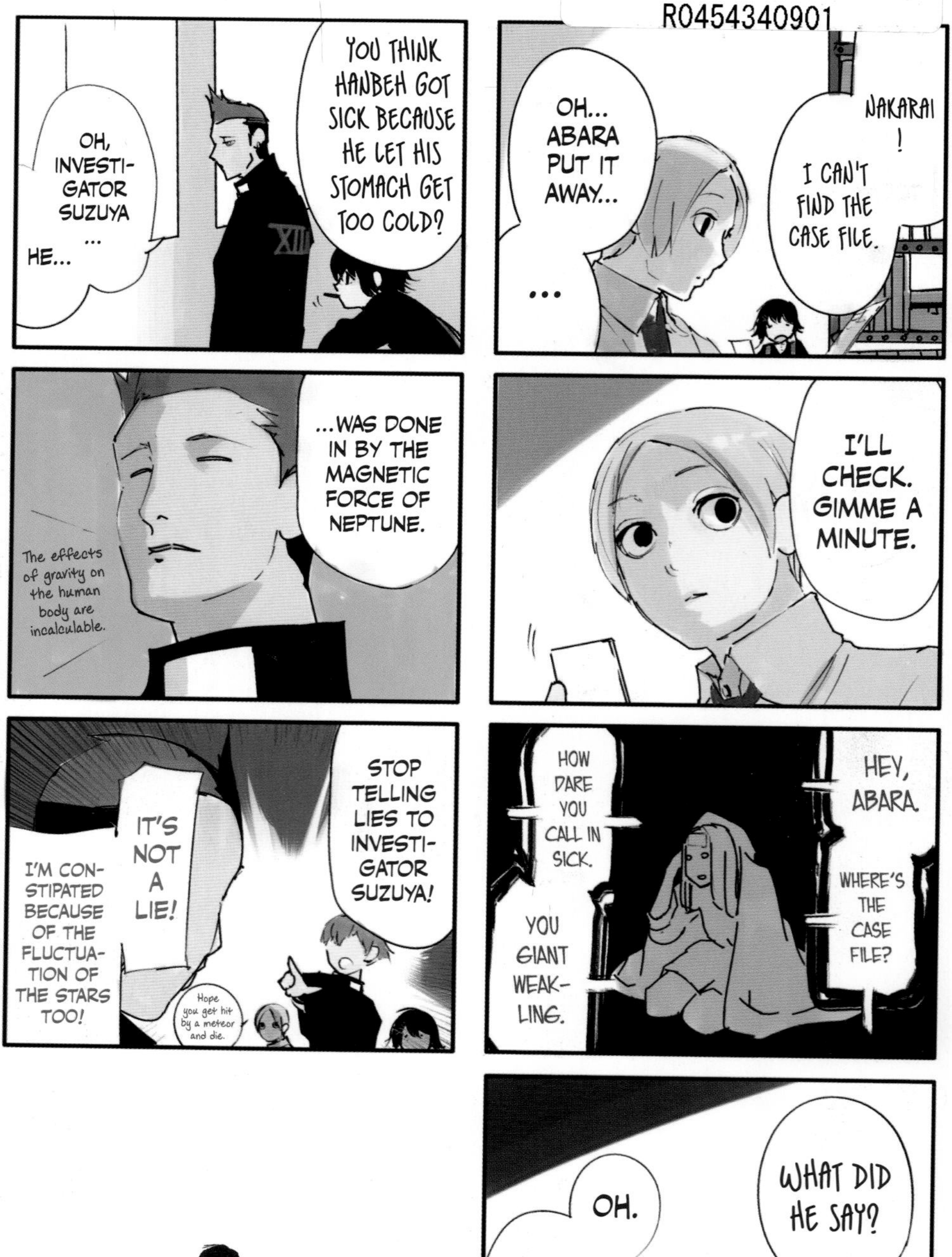
NAKARAI!
I CAN'T FIND THE CASE FILE.
OH... ABARA PUT IT AWAY...
...
I'LL CHECK. GIMME A MINUTE.
HEY, ABARA.
WHERE'S THE CASE FILE?
HOW DARE YOU CALL IN SICK.
YOU GIANT WEAKLING.
WHAT DID HE SAY?
OH.
HE WAS CRYING AND SAID HE'D LOOK FOR IT.
Coffee break?
YOU THINK HANBEH GOT SICK BECAUSE HE LET HIS STOMACH GET TOO COLD?
OH, INVESTIGATOR SUZUYA... HE...
...WAS DONE IN BY THE MAGNETIC FORCE OF NEPTUNE.
The effects of gravity on the human body are incalculable.
STOP TELLING LIES TO INVESTIGATOR SUZUYA!
IT'S NOT A LIE!
I'M CONSTIPATED BECAUSE OF THE FLUCTUATION OF THE STARS TOO!
Hope you get hit by a meteor and die.

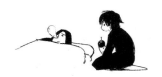

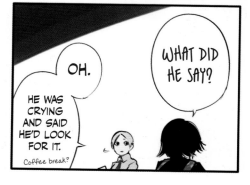

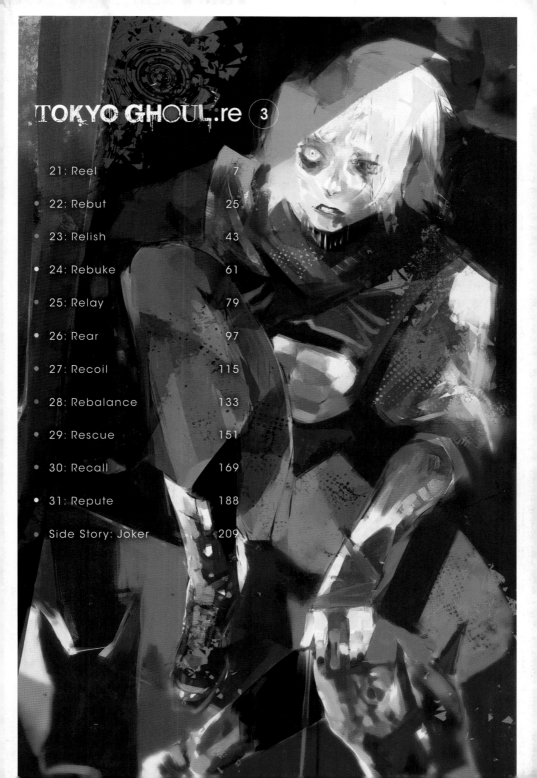

TOKYO GHOUL:re ③

CCG Ghoul Investigators / Tokyo Ghoul :re

The CCG is the only organization in the world that investigates and solves Ghoul-related crimes. Founded by the Washu Family, the CCG developed and evolved Quinques, a type of weapon derived from Ghouls' Kagune. Quinx, an advanced, next-generation technology in which humans are implanted with Quinques is currently under development.

Mado Squad

Qs (Quinx) • Investigators implanted with Quinques. They all live together in a house called the **Chateau** with Investigator Sasaki.

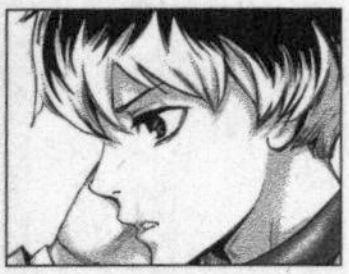

● Haise Sasaki
佐々木琲世

Rank 1 Investigator
Mentor to the Quinx Squad. Despite being half-Ghoul, he is passionate about guiding his squad members. He has no memory of his past. And whose voice sometimes echoes in his head...?!

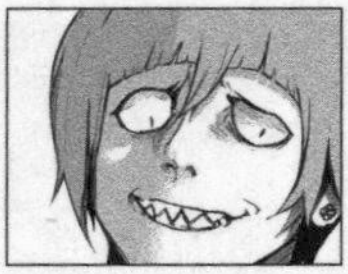

● Ginshi Shirazu
不知吟士

Rank 3 Investigator
Current Qs squad leader. Agreed to the Quinx procedure for mainly financial reasons. Despite a thuggish appearance, he has a caring side. Trying desperately to be a leader, although he is totally unaccustomed to the role.

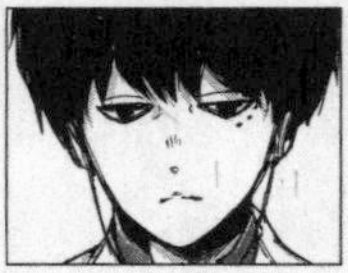

● Kuki Urie
瓜江久生

Rank 2 Investigator
Former Qs squad leader. The most talented fighter in the squad. He seeks to avenge his father's death. On his own authority he recently underwent the Frame Release procedure, with unknown results...

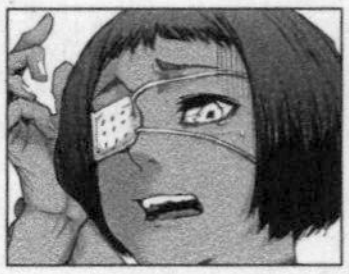

● Toru Mutsuki
六月 透

Rank 3 Investigator
Both his parents were killed by a Ghoul and he decided to become a Ghoul Investigator. Assigned female at birth, he decides to transition after undergoing the Quinx procedure. Skilled with knives.

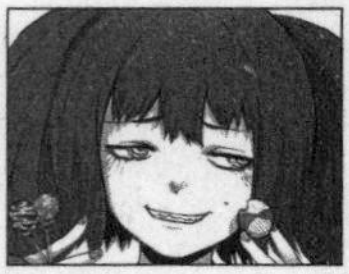

● Saiko Yonebayashi
米林才子

Rank 3 Investigator
Has little aptitude as an investigator, but she was by far the most suitable candidate for the Quinx procedure. Very bad at time management. A sucker for games and snacks.

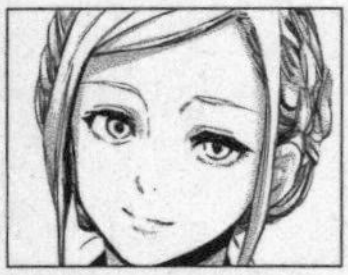

● Akira Mado
真戸 暁

Senior Investigator
Mentors Haise. Takes after her father, Kureo, and is determined to eradicate Ghouls. Investigating the Aogiri Tree.

Hirako Squad

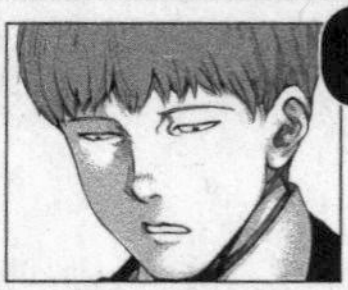

● Take Hirako
平子 丈

Senior Investigator
In pursuit of the Orochi. A reticent investigator.

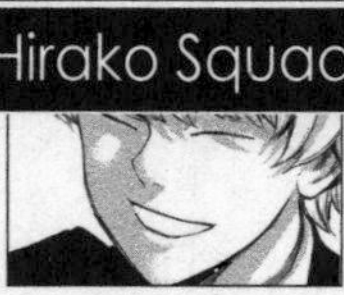

● Kuramoto Ito
伊東倉元

Rank 1 Investigator
Member of the Hirako Squad. Has a cheerful disposition.

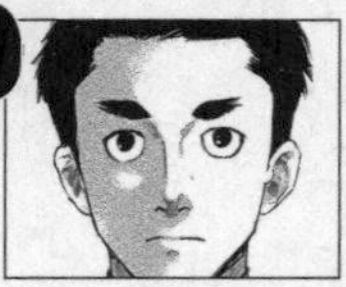

● Takeomi Kuroiwa
黒磐武臣

Rank 2 Investigator
The son of Special Investigator Iwao Kuroiwa.

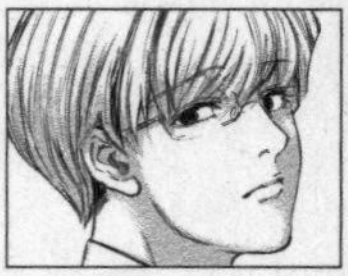

● Kisho Arima
有馬貴将

Special Investigator
An undefeated investigator respected by many at the CCG.

Suzuya Squad

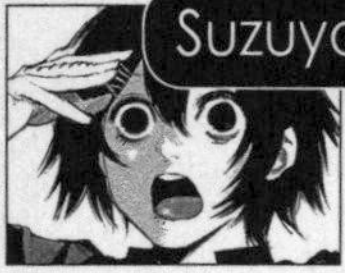

● Juzo Suzuya
鈴屋什造

Assistant Special Investigator
An eccentric who quickly climbed the ranks at a young age. He fights with knives he keeps concealed in his artificial leg. How is he connected to the Big Madam?

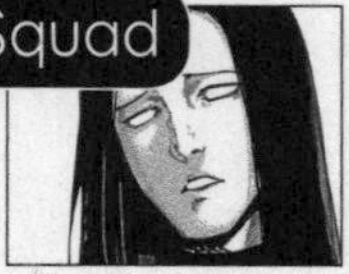

● Hanbeh Abara
阿原半兵衛

Rank 2 Investigator
Suzuya's right-hand man. A tall and gentle person.

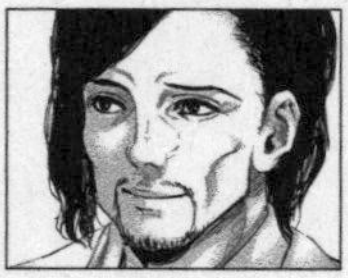

● Yoshitoki Washu
和修吉時

CCG Bureau Chief
Supervisor of the Quinx Project. A member of the CCG's founding family, but he still has an approachable side.

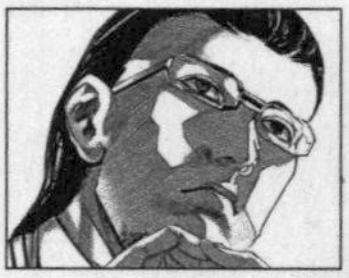

● Matsuri Washu
和修 政

Assistant Special Investigator
Yoshitoki's son. A Washu supremacist who takes pride in his lineage. He is skeptical of Quinxes. Commander of Operation Auction Sweep.

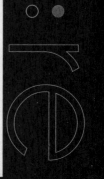

T ● K Y ● G H ● U L

Tokyo Ghoul :re

Ghouls

They appear human, but have a unique predation organ called Kagune and can only survive by feeding on human flesh. They are the nemesis of humanity. Besides human flesh, the only other thing they can ingest is coffee. Ghouls can only be wounded by Kagune or a Quinque made from a Kagune. One of the most prominent Ghoul factions is the Aogiri Tree, a hostile organization that is expanding its numbers.

Aogiri Tree

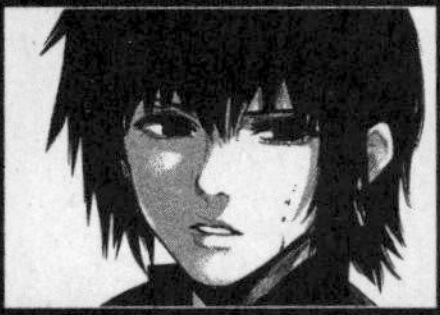

Ayato アヤト
A leading member of the Aogiri Tree. A Rate SS Ghoul known as the Rabbit. But…?!

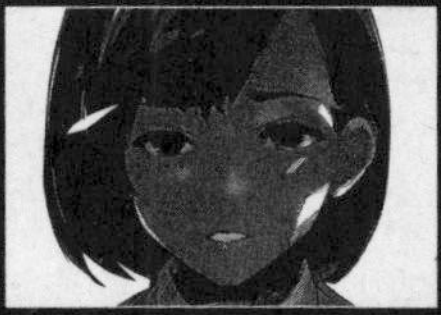

Hinami ヒナミ
Member of the Aogiri Tree. Also known as Yotsume. In charge of analyzing sounds.

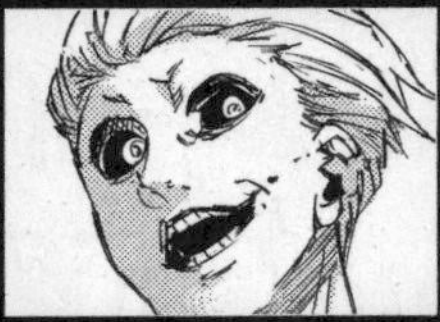

Naki ナキ
Member of the Aogiri Tree. Rate S. Frequently flips out of control.

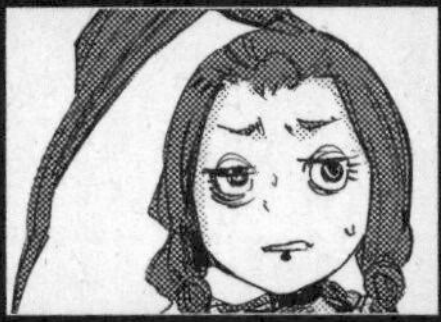

Miza ミザ
Member of the Aogiri Tree. Rate S. Known as the Triple Blade.

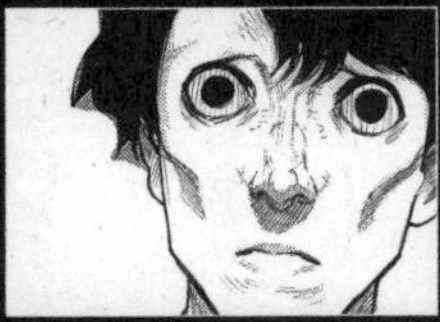

The Torso (Karao Saeki) トルソー（冴木空男）
Rate A Ghoul. Preyed on multiple women with scars. Currently part of the Aogiri Tree.

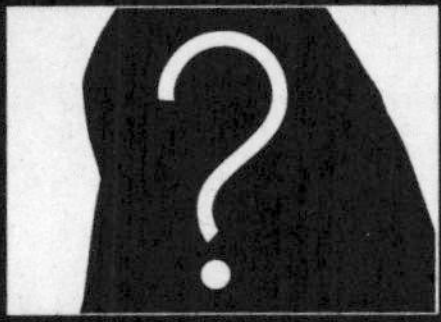

The Owl オウル
Unknown

Eradication Targets

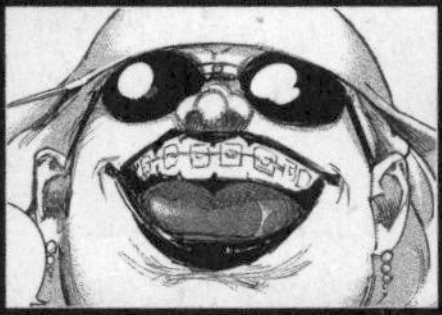

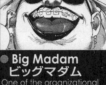

Big Madam ビッグマダム
One of the organizational chairs of the auction. An infamous Ghoul seeking beautiful human pets.

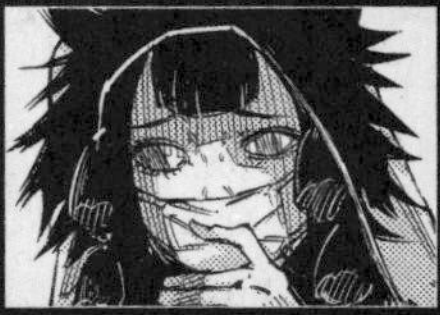

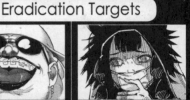

Nutcracker ナッツクラッカー
Rate ≥A Ghoul with a fetish for crushing testicles. Next target of the Quinx Squad.

The Clown Masks

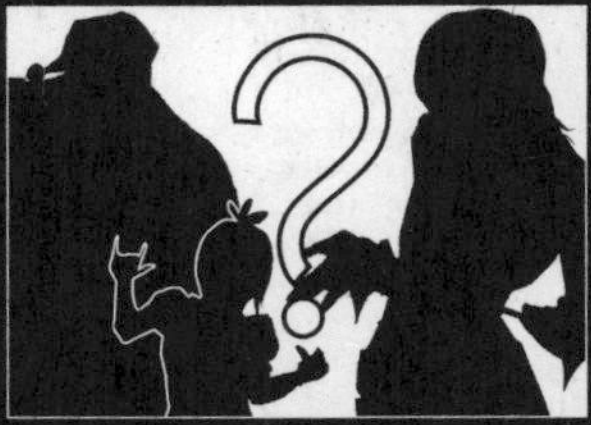

Unknown

Others

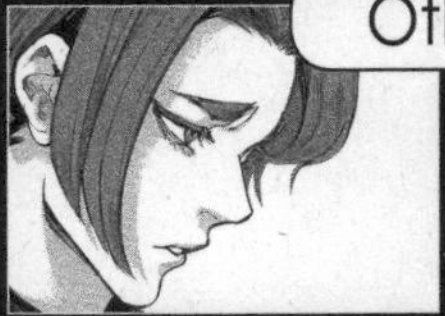

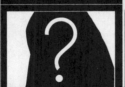

Kanae von Rosewald カナエ＝フォン・ロゼヴァルト
Tsukiyama family retainer. At the auction on behalf of Shu Tsukiyama.

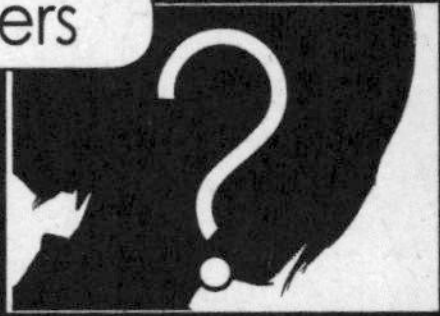

Matsumae 松前
Unknown

So far in :re

T ● K Y ● G H ● U L

The Quinx Project was implemented to develop investigators to surpass Kisho Arima in order to combat the growing strength of Ghoul organizations. Some in the CCG view these unusual investigators who fight using Ghoul abilities with suspicion. The Qs' mentor, Haise Sasaki, is leading them in the Nutcracker investigation. Mutsuki's undercover infiltration and Suzuya Squad's investigation reveal that a Ghoul targeted for eradication is going to be at the auction. Then the Aogiri Tree shows up and the situation intensifies!

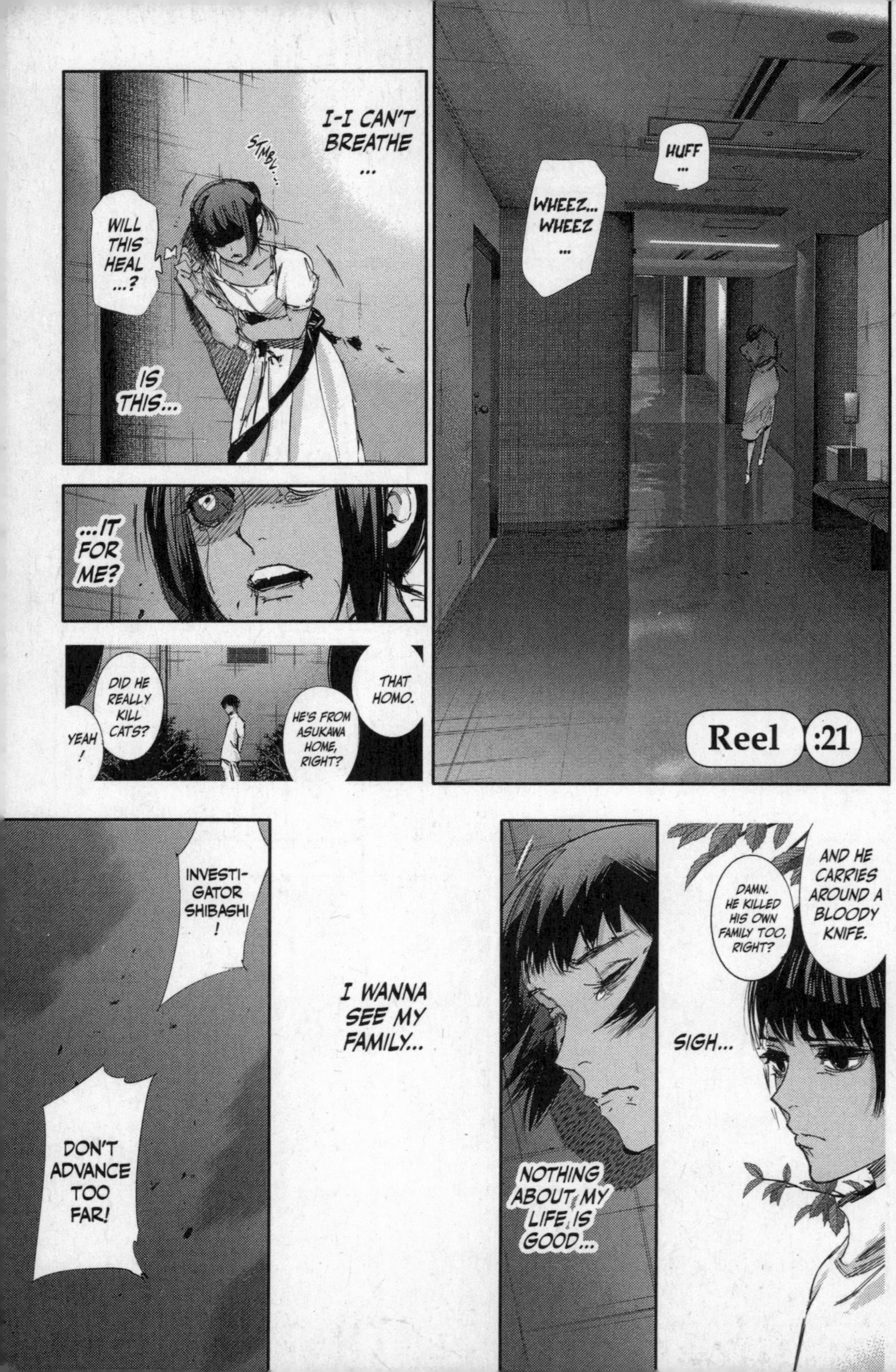
HUFF...
WHEEZ... WHEEZ...
Reel :21
I-I CAN'T BREATHE...
STMBL
WILL THIS HEAL...?
IS THIS...
...IT FOR ME?
THAT HOMO.
HE'S FROM ASUKAWA HOME, RIGHT?
DID HE REALLY KILL CATS?
YEAH!
AND HE CARRIES AROUND A BLOODY KNIFE.
DAMN. HE KILLED HIS OWN FAMILY TOO, RIGHT?
SIGH...
NOTHING ABOUT MY LIFE IS GOOD...
I WANNA SEE MY FAMILY...
INVESTIGATOR SHIBASHI!
DON'T ADVANCE TOO FAR!

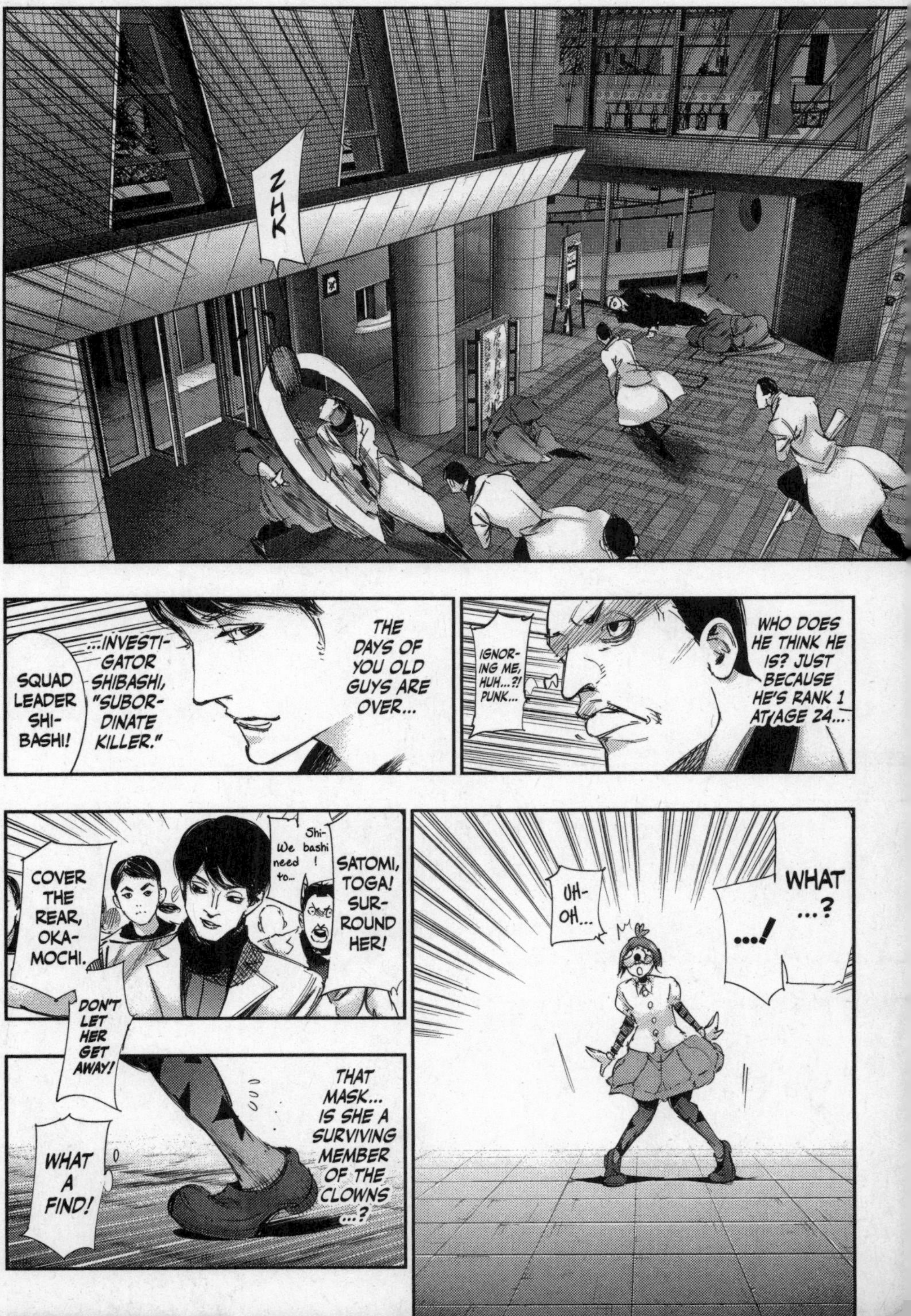
ZHK
WHO DOES HE THINK HE IS? JUST BECAUSE HE'S RANK 1 AT AGE 24...
IGNORING ME, HUH...?! PUNK...
THE DAYS OF YOU OLD GUYS ARE OVER...
...INVESTIGATOR SHIBASHI, "SUBORDINATE KILLER."
SQUAD LEADER SHIBASHI!
WHAT ...?
...!
UH-OH...
SATOMI, TOGA! SURROUND HER!
Shibashi!
We need to...
COVER THE REAR, OKAMOCHI.
DON'T LET HER GET AWAY!
THAT MASK... IS SHE A SURVIVING MEMBER OF THE CLOWNS ...?
WHAT A FIND!

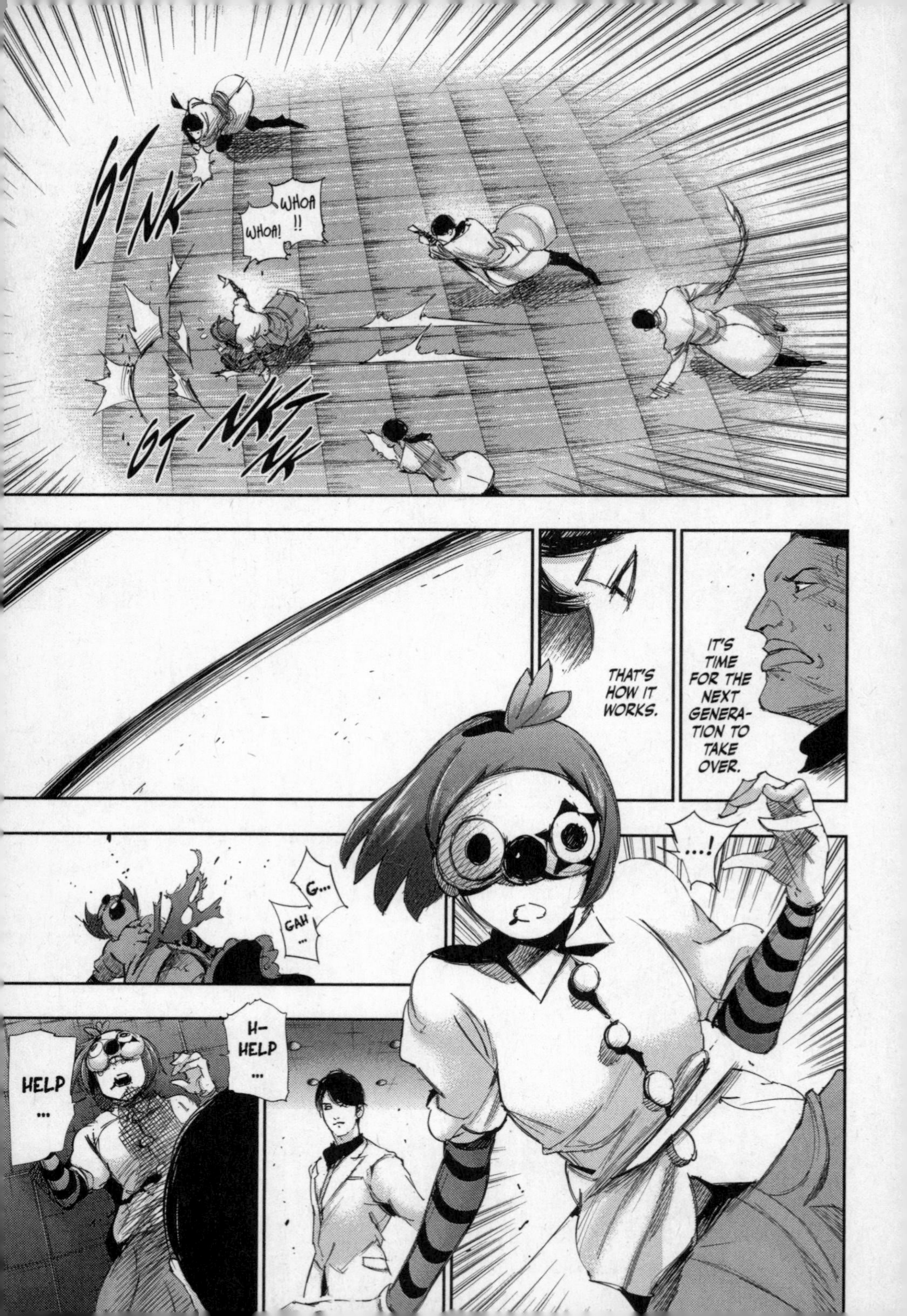
WHOA !!
WHOA!
GT NK
GT NKT NK
IT'S TIME FOR THE NEXT GENERATION TO TAKE OVER.
THAT'S HOW IT WORKS.
...!
G...
GAH ...
H-HELP ...
HELP ...

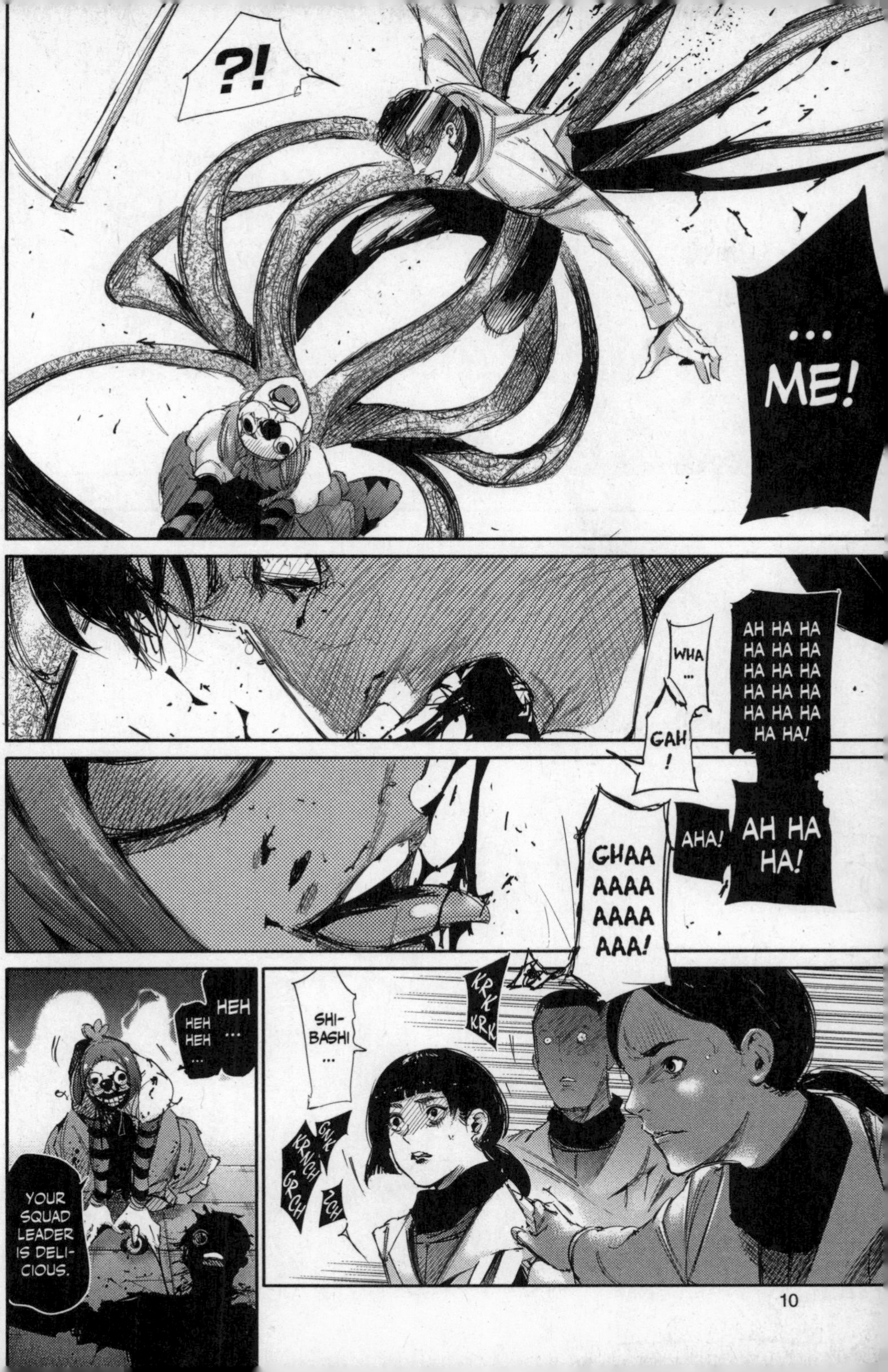

... ME!
?!
AH HA HA HA HA HA HA HA HA HA HA HA HA HA HA HA HA!
WHA... GAH!
AH HA HA!
AHA!
GHAA AAAA AAAA AAA!
KRK KRK
SHI-BASHI...
GNK KRNCH GRCH ZCH
HEH HEH HEH...
YOUR SQUAD LEADER IS DELICIOUS.

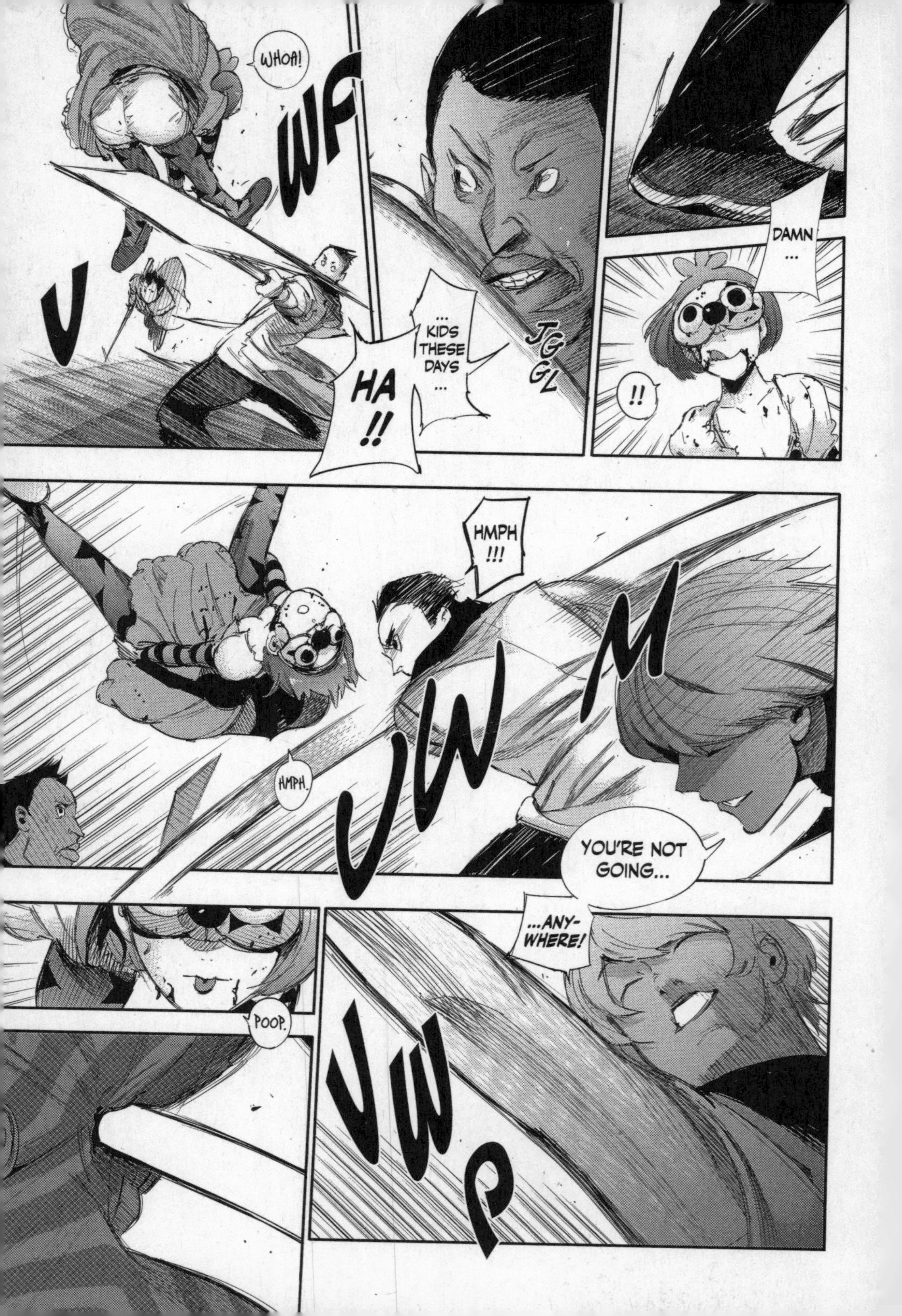
DAMN ...
!!
... KIDS THESE DAYS ...
JGGL
HA !!
WHOA!
WF
V
HMPH !!!
VWM
HMPH.
YOU'RE NOT GOING...
...ANY-WHERE!
POOP.

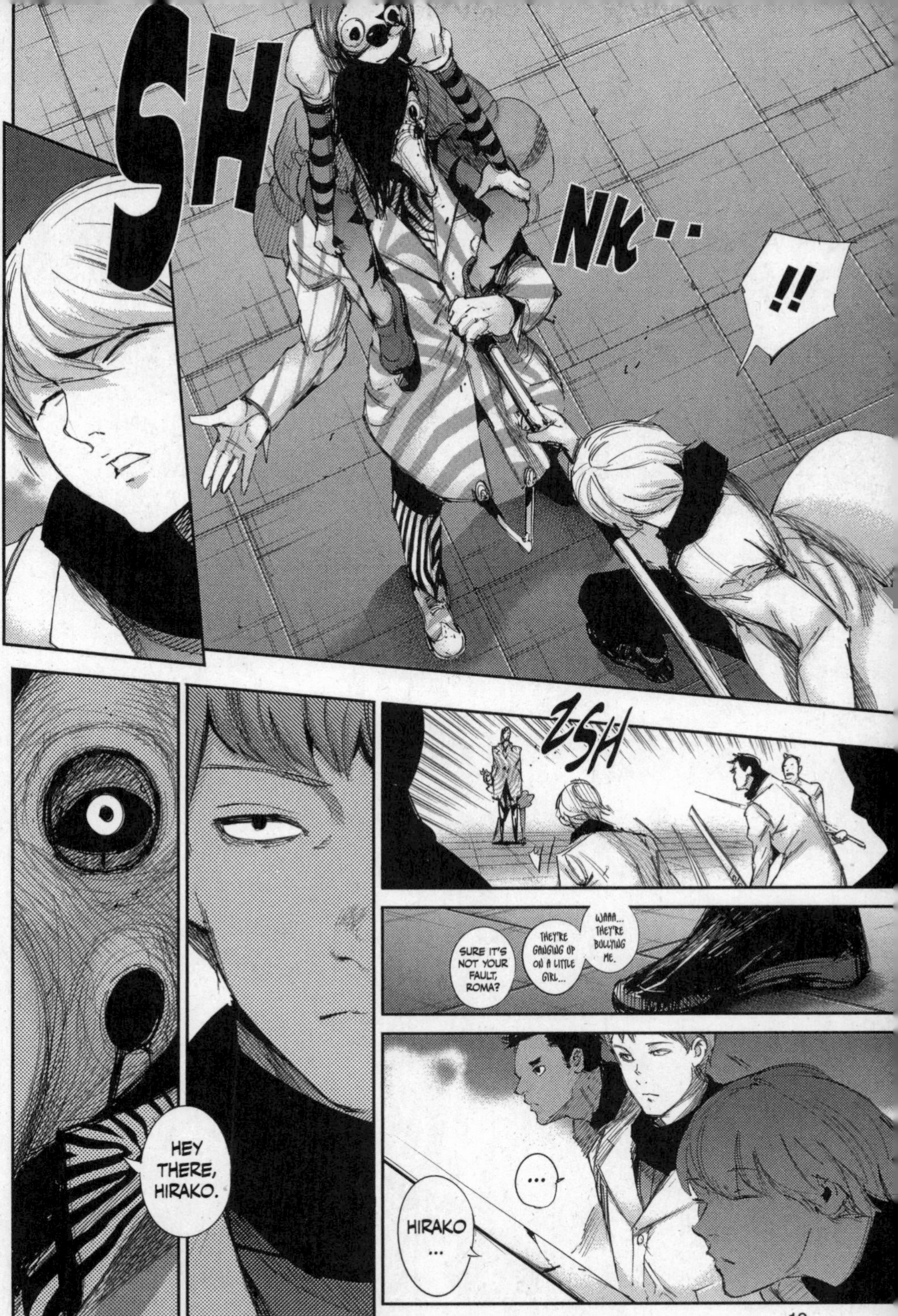
SH
NK . .
!!
ZSH
WAAA... THEY'RE BULLYING ME.
THEY'RE GANGING UP ON A LITTLE GIRL...
SURE IT'S NOT YOUR FAULT, ROMA?
...
HIRAKO ...
HEY THERE, HIRAKO.

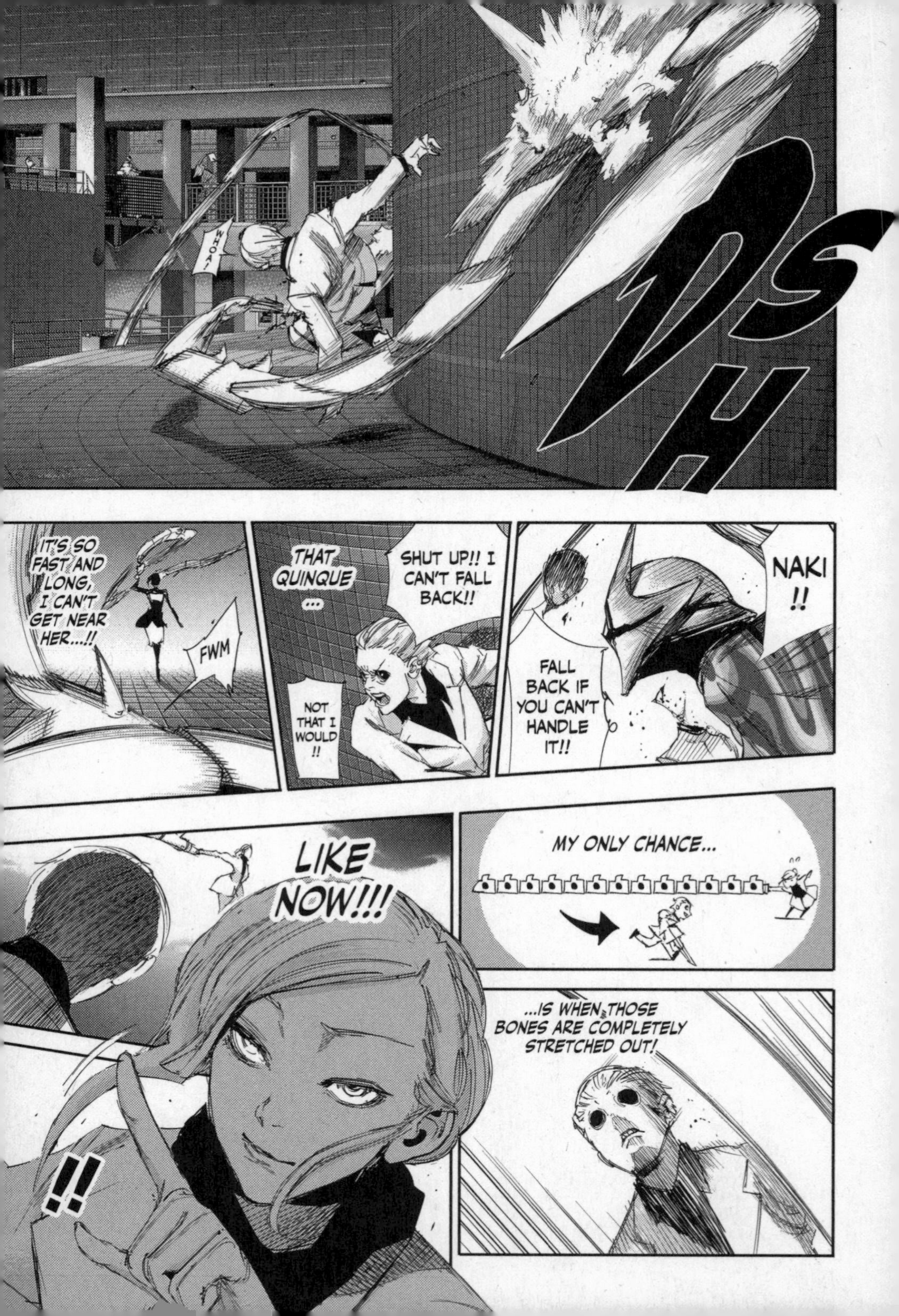
WHOA!
NAKI !!
FALL BACK IF YOU CAN'T HANDLE IT!!
SHUT UP!! I CAN'T FALL BACK!!
THAT QUINQUE ...
NOT THAT I WOULD !!
IT'S SO FAST AND LONG, I CAN'T GET NEAR HER...!!
FWM
MY ONLY CHANCE...
...IS WHEN THOSE BONES ARE COMPLETELY STRETCHED OUT!
LIKE NOW!!!
!!

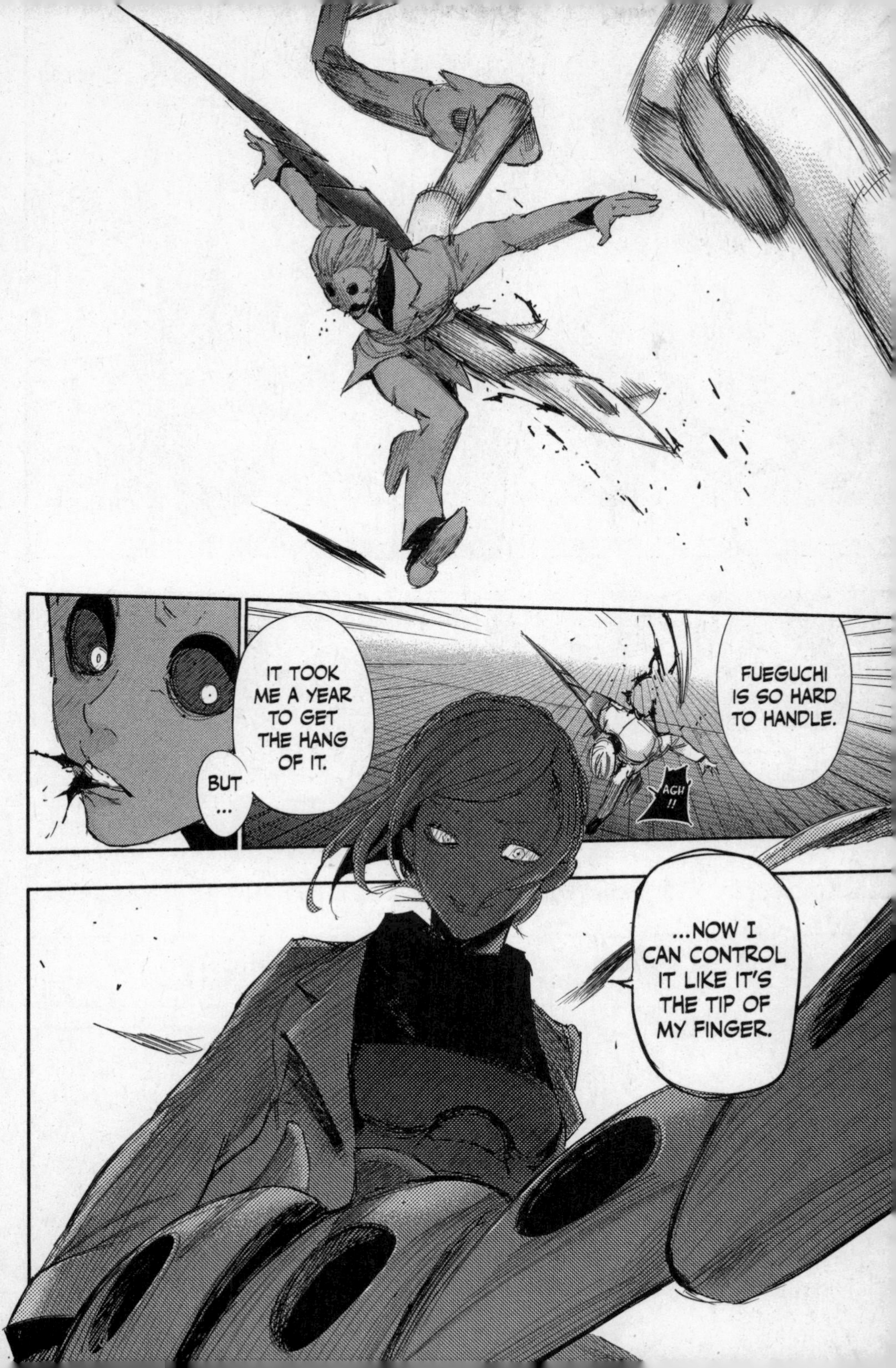
FUEGUCHI IS SO HARD TO HANDLE.
AGH!!
IT TOOK ME A YEAR TO GET THE HANG OF IT.
BUT ...
...NOW I CAN CONTROL IT LIKE IT'S THE TIP OF MY FINGER.

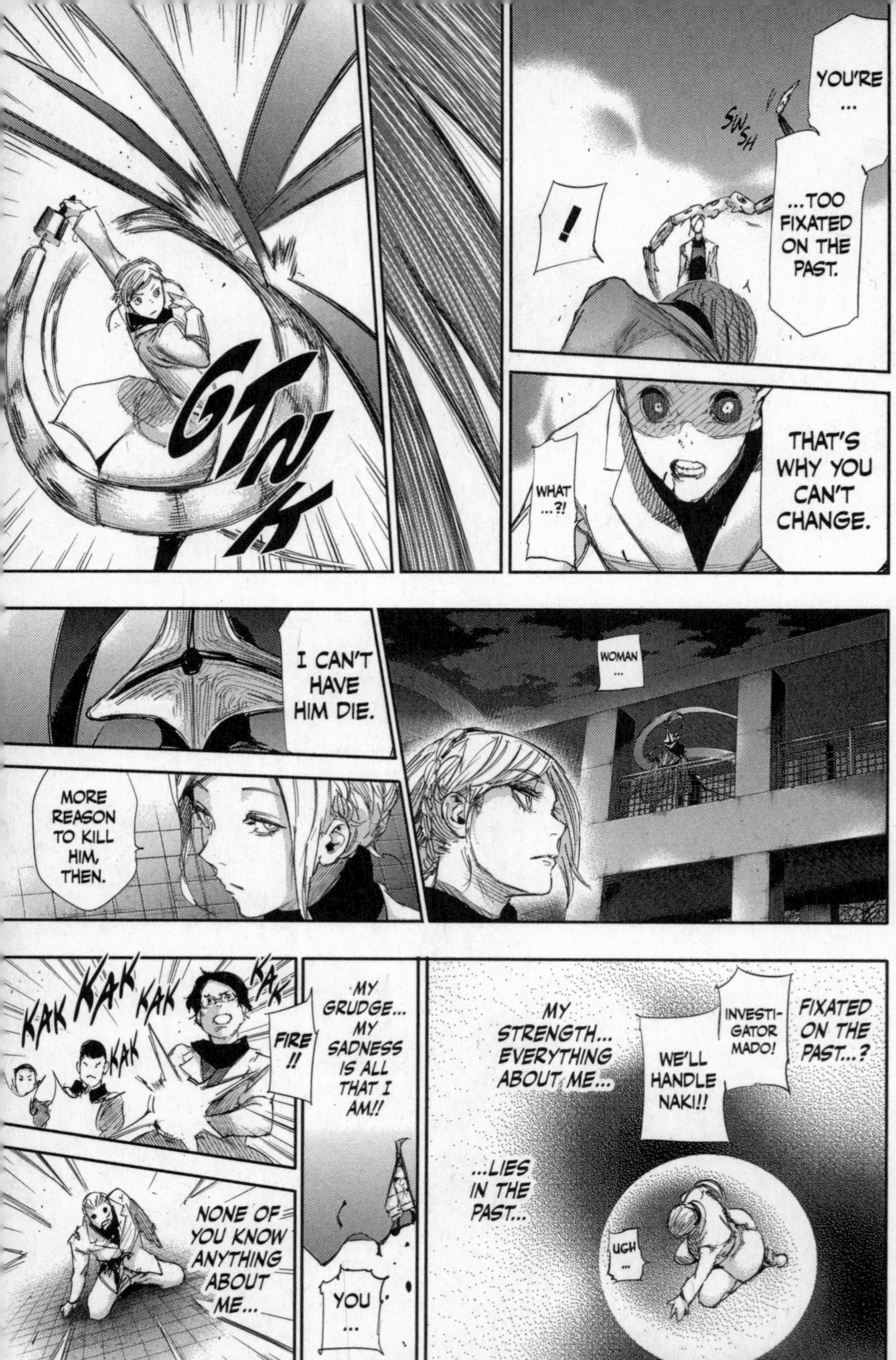
YOU'RE ...
SWSH
...TOO FIXATED ON THE PAST.
!
THAT'S WHY YOU CAN'T CHANGE.
WHAT ...?!
GTNK
WOMAN ...
I CAN'T HAVE HIM DIE.
MORE REASON TO KILL HIM, THEN.
FIXATED ON THE PAST...?
INVESTI-GATOR MADO!
WE'LL HANDLE NAKI!!
MY STRENGTH... EVERYTHING ABOUT ME...
...LIES IN THE PAST...
UGH ...
MY GRUDGE... MY SADNESS IS ALL THAT I AM!!
YOU ...
FIRE !!
KAK KAK KAK KAK KAK KAK
NONE OF YOU KNOW ANYTHING ABOUT ME...

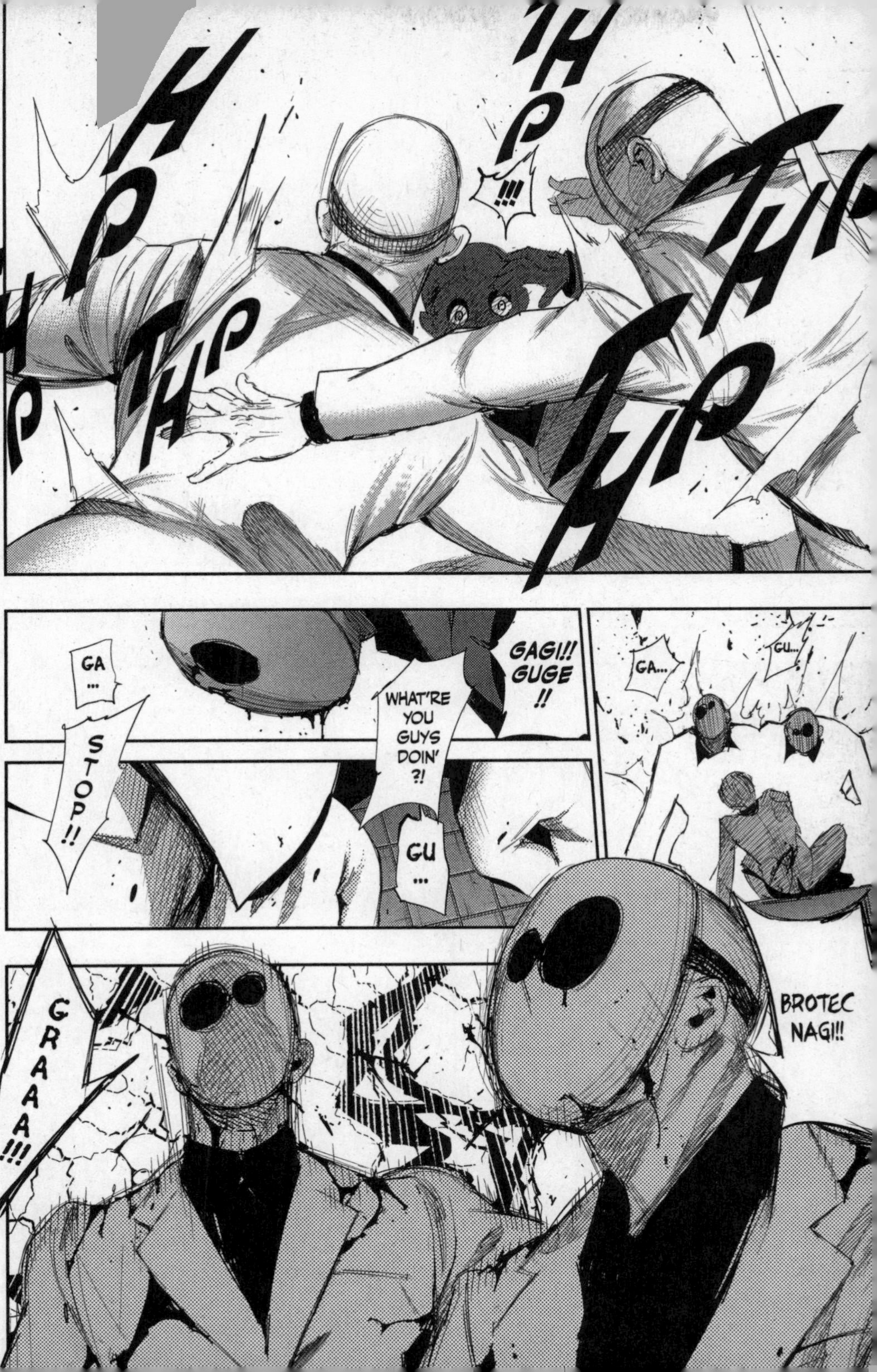
THP!!!
THP
THP
THP
THP
THP
GA...
GU...
GAGI!! GUGE!!
WHAT'RE YOU GUYS DOIN'?!
GA ...
GU ...
STOP!!
BROTEC NAGI!!
GRAAAA!!!

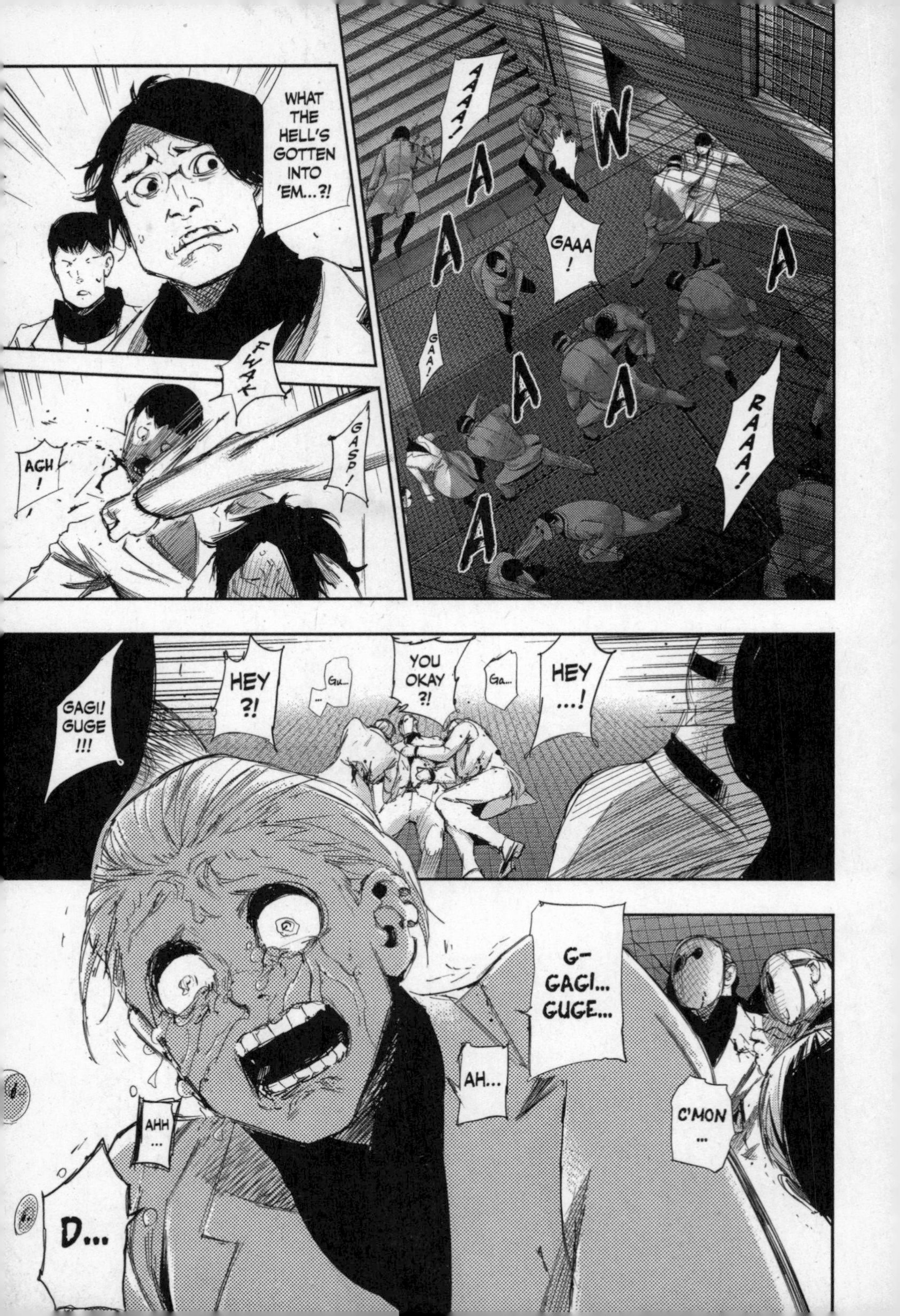
AAAAA!
W
A
A
A
A
A
A
A
GAAA!
GAA!
RAAAA!
WHAT THE HELL'S GOTTEN INTO 'EM...?!
FWAK
GASP!
AGH!
HEY...!
Ga...
YOU OKAY?!
Gu......
HEY?!
GAGI! GUGE!!!
G-GAGI... GUGE...
C'MON...
AH...
AHH...
D...

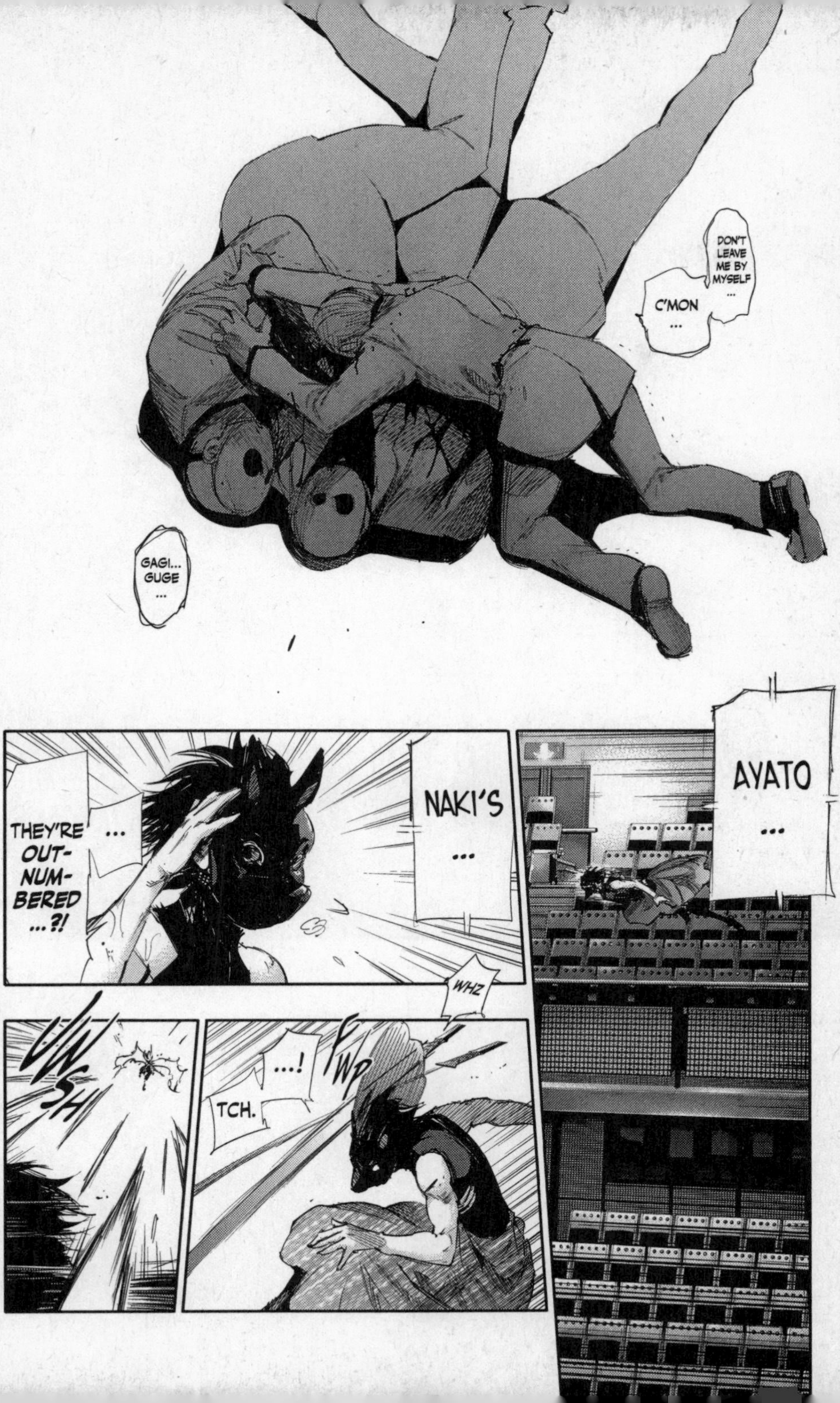
DON'T LEAVE ME BY MYSELF ...
C'MON ...
GAGI... GUGE ...
AYATO ...
NAKI'S ...
...
THEY'RE OUT-NUMBERED ...?!
WHZ
FWP
...!
TCH.
WNSH

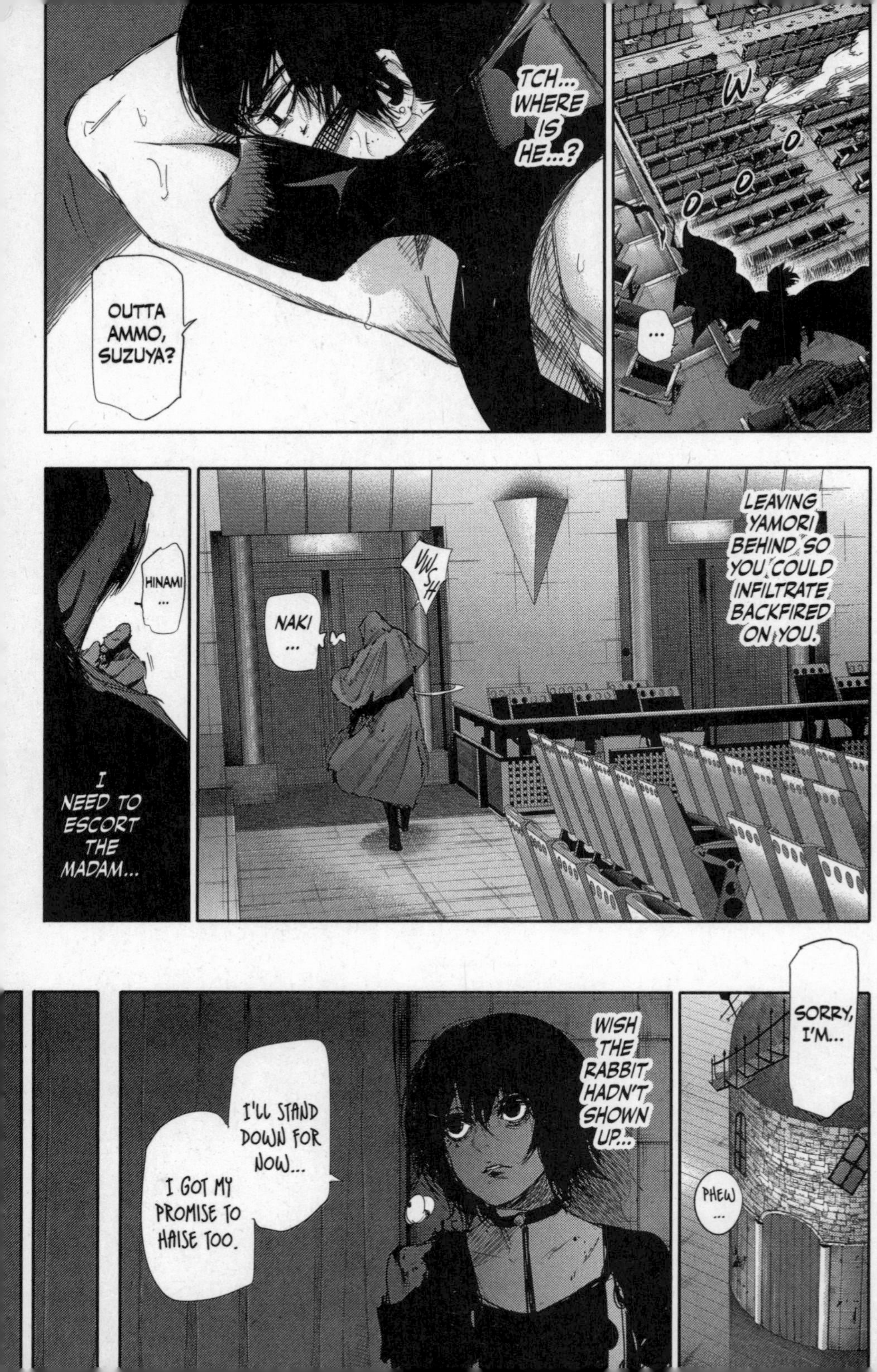
WOOOO
...
TCH... WHERE IS HE...?
OUTTA AMMO, SUZUYA?
LEAVING YAMORI BEHIND SO YOU COULD INFILTRATE BACKFIRED ON YOU.
VWSH
NAKI ...
HINAMI ...
I NEED TO ESCORT THE MADAM...
SORRY, I'M...
PHEW ...
WISH THE RABBIT HADN'T SHOWN UP...
I'LL STAND DOWN FOR NOW...
I GOT MY PROMISE TO HAISE TOO.

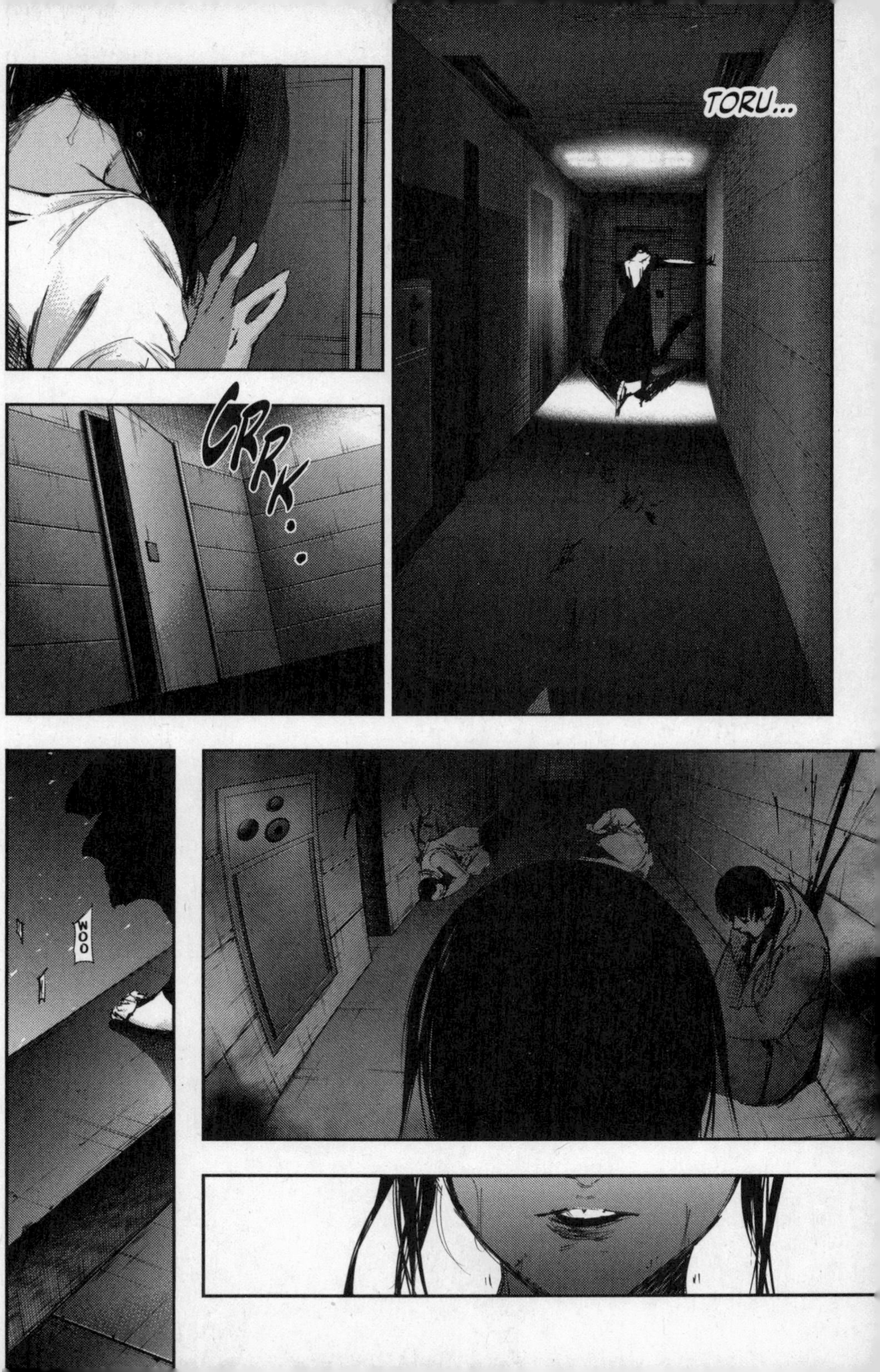
TORU...
CRRK..
WOO

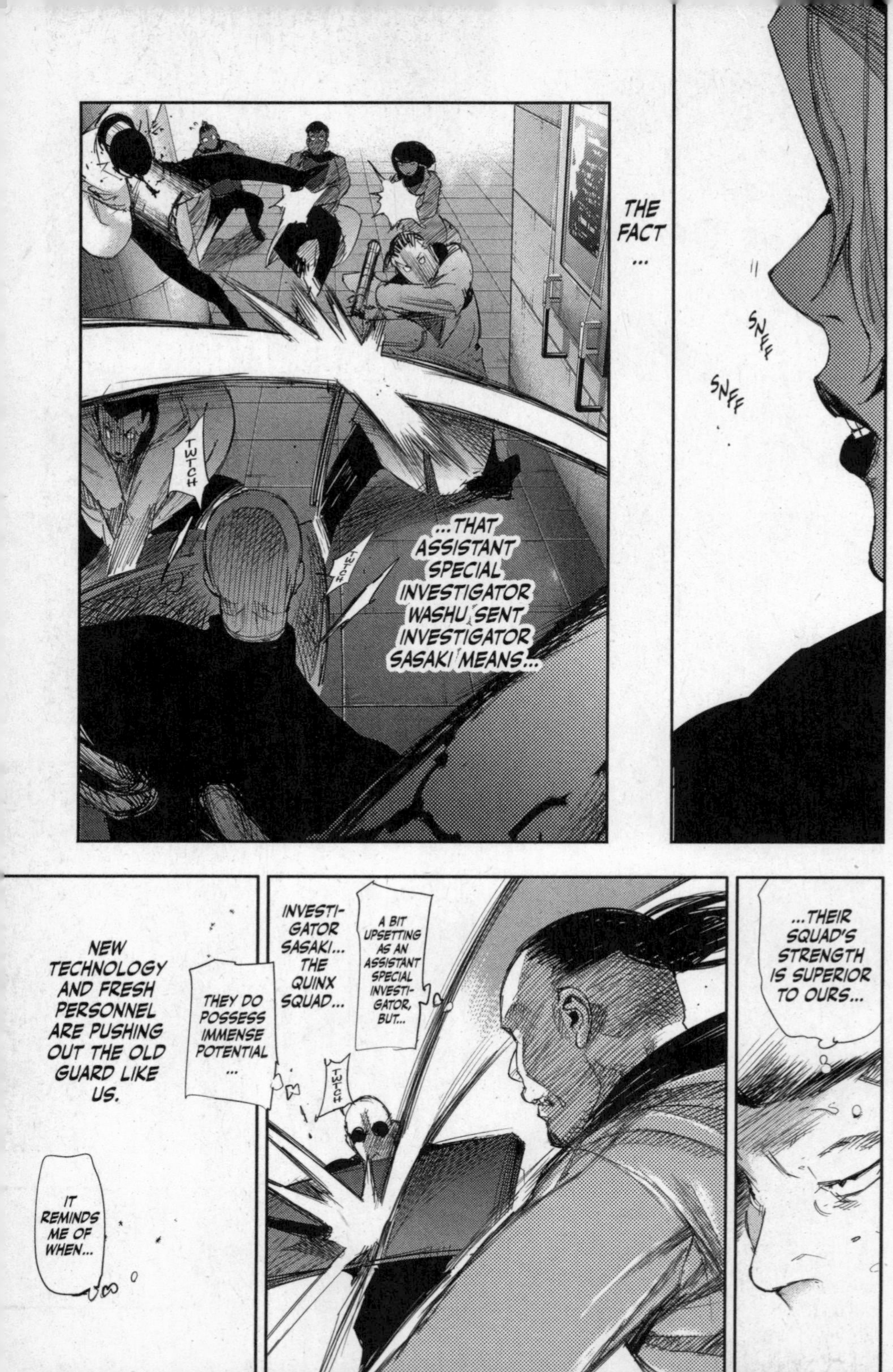
THE FACT...
SNFF
SNFF
TWTCH
TWTCH
...THAT ASSISTANT SPECIAL INVESTIGATOR WASHU SENT INVESTIGATOR SASAKI MEANS...
...THEIR SQUAD'S STRENGTH IS SUPERIOR TO OURS...
A BIT UPSETTING AS AN ASSISTANT SPECIAL INVESTI-GATOR, BUT...
INVESTI-GATOR SASAKI... THE QUINX SQUAD...
THEY DO POSSESS IMMENSE POTENTIAL...
TWTCH
NEW TECHNOLOGY AND FRESH PERSONNEL ARE PUSHING OUT THE OLD GUARD LIKE US.
IT REMINDS ME OF WHEN...

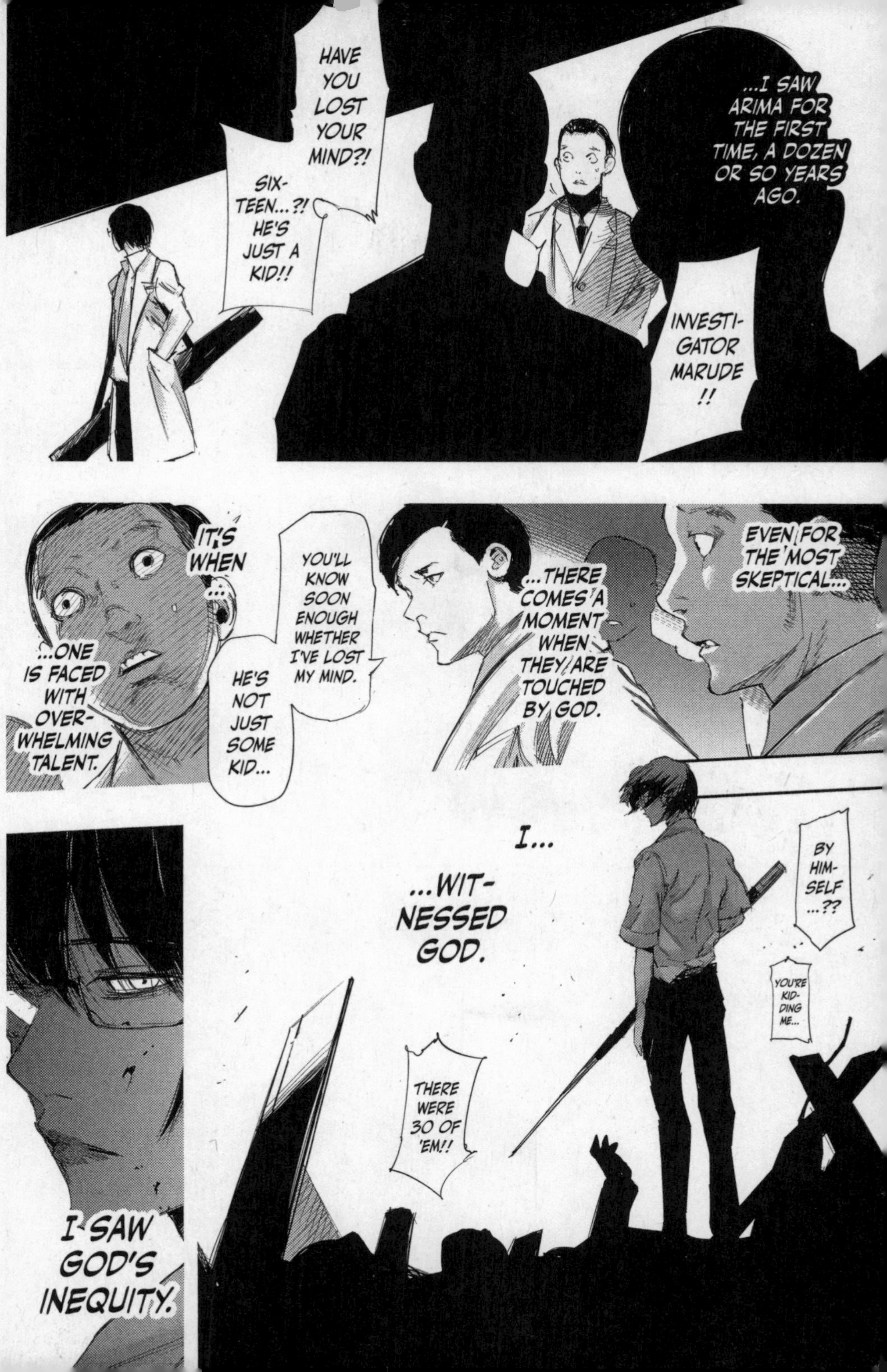
...I SAW ARIMA FOR THE FIRST TIME, A DOZEN OR SO YEARS AGO.
INVESTI-GATOR MARUDE!!
HAVE YOU LOST YOUR MIND?!
SIX-TEEN...?! HE'S JUST A KID!!
EVEN FOR THE MOST SKEPTICAL...
...THERE COMES A MOMENT WHEN THEY ARE TOUCHED BY GOD.
YOU'LL KNOW SOON ENOUGH WHETHER I'VE LOST MY MIND.
HE'S NOT JUST SOME KID...
IT'S WHEN...
...ONE IS FACED WITH OVER-WHELMING TALENT.
BY HIM-SELF...??
YOU'RE KID-DING ME...
I...
...WIT-NESSED GOD.
THERE WERE 30 OF 'EM!!
I SAW GOD'S INEQUITY.

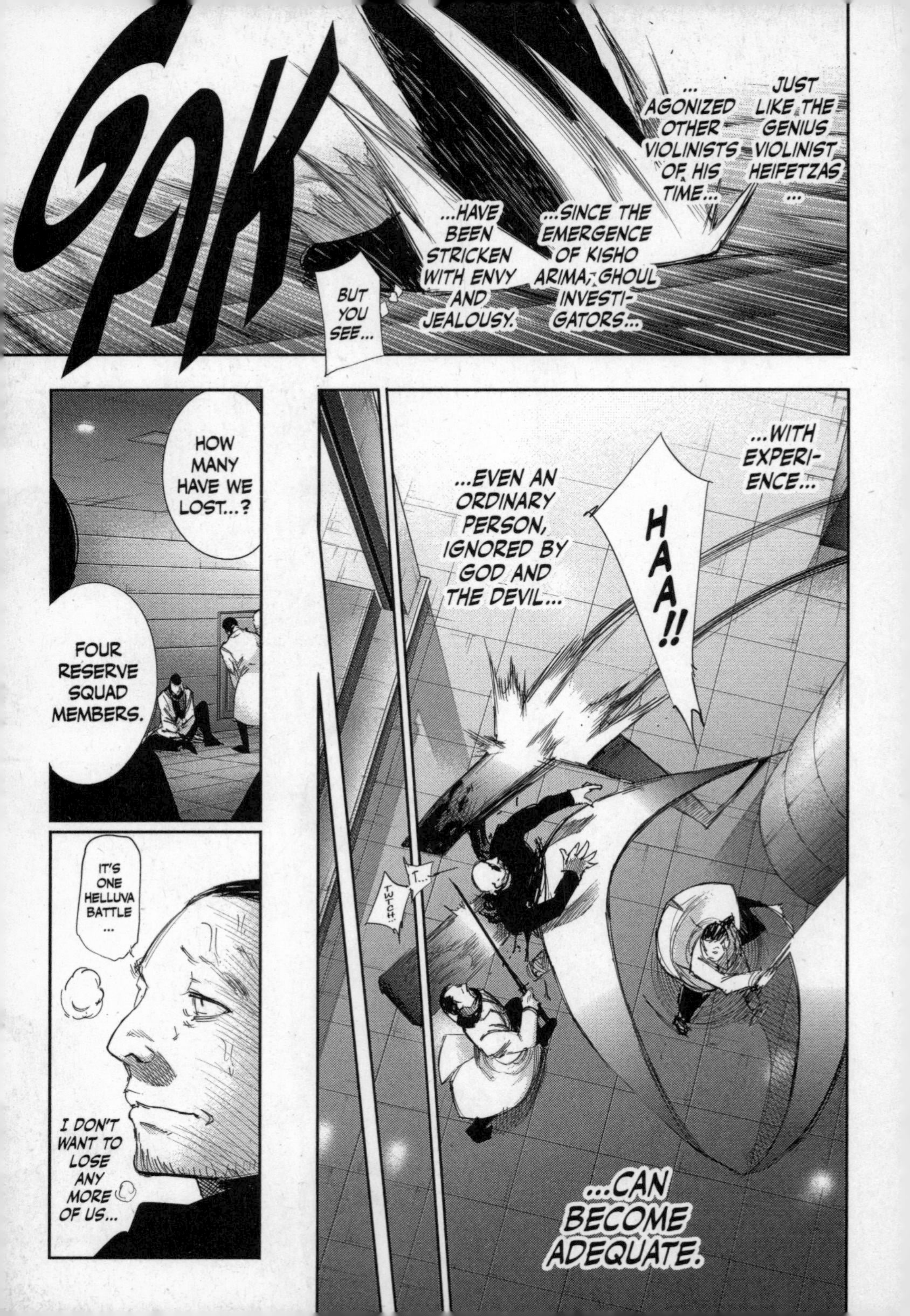
JUST LIKE THE GENIUS VIOLINIST HEIFETZAS ...
... AGONIZED OTHER VIOLINISTS OF HIS TIME...
...SINCE THE EMERGENCE OF KISHO ARIMA, GHOUL INVESTIGATORS...
...HAVE BEEN STRICKEN WITH ENVY AND JEALOUSY.
BUT YOU SEE...
GAK
...WITH EXPERIENCE...
HAAA!!
...EVEN AN ORDINARY PERSON, IGNORED BY GOD AND THE DEVIL...
T...
TWITCH
...CAN BECOME ADEQUATE.
HOW MANY HAVE WE LOST...?
FOUR RESERVE SQUAD MEMBERS.
IT'S ONE HELLUVA BATTLE ...
I DON'T WANT TO LOSE ANY MORE OF US...

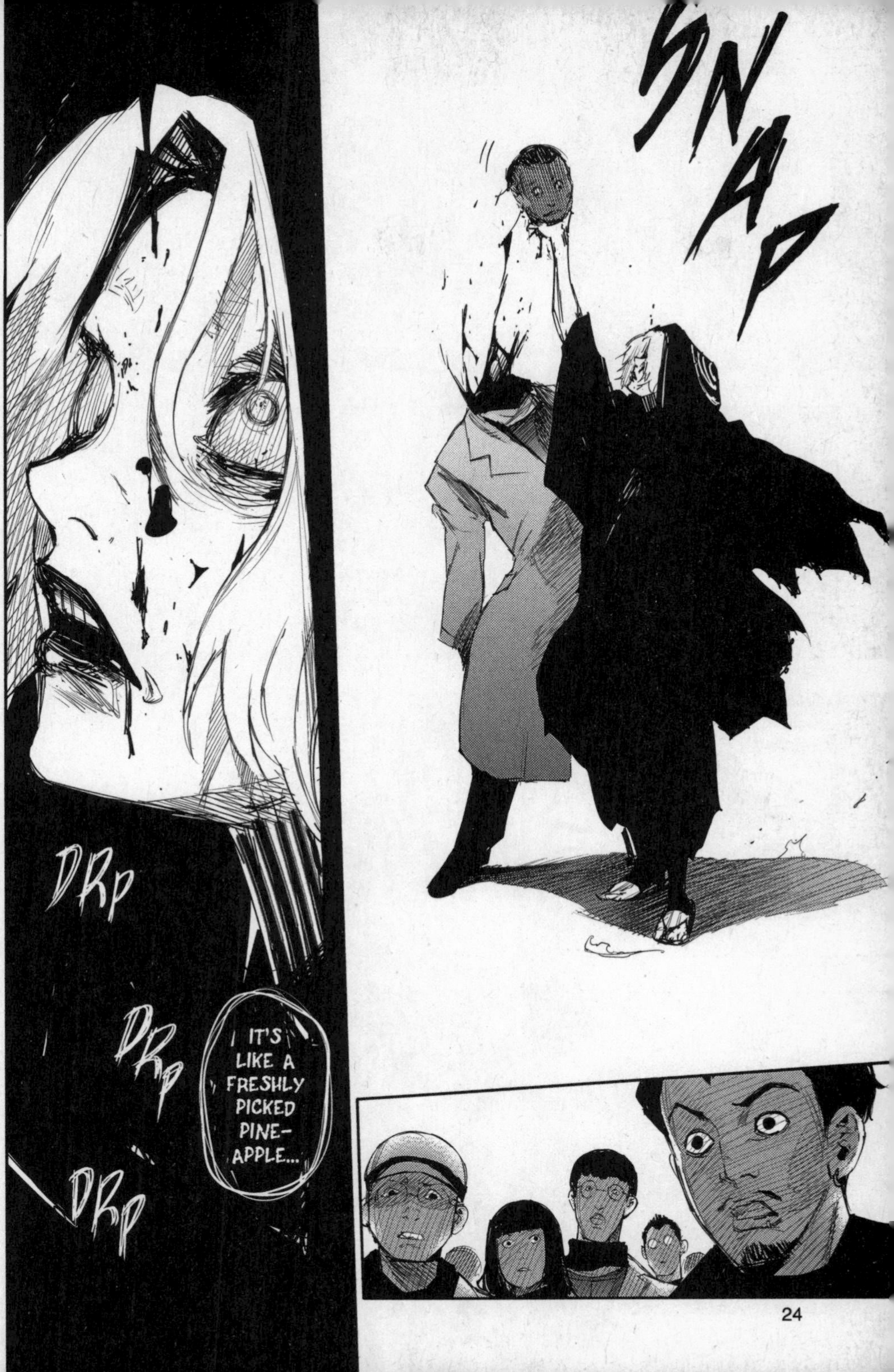
SNAP
DRP
IT'S LIKE A FRESHLY PICKED PINE-APPLE...
DRP
DRP

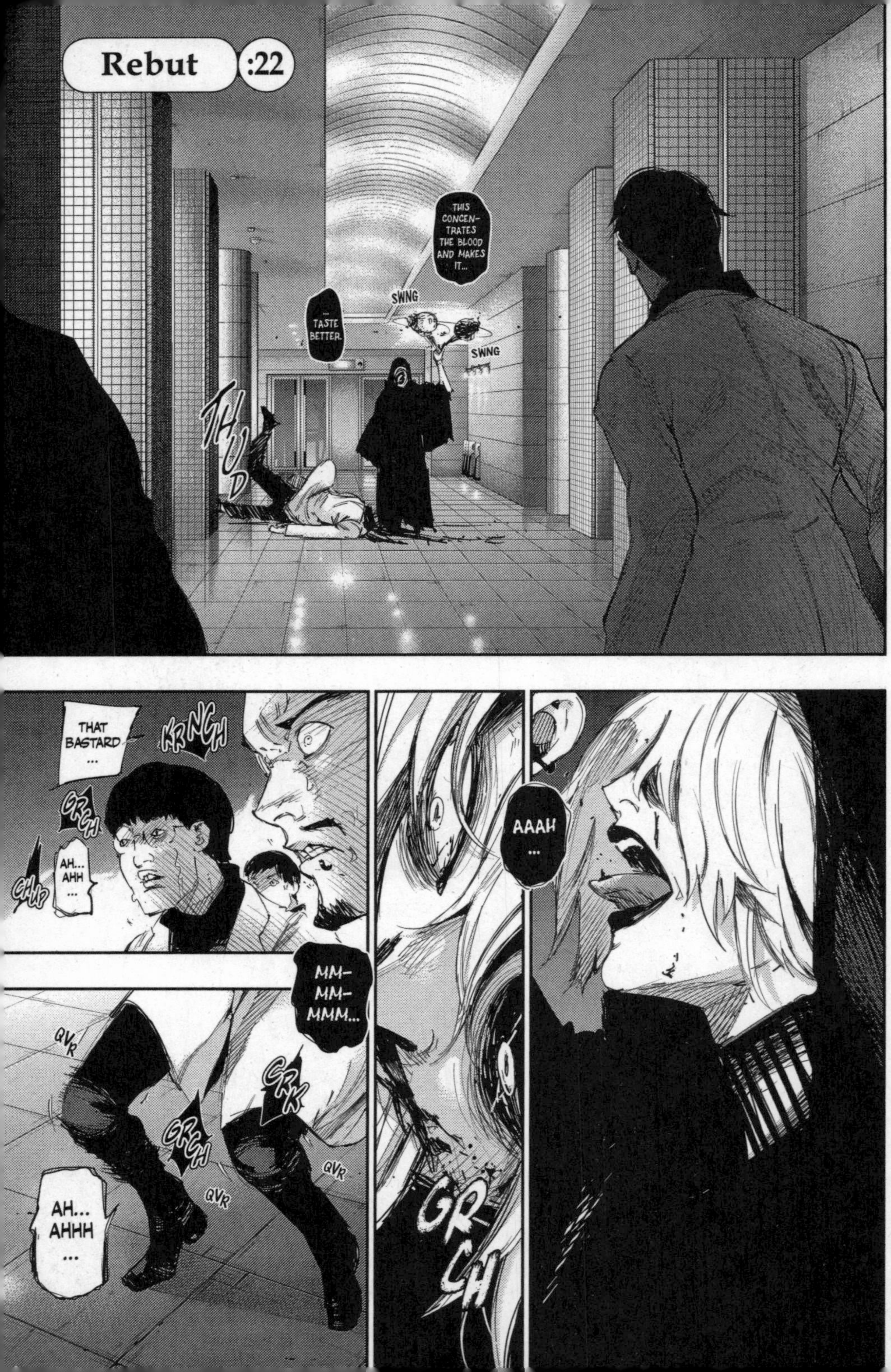
Rebut :22
THIS CONCENTRATES THE BLOOD AND MAKES IT...
...TASTE BETTER.
SWNG
SWNG
THUD
AAAH...
MM-MM-MMM...
GRCH
THAT BASTARD...
KRNCH
GRCH
AH... AHH...
CHUP
GRK
GRCH
QVR
QVR
QVR
AH... AHHH...

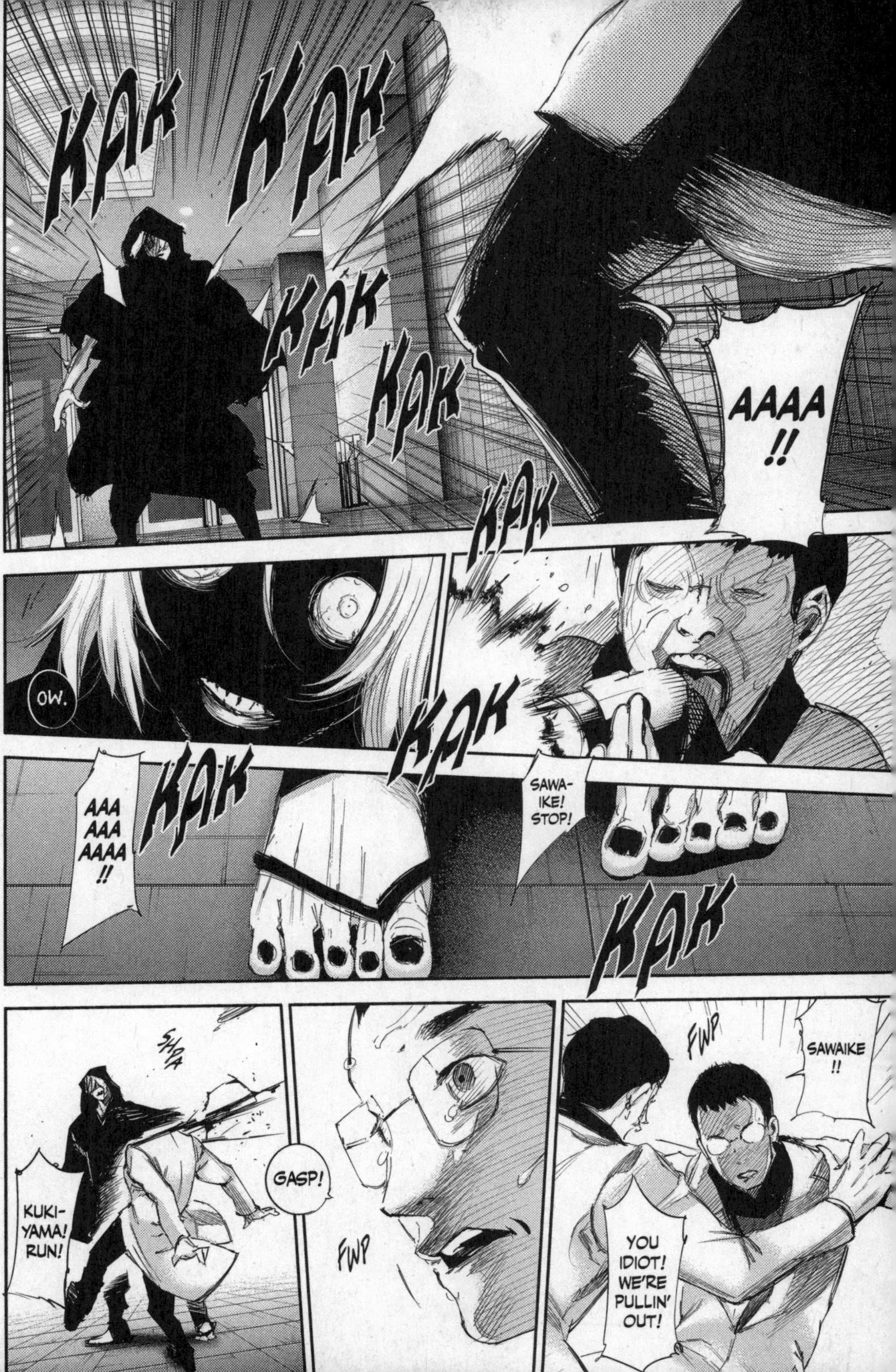
AAAA!!
KAK
KAK
KAK
KAK
KAK
KAK
OW.
SAWAIKE! STOP!
KAK
AAA AAA AAAA!!
KAK
SAWAIKE!!
FWP
YOU IDIOT! WE'RE PULLIN' OUT!
GASP!
FWP
KUKIYAMA! RUN!

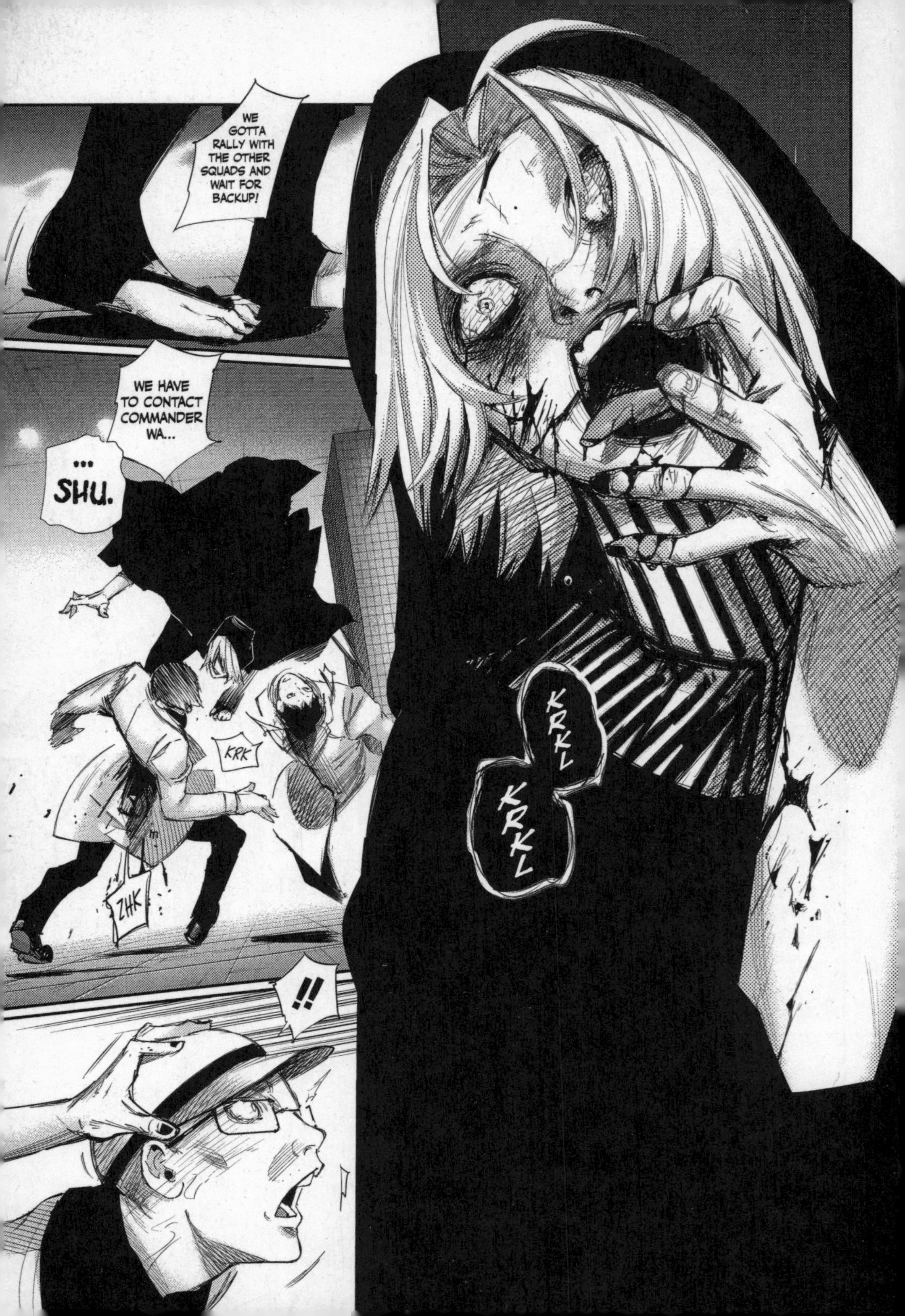
KRKL
KRKL
WE GOTTA RALLY WITH THE OTHER SQUADS AND WAIT FOR BACKUP!
WE HAVE TO CONTACT COMMANDER WA...
...SHU.
KRK
ZHK
!!

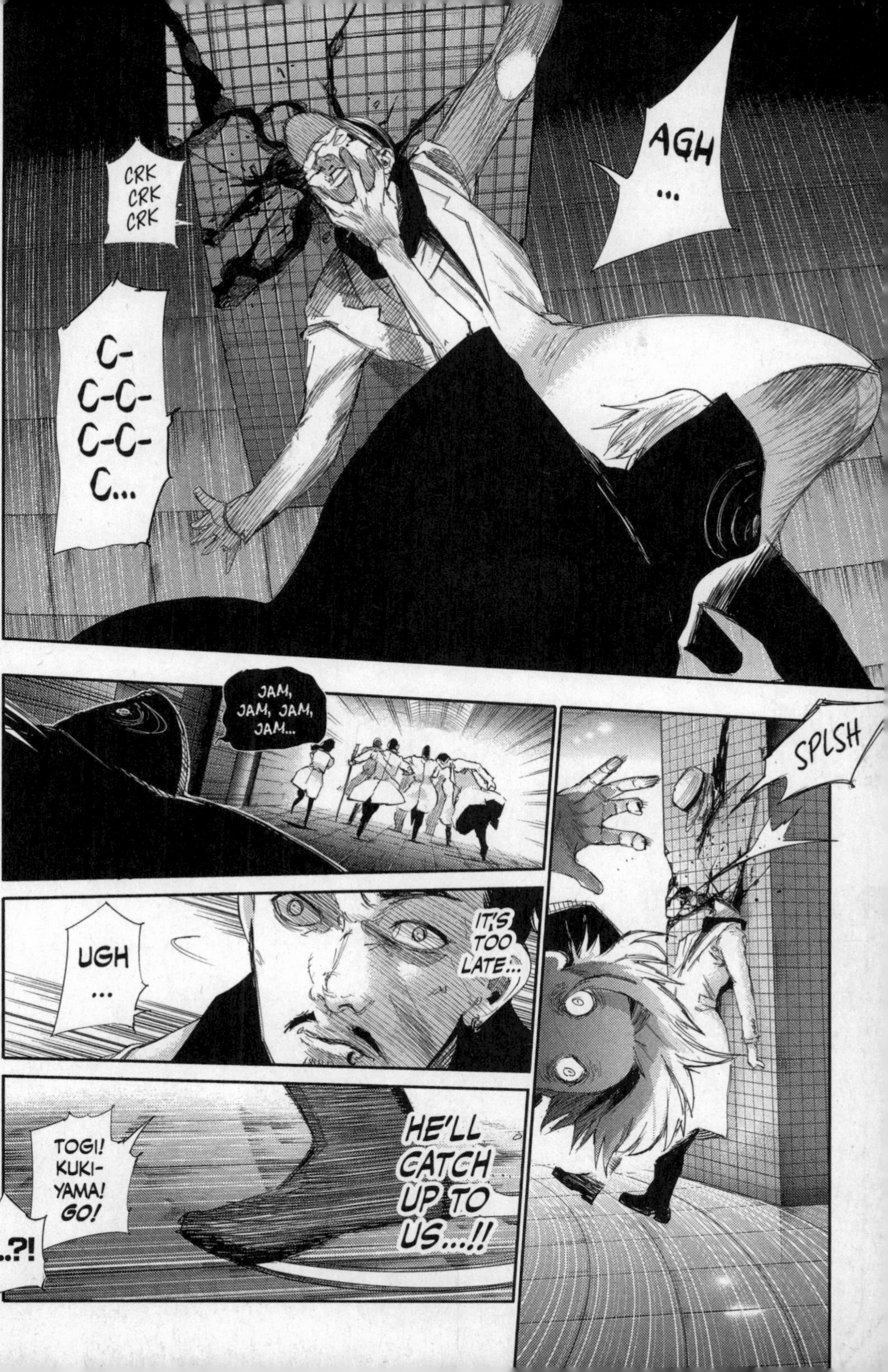
AGH ...
CRK CRK CRK
C- C-C- C-C- C...
SPLSH
IT'S TOO LATE...
HE'LL CATCH UP TO US...!!
JAM, JAM, JAM, JAM...
UGH ...
TOGI! KUKI-YAMA! GO!
...?!

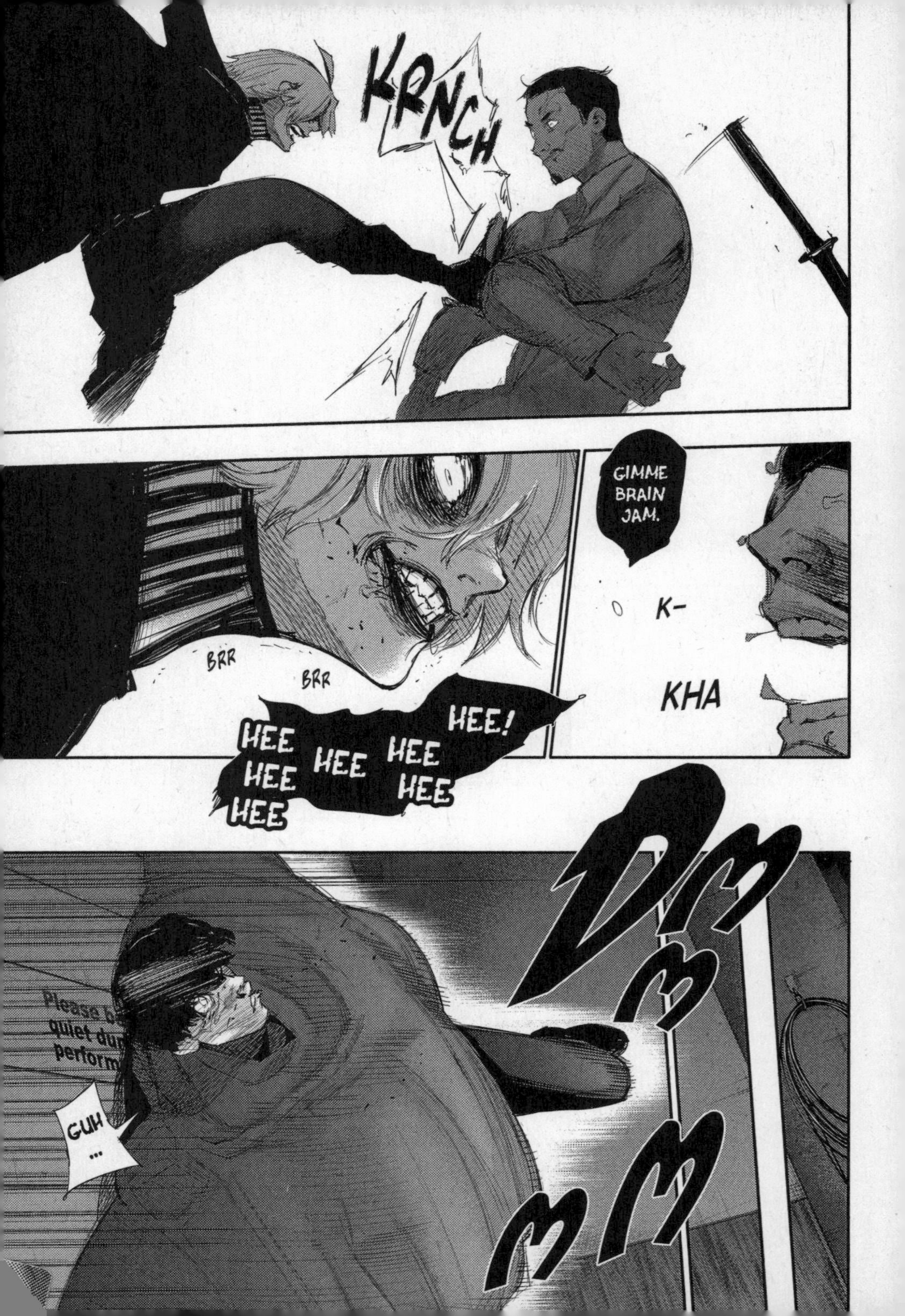
KRNCH
GIMME BRAIN JAM.
K-
KHA
BRR
BRR
HEE! HEE HEE HEE HEE HEE HEE HEE
DMMMMM
Please b
quiet du
perform
GUH ...

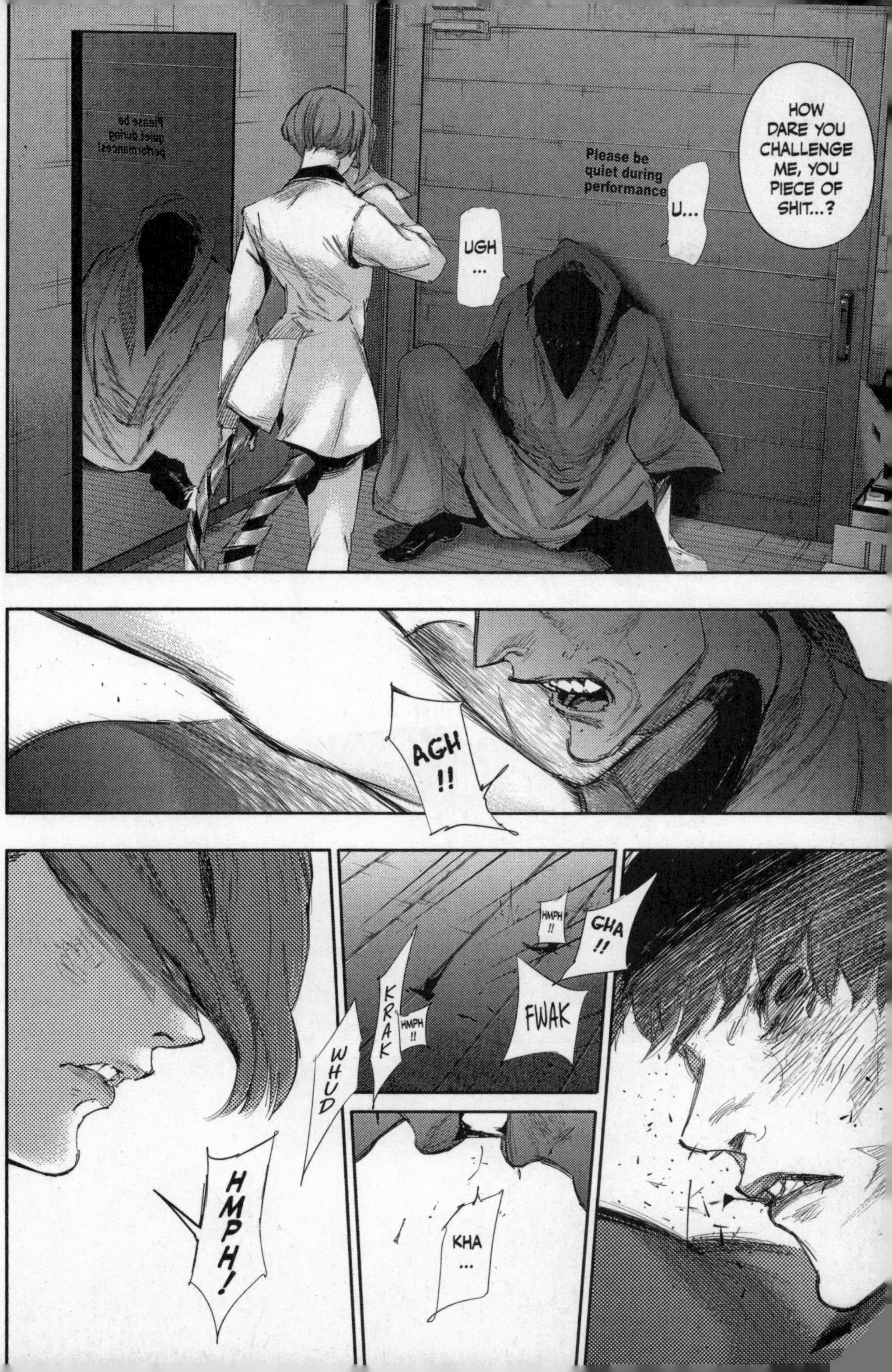
HOW DARE YOU CHALLENGE ME, YOU PIECE OF SHIT...?
Please be quiet during performance
U...
UGH ...
Please be quiet during performances!
AGH !!
GHA !!
HMPH !!
FWAK
HMPH !!
KRAK
WHUD
KHA ...
HMPH!

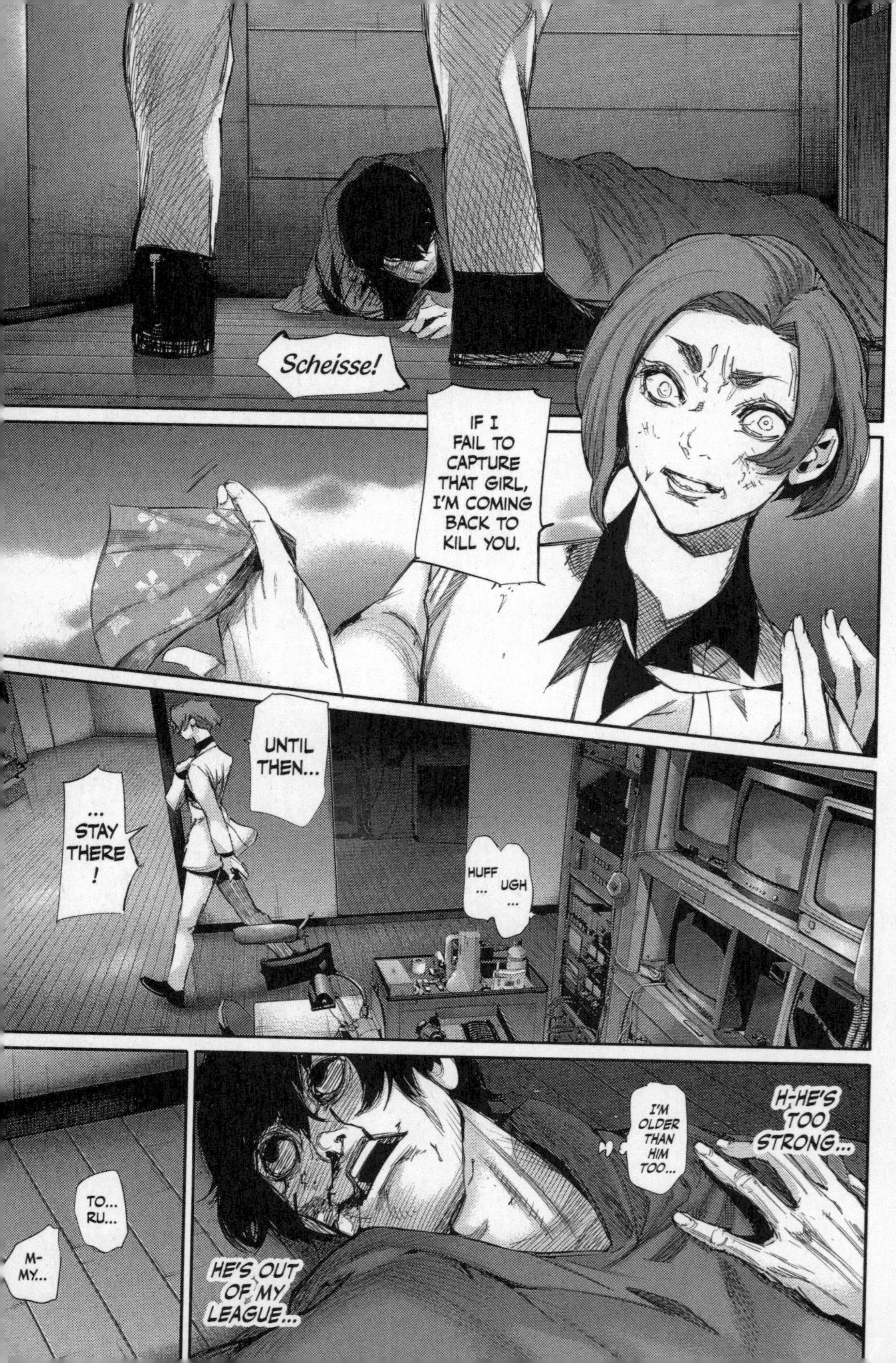
Scheisse!
IF I FAIL TO CAPTURE THAT GIRL, I'M COMING BACK TO KILL YOU.
UNTIL THEN...
... STAY THERE !
HUFF ... UGH ...
H-HE'S TOO STRONG...
I'M OLDER THAN HIM TOO...
HE'S OUT OF MY LEAGUE...
TO... RU...
M-MY...

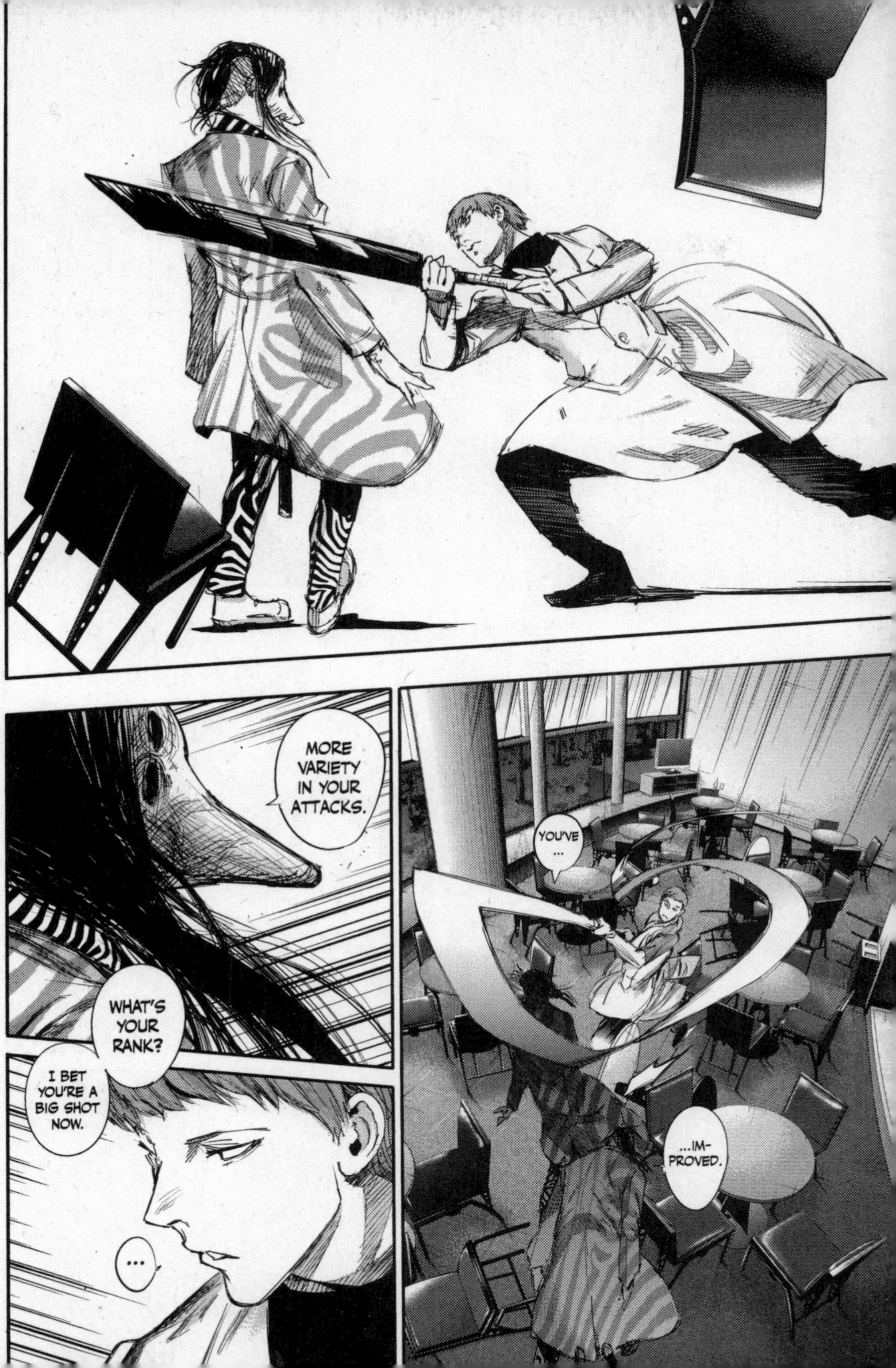
YOU'VE ...
...IM-PROVED.
MORE VARIETY IN YOUR ATTACKS.
WHAT'S YOUR RANK?
I BET YOU'RE A BIG SHOT NOW.
...

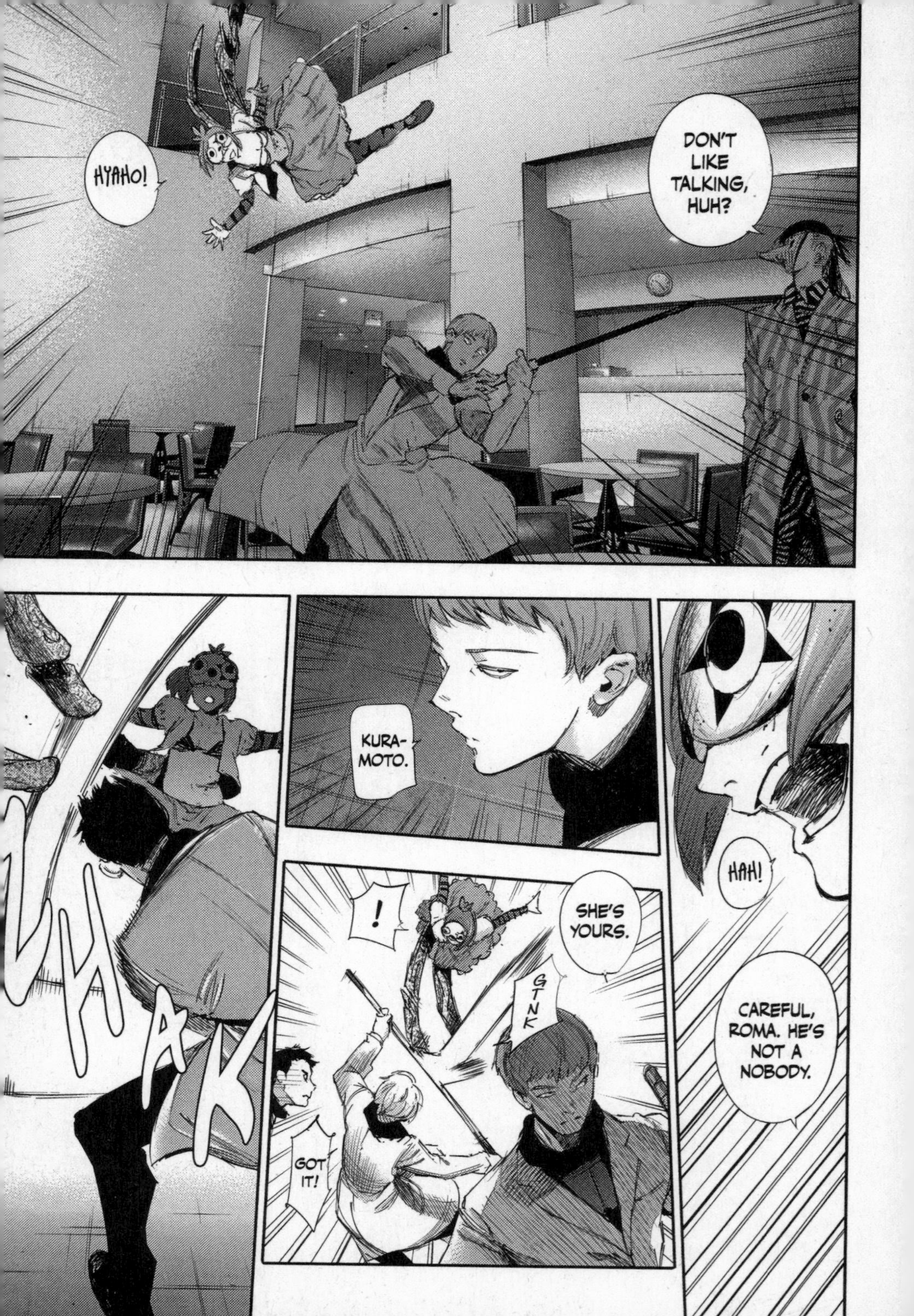
DON'T LIKE TALKING, HUH?
HYAHO!
HAH!
CAREFUL, ROMA. HE'S NOT A NOBODY.
KURA-MOTO.
!
SHE'S YOURS.
GTNK
GOT IT!
WHAK

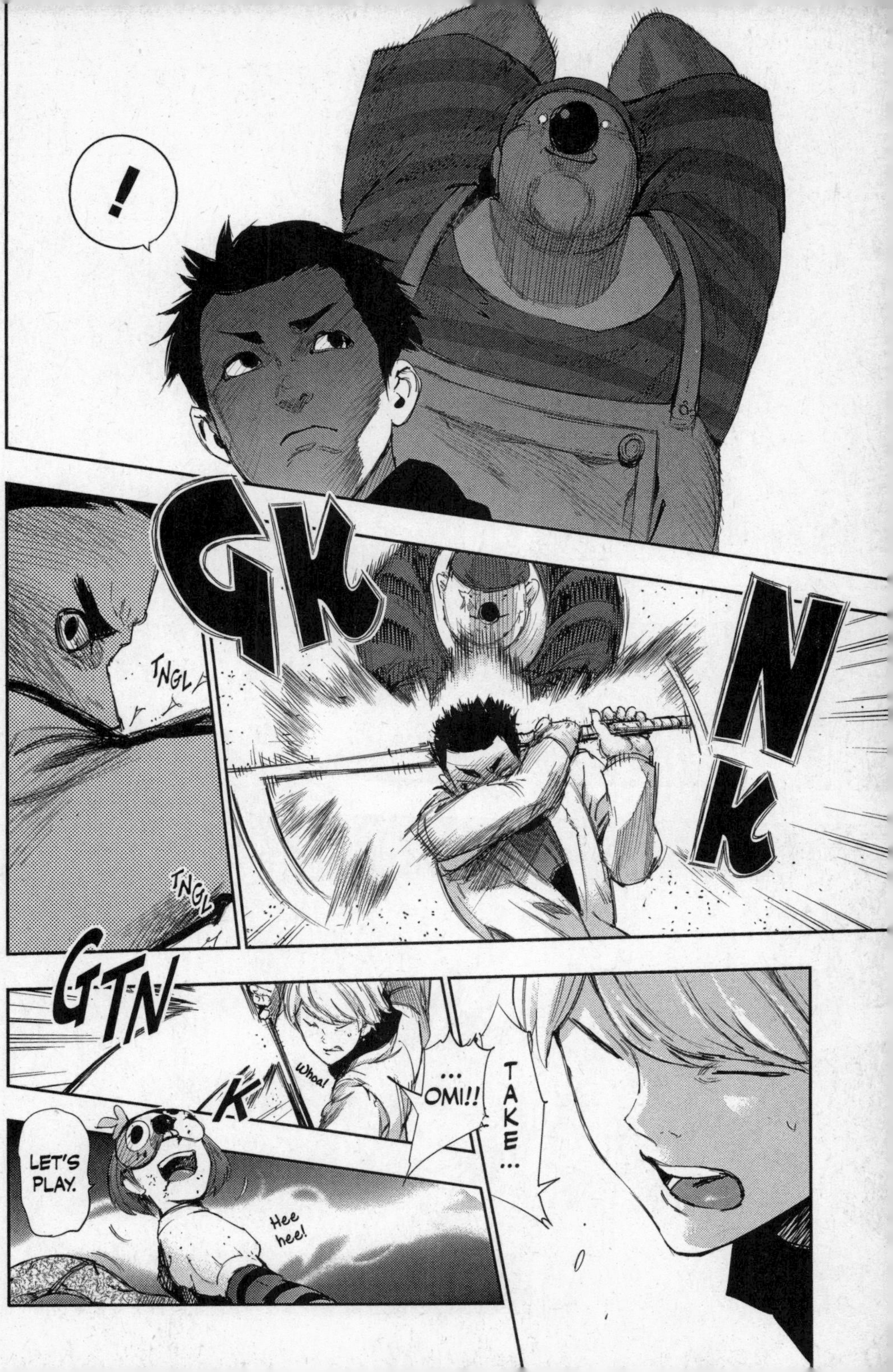
!
GK
NNK
TNGL
TNGL
TAKE...
...OMI!!
GTN
K
Whoa!
LET'S PLAY.
Hee hee!

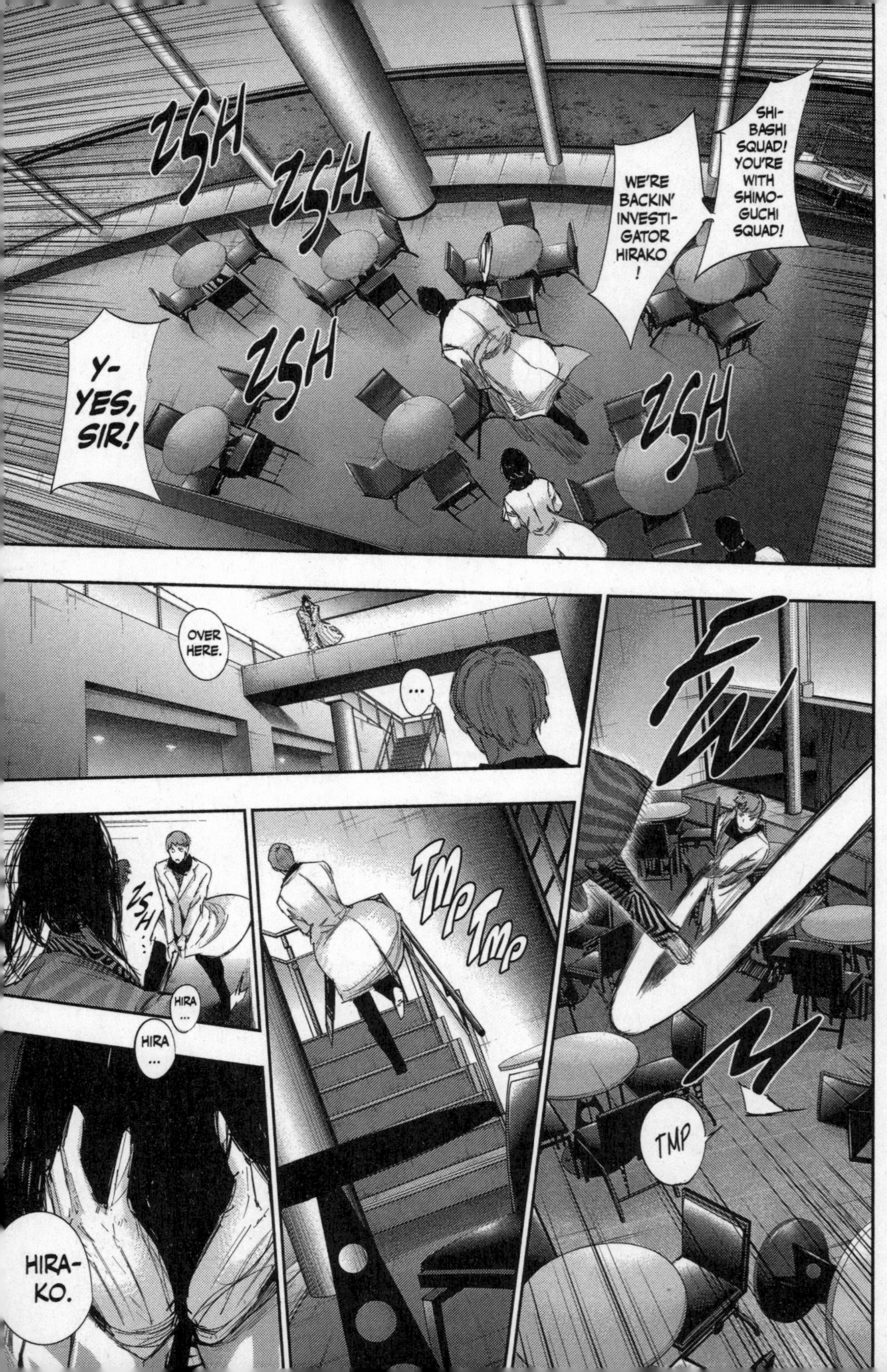
SHI-BASHI SQUAD! YOU'RE WITH SHIMO-GUCHI SQUAD!
WE'RE BACKIN' INVESTI-GATOR HIRAKO!
ZSH
ZSH
ZSH
ZSH
Y-YES, SIR!
FWM
TMP
OVER HERE.
...
TMP TMP
ZSH...
HIRA...
HIRA...
HIRA-KO.

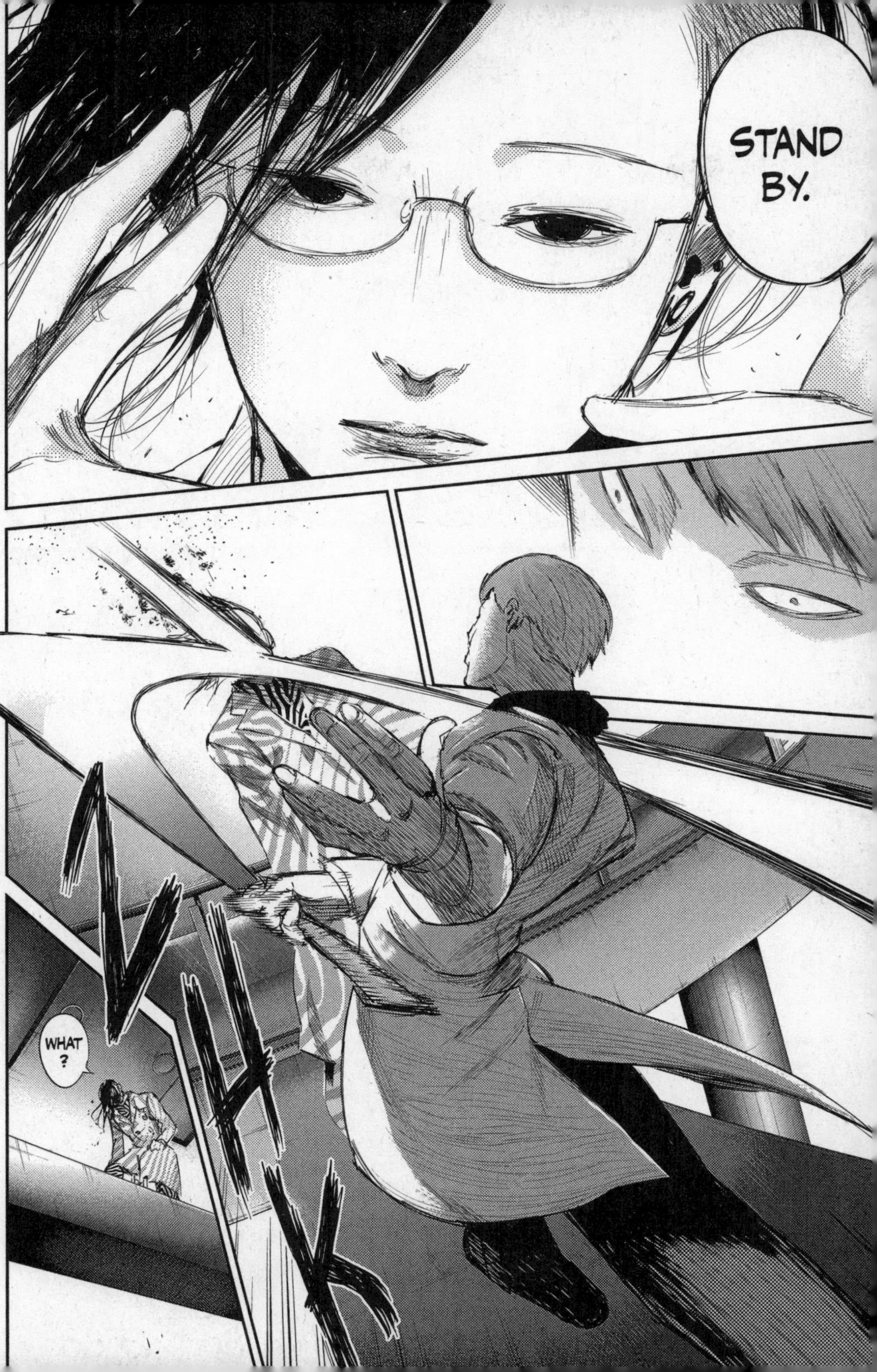
STAND BY.
WHAT?
NHK

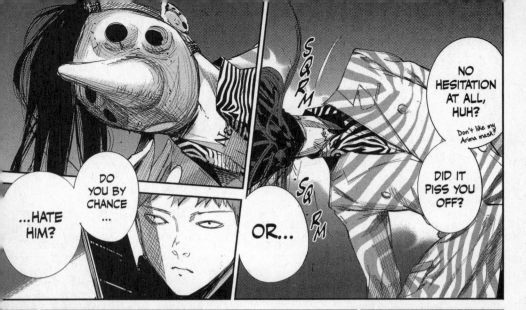

NO HESITATION AT ALL, HUH?

Don't like my Arina mask?

DID IT PISS YOU OFF?

DO YOU BY CHANCE...

...HATE HIM?

OR...

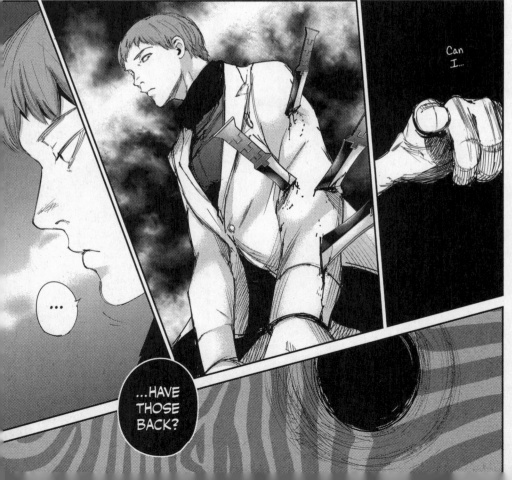

Can I...

...

...HAVE THOSE BACK?

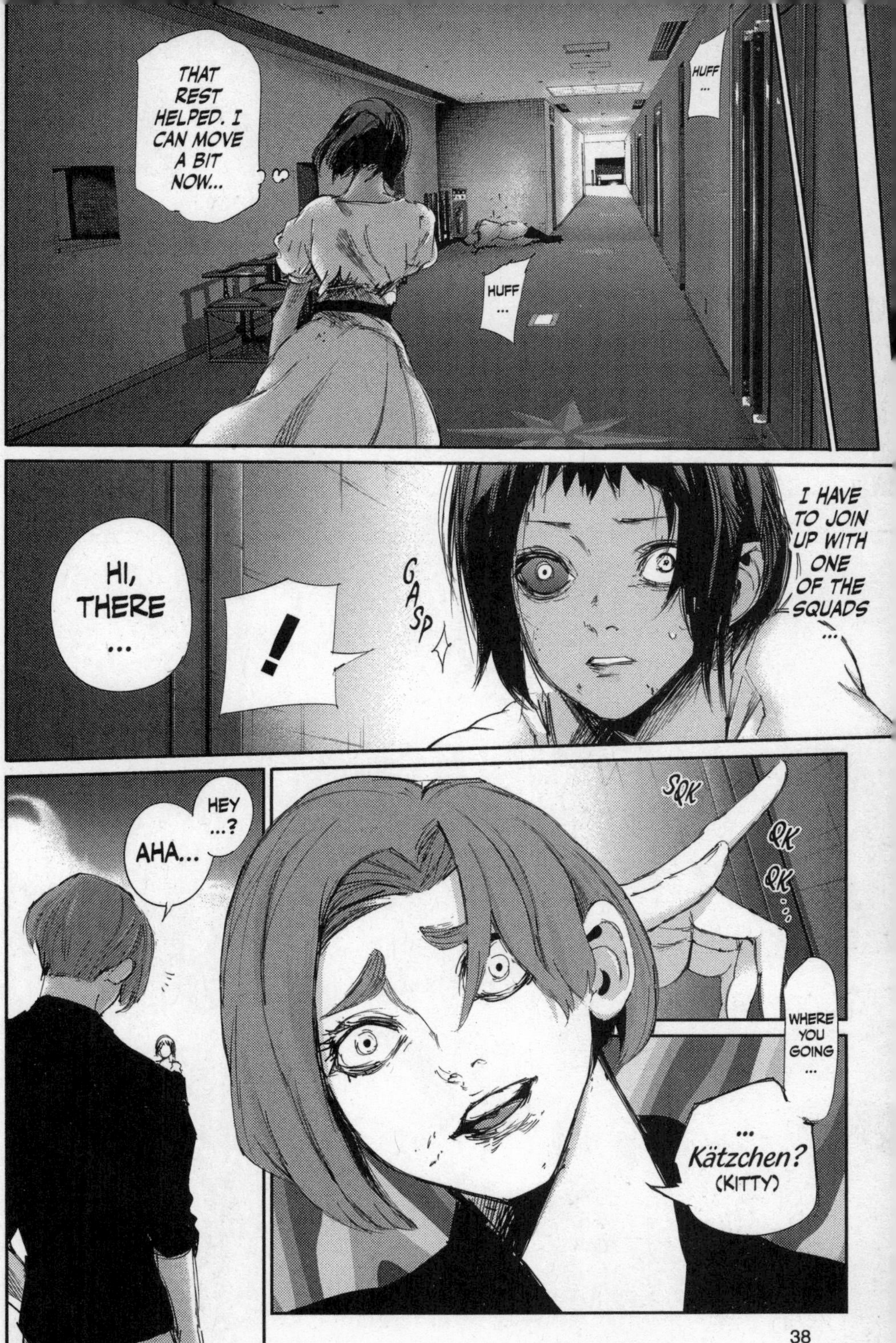
HUFF ...
THAT REST HELPED. I CAN MOVE A BIT NOW...
HUFF ...
I HAVE TO JOIN UP WITH ONE OF THE SQUADS ...
GASP
!
HI, THERE ...
SQK
QK
QK
WHERE YOU GOING ...
... Kätzchen? (KITTY)
HEY ...?
AHA...

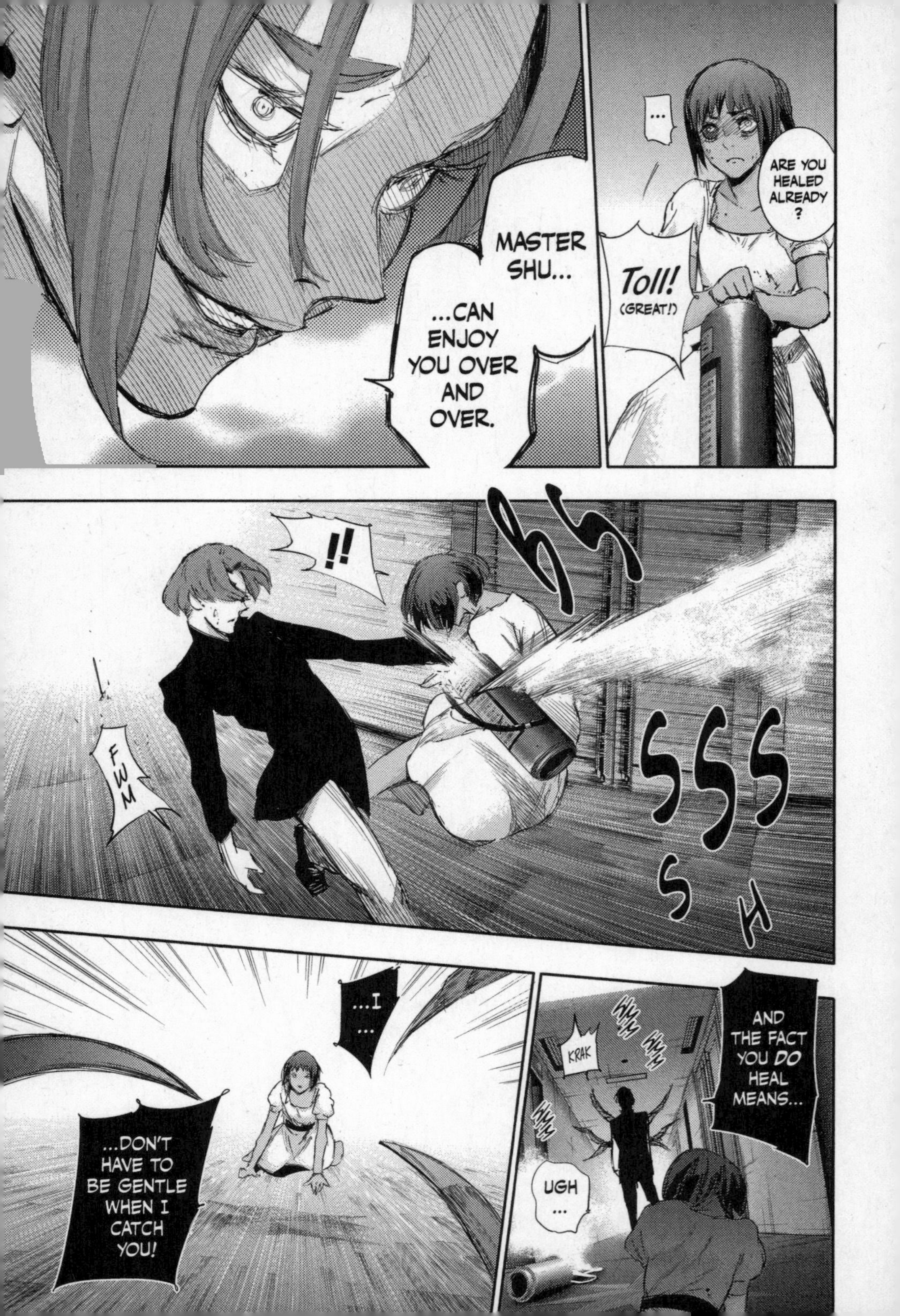
...
ARE YOU HEALED ALREADY ?
Toll! (GREAT!)
MASTER SHU...
...CAN ENJOY YOU OVER AND OVER.
SSSSH
!!
FWM
AND THE FACT YOU DO HEAL MEANS...
WMM
WMM
KRAK
WMM
UGH ...
...I ...
...DON'T HAVE TO BE GENTLE WHEN I CATCH YOU!

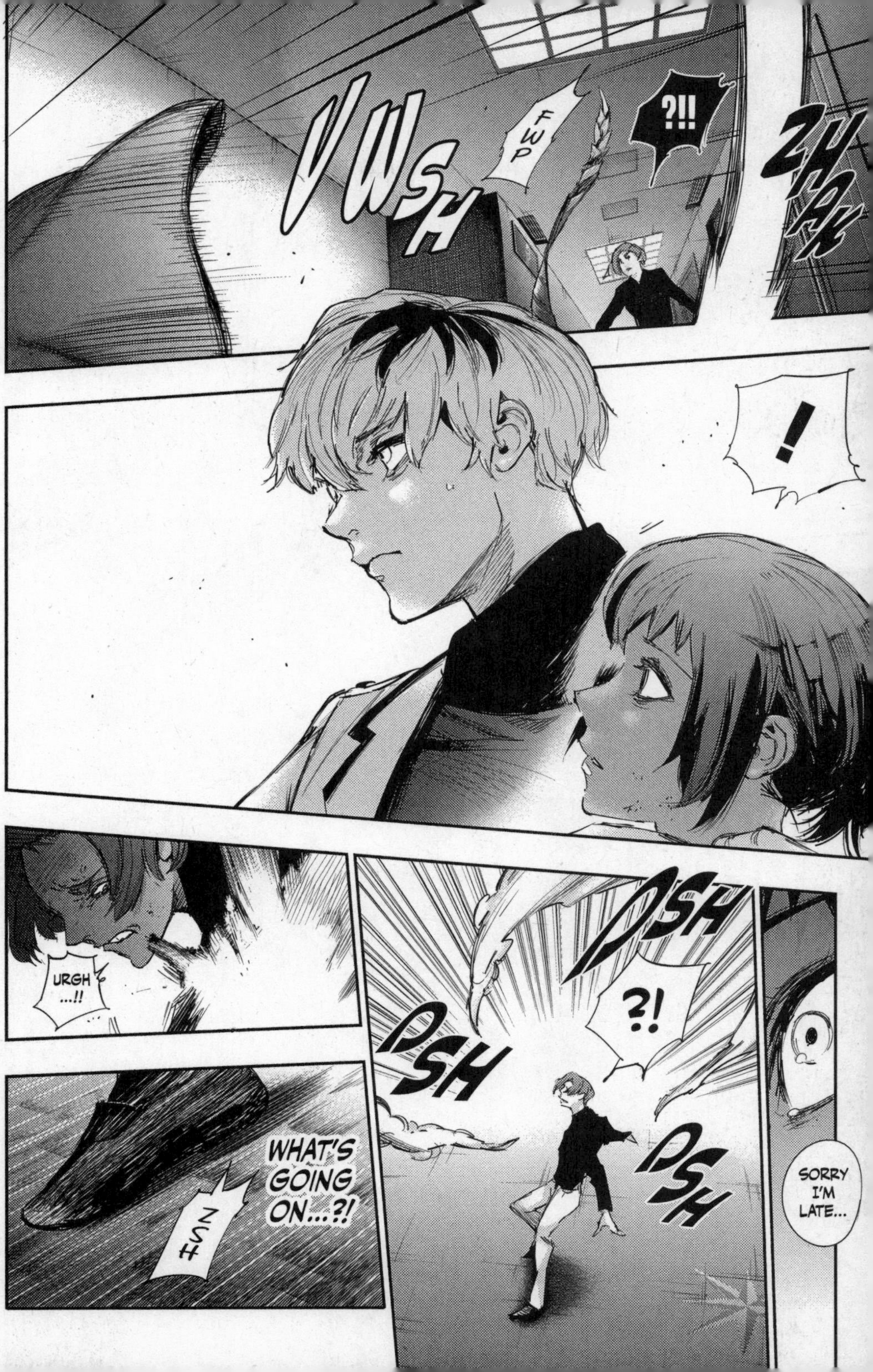
ZHAK
?!!
FWP
VWSH
!
SORRY I'M LATE...
DSH
?!
DSH
DSH
URGH ...!!
WHAT'S GOING ON...?!
ZSH

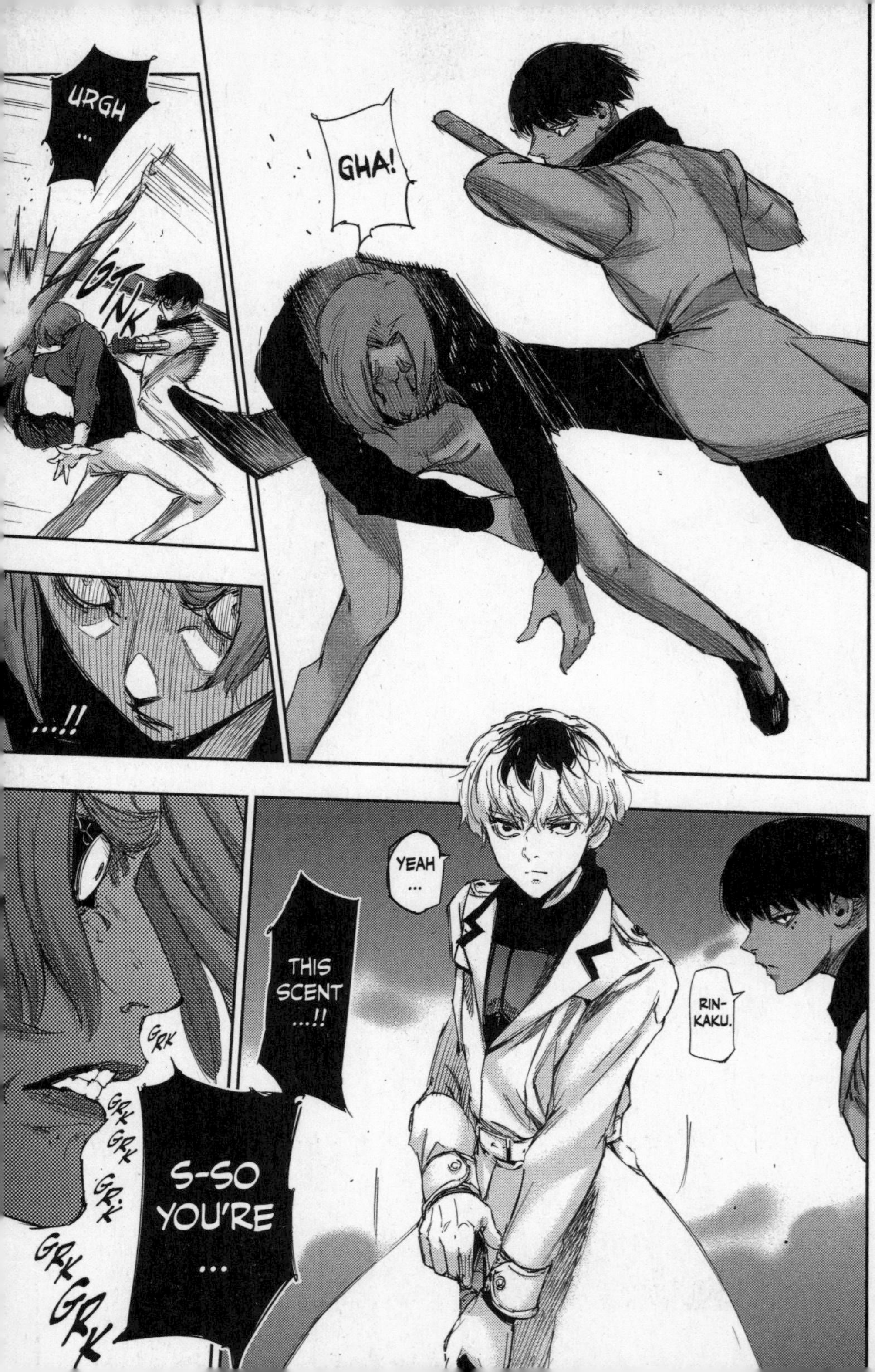
GHA!
URGH ...
GTNK
...!!
RIN-KAKU.
YEAH ...
THIS SCENT ...!!
GRK
GRK GRK GRK GRK GRK
S-SO YOU'RE ...

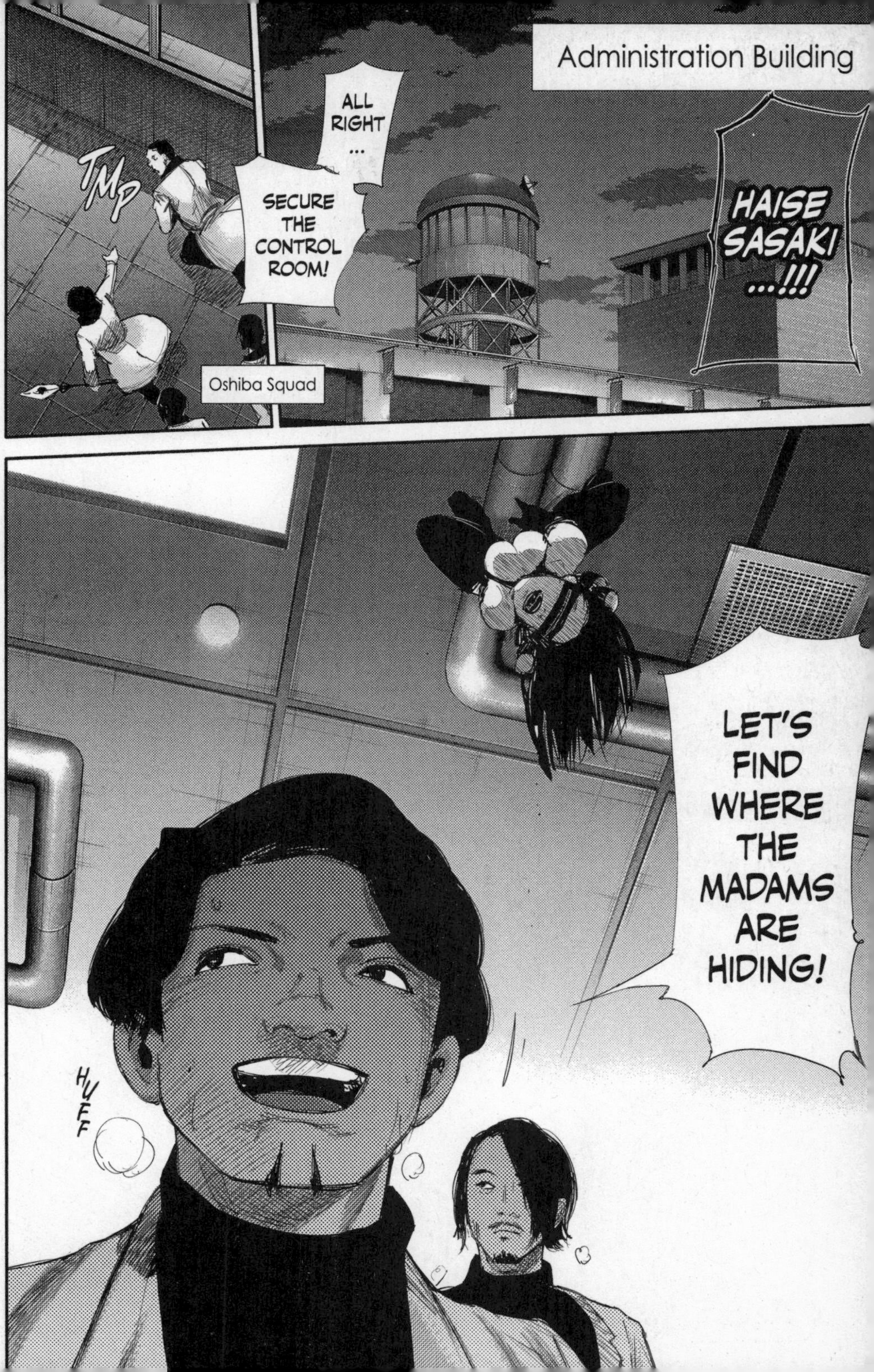
Administration Building
HAISE SASAKI ...!!!
ALL RIGHT ...
SECURE THE CONTROL ROOM!
TMP
Oshiba Squad
LET'S FIND WHERE THE MADAMS ARE HIDING!
HUFF

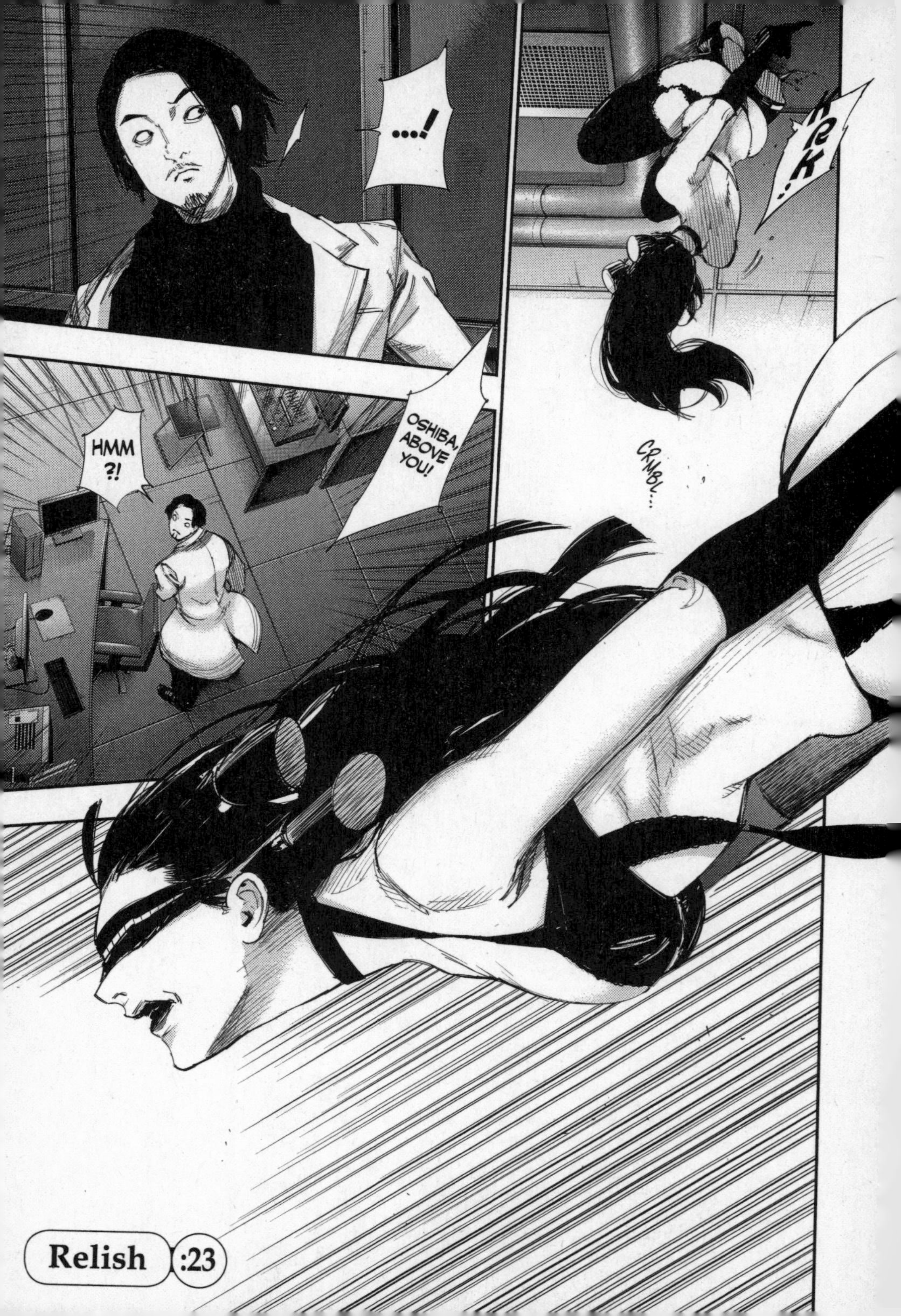
KRK...
...!
OSHIBA, ABOVE YOU!
HMM ?!
CRMBL...

Relish :23

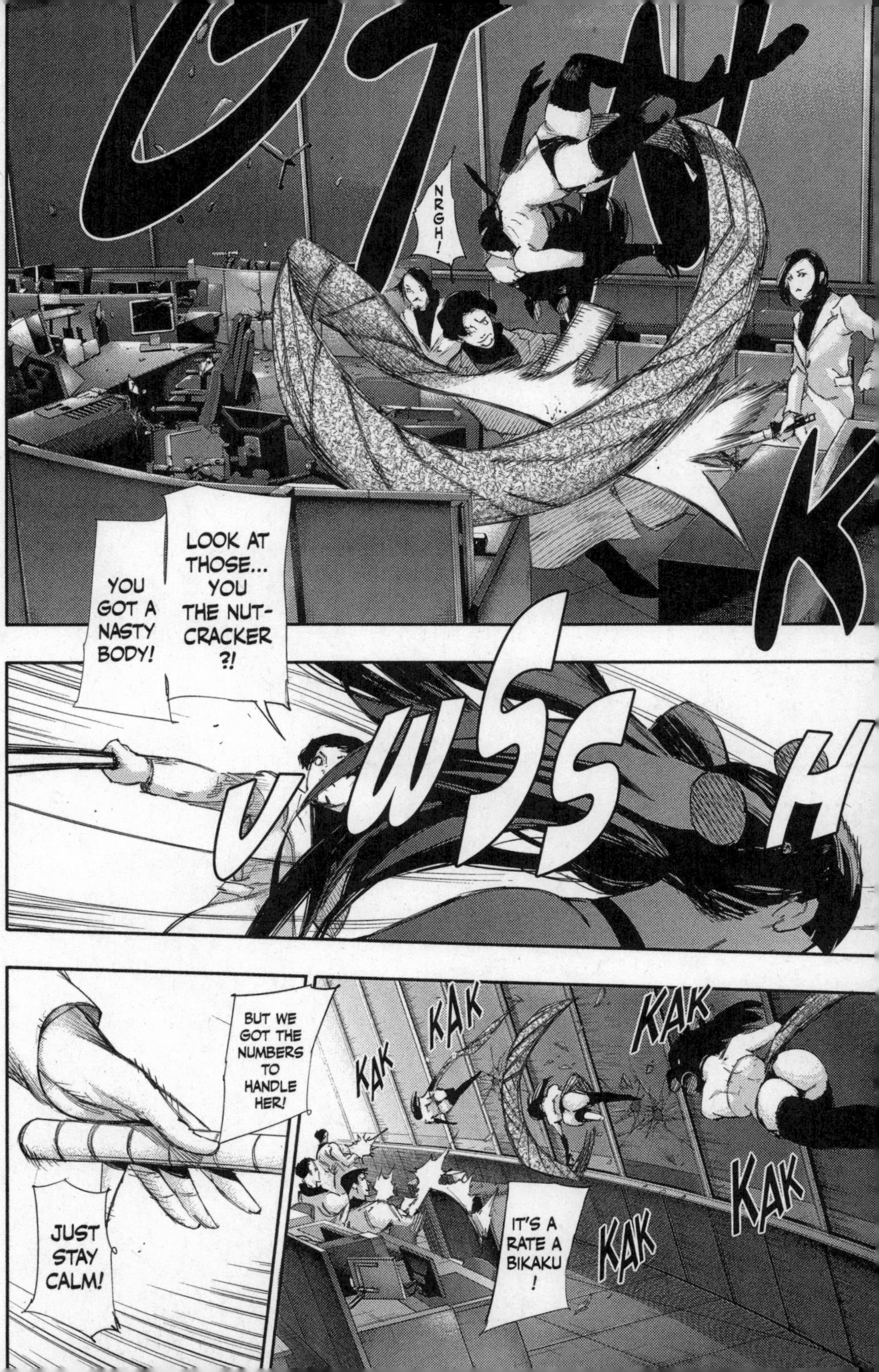
NRGH!
LOOK AT THOSE... YOU THE NUT-CRACKER?!
YOU GOT A NASTY BODY!
VWSSH
KAK
KAK
KAK
BUT WE GOT THE NUMBERS TO HANDLE HER!
KAK
KAK
IT'S A RATE A BIKAKU!
JUST STAY CALM!

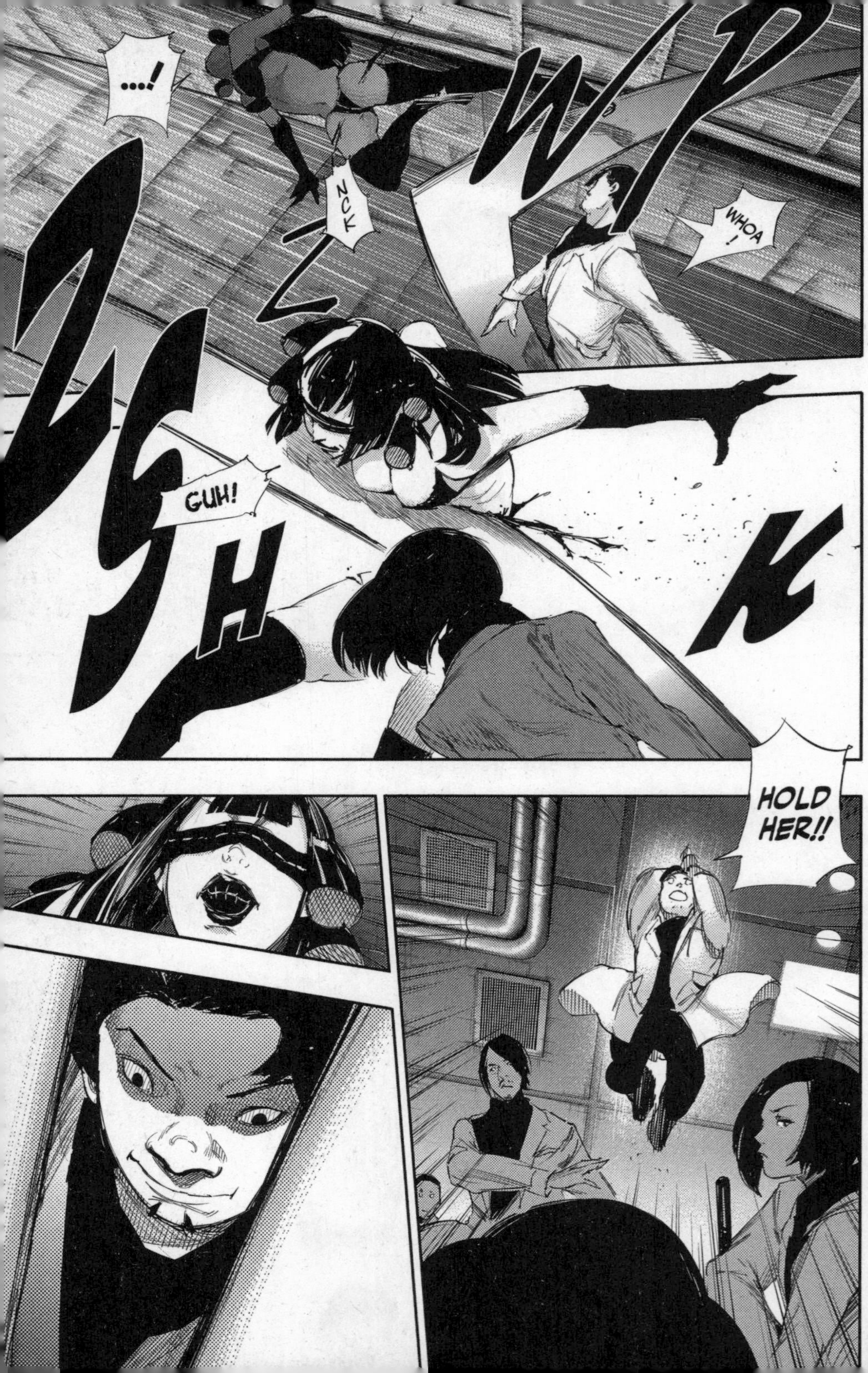

WIP
WHOA!
NCK
...!
GUH!
HOLD HER!!

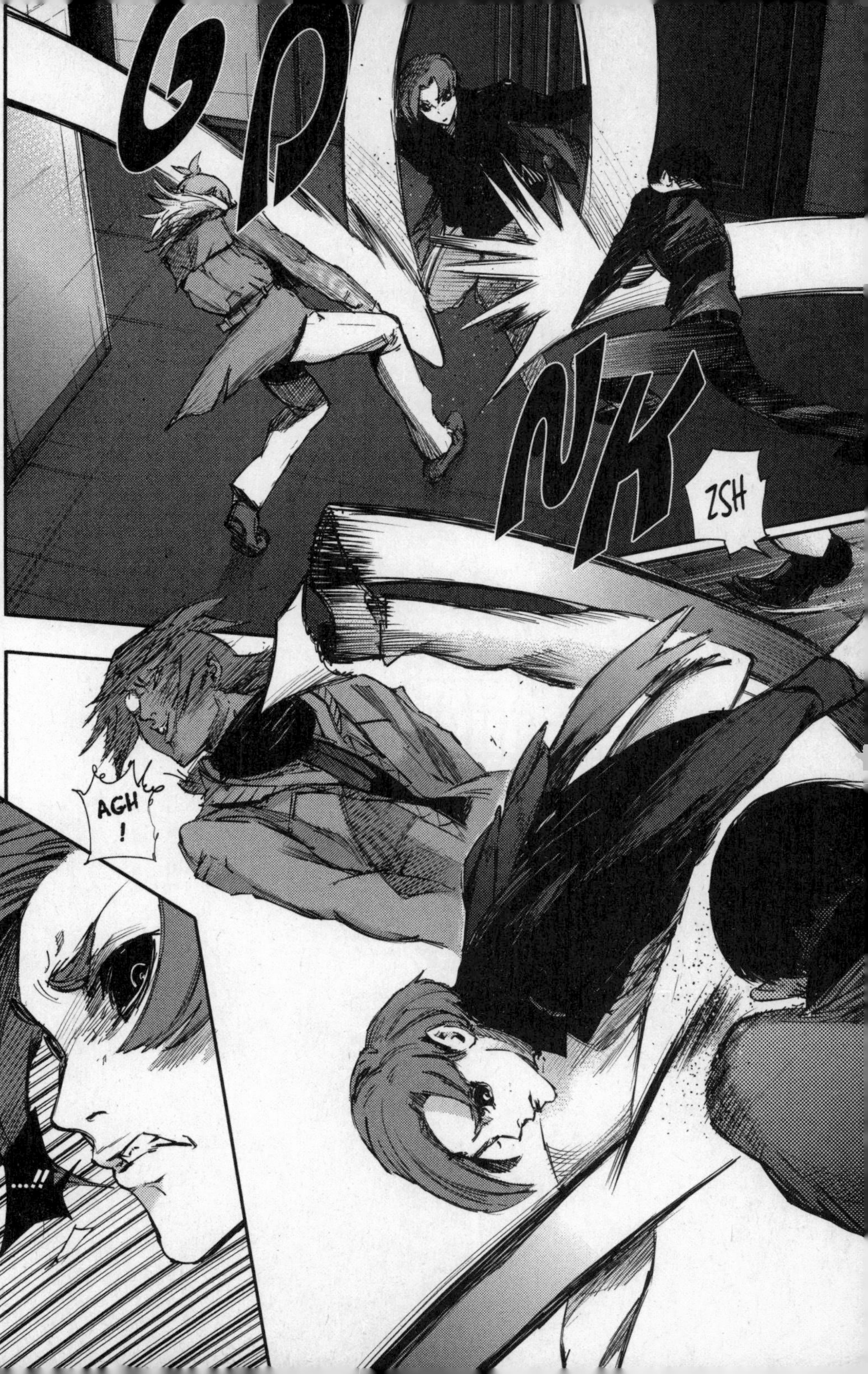
GO
NK
ZSH
AGH !
....!!

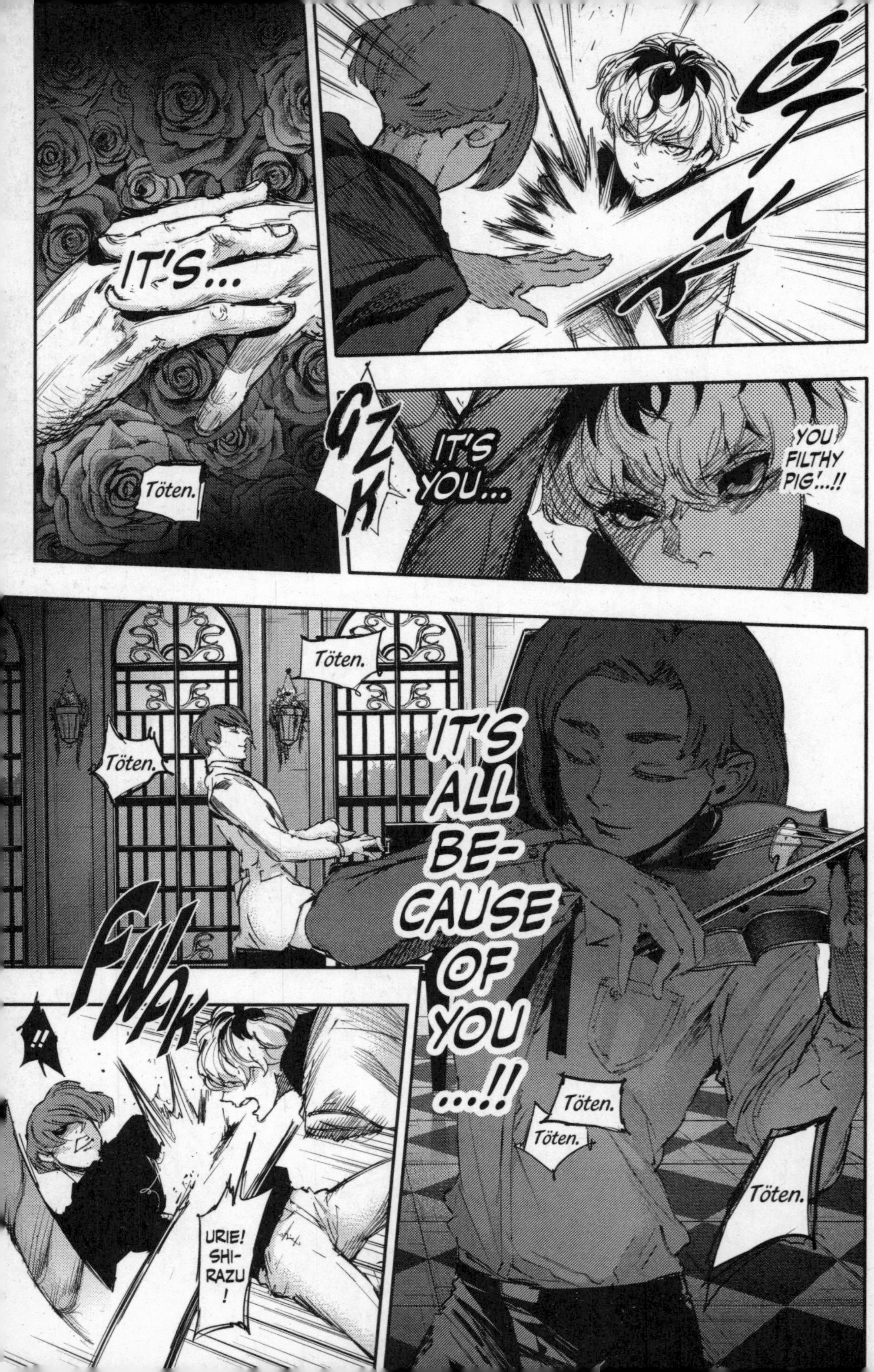
GINK
YOU FILTHY PIG...!!
IT'S YOU...
GZK
IT'S...
Töten.
IT'S ALL BE-CAUSE OF YOU...!!
Töten.
Töten.
Töten.
Töten.
Töten.
FWAK
!!
URIE! SHI-RAZU!

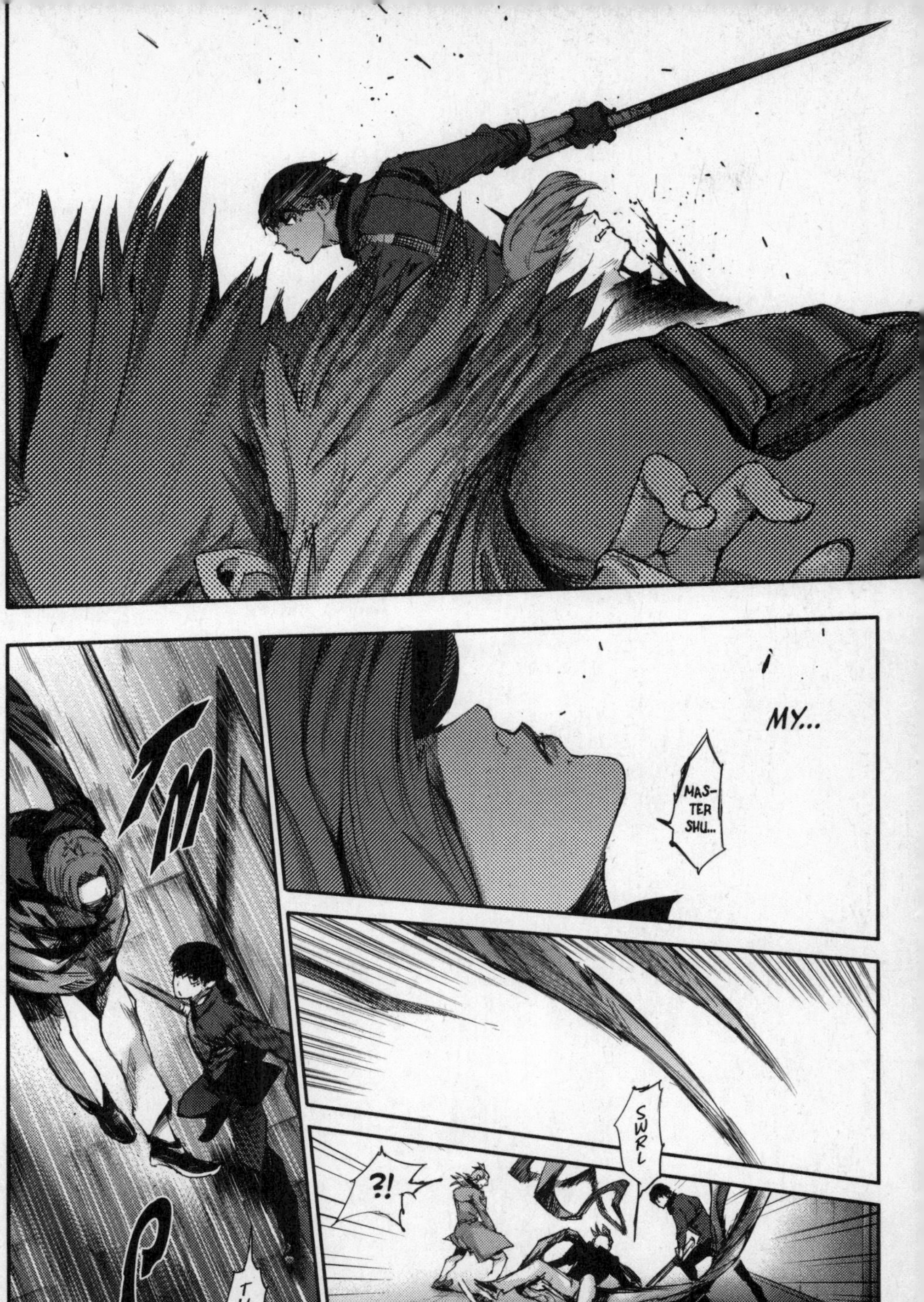
MY...
MAS-TER SHU...
SWRL
?!
TUG

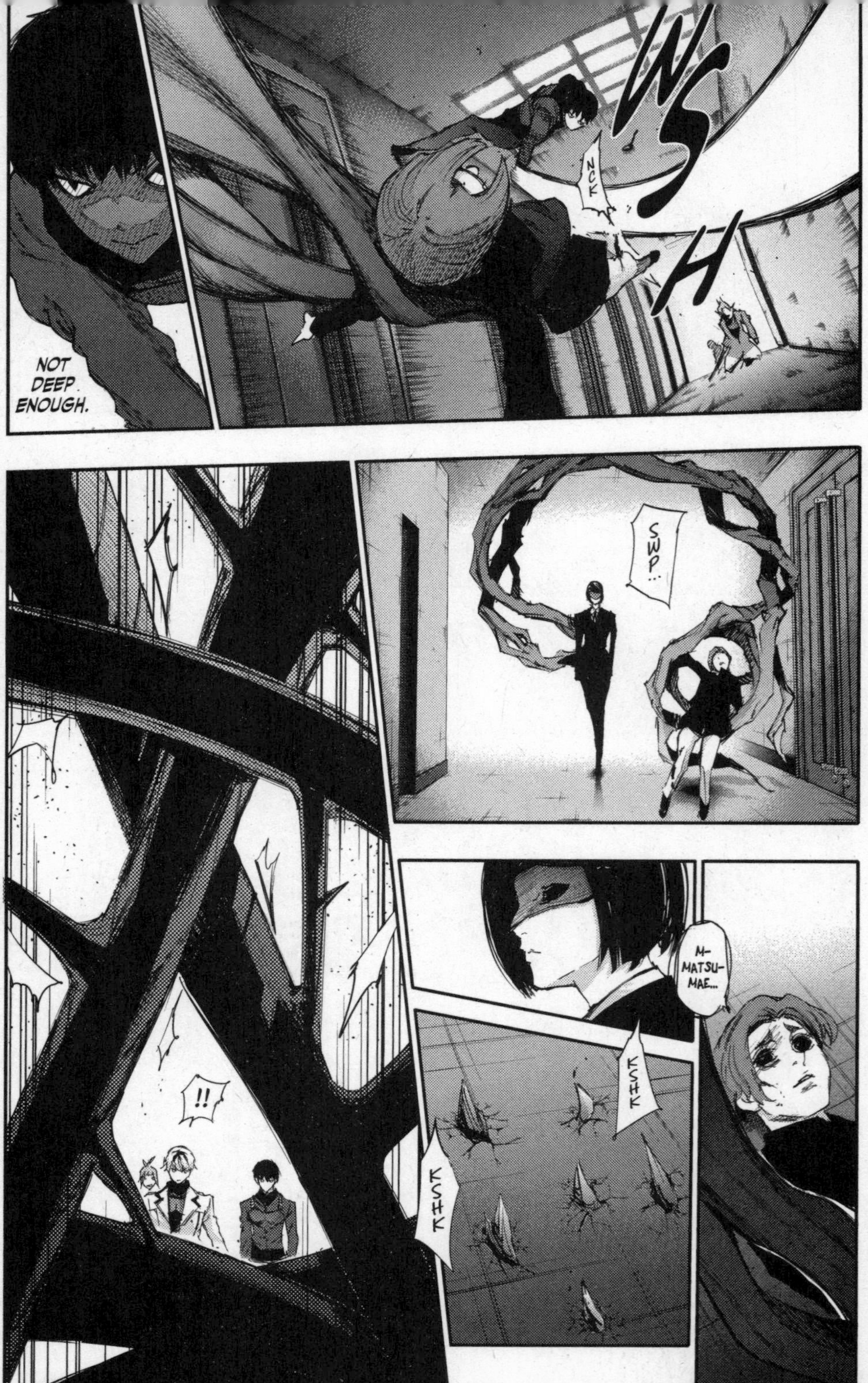
WSH
NCK
NOT DEEP ENOUGH.
SWP...
M-MATSU-MAE...
KSHK
KSHK
!!

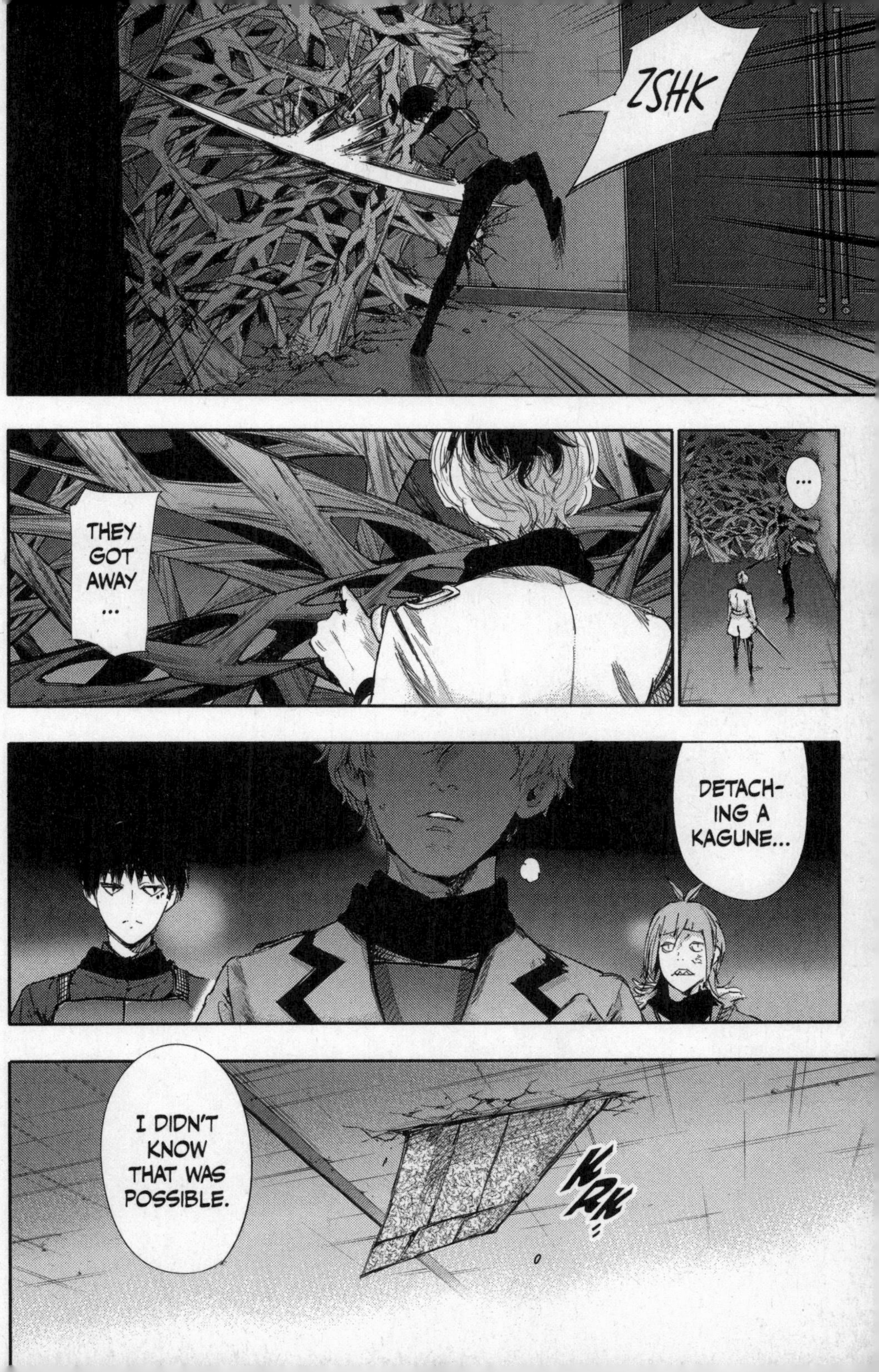
ZSHK
...
THEY GOT AWAY ...
DETACHING A KAGUNE...
I DIDN'T KNOW THAT WAS POSSIBLE.

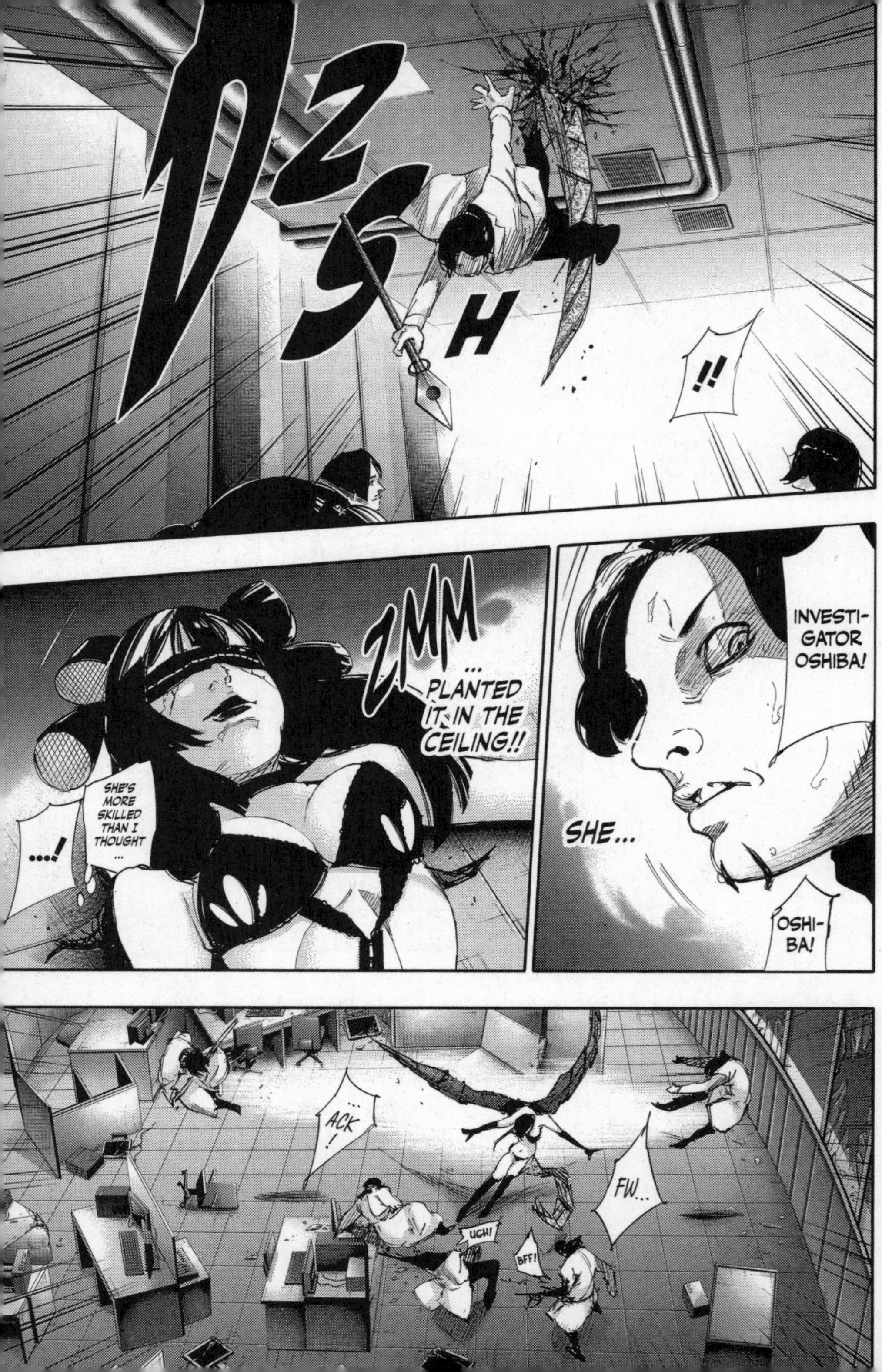
DZSH
!!
INVESTI-GATOR OSHIBA!
SHE...
OSHI-BA!
ZMM
...PLANTED IT IN THE CEILING!!
SHE'S MORE SKILLED THAN I THOUGHT...
...!
FW...
...ACK!
UGH!
BFF!

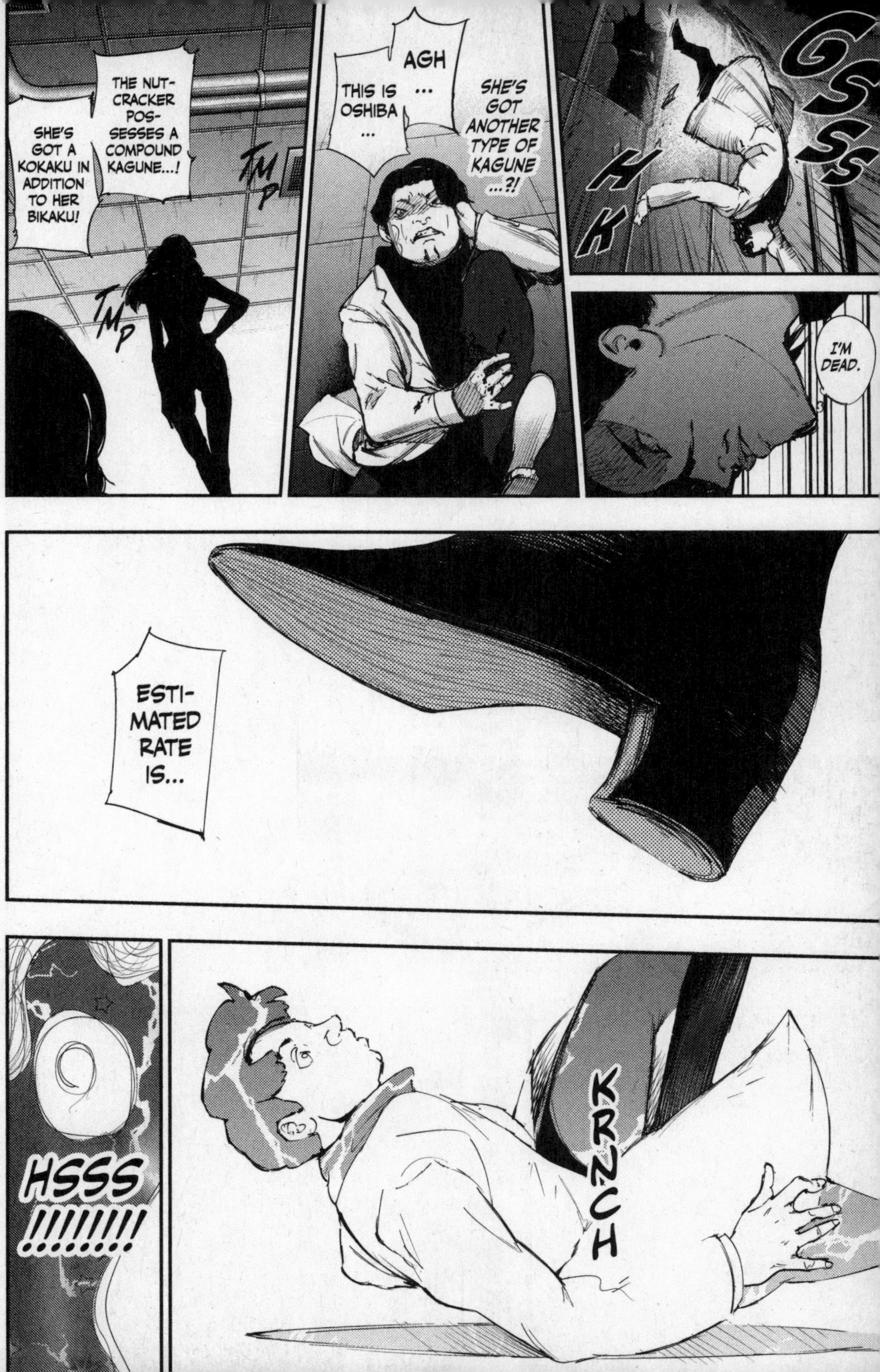
GSSSS
HKK
I'M DEAD.
AGH ...
THIS IS OSHIBA ...
SHE'S GOT ANOTHER TYPE OF KAGUNE ...?!
THE NUT-CRACKER POS-SESSES A COMPOUND KAGUNE...!
SHE'S GOT A KOKAKU IN ADDITION TO HER BIKAKU!
TMP
TMP
ESTI-MATED RATE IS...
KRNCH
HSSS !!!!!!!!

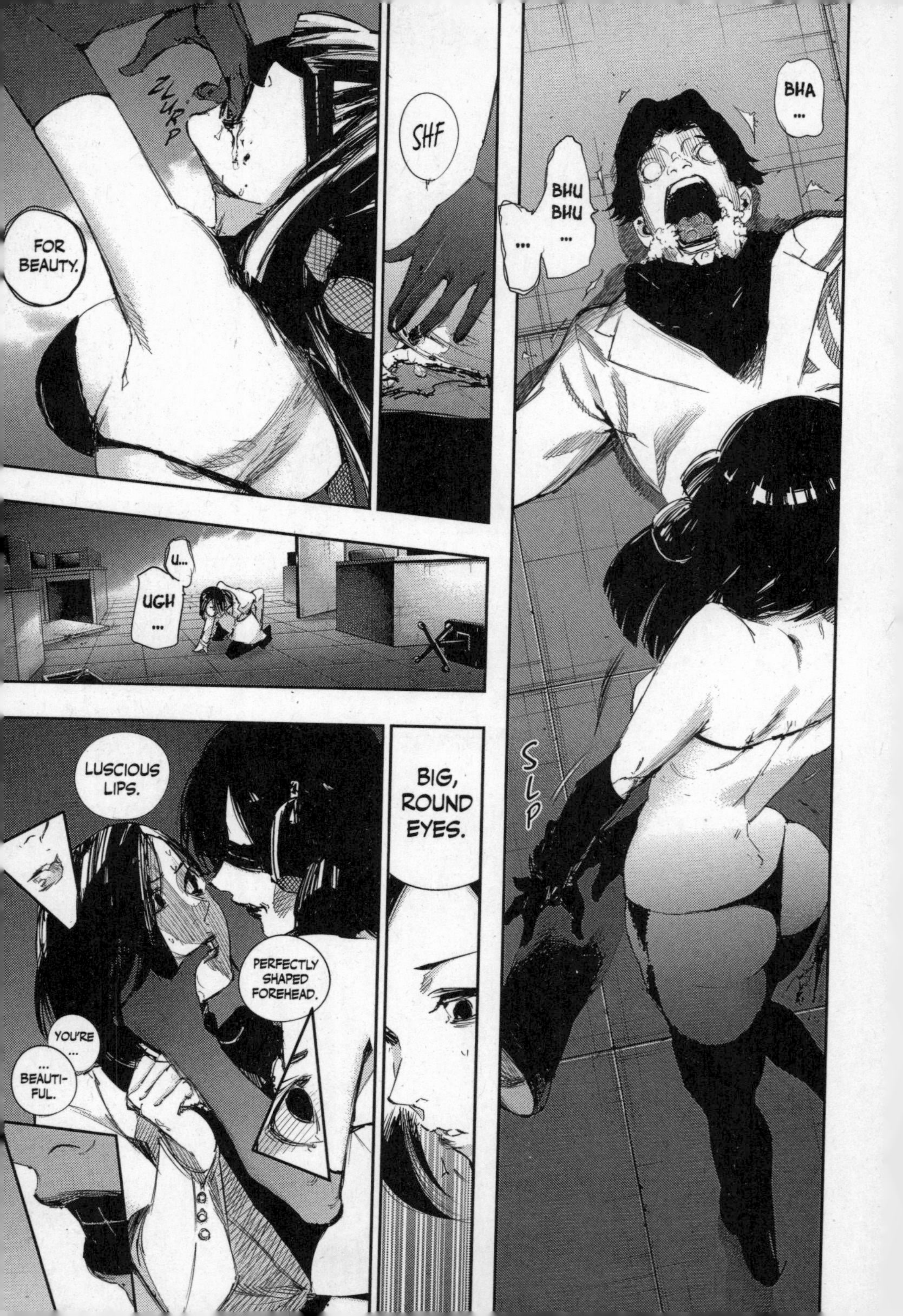
BHA ...
BHU BHU ... ...
SLP
SHF
ZLURP
FOR BEAUTY.
U...
UGH ...
BIG, ROUND EYES.
LUSCIOUS LIPS.
PERFECTLY SHAPED FOREHEAD.
YOU'RE ...
... BEAUTI-FUL.

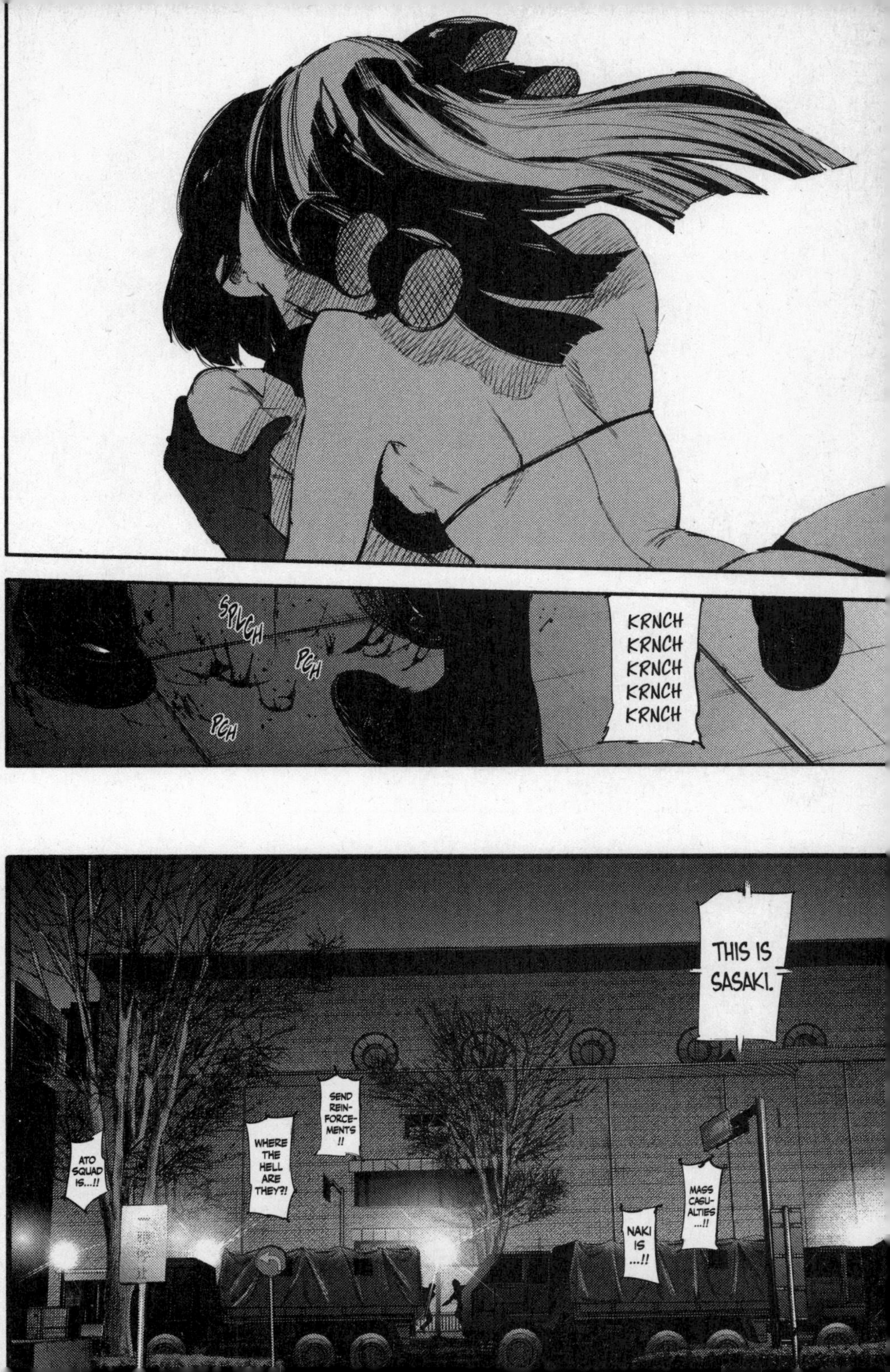
KRNCH KRNCH KRNCH KRNCH KRNCH
SPLUCH
PCH
PCH
THIS IS SASAKI.
MASS CASUALTIES ...!!
NAKI IS ...!!
SEND REINFORCEMENTS !!
WHERE THE HELL ARE THEY?!
ATO SQUAD IS...!!

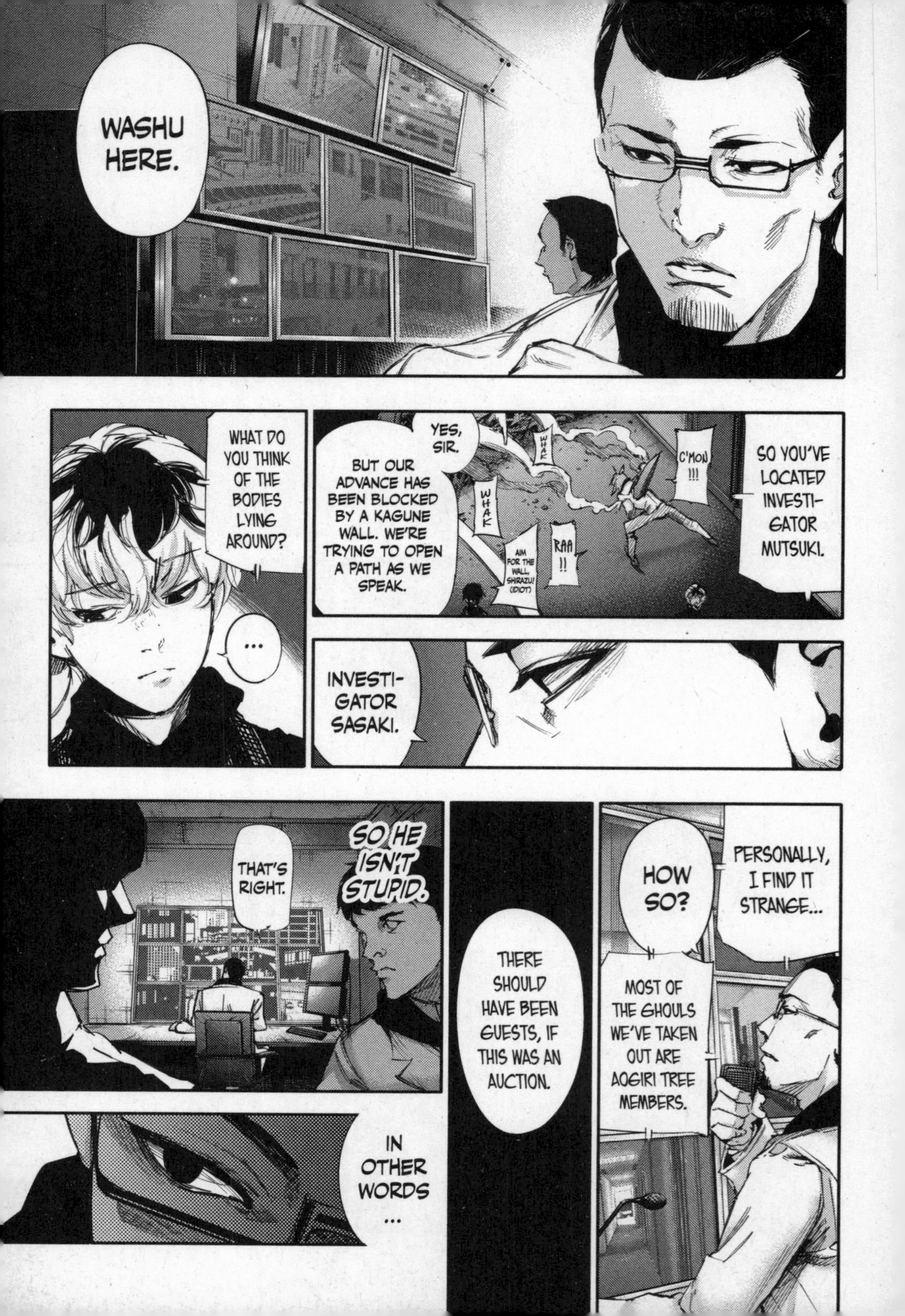
WASHU HERE.
SO YOU'VE LOCATED INVESTI-GATOR MUTSUKI.
C'MON!!!
WHAK
WHAK
RAA!!
AIM FOR THE WALL, SHIRAZU! (IDIOT)
YES, SIR.
BUT OUR ADVANCE HAS BEEN BLOCKED BY A KAGUNE WALL. WE'RE TRYING TO OPEN A PATH AS WE SPEAK.
INVESTI-GATOR SASAKI.
WHAT DO YOU THINK OF THE BODIES LYING AROUND?
...
PERSONALLY, I FIND IT STRANGE...
HOW SO?
MOST OF THE GHOULS WE'VE TAKEN OUT ARE AOGIRI TREE MEMBERS.
THERE SHOULD HAVE BEEN GUESTS, IF THIS WAS AN AUCTION.
SO HE ISN'T STUPID.
THAT'S RIGHT.
IN OTHER WORDS ...

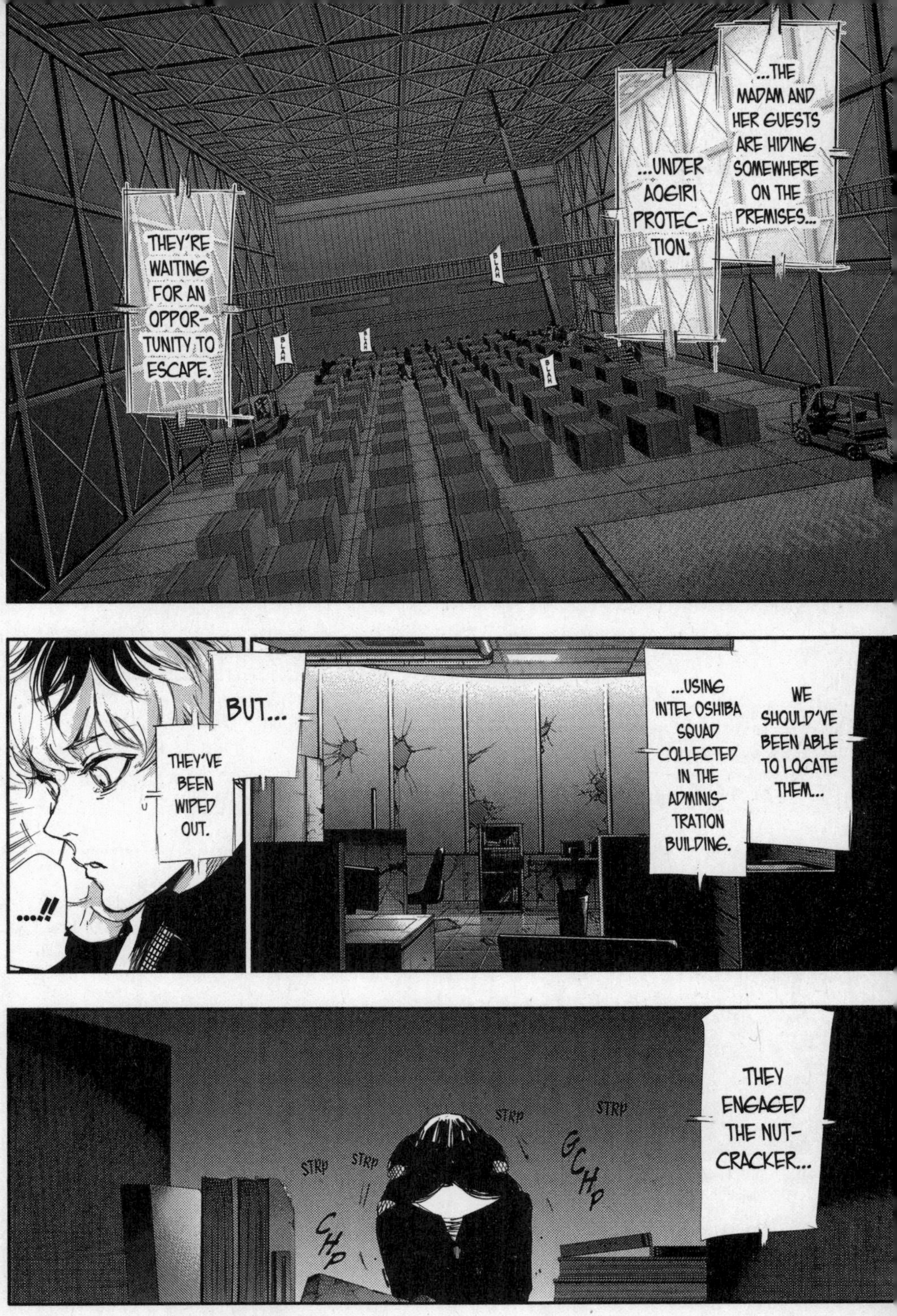
...THE MADAM AND HER GUESTS ARE HIDING SOMEWHERE ON THE PREMISES...
...UNDER AOGIRI PROTEC-TION.
BLAH
BLAH
BLAH
BLAH
THEY'RE WAITING FOR AN OPPOR-TUNITY TO ESCAPE.
WE SHOULD'VE BEEN ABLE TO LOCATE THEM...
...USING INTEL OSHIBA SQUAD COLLECTED IN THE ADMINIS-TRATION BUILDING.
BUT...
THEY'VE BEEN WIPED OUT.
...!!
THEY ENGAGED THE NUT-CRACKER...
STRP
STRP
GCHA
STRP
STRP
CHA

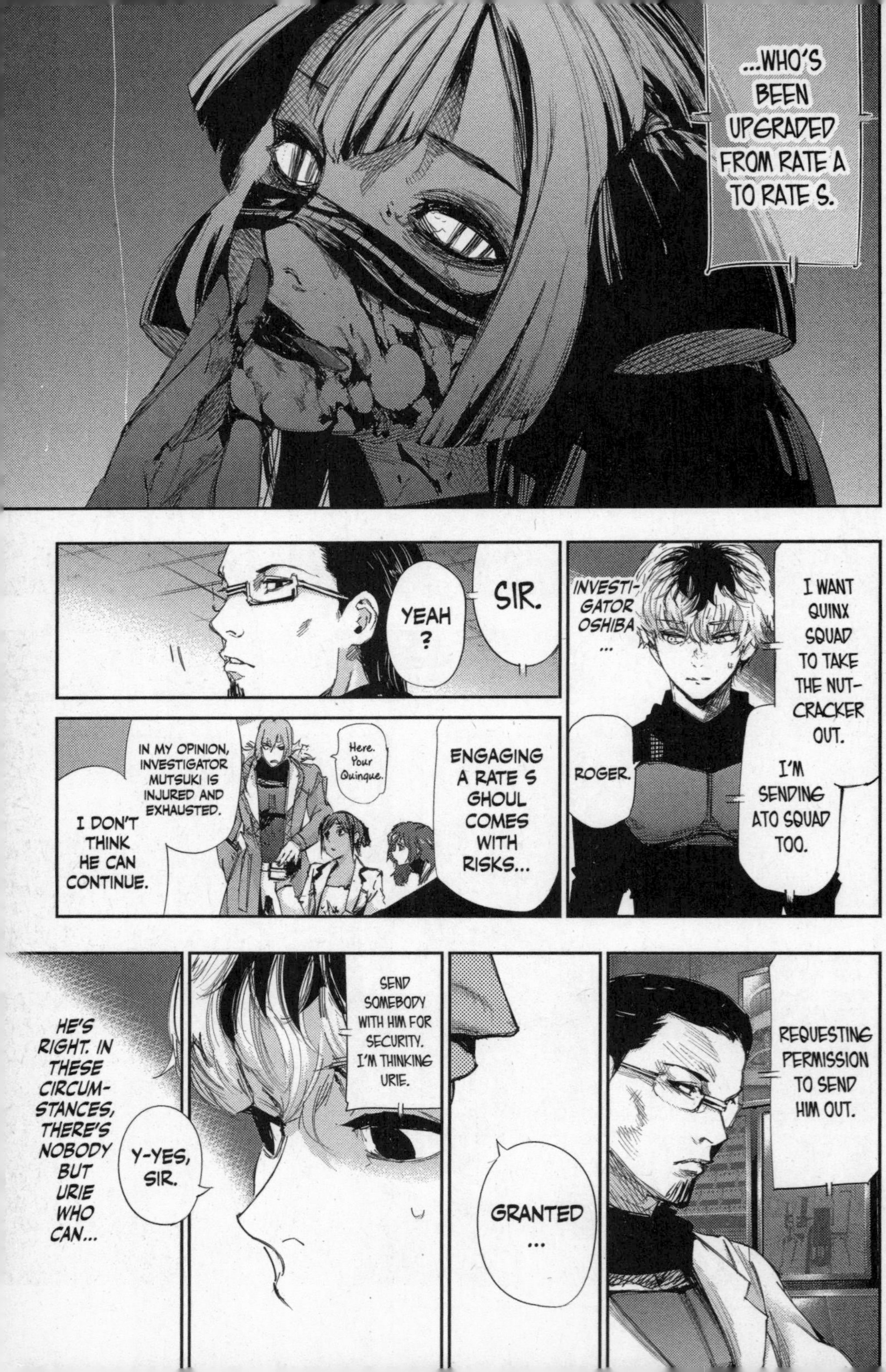
...WHO'S BEEN UPGRADED FROM RATE A TO RATE S.
I WANT QUINX SQUAD TO TAKE THE NUT-CRACKER OUT.
INVESTI-GATOR OSHIBA...
I'M SENDING ATO SQUAD TOO.
ROGER.
SIR.
YEAH?
ENGAGING A RATE S GHOUL COMES WITH RISKS...
Here. Your Quinque.
IN MY OPINION, INVESTIGATOR MUTSUKI IS INJURED AND EXHAUSTED.
I DON'T THINK HE CAN CONTINUE.
REQUESTING PERMISSION TO SEND HIM OUT.
GRANTED...
SEND SOMEBODY WITH HIM FOR SECURITY. I'M THINKING URIE.
Y-YES, SIR.
HE'S RIGHT. IN THESE CIRCUM-STANCES, THERE'S NOBODY BUT URIE WHO CAN...

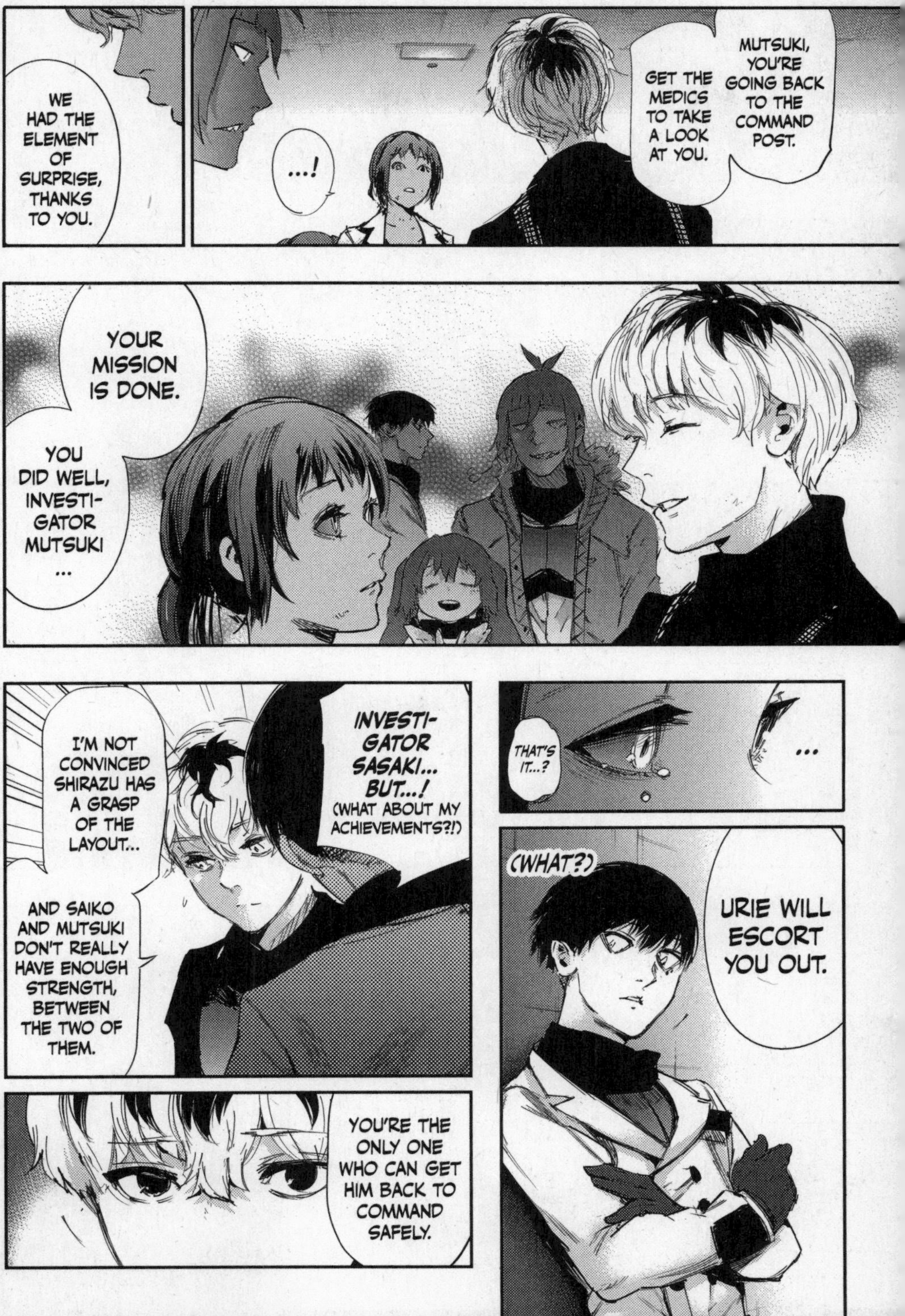
MUTSUKI, YOU'RE GOING BACK TO THE COMMAND POST.
GET THE MEDICS TO TAKE A LOOK AT YOU.
...!
WE HAD THE ELEMENT OF SURPRISE, THANKS TO YOU.
YOUR MISSION IS DONE.
YOU DID WELL, INVESTI-GATOR MUTSUKI ...
...
THAT'S IT...?
(WHAT?)
URIE WILL ESCORT YOU OUT.
INVESTI-GATOR SASAKI... BUT...!
(WHAT ABOUT MY ACHIEVEMENTS?!)
I'M NOT CONVINCED SHIRAZU HAS A GRASP OF THE LAYOUT...
AND SAIKO AND MUTSUKI DON'T REALLY HAVE ENOUGH STRENGTH, BETWEEN THE TWO OF THEM.
YOU'RE THE ONLY ONE WHO CAN GET HIM BACK TO COMMAND SAFELY.

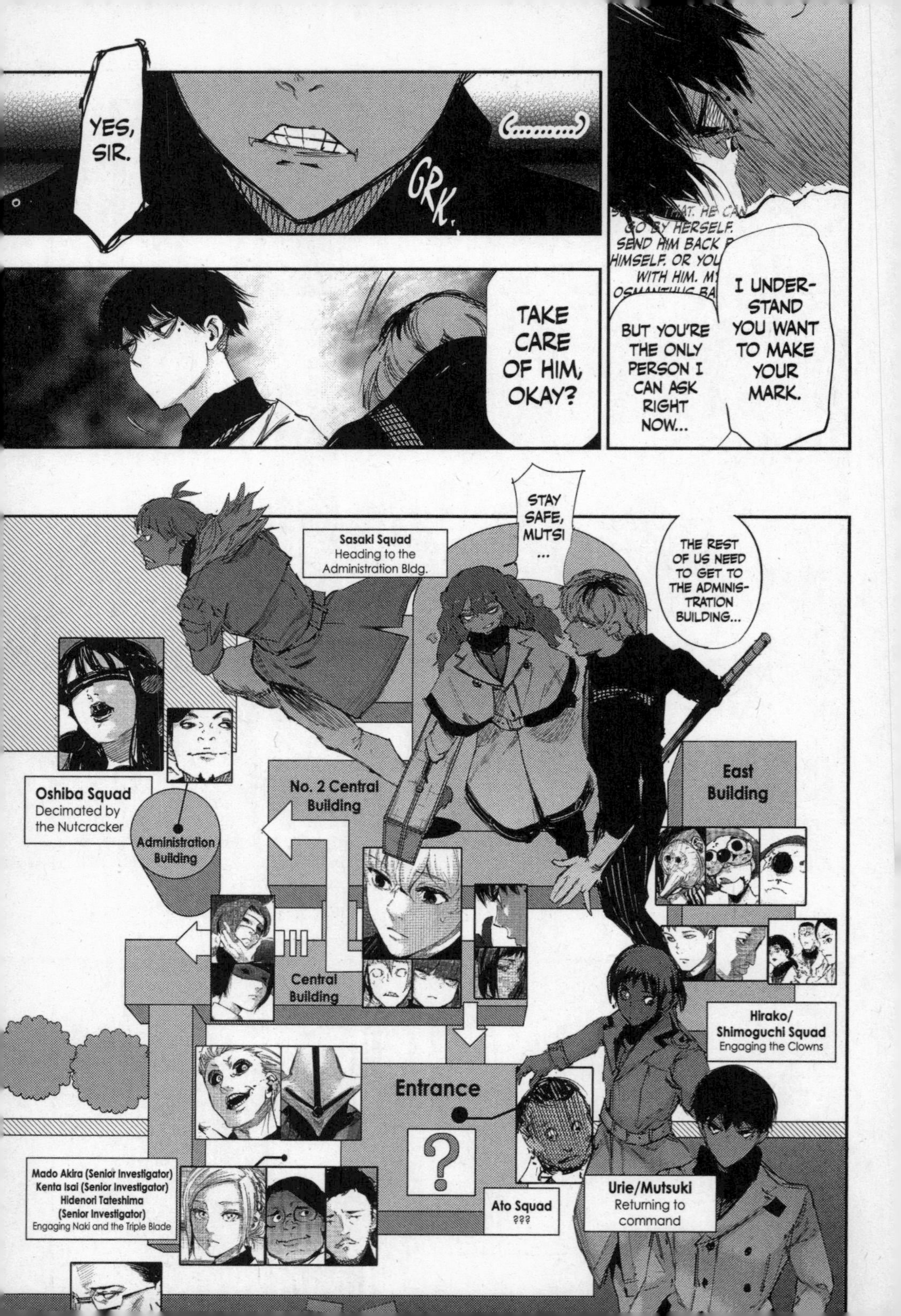

AT. HE CA
GO BY HERSELF.
SEND HIM BACK
HIMSELF. OR YOU
WITH HIM.
I UNDERSTAND YOU WANT TO MAKE YOUR MARK.
BUT YOU'RE THE ONLY PERSON I CAN ASK RIGHT NOW...
(........)
YES, SIR.
GRK.
TAKE CARE OF HIM, OKAY?
STAY SAFE, MUTSI ...
THE REST OF US NEED TO GET TO THE ADMINISTRATION BUILDING...
Sasaki Squad
Heading to the Administration Bldg.
East Building
No. 2 Central Building
Oshiba Squad
Decimated by the Nutcracker
Administration Building
Central Building
Hirako/ Shimoguchi Squad
Engaging the Clowns
Entrance
?
Mado Akira (Senior Investigator)
Kenta Isai (Senior Investigator)
Hidenori Tateshima (Senior Investigator)
Engaging Naki and the Triple Blade
Ato Squad
???
Urie/Mutsuki
Returning to command

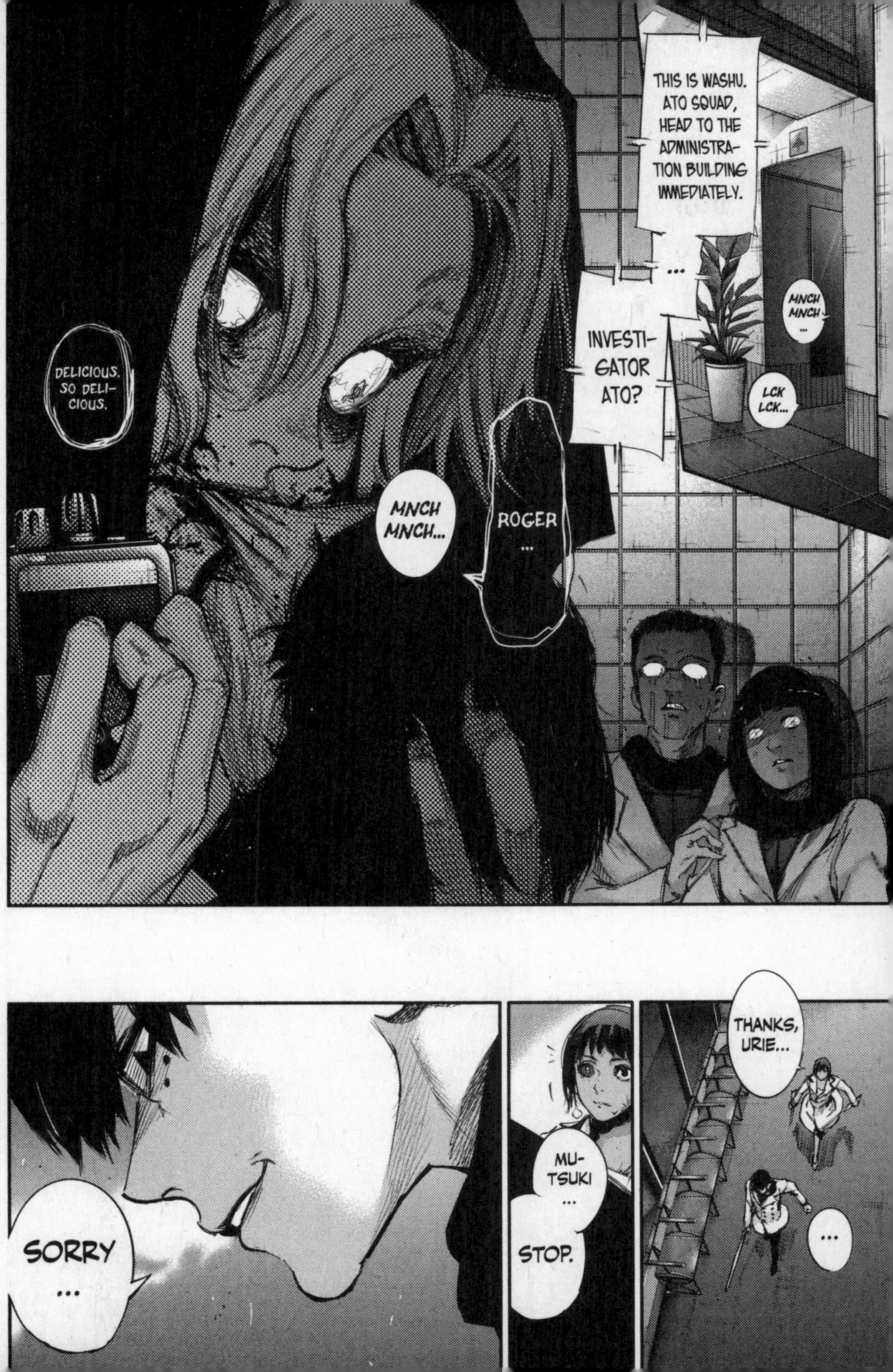
THIS IS WASHU. ATO SQUAD, HEAD TO THE ADMINISTRATION BUILDING IMMEDIATELY.
MNCH MNCH...
LCK LCK...
...
INVESTIGATOR ATO?
ROGER...
MNCH MNCH...
DELICIOUS. SO DELICIOUS.
THANKS, URIE...
...
MUTSUKI...
STOP.
SORRY...

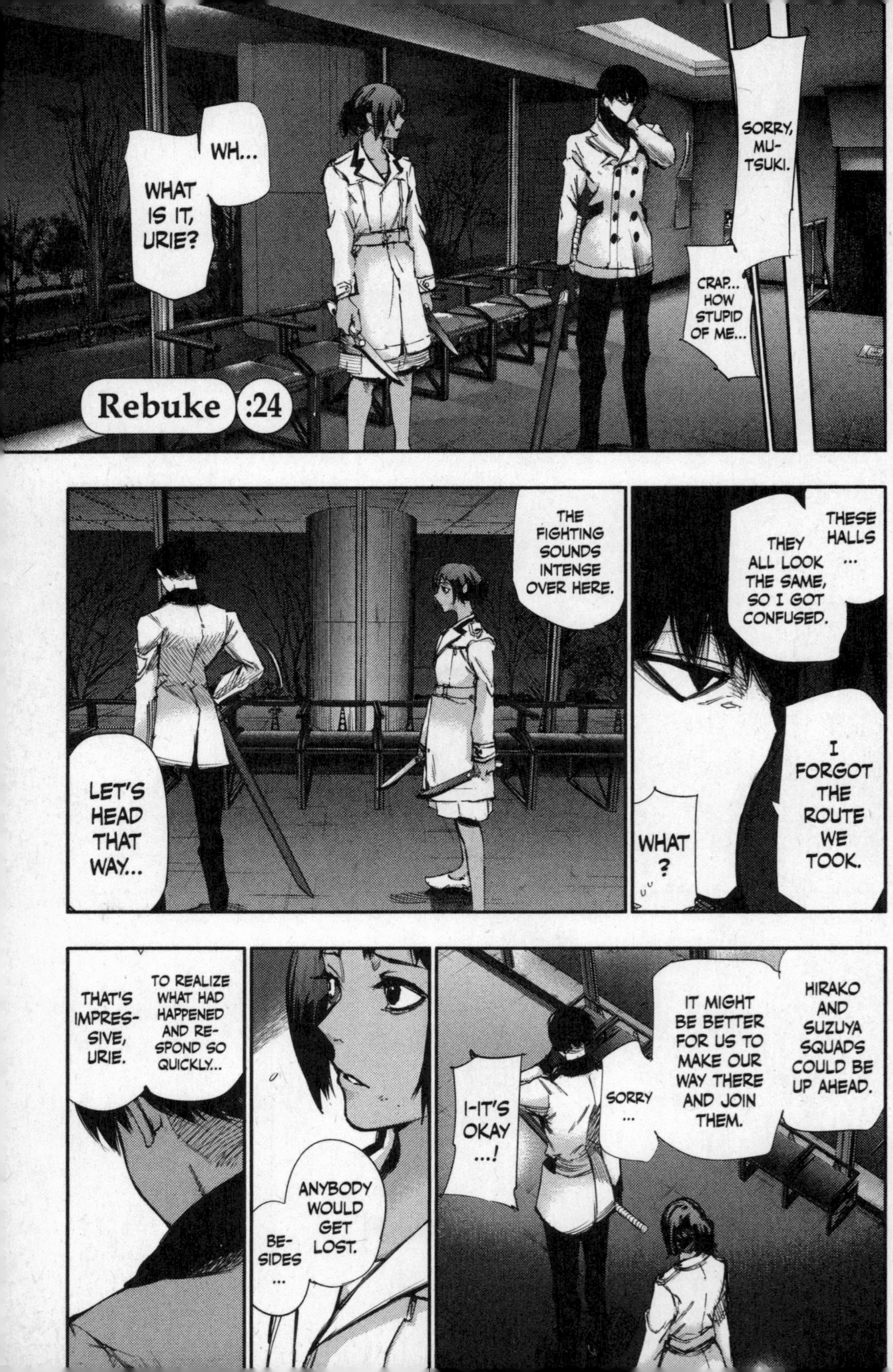
SORRY, MUTSUKI.
CRAP... HOW STUPID OF ME...
WH...
WHAT IS IT, URIE?
Rebuke :24
THESE HALLS ...
THEY ALL LOOK THE SAME, SO I GOT CONFUSED.
I FORGOT THE ROUTE WE TOOK.
WHAT ?
THE FIGHTING SOUNDS INTENSE OVER HERE.
LET'S HEAD THAT WAY...
HIRAKO AND SUZUYA SQUADS COULD BE UP AHEAD.
IT MIGHT BE BETTER FOR US TO MAKE OUR WAY THERE AND JOIN THEM.
SORRY ...
I-IT'S OKAY ...!
ANYBODY WOULD GET LOST.
BESIDES ...
TO REALIZE WHAT HAD HAPPENED AND RESPOND SO QUICKLY...
THAT'S IMPRESSIVE, URIE.

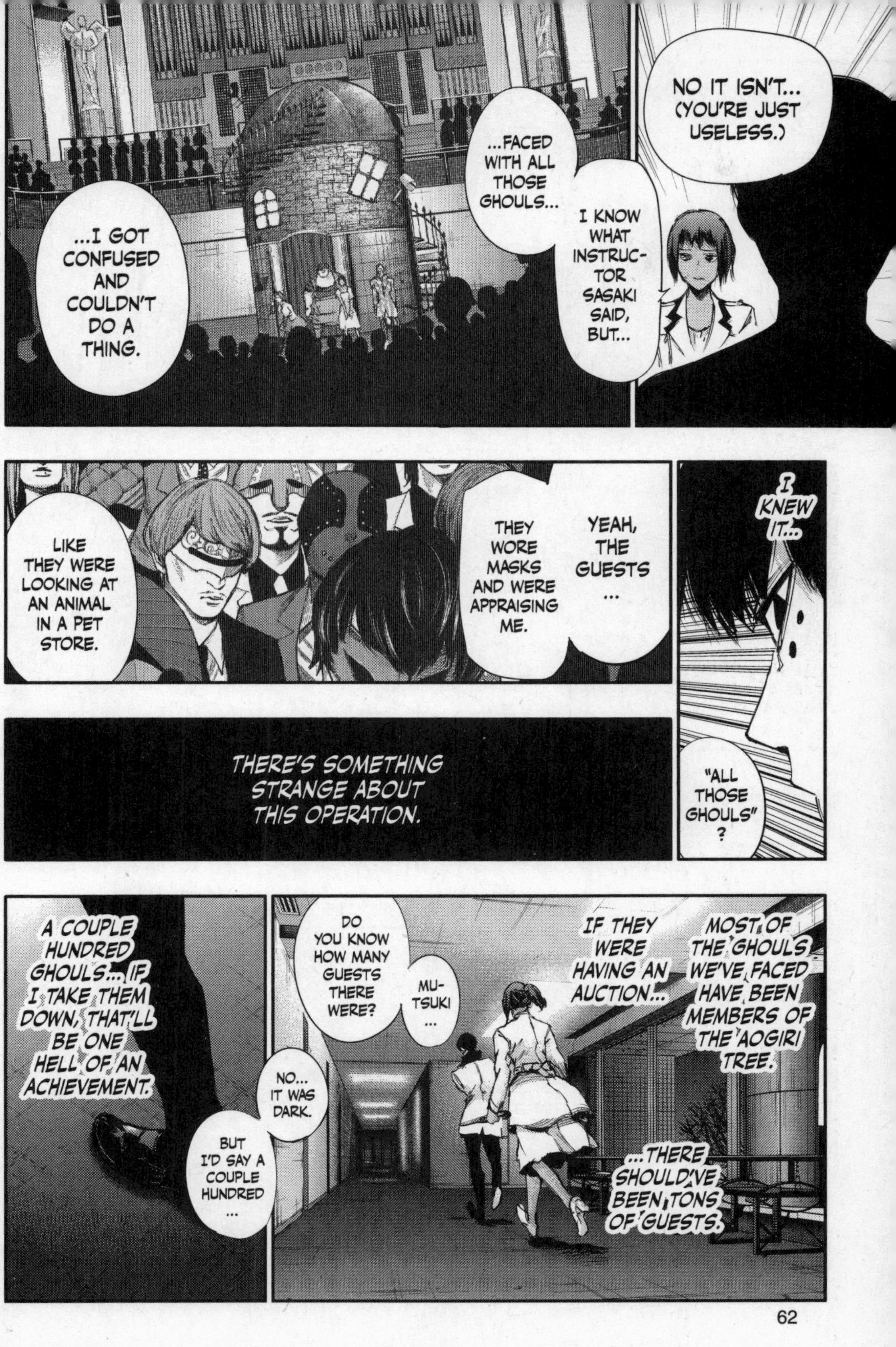
NO IT ISN'T... (YOU'RE JUST USELESS.)
I KNOW WHAT INSTRUCTOR SASAKI SAID, BUT...
...FACED WITH ALL THOSE GHOULS...
...I GOT CONFUSED AND COULDN'T DO A THING.
I KNEW IT...
"ALL THOSE GHOULS"?
YEAH, THE GUESTS ...
THEY WORE MASKS AND WERE APPRAISING ME.
LIKE THEY WERE LOOKING AT AN ANIMAL IN A PET STORE.
THERE'S SOMETHING STRANGE ABOUT THIS OPERATION.
MOST OF THE GHOULS WE'VE FACED HAVE BEEN MEMBERS OF THE AOGIRI TREE.
IF THEY WERE HAVING AN AUCTION...
MU-TSUKI ...
DO YOU KNOW HOW MANY GUESTS THERE WERE?
NO... IT WAS DARK.
BUT I'D SAY A COUPLE HUNDRED ...
...THERE SHOULD'VE BEEN TONS OF GUESTS.
A COUPLE HUNDRED GHOULS... IF I TAKE THEM DOWN, THAT'LL BE ONE HELL OF AN ACHIEVEMENT.

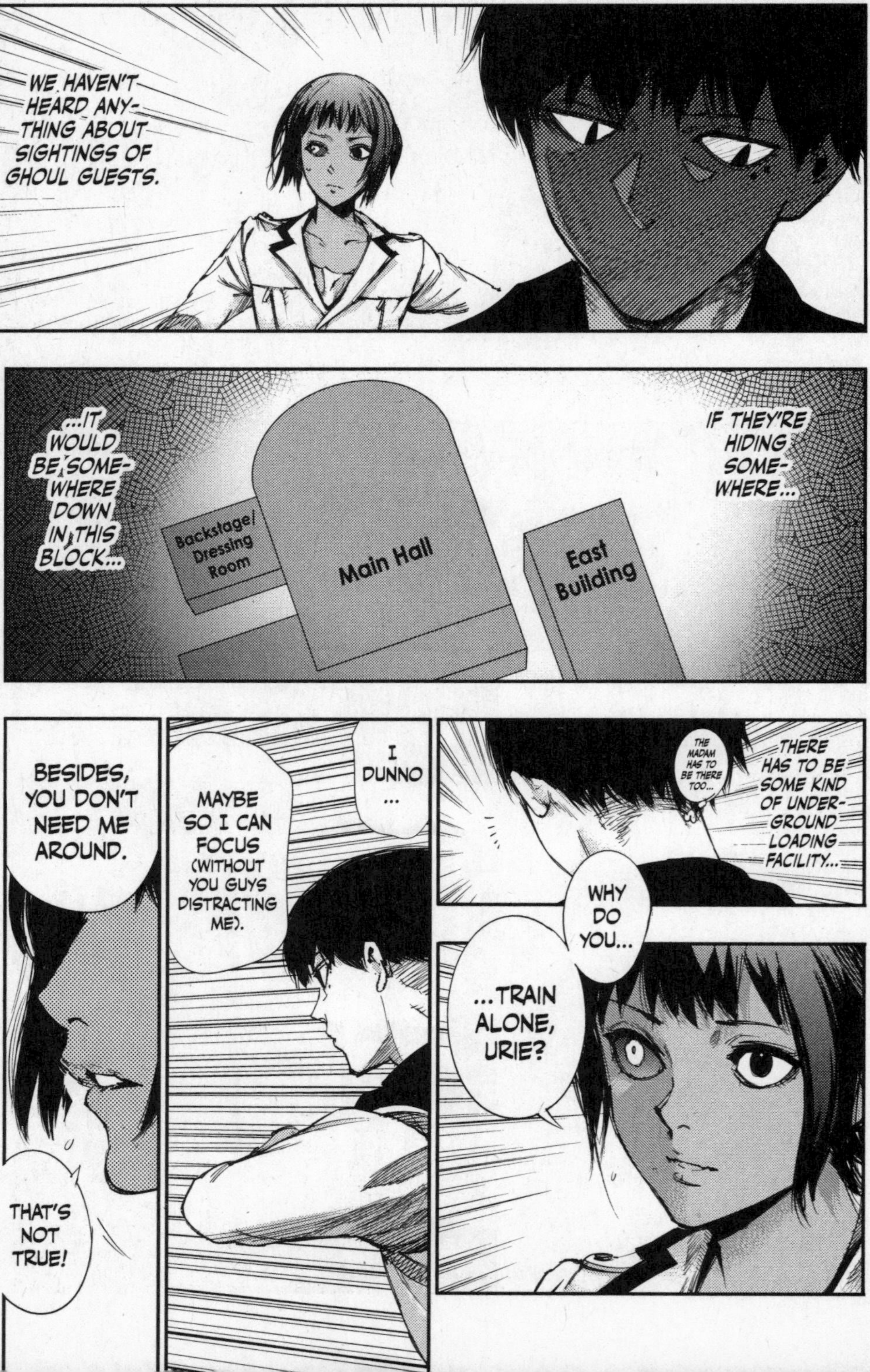
WE HAVEN'T HEARD ANYTHING ABOUT SIGHTINGS OF GHOUL GUESTS.
IF THEY'RE HIDING SOMEWHERE...
...IT WOULD BE SOMEWHERE DOWN IN THIS BLOCK...
East Building
Main Hall
Backstage/ Dressing Room
THERE HAS TO BE SOME KIND OF UNDERGROUND LOADING FACILITY...
THE MADAM HAS TO BE THERE TOO...
WHY DO YOU...
...TRAIN ALONE, URIE?
I DUNNO...
MAYBE SO I CAN FOCUS (WITHOUT YOU GUYS DISTRACTING ME).
BESIDES, YOU DON'T NEED ME AROUND.
THAT'S NOT TRUE!

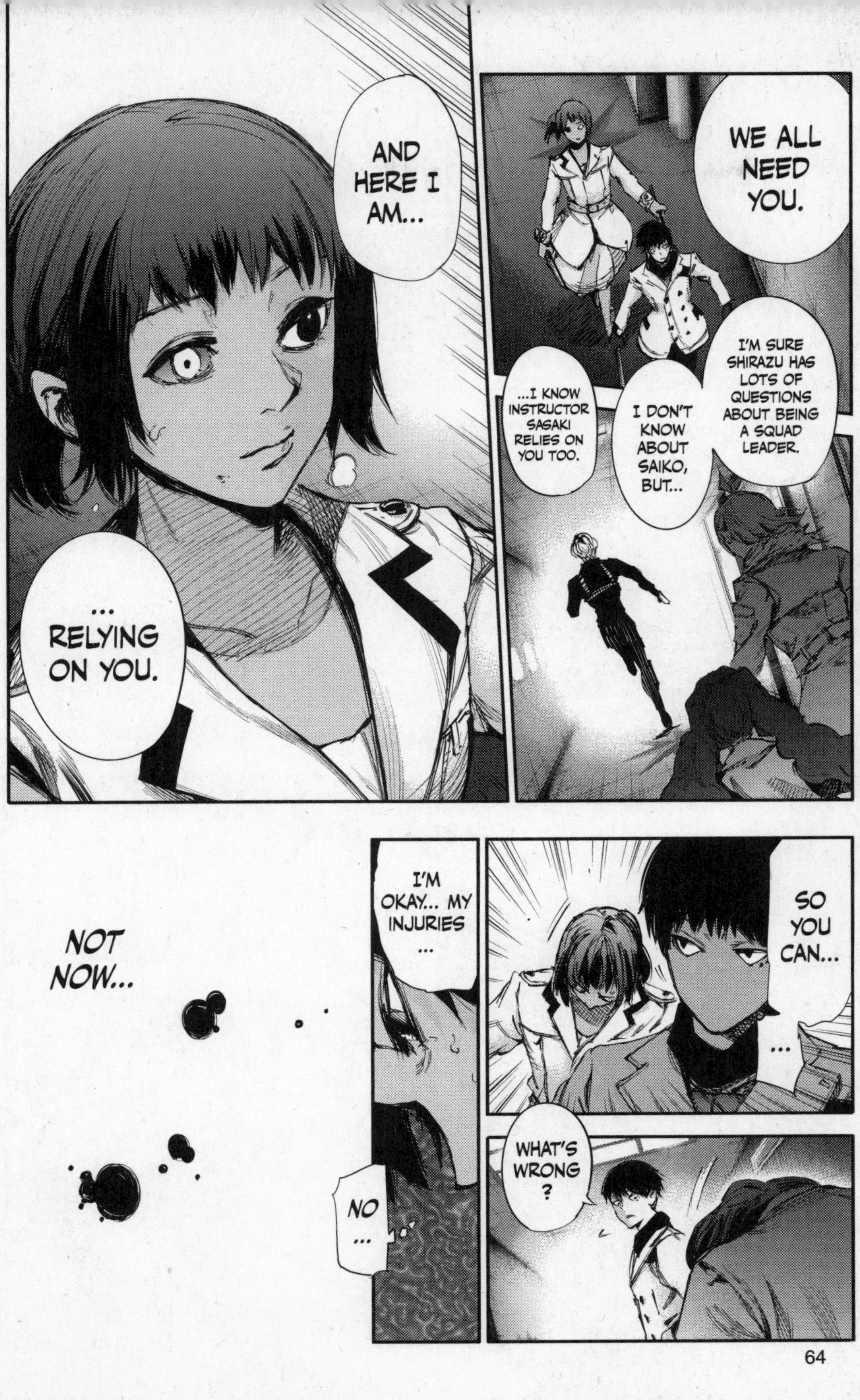
WE ALL NEED YOU.
I'M SURE SHIRAZU HAS LOTS OF QUESTIONS ABOUT BEING A SQUAD LEADER.
I DON'T KNOW ABOUT SAIKO, BUT...
...I KNOW INSTRUCTOR SASAKI RELIES ON YOU TOO.
AND HERE I AM...
...RELYING ON YOU.
SO YOU CAN...
...
WHAT'S WRONG?
I'M OKAY... MY INJURIES...
NO...
NOT NOW...

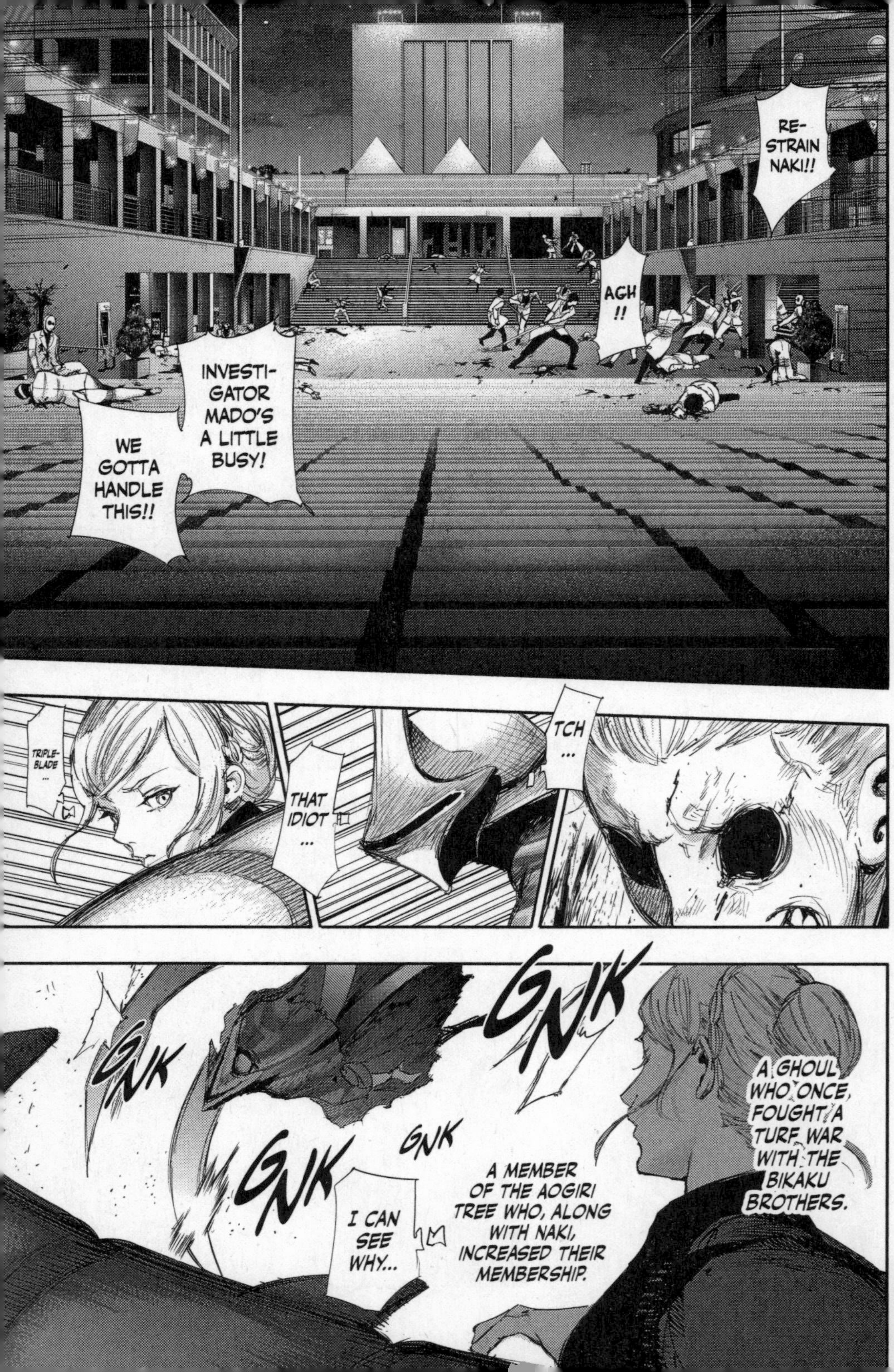
RE-
STRAIN
NAKI!!
AGH
!!
INVESTI-
GATOR
MADO'S
A LITTLE
BUSY!
WE
GOTTA
HANDLE
THIS!!
TCH
...
THAT
IDIOT
...
TRIPLE-
BLADE
...
GNK
GNK
A GHOUL WHO ONCE FOUGHT A TURF WAR WITH THE BIKAKU BROTHERS.
A MEMBER OF THE AOGIRI TREE WHO, ALONG WITH NAKI, INCREASED THEIR MEMBERSHIP.
GNK
GNK
I CAN SEE WHY...
-!!

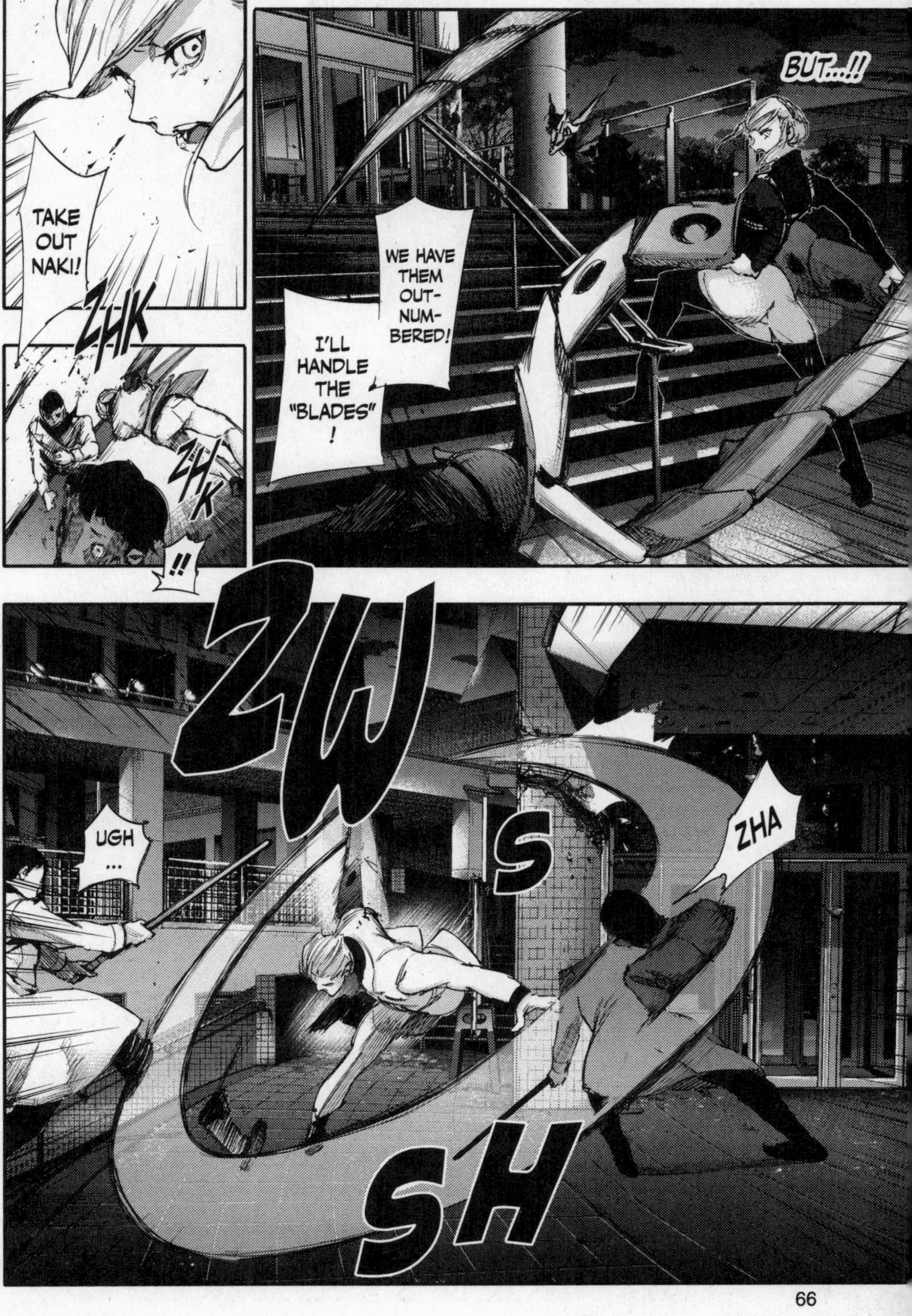
BUT...!!
WE HAVE THEM OUT-NUMBERED!
I'LL HANDLE THE "BLADES" !
TAKE OUT NAKI!
ZHK
ZHK
!!
ZHA
ZWSSH
UGH ...

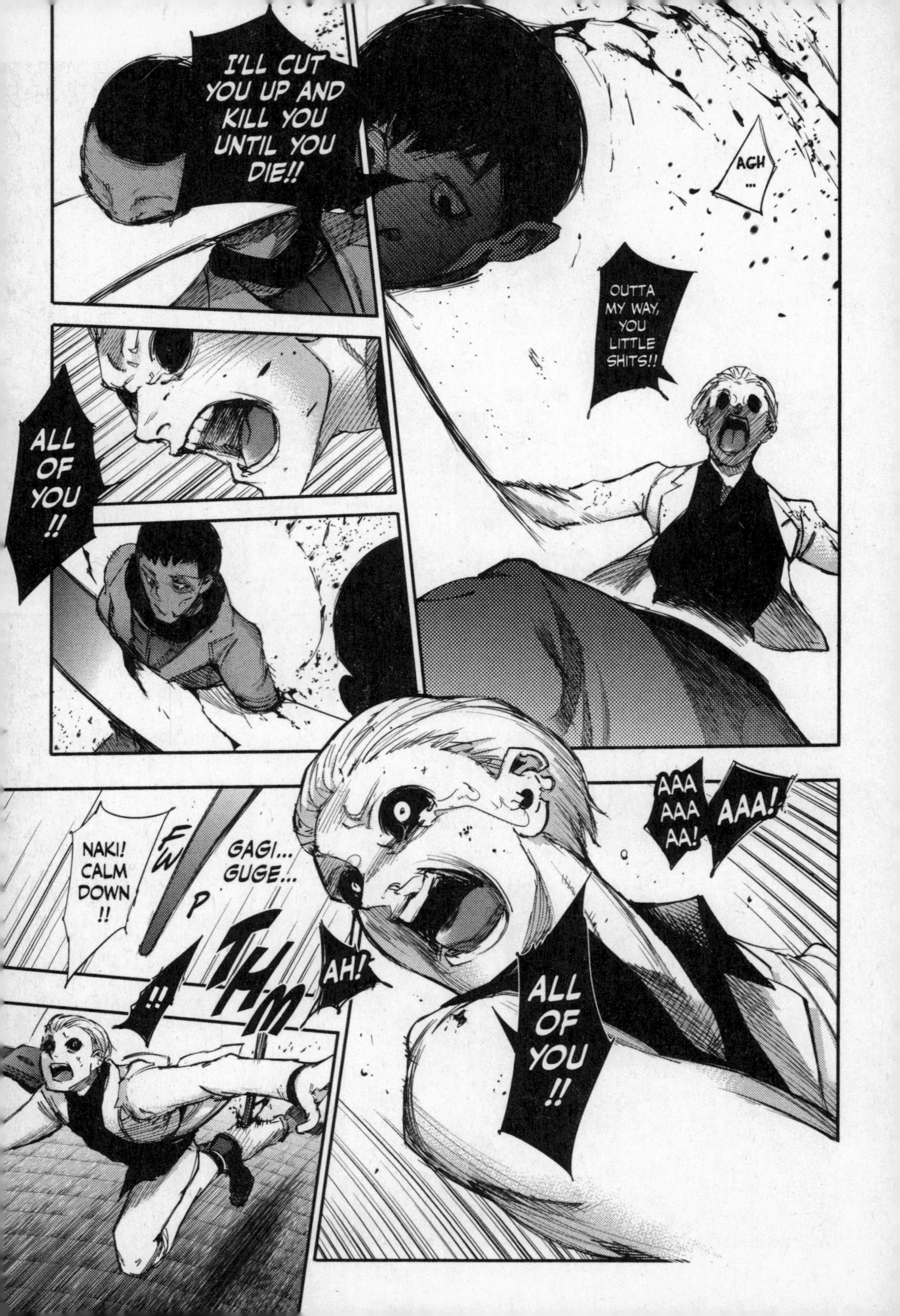
AGH ...
OUTTA MY WAY, YOU LITTLE SHITS!!
I'LL CUT YOU UP AND KILL YOU UNTIL YOU DIE!!
ALL OF YOU !!
AAA AAA AA!
AAA!
ALL OF YOU !!
AH!
THM
GAGI... GUGE...
FWP
NAKI! CALM DOWN !!
!!

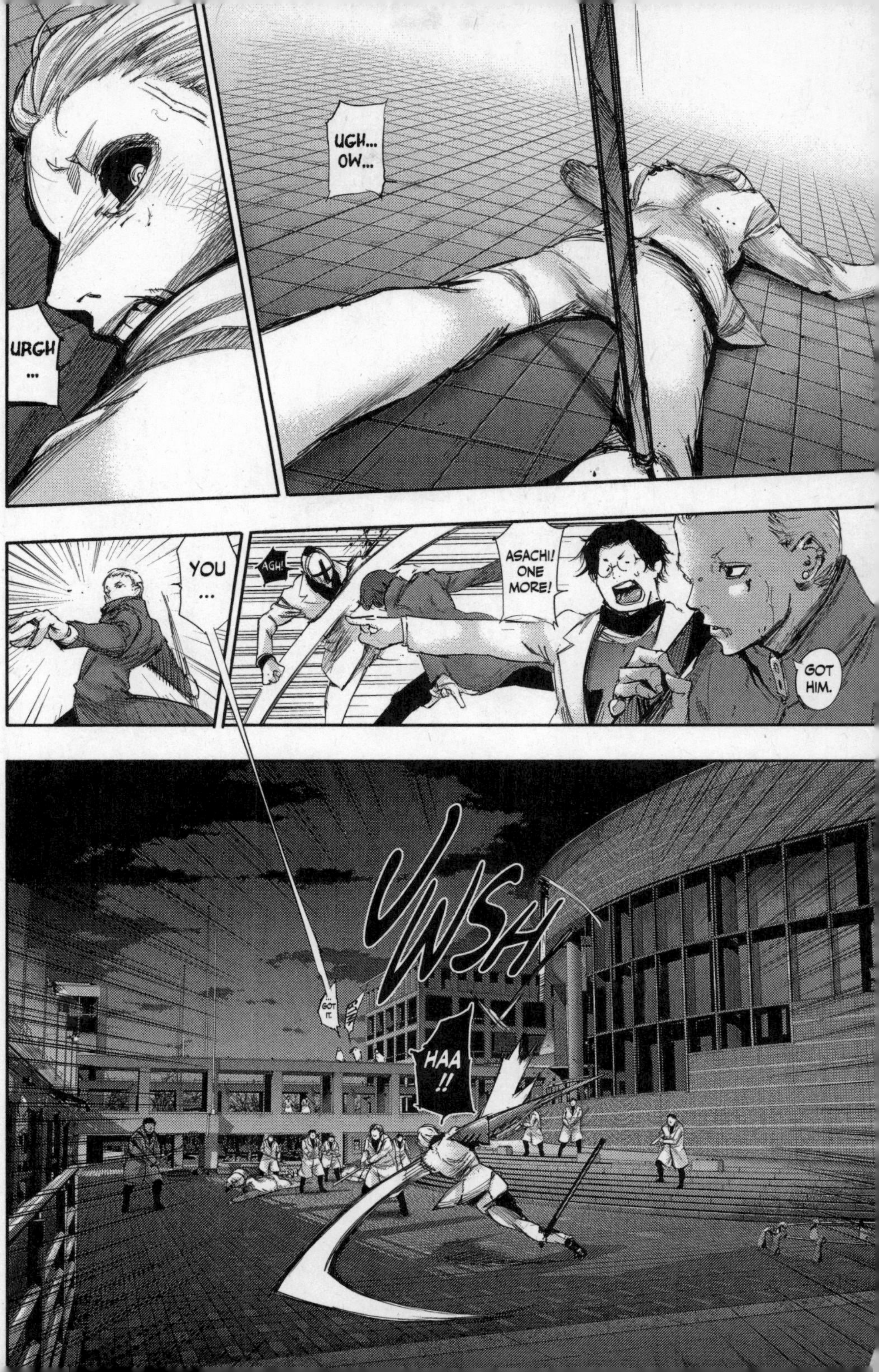
UGH... OW...
URGH ...
ASACHI! ONE MORE!
GOT HIM.
AGH!
YOU ...
VWSH
... GOT IT.
HAA !!

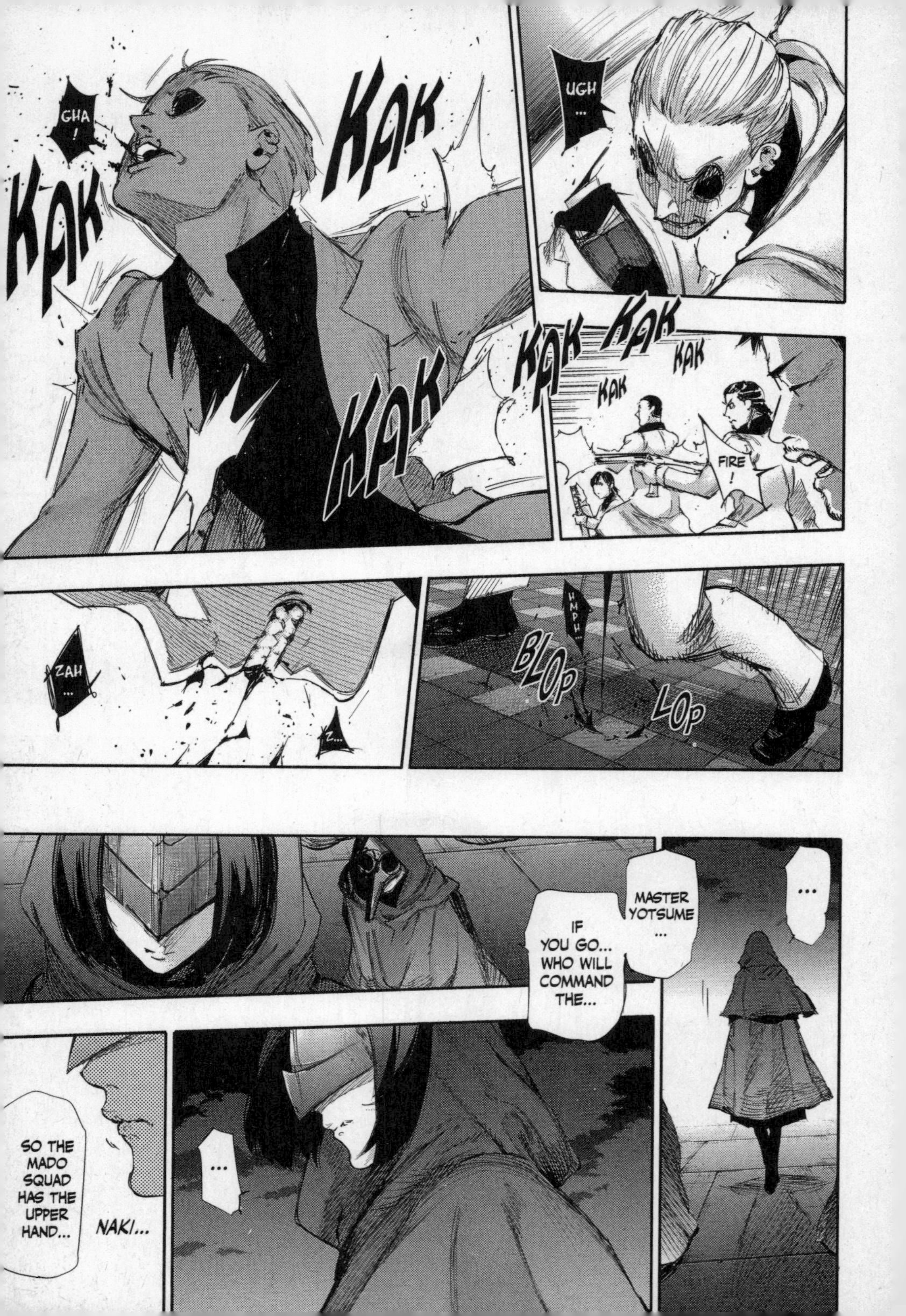
UGH ...
KAK
KAK
KAK
KAK
FIRE!
GHA!
KAK
KAK
KAK
HMPH...
BLOP
LOP
ZAH ...
Z...
...
MASTER YOTSUME ...
IF YOU GO... WHO WILL COMMAND THE...
...
SO THE MADO SQUAD HAS THE UPPER HAND...
NAKI...

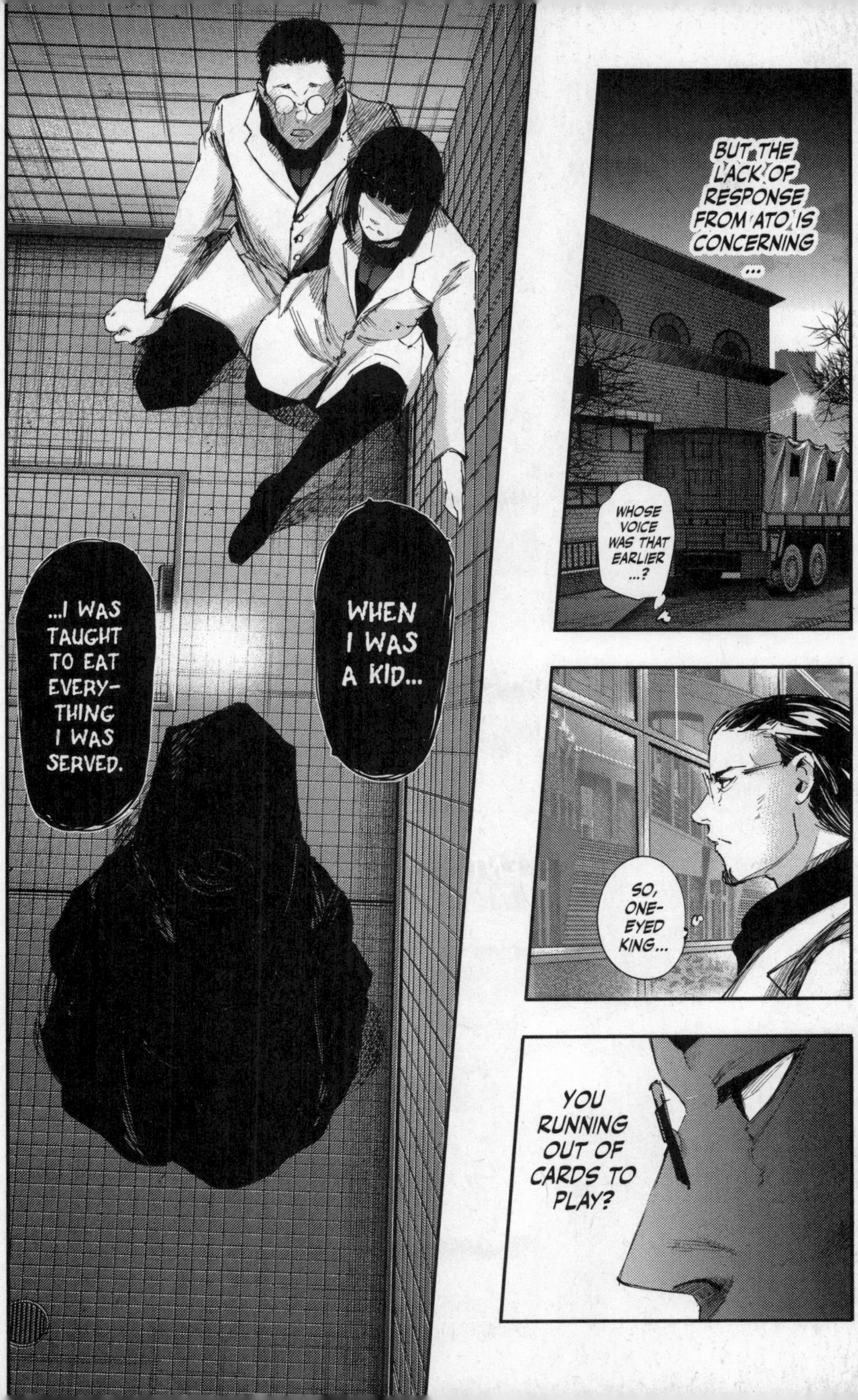
BUT THE LACK OF RESPONSE FROM ATO IS CONCERNING ...
WHOSE VOICE WAS THAT EARLIER ...?
SO, ONE-EYED KING...
YOU RUNNING OUT OF CARDS TO PLAY?
WHEN I WAS A KID...
...I WAS TAUGHT TO EAT EVERY-THING I WAS SERVED.

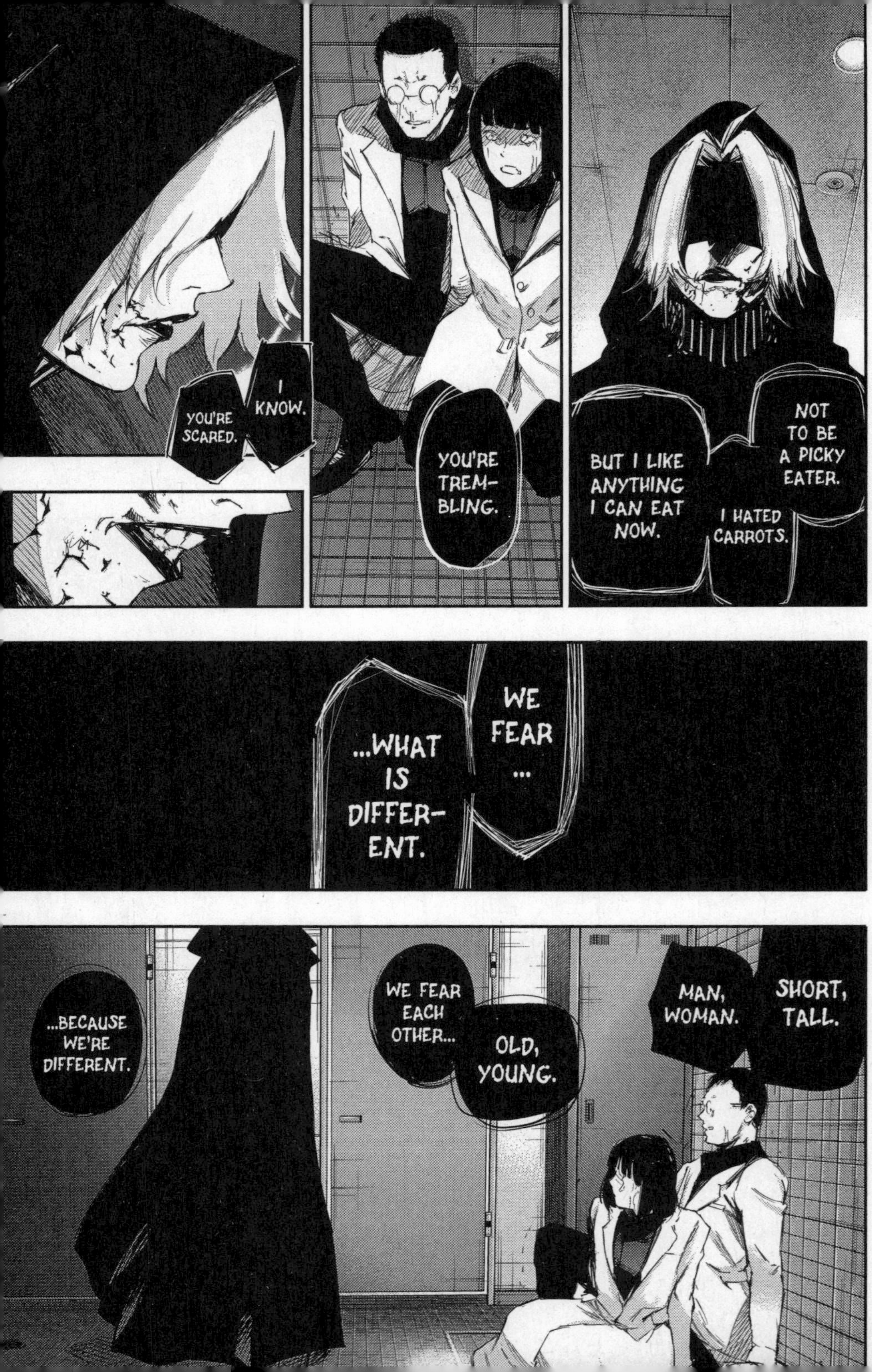
NOT TO BE A PICKY EATER.
I HATED CARROTS.
BUT I LIKE ANYTHING I CAN EAT NOW.
YOU'RE TREM-BLING.
I KNOW.
YOU'RE SCARED.
WE FEAR...
...WHAT IS DIFFER-ENT.
SHORT, TALL.
MAN, WOMAN.
OLD, YOUNG.
WE FEAR EACH OTHER...
...BECAUSE WE'RE DIFFERENT.

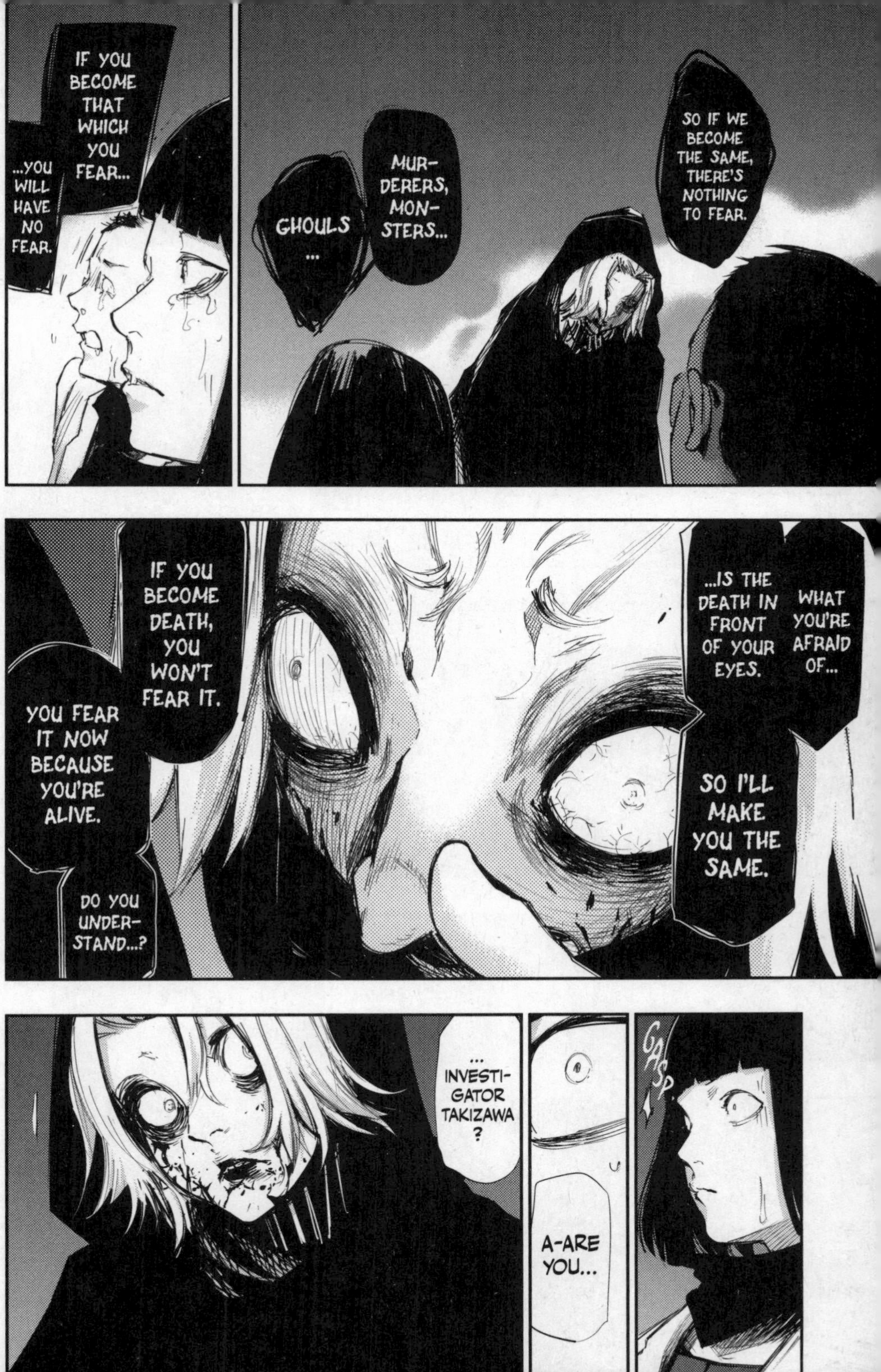
SO IF WE BECOME THE SAME, THERE'S NOTHING TO FEAR.
MURDERERS, MONSTERS...
GHOULS ...
IF YOU BECOME THAT WHICH YOU FEAR...
...YOU WILL HAVE NO FEAR.
WHAT YOU'RE AFRAID OF...
...IS THE DEATH IN FRONT OF YOUR EYES.
SO I'LL MAKE YOU THE SAME.
IF YOU BECOME DEATH, YOU WON'T FEAR IT.
YOU FEAR IT NOW BECAUSE YOU'RE ALIVE.
DO YOU UNDERSTAND...?
GASP
... INVESTIGATOR TAKIZAWA ?
A-ARE YOU...

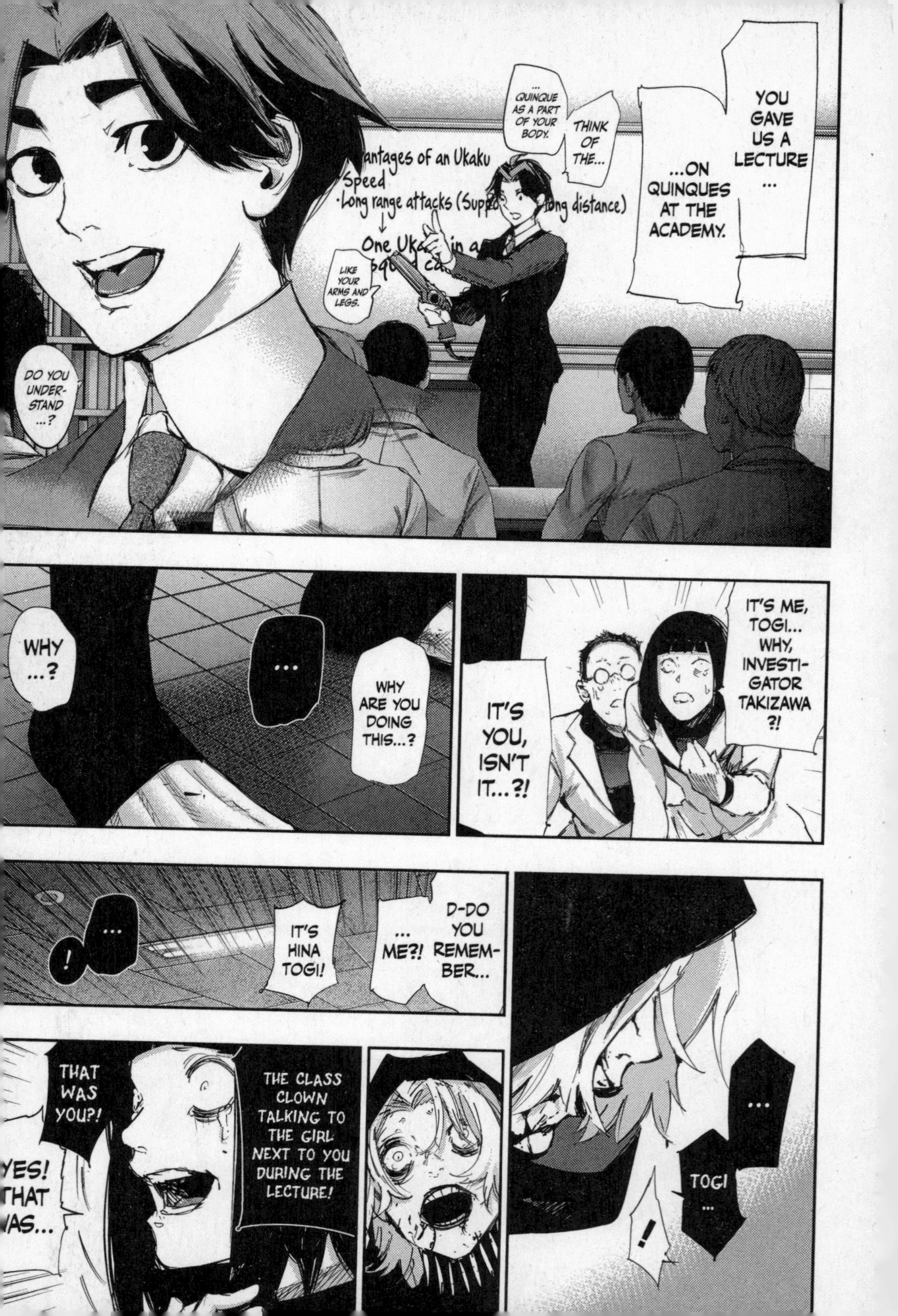
YOU GAVE US A LECTURE ...
...ON QUINQUES AT THE ACADEMY.
THINK OF THE...
... QUINQUE AS A PART OF YOUR BODY.
antages of an Ukaku
·Speed
·Long range attacks (Suppo ong distance)
LIKE YOUR ARMS AND LEGS.
DO YOU UNDER-STAND ...?
IT'S ME, TOGI... WHY, INVESTI-GATOR TAKIZAWA ?!
IT'S YOU, ISN'T IT...?!
WHY ARE YOU DOING THIS...?
...
WHY ...?
...
TOGI ...
!
D-DO YOU REMEM-BER...
... ME?!
IT'S HINA TOGI!
...
!
THE CLASS CLOWN TALKING TO THE GIRL NEXT TO YOU DURING THE LECTURE!
THAT WAS YOU?!
YES! THAT WAS...

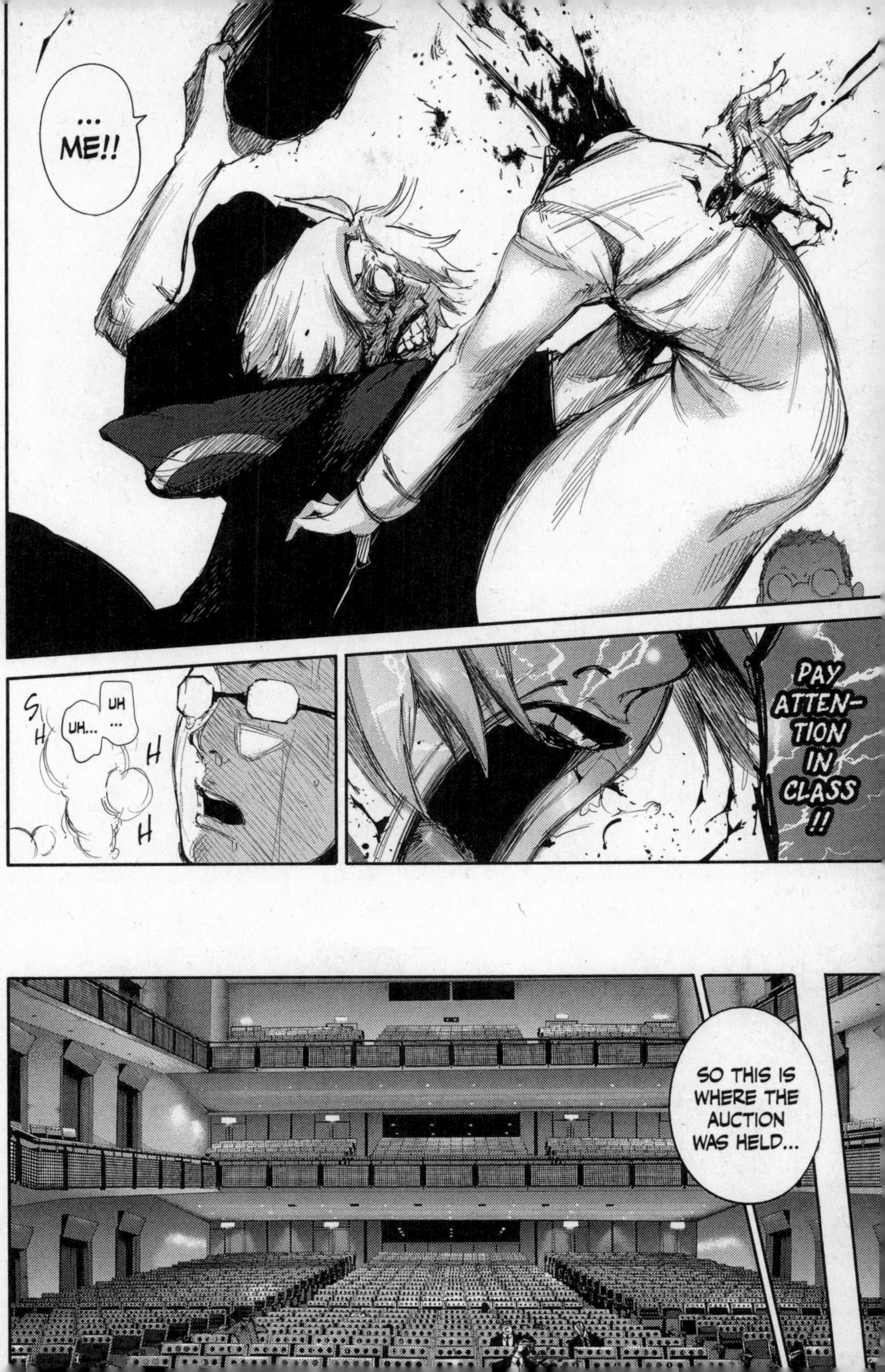
... ME!!
PAY ATTEN-TION IN CLASS!!
UH ...
UH...
SHHH
SO THIS IS WHERE THE AUCTION WAS HELD...

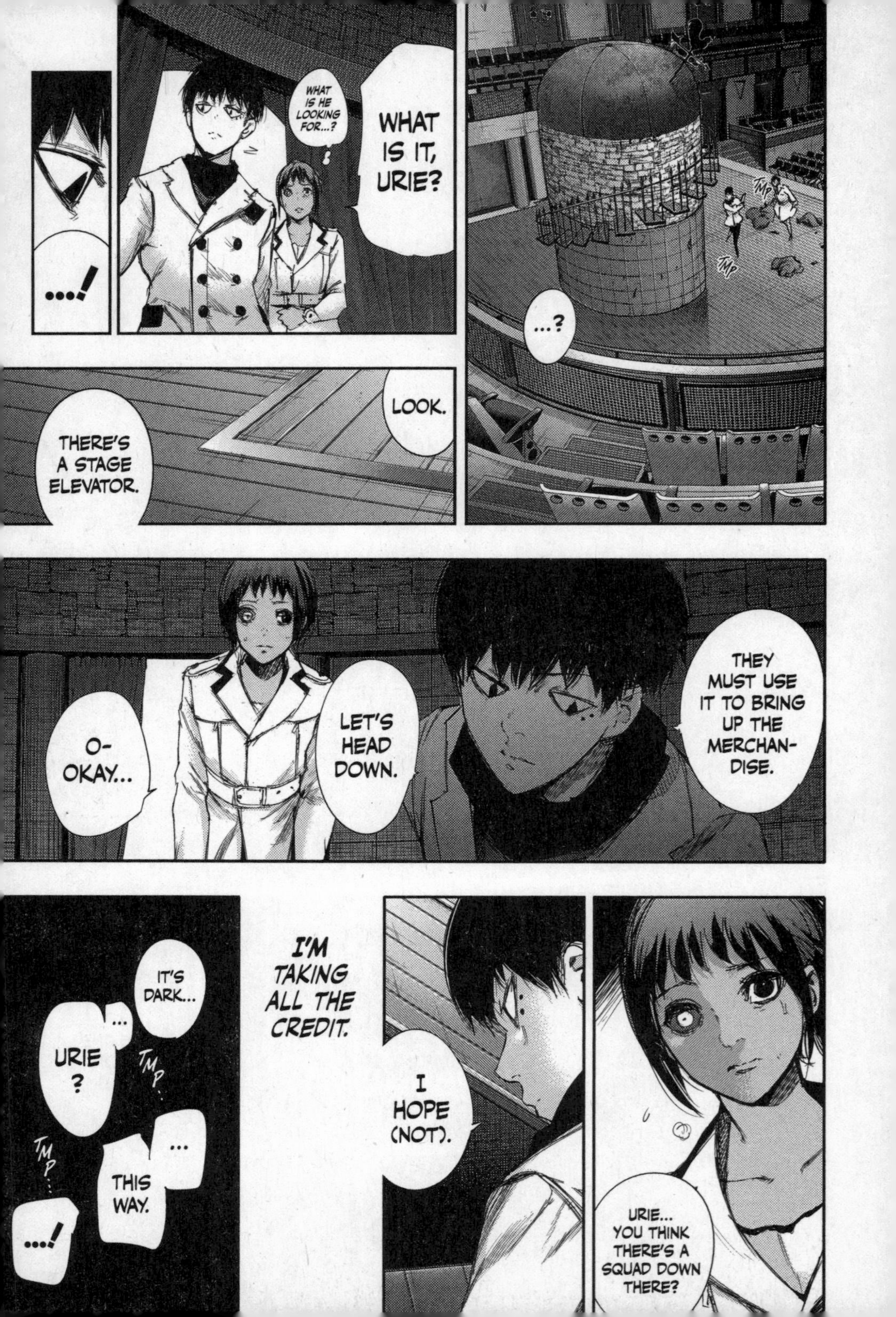
TMP
TMP
...?
WHAT IS IT, URIE?
WHAT IS HE LOOKING FOR...?
...!
LOOK.
THERE'S A STAGE ELEVATOR.
THEY MUST USE IT TO BRING UP THE MERCHAN-DISE.
LET'S HEAD DOWN.
O-OKAY...
URIE... YOU THINK THERE'S A SQUAD DOWN THERE?
I HOPE (NOT).
I'M TAKING ALL THE CREDIT.
IT'S DARK...
...
URIE ?
TMP...
...
THIS WAY.
TMP...
...!

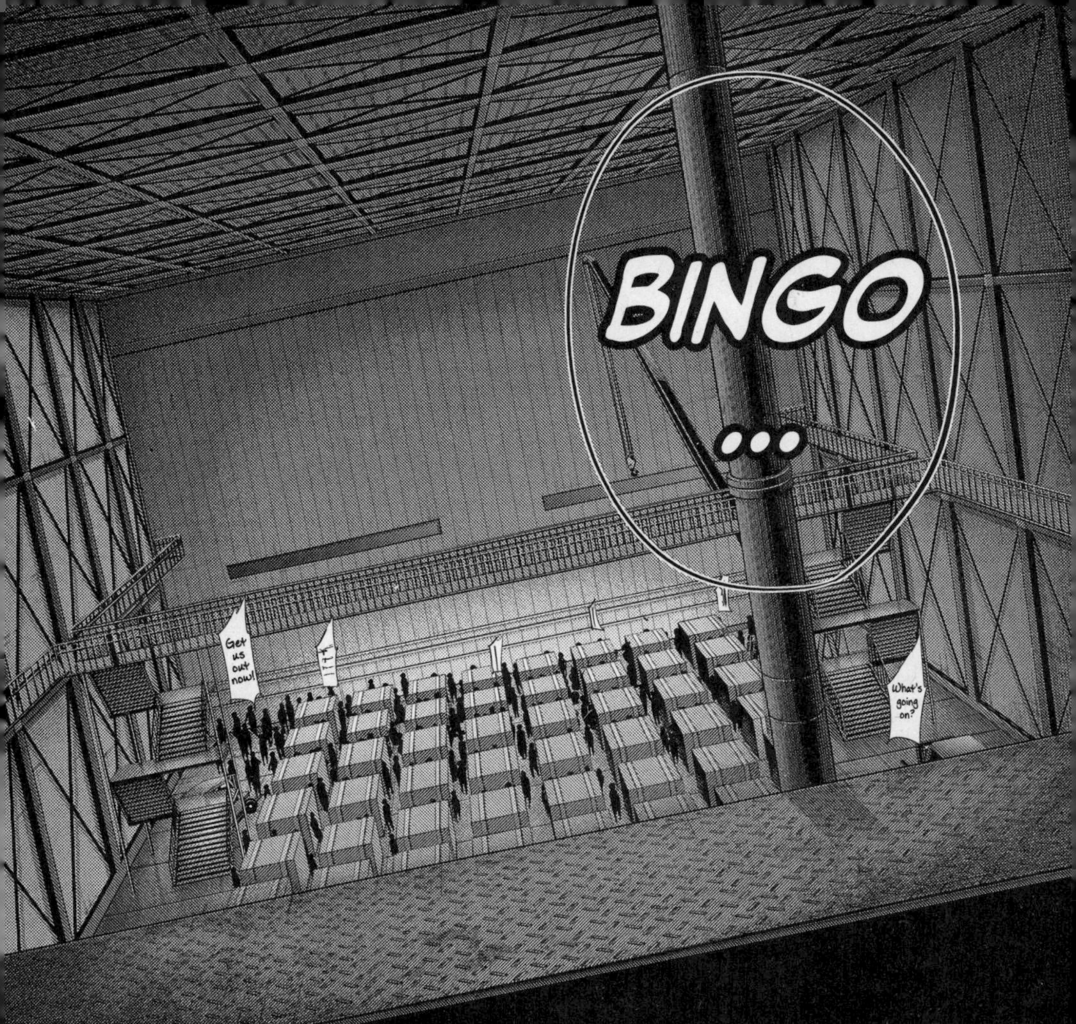
BINGO
...
What's going on?
Get us out now!
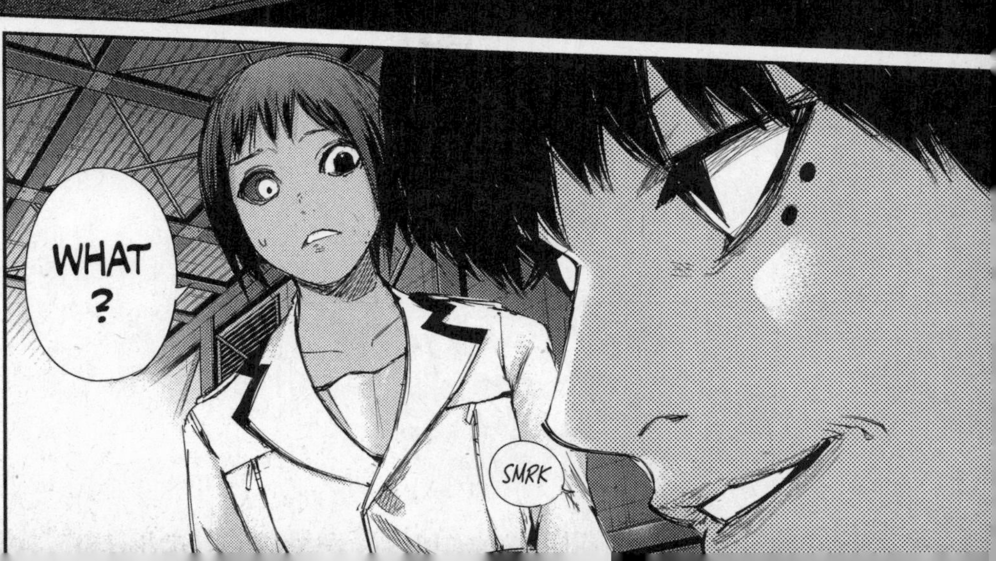
SMRK
WHAT
?

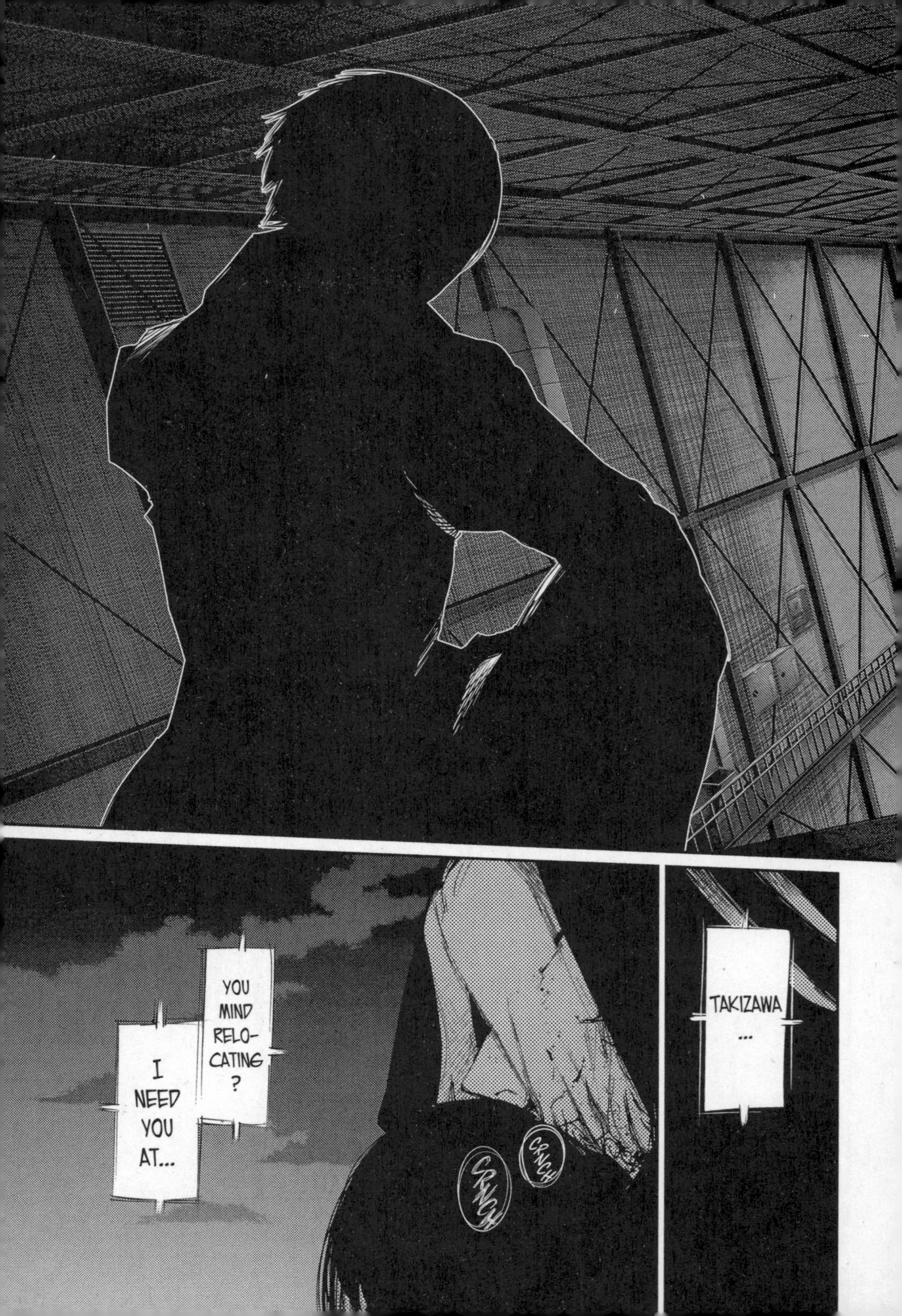
TAKIZAWA ...
YOU MIND RELO-CATING?
I NEED YOU AT...
CRNCH
CRNCH

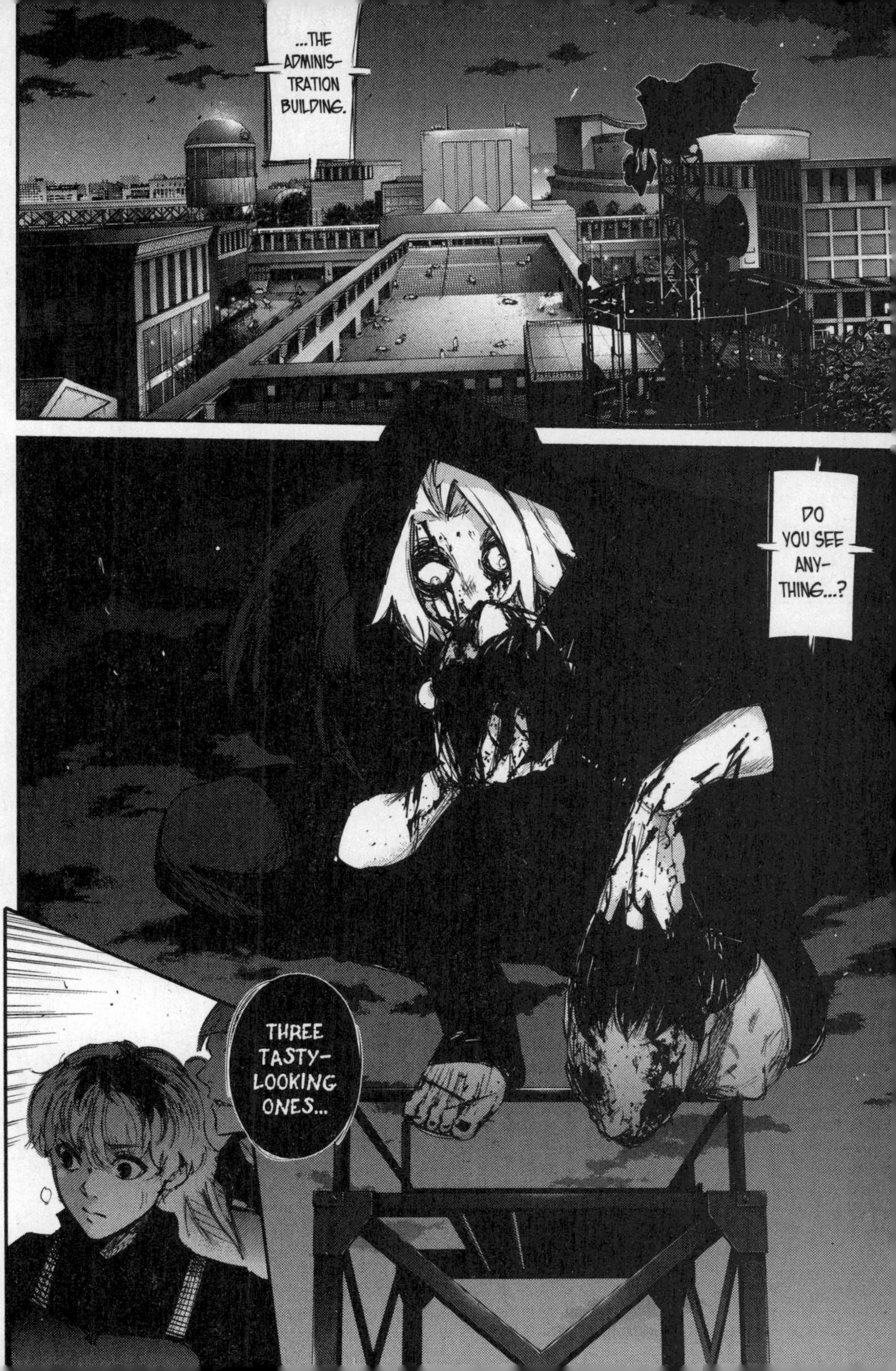
...THE ADMINIS-TRATION BUILDING.
DO YOU SEE ANY-THING...?
THREE TASTY-LOOKING ONES...

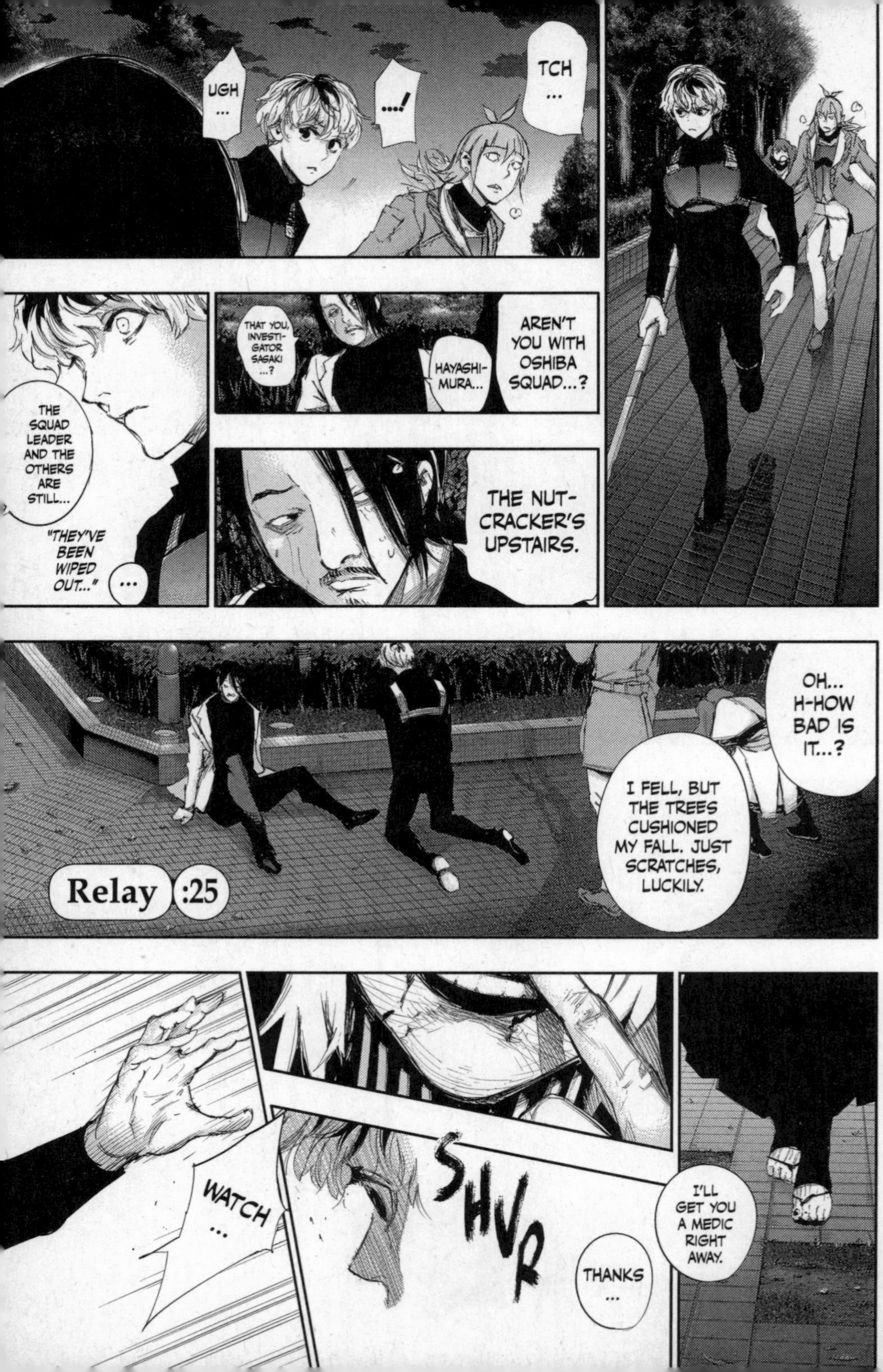
TCH ...
...!
UGH ...
AREN'T YOU WITH OSHIBA SQUAD...?
HAYASHIMURA...
THAT YOU, INVESTIGATOR SAGAKI ...?
THE NUTCRACKER'S UPSTAIRS.
THE SQUAD LEADER AND THE OTHERS ARE STILL...
"THEY'VE BEEN WIPED OUT..."
...
OH... H-HOW BAD IS IT...?
I FELL, BUT THE TREES CUSHIONED MY FALL. JUST SCRATCHES, LUCKILY.
Relay :25
I'LL GET YOU A MEDIC RIGHT AWAY.
THANKS ...
SHVR
WATCH ...

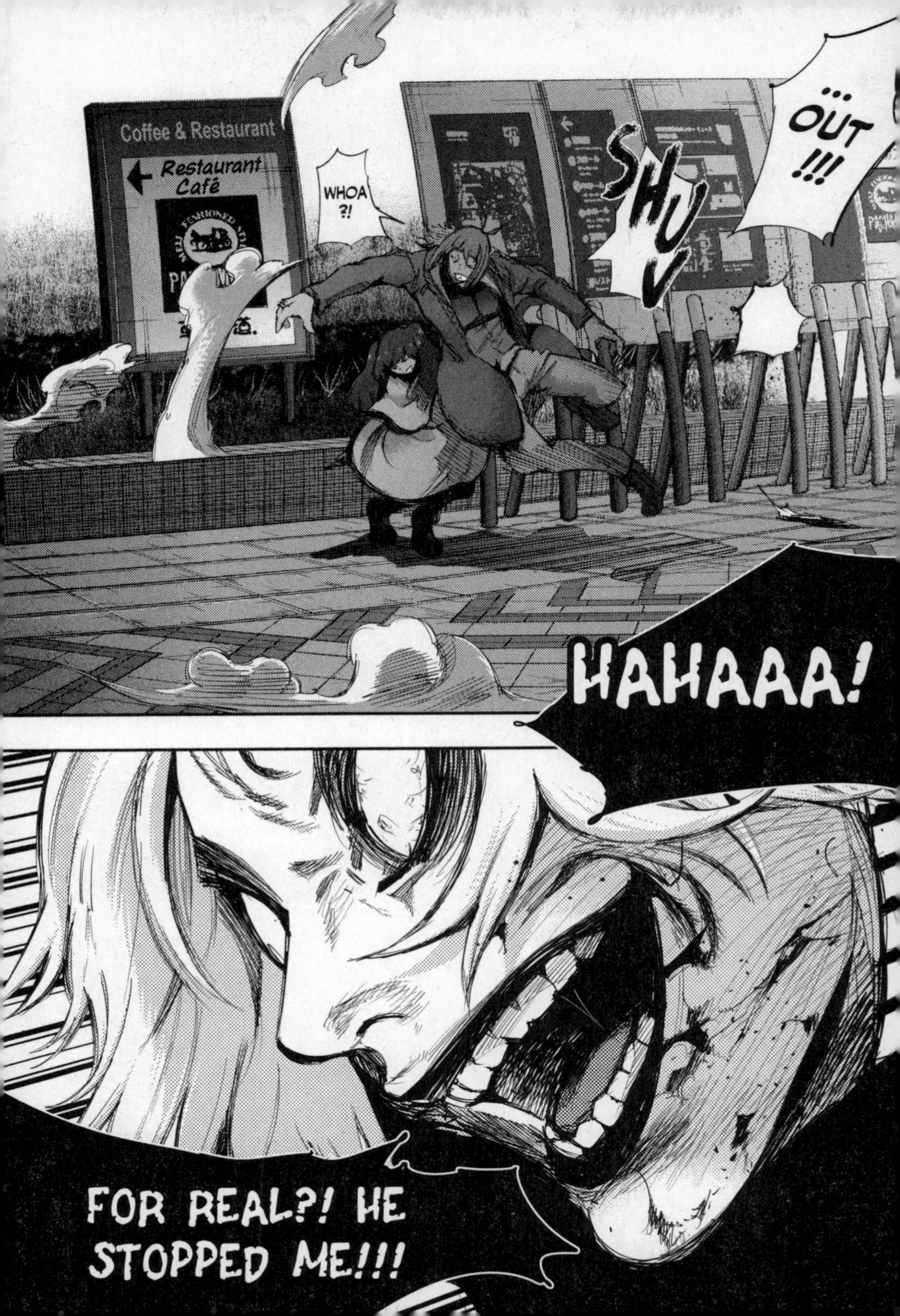

...OUT!!!
SHUV
WHOA ?!
Coffee & Restaurant
Restaurant Café
HAHAAA!
FOR REAL?! HE STOPPED ME!!!

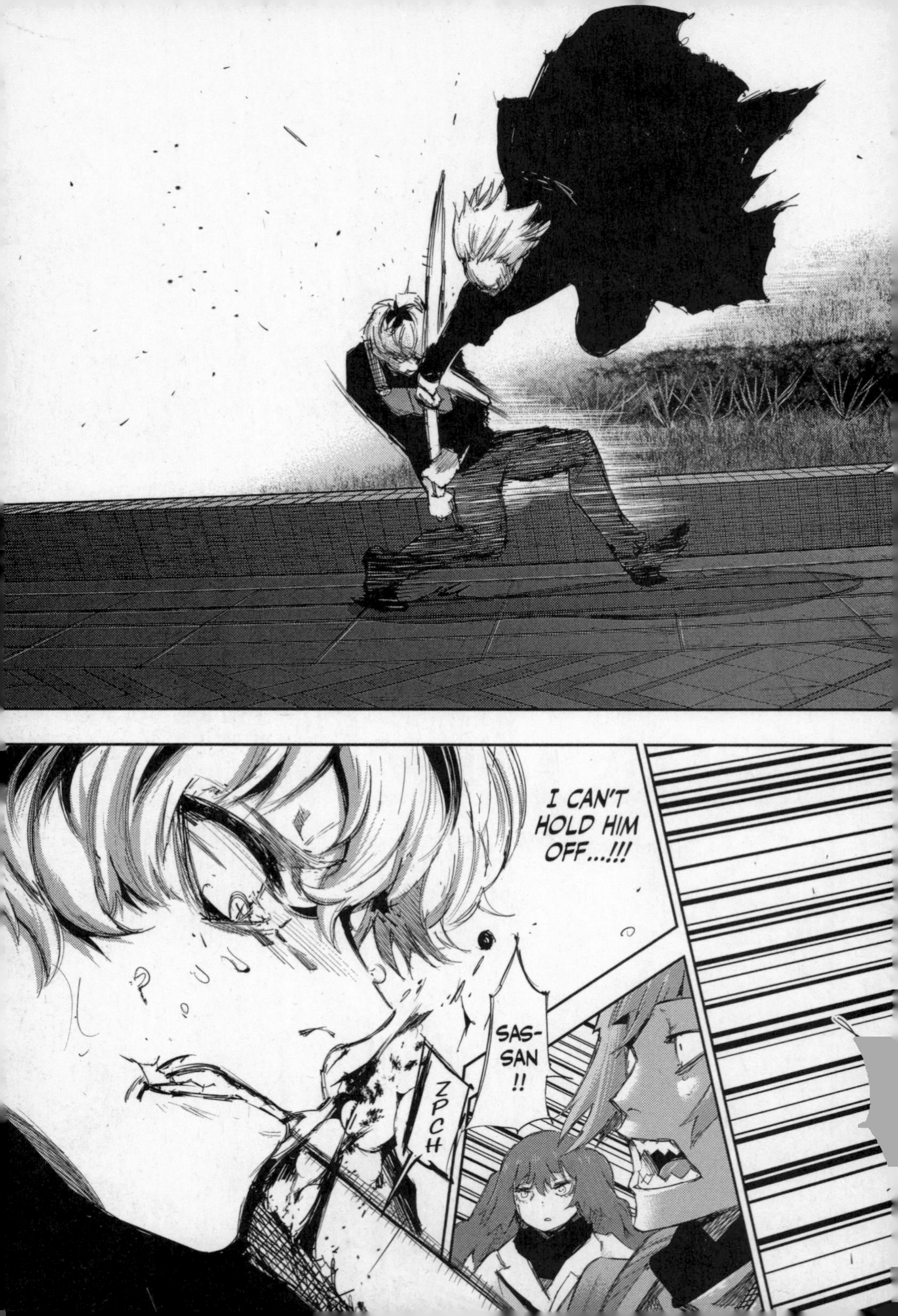
I CAN'T HOLD HIM OFF...!!!
SAS-SAN!!
ZPCH

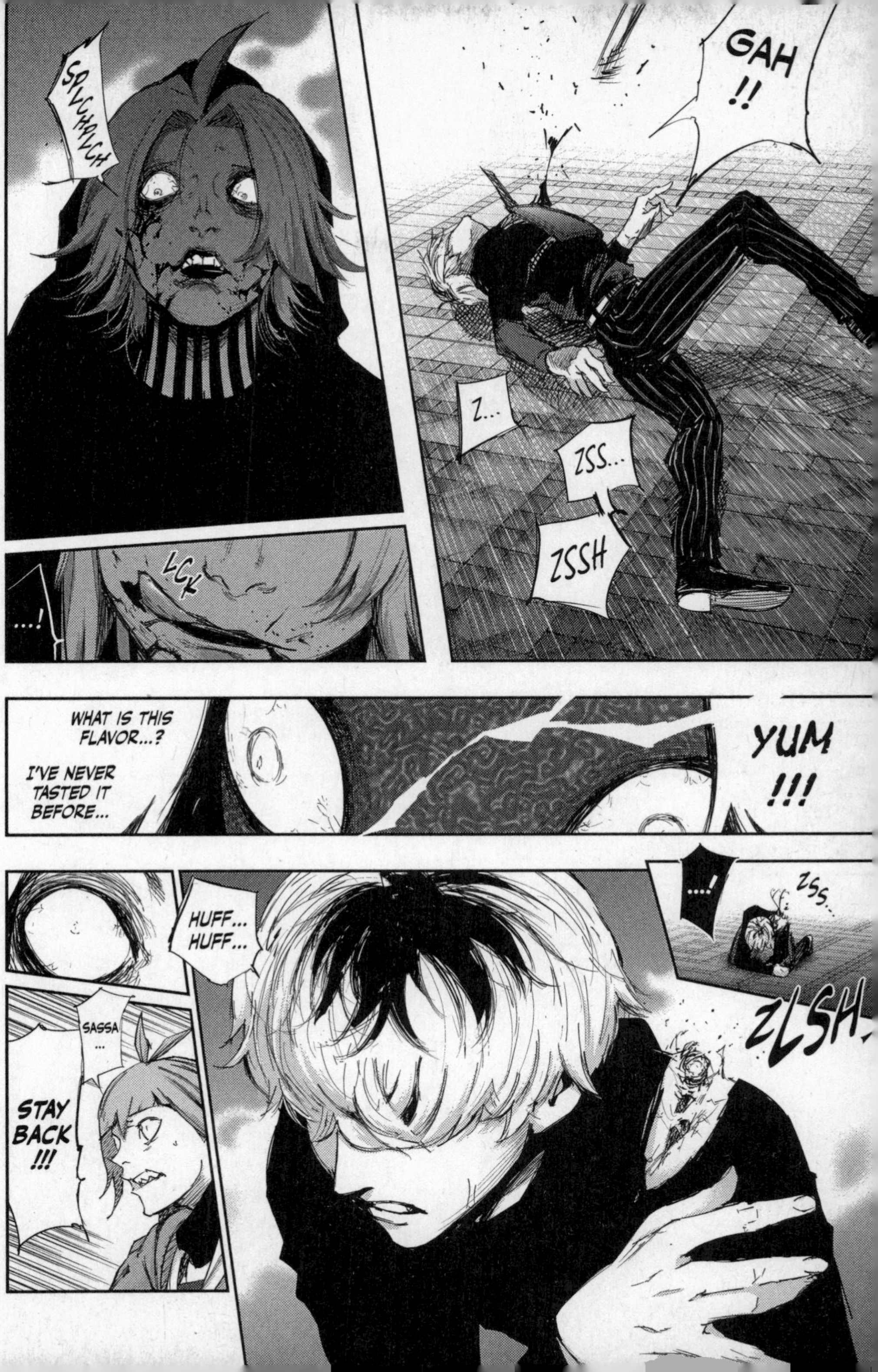
GAH !!
Z...
ZSS...
ZSSH
SPLCHLCH
LCK
...!
YUM !!!
WHAT IS THIS FLAVOR...?
I'VE NEVER TASTED IT BEFORE...
....!
ZSS...
ZLSH
HUFF... HUFF...
SASSA ...
STAY BACK !!!

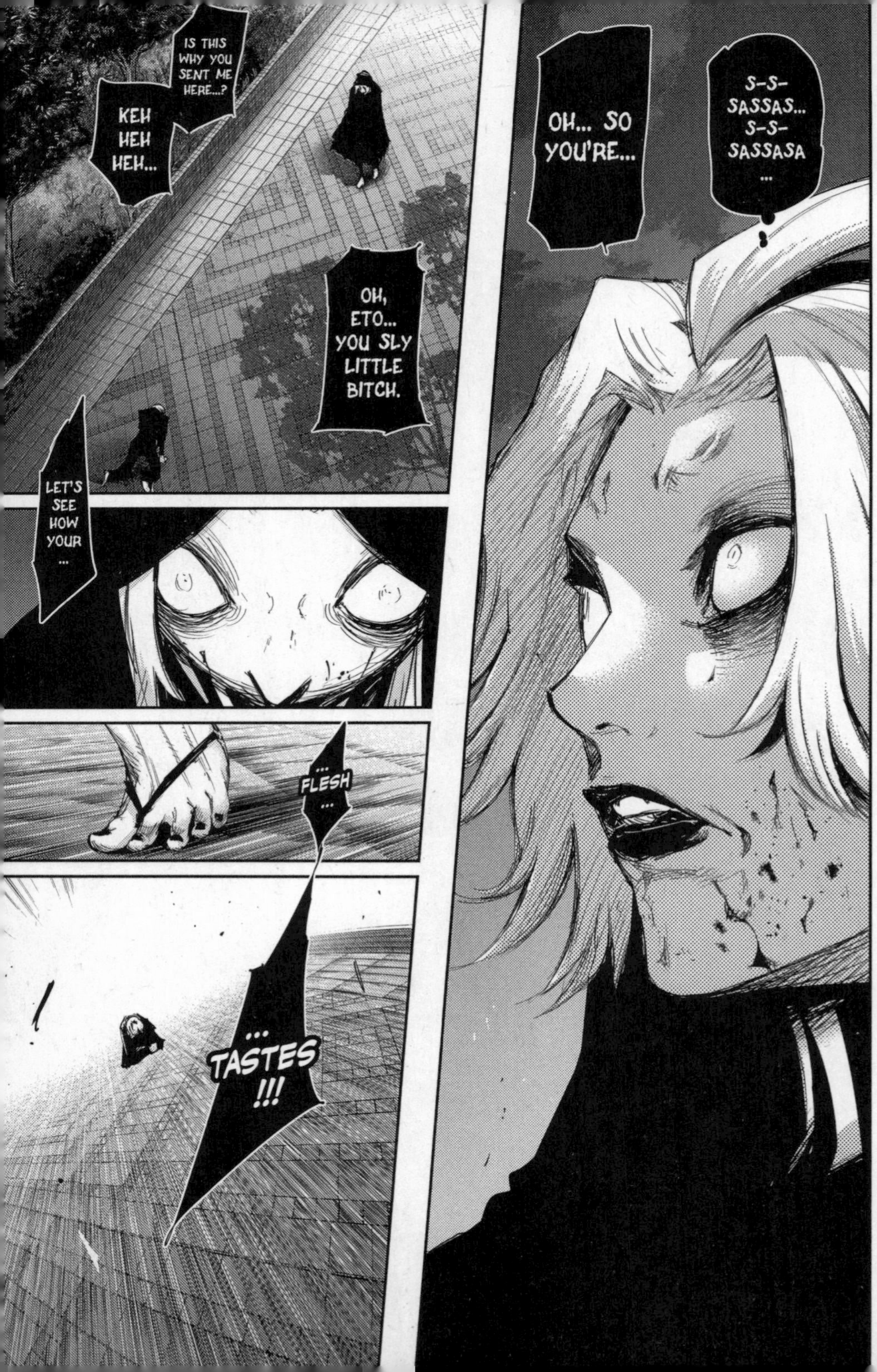
S-S-SASSAS... S-S-SASSASA ...
OH... SO YOU'RE...
IS THIS WHY YOU SENT ME HERE...?
KEH HEH HEH...
OH, ETO... YOU SLY LITTLE BITCH.
LET'S SEE HOW YOUR ...
... FLESH ...
... TASTES !!!

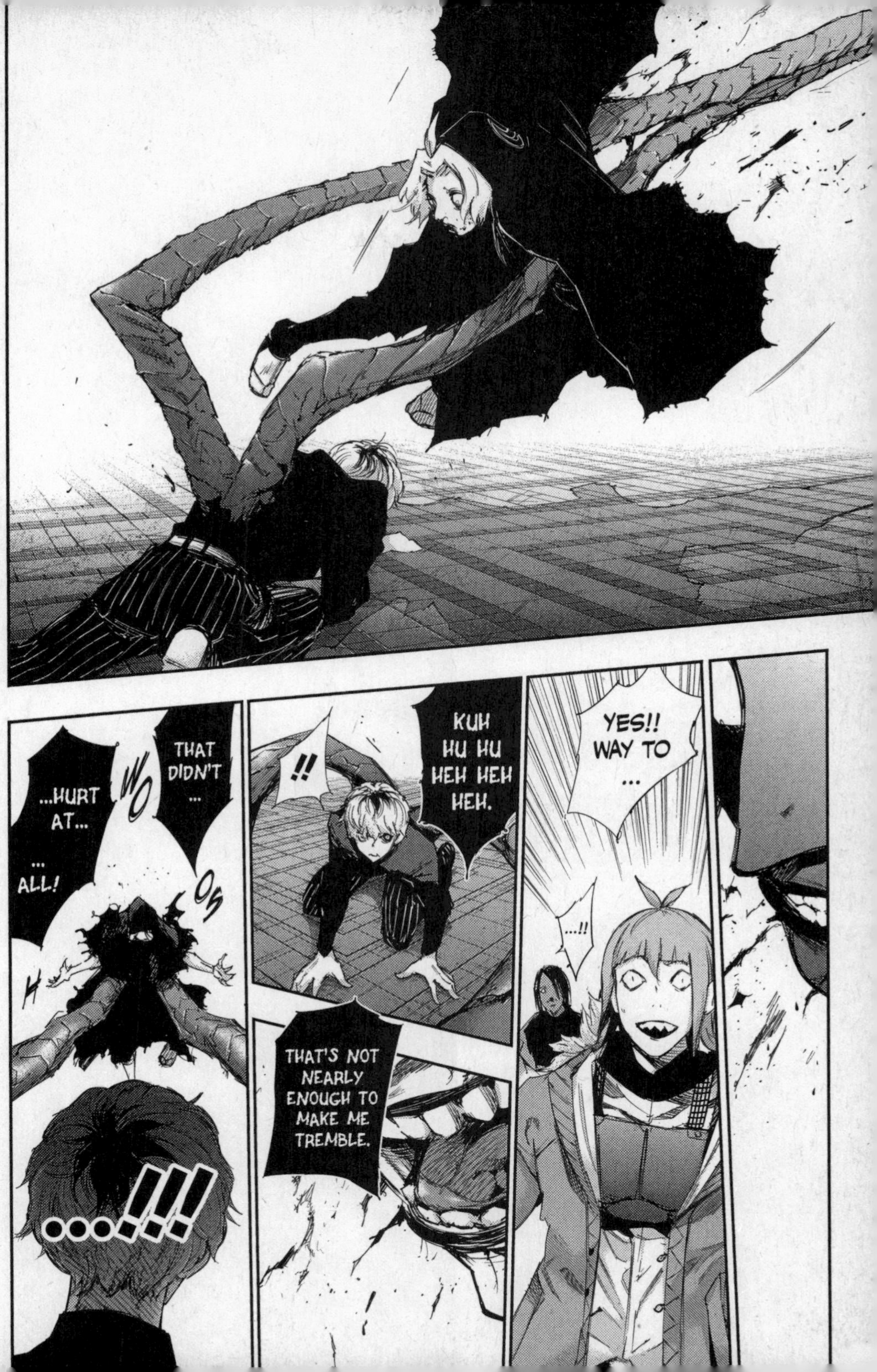
YES!! WAY TO ...
...!!
!!
KUH HU HU HEH HEH HEH.
THAT'S NOT NEARLY ENOUGH TO MAKE ME TREMBLE.
THAT DIDN'T ...
...HURT AT...
... ALL!
...!!!

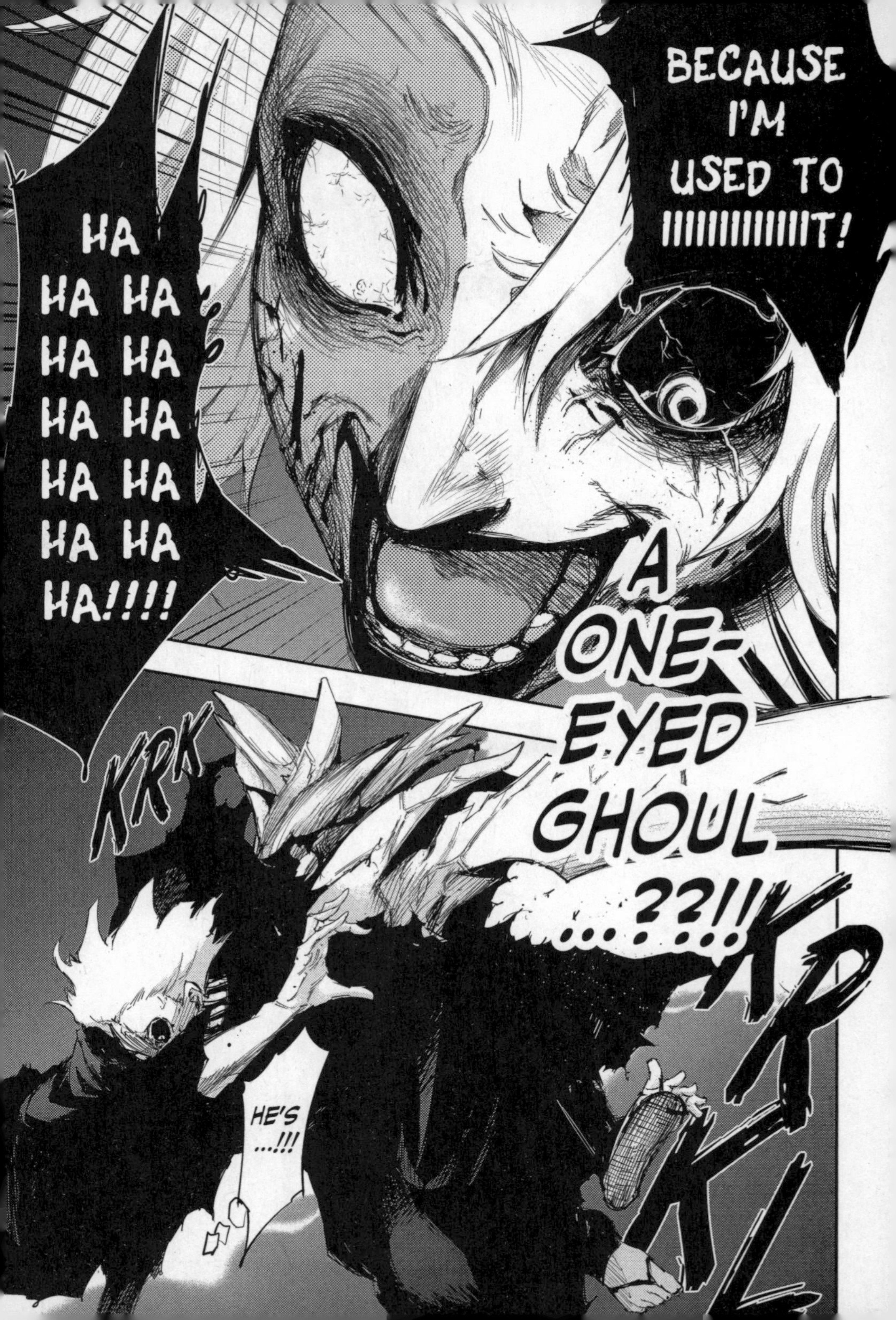

BECAUSE I'M USED TO IIIIIIIIIIIIT!
HA HA HA HA HA HA HA HA HA HA HA HA HA HA!!!!
A ONE-EYED GHOUL ...??!!
KRK
KRK
HE'S ...!!!

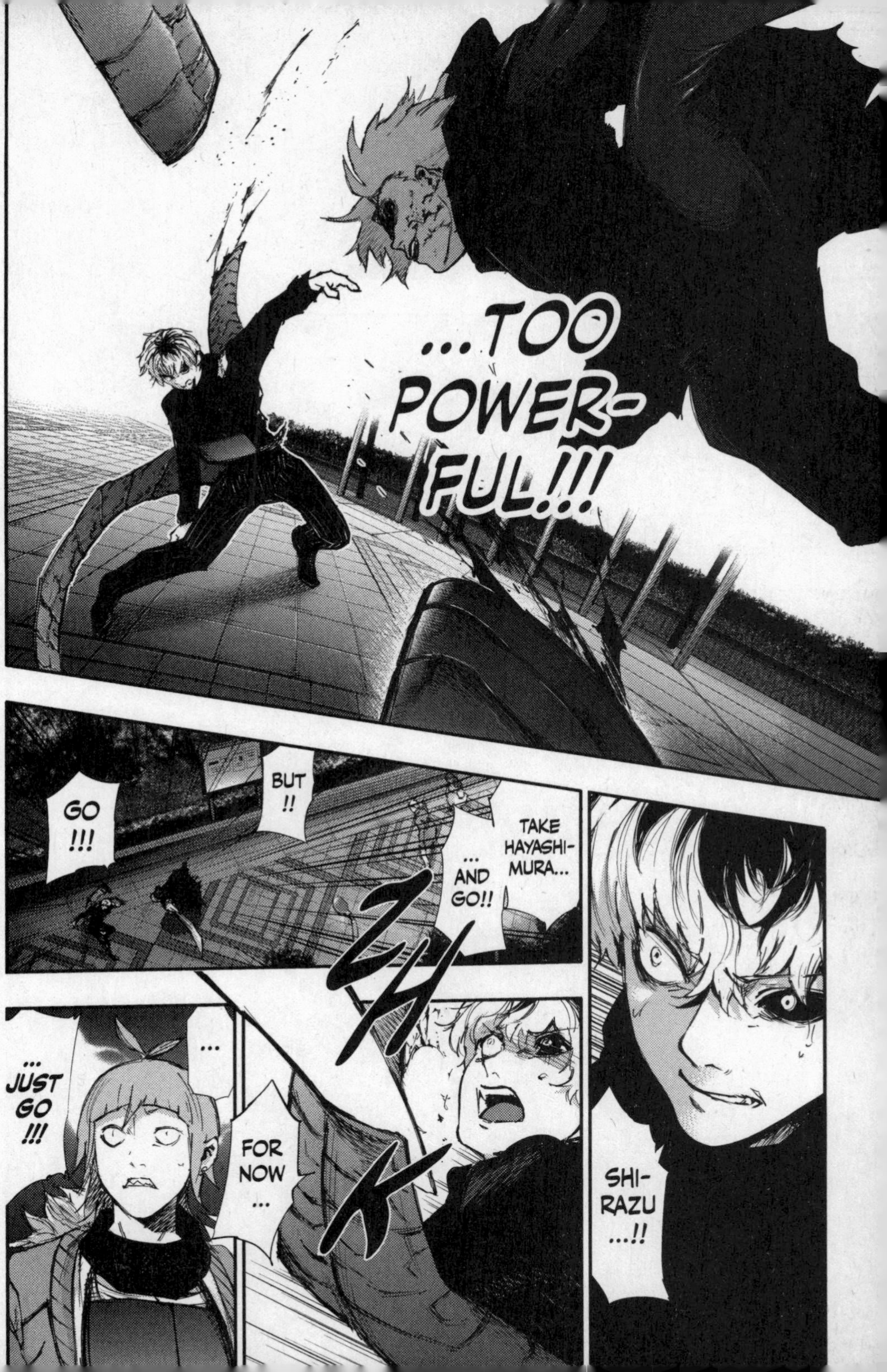
...TOO POWER-FUL!!!
SHI-RAZU ...!!
TAKE HAYASHI-MURA...
... AND GO!!
BUT !!
GO !!!
ZAK
FOR NOW ...
...
... JUST GO !!!

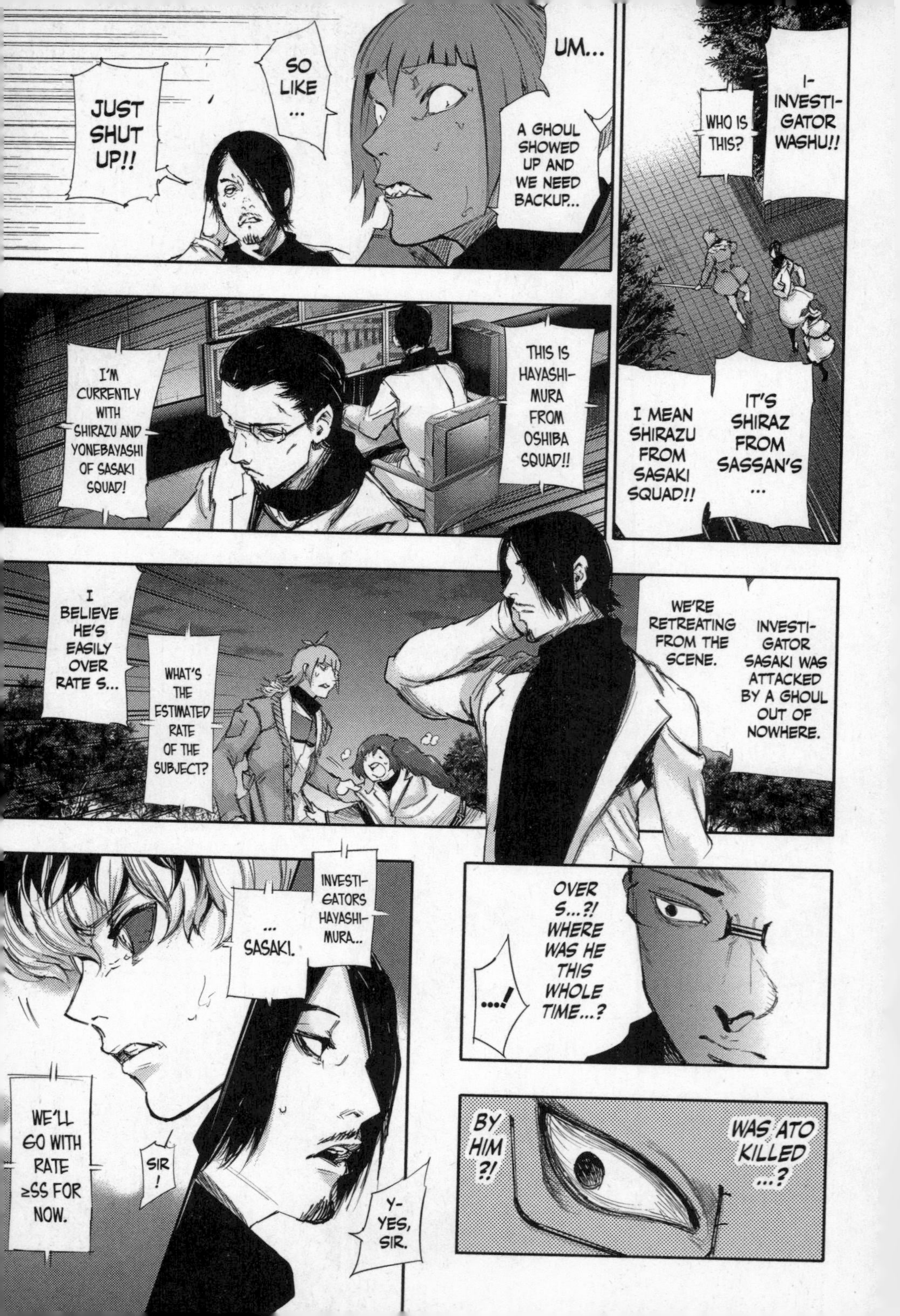
I-INVESTIGATOR WASHU!!
WHO IS THIS?
IT'S SHIRAZ FROM SASSAN'S...
I MEAN SHIRAZU FROM SASAKI SQUAD!!
UM...
A GHOUL SHOWED UP AND WE NEED BACKUP...
SO LIKE...
JUST SHUT UP!!
THIS IS HAYASHIMURA FROM OSHIBA SQUAD!!
I'M CURRENTLY WITH SHIRAZU AND YONEBAYASHI OF SASAKI SQUAD!
INVESTIGATOR SASAKI WAS ATTACKED BY A GHOUL OUT OF NOWHERE.
WE'RE RETREATING FROM THE SCENE.
WHAT'S THE ESTIMATED RATE OF THE SUBJECT?
I BELIEVE HE'S EASILY OVER RATE S...
OVER S...?! WHERE WAS HE THIS WHOLE TIME...?
...!
WAS ATO KILLED...?
BY HIM?!
INVESTIGATORS HAYASHIMURA...
...SASAKI.
WE'LL GO WITH RATE ≥SS FOR NOW.
SIR!
Y-YES, SIR.

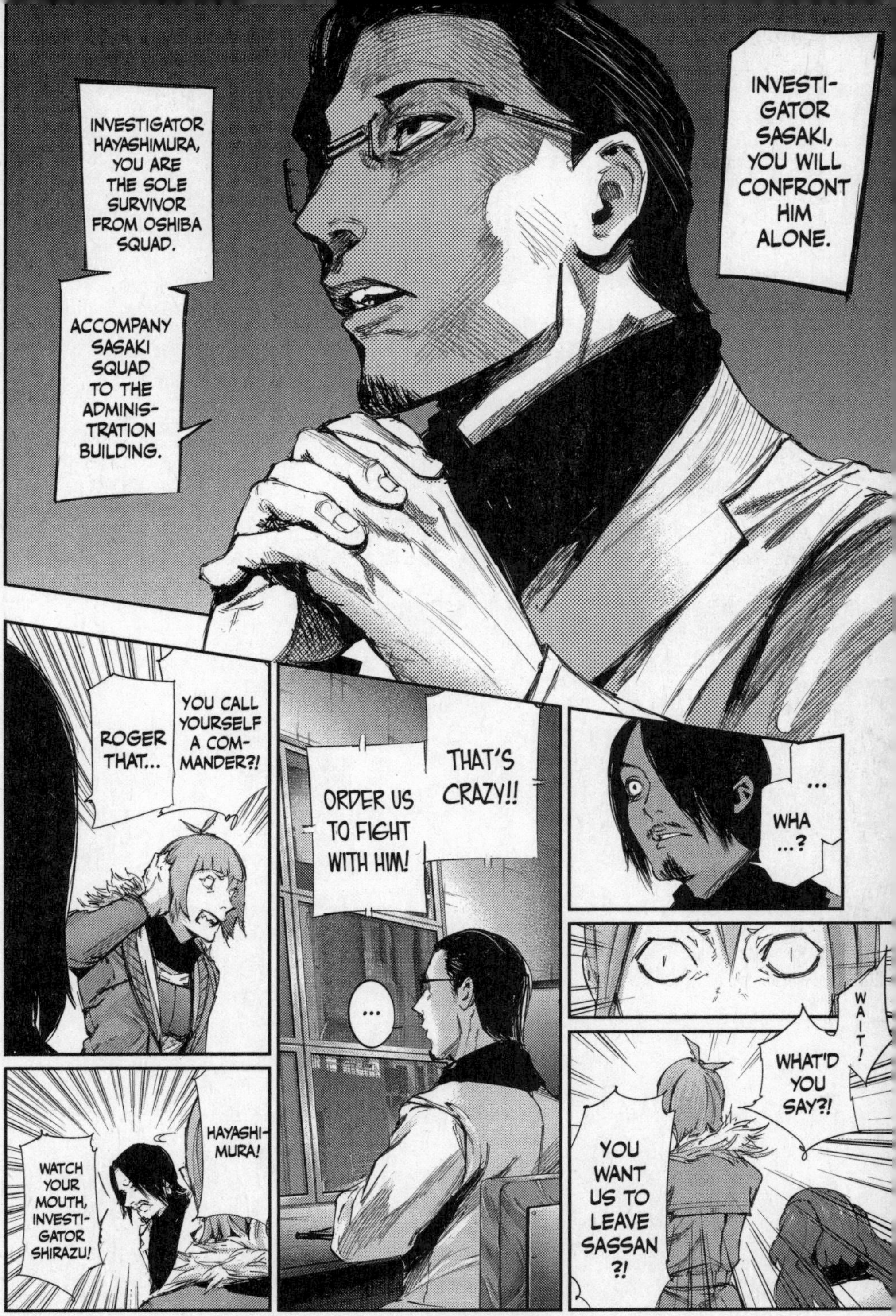
INVESTIGATOR SASAKI, YOU WILL CONFRONT HIM ALONE.
INVESTIGATOR HAYASHIMURA, YOU ARE THE SOLE SURVIVOR FROM OSHIBA SQUAD.
ACCOMPANY SASAKI SQUAD TO THE ADMINISTRATION BUILDING.
... WHA ...?
WAIT!
WHAT'D YOU SAY?!
YOU WANT US TO LEAVE SASSAN?!
THAT'S CRAZY!!
ORDER US TO FIGHT WITH HIM!
...
YOU CALL YOURSELF A COMMANDER?!
ROGER THAT...
HAYASHIMURA!
WATCH YOUR MOUTH, INVESTIGATOR SHIRAZU!

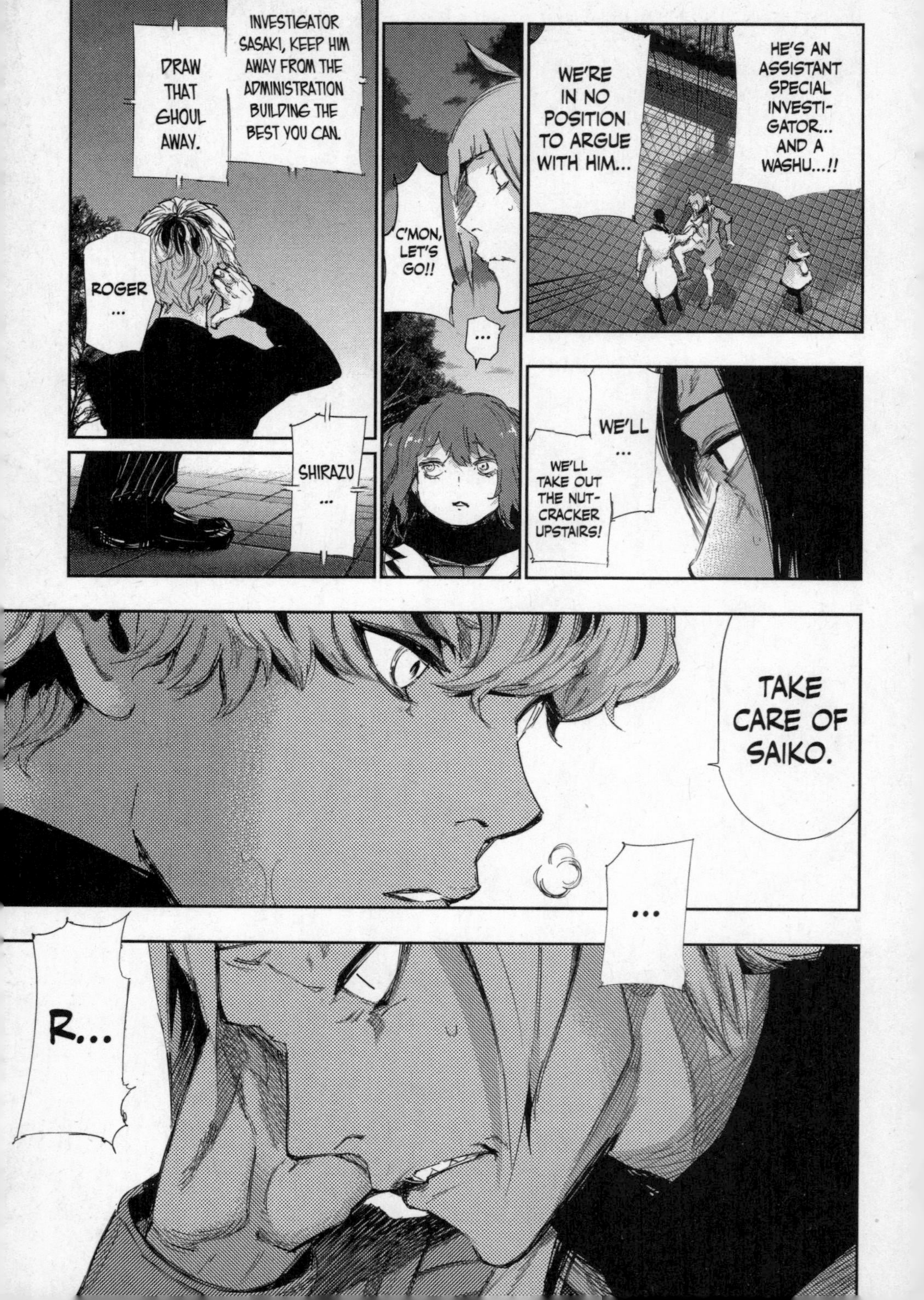
HE'S AN ASSISTANT SPECIAL INVESTI-GATOR... AND A WASHU...!!
WE'RE IN NO POSITION TO ARGUE WITH HIM...
WE'LL...
WE'LL TAKE OUT THE NUT-CRACKER UPSTAIRS!
C'MON, LET'S GO!!
...
INVESTIGATOR SASAKI, KEEP HIM AWAY FROM THE ADMINISTRATION BUILDING THE BEST YOU CAN.
DRAW THAT GHOUL AWAY.
ROGER...
SHIRAZU...
TAKE CARE OF SAIKO.
...
R...

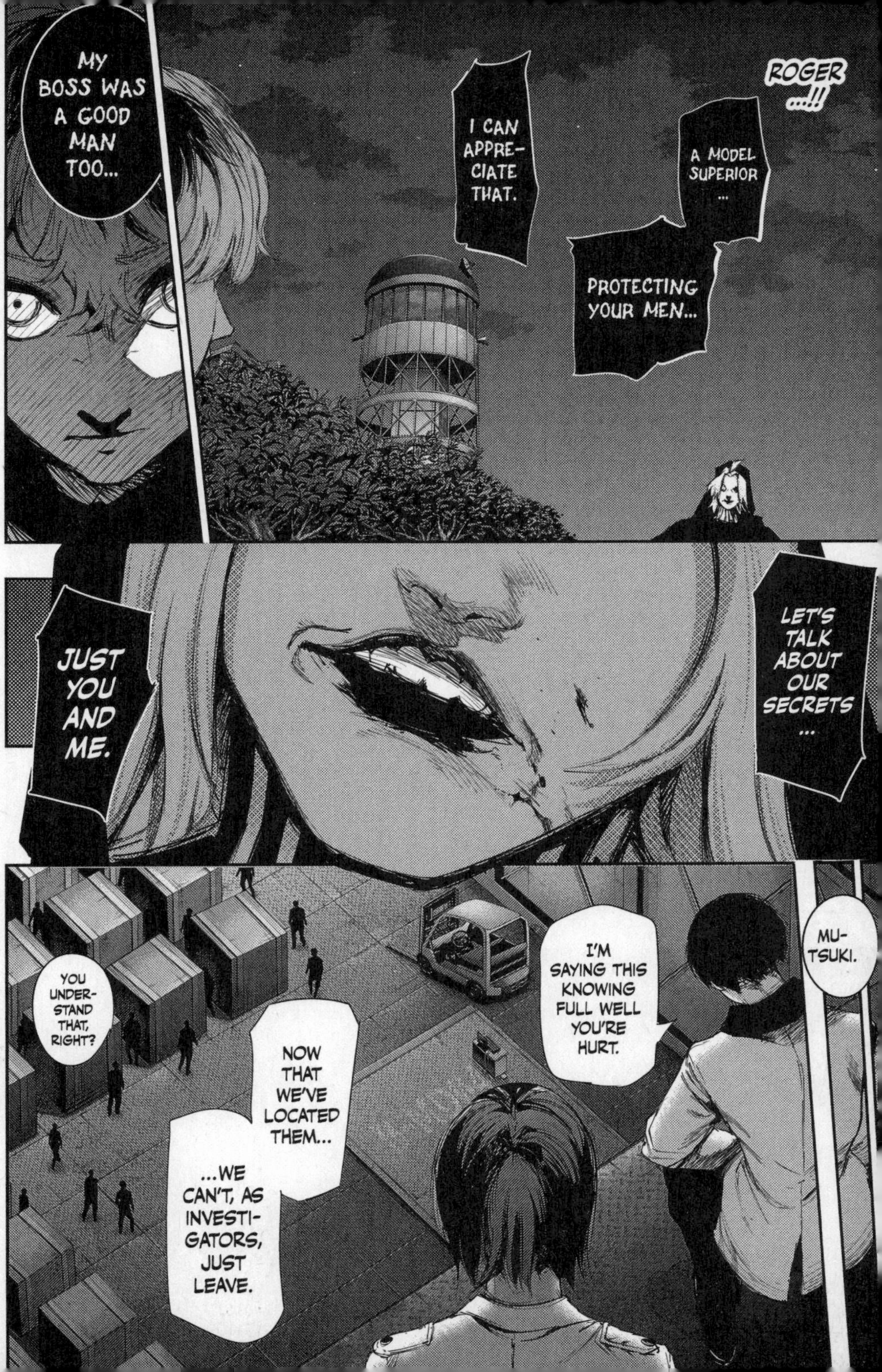
ROGER ...!!
A MODEL SUPERIOR ...
PROTECTING YOUR MEN...
I CAN APPRECIATE THAT.
MY BOSS WAS A GOOD MAN TOO...
LET'S TALK ABOUT OUR SECRETS ...
JUST YOU AND ME.
MUTSUKI.
I'M SAYING THIS KNOWING FULL WELL YOU'RE HURT.
NOW THAT WE'VE LOCATED THEM...
...WE CAN'T, AS INVESTIGATORS, JUST LEAVE.
YOU UNDERSTAND THAT, RIGHT?

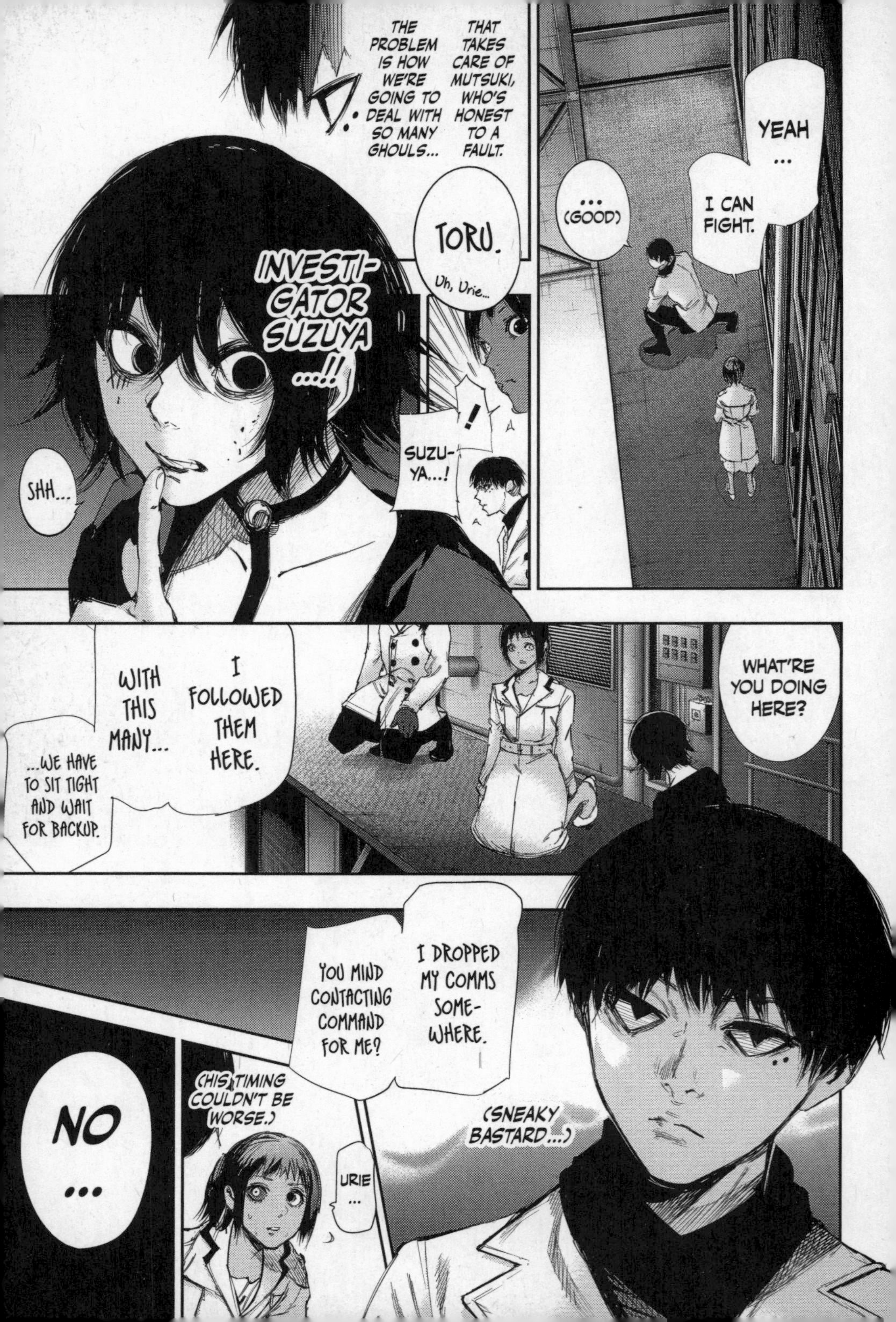
YEAH ... I CAN FIGHT.
... (GOOD)
THAT TAKES CARE OF MUTSUKI, WHO'S HONEST TO A FAULT.
THE PROBLEM IS HOW WE'RE GOING TO DEAL WITH SO MANY GHOULS...
TORU.
Uh, Urie...
INVESTI-GATOR SUZUYA ...!!
!
SUZU-YA...!
SHH...
WHAT'RE YOU DOING HERE?
I FOLLOWED THEM HERE.
WITH THIS MANY...
...WE HAVE TO SIT TIGHT AND WAIT FOR BACKUP.
I DROPPED MY COMMS SOME-WHERE.
YOU MIND CONTACTING COMMAND FOR ME?
(SNEAKY BASTARD...)
(THIS TIMING COULDN'T BE WORSE.)
URIE ...
NO ...

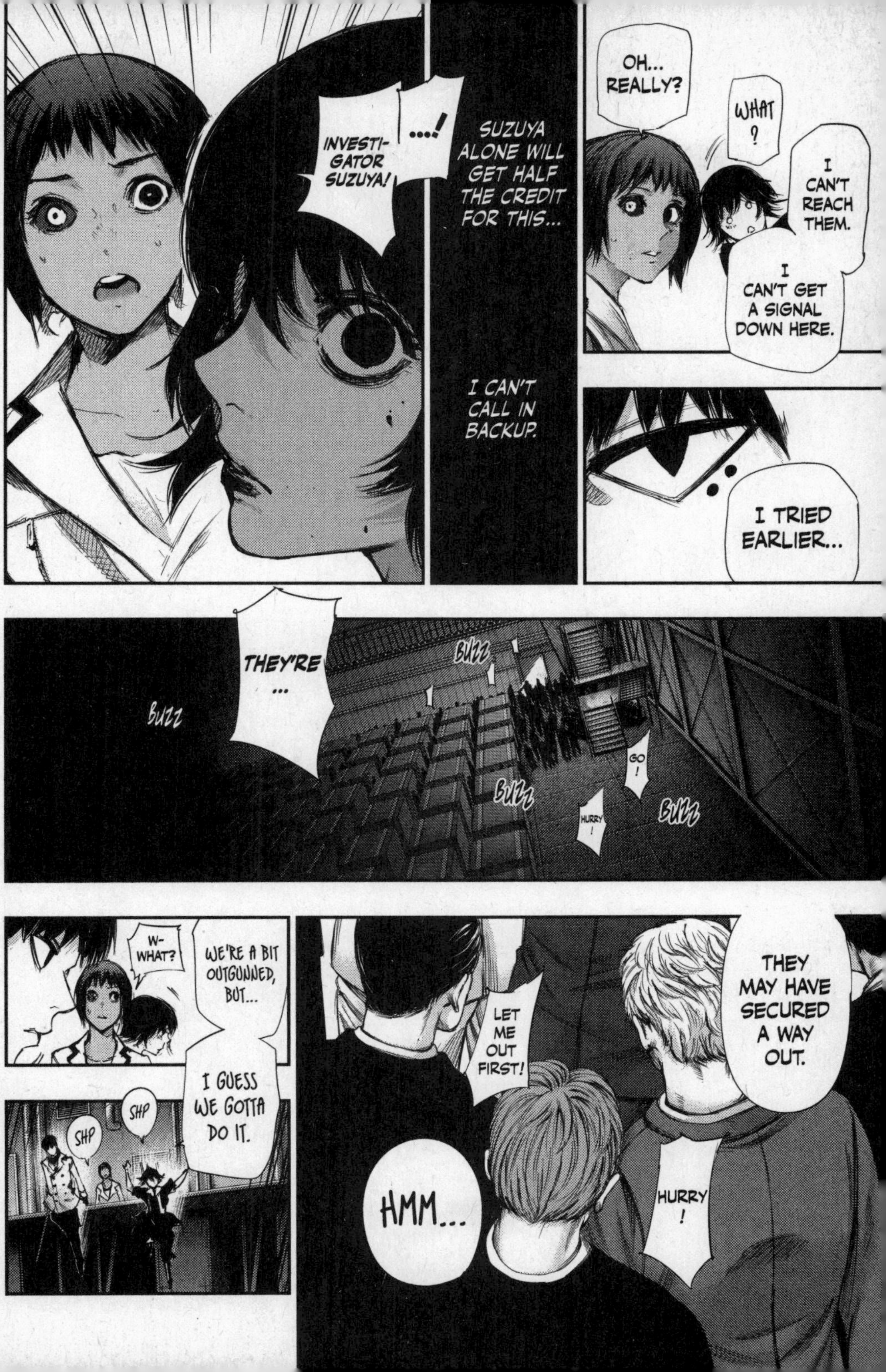
OH... REALLY?
WHAT ?
I CAN'T REACH THEM.
I CAN'T GET A SIGNAL DOWN HERE.
I TRIED EARLIER...
SUZUYA ALONE WILL GET HALF THE CREDIT FOR THIS...
I CAN'T CALL IN BACKUP.
...!
INVESTI-GATOR SUZUYA!
THEY'RE ...
BUZZ
BUZZ
GO !
BUZZ
BUZZ
HURRY !
THEY MAY HAVE SECURED A WAY OUT.
LET ME OUT FIRST!
HURRY !
HMM...
W-WHAT?
WE'RE A BIT OUTGUNNED, BUT...
I GUESS WE GOTTA DO IT.
SHP
SHP

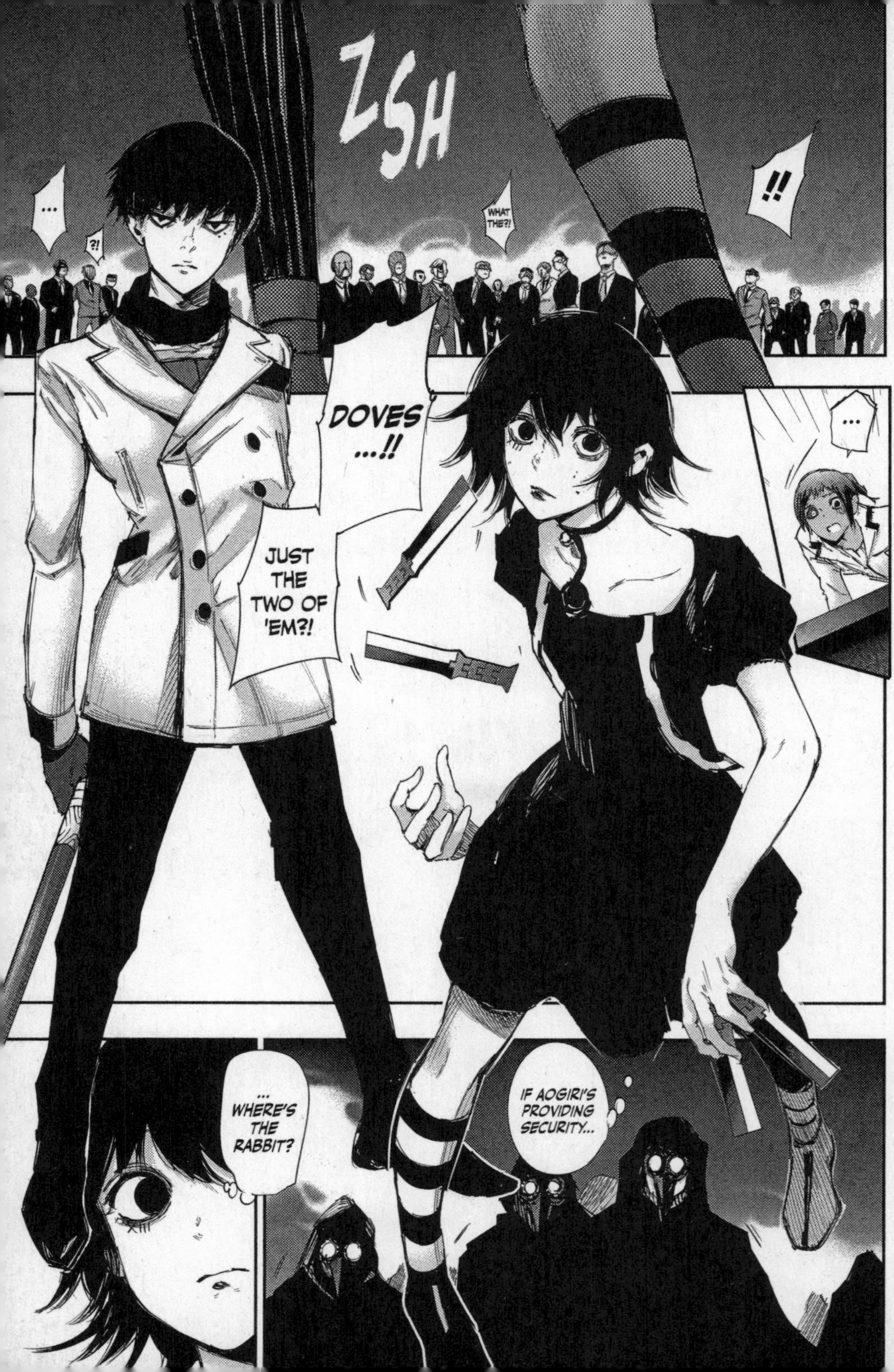
ZSH
!!
WHAT THE?!
?!
...
...
DOVES ...!!
JUST THE TWO OF 'EM?!
IF AOGIRI'S PROVIDING SECURITY...
... WHERE'S THE RABBIT?

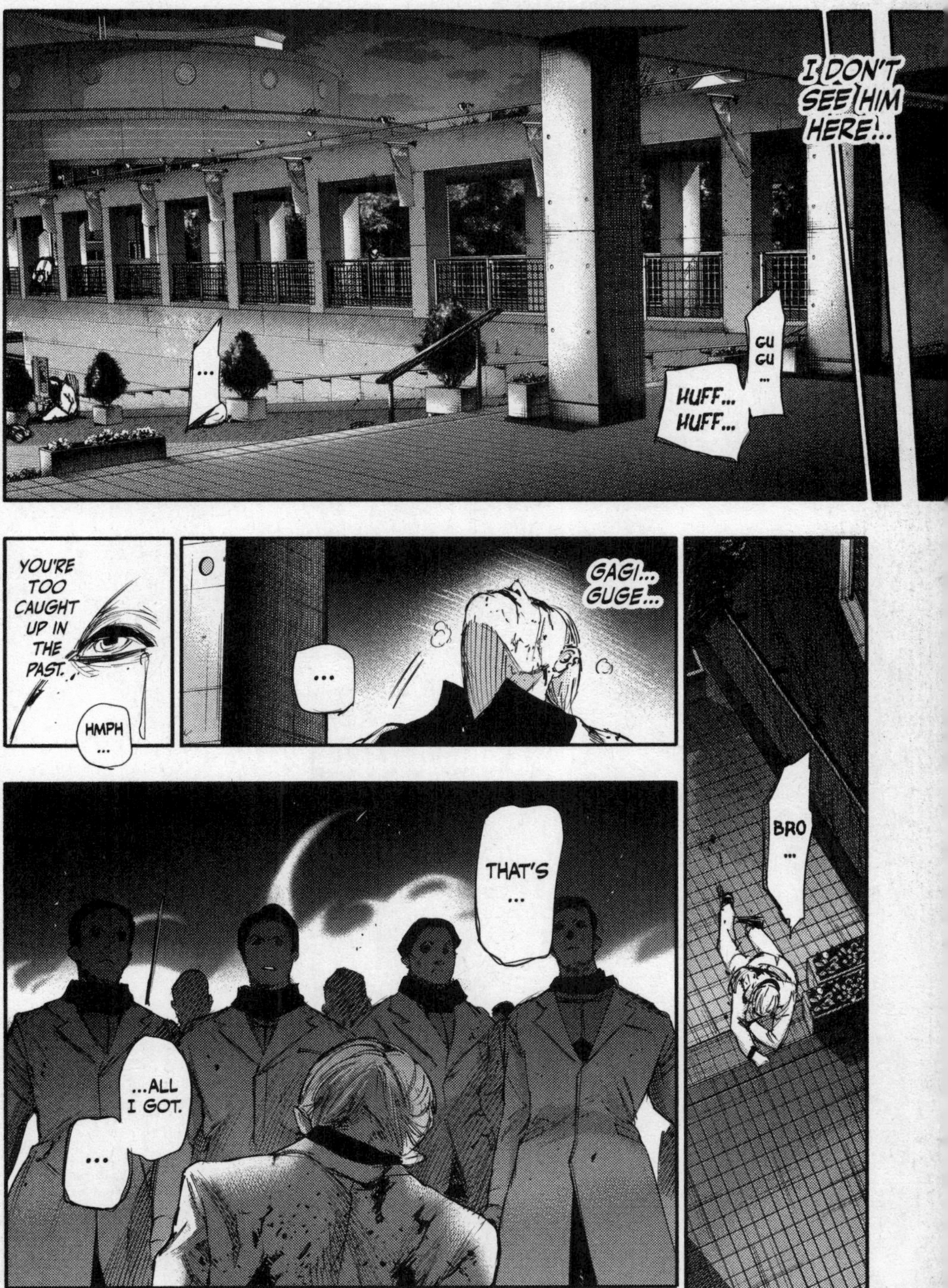
I DON'T SEE HIM HERE...
GU GU ...
HUFF... HUFF...
...
BRO ...
GAGI... GUGE...
...
YOU'RE TOO CAUGHT UP IN THE PAST.
HMPH ...
THAT'S ...
...ALL I GOT.
...

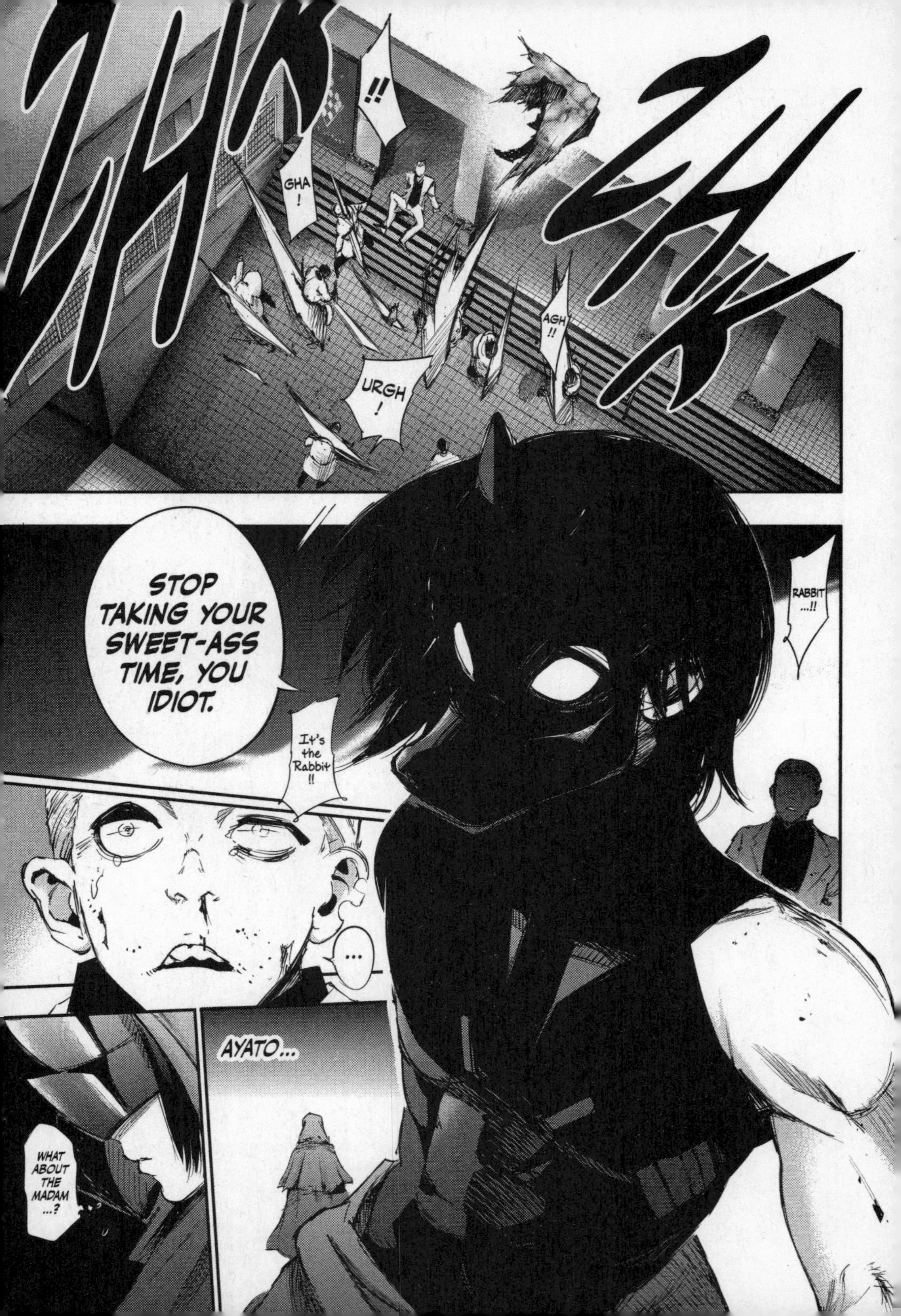
!!
AGH !!
GHA !
URGH !
RABBIT ...!!
STOP TAKING YOUR SWEET-ASS TIME, YOU IDIOT.
It's the Rabbit !!
...
AYATO...
WHAT ABOUT THE MADAM ...?

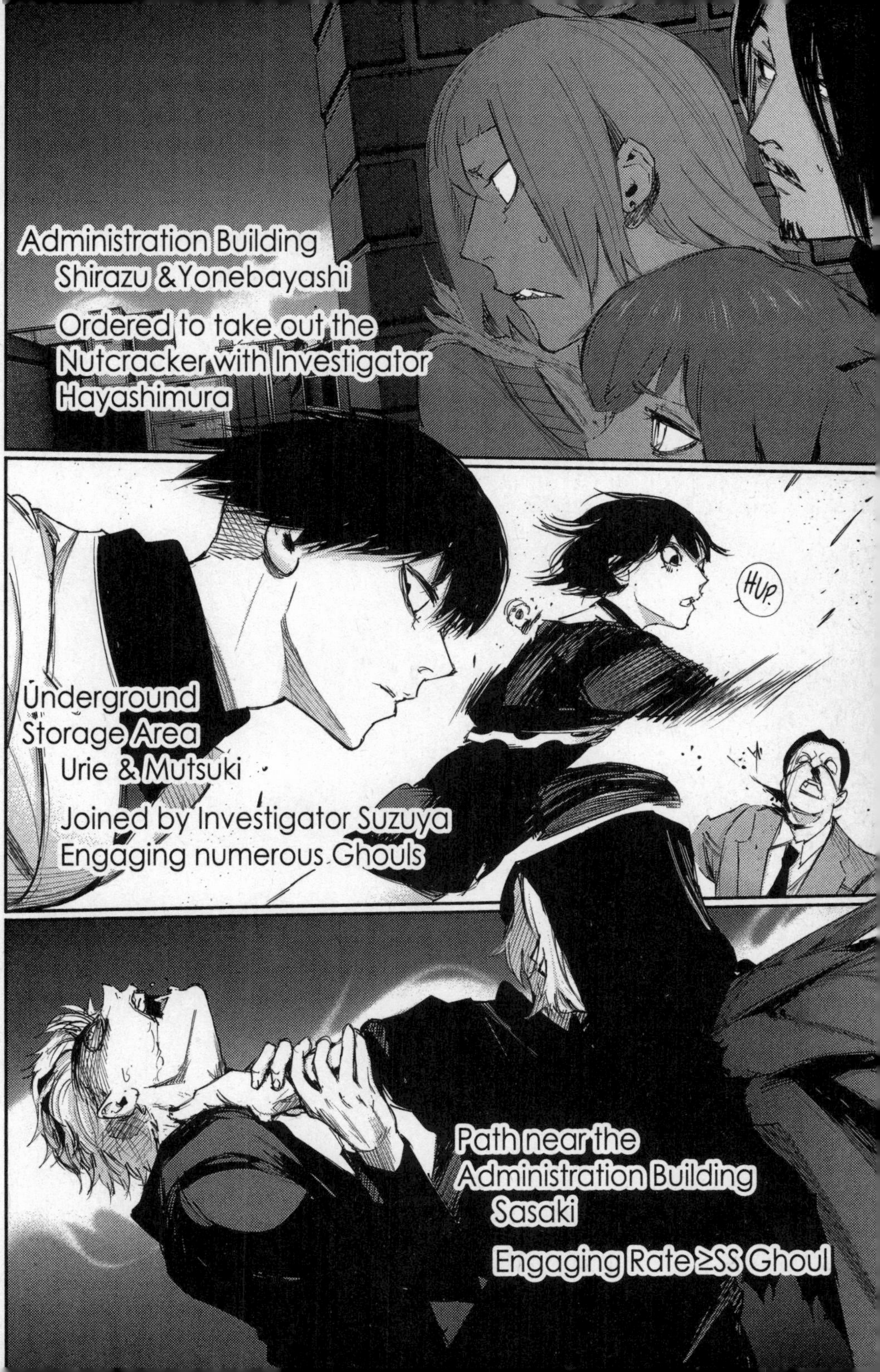
Administration Building
Shirazu & Yonebayashi
Ordered to take out the Nutcracker with Investigator Hayashimura
HUP.
Underground Storage Area
Urie & Mutsuki
Joined by Investigator Suzuya
Engaging numerous Ghouls
Path near the Administration Building
Sasaki
Engaging Rate ≥SS Ghoul

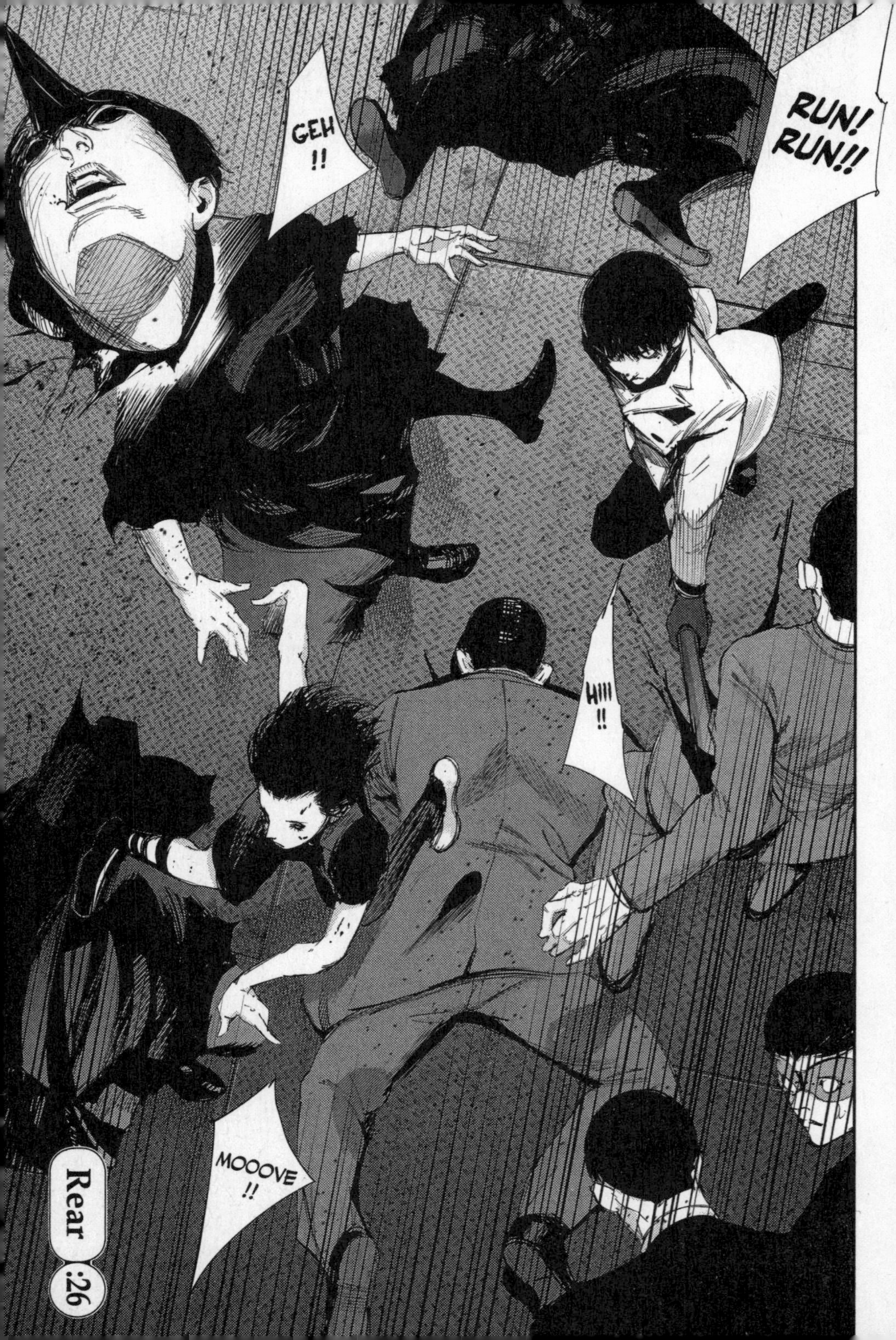
RUN! RUN!!
GEH !!
HI!! !!
MOOOVE !!

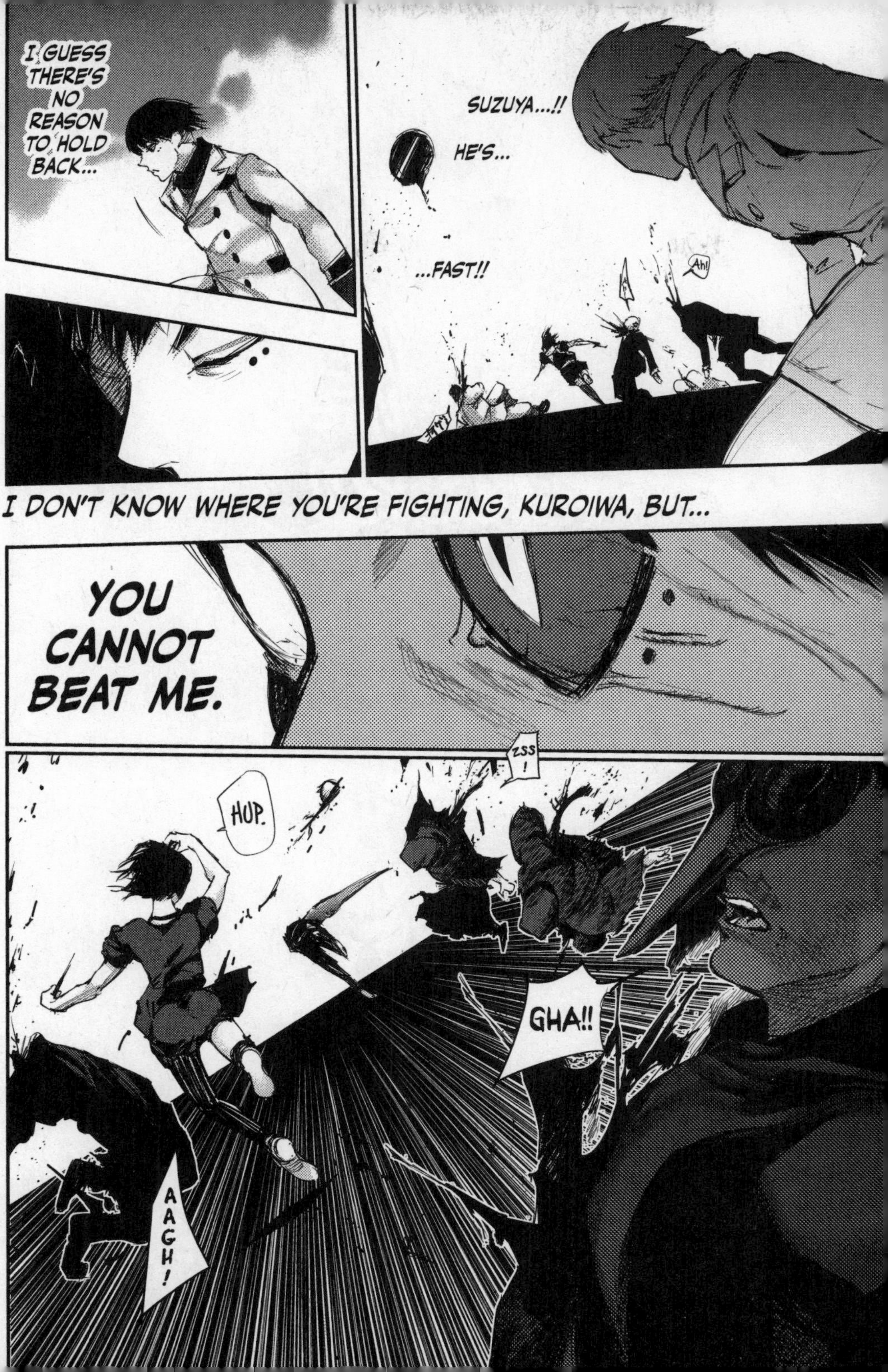
SUZUYA...!!
HE'S...
Ah!
...FAST!!
I GUESS THERE'S NO REASON TO HOLD BACK...
I DON'T KNOW WHERE YOU'RE FIGHTING, KUROIWA, BUT...
YOU CANNOT BEAT ME.
ZSS!
HUP.
GHA!!
AAGH!

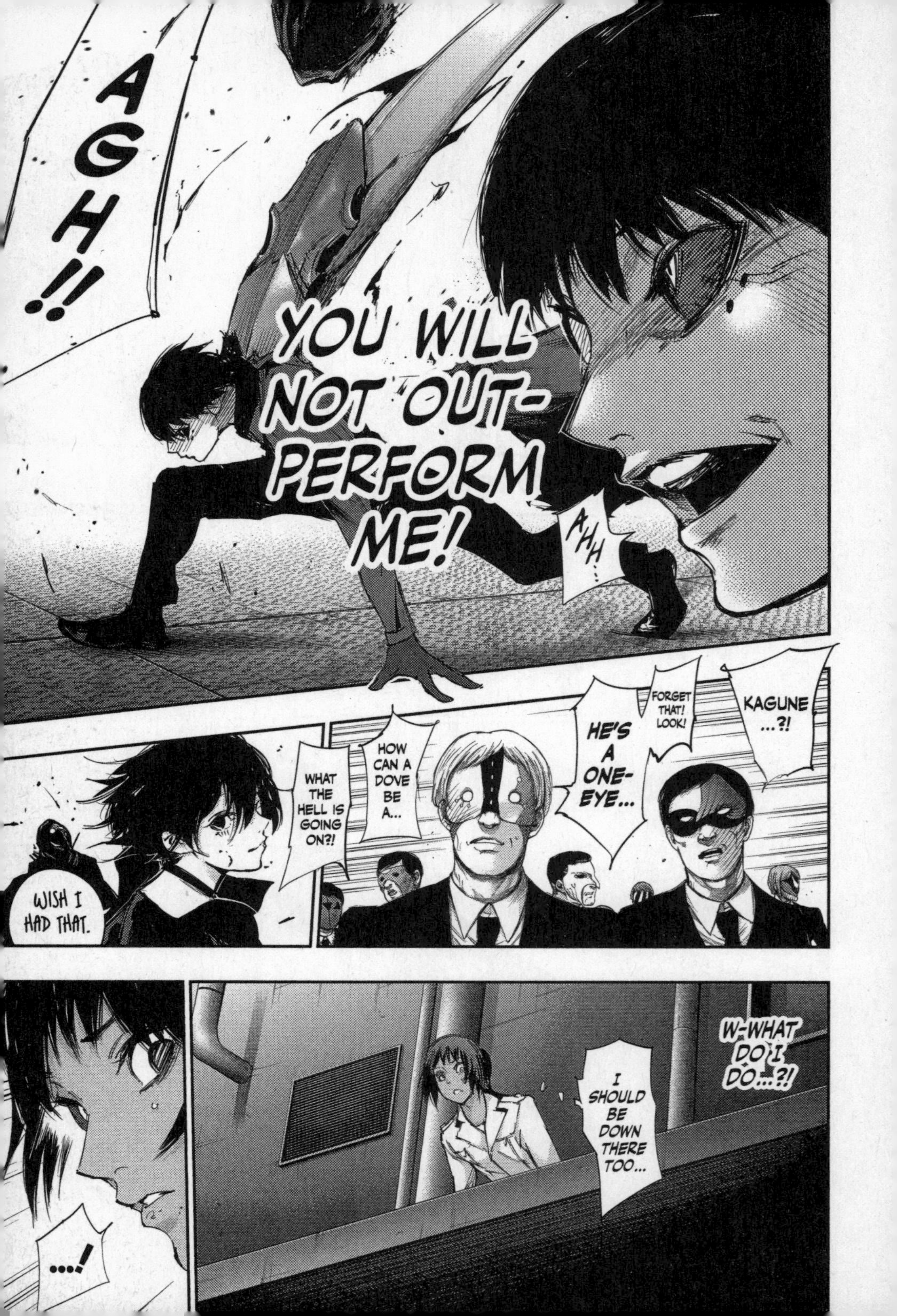
AGH!!
YOU WILL NOT OUT-PERFORM ME!
AHH...
KAGUNE ...?!
FORGET THAT! LOOK!
HE'S A ONE-EYE...
HOW CAN A DOVE BE A...
WHAT THE HELL IS GOING ON?!
WISH I HAD THAT.
W-WHAT DO I DO...?!
I SHOULD BE DOWN THERE TOO...
...!

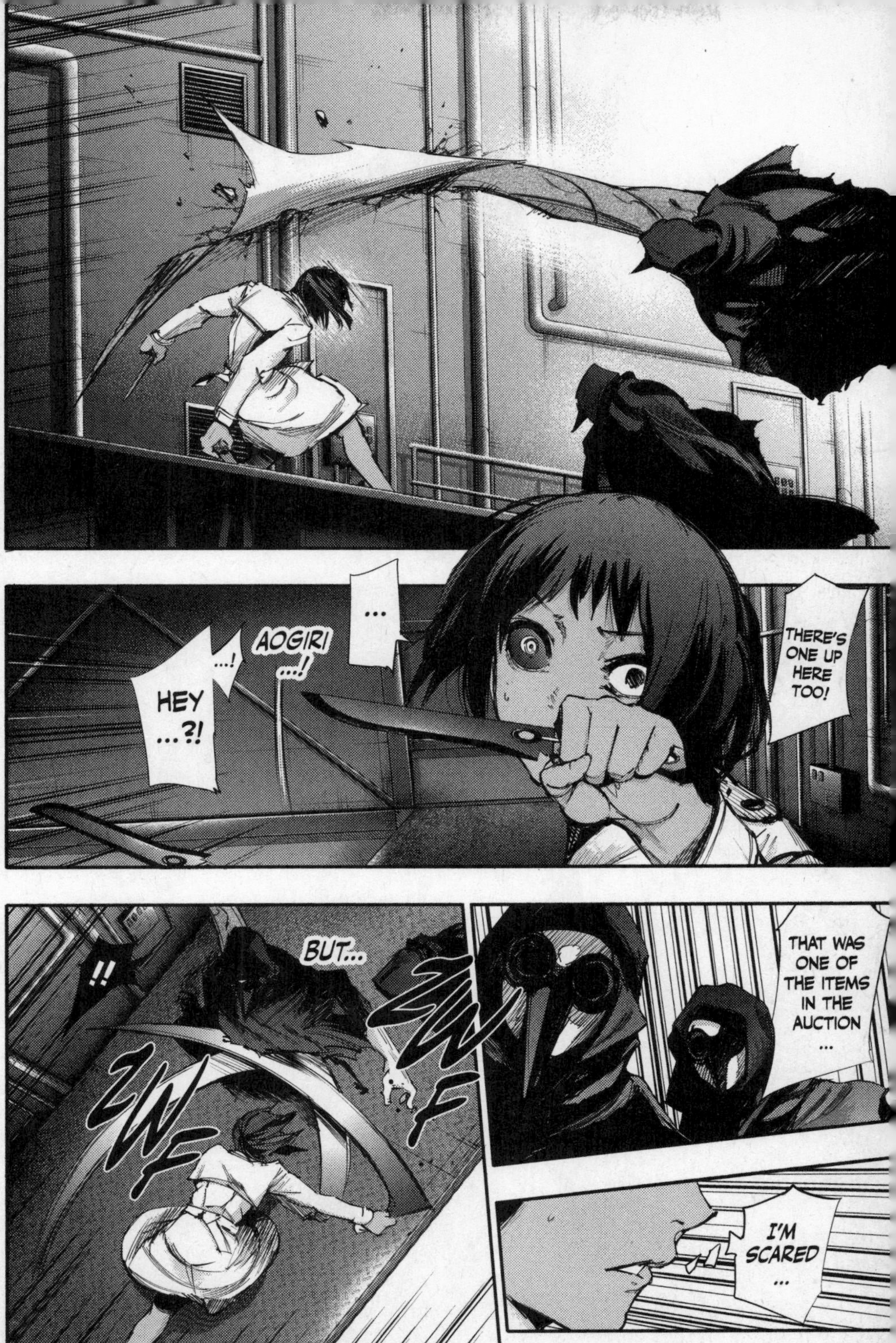
THERE'S ONE UP HERE TOO!
...
AOGIRI ...!
...!
HEY ...?!
THAT WAS ONE OF THE ITEMS IN THE AUCTION ...
I'M SCARED ...
BUT...
!!

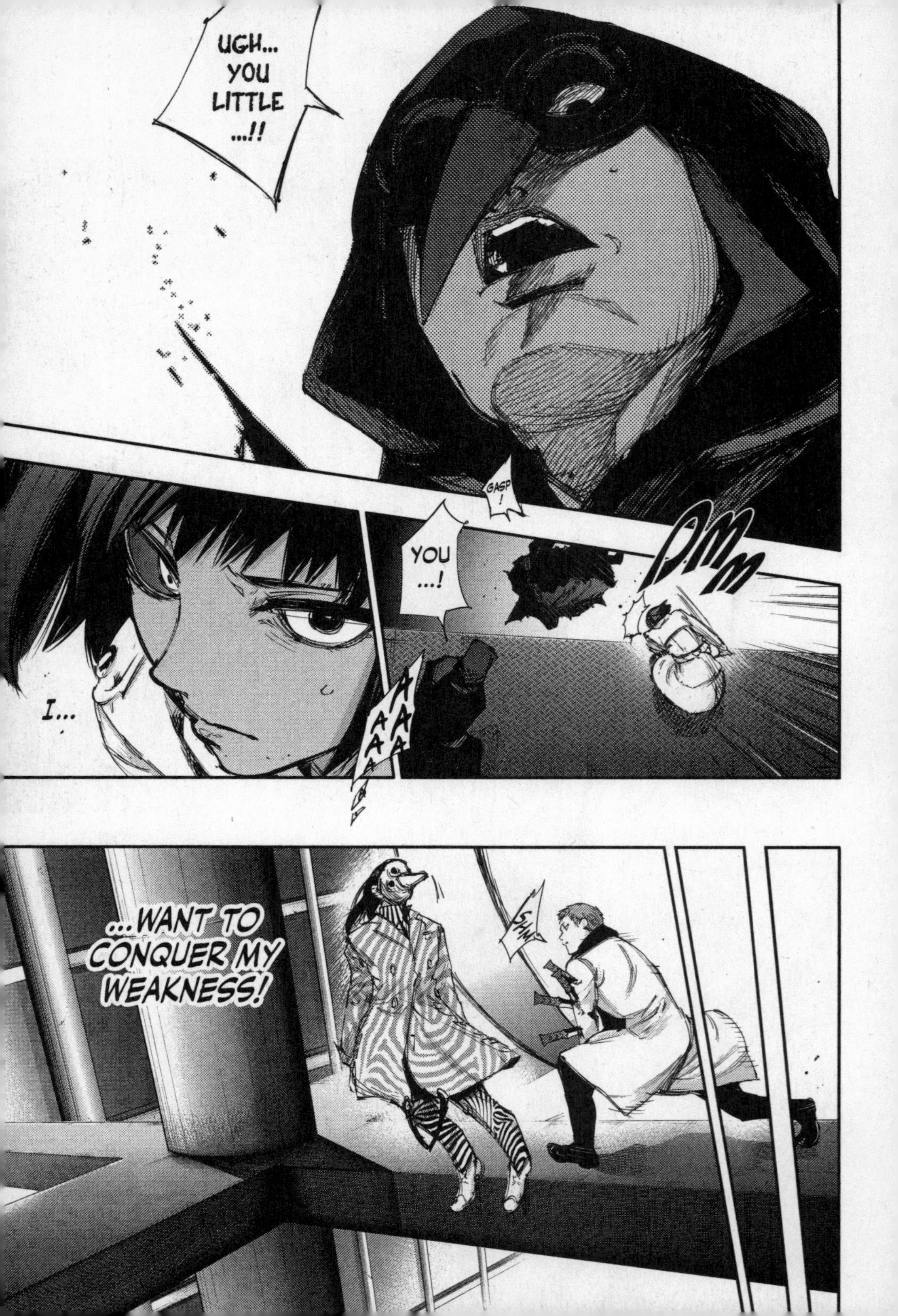
UGH... YOU LITTLE ...!!
GASP!
DMM
YOU ...!
I...
...WANT TO CONQUER MY WEAKNESS!
SHM

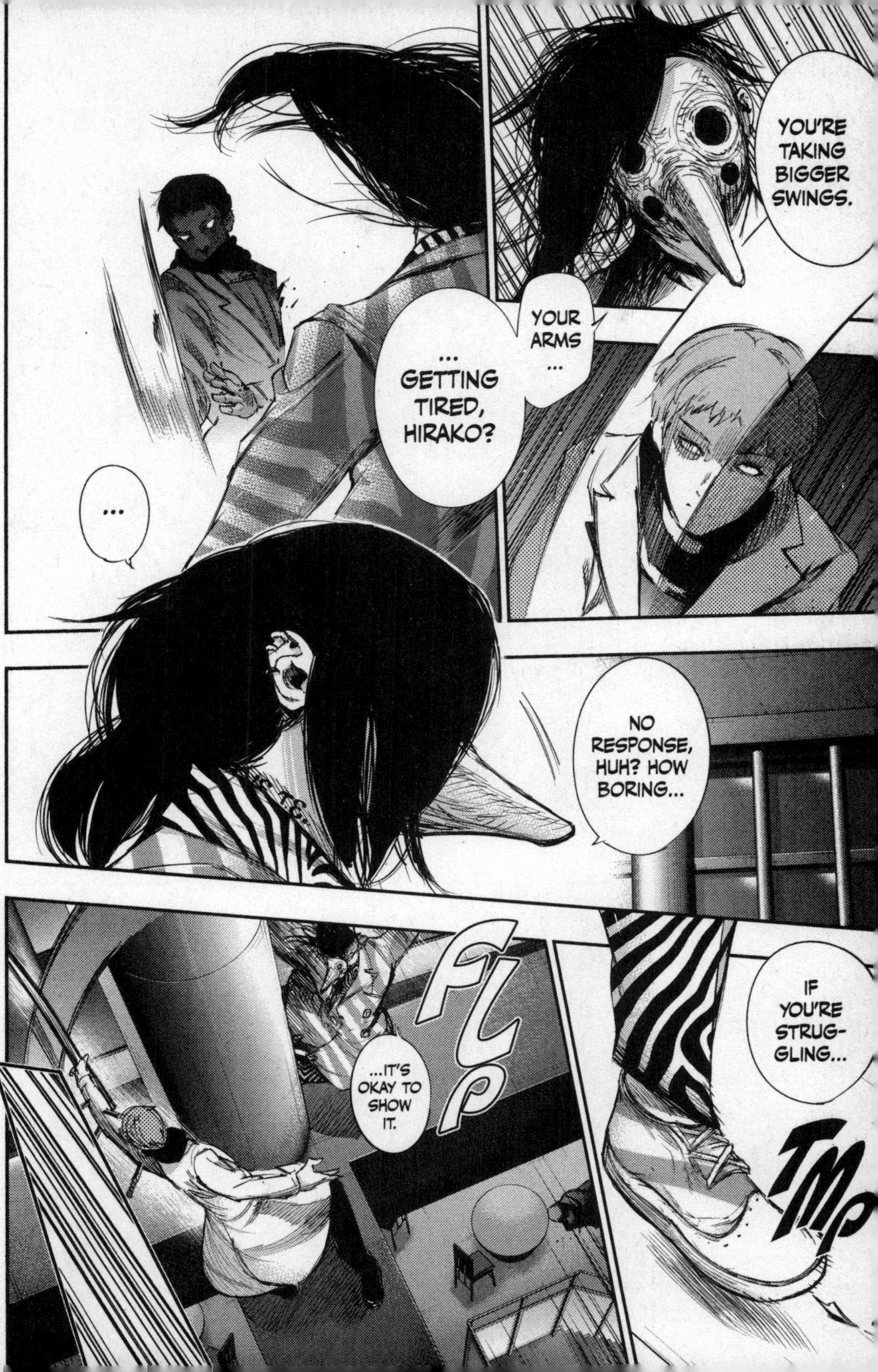
YOU'RE TAKING BIGGER SWINGS.
YOUR ARMS ...
... GETTING TIRED, HIRAKO?
...
NO RESPONSE, HUH? HOW BORING...
IF YOU'RE STRUG-GLING...
TMP
FLIP
...IT'S OKAY TO SHOW IT.

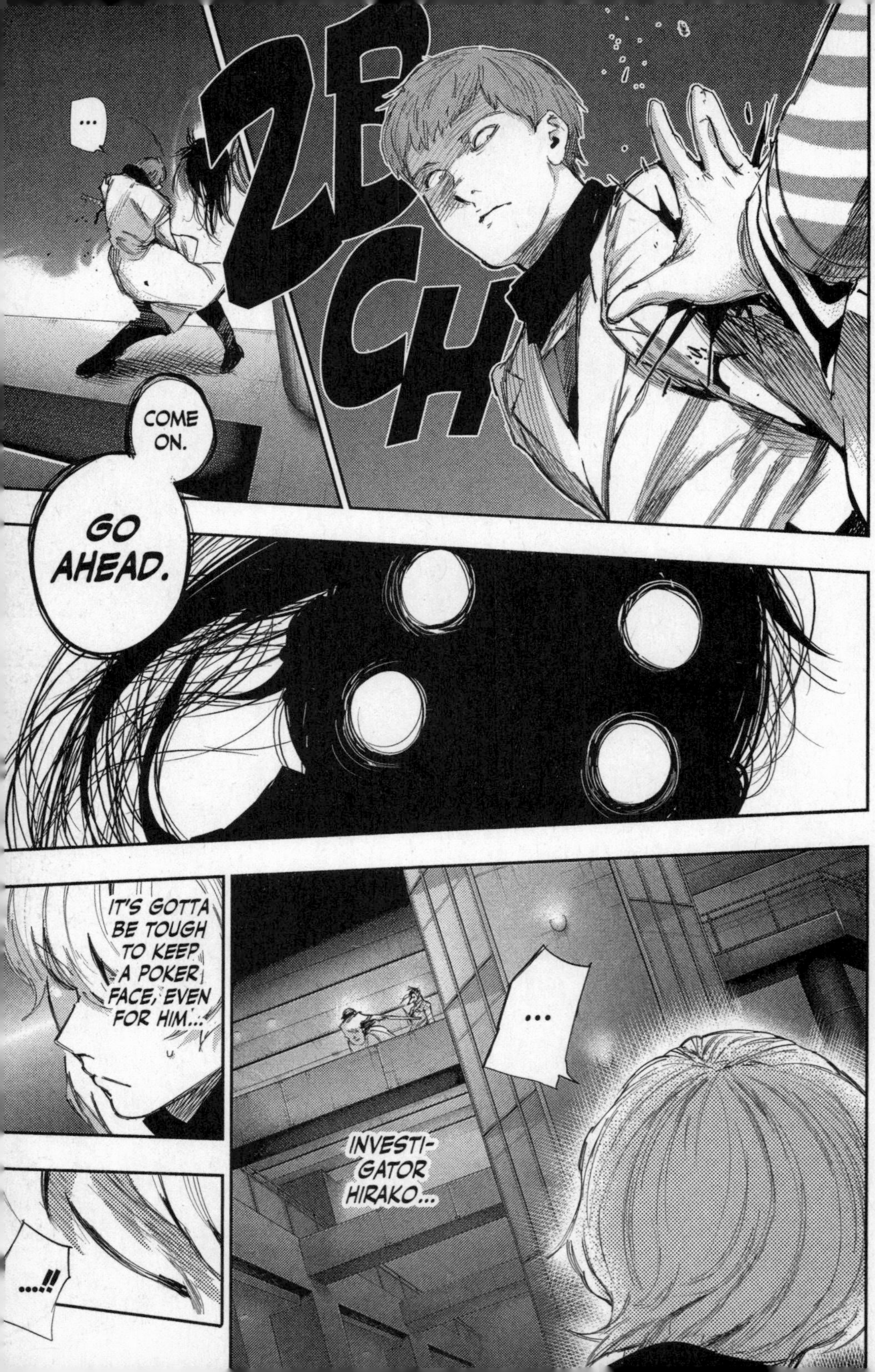
ZBCH
...
COME ON.
GO AHEAD.
...
INVESTI-GATOR HIRAKO...
IT'S GOTTA BE TOUGH TO KEEP A POKER FACE, EVEN FOR HIM...
...!!

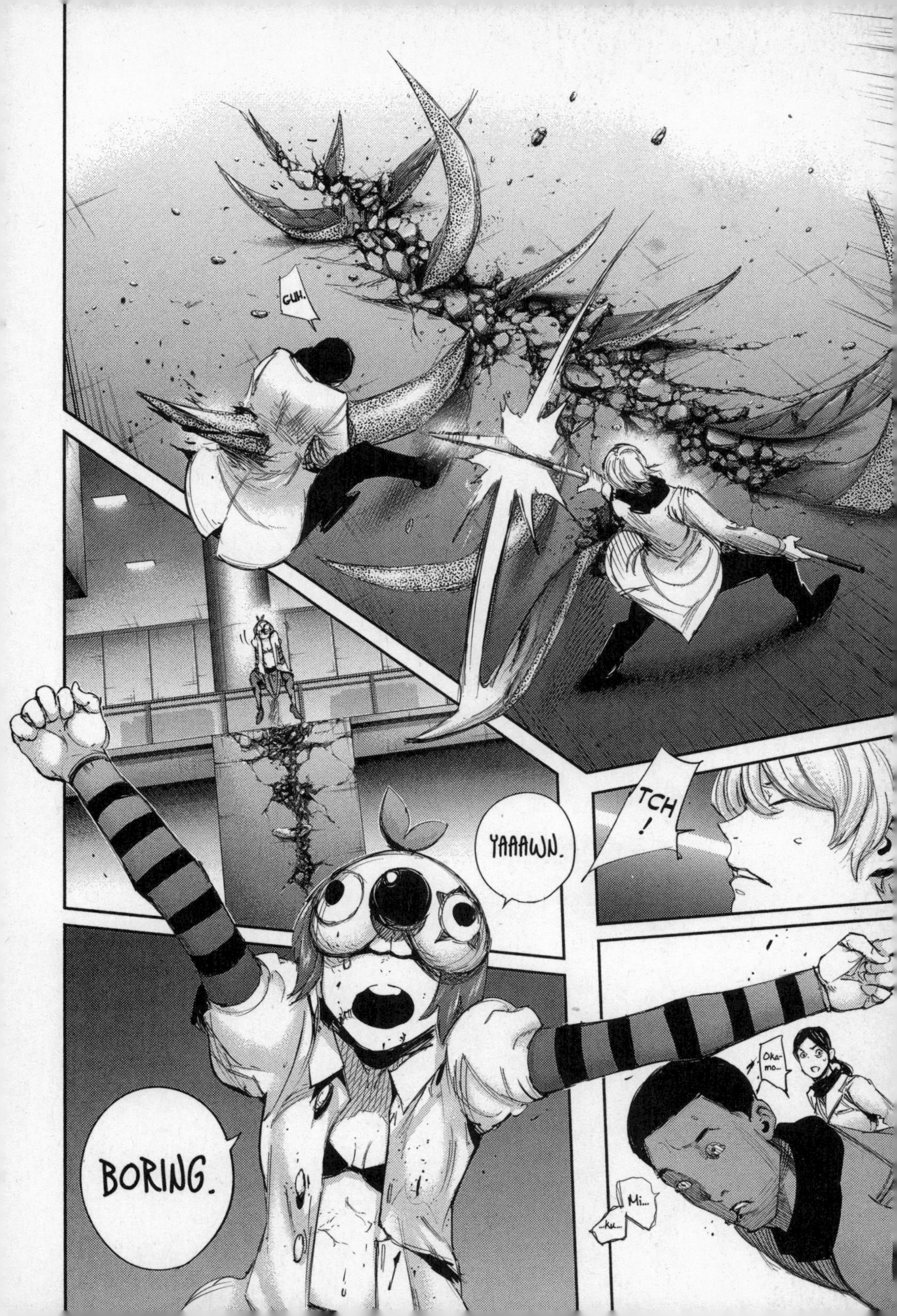
GUH.
TCH!
YAAAWN.
Oka-mo...
Mi...
...ku...
BORING.

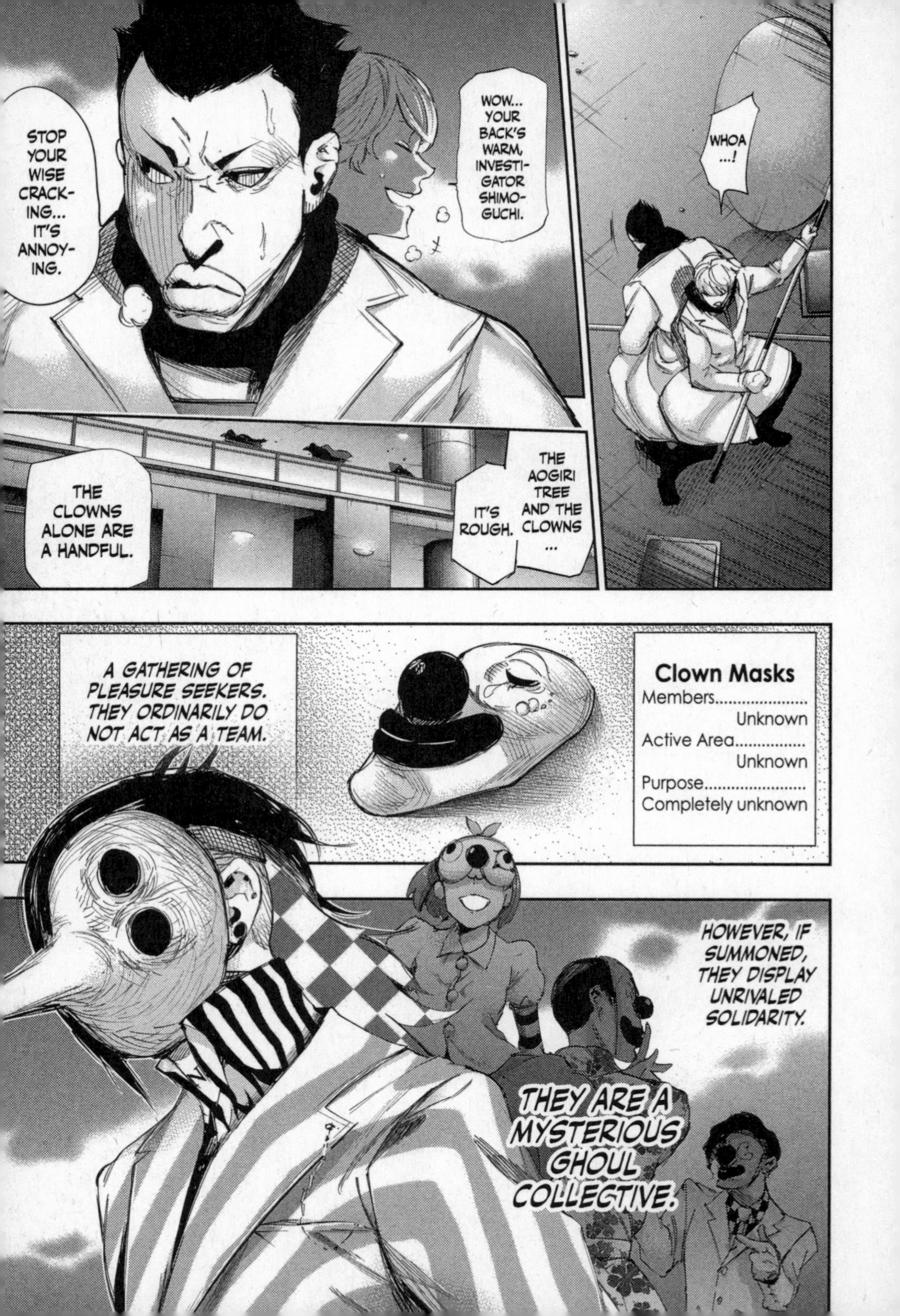
WHOA ...!
WOW... YOUR BACK'S WARM, INVESTIGATOR SHIMOGUCHI.
STOP YOUR WISE CRACKING... IT'S ANNOYING.
THE AOGIRI TREE AND THE CLOWNS ...
IT'S ROUGH.
THE CLOWNS ALONE ARE A HANDFUL.
Clown Masks
Members................... Unknown
Active Area............... Unknown
Purpose.................... Completely unknown
A GATHERING OF PLEASURE SEEKERS. THEY ORDINARILY DO NOT ACT AS A TEAM.
HOWEVER, IF SUMMONED, THEY DISPLAY UNRIVALED SOLIDARITY.
THEY ARE A MYSTERIOUS GHOUL COLLECTIVE.

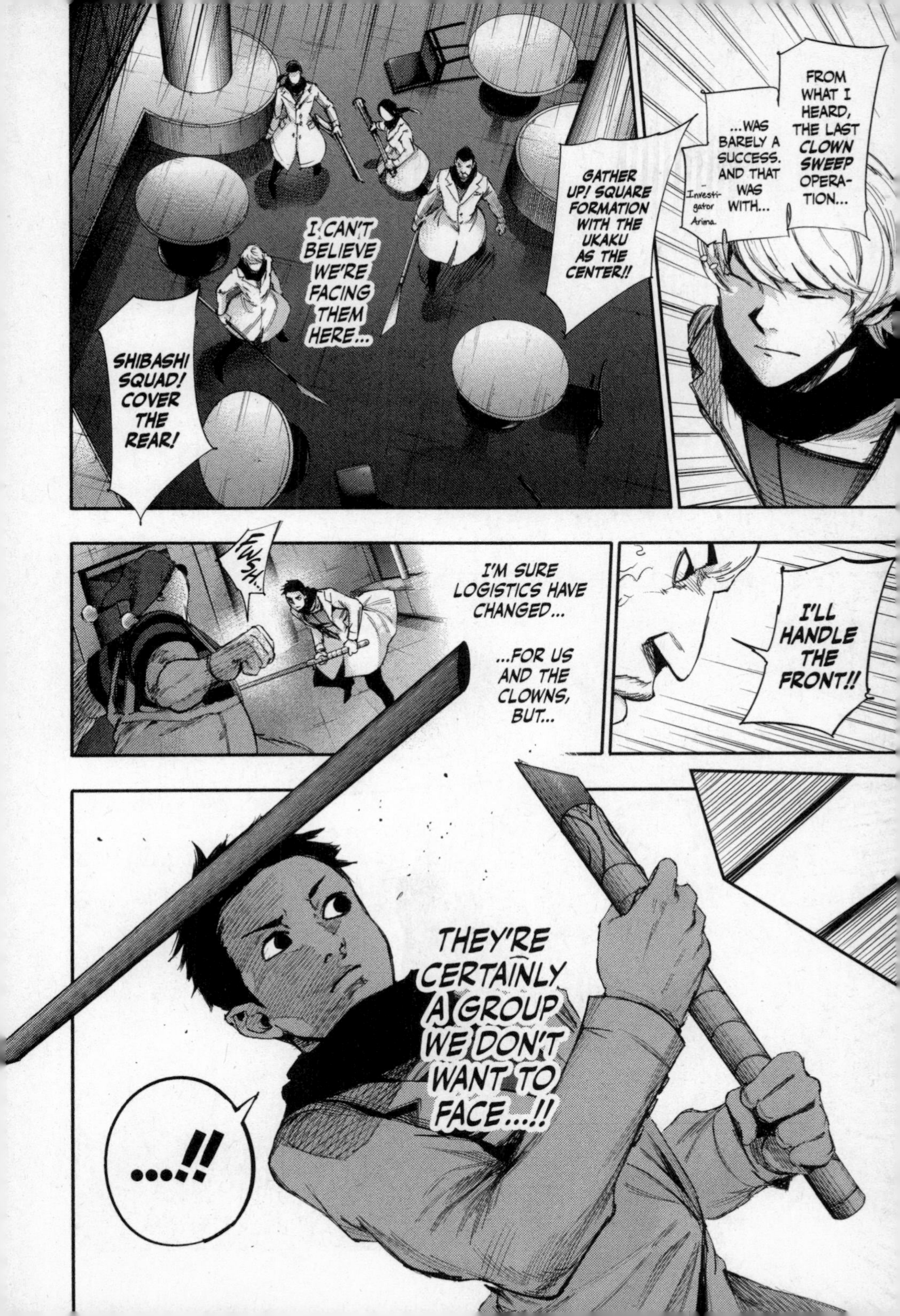
FROM WHAT I HEARD, THE LAST CLOWN SWEEP OPERATION...
...WAS BARELY A SUCCESS. AND THAT WAS WITH...
—Investigator Arima.
GATHER UP! SQUARE FORMATION WITH THE UKAKU AS THE CENTER!!
I CAN'T BELIEVE WE'RE FACING THEM HERE...
SHIBASHI SQUAD! COVER THE REAR!
I'LL HANDLE THE FRONT!!
I'M SURE LOGISTICS HAVE CHANGED...
...FOR US AND THE CLOWNS, BUT...
FWSH...
THEY'RE CERTAINLY A GROUP WE DON'T WANT TO FACE...!!
...!!

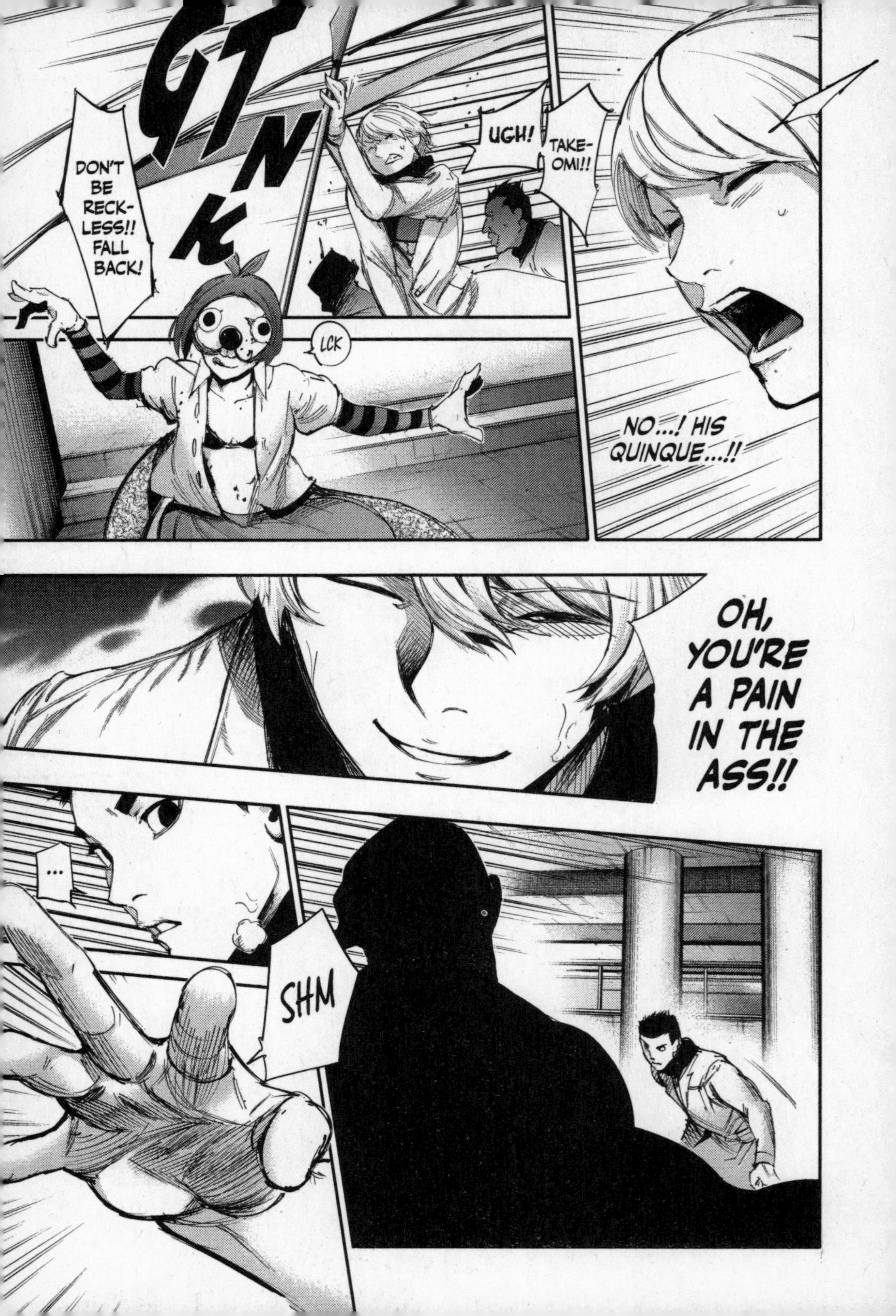
NO...! HIS QUINQUE...!!
TAKE-OMI!!
UGH!
GTNK
DON'T BE RECK-LESS!! FALL BACK!
LCK
OH, YOU'RE A PAIN IN THE ASS!!
SHM
...

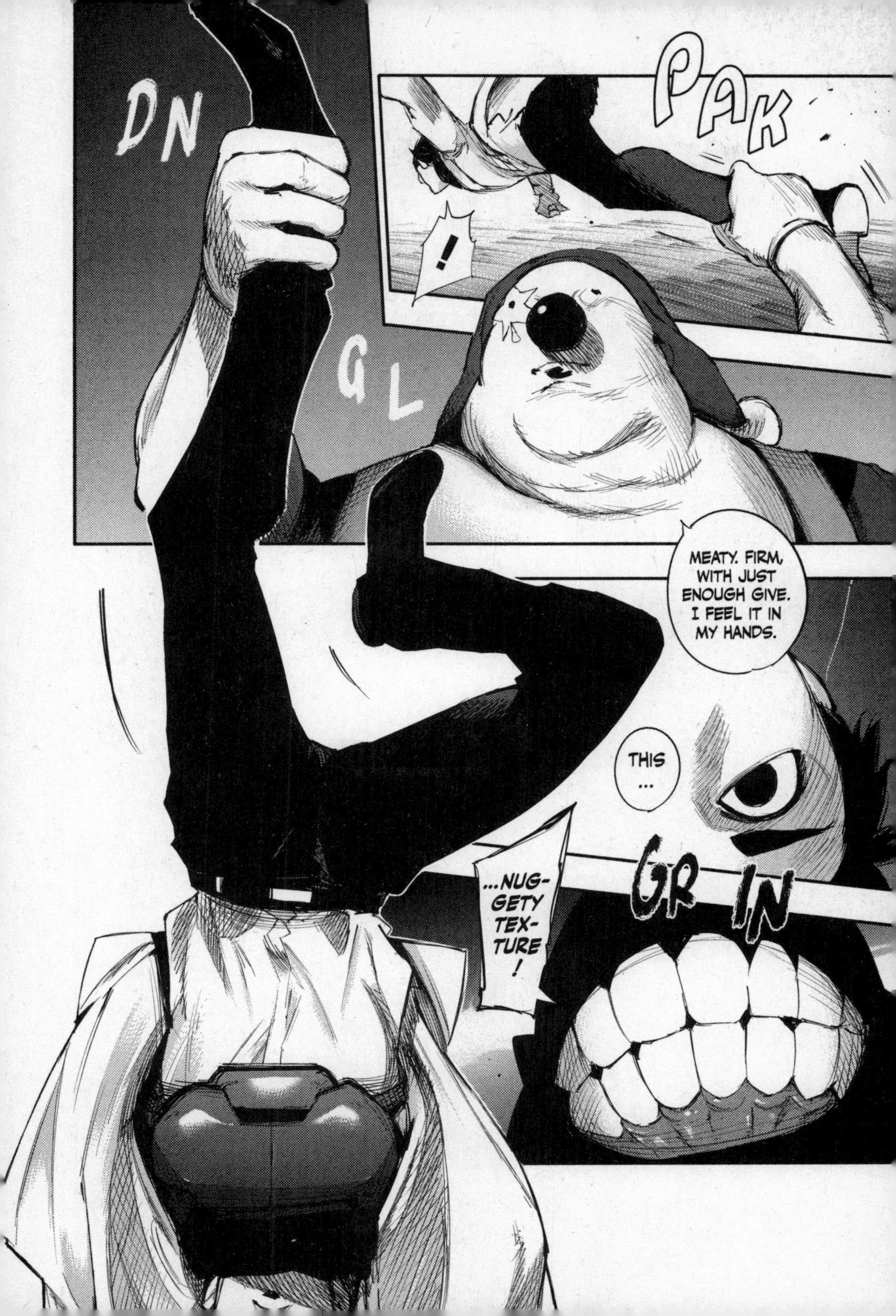
PAK
!
DN
GL
MEATY. FIRM, WITH JUST ENOUGH GIVE. I FEEL IT IN MY HANDS.
THIS ...
...NUG-GETY TEX-TURE!
GR IN

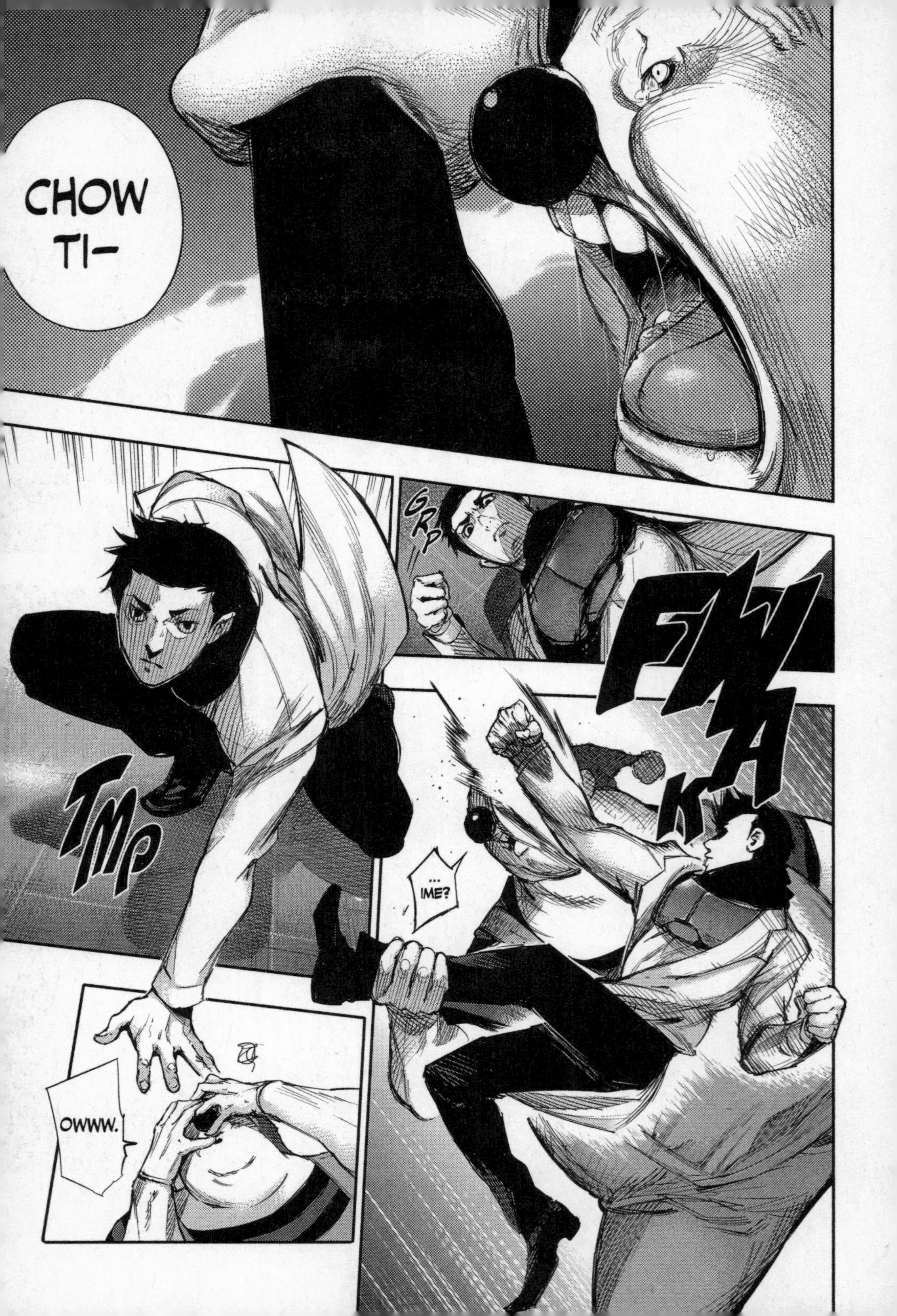
CHOW TI-
GRP
TMP
FWAKA
...IME?
OWWW.

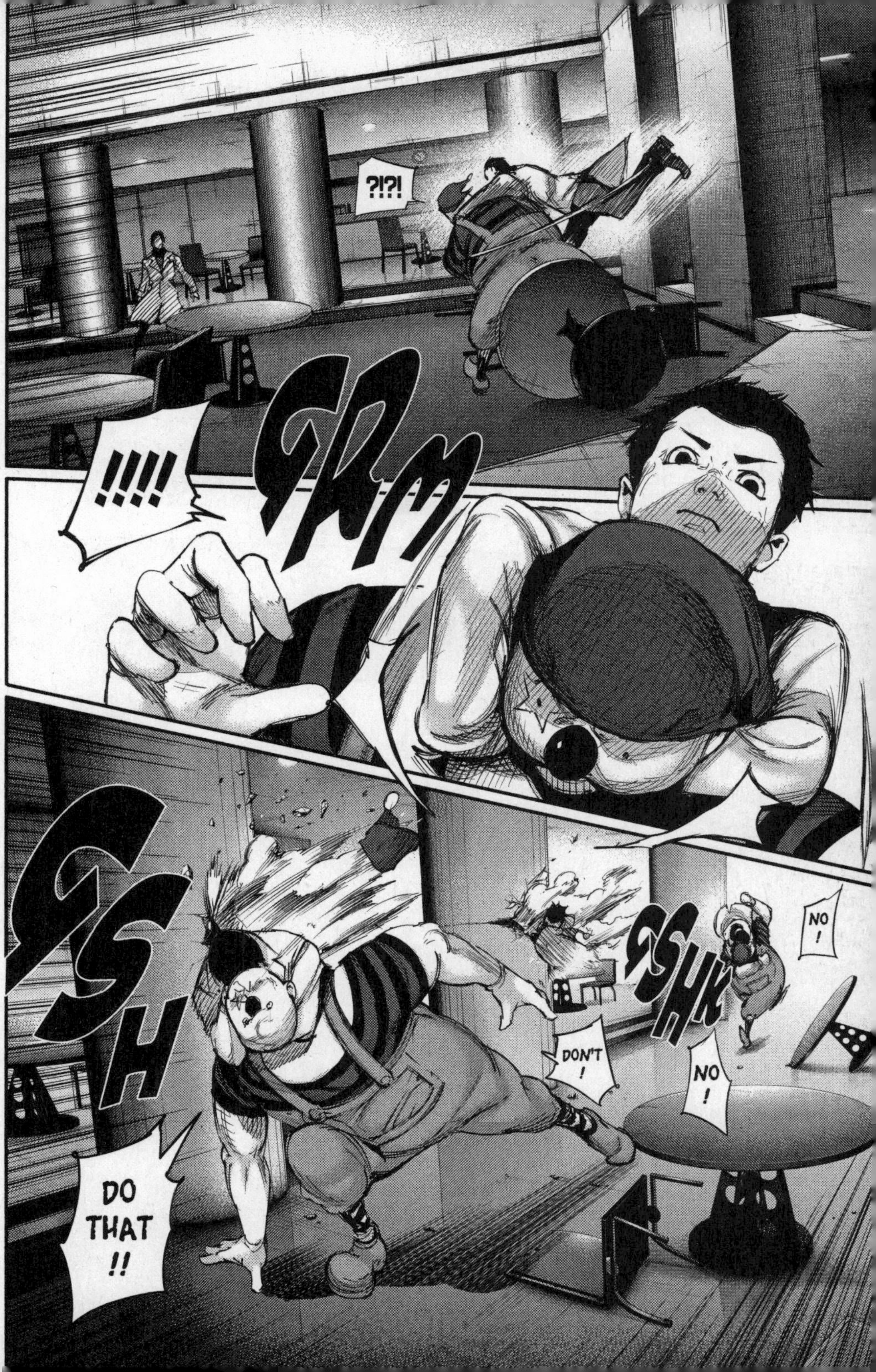
?!?!
!!!!
GRM
NO!
GSHK
NO!
DON'T!
GSH
DO THAT!!

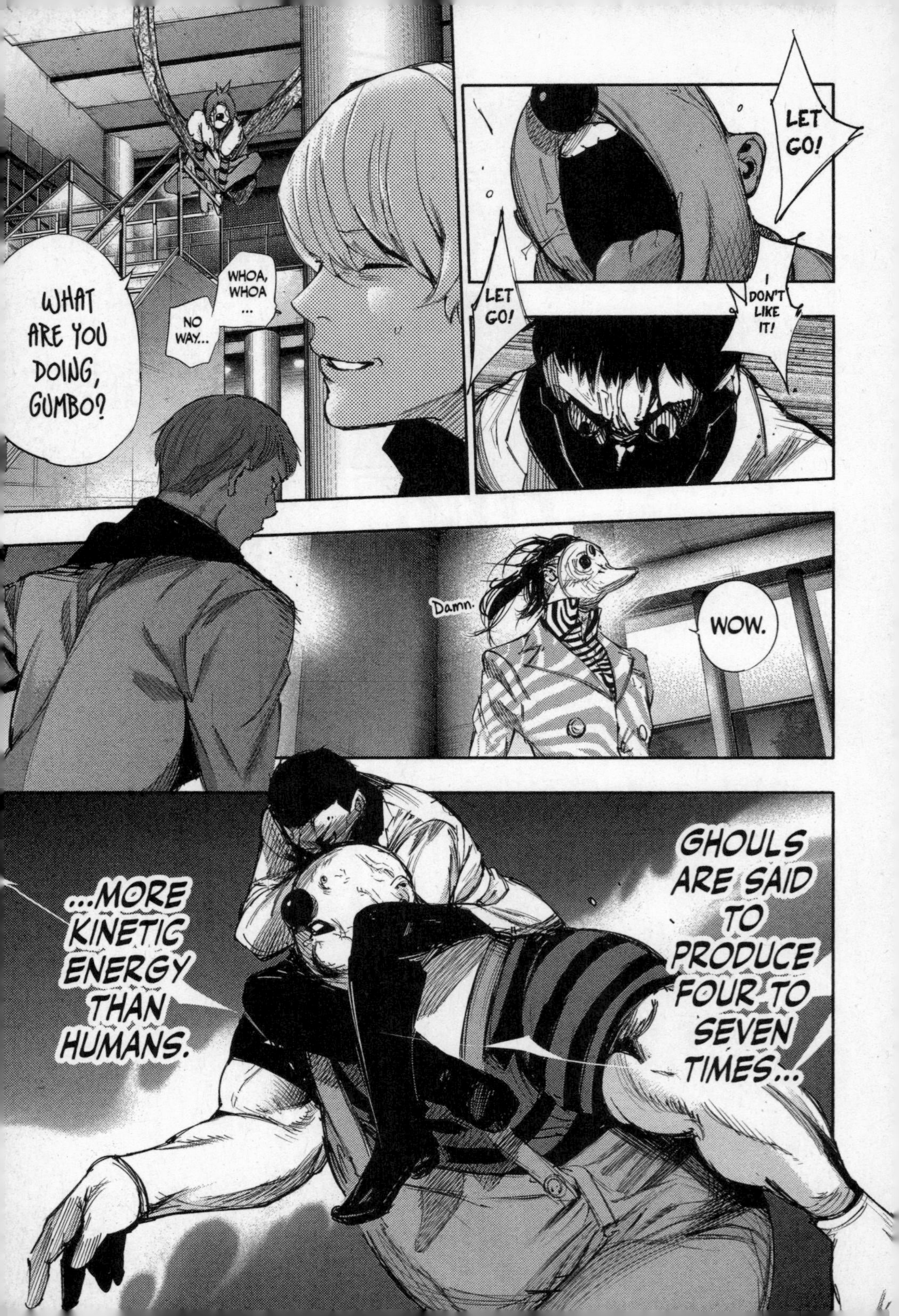
LET GO!
I DON'T LIKE IT!
LET GO!
WHOA, WHOA ...
NO WAY...
WHAT ARE YOU DOING, GUMBO?
WOW.
Damn.
GHOULS ARE SAID TO PRODUCE FOUR TO SEVEN TIMES...
...MORE KINETIC ENERGY THAN HUMANS.

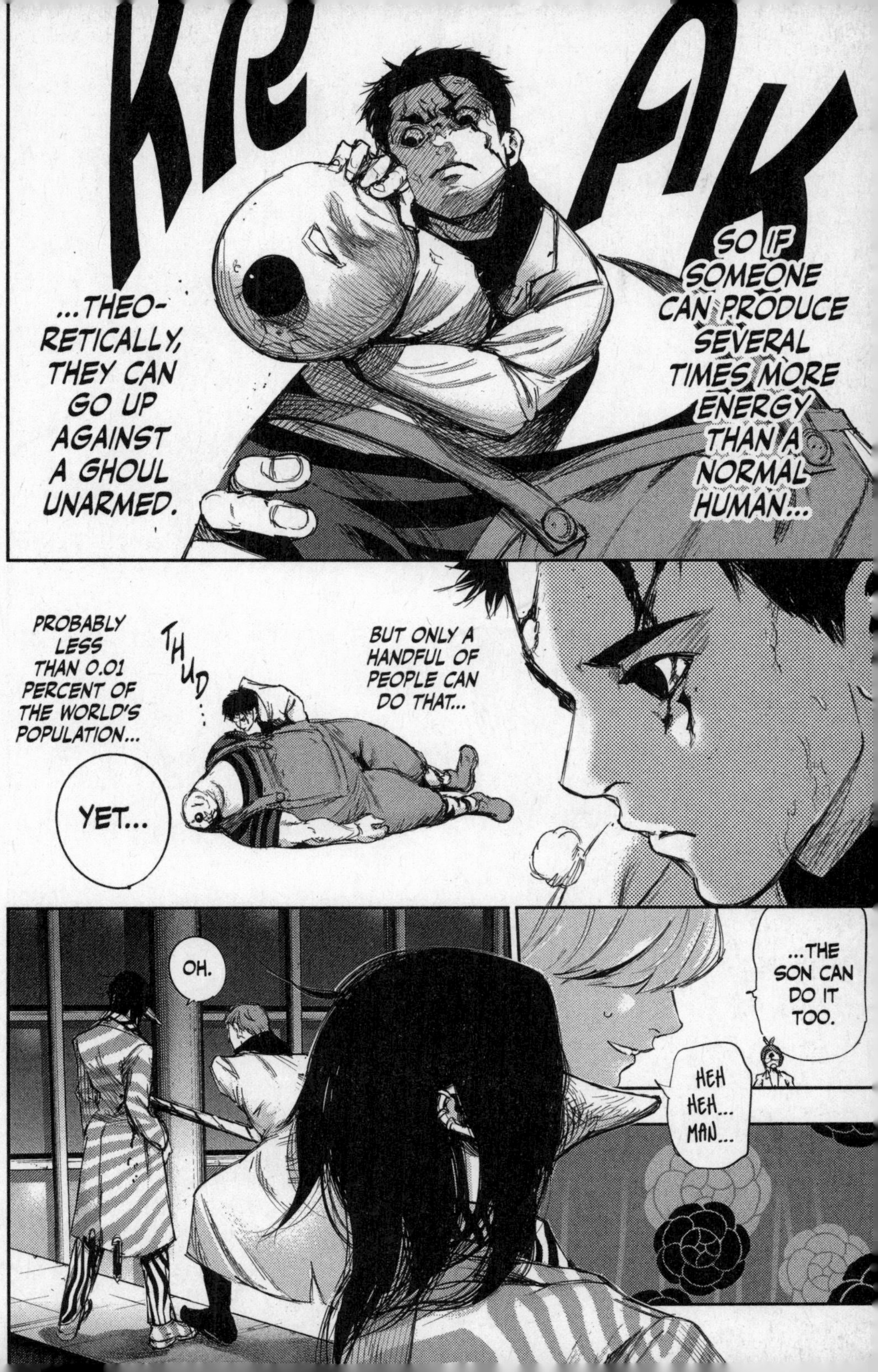
KRAK
SO IF SOMEONE CAN PRODUCE SEVERAL TIMES MORE ENERGY THAN A NORMAL HUMAN...
...THEO-RETICALLY, THEY CAN GO UP AGAINST A GHOUL UNARMED.
BUT ONLY A HANDFUL OF PEOPLE CAN DO THAT...
THUD
PROBABLY LESS THAN 0.01 PERCENT OF THE WORLD'S POPULATION...
YET...
...THE SON CAN DO IT TOO.
HEH HEH... MAN...
OH.

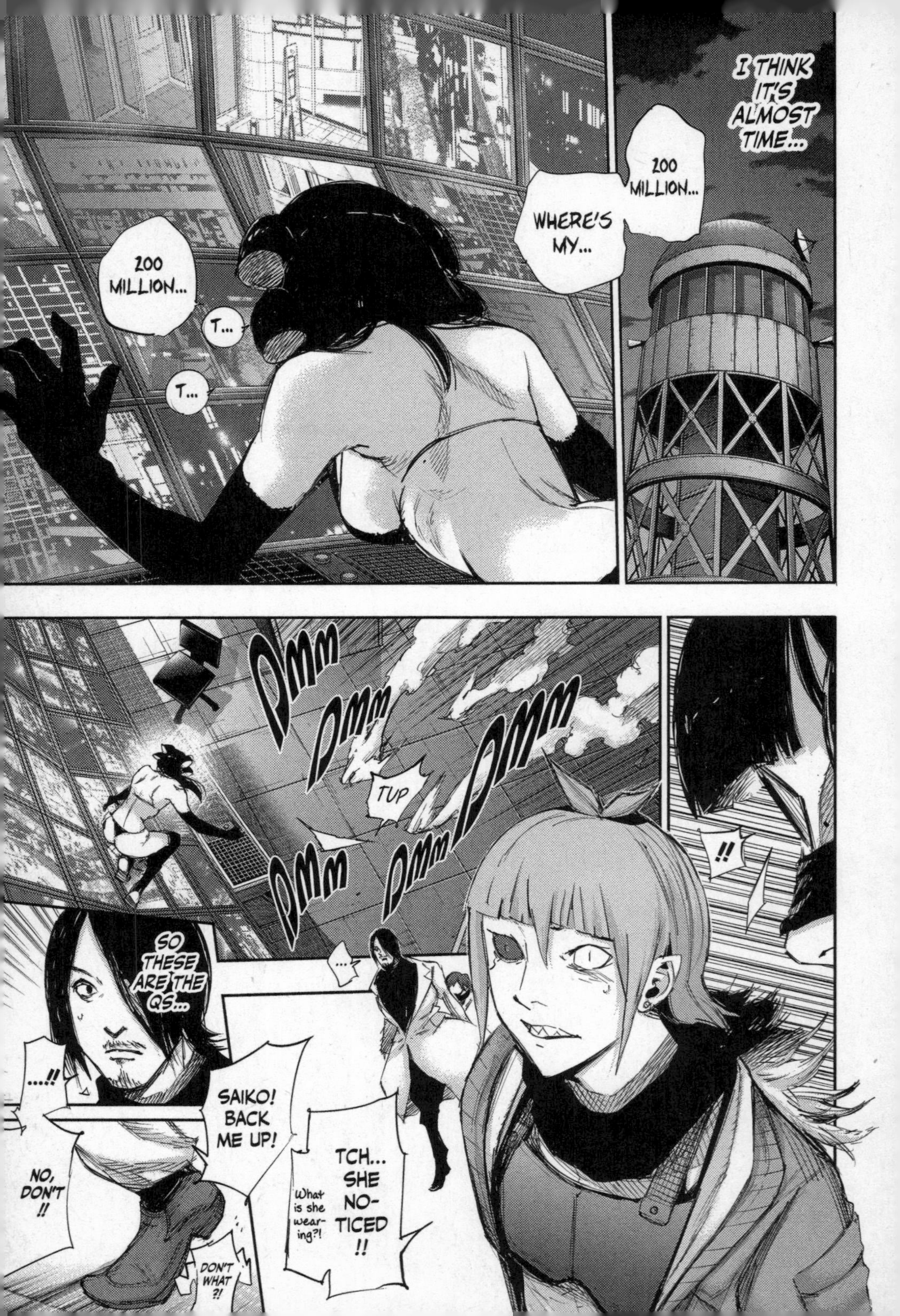
I THINK IT'S ALMOST TIME...
200 MILLION...
WHERE'S MY...
200 MILLION...
T...
T...
!!
DMM DMM DMM DMM DMM DMM DMM
TUP
TCH... SHE NO-TICED !!
What is she wearing?!
...
SO THESE ARE THE QS...
....!!
SAIKO! BACK ME UP!
NO, DON'T !!
DON'T WHAT ?!

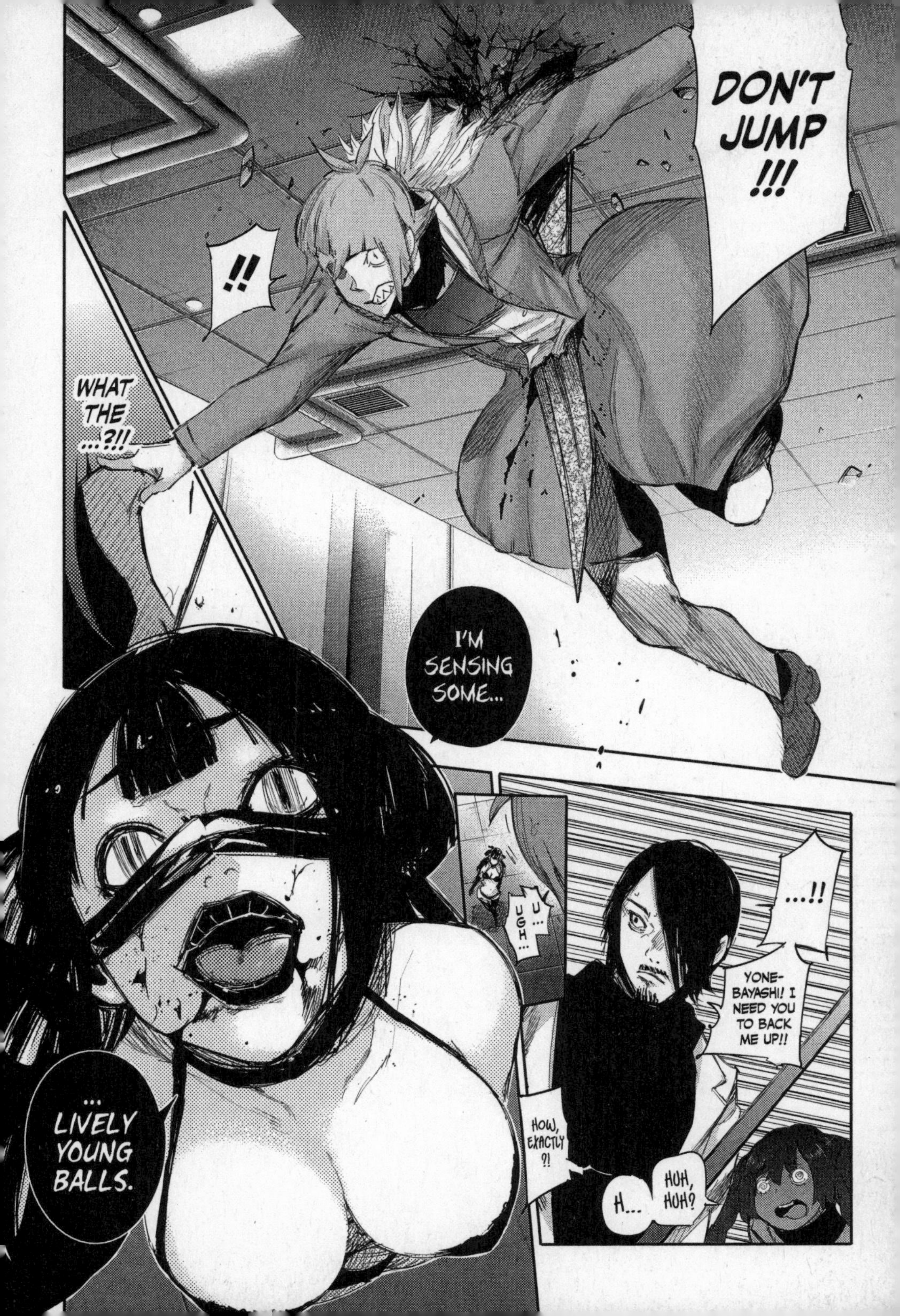
DON'T JUMP !!!
!!
WHAT THE ...?!!
...!!
YONE-BAYASHI! I NEED YOU TO BACK ME UP!!
U... UGH...
HOW, EXACTLY ?!
HUH, HUH?
H...
I'M SENSING SOME...
... LIVELY YOUNG BALLS.

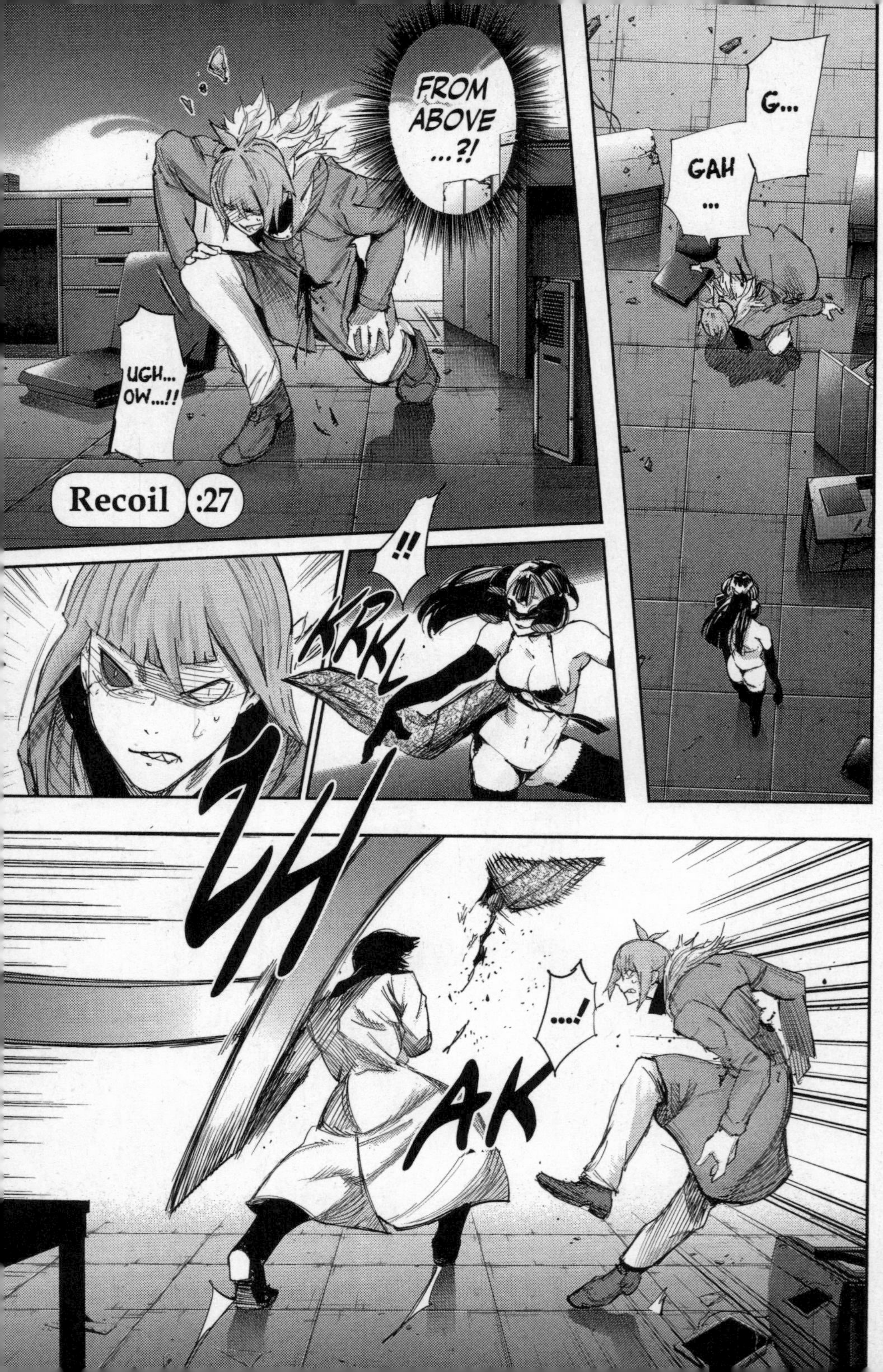
G...
GAH...
FROM ABOVE ...?!
UGH... OW...!!
Recoil :27
!!
KRKL
ZH
...!
AK

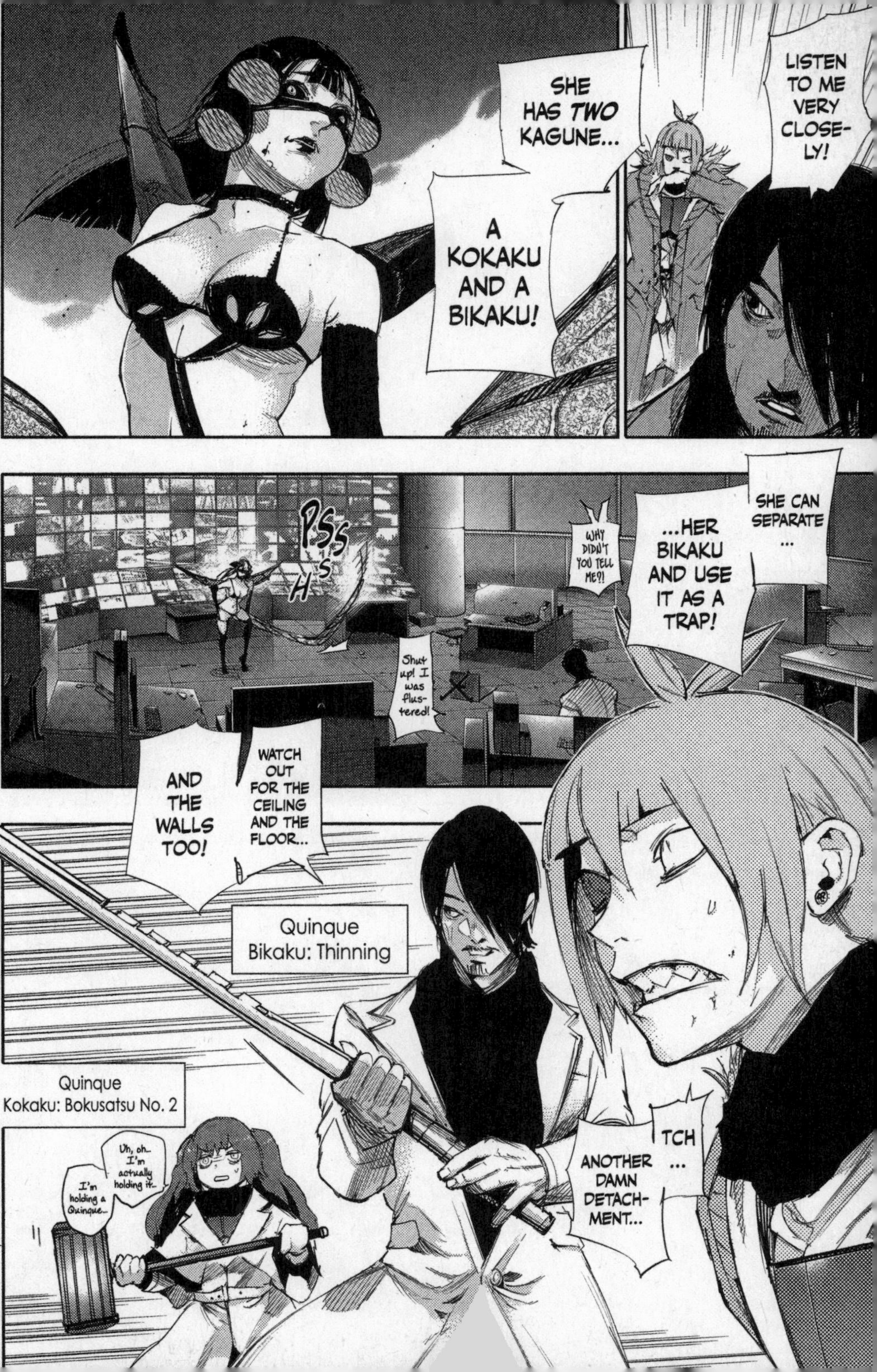
LISTEN TO ME VERY CLOSE-LY!
SHE HAS TWO KAGUNE...
A KOKAKU AND A BIKAKU!
SHE CAN SEPARATE ...
...HER BIKAKU AND USE IT AS A TRAP!
WHY DIDN'T YOU TELL ME?!
Shut up! I was flus-tered!
PSSSH
WATCH OUT FOR THE CEILING AND THE FLOOR...
AND THE WALLS TOO!
Quinque Bikaku: Thinning
TCH ...
ANOTHER DAMN DETACH-MENT...
Quinque Kokaku: Bokusatsu No. 2
Uh, oh... I'm actually holding it...
I'm holding a Quinque...

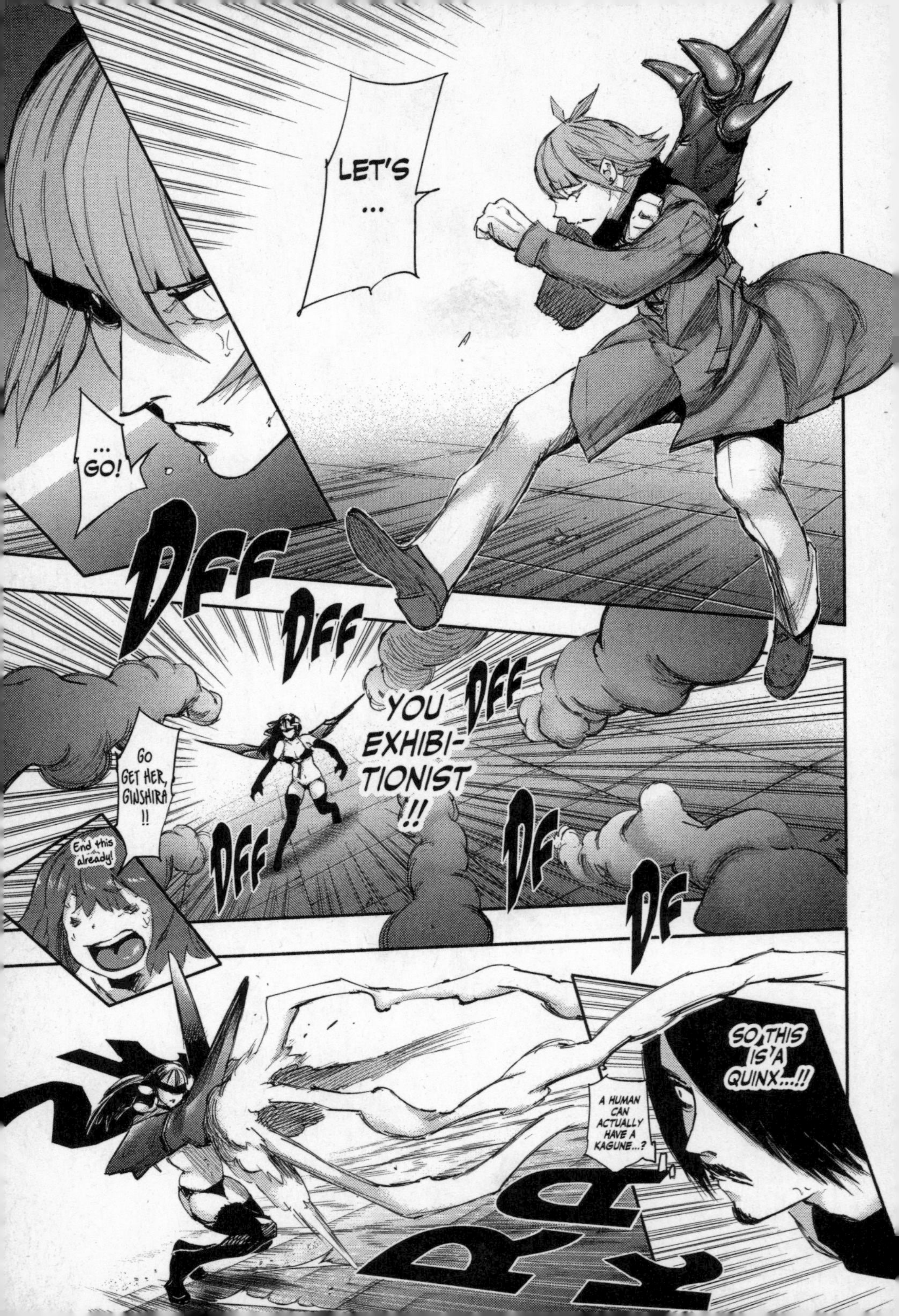
LET'S ...
... GO!
DFF
DFF
YOU EXHIBITIONIST!!
DFF
GO GET HER, GINSHIRA!!
End this already!
DFF
DF
DF
SO THIS IS A QUINX...!!
A HUMAN CAN ACTUALLY HAVE A KAGUNE...?

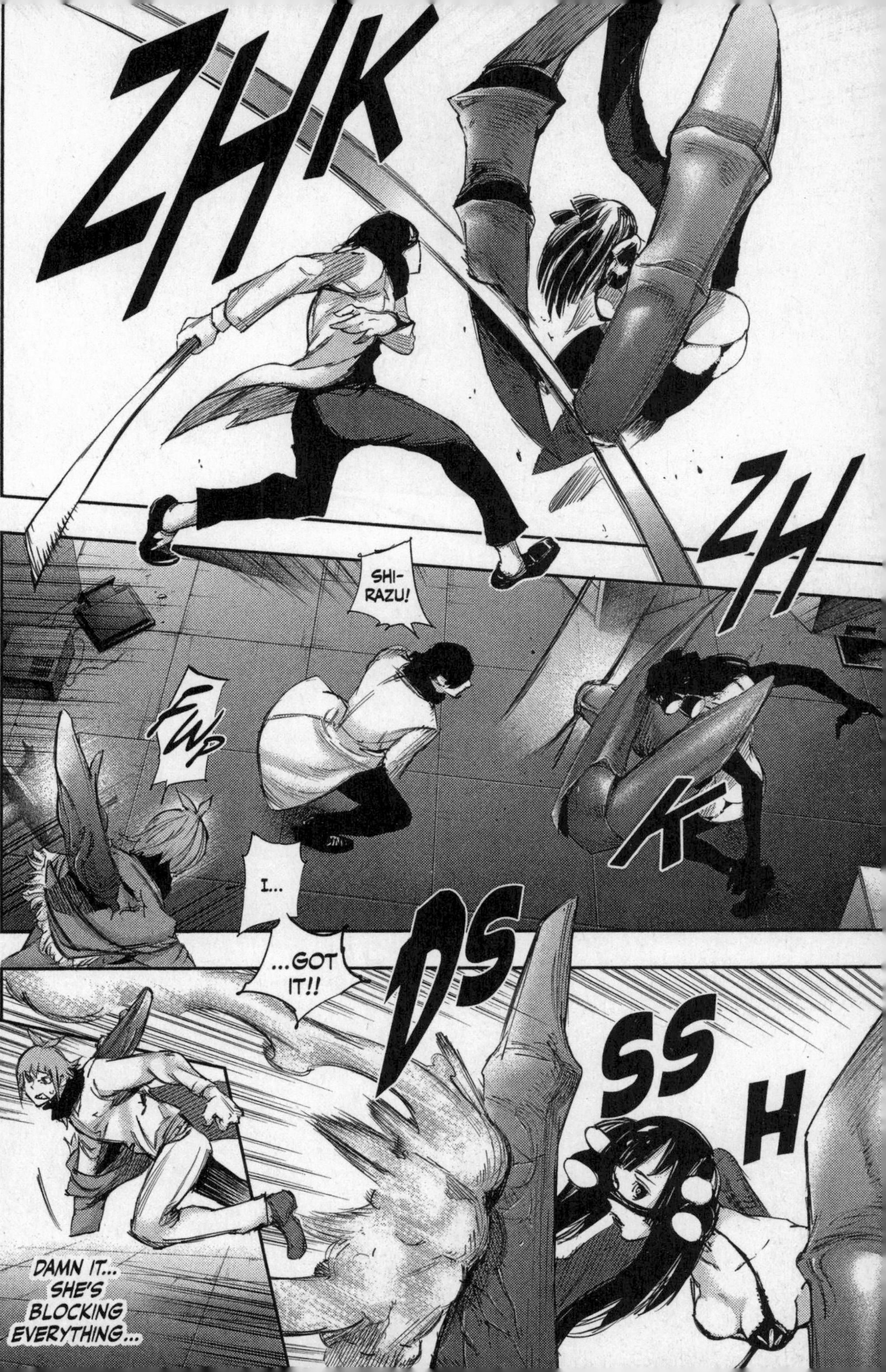
ZHK
ZHK
SHI-RAZU!
FWP
I...
DSSSH
...GOT IT!!
DAMN IT... SHE'S BLOCKING EVERYTHING...

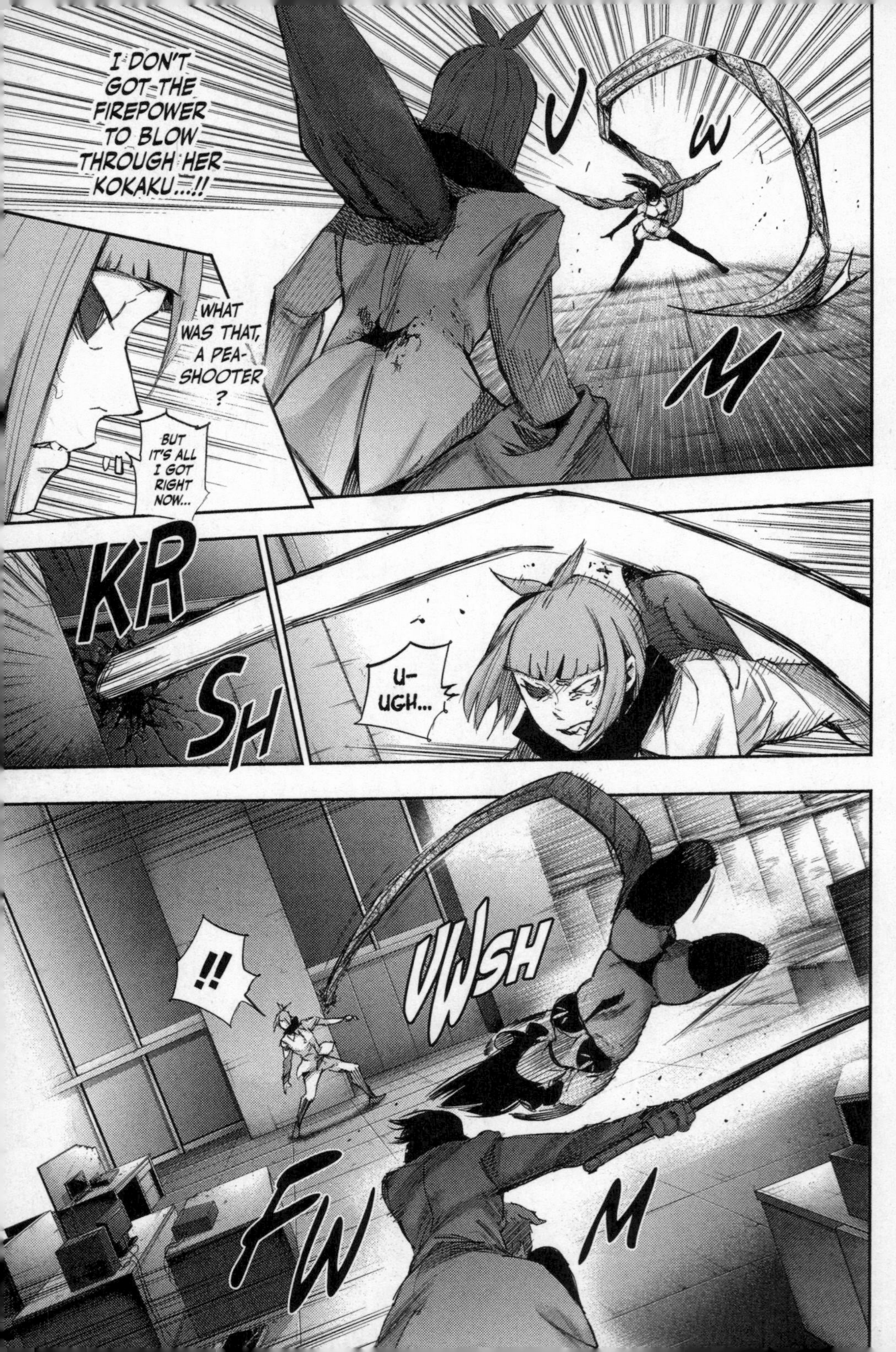
JWWM
I DON'T GOT THE FIREPOWER TO BLOW THROUGH HER KOKAKU...!!
WHAT WAS THAT, A PEA-SHOOTER?
BUT IT'S ALL I GOT RIGHT NOW...
U-UGH...
KR
SH
!!
VWSH
FWM

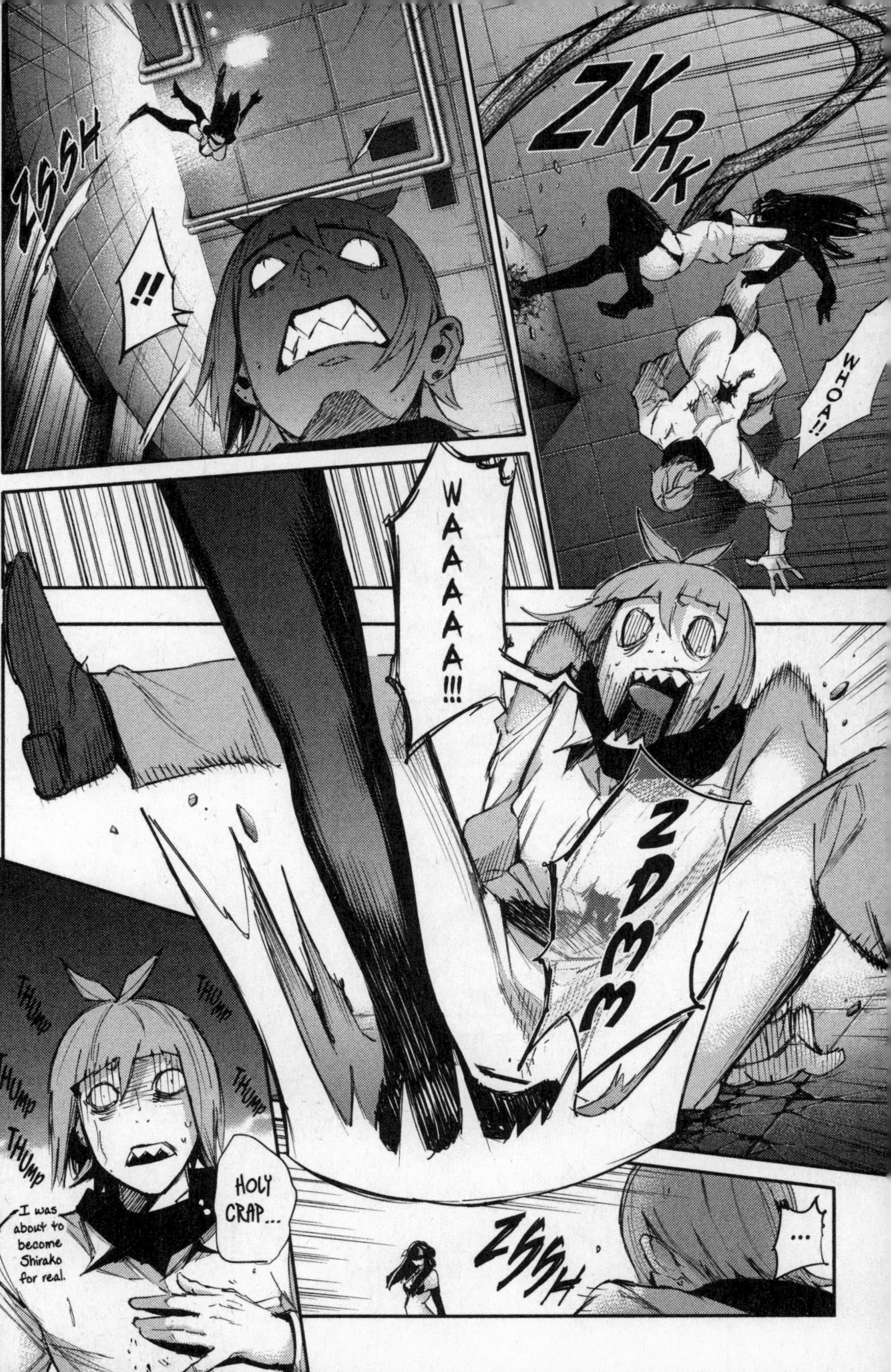
ZKRK
WHOA!!
ZSSH
!!
WAAAAAA!!!
ZDMM
...
ZSSK
THUMP THUMP THUMP THUMP THUMP
HOLY CRAP...
I was about to become Shirako for real.

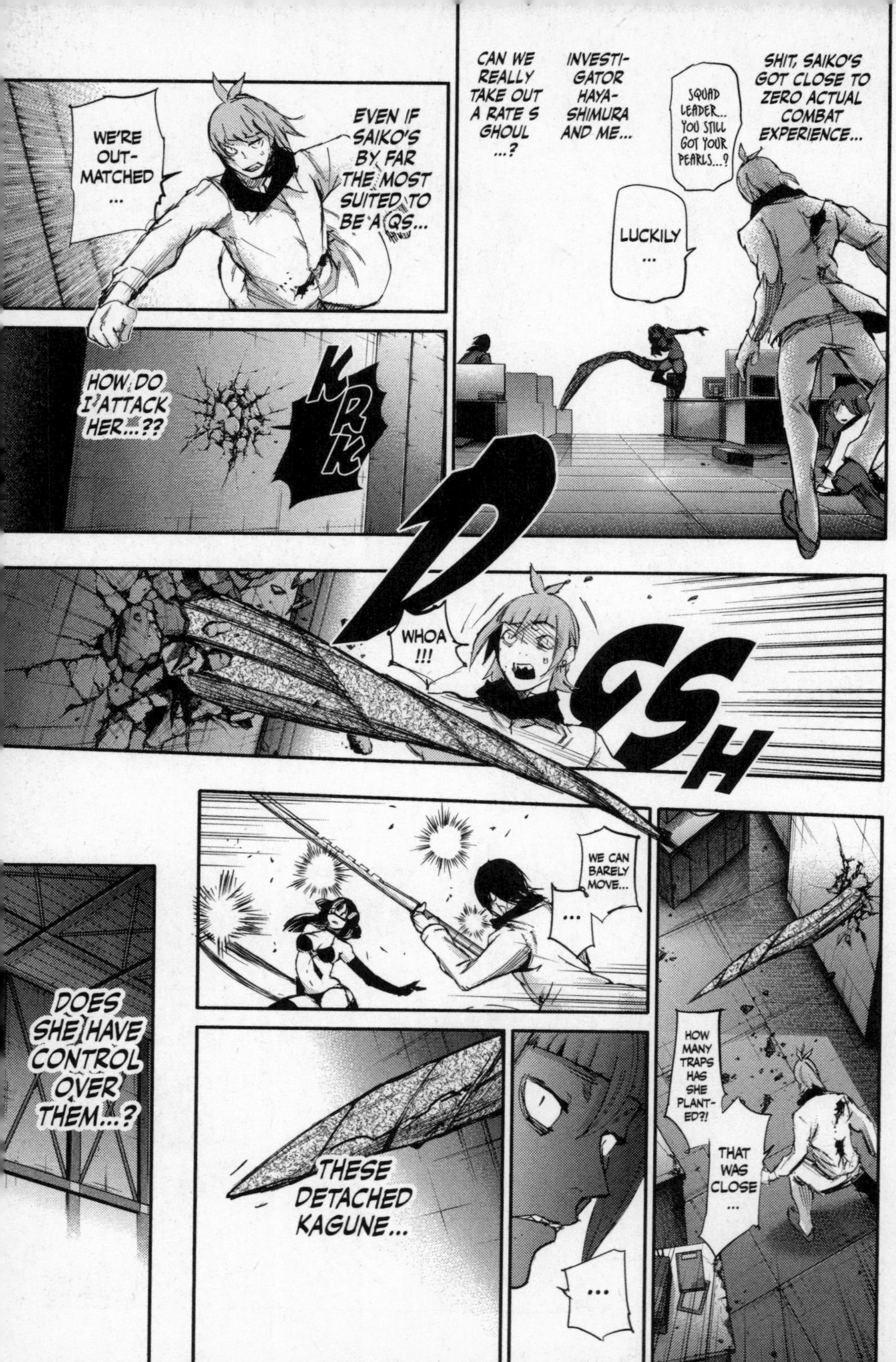
SHIT, SAIKO'S GOT CLOSE TO ZERO ACTUAL COMBAT EXPERIENCE...
SQUAD LEADER... YOU STILL GOT YOUR PEARLS...?
INVESTI-GATOR HAYA-SHIMURA AND ME...
CAN WE REALLY TAKE OUT A RATE S GHOUL ...?
LUCKILY ...
EVEN IF SAIKO'S BY FAR THE MOST SUITED TO BE A QS...
WE'RE OUT-MATCHED ...
KRK
HOW DO I ATTACK HER...??
D
WHOA !!!
GSH
HOW MANY TRAPS HAS SHE PLANT-ED?!
THAT WAS CLOSE ...
WE CAN BARELY MOVE...
...
...
THESE DETACHED KAGUNE...
DOES SHE HAVE CONTROL OVER THEM...?

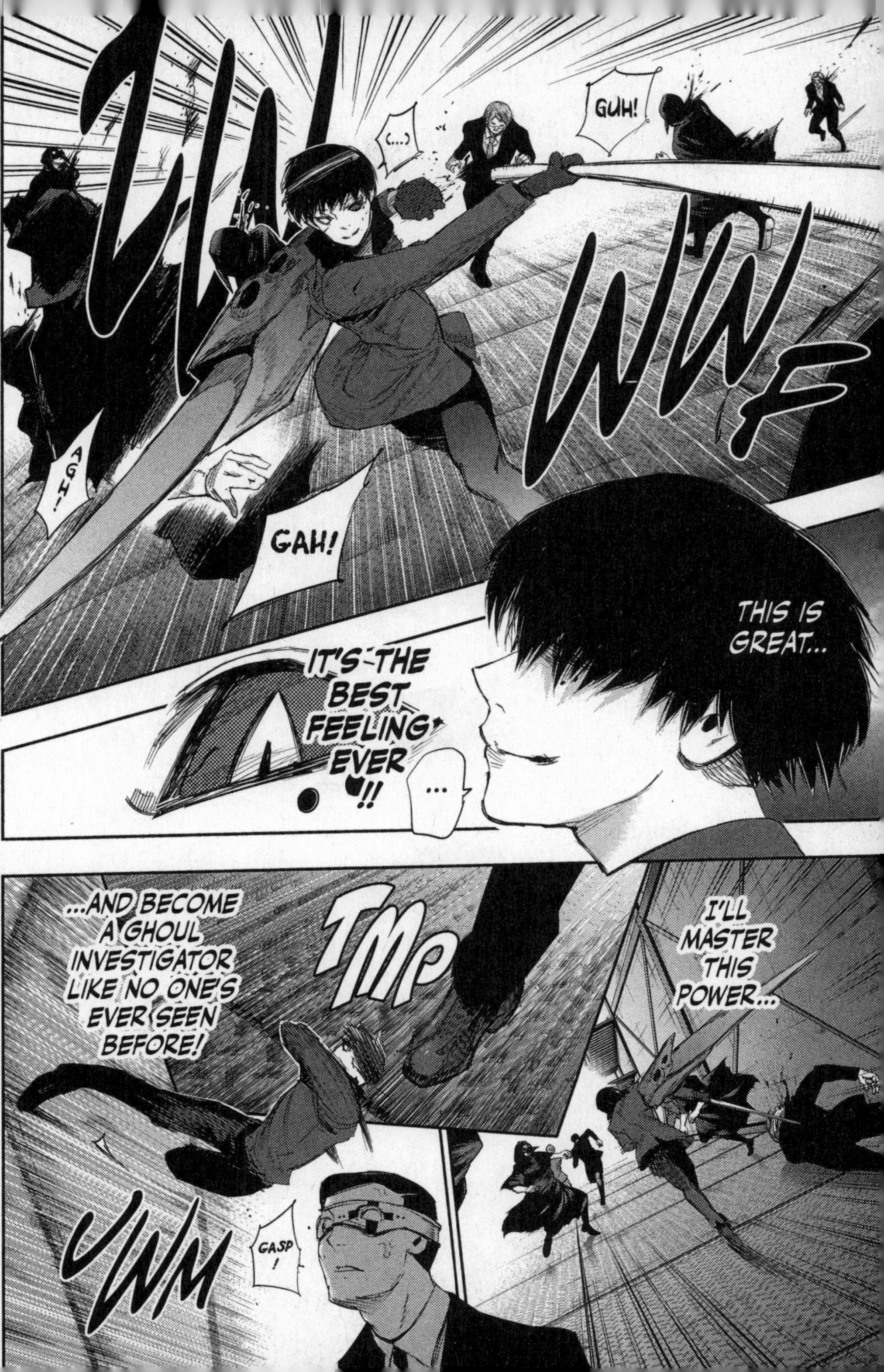
GUH!
(...)
AGH!
GAH!
THIS IS GREAT...
IT'S THE BEST FEELING EVER!!
...
I'LL MASTER THIS POWER...
...AND BECOME A GHOUL INVESTIGATOR LIKE NO ONE'S EVER SEEN BEFORE!
TMP
GASP!

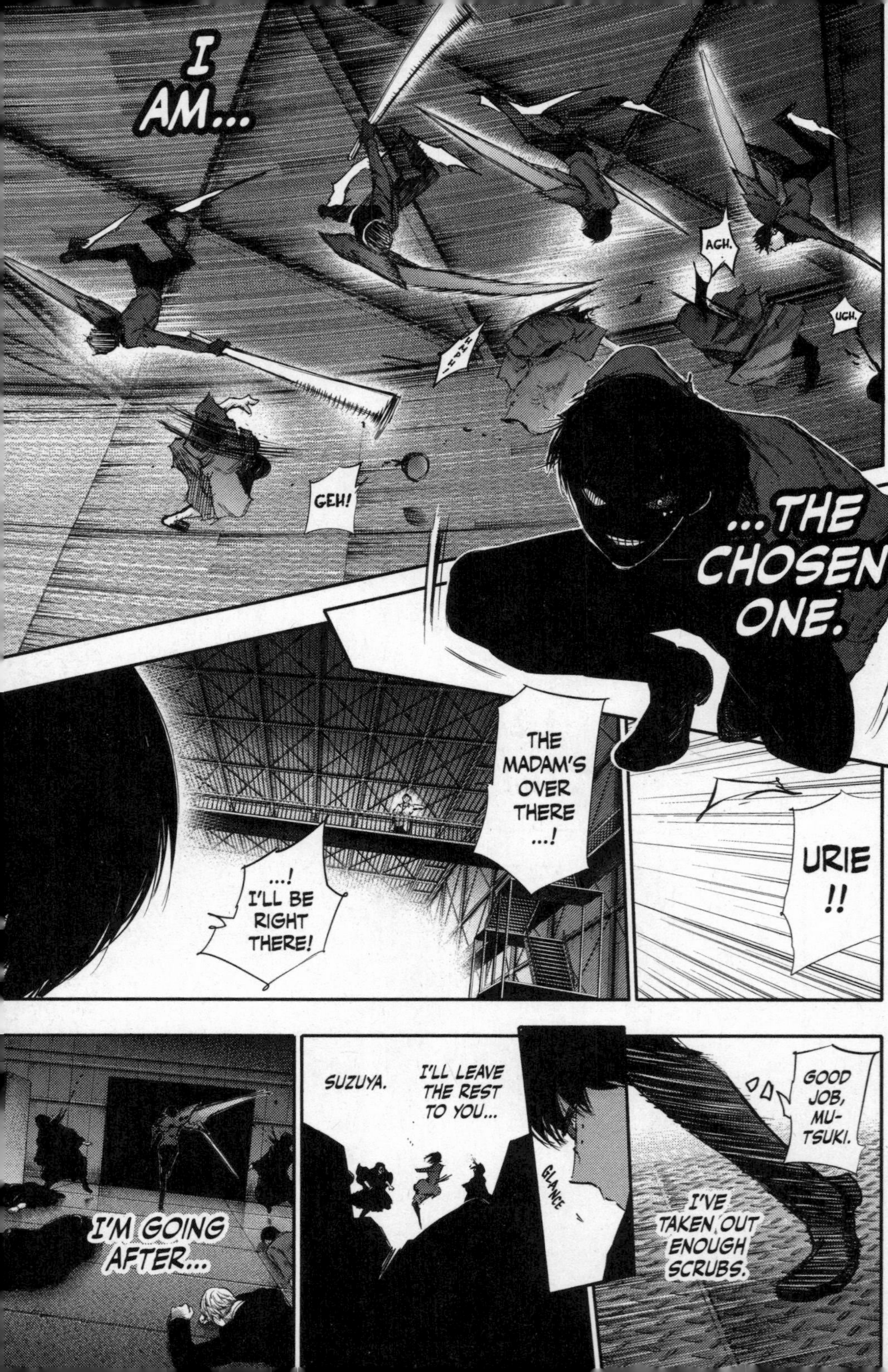
AGH.
UGH.
I AM...
GEH!
...THE CHOSEN ONE.
URIE !!
THE MADAM'S OVER THERE ...!
...! I'LL BE RIGHT THERE!
GOOD JOB, MU-TSUKI.
GLANCE
I'VE TAKEN OUT ENOUGH SCRUBS.
SUZUYA.
I'LL LEAVE THE REST TO YOU...
I'M GOING AFTER...

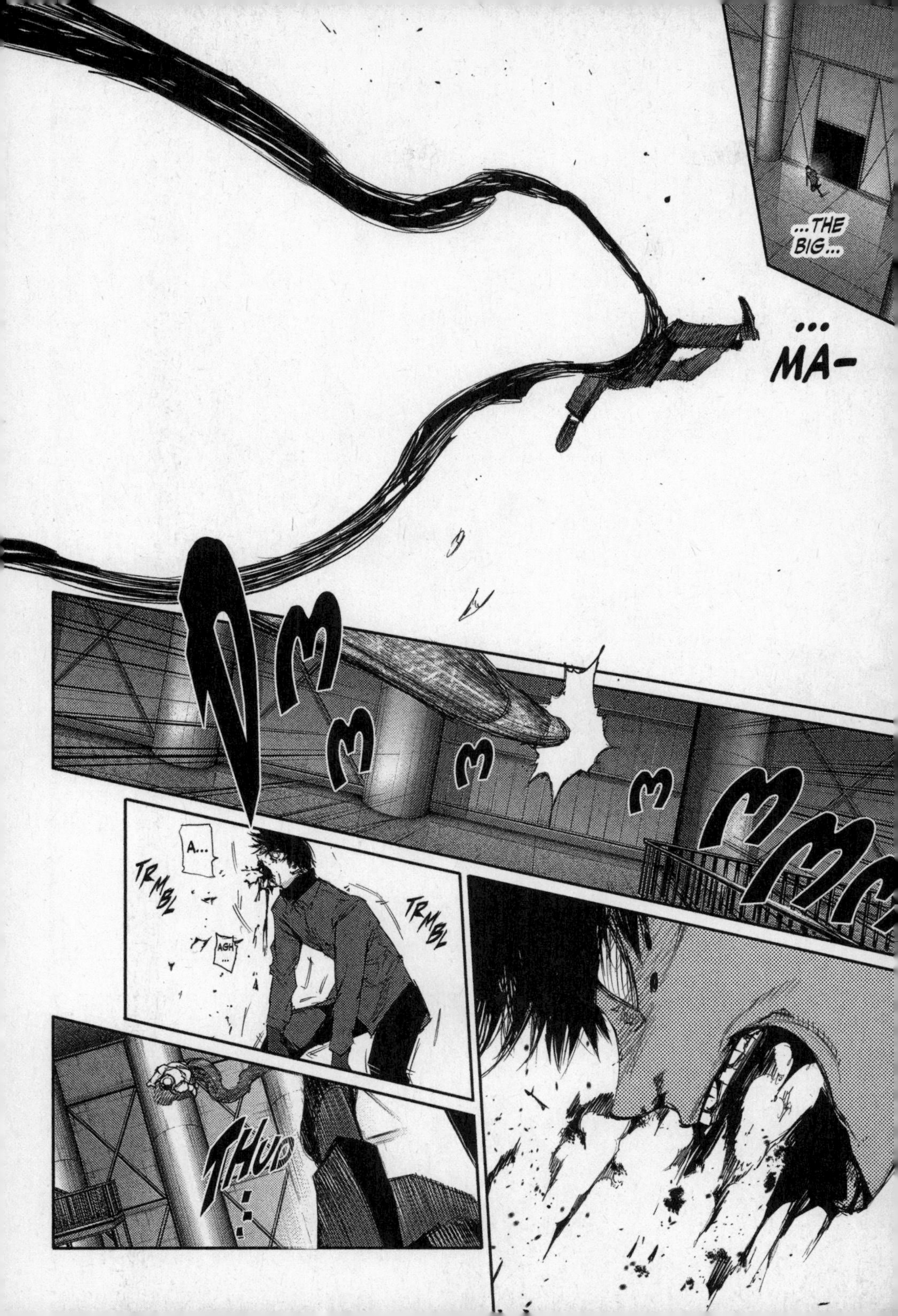
...THE BIG...
...
MA-
A...
TRMBL
TRMBL
AGH...
THUD

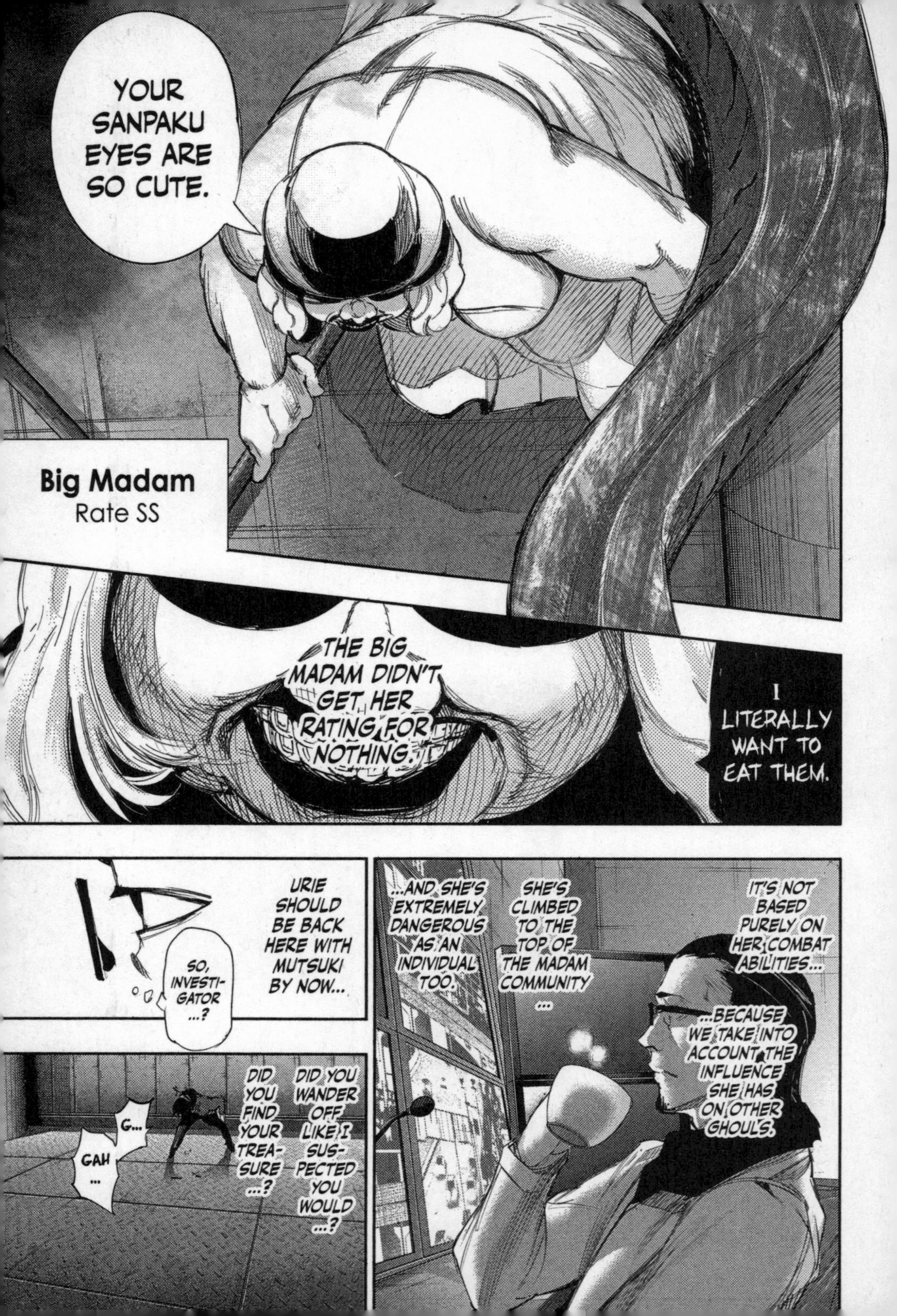

YOUR SANPAKU EYES ARE SO CUTE.
Big Madam
Rate SS
I LITERALLY WANT TO EAT THEM.
THE BIG MADAM DIDN'T GET HER RATING FOR NOTHING.
IT'S NOT BASED PURELY ON HER COMBAT ABILITIES...
...BECAUSE WE TAKE INTO ACCOUNT THE INFLUENCE SHE HAS ON OTHER GHOULS.
SHE'S CLIMBED TO THE TOP OF THE MADAM COMMUNITY...
...AND SHE'S EXTREMELY DANGEROUS AS AN INDIVIDUAL TOO.
URIE SHOULD BE BACK HERE WITH MUTSUKI BY NOW...
SO, INVESTI-GATOR...?
DID YOU WANDER OFF LIKE I SUS-PECTED YOU WOULD...?
DID YOU FIND YOUR TREA-SURE...?
G...
GAH...

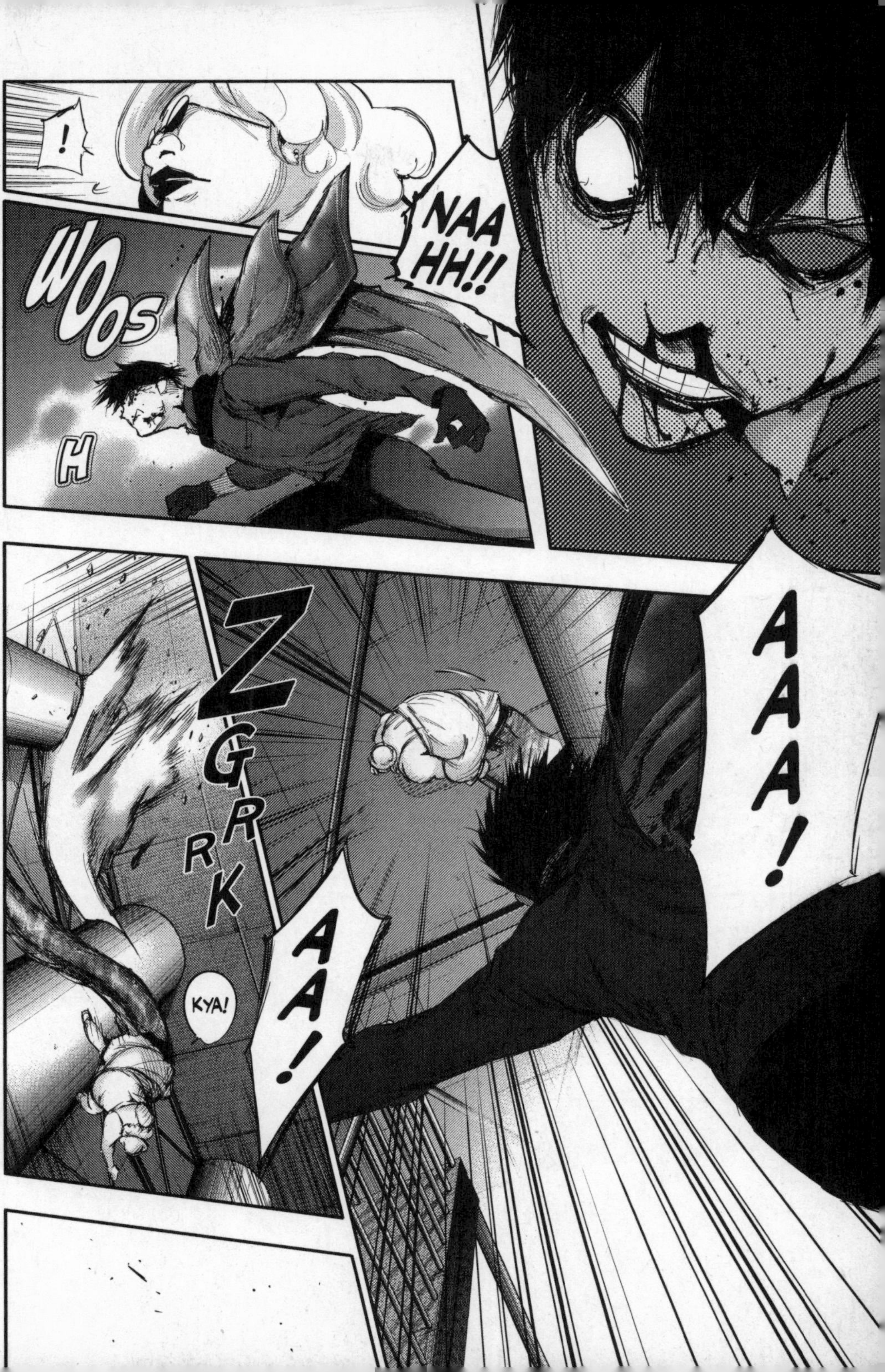
NAAHH!!
!
WOOSH
AAAA!
ZGRRK
AAA!
KYA!

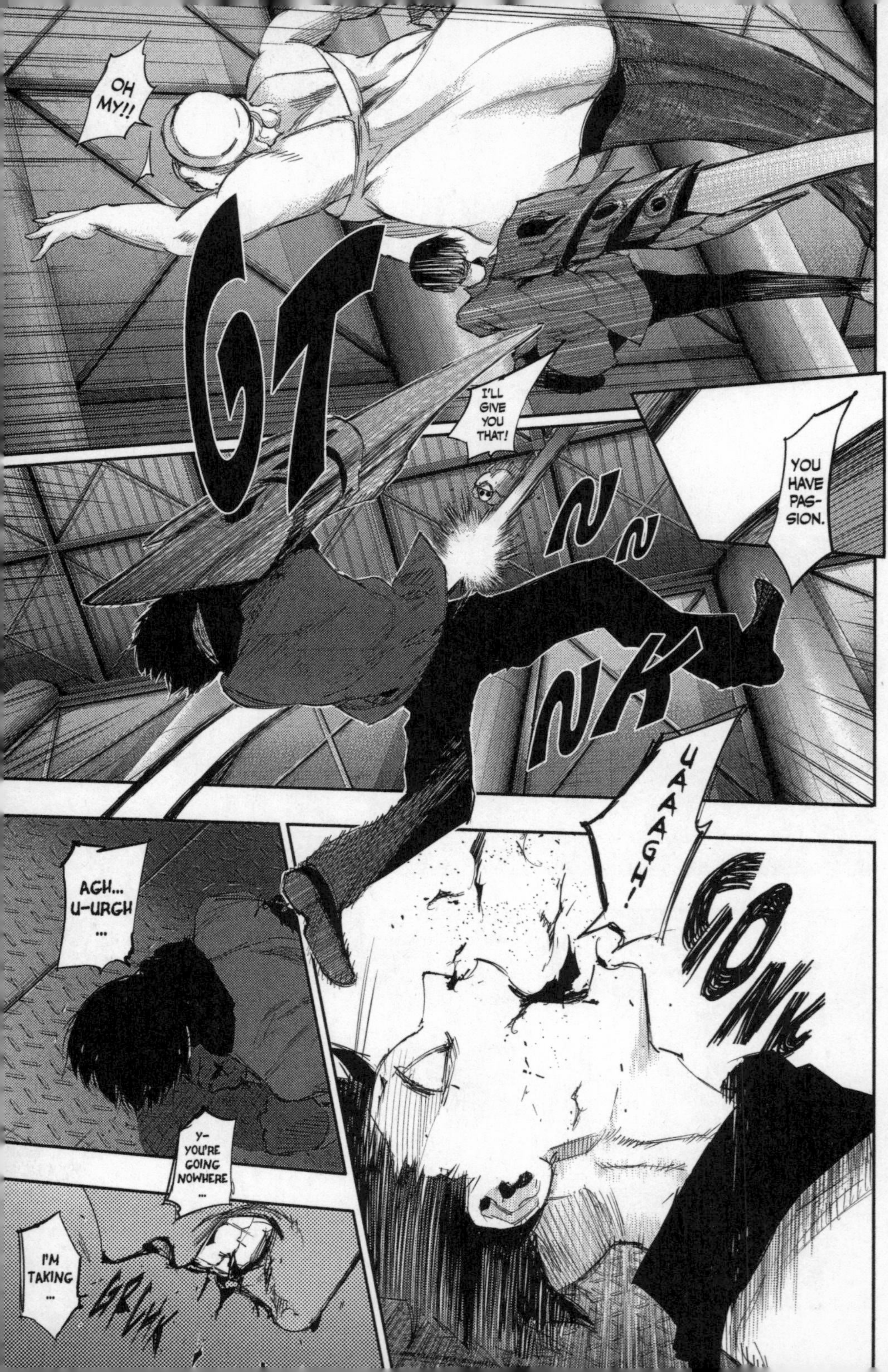
OH MY!!
YOU HAVE PAS-SION.
I'LL GIVE YOU THAT!
UAAAGH!
GONK
AGH... U-URGH ...
Y- YOU'RE GOING NOWHERE ...
I'M TAKING ...

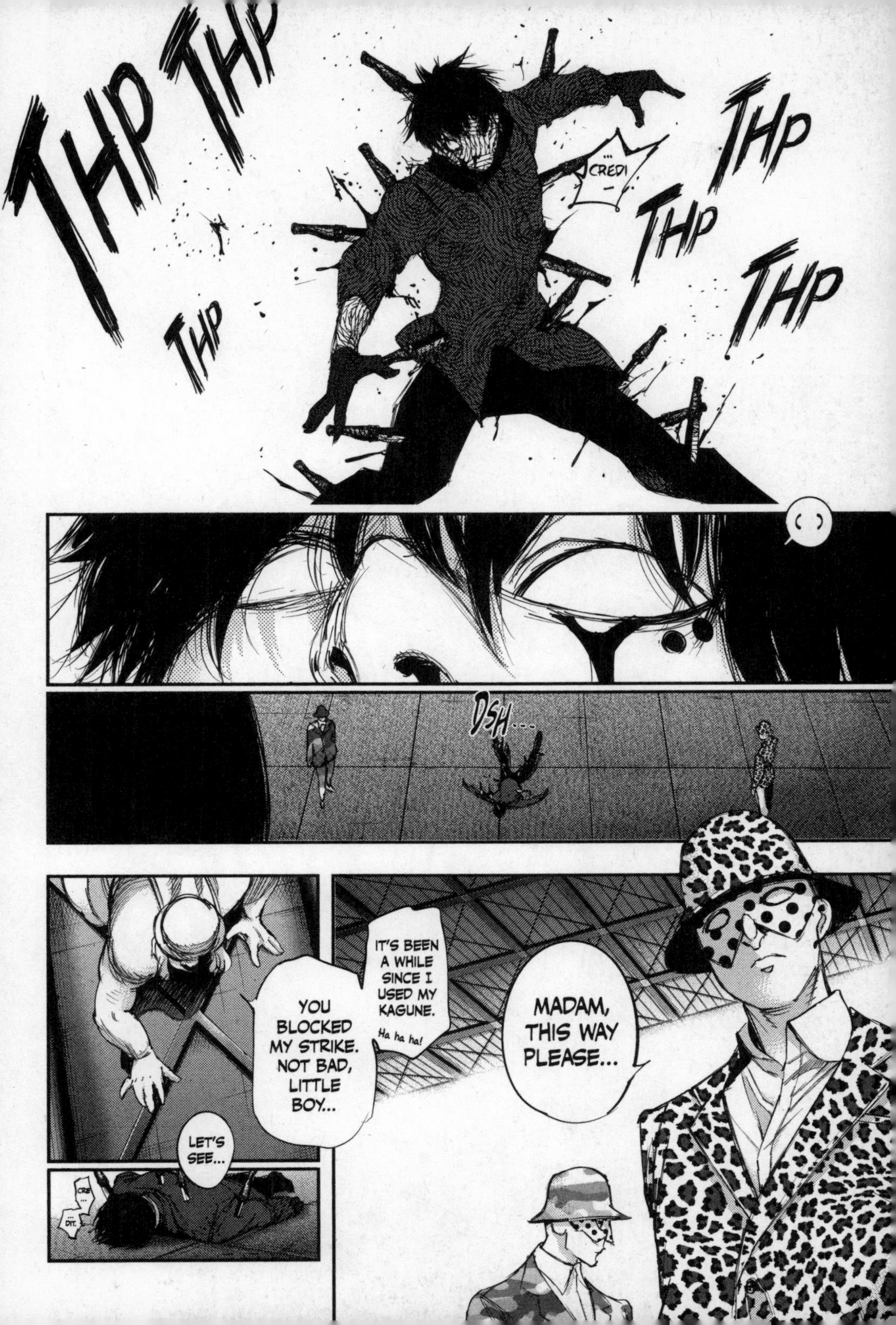
THP
THP
THP
...CREDI—
THP
THP
THP
THP
( )
DSH...
MADAM, THIS WAY PLEASE...
IT'S BEEN A WHILE SINCE I USED MY KAGUNE.
Ha ha ha!
YOU BLOCKED MY STRIKE. NOT BAD, LITTLE BOY...
LET'S SEE...
CRE...
...DIT.

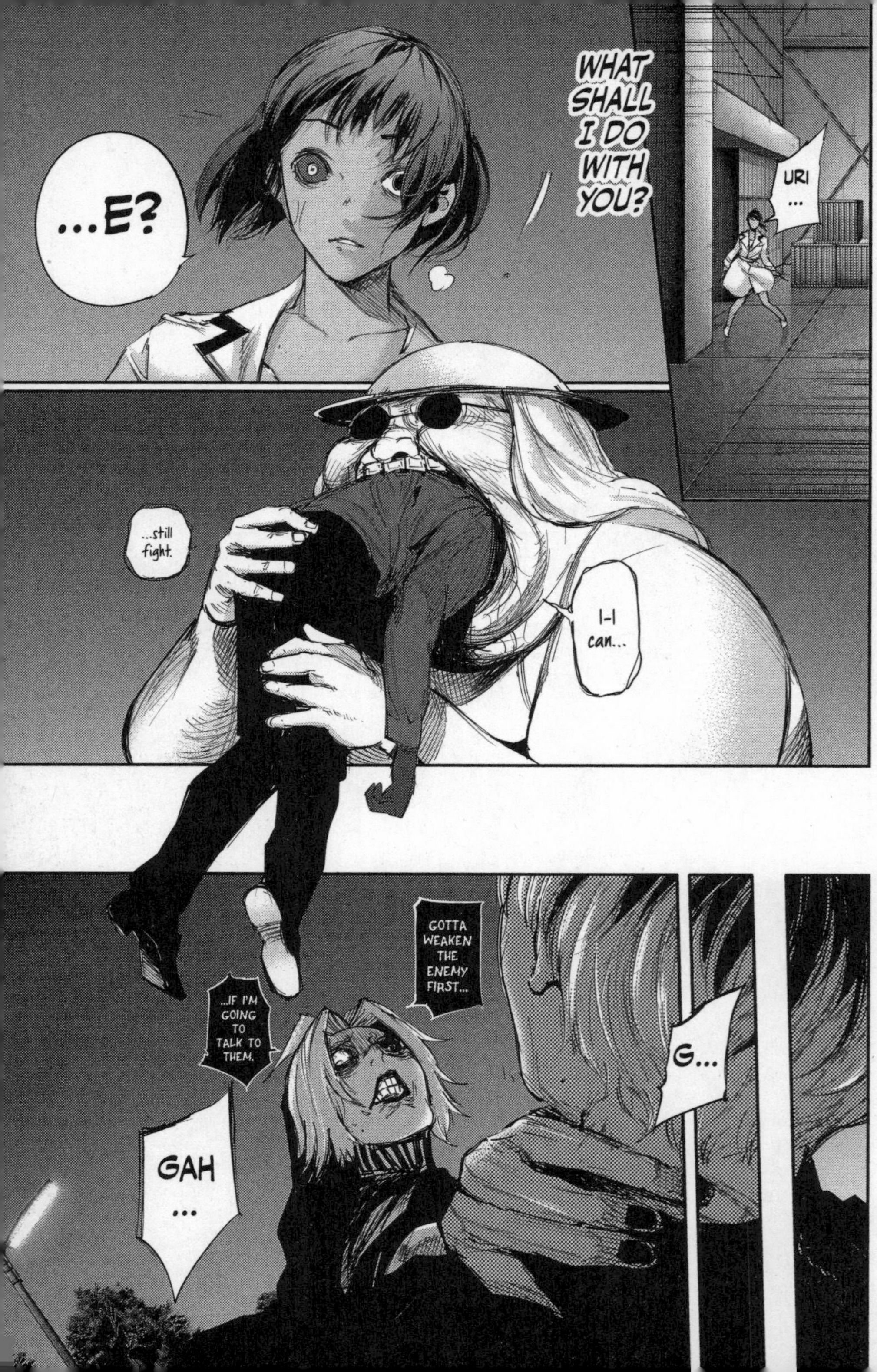
URI ...
WHAT SHALL I DO WITH YOU?
...E?
I-I can...
...still fight.
G...
GOTTA WEAKEN THE ENEMY FIRST...
...IF I'M GOING TO TALK TO THEM.
GAH ...

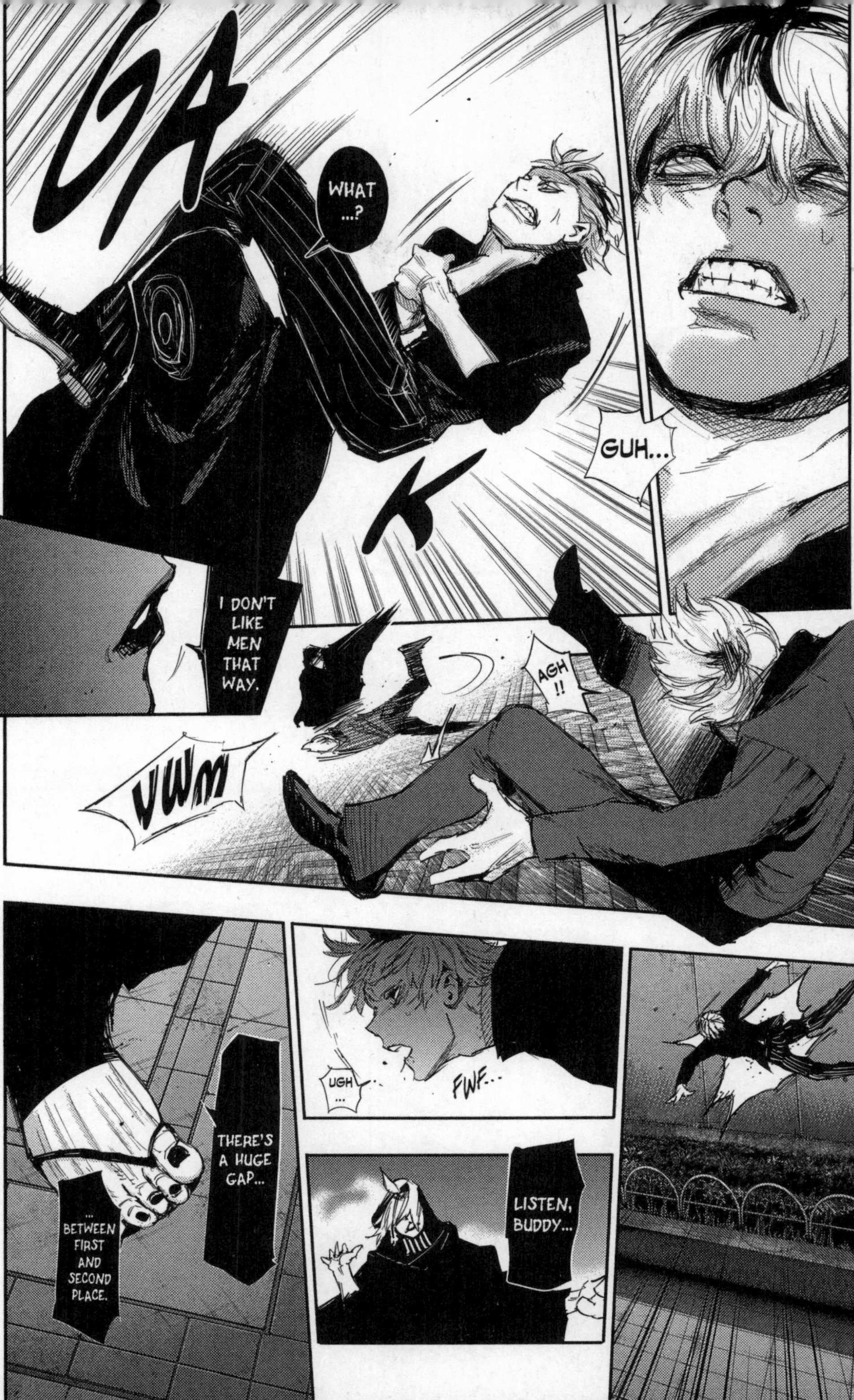
GUH...
GA
WHAT ...?
K
AGH !!
VWM
I DON'T LIKE MEN THAT WAY.
UGH ...
FWF...
LISTEN, BUDDY...
THERE'S A HUGE GAP...
... BETWEEN FIRST AND SECOND PLACE.

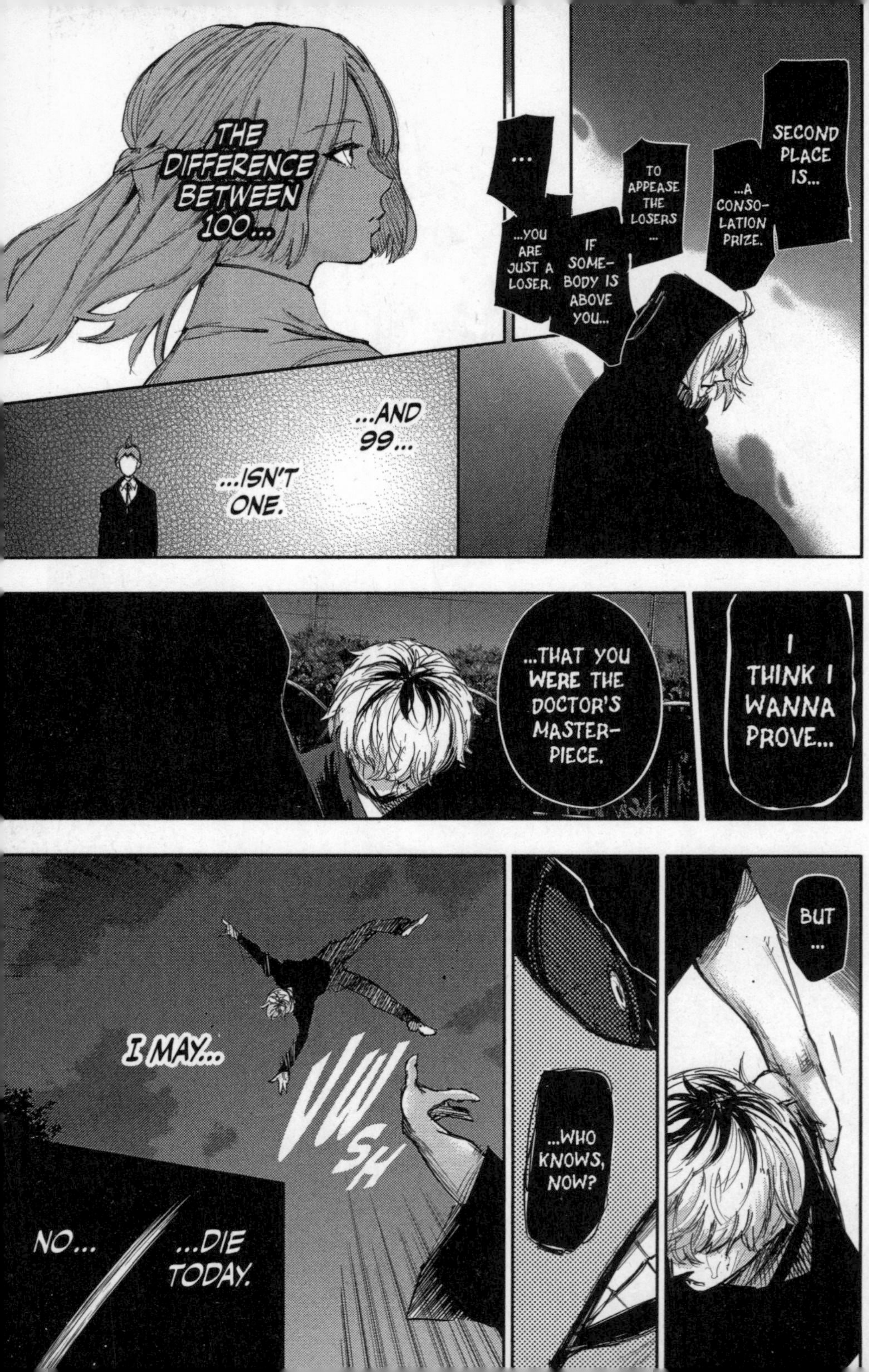
SECOND PLACE IS...
...A CONSOLATION PRIZE.
TO APPEASE THE LOSERS...
IF SOMEBODY IS ABOVE YOU...
...
...YOU ARE JUST A LOSER.
THE DIFFERENCE BETWEEN 100...
...AND 99...
...ISN'T ONE.
I THINK I WANNA PROVE...
...THAT YOU WERE THE DOCTOR'S MASTERPIECE.
BUT...
...WHO KNOWS, NOW?
I MAY...
VWSH
NO...
...DIE TODAY.

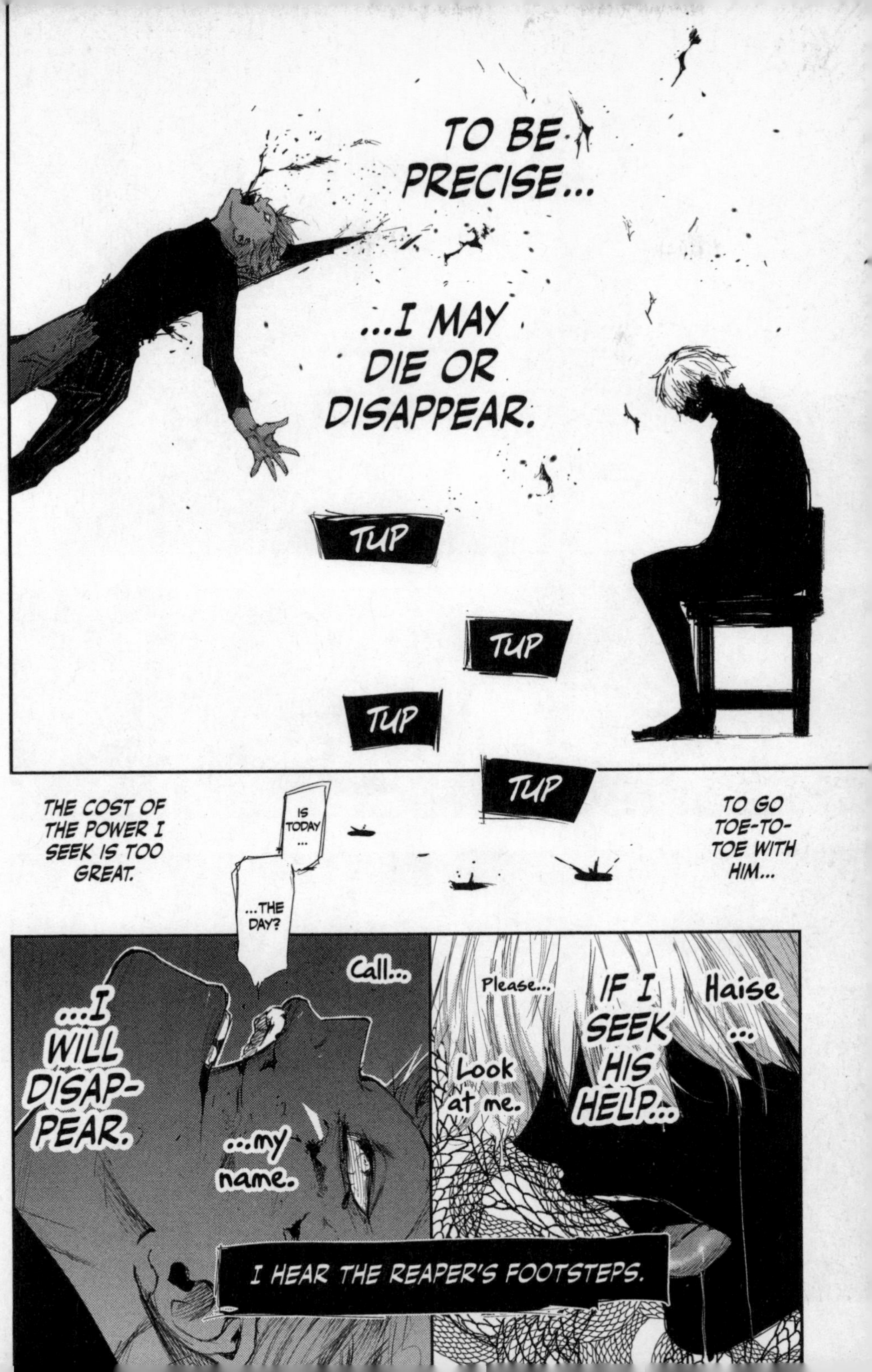
TO BE PRECISE...
...I MAY DIE OR DISAPPEAR.
TUP
TUP
TUP
TUP
TO GO TOE-TO-TOE WITH HIM...
IS TODAY...
...THE DAY?
THE COST OF THE POWER I SEEK IS TOO GREAT.
Haise...
IF I SEEK HIS HELP...
Please...
Look at me.
Call...
...I WILL DISAP-PEAR.
...my name.
I HEAR THE REAPER'S FOOTSTEPS.

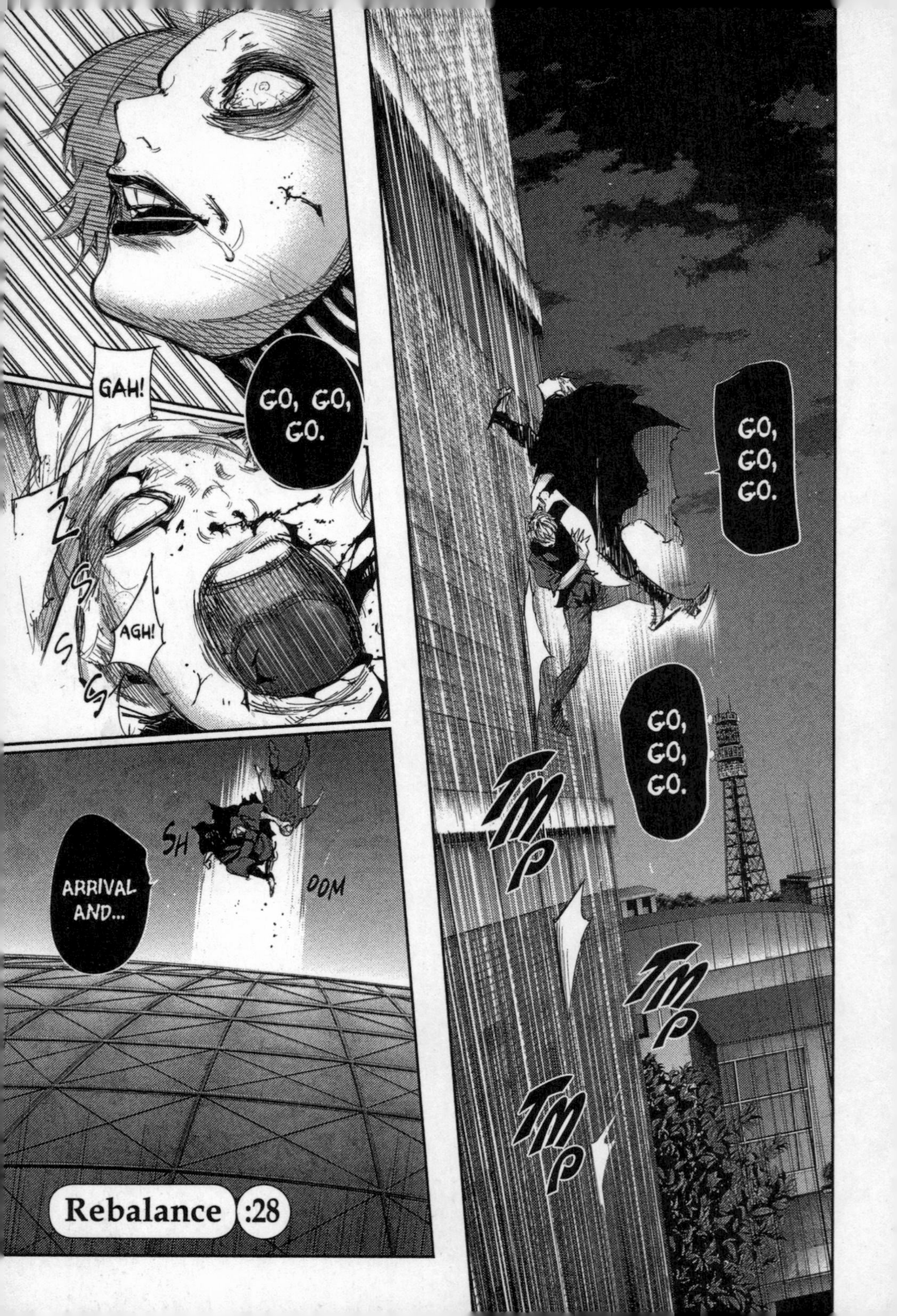
GO, GO, GO.
GO, GO, GO.
TMP
TMP
TMP
GO, GO, GO.
GAH!
ZSSSS
AGH!
ARRIVAL AND...
SH
OOM
Rebalance :28

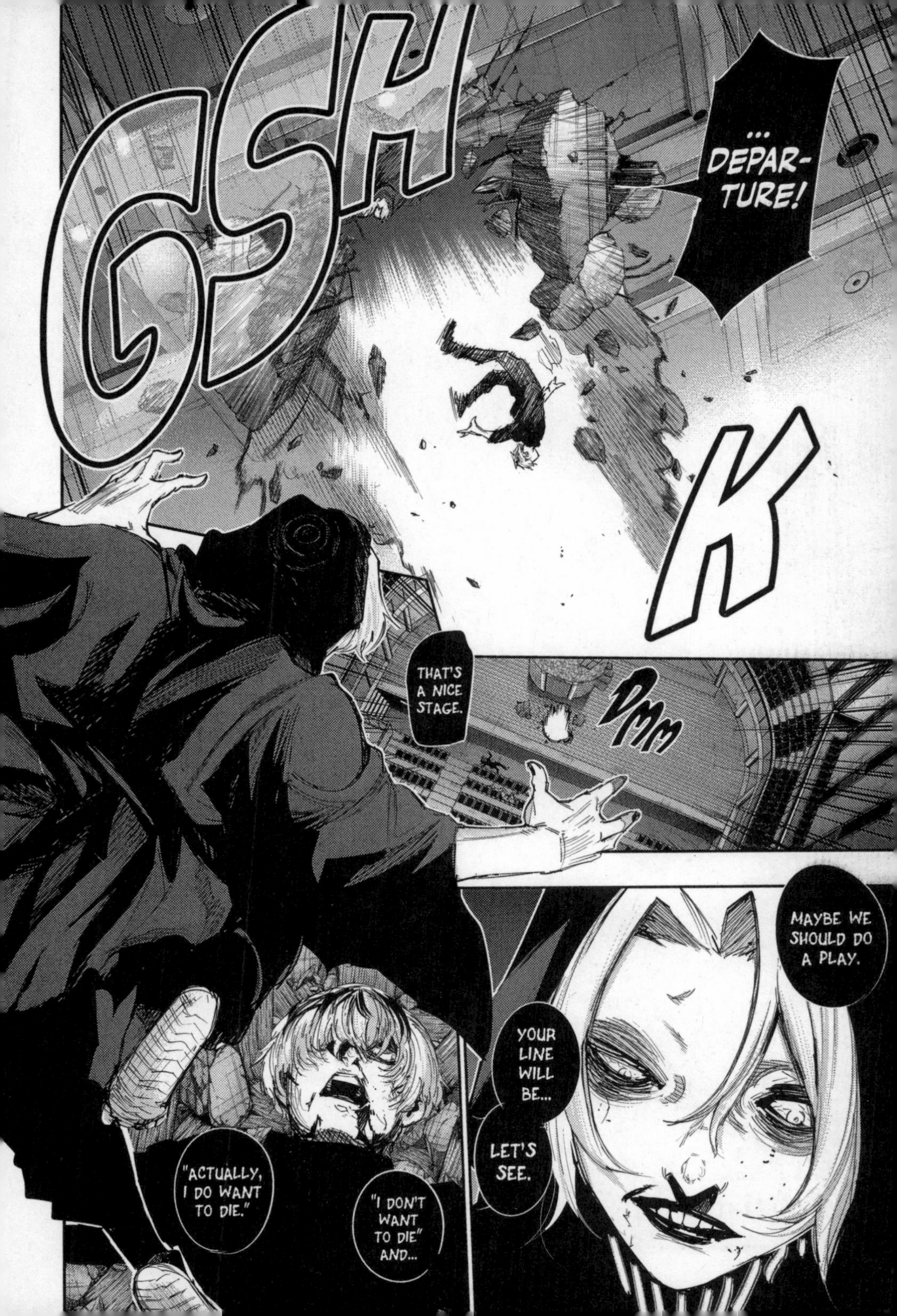
... DEPARTURE!
GSHK
THAT'S A NICE STAGE.
DMM
MAYBE WE SHOULD DO A PLAY.
YOUR LINE WILL BE...
LET'S SEE.
"I DON'T WANT TO DIE" AND...
"ACTUALLY, I DO WANT TO DIE."

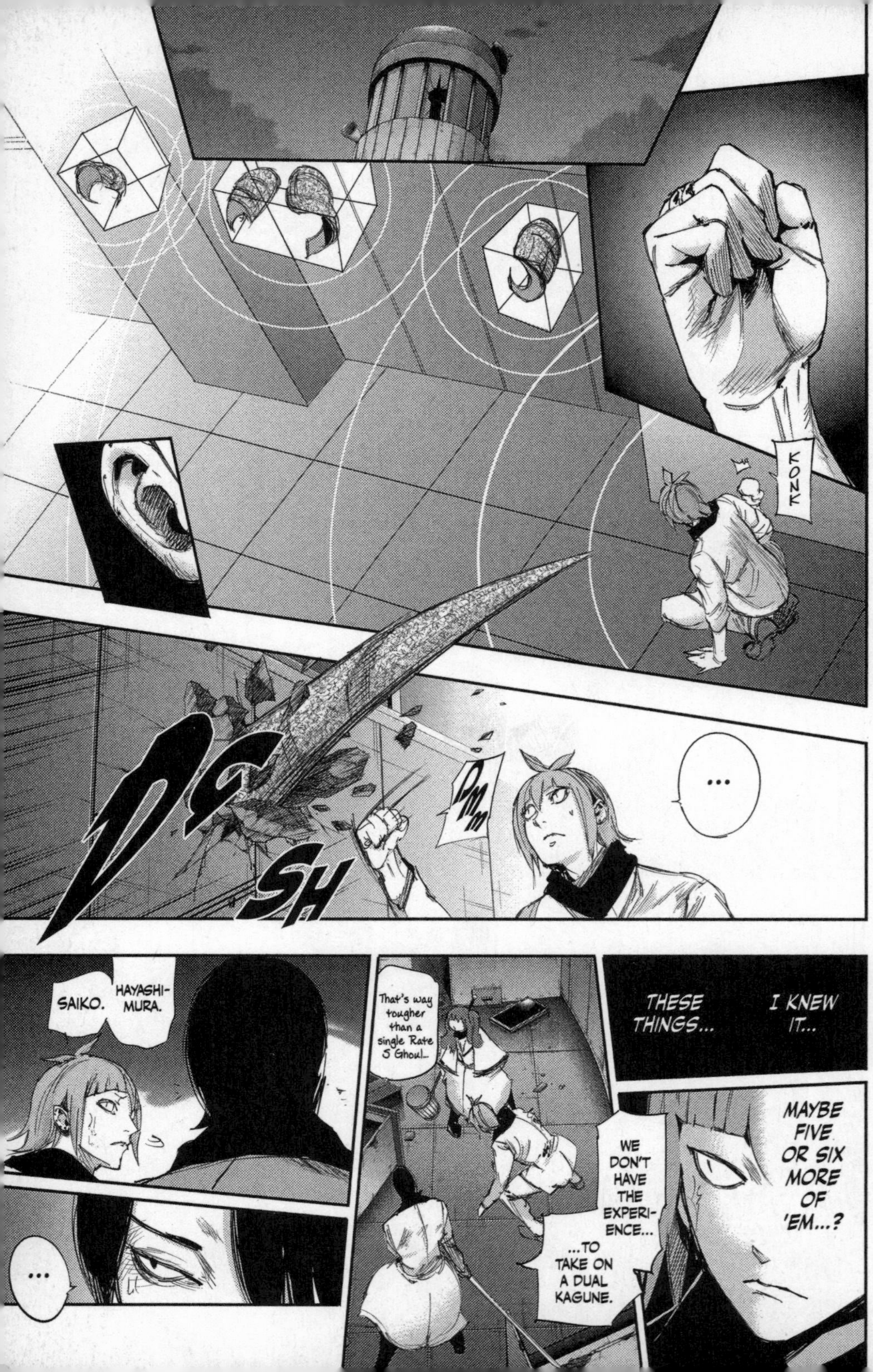
KONK
...
DMM
DGSH
I KNEW IT...
THESE THINGS...
MAYBE FIVE OR SIX MORE OF 'EM...?
That's way tougher than a single Rate S Ghoul...
WE DON'T HAVE THE EXPERIENCE...
...TO TAKE ON A DUAL KAGUNE.
HAYASHIMURA.
SAIKO.
...

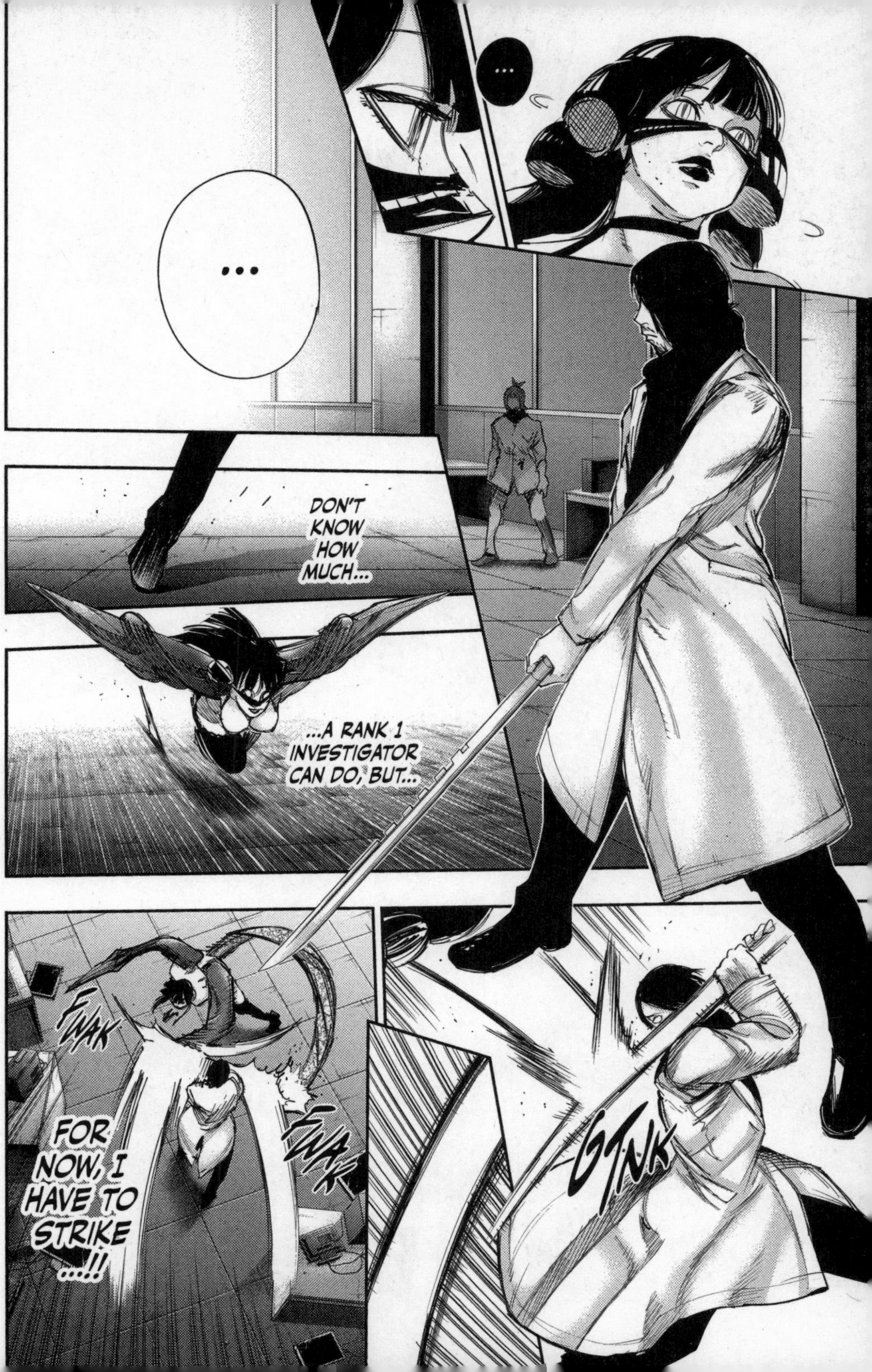
...
...
DON'T KNOW HOW MUCH...
...A RANK 1 INVESTIGATOR CAN DO, BUT...
GTNK
FWAK
FWAK
FOR NOW, I HAVE TO STRIKE ...!!

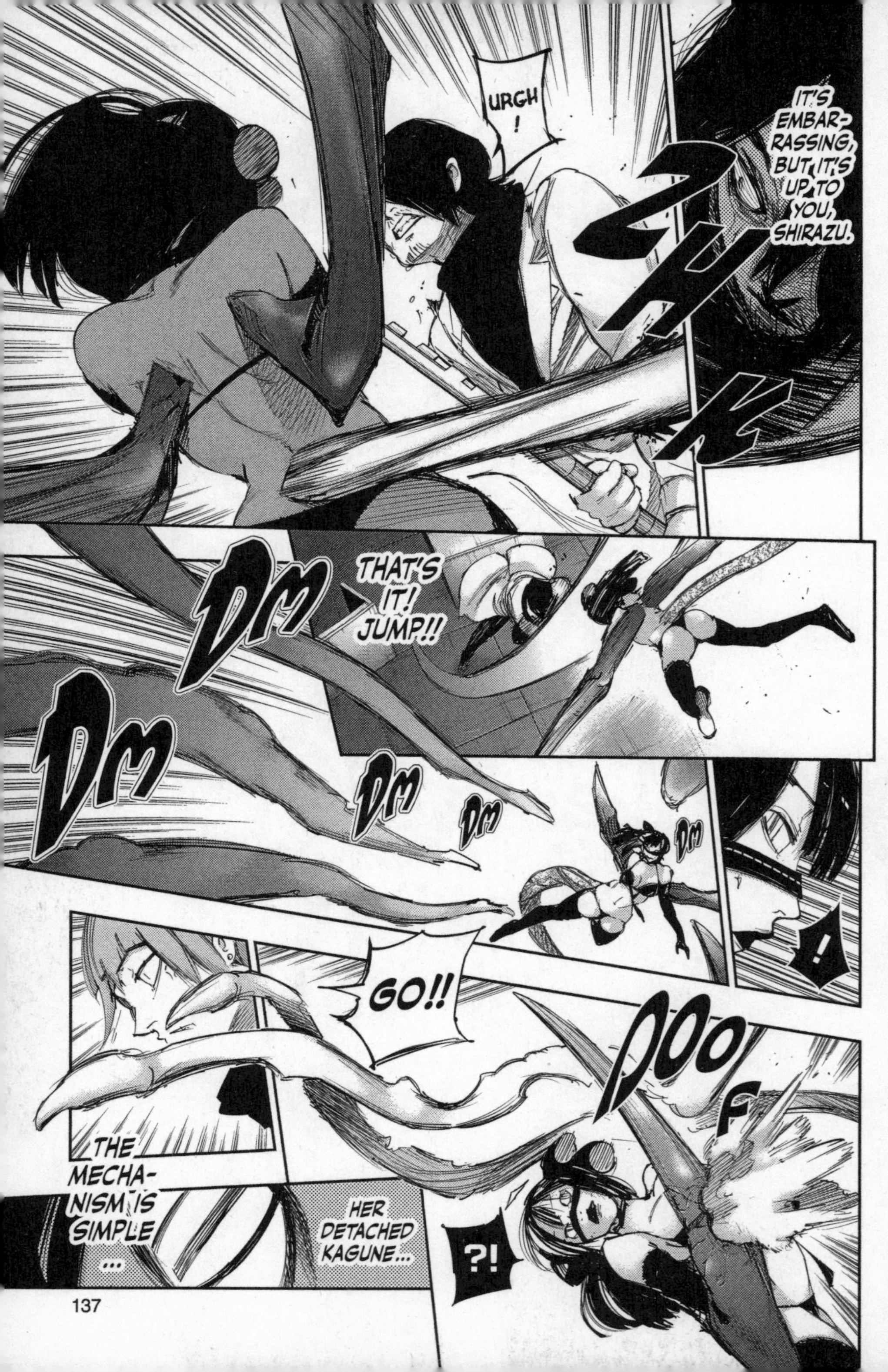
IT'S EMBAR-RASSING, BUT IT'S UP TO YOU, SHIRAZU.
URGH!
CHKK
THAT'S IT! JUMP!!
DM
DM
DM
DM
DM
!
GO!!
DOOF
?!
HER DETACHED KAGUNE...
THE MECHA-NISM IS SIMPLE...

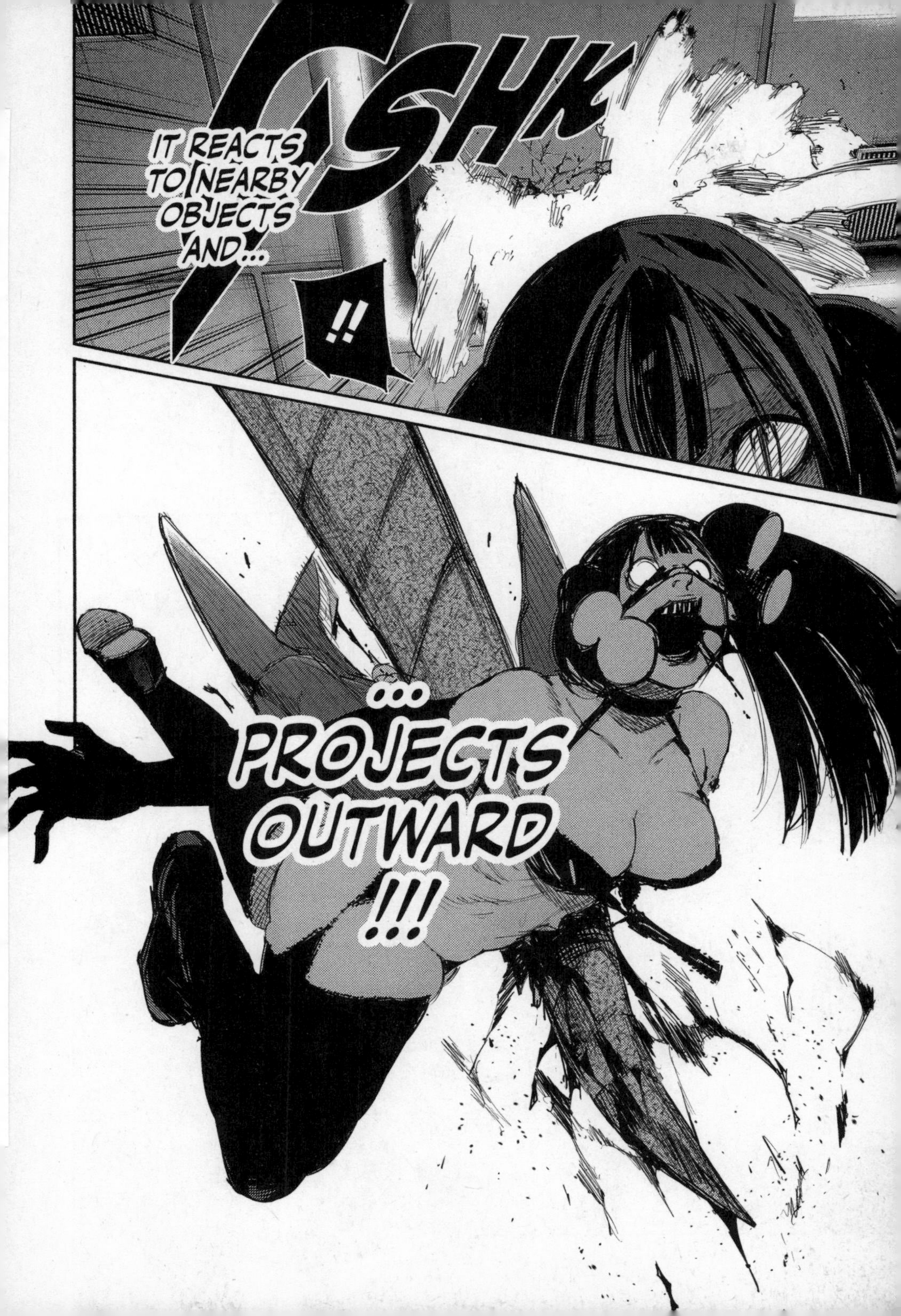
SHK
IT REACTS TO NEARBY OBJECTS AND...
!!
...PROJECTS OUTWARD!!!

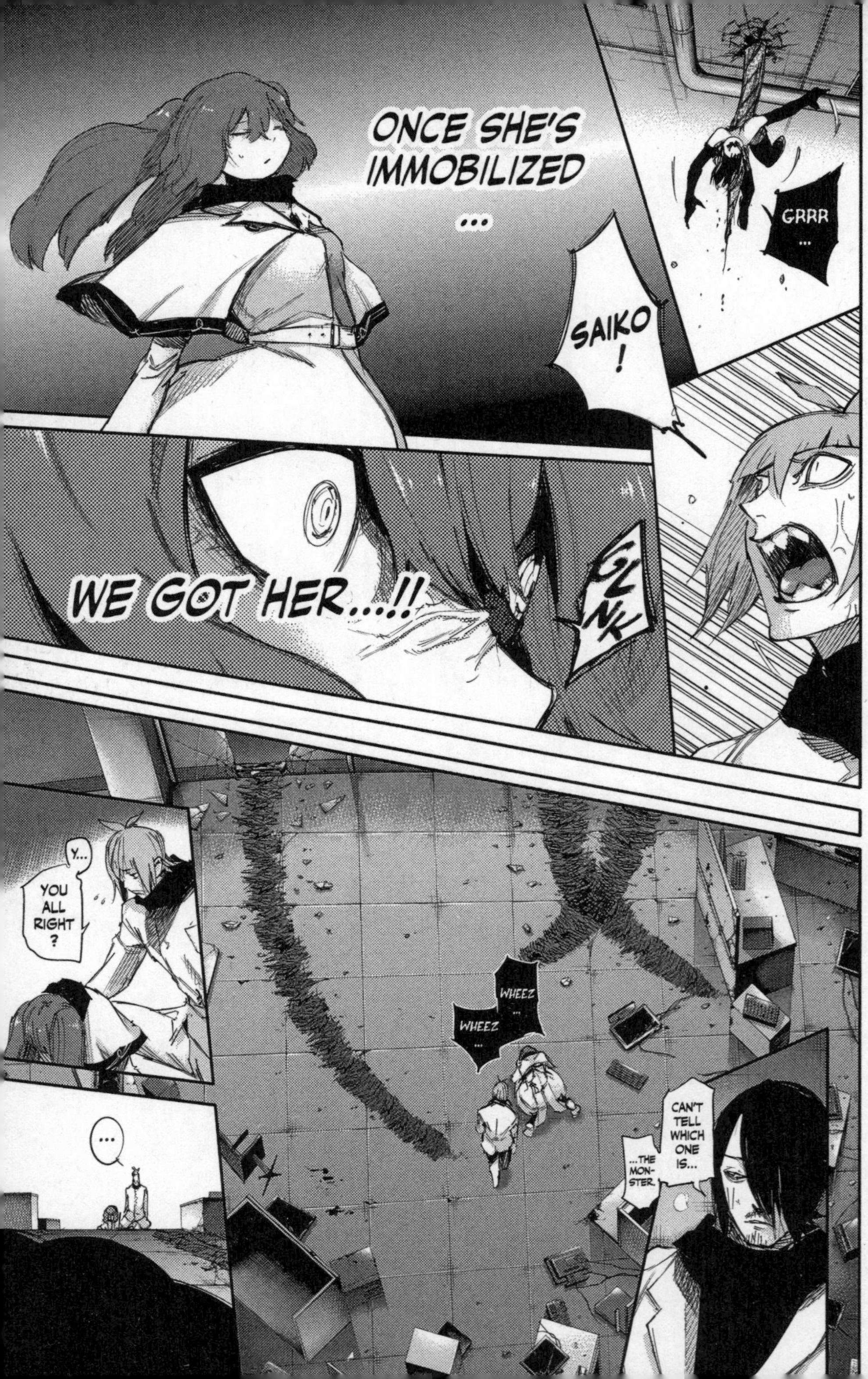
GRRR ...
SAIKO !
ONCE SHE'S IMMOBILIZED ...
GUNK
WE GOT HER...!!
CAN'T TELL WHICH ONE IS...
...THE MONSTER.
WHEEZ ...
WHEEZ ...
Y...
YOU ALL RIGHT ?
...

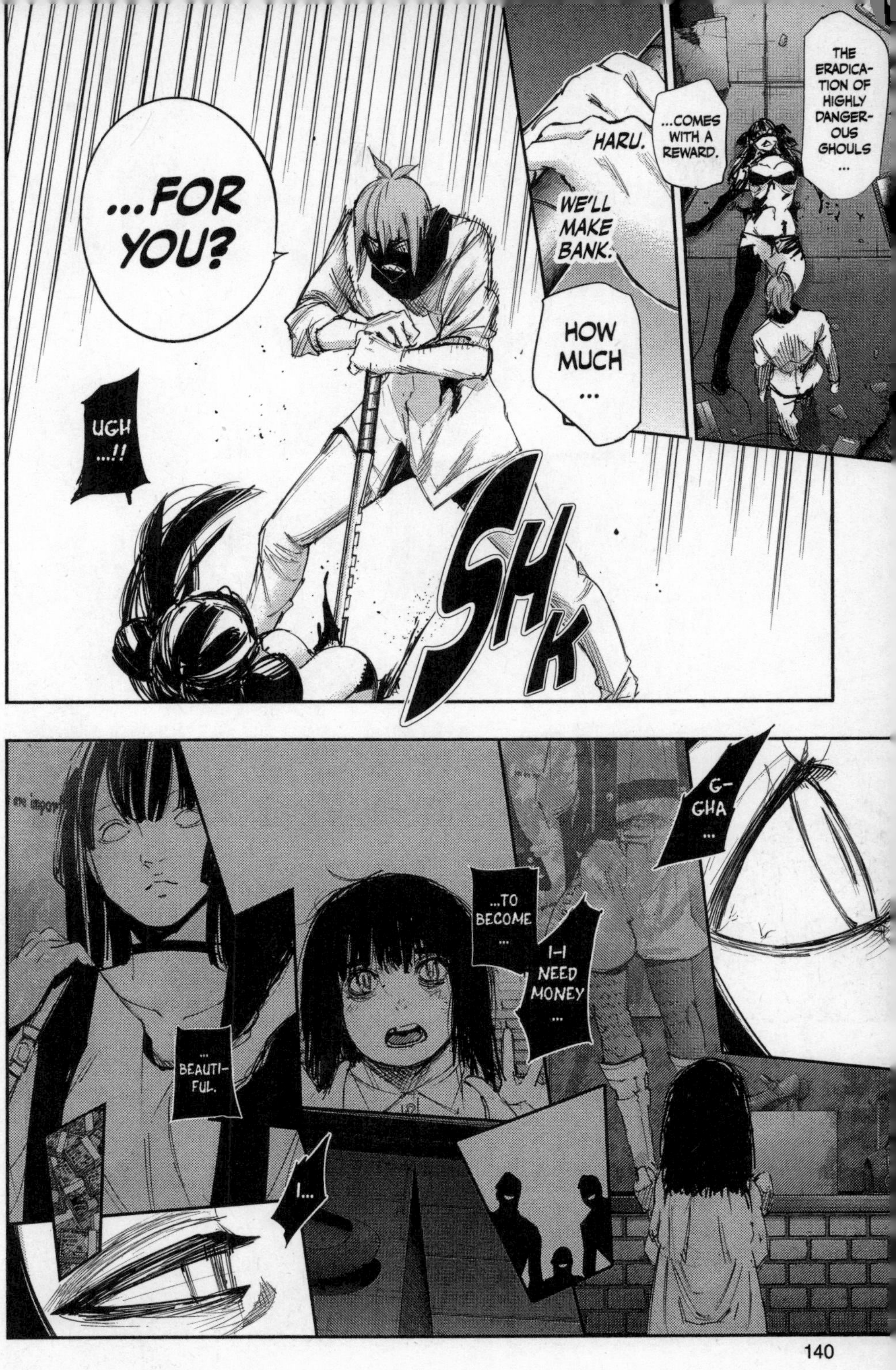
THE ERADICATION OF HIGHLY DANGEROUS GHOULS ...
...COMES WITH A REWARD.
HARU.
WE'LL MAKE BANK.
HOW MUCH ...
...FOR YOU?
SHK
UGH ...!!
G-GHA ...
I-I NEED MONEY ...
...TO BECOME ...
... BEAUTIFUL.
I...

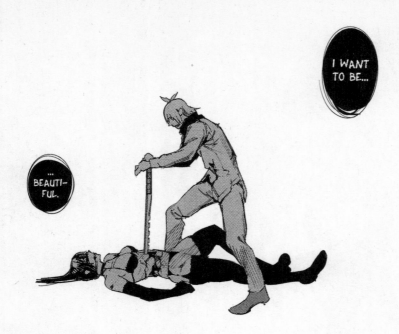

I WANT
TO BE...

...
BEAUTI-
FUL.

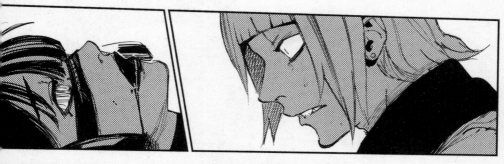

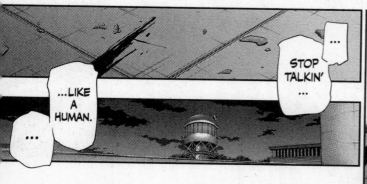

...LIKE
A
HUMAN.

...

STOP
TALKIN'
...

...

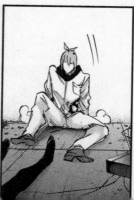

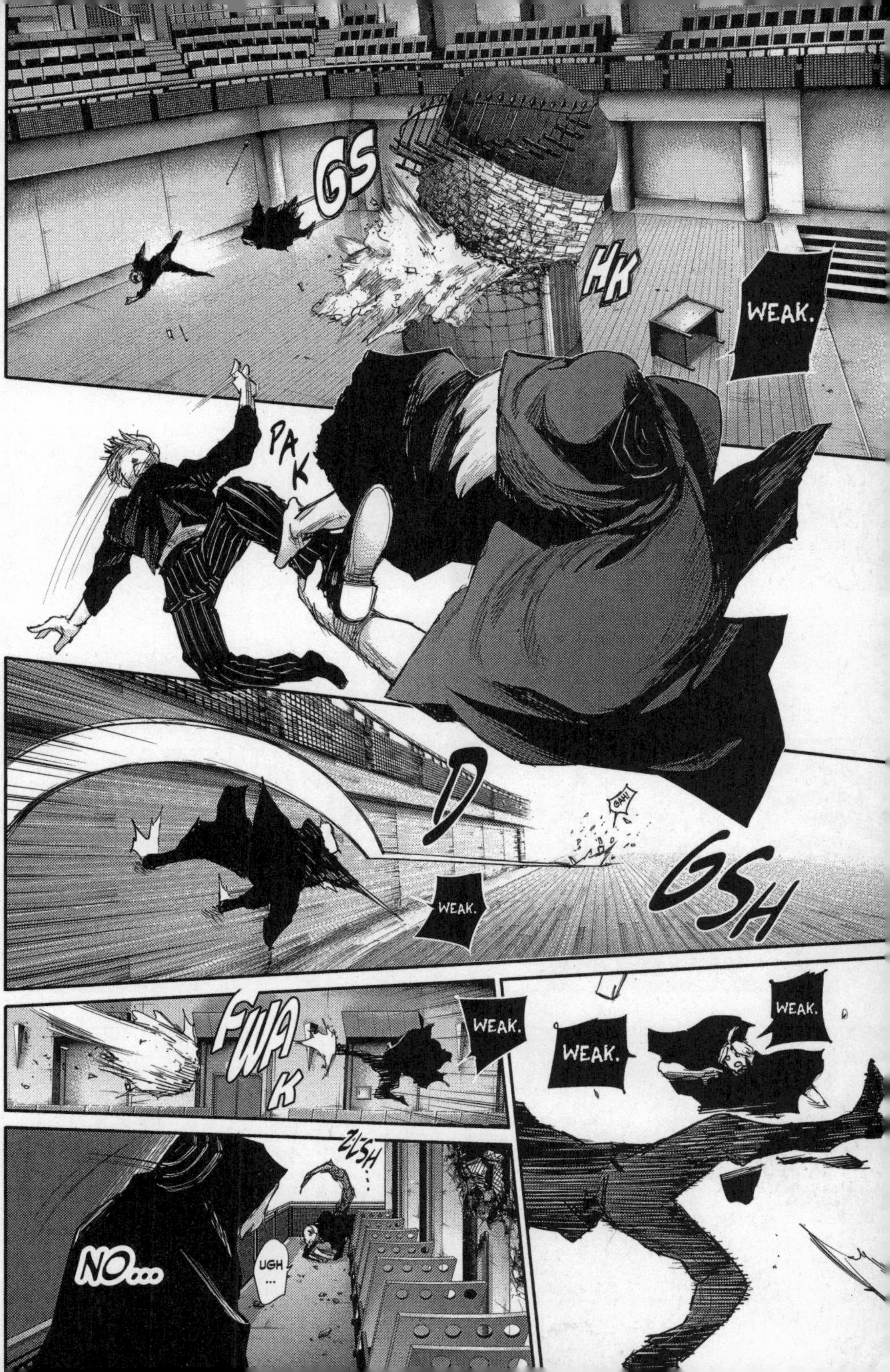
WEAK.
HK
GS
PAK
GSH
GAH!
D
WEAK.
WEAK.
WEAK.
WEAK.
FWAK
ZZSH...
UGH...
NO...

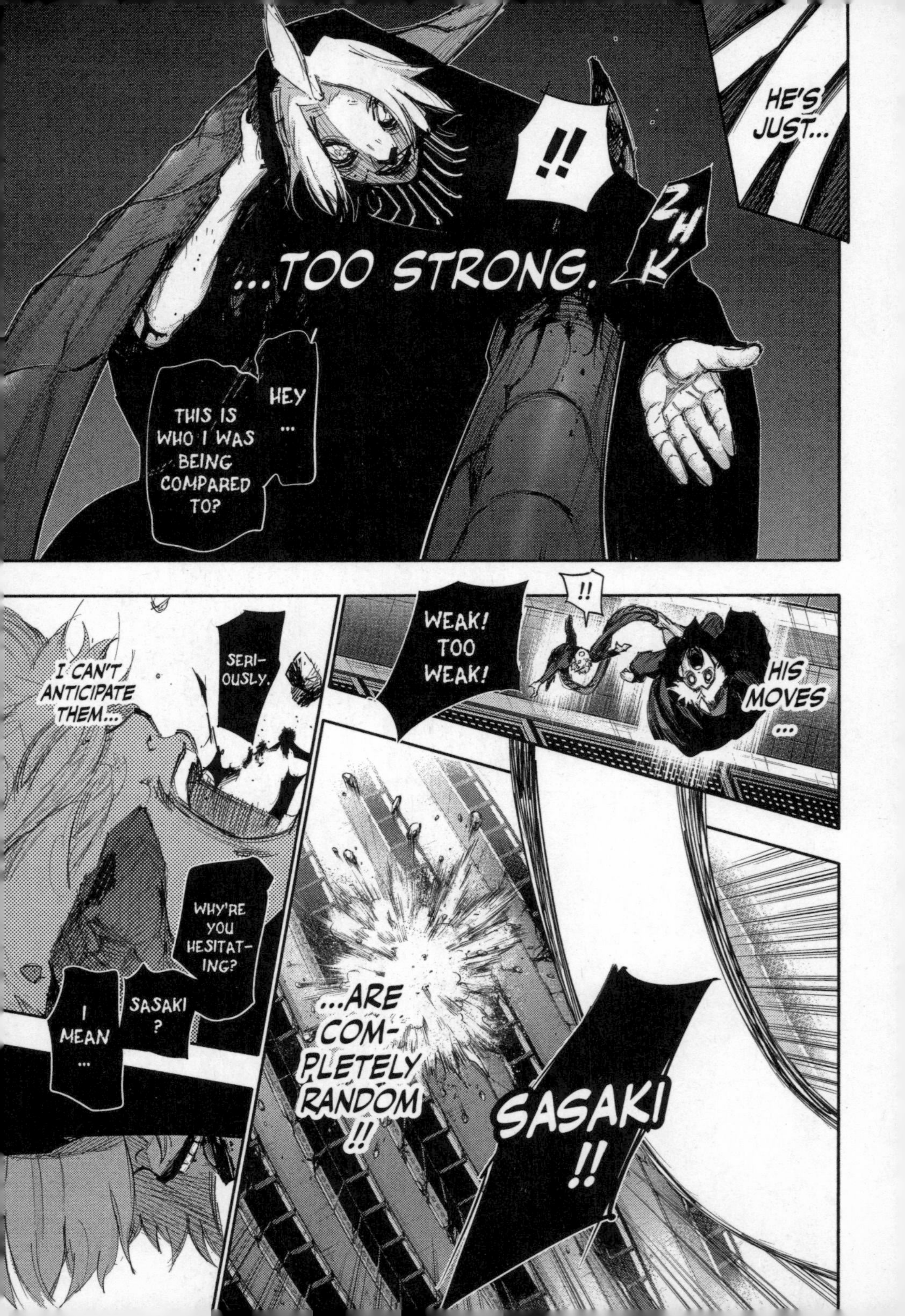
HE'S JUST...
!!
ZHK
...TOO STRONG.
HEY ...
THIS IS WHO I WAS BEING COMPARED TO?
!!
HIS MOVES ...
WEAK! TOO WEAK!
...ARE COM-PLETELY RANDOM !!
SASAKI !!
SERI-OUSLY.
I CAN'T ANTICIPATE THEM...
WHY'RE YOU HESITAT-ING?
SASAKI ?
I MEAN ...

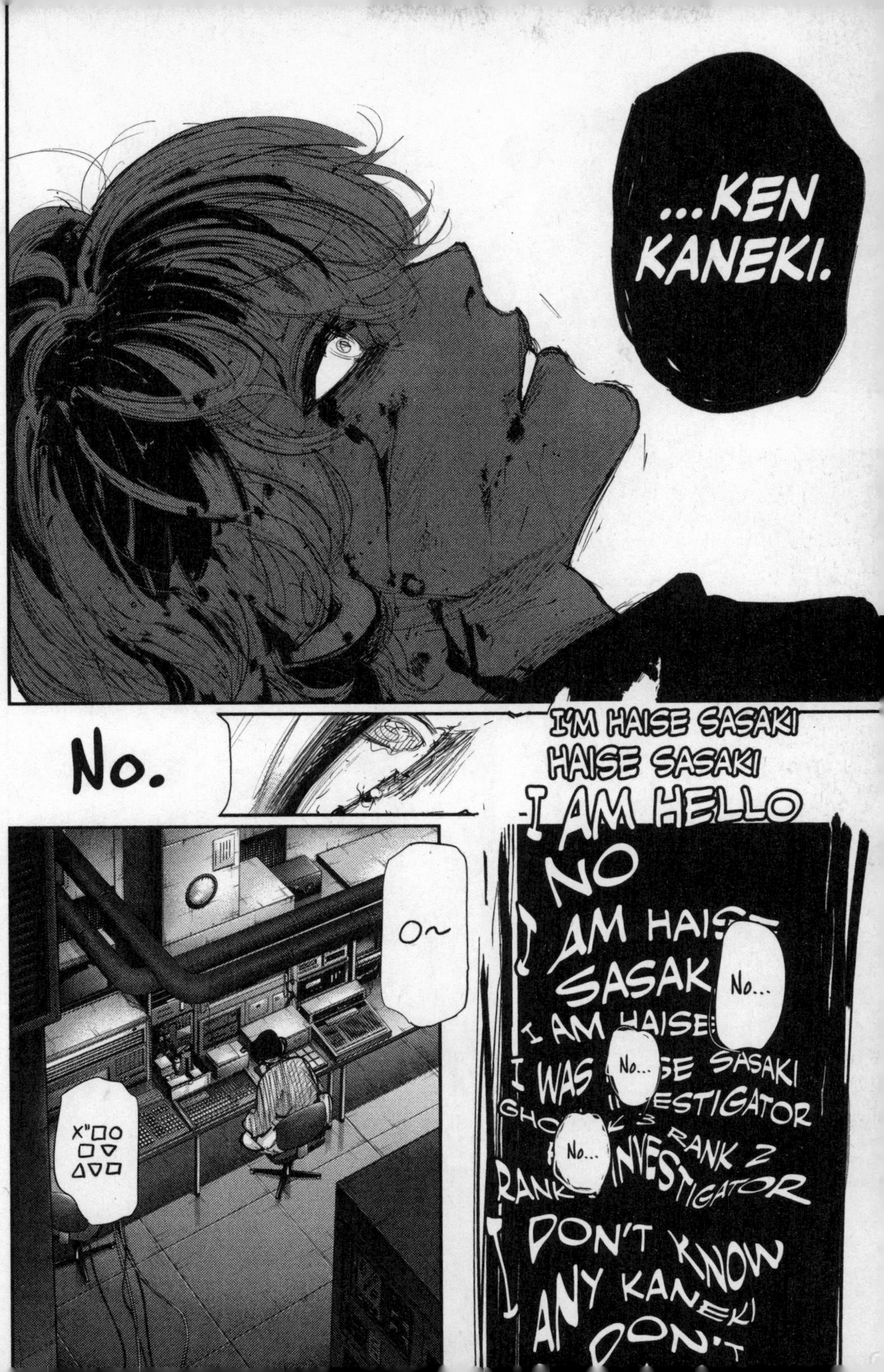
...KEN KANEKI.
I'M HAISE SASAKI
HAISE SASAKI
I AM HELLO
No.
NO
I AM HAIS
SASAK
No...
I AM HAISE
No...
I WAS SE SASAKI
ESTIGATOR
No...
RANK 2
RANK INVESTIGATOR
I DON'T KNOW
ANY KANEKI
DON'T
O~
X"□O
□▽
△▽□

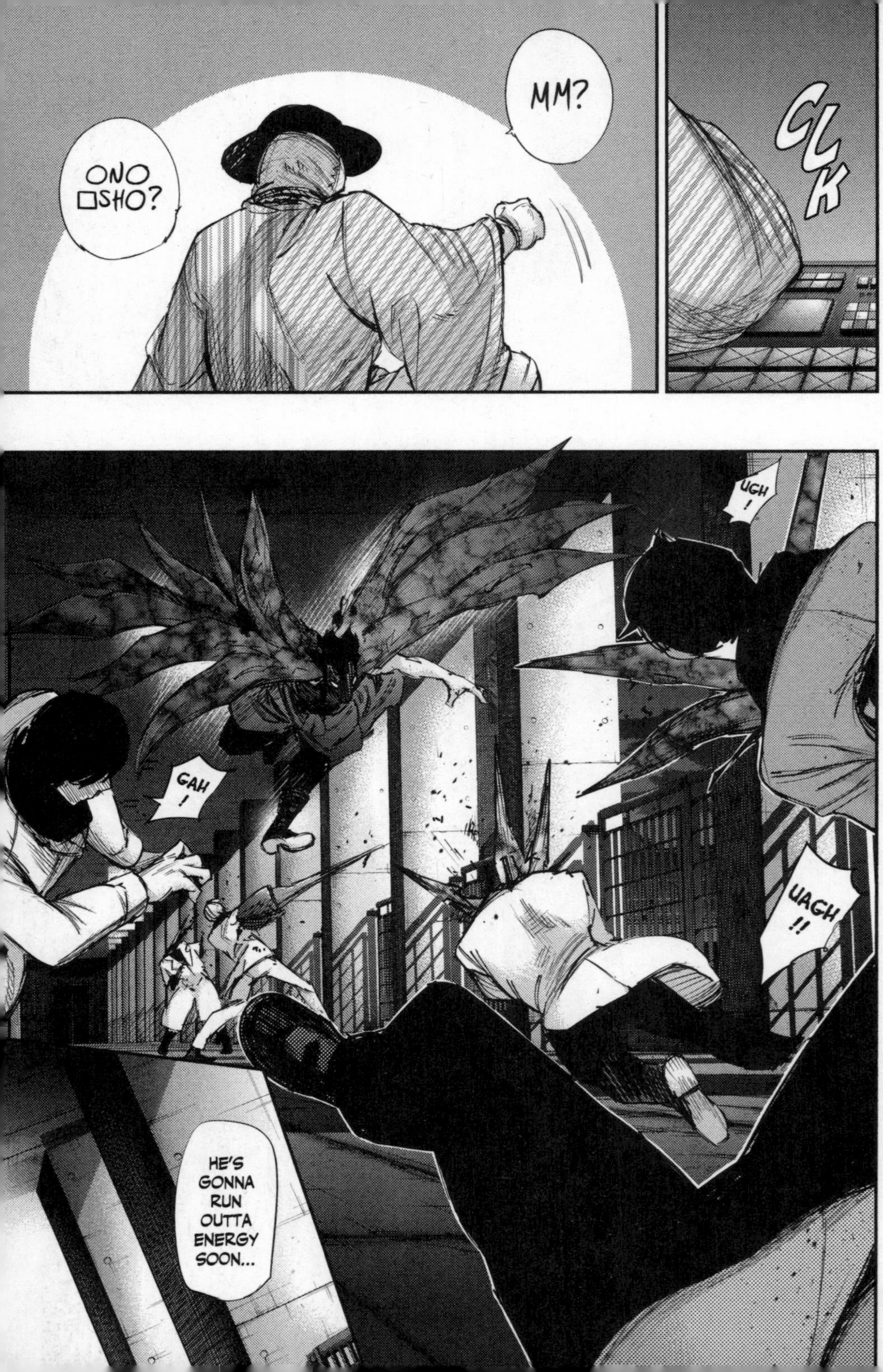
CLK
MM?
ONO□SHO?
UGH!
UAGH!!
GAH!
HE'S GONNA RUN OUTTA ENERGY SOON...

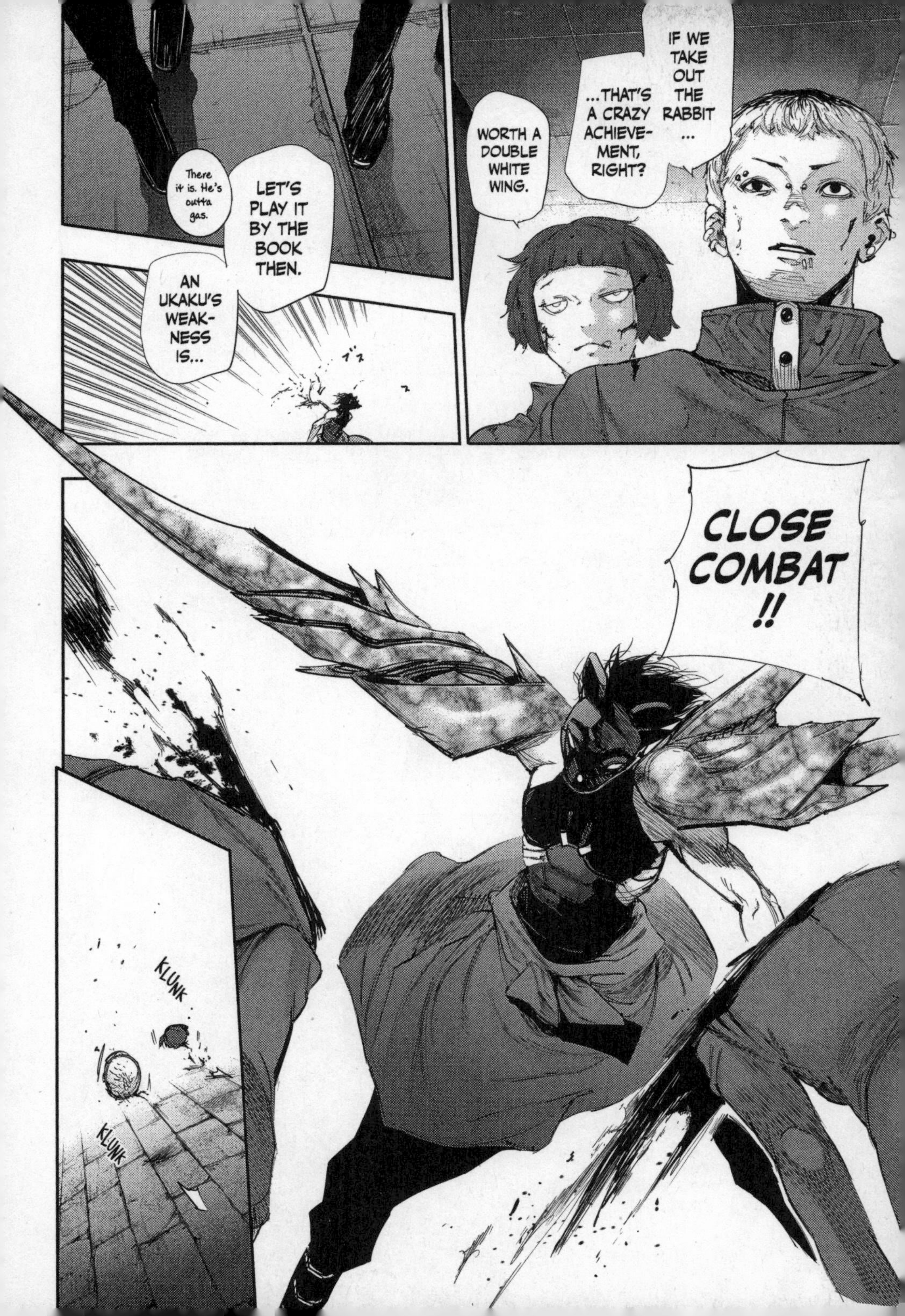

IF WE TAKE OUT THE RABBIT...
...THAT'S A CRAZY ACHIEVEMENT, RIGHT?
WORTH A DOUBLE WHITE WING.
LET'S PLAY IT BY THE BOOK THEN.
There it is. He's outta gas.
AN UKAKU'S WEAKNESS IS...
CLOSE COMBAT!!
KLUNK
KLUNK

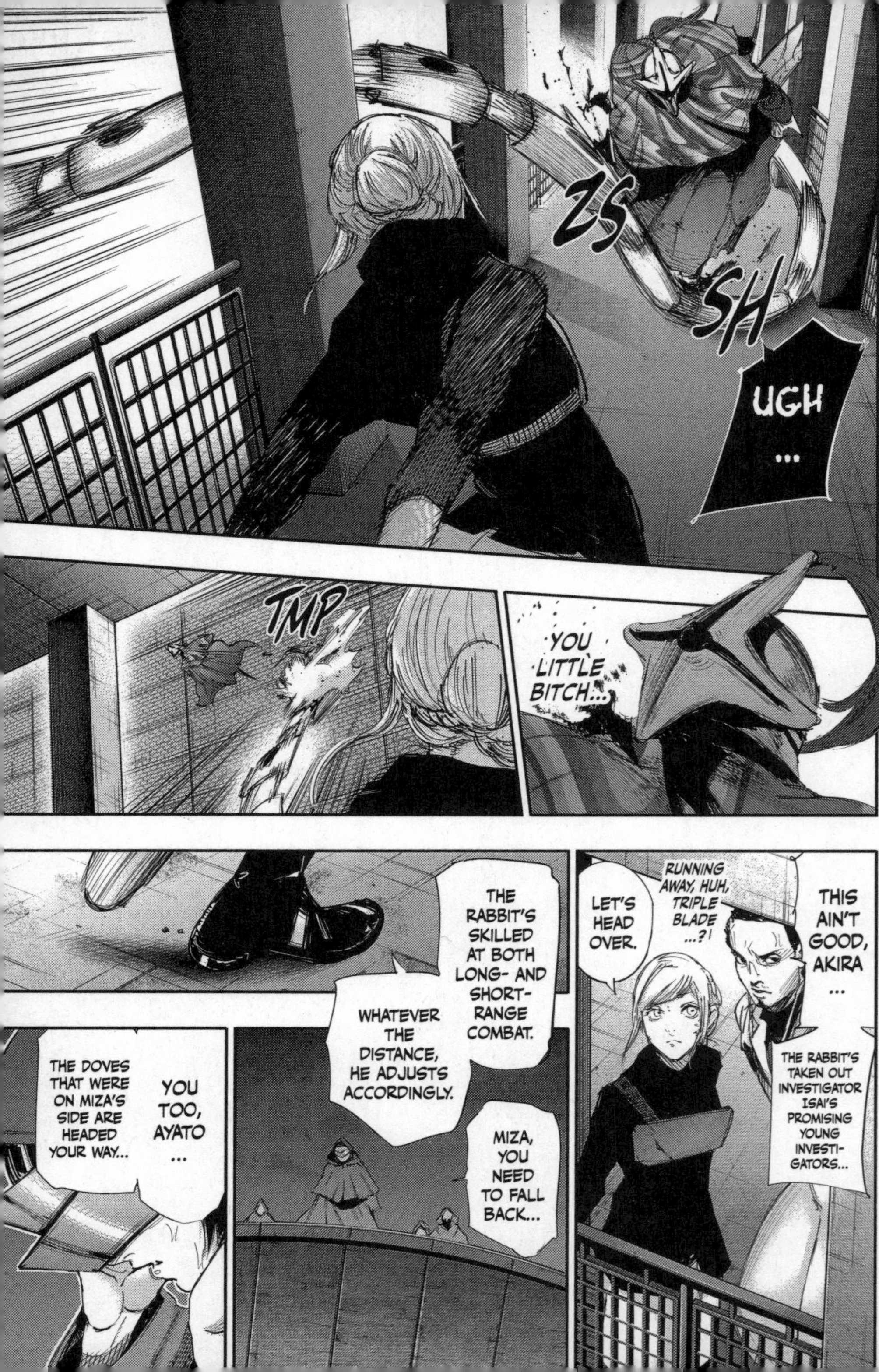
ZS
SH
UGH...
YOU LITTLE BITCH...
TMP
THIS AIN'T GOOD, AKIRA...
RUNNING AWAY, HUH, TRIPLE BLADE...?!
LET'S HEAD OVER.
THE RABBIT'S TAKEN OUT INVESTIGATOR ISAI'S PROMISING YOUNG INVESTIGATORS...
THE RABBIT'S SKILLED AT BOTH LONG- AND SHORT-RANGE COMBAT.
WHATEVER THE DISTANCE, HE ADJUSTS ACCORDINGLY.
MIZA, YOU NEED TO FALL BACK...
YOU TOO, AYATO...
THE DOVES THAT WERE ON MIZA'S SIDE ARE HEADED YOUR WAY...

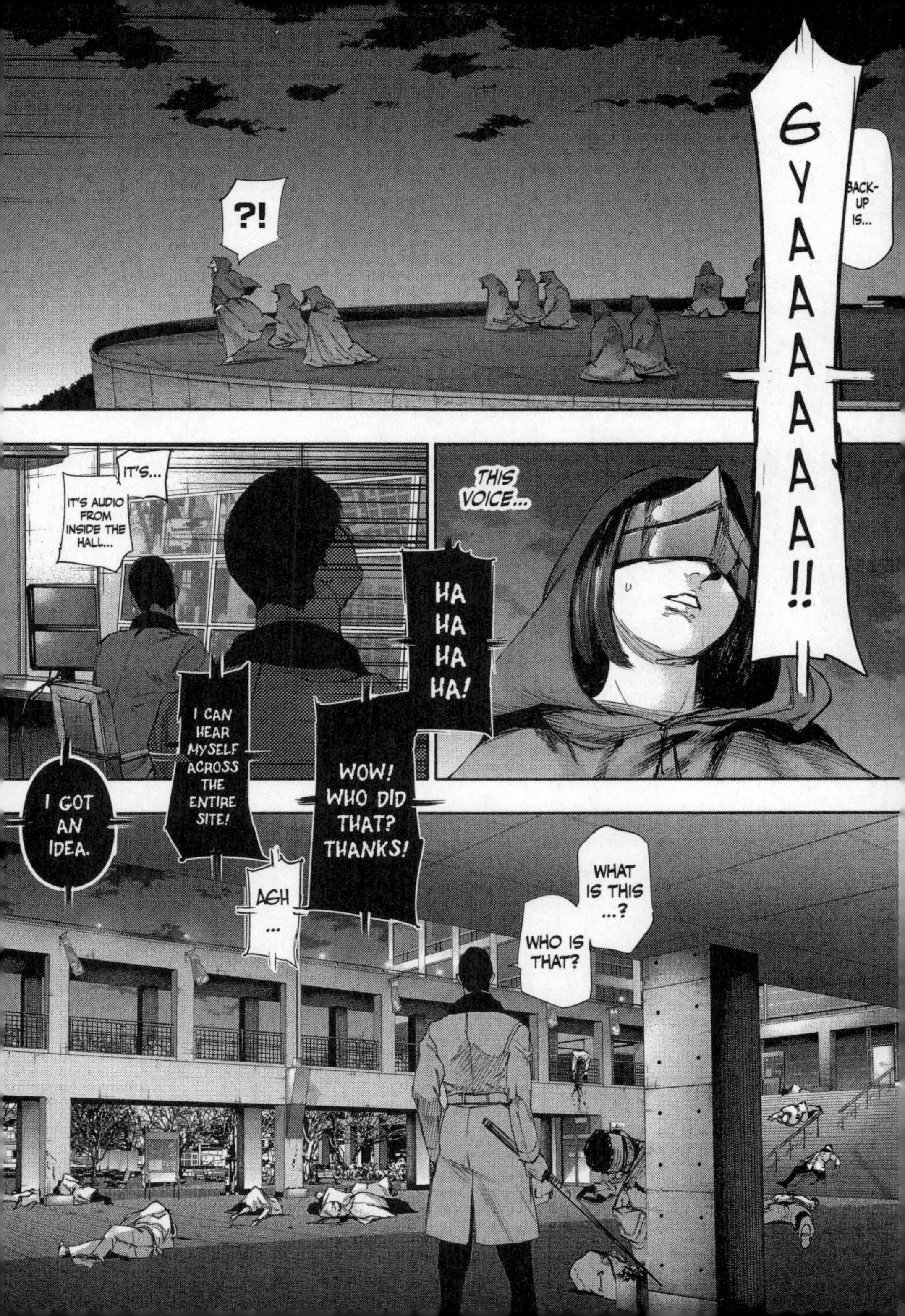
BACK-UP IS...
GYAAAAAA!!
?!
THIS VOICE...
IT'S...
IT'S AUDIO FROM INSIDE THE HALL...
HA HA HA HA!
I CAN HEAR MYSELF ACROSS THE ENTIRE SITE!
WHAT IS THIS ...?
WHO IS THAT?
WOW! WHO DID THAT? THANKS!
AGH ...
I GOT AN IDEA.

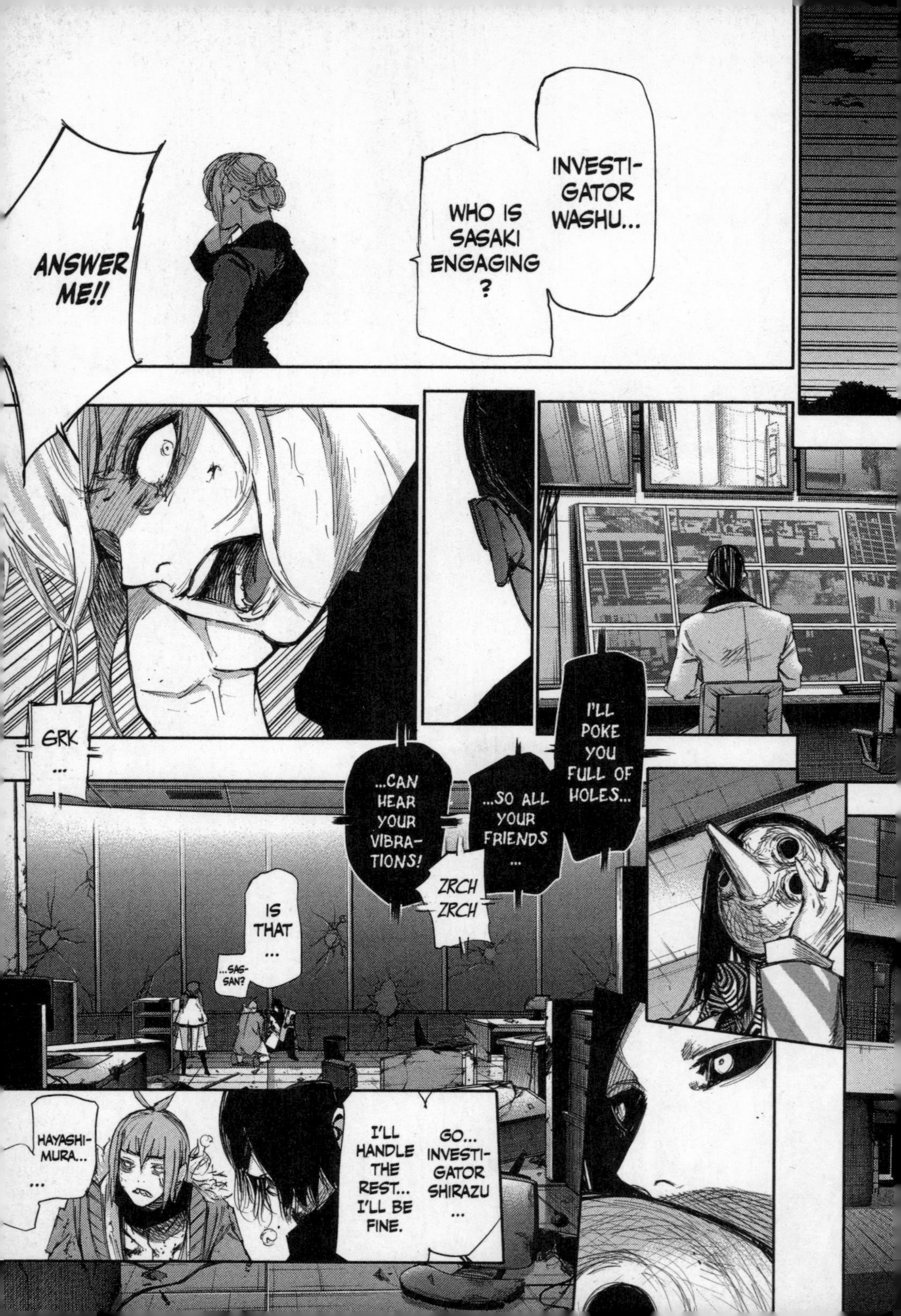
INVESTI-
GATOR
WASHU...
WHO IS
SASAKI
ENGAGING
?
ANSWER
ME!!
GRK
...
I'LL
POKE
YOU
FULL OF
HOLES...
...SO ALL
YOUR
FRIENDS
...
...CAN
HEAR
YOUR
VIBRA-
TIONS!
ZRCH
ZRCH
IS
THAT
...
...SAS-
SAN?
GO...
INVESTI-
GATOR
SHIRAZU
...
I'LL
HANDLE
THE
REST...
I'LL BE
FINE.
HAYASHI-
MURA...
...

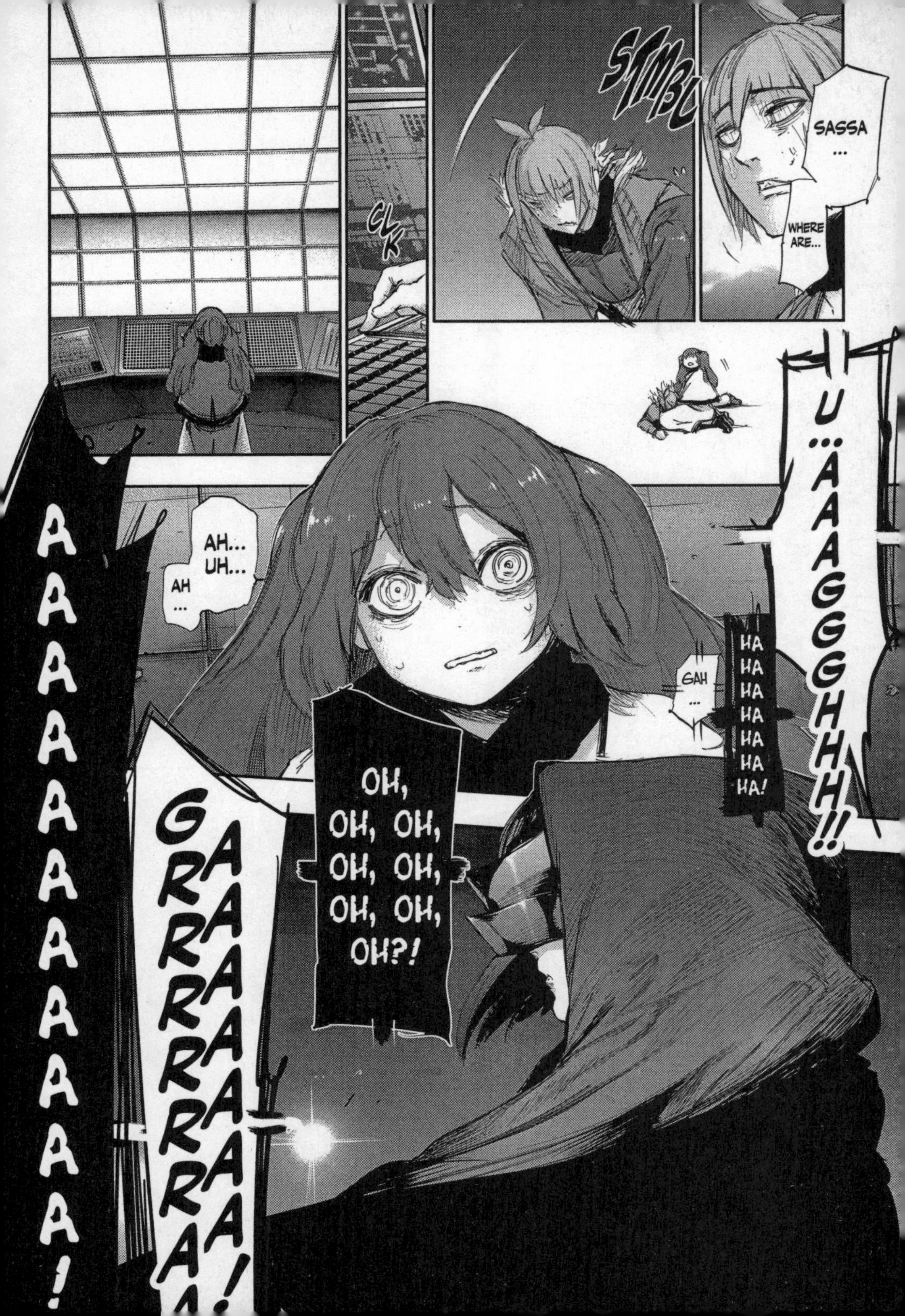

SASSA ...
WHERE ARE...
STMBL
CLK
U...ÄAAAGGGHHH!!
HA HA HA HA HA HA HA!
GAH ...
AH... UH...
AH ...
OH, OH, OH, OH, OH, OH, OH, OH, OH?!
GARARARARARAAA!
AAAAAAAAAAA!

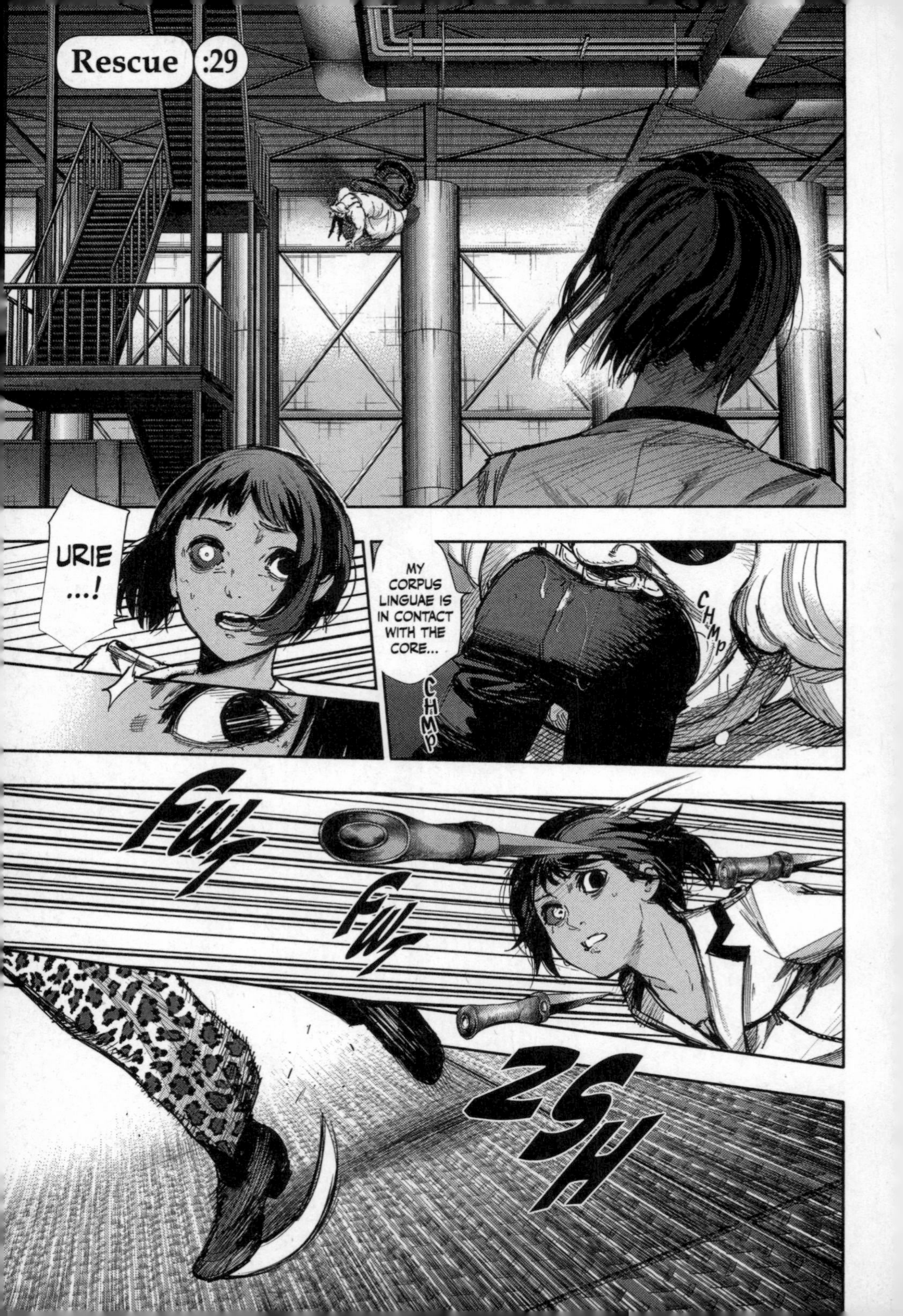
Rescue :29
MY CORPUS LINGUAE IS IN CONTACT WITH THE CORE...
CHMP
CHMP
URIE ...!
FWT
FWT
ZSH

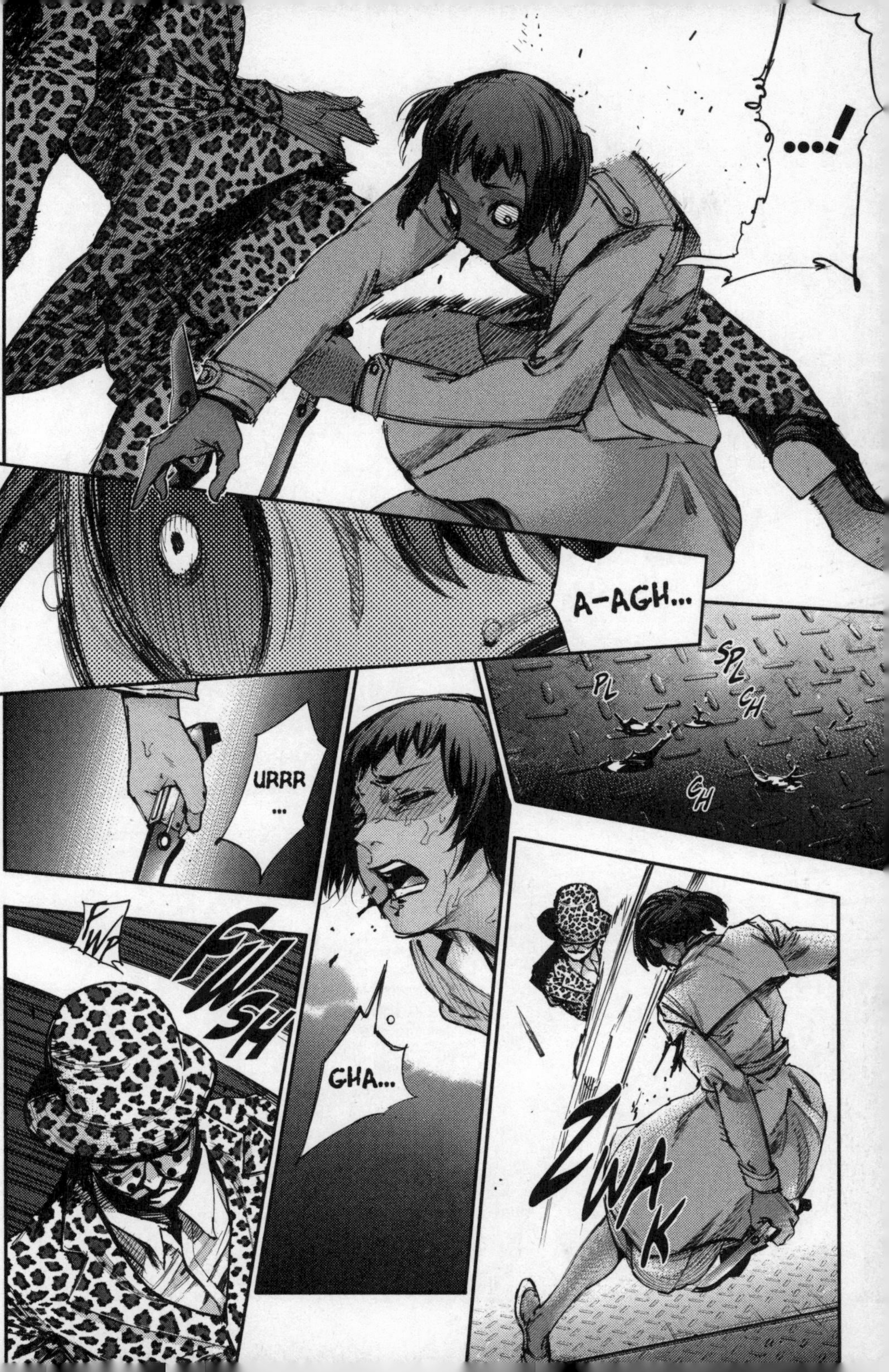
...!
A-AGH...
SPLCH
PL
CH
ZWAK
GHA...
URRR ...
PWP
FWSH

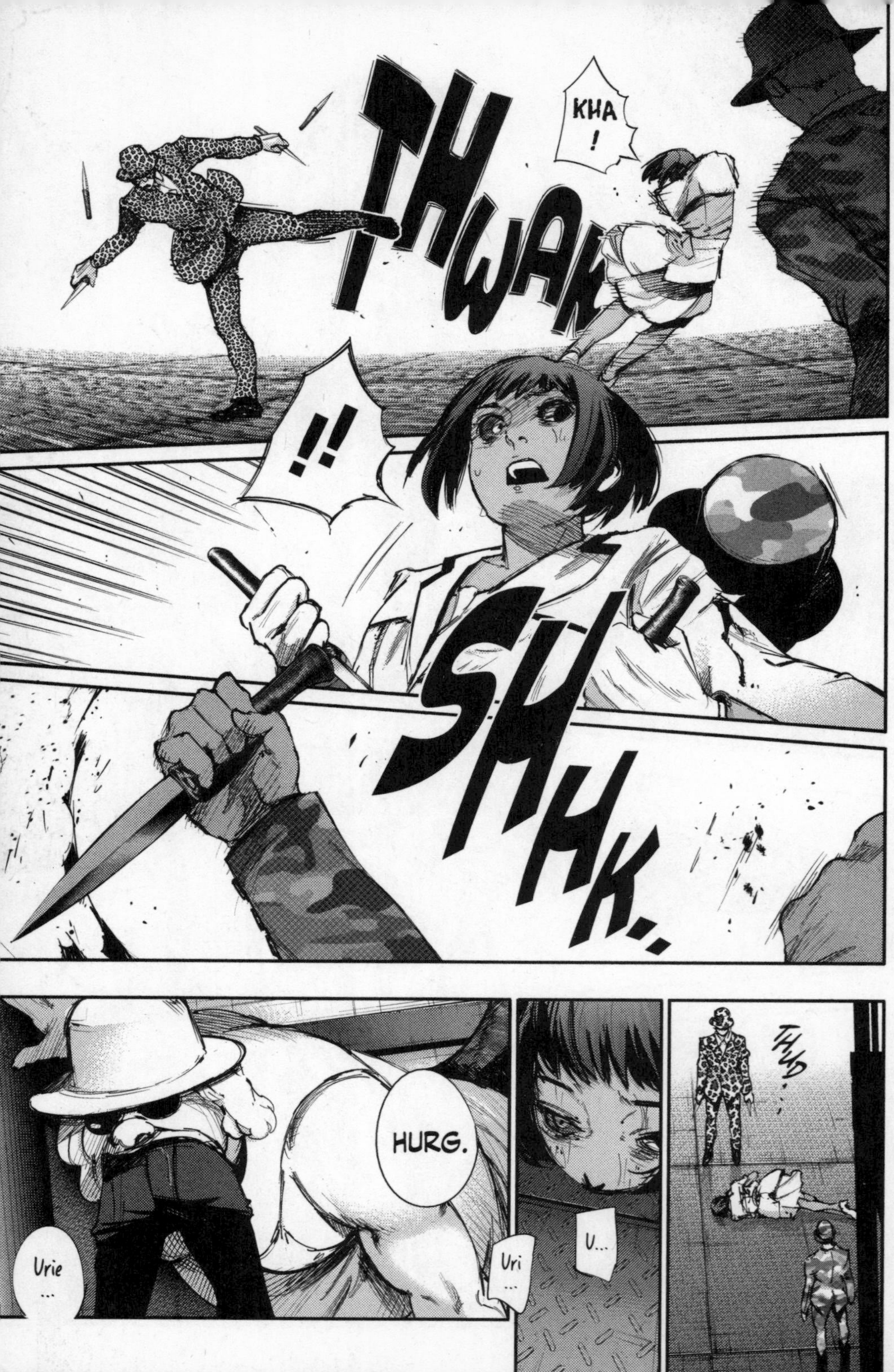
KHA!
THWAK
!!
SHHK..
THUD
U...
HURG.
Uri...
Urie...

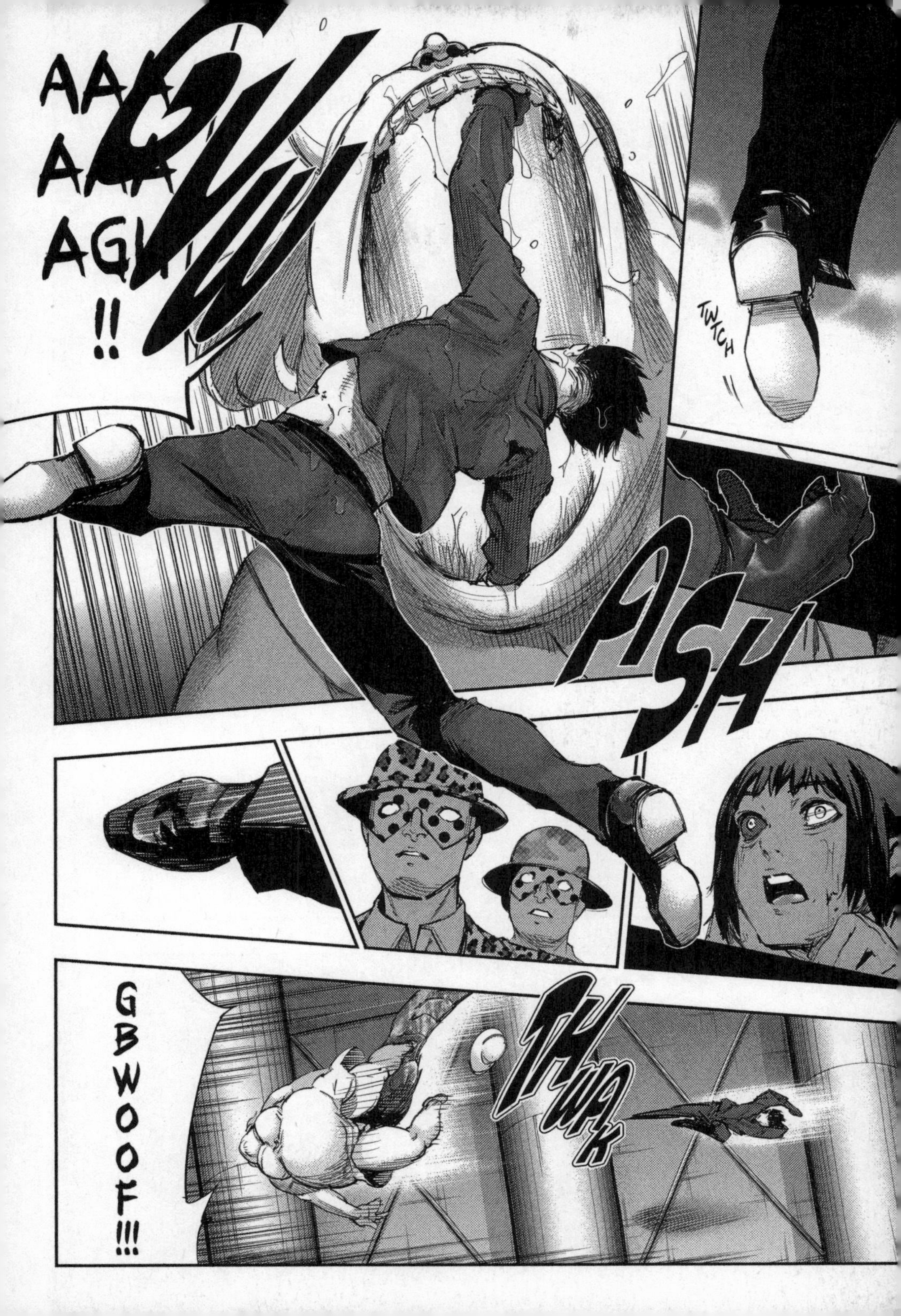
TWITCH
AA
AA
AG
!!
ASH
GBWOOF!!!
THUNK

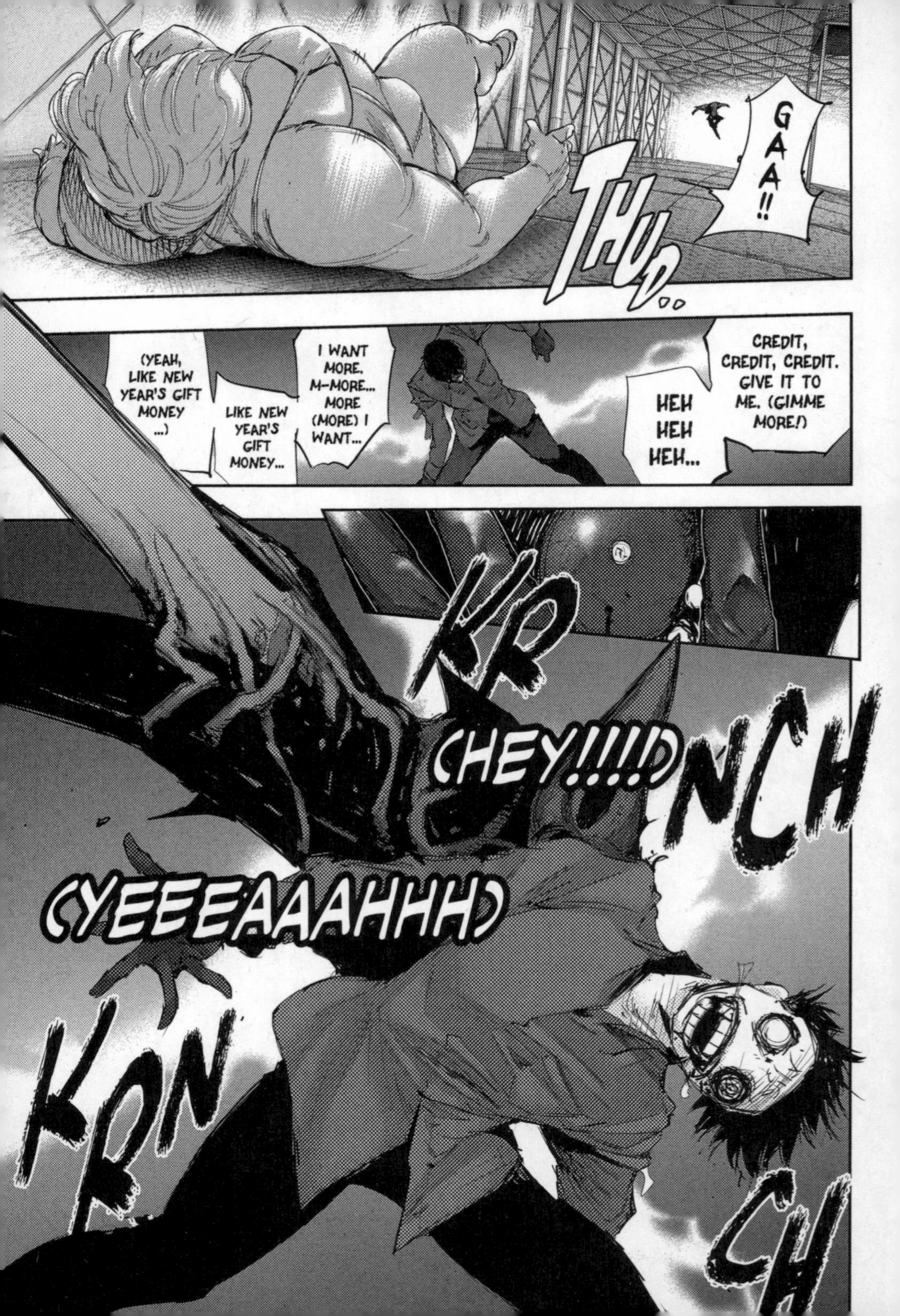
GAA!!
THUD..
CREDIT, CREDIT, CREDIT. GIVE IT TO ME. (GIMME MORE!)
HEH HEH HEH...
I WANT MORE. M-MORE... MORE (MORE) I WANT...
LIKE NEW YEAR'S GIFT MONEY...
(YEAH, LIKE NEW YEAR'S GIFT MONEY ...)
KR
NCH
(HEY!!!!)
(YEEEAAAHHH)
KRN
CH

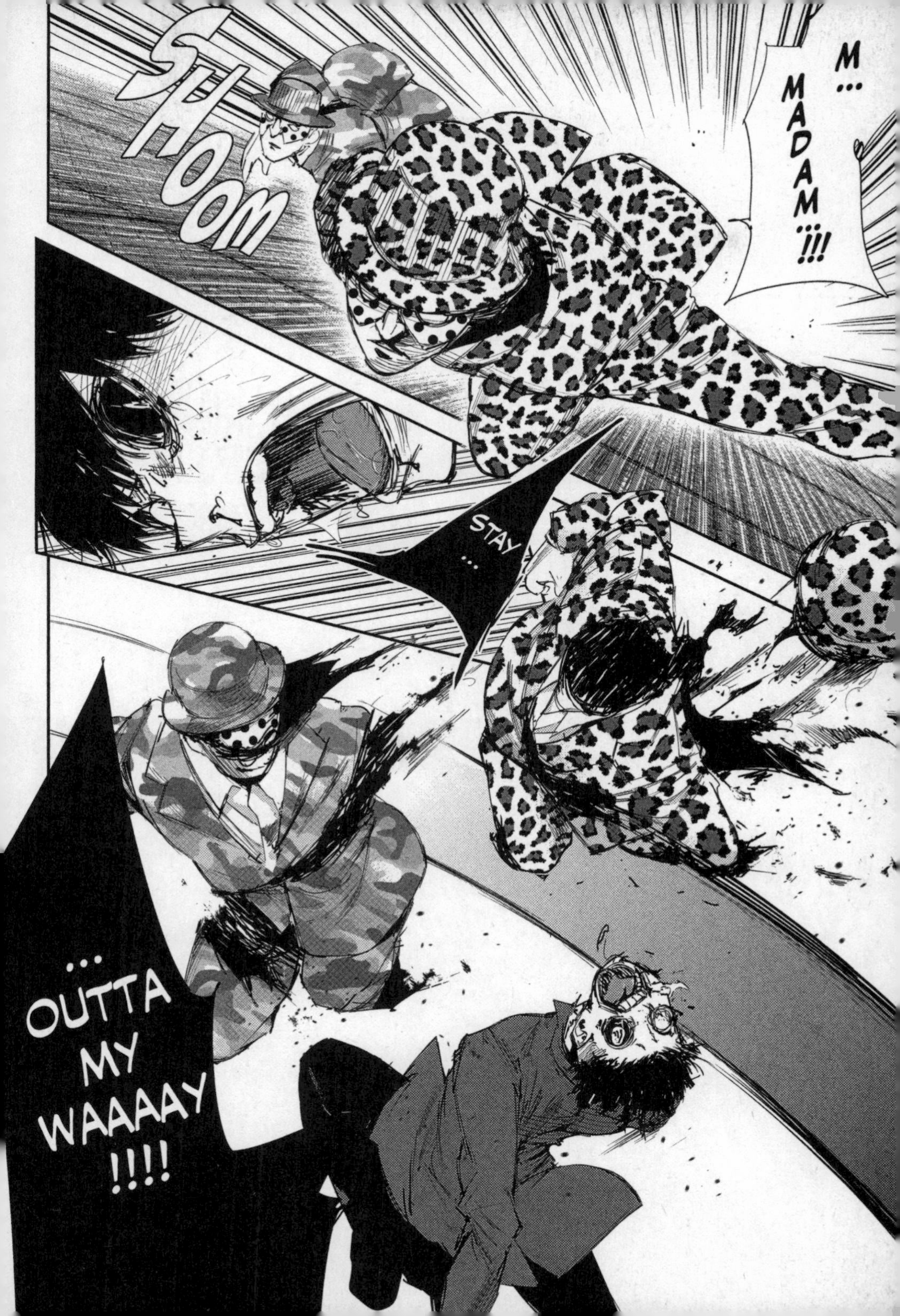
M... MADAM...!!!
SHOOM
STAY...
...OUTTA MY WAAAAY!!!!

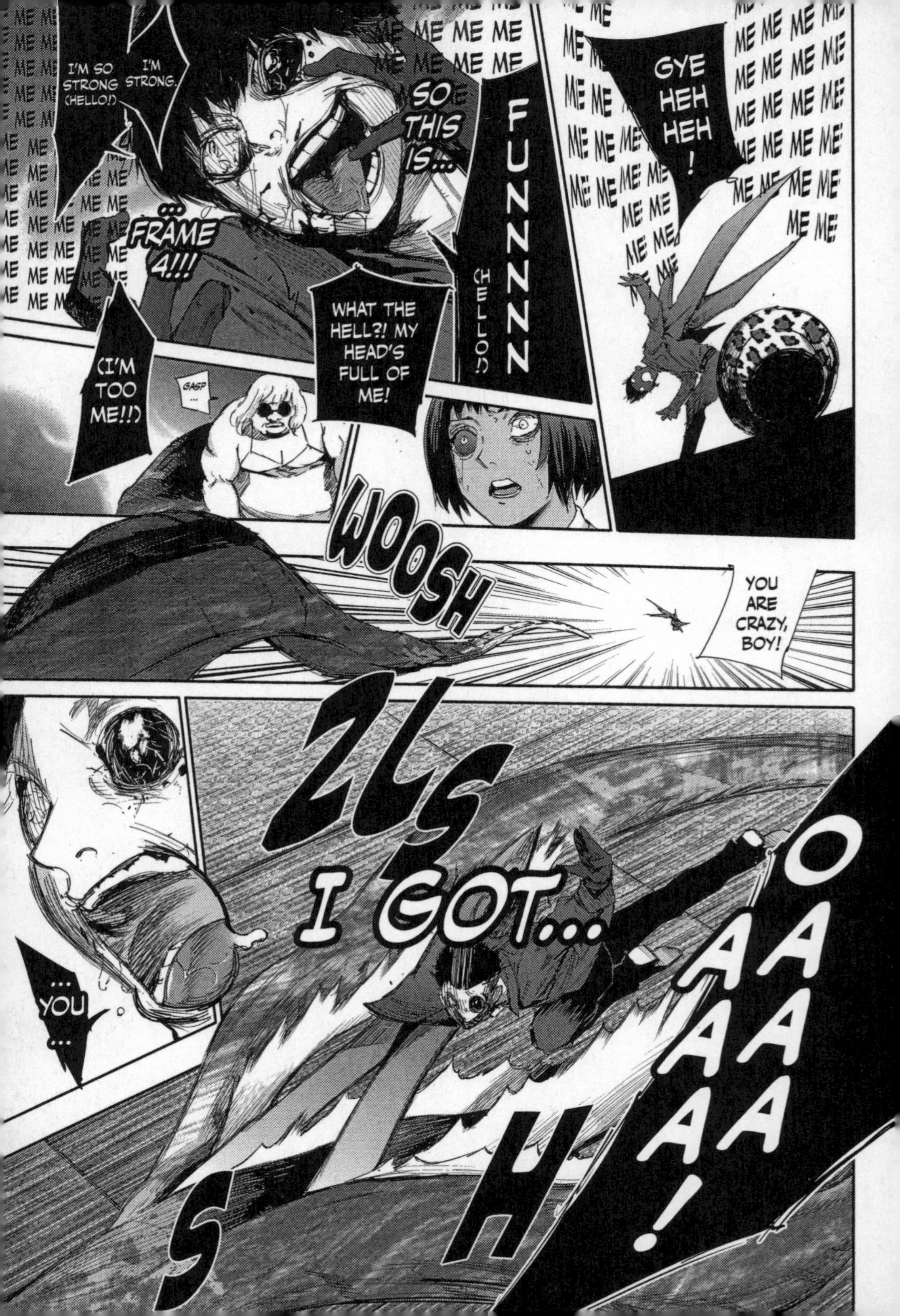

ME ME ME ME
GYE HEH HEH!
SO THIS IS...
FUNNNNN (HELLO!)
I'M STRONG.
I'M SO STRONG (HELLO!)
...FRAME 4!!!
WHAT THE HELL?! MY HEAD'S FULL OF ME!
GASP...
(I'M TOO ME!!)
WOOSH
YOU ARE CRAZY, BOY!
OAAAAAAAAA!
ZUS
I GOT...
SH
...YOU...

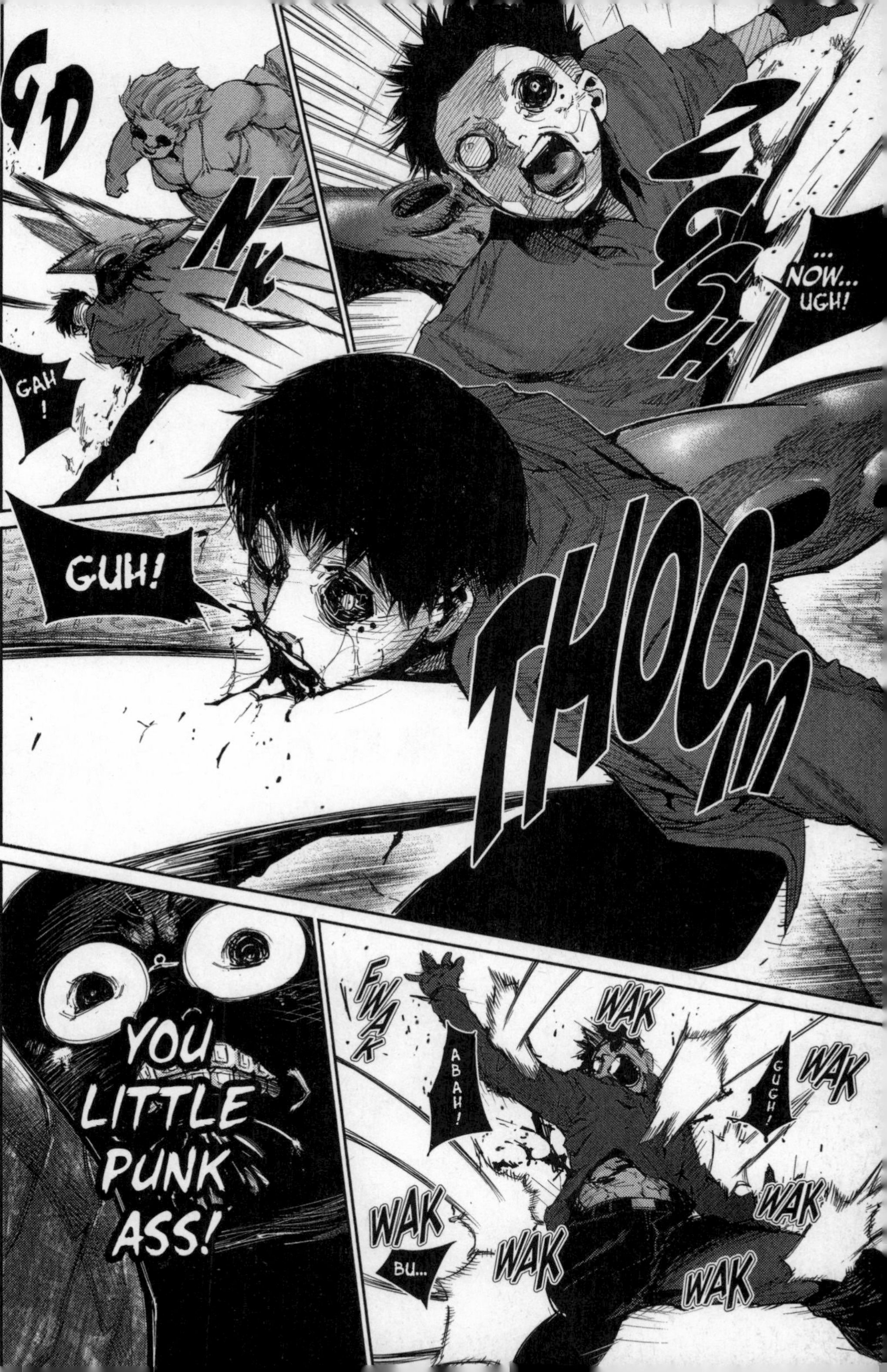
ZUGSH
...NOW... UGH!
GDNK
GAH!
GUH!
THOOM
FWAK
WAK
ABAH!
WAK
GUGH!
WAK
WAK
WAK
BU...
WAK
YOU LITTLE PUNK ASS!

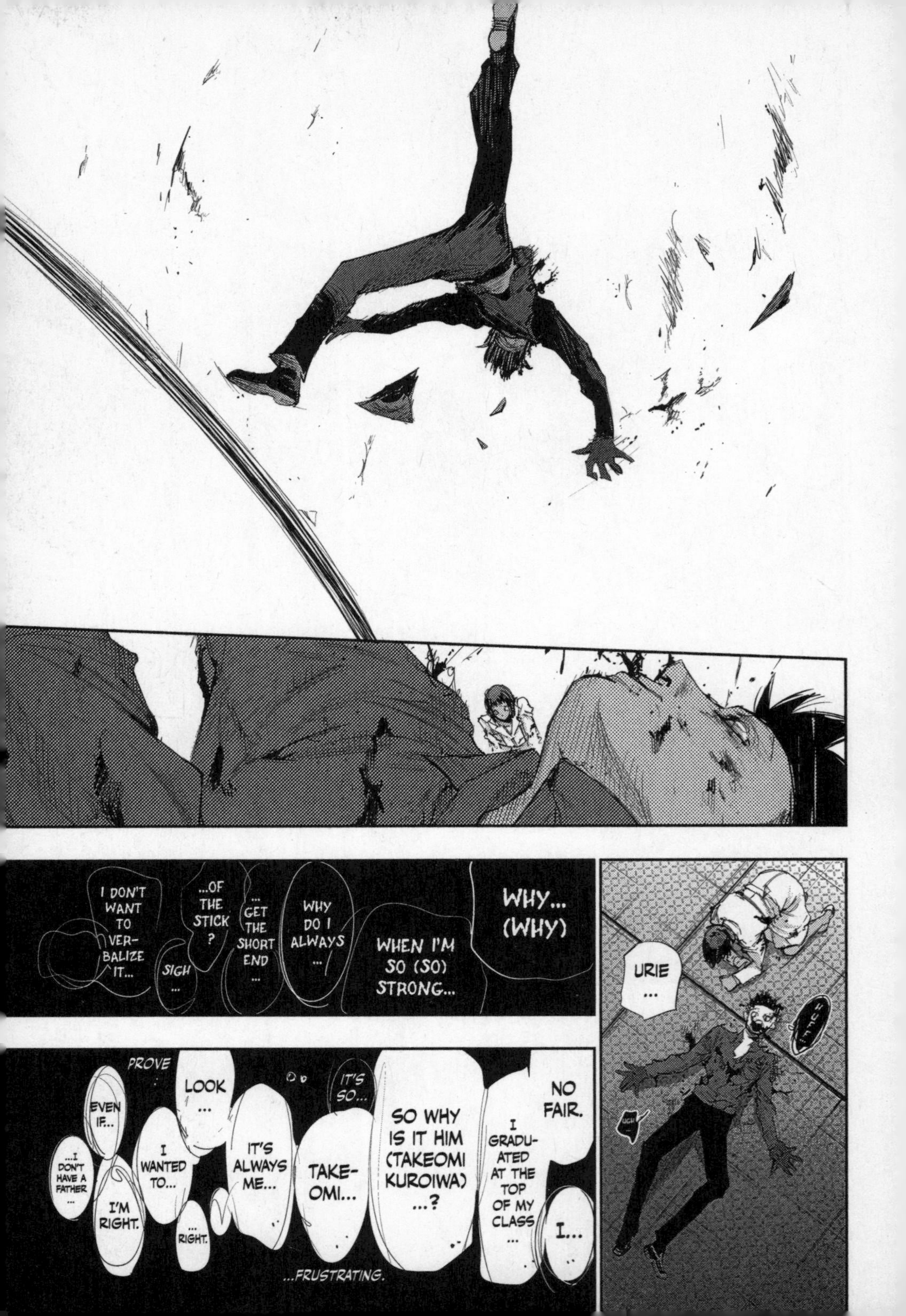
URIE ...
UGH
WHY... (WHY)
WHEN I'M SO (SO) STRONG...
WHY DO I ALWAYS ...
... GET THE SHORT END ...
...OF THE STICK ?
SIGH ...
I DON'T WANT TO VER-BALIZE IT...
NO FAIR.
I...
I GRADUATED AT THE TOP OF MY CLASS ...
SO WHY IS IT HIM (TAKEOMI KUROIWA) ...?
IT'S SO...
TAKE-OMI...
IT'S ALWAYS ME...
LOOK ...
PROVE :
... RIGHT.
I WANTED TO...
EVEN IF...
I'M RIGHT.
...I DON'T HAVE A FATHER ...
...FRUSTRATING.

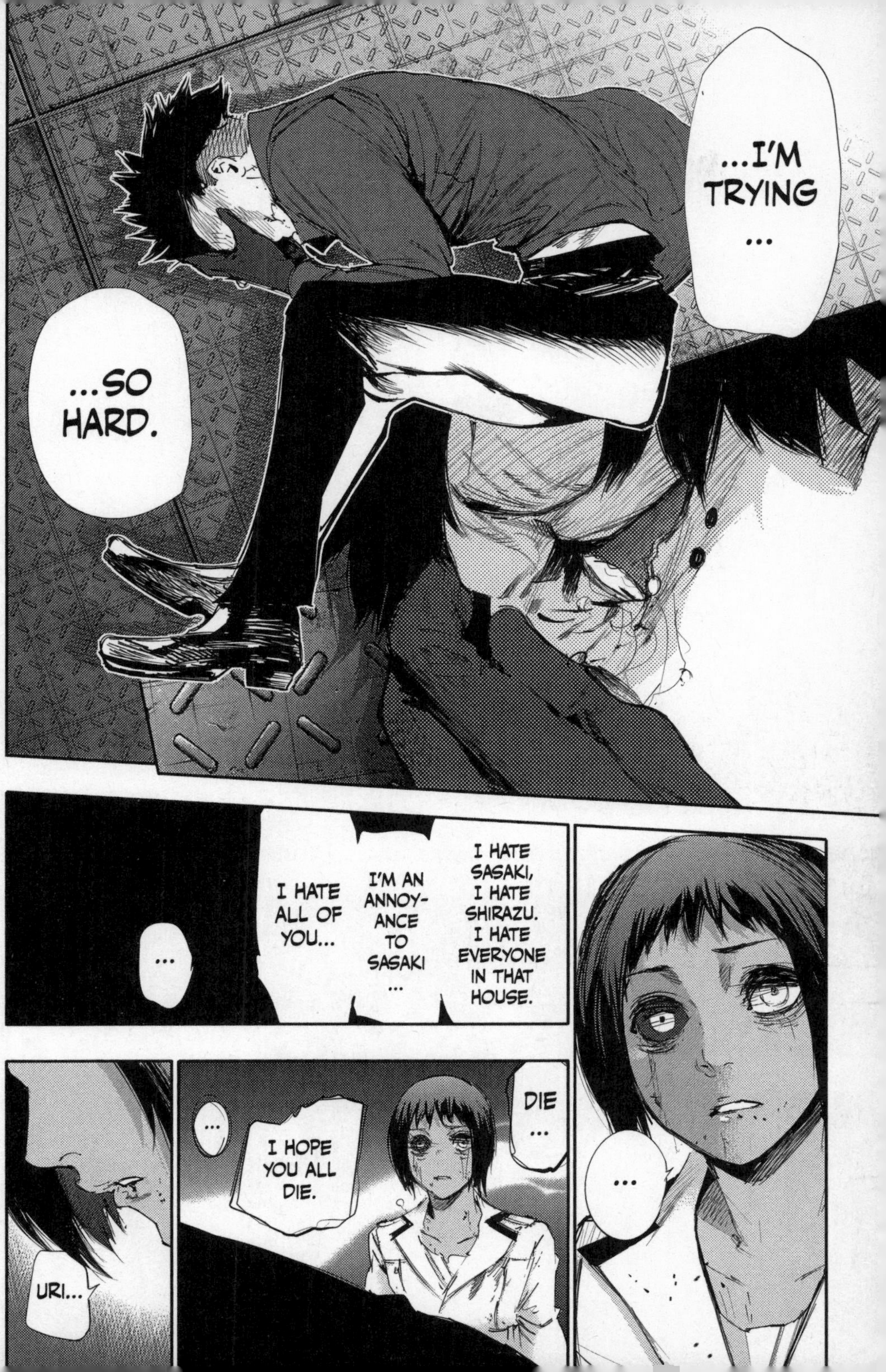
...I'M TRYING ...
...SO HARD.
...
I HATE SASAKI, I HATE SHIRAZU. I HATE EVERYONE IN THAT HOUSE.
I'M AN ANNOY-ANCE TO SASAKI ...
I HATE ALL OF YOU...
...
DIE ...
I HOPE YOU ALL DIE.
...
URI...

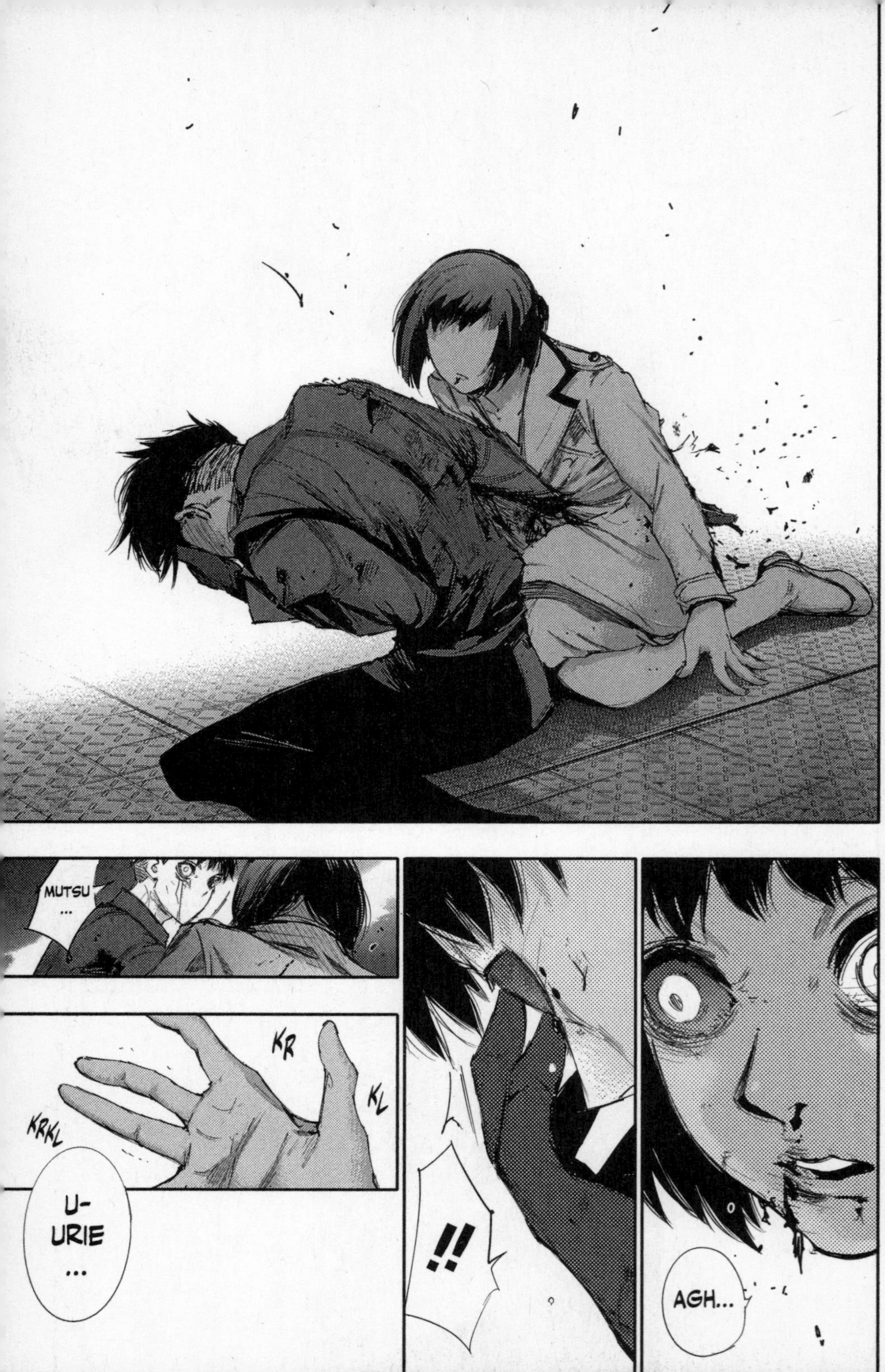
AGH...
!!
MUTSU ...
KR
KL
KRKL
U- URIE ...

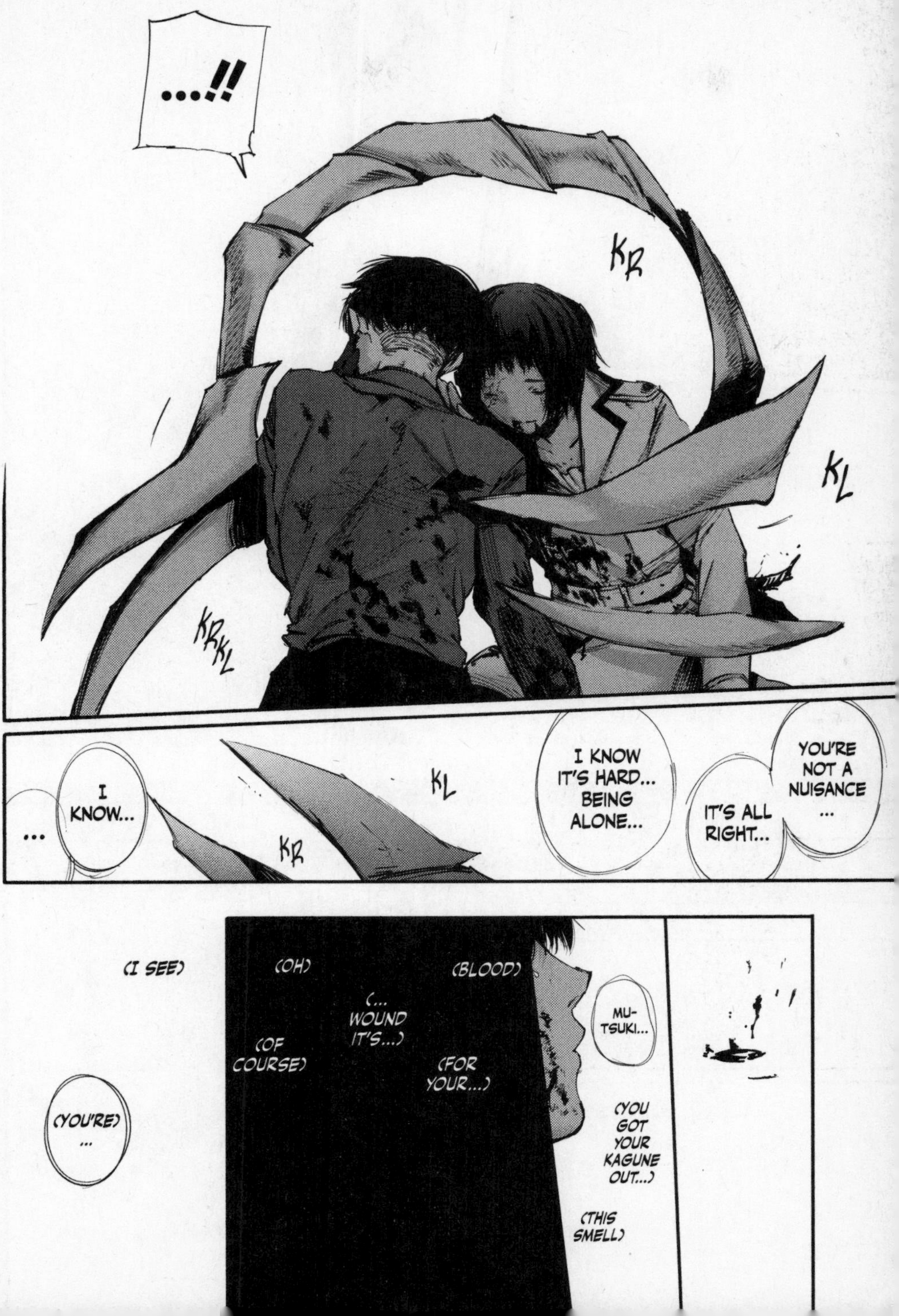
...!!
KR
KL
KRKL
YOU'RE NOT A NUISANCE ...
IT'S ALL RIGHT...
I KNOW IT'S HARD... BEING ALONE...
KL
KR
I KNOW...
...
MU-TSUKI...
(BLOOD)
(... WOUND IT'S...)
(OH)
(FOR YOUR...)
(OF COURSE)
(I SEE)
(YOU GOT YOUR KAGUNE OUT...)
(THIS SMELL)
(YOU'RE) ...

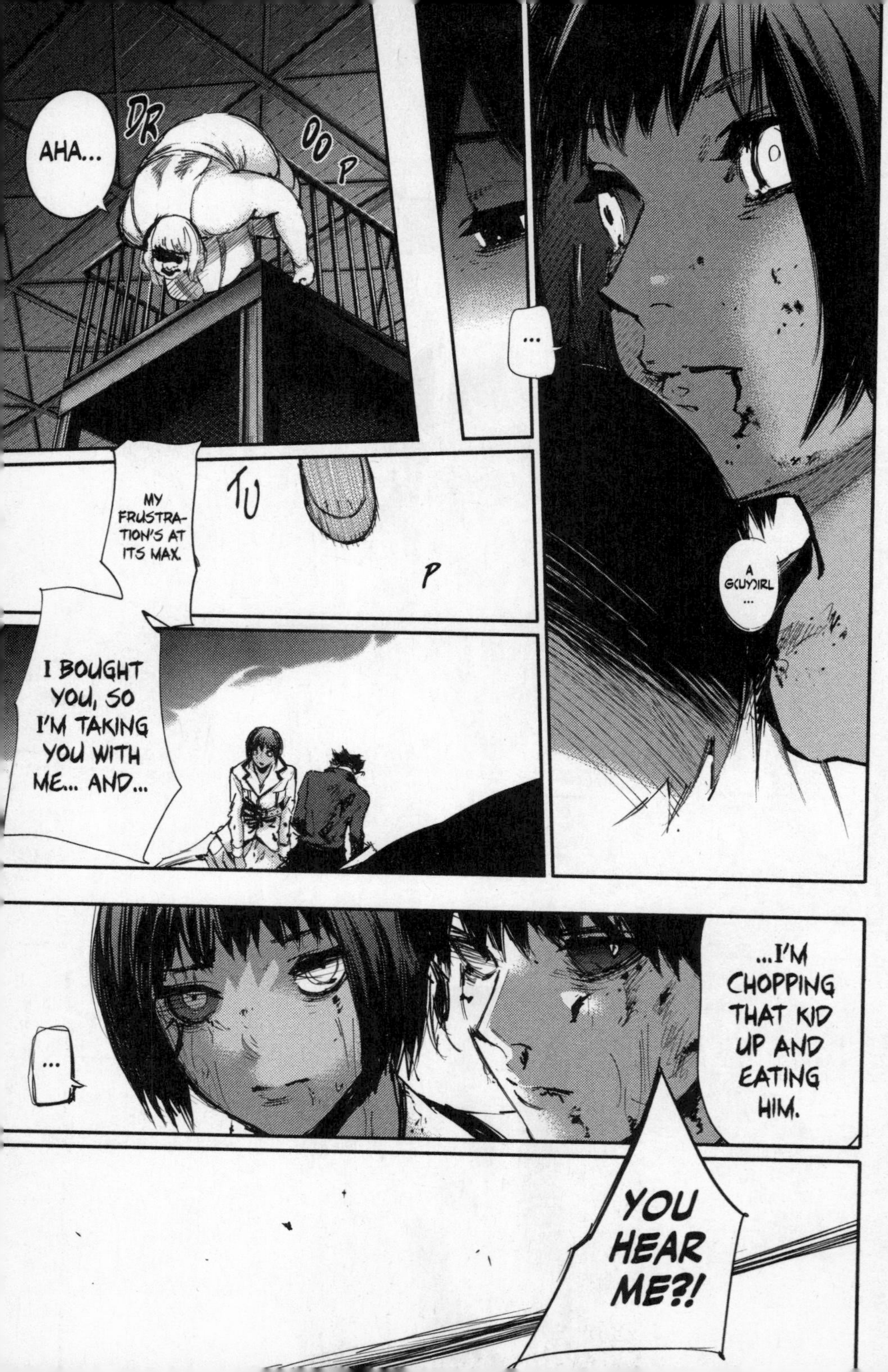
...
A G(UY)IRL ...
AHA...
DROOP
MY FRUSTRATION'S AT ITS MAX.
TUP
I BOUGHT YOU, SO I'M TAKING YOU WITH ME... AND...
...I'M CHOPPING THAT KID UP AND EATING HIM.
...
YOU HEAR ME?!

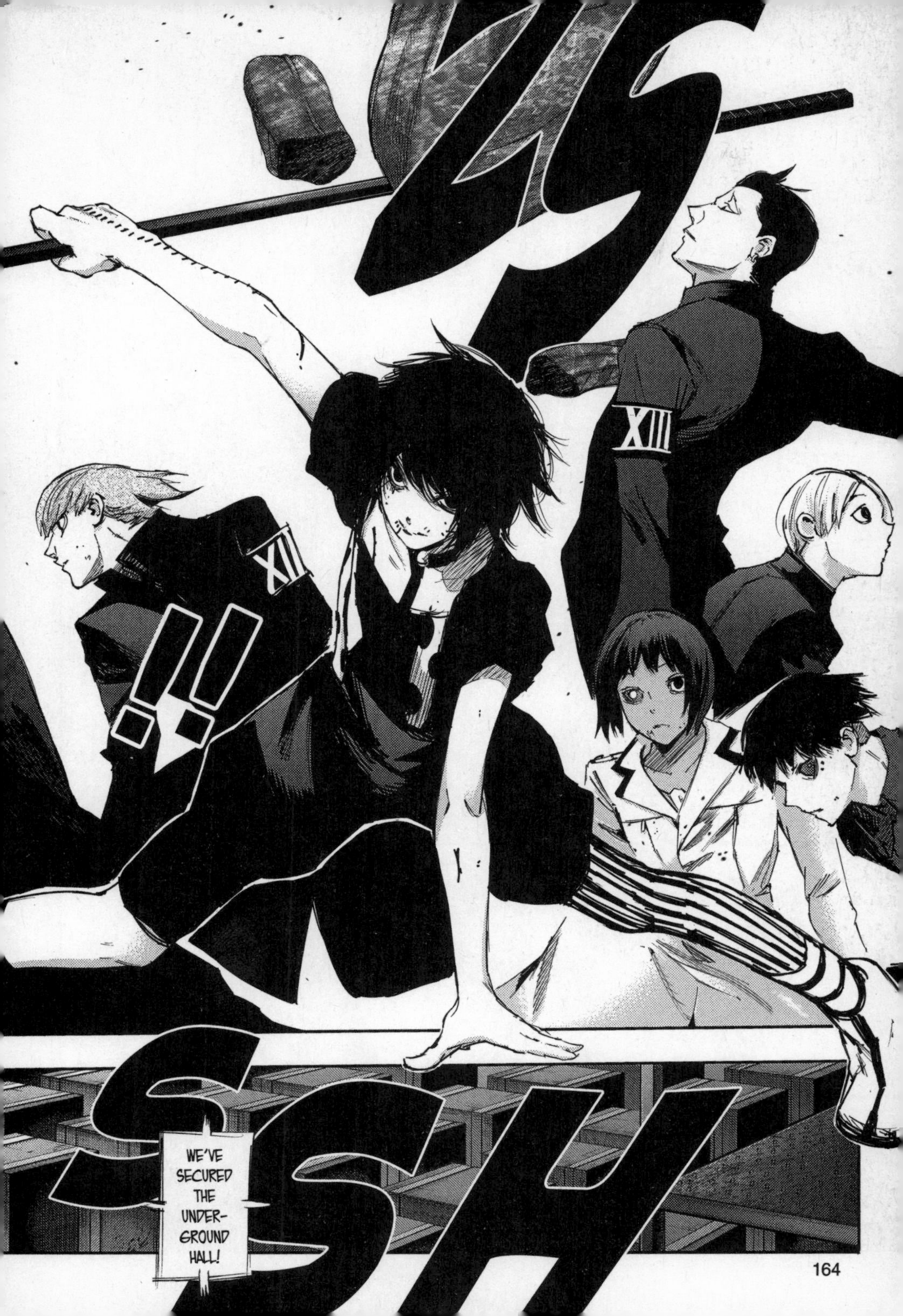

WE'VE SECURED THE UNDER-GROUND HALL!

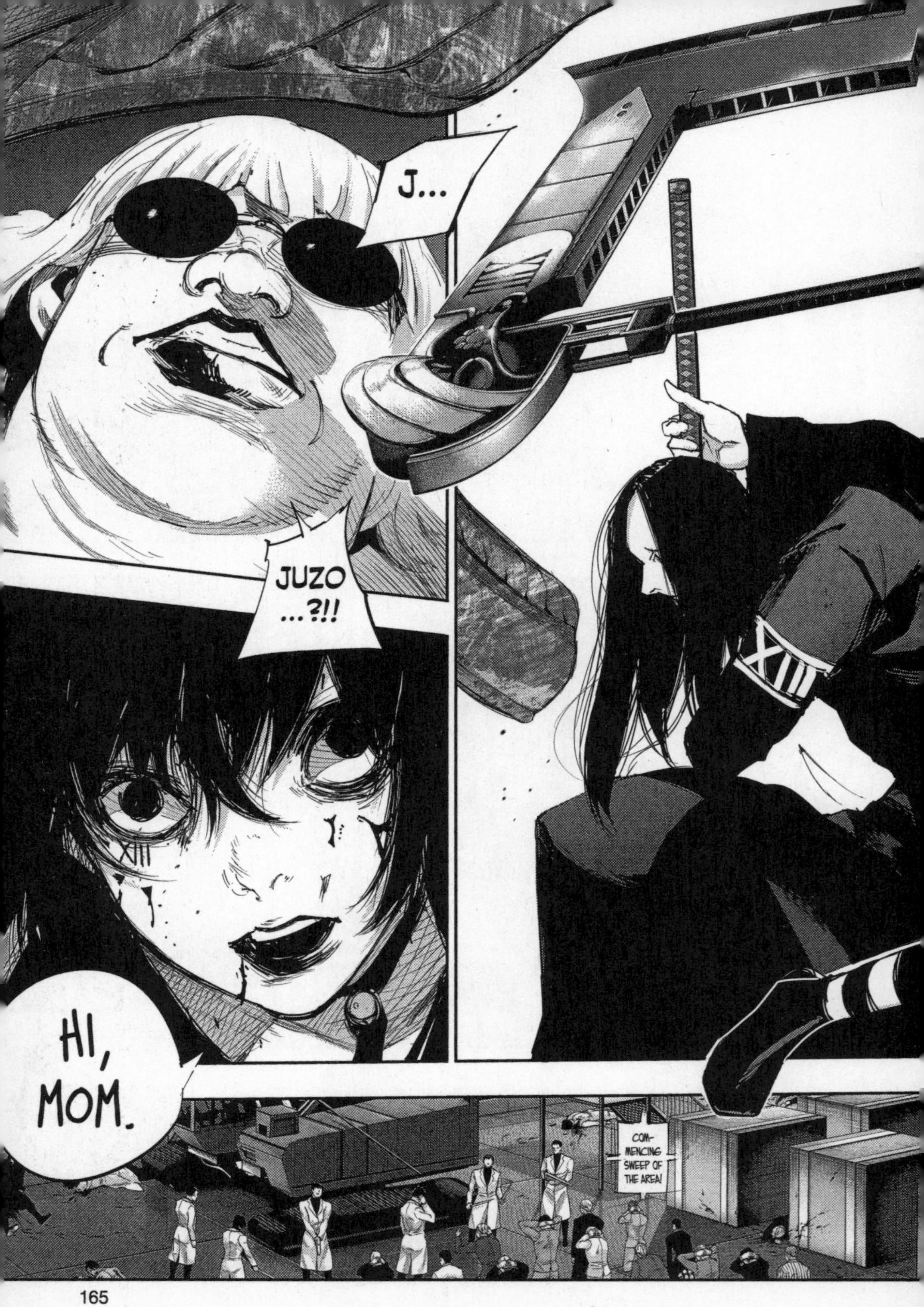
J...
JUZO ...?!!
HI, MOM.
COM-MENCING SWEEP OF THE AREA!

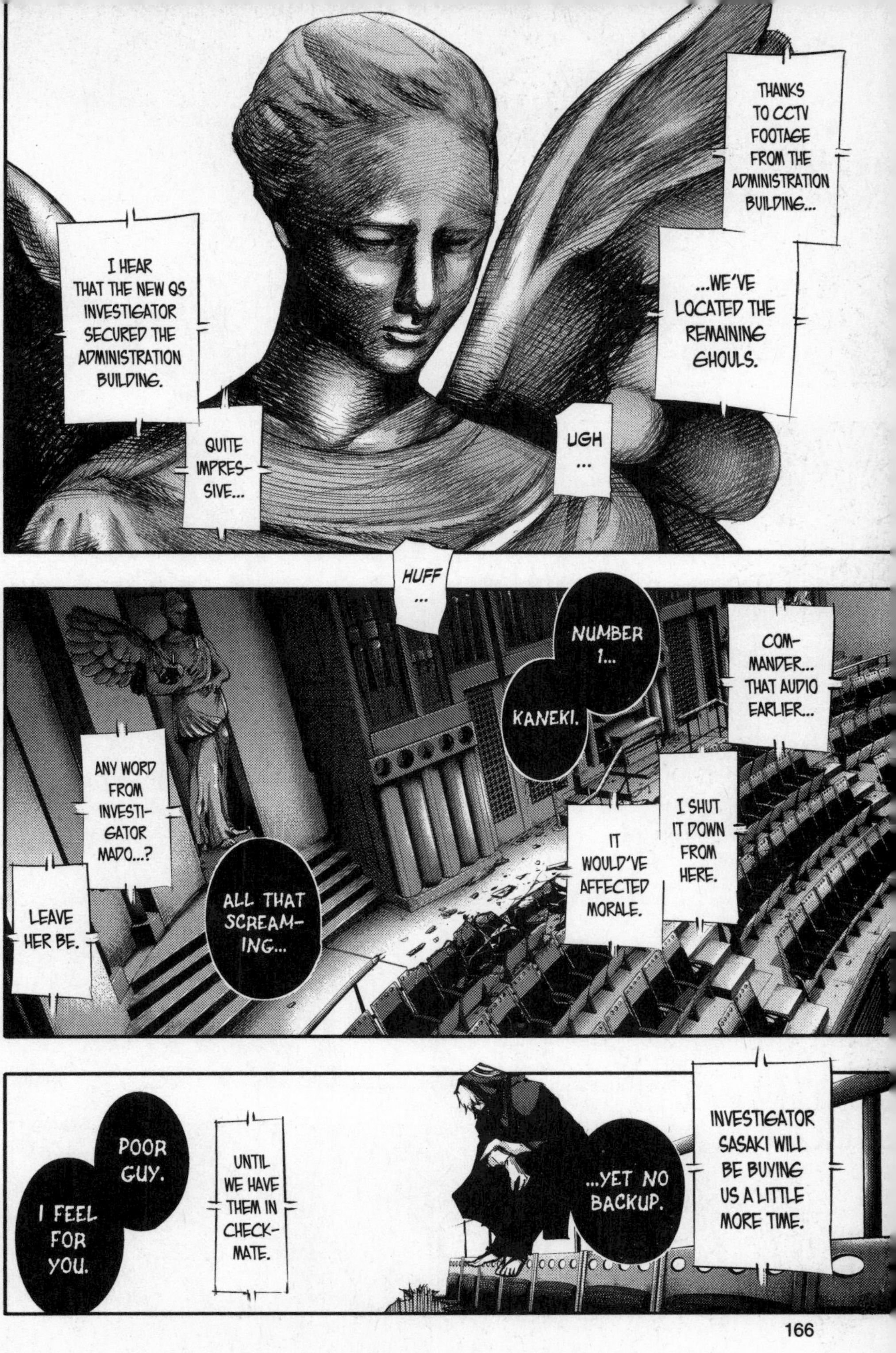
THANKS TO CCTV FOOTAGE FROM THE ADMINISTRATION BUILDING...
...WE'VE LOCATED THE REMAINING GHOULS.
UGH ...
I HEAR THAT THE NEW QS INVESTIGATOR SECURED THE ADMINISTRATION BUILDING.
QUITE IMPRES-SIVE...
HUFF ...
COM-MANDER... THAT AUDIO EARLIER...
NUMBER 1...
KANEKI.
I SHUT IT DOWN FROM HERE.
IT WOULD'VE AFFECTED MORALE.
ALL THAT SCREAM-ING...
ANY WORD FROM INVESTI-GATOR MADO...?
LEAVE HER BE.
INVESTIGATOR SASAKI WILL BE BUYING US A LITTLE MORE TIME.
...YET NO BACKUP.
UNTIL WE HAVE THEM IN CHECK-MATE.
POOR GUY.
I FEEL FOR YOU.

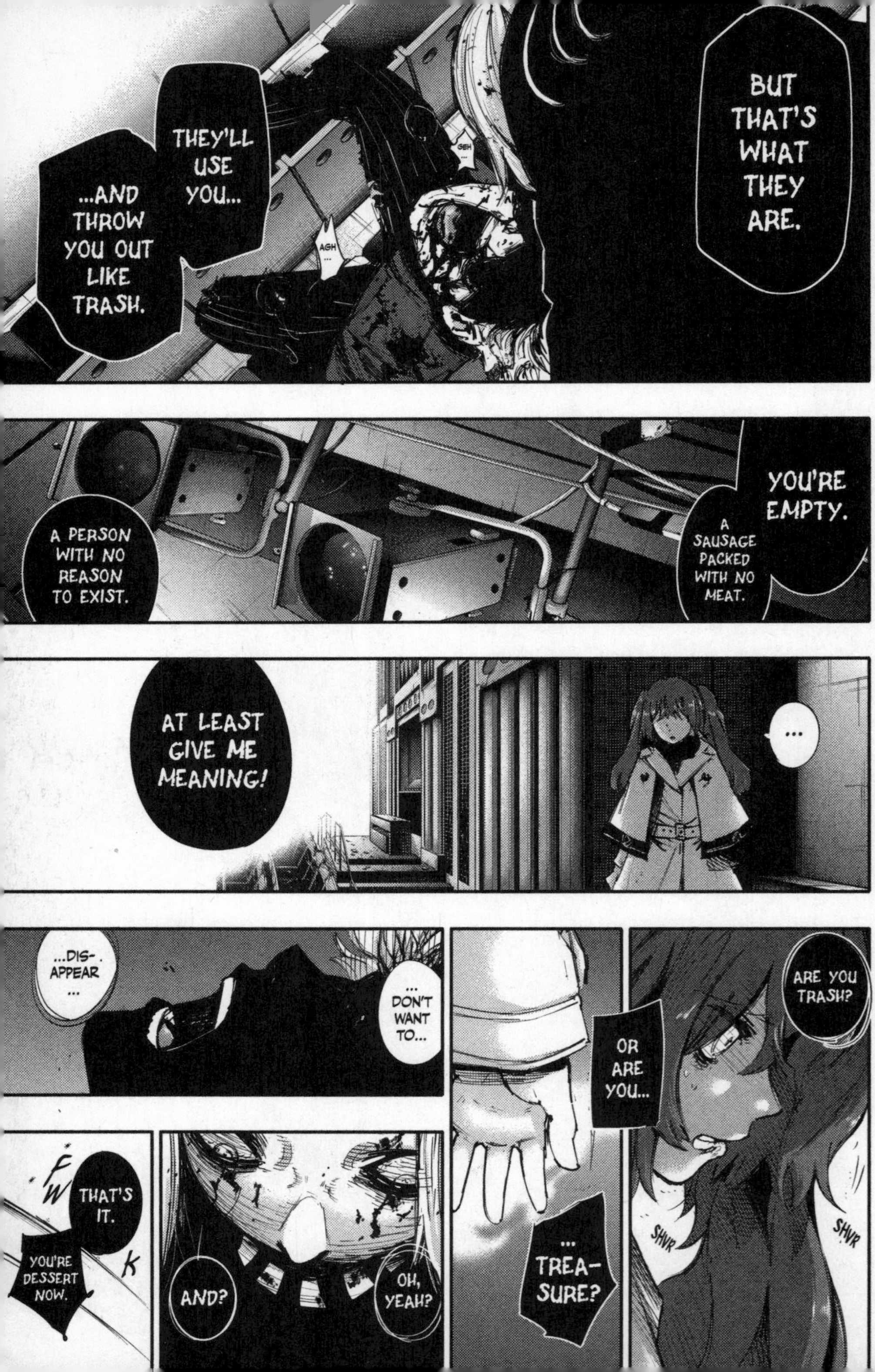
BUT THAT'S WHAT THEY ARE.
GEH...
THEY'LL USE YOU...
AGH...
...AND THROW YOU OUT LIKE TRASH.
YOU'RE EMPTY.
A SAUSAGE PACKED WITH NO MEAT.
A PERSON WITH NO REASON TO EXIST.
...
AT LEAST GIVE ME MEANING!
ARE YOU TRASH?
OR ARE YOU...
SHVR
SHVR
...TREASURE?
...DON'T WANT TO...
...DIS-APPEAR...
OH, YEAH?
AND?
THAT'S IT.
FWK
YOU'RE DESSERT NOW.

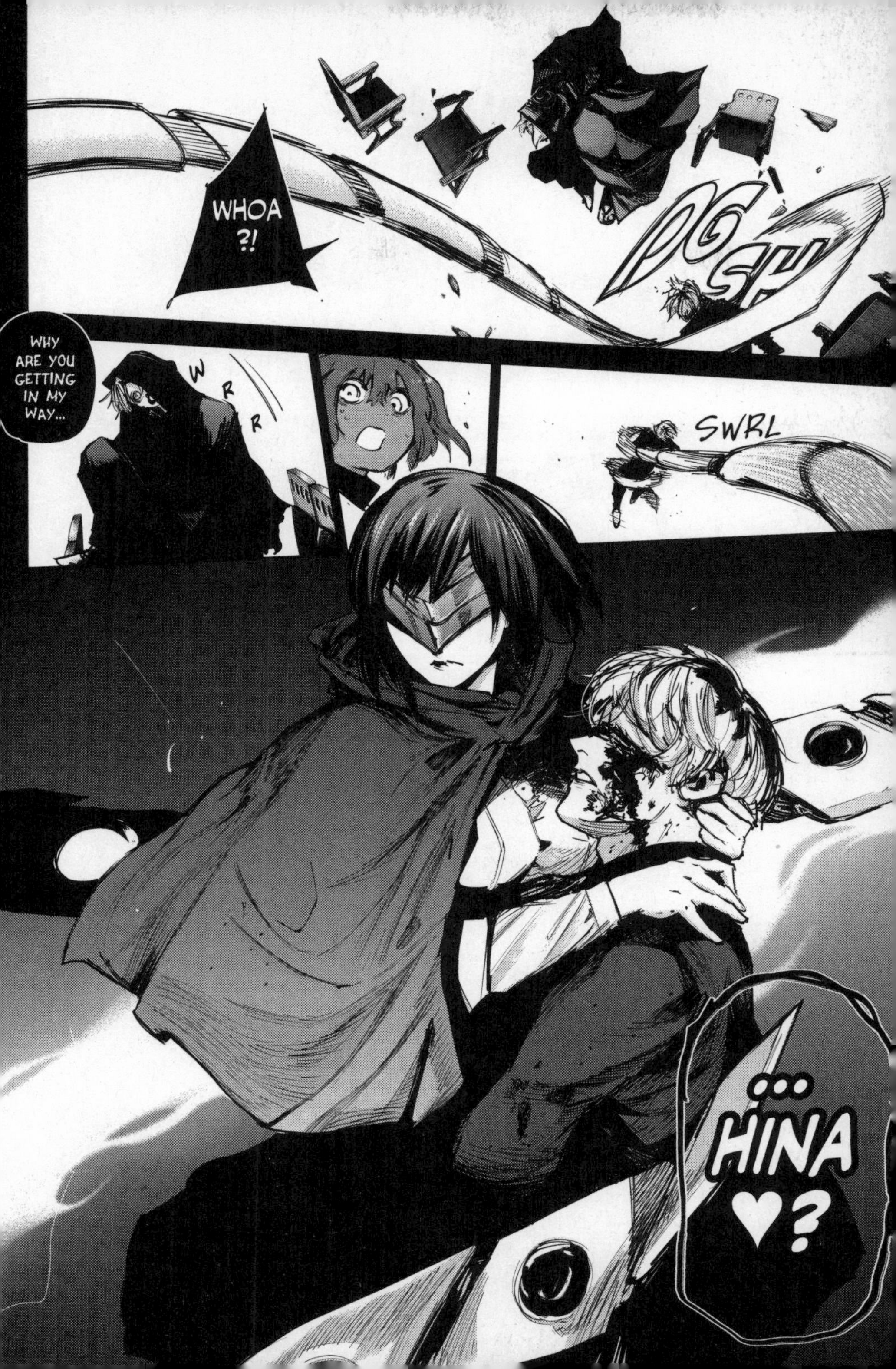
WHOA ?!
SWRL
WHY ARE YOU GETTING IN MY WAY...
WRR
...HINA ♥?

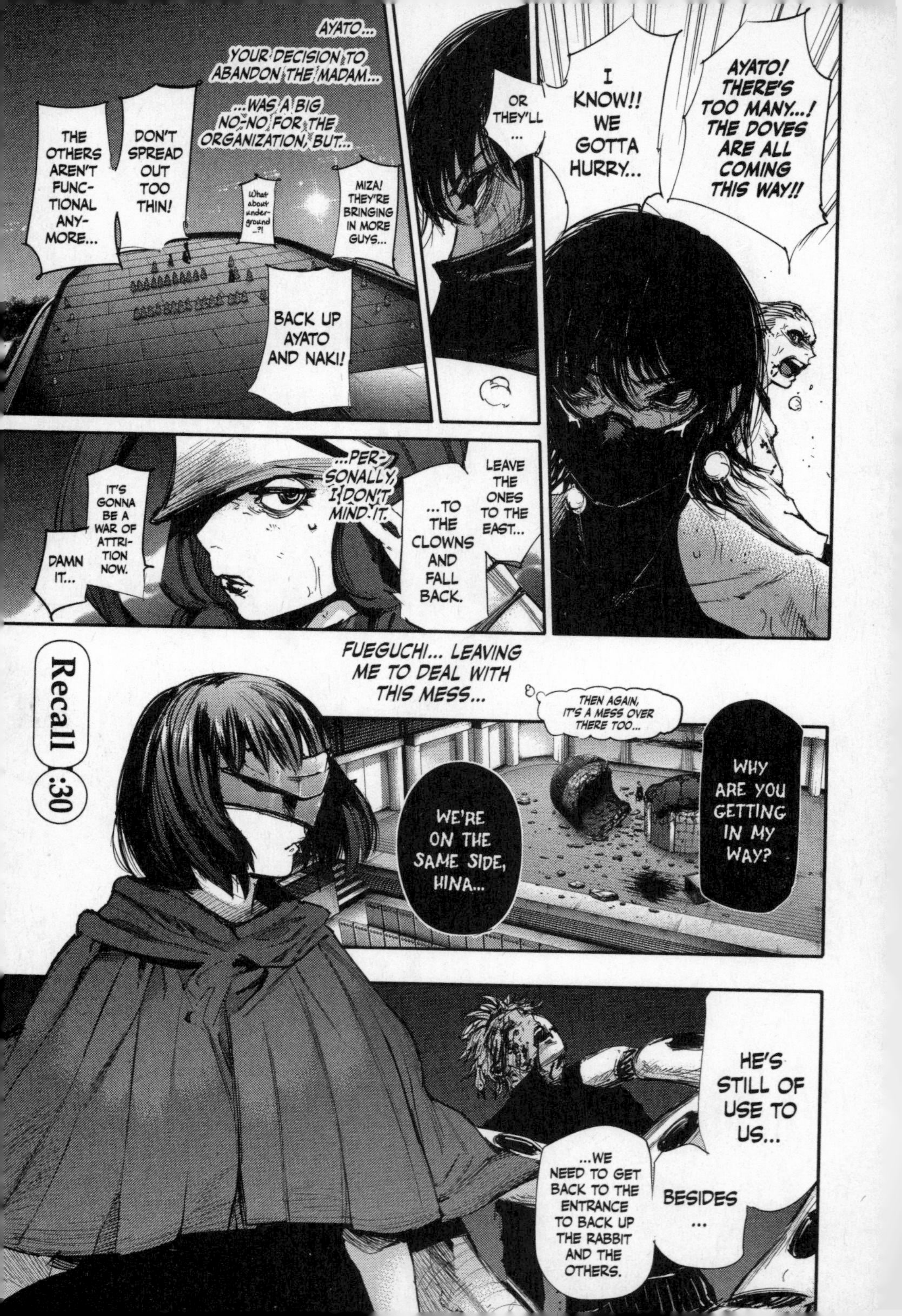
AYATO! THERE'S TOO MANY...! THE DOVES ARE ALL COMING THIS WAY!!
I KNOW!! WE GOTTA HURRY...
OR THEY'LL ...
AYATO... YOUR DECISION TO ABANDON THE MADAM... ...WAS A BIG NO-NO FOR THE ORGANIZATION, BUT...
MIZA! THEY'RE BRINGING IN MORE GUYS...
What about underground...?!
BACK UP AYATO AND NAKI!
DON'T SPREAD OUT TOO THIN!
THE OTHERS AREN'T FUNCTIONAL ANYMORE...
LEAVE THE ONES TO THE EAST...
...TO THE CLOWNS AND FALL BACK.
...PERSONALLY, I DON'T MIND IT.
IT'S GONNA BE A WAR OF ATTRITION NOW.
DAMN IT...
WHY ARE YOU GETTING IN MY WAY?
WE'RE ON THE SAME SIDE, HINA...
HE'S STILL OF USE TO US...
BESIDES ...
...WE NEED TO GET BACK TO THE ENTRANCE TO BACK UP THE RABBIT AND THE OTHERS.
FUEGUCHI... LEAVING ME TO DEAL WITH THIS MESS...
THEN AGAIN, IT'S A MESS OVER THERE TOO...
Recall :30

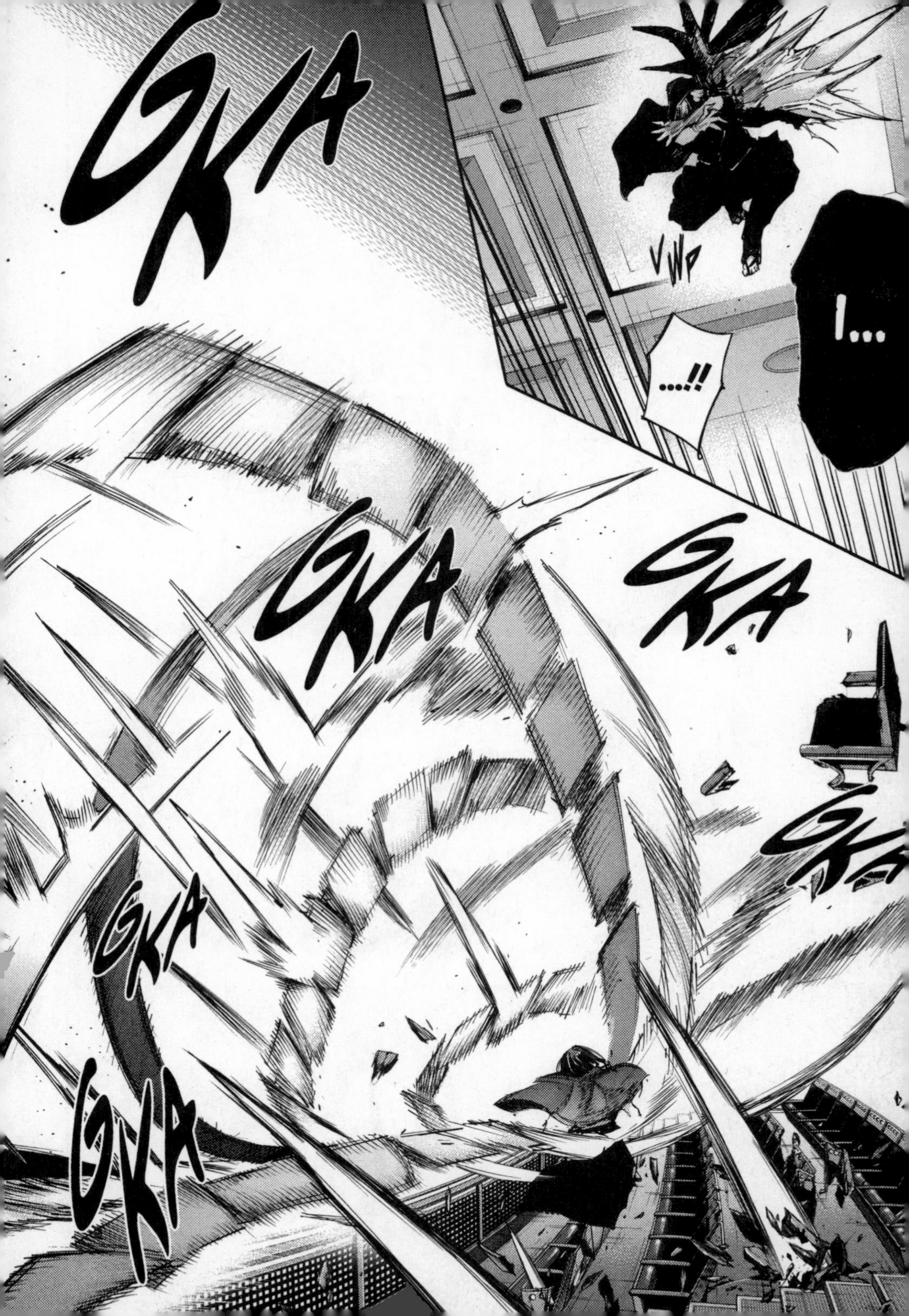

VWP
I...
...!!
GKA
GKA
GKA
GKA
GKA
GKA

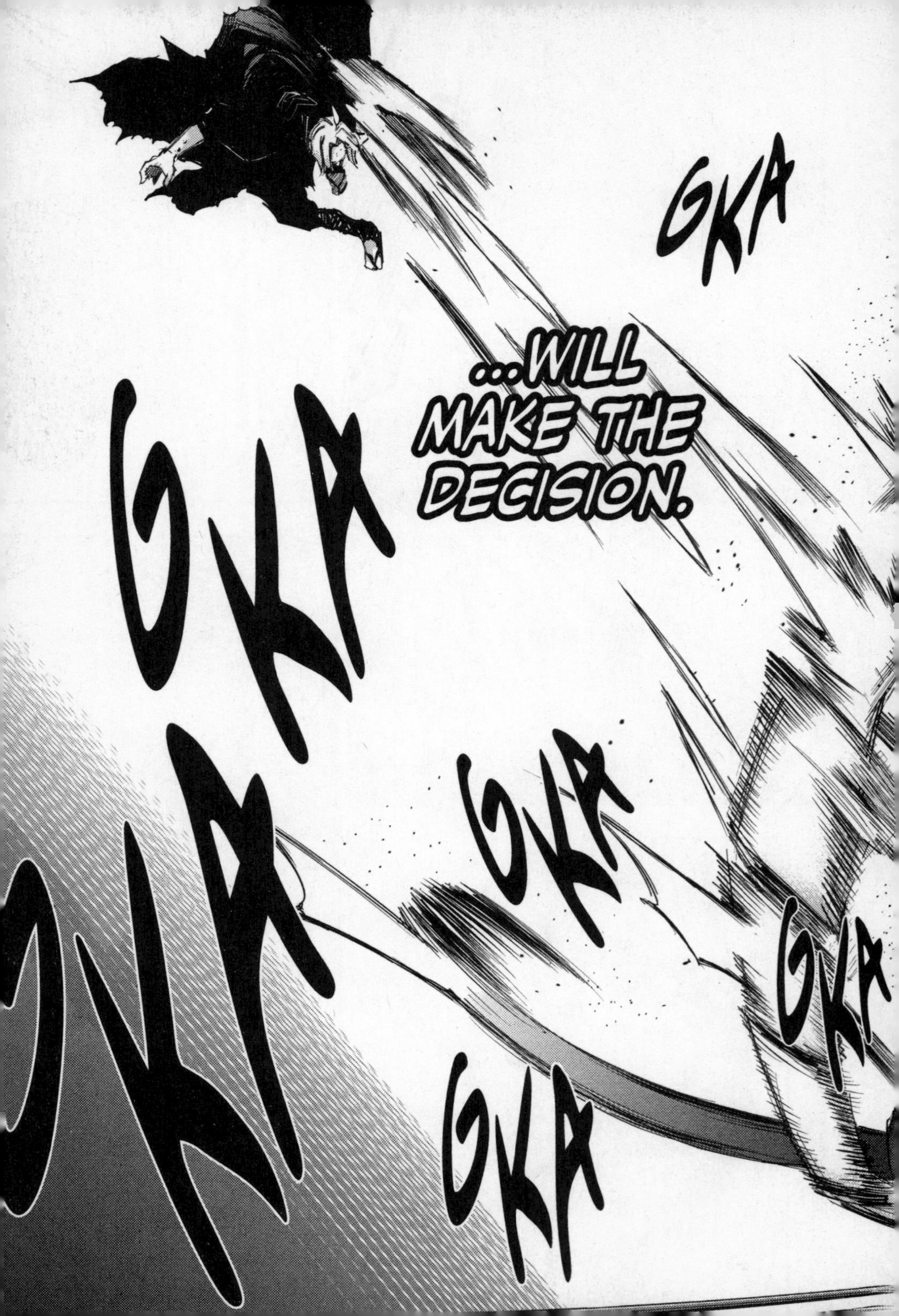
GKA
...WILL MAKE THE DECISION.
GKA
GKA
GKA
GKA

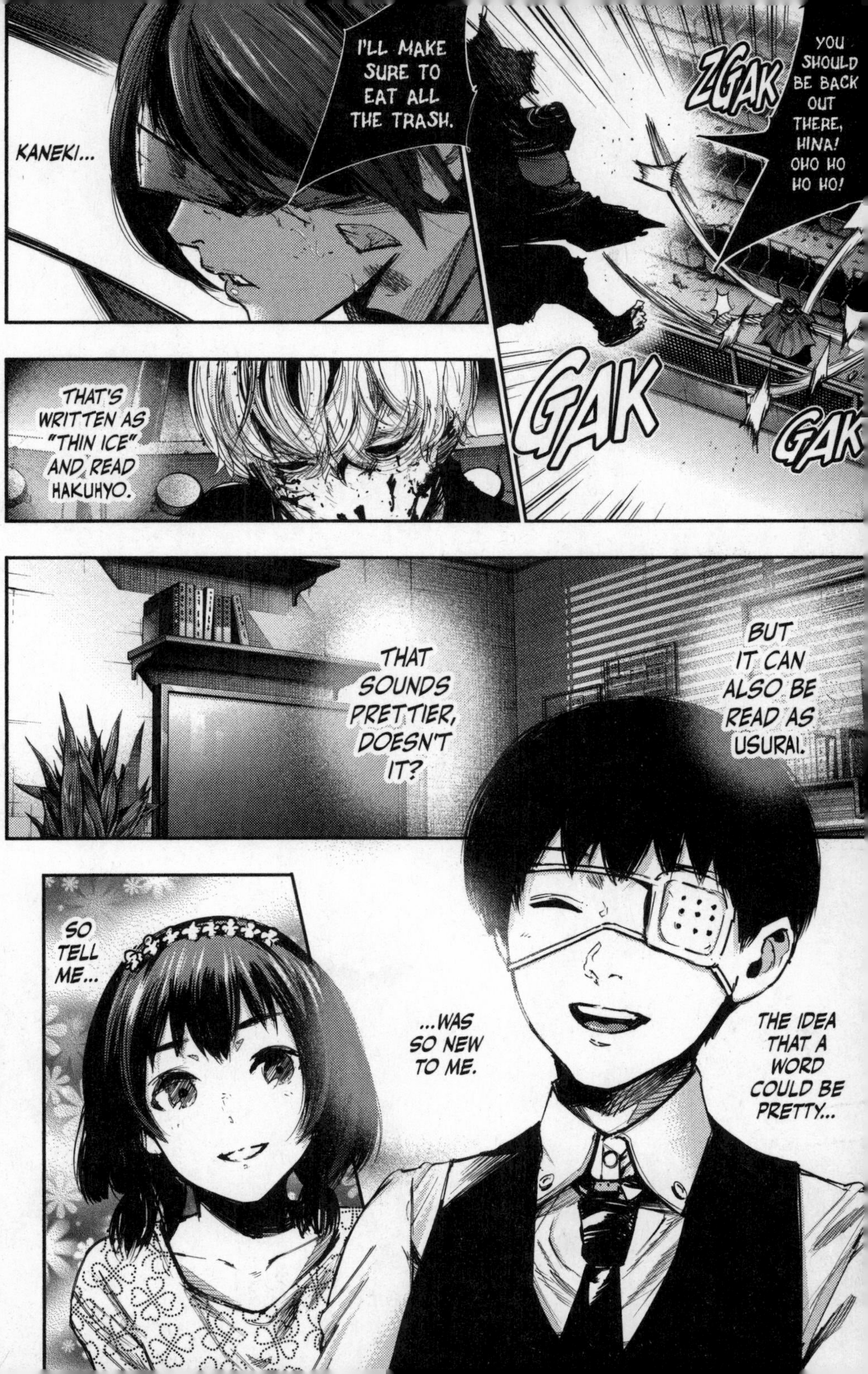

ZGAK
YOU SHOULD BE BACK OUT THERE, HINA! OHO HO HO HO!
GAK
GAK
I'LL MAKE SURE TO EAT ALL THE TRASH.
KANEKI...
THAT'S WRITTEN AS "THIN ICE" AND READ HAKUHYO.
BUT IT CAN ALSO BE READ AS USURAI.
THAT SOUNDS PRETTIER, DOESN'T IT?
THE IDEA THAT A WORD COULD BE PRETTY...
...WAS SO NEW TO ME.
SO TELL ME...

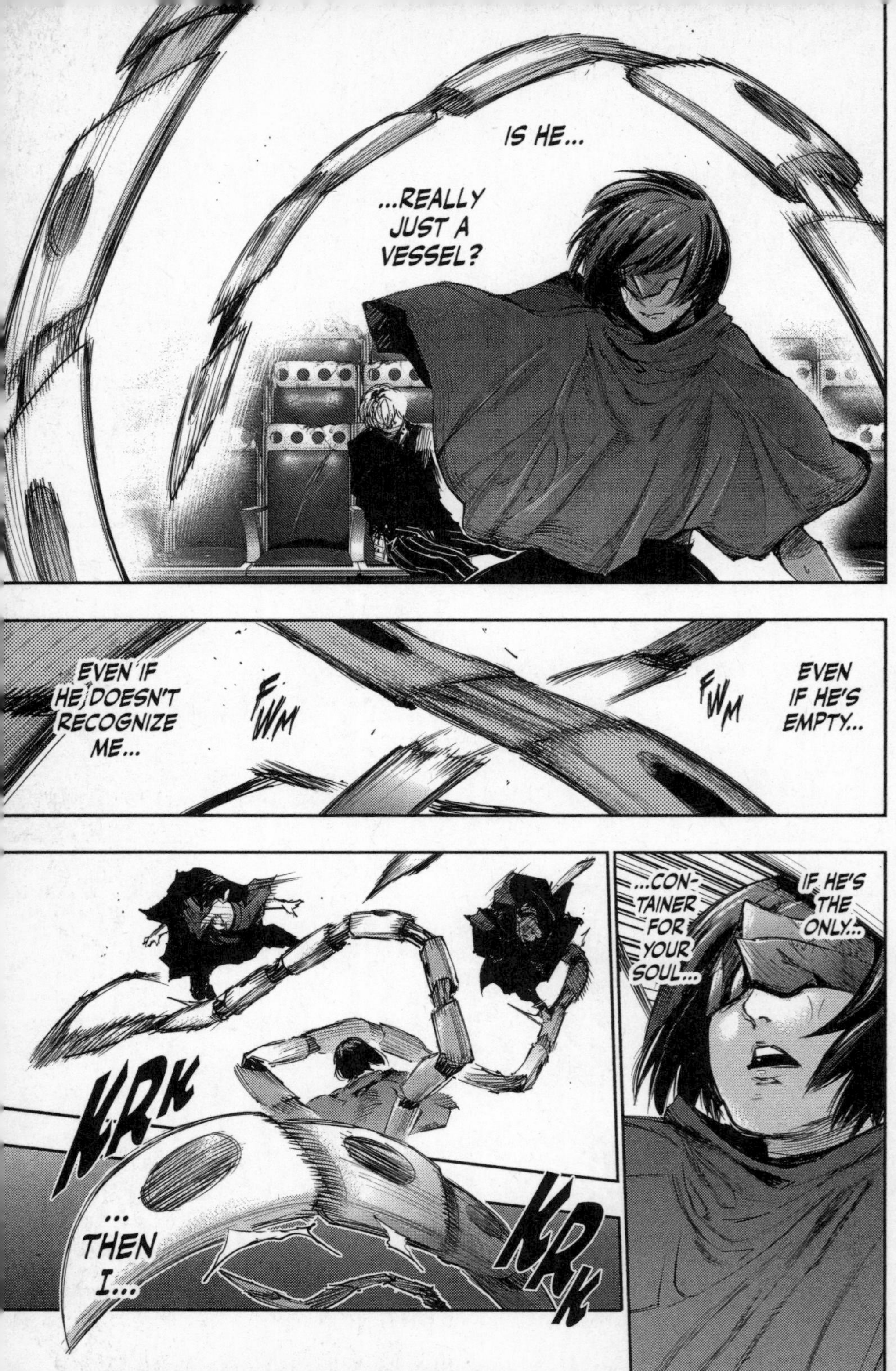
IS HE...
...REALLY JUST A VESSEL?
EVEN IF HE'S EMPTY...
FWM
FWM
EVEN IF HE DOESN'T RECOGNIZE ME...
IF HE'S THE ONLY...
...CON-TAINER FOR YOUR SOUL...
KRK
KRK
... THEN I...

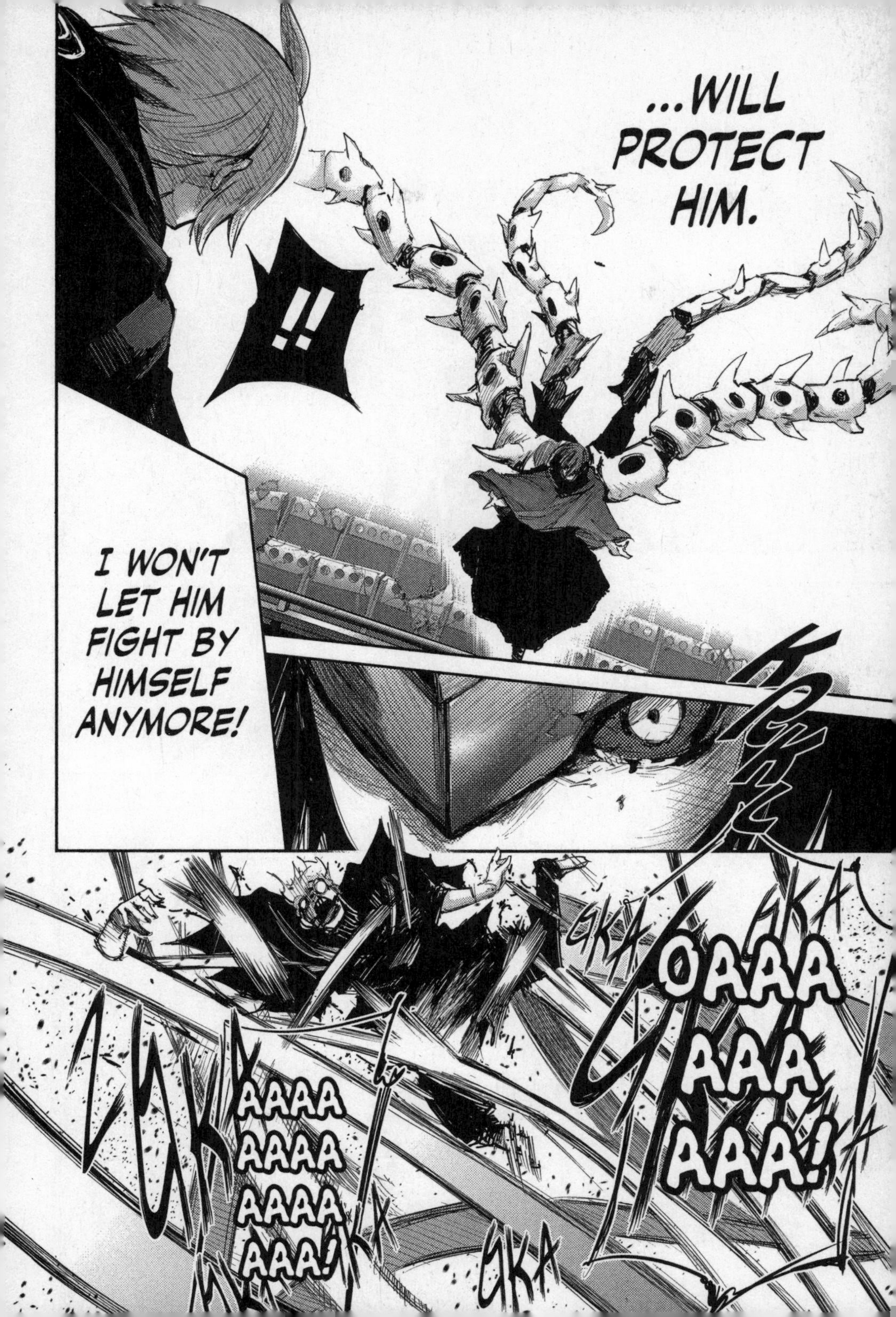
...WILL PROTECT HIM.
!!
I WON'T LET HIM FIGHT BY HIMSELF ANYMORE!
GKA
GKA
OAAA AAA AAA!
AAAA AAAA AAAA AAA!
GKA

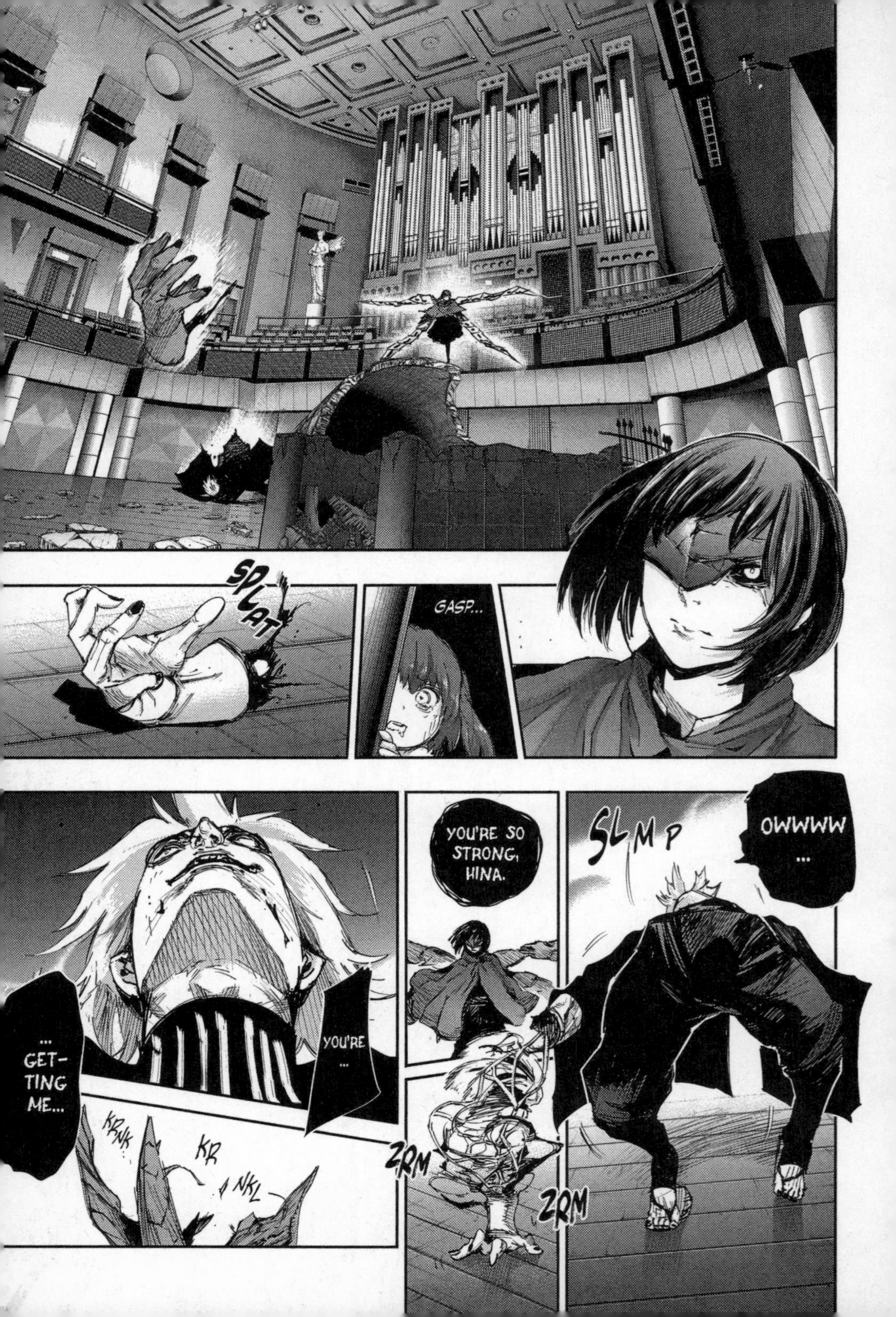
GASP...
SPLAT
OWWWW ...
SLMP
YOU'RE SO STRONG, HINA.
ZRM
ZRM
YOU'RE ...
... GET-TING ME...
KRNK
KR
NKL

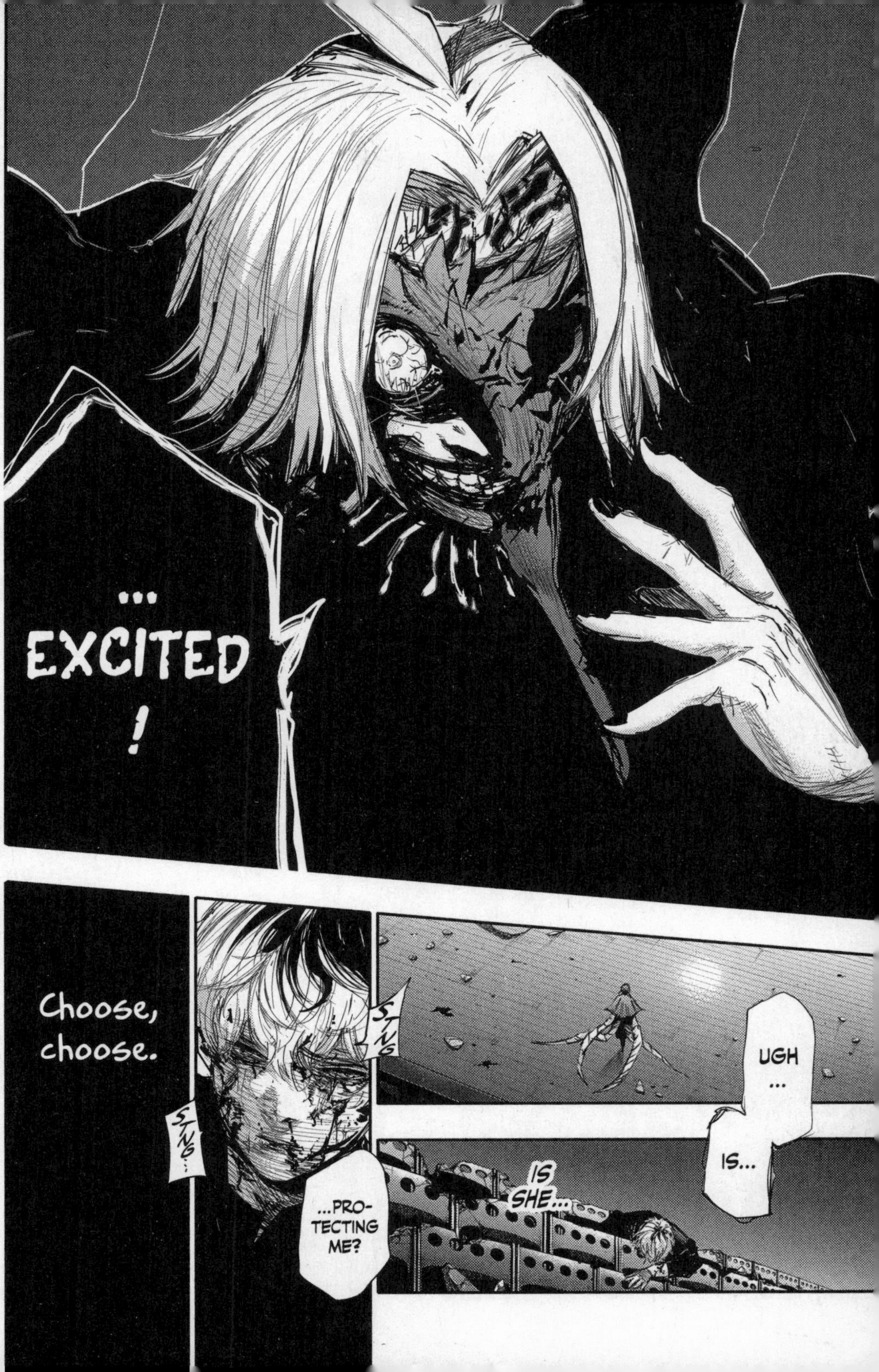
...EXCITED!
UGH...
IS...
IS SHE...
STING
STING...
...PROTECTING ME?
Choose, choose.

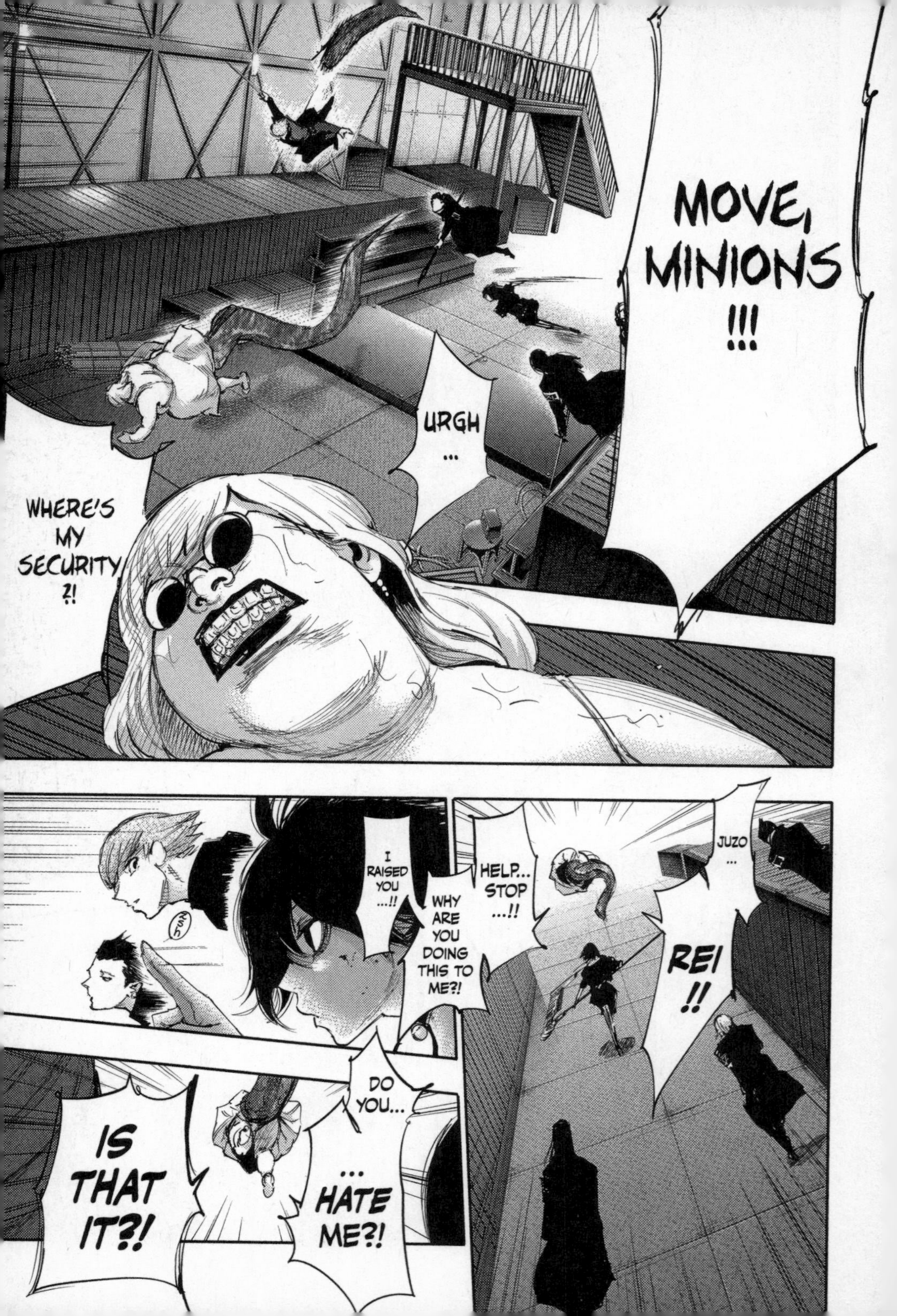
MOVE, MINIONS !!!
URGH ...
WHERE'S MY SECURITY ?!
JUZO ...
REI !!
HELP... STOP ...!!
WHY ARE YOU DOING THIS TO ME?!
I RAISED YOU ...!!
DO YOU...
... HATE ME?!
IS THAT IT?!

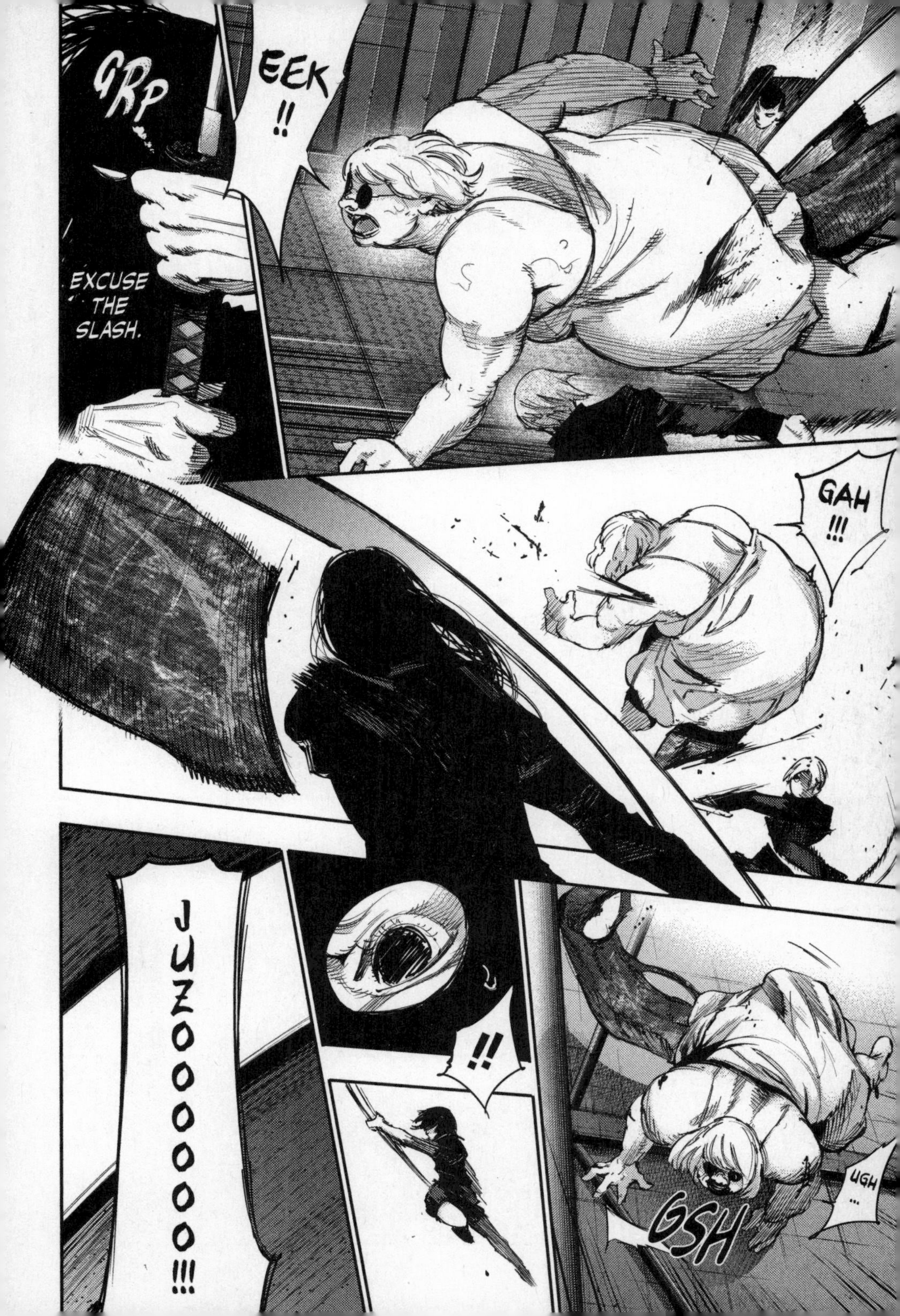
EEK !!
GRP
EXCUSE THE SLASH.
GAH !!!
UGH ...
GSH
!!
JUZOOOOOO!!!

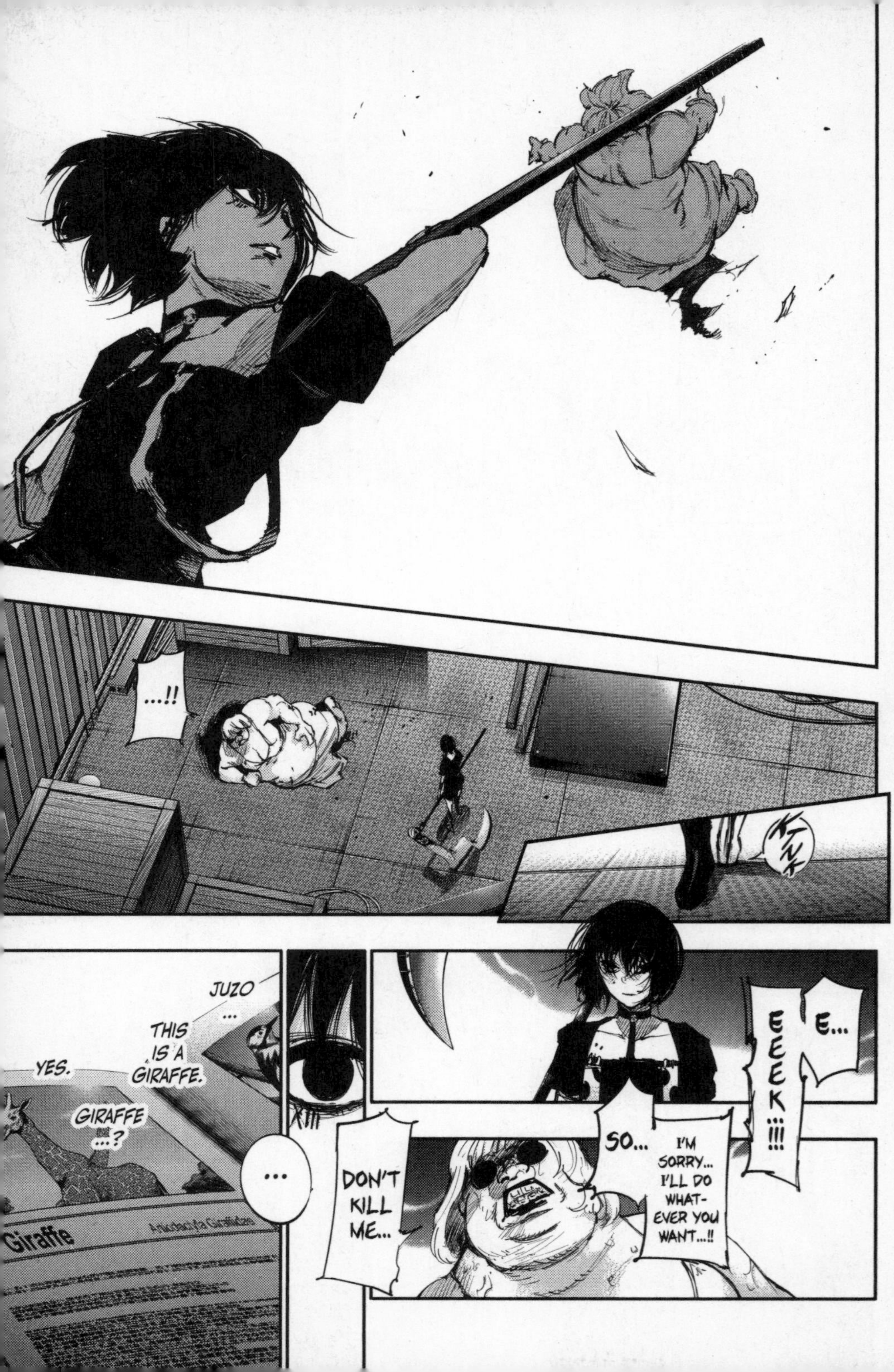
...!!
KINK
E...
EEEK!!!
SO...
I'M SORRY... I'LL DO WHAT-EVER YOU WANT...!!
DON'T KILL ME...
...
JUZO ...
THIS IS A GIRAFFE.
YES.
GIRAFFE ...?
Giraffe

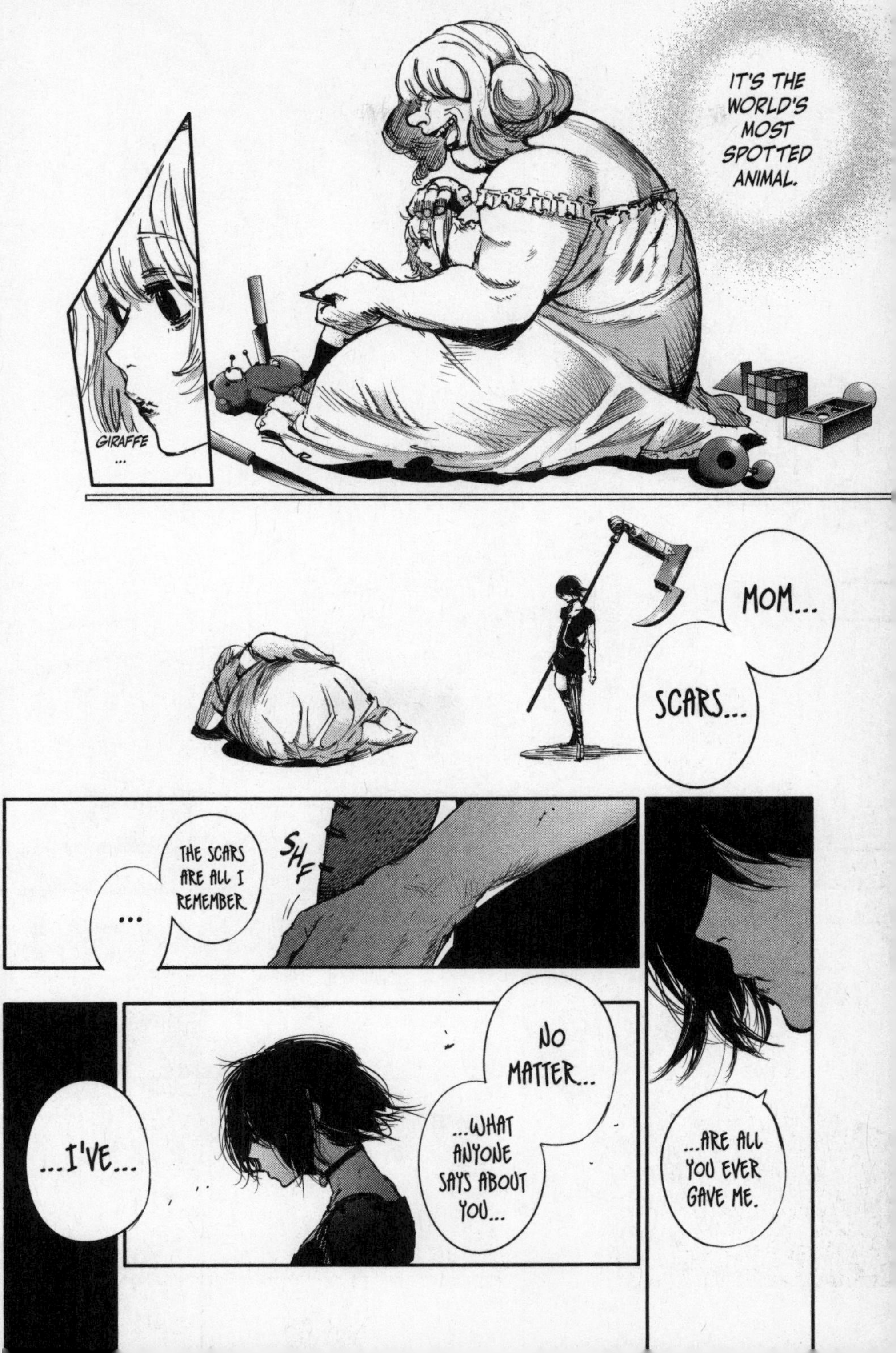
IT'S THE WORLD'S MOST SPOTTED ANIMAL.
GIRAFFE ...
MOM...
SCARS...
SHF
THE SCARS ARE ALL I REMEMBER
...
NO MATTER...
...WHAT ANYONE SAYS ABOUT YOU...
...ARE ALL YOU EVER GAVE ME.
...I'VE...

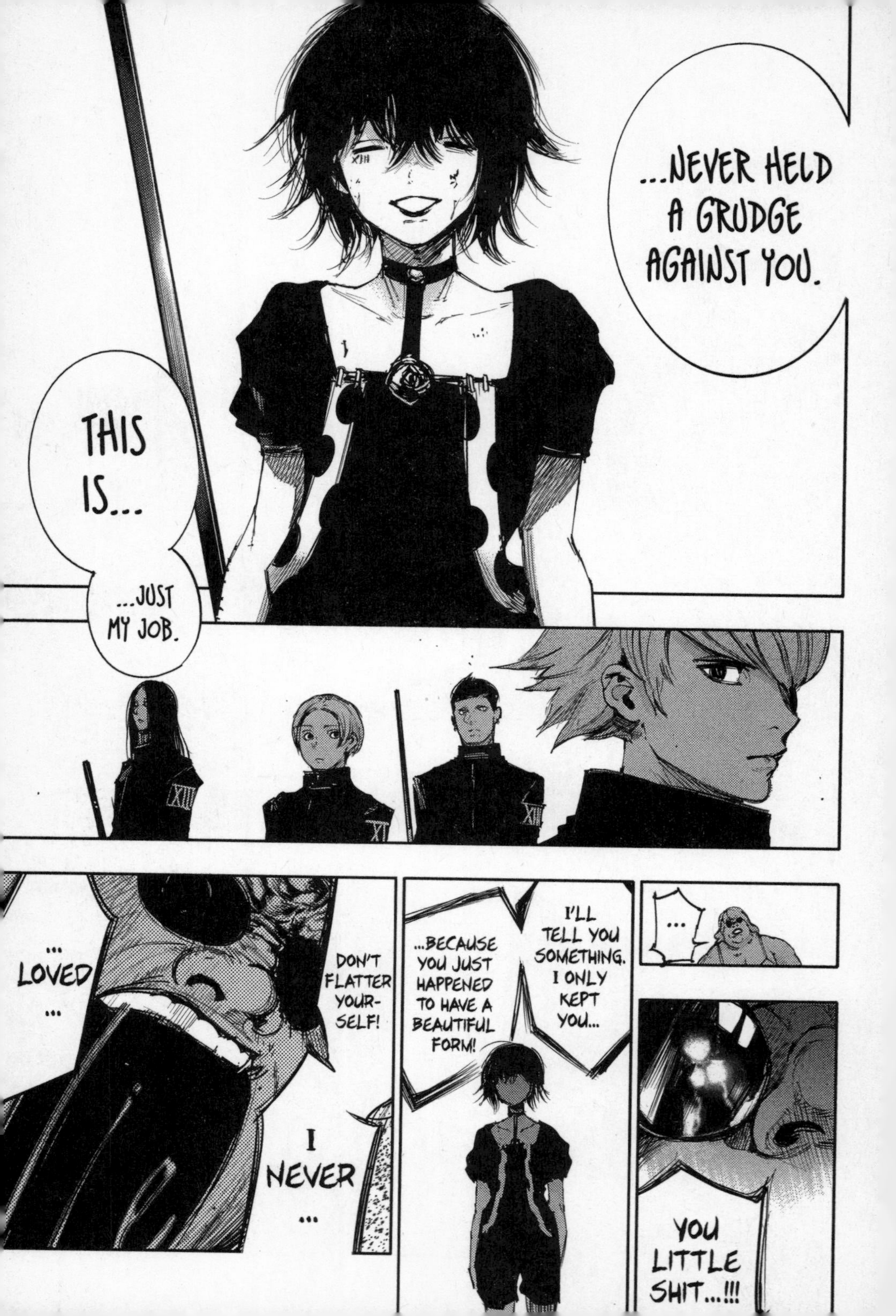
...NEVER HELD A GRUDGE AGAINST YOU.
THIS IS...
...JUST MY JOB.
...
YOU LITTLE SHIT...!!!
I'LL TELL YOU SOMETHING. I ONLY KEPT YOU...
...BECAUSE YOU JUST HAPPENED TO HAVE A BEAUTIFUL FORM!
DON'T FLATTER YOURSELF!
I NEVER...
...LOVED...

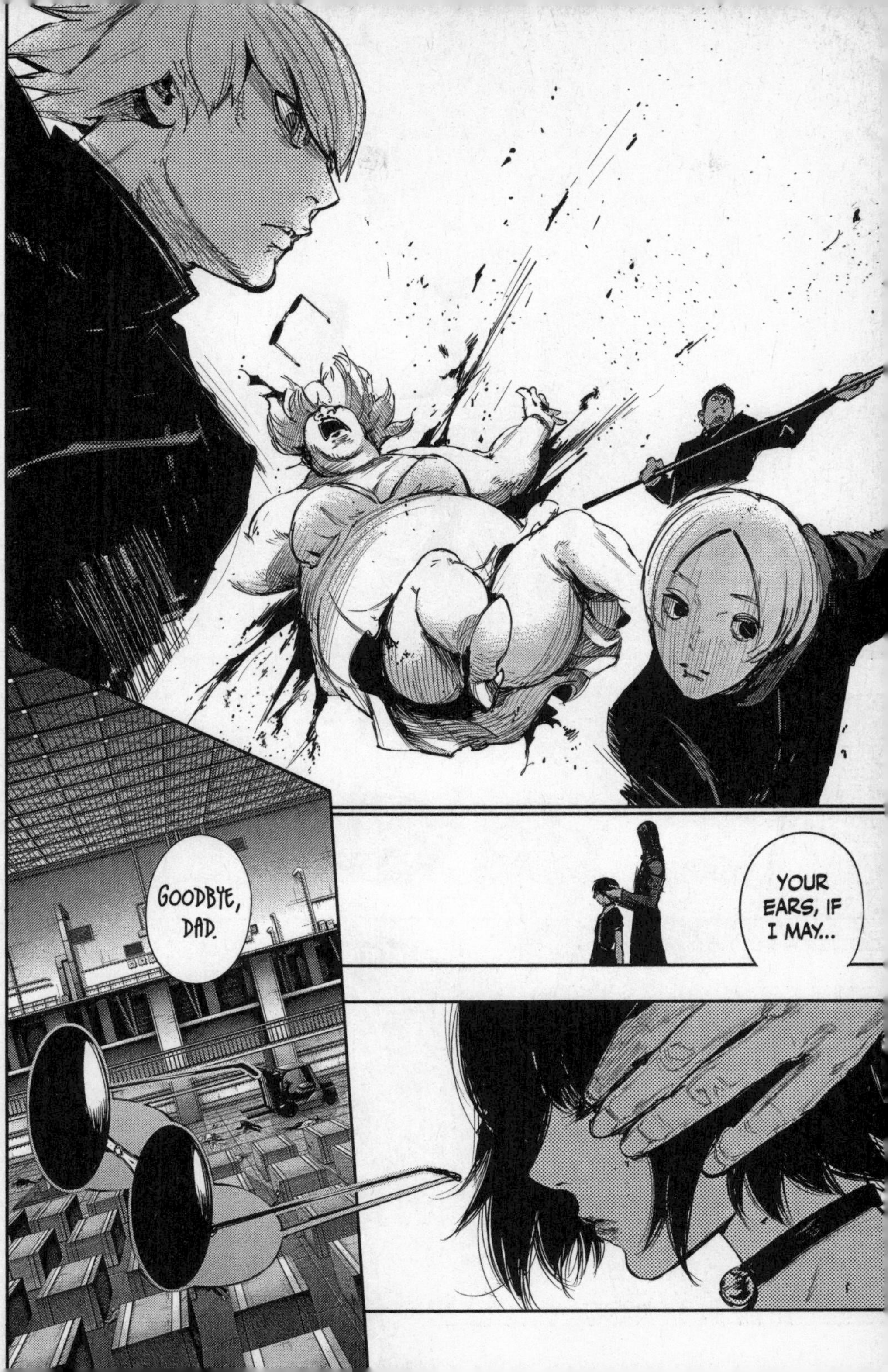
YOUR EARS, IF I MAY...
GOODBYE, DAD.

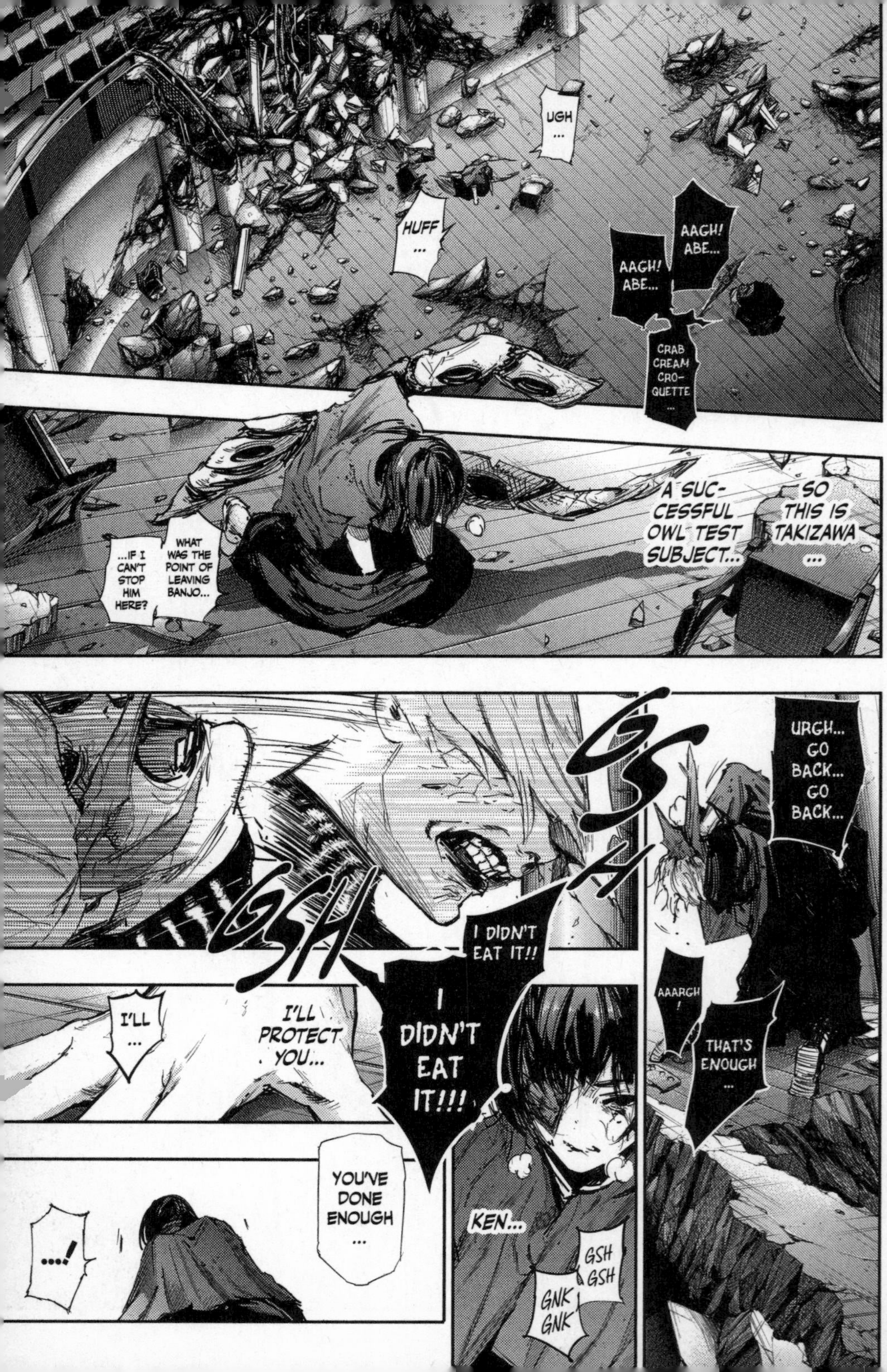
AAGH! ABE...
AAGH! ABE...
CRAB CREAM CRO-QUETTE...
UGH...
HUFF...
SO THIS IS TAKIZAWA...
A SUC-CESSFUL OWL TEST SUBJECT...
WHAT WAS THE POINT OF LEAVING BANJO...
...IF I CAN'T STOP HIM HERE?
URGH... GO BACK... GO BACK...
GSH
GSH
I DIDN'T EAT IT!!
AAARGH!
THAT'S ENOUGH...
I DIDN'T EAT IT!!!
I'LL PROTECT YOU...
I'LL...
KEN...
GSH GSH
GNK GNK
YOU'VE DONE ENOUGH...
...!

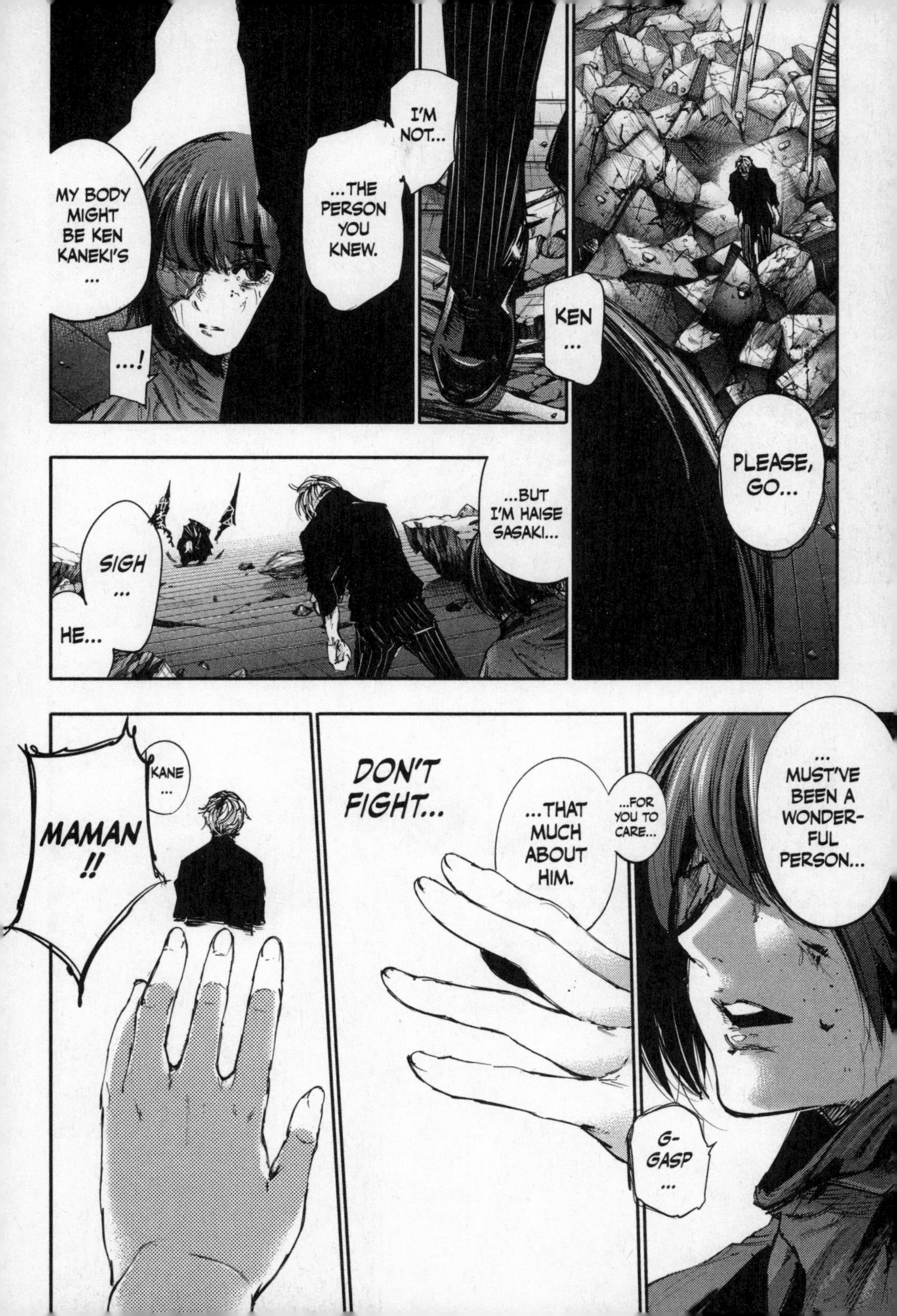
KEN ...
PLEASE, GO...
I'M NOT...
...THE PERSON YOU KNEW.
MY BODY MIGHT BE KEN KANEKI'S ...
...!
...BUT I'M HAISE SASAKI...
SIGH ...
HE...
... MUST'VE BEEN A WONDERFUL PERSON...
...FOR YOU TO CARE...
...THAT MUCH ABOUT HIM.
G-GASP ...
DON'T FIGHT...
KANE ...
MAMAN !!

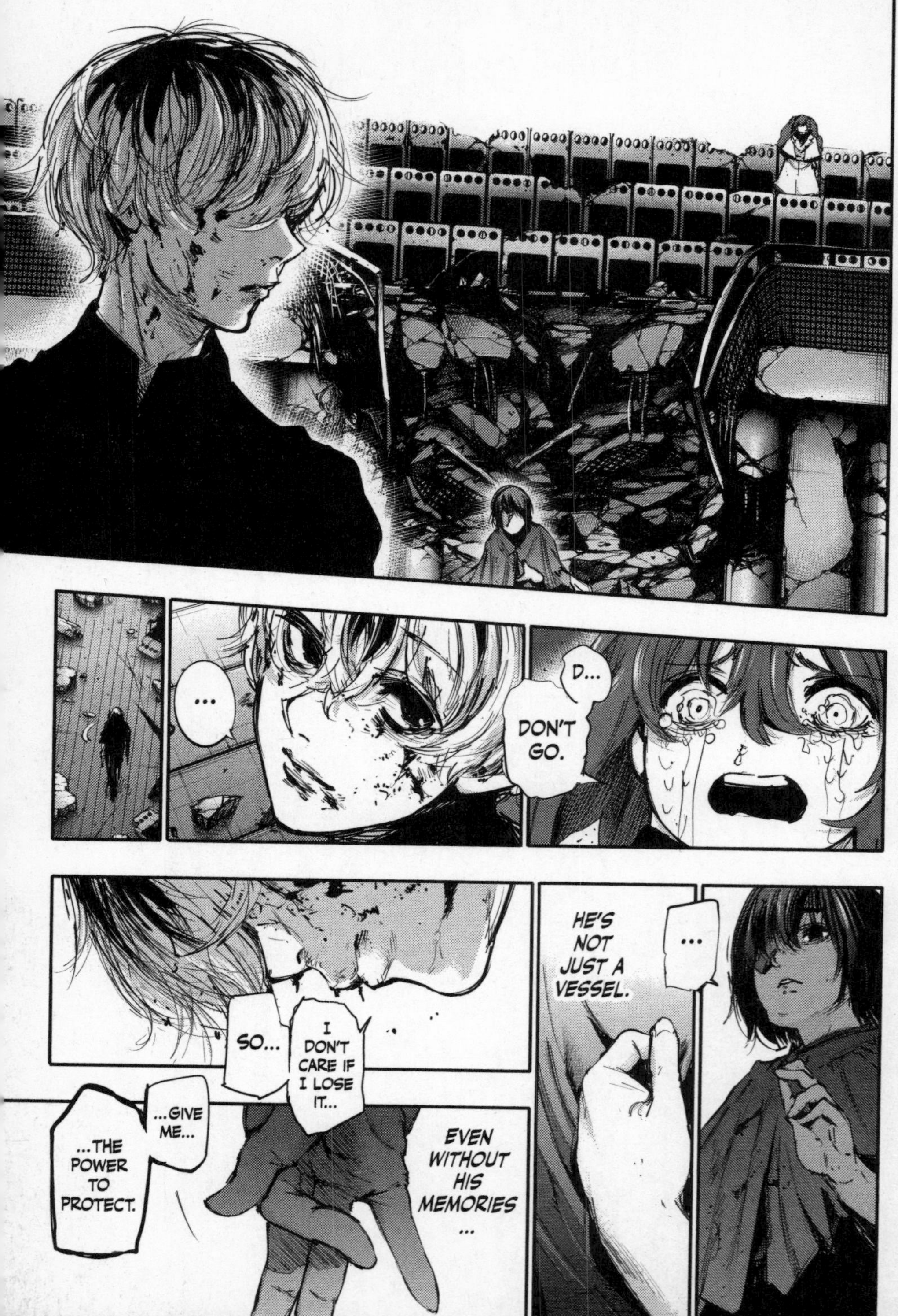
D...
DON'T GO.
...
...
HE'S NOT JUST A VESSEL.
EVEN WITHOUT HIS MEMORIES ...
I DON'T CARE IF I LOSE IT...
SO...
...GIVE ME...
...THE POWER TO PROTECT.

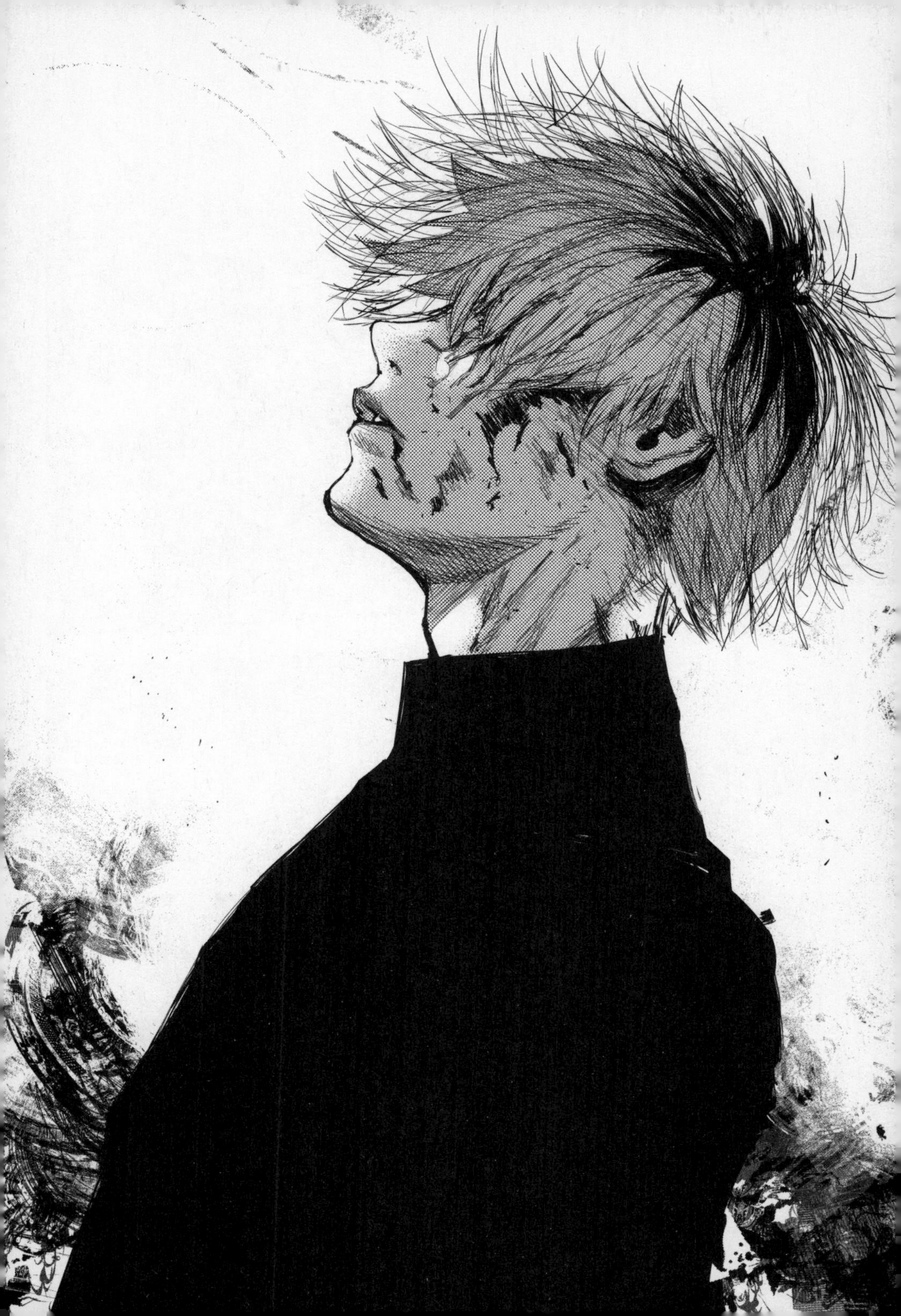

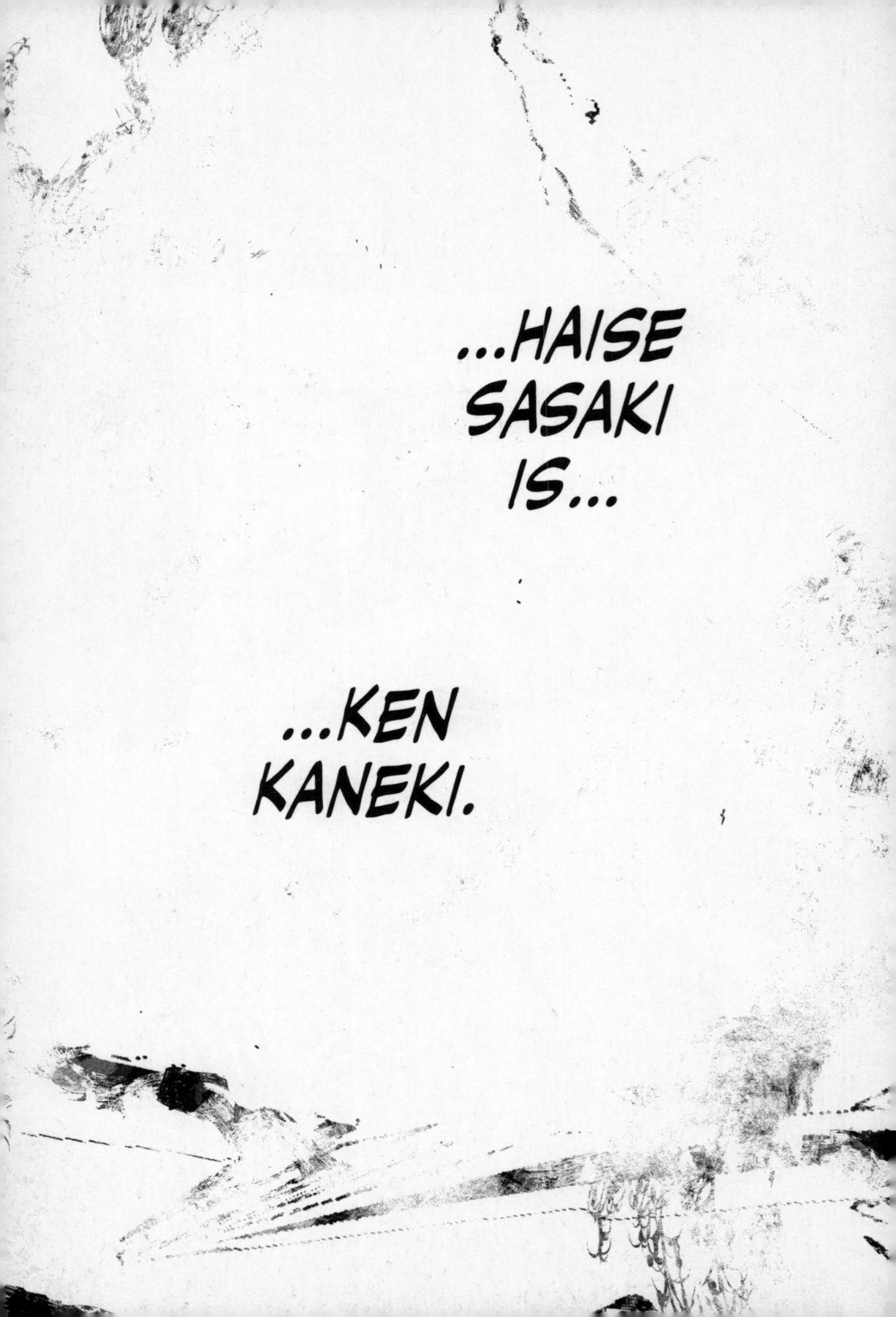
...HAISE SASAKI IS...
...KEN KANEKI.

Haise.

Are you afraid of me?

YEAH...

I–I'M SORRY MOM. SORRY, DAD. I HAD TO. I HAD TO...

AAAA AAAA AAAA AAAA!

Why?

WELL, BECAUSE...

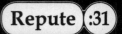
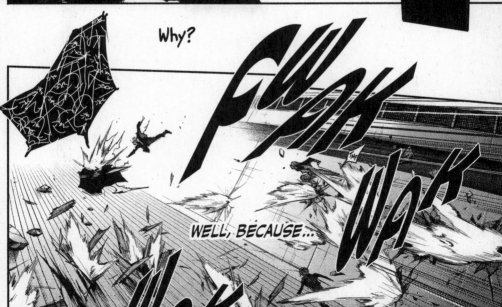
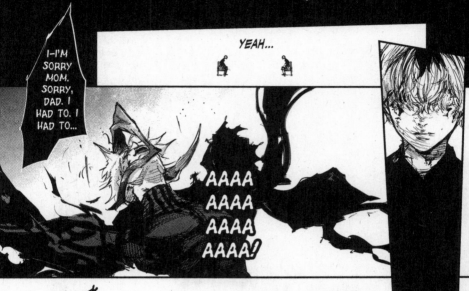

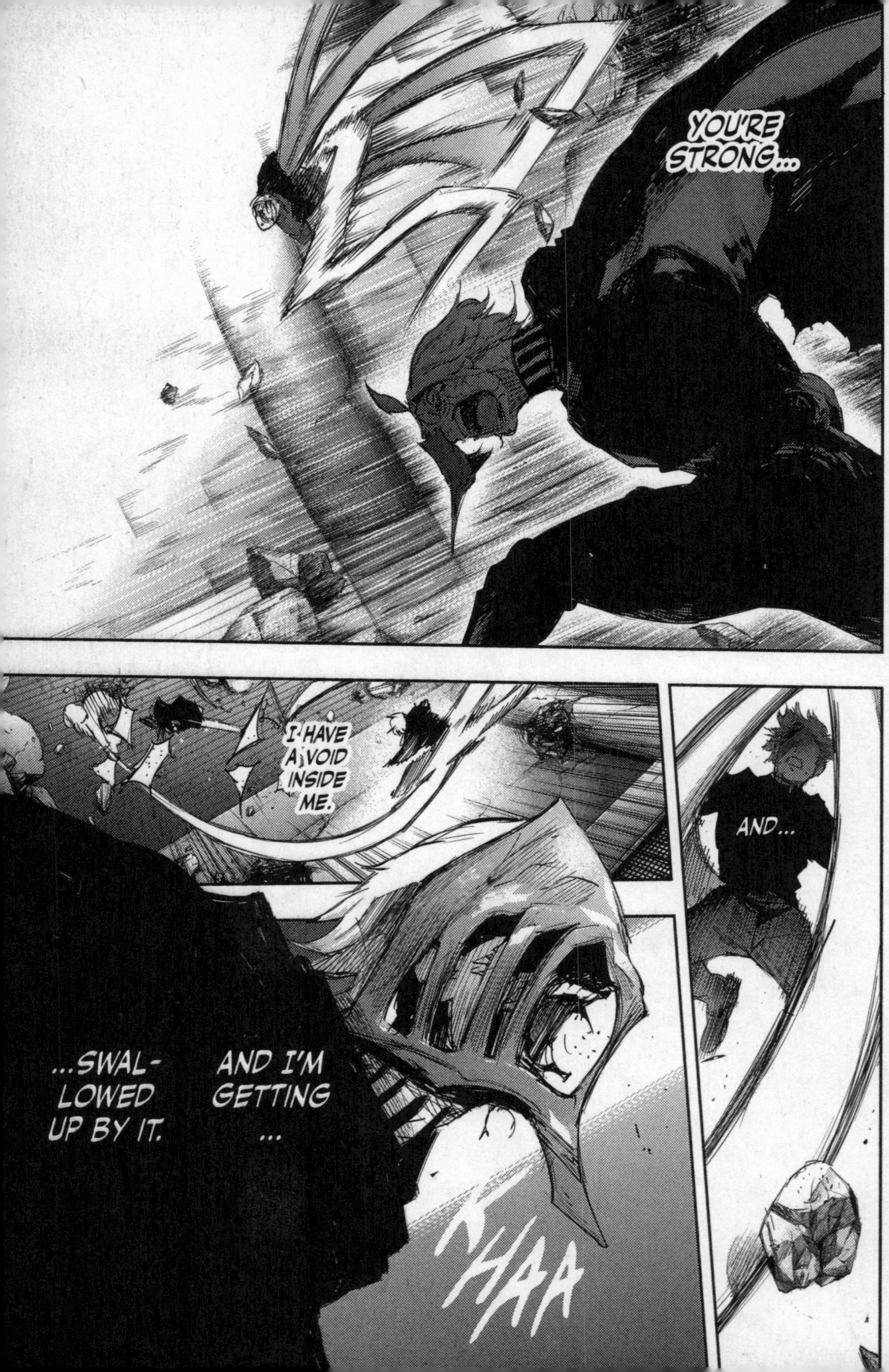
YOU'RE STRONG...
AND...
I HAVE A VOID INSIDE ME.
AND I'M GETTING ...
...SWAL-LOWED UP BY IT.
KHAA

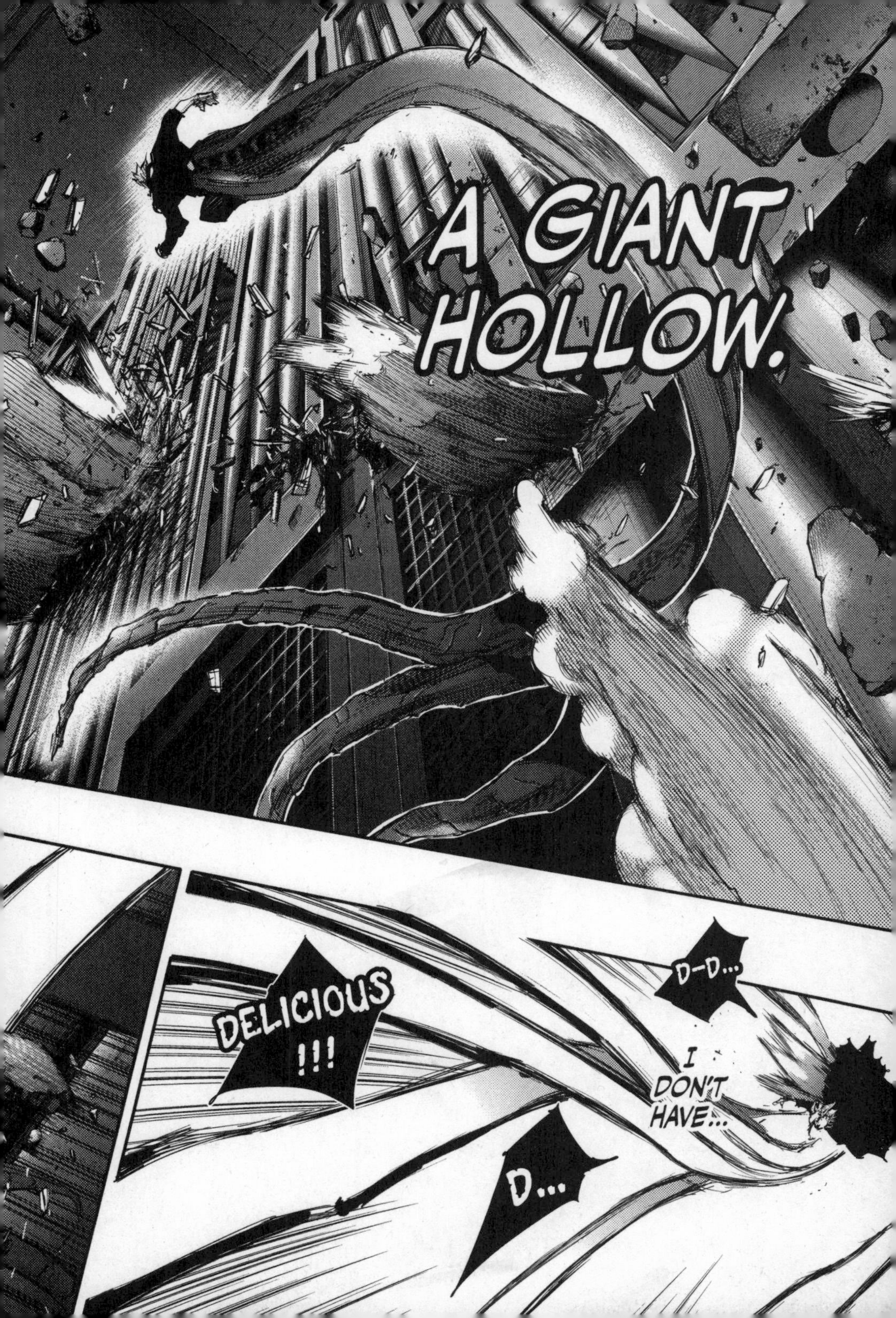
A GIANT HOLLOW.
D-D...
I DON'T HAVE...
DELICIOUS !!!
D...

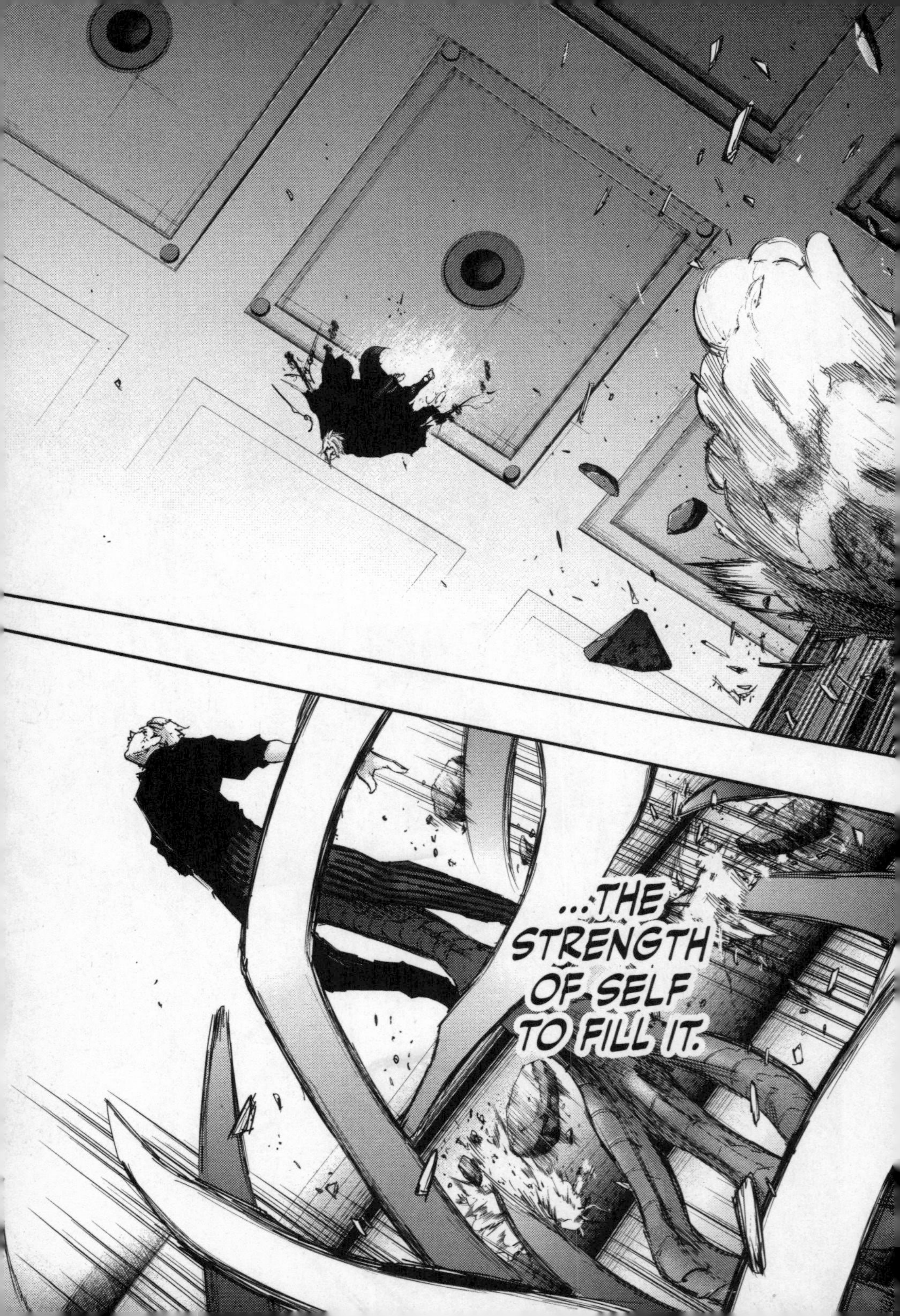
...THE STRENGTH OF SELF TO FILL IT.

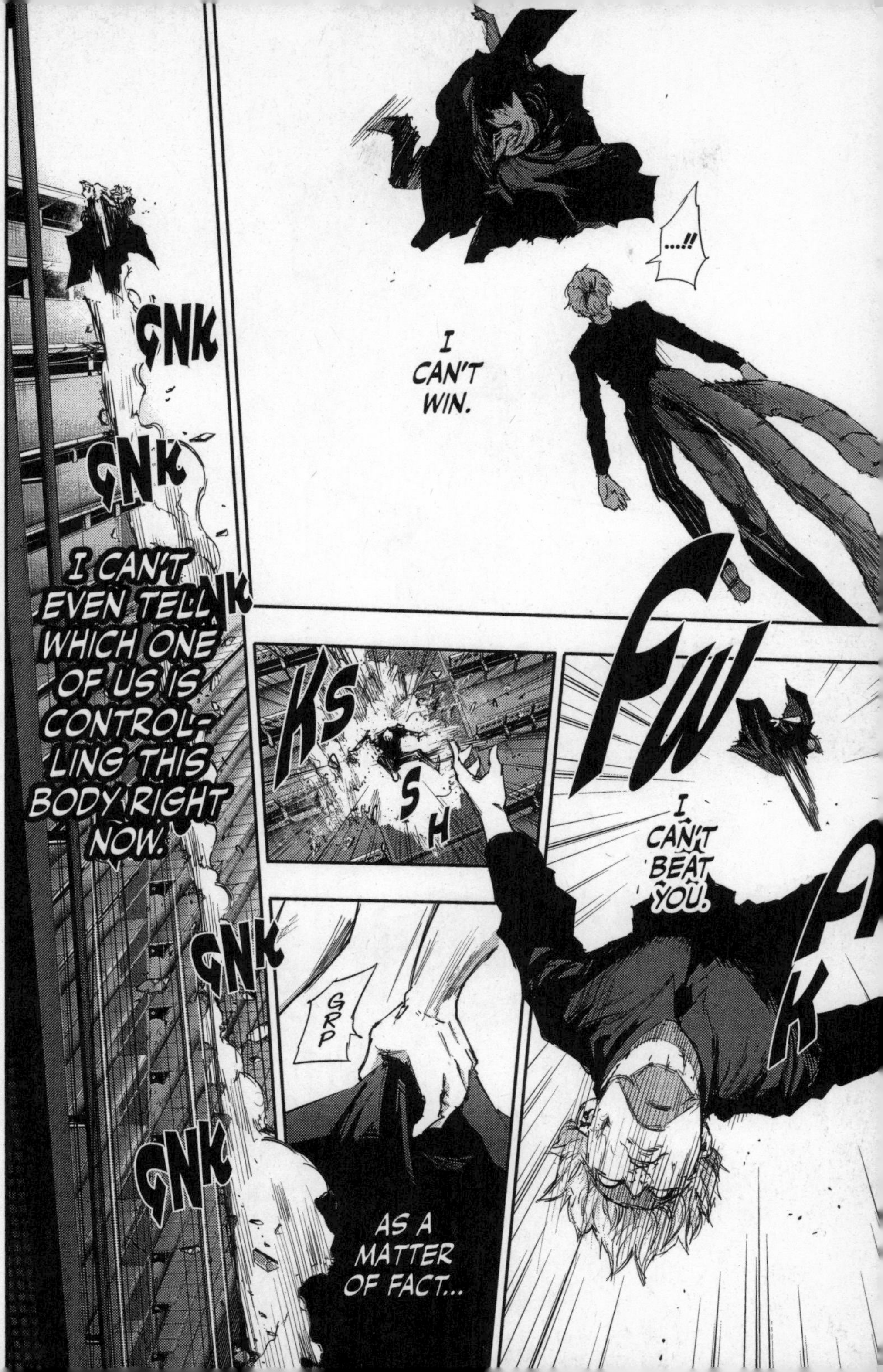

...!!
I CAN'T WIN.
FW
I CAN'T BEAT YOU.
K
KS
SH
GRP
AS A MATTER OF FACT...
GNK
GNK
I CAN'T EVEN TELL WHICH ONE OF US IS CONTROL-LING THIS BODY RIGHT NOW.
GNK
GNK

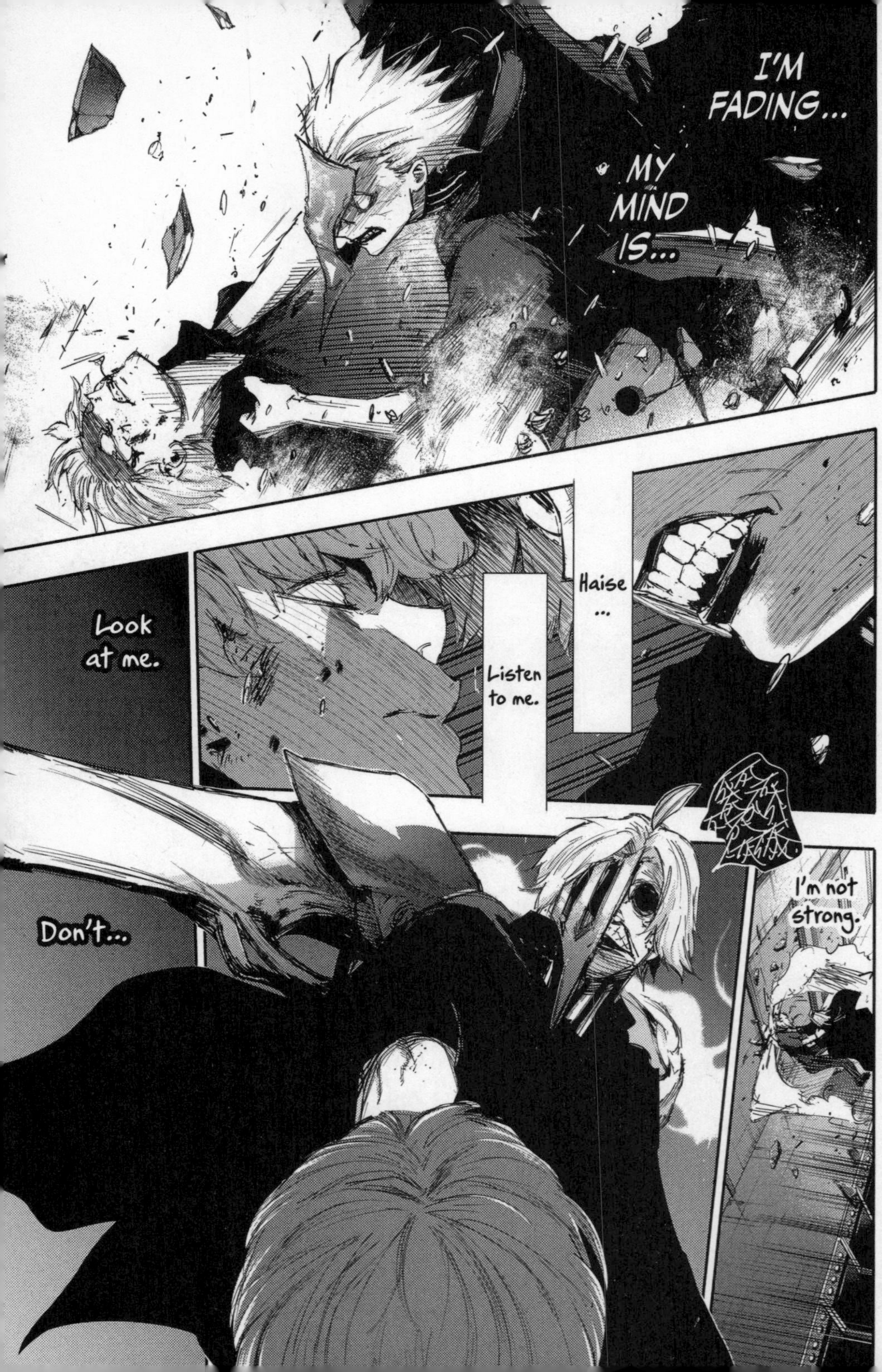
I'M FADING...
MY MIND IS...
Haise...
Listen to me.
Look at me.
I'm not strong.
Don't...

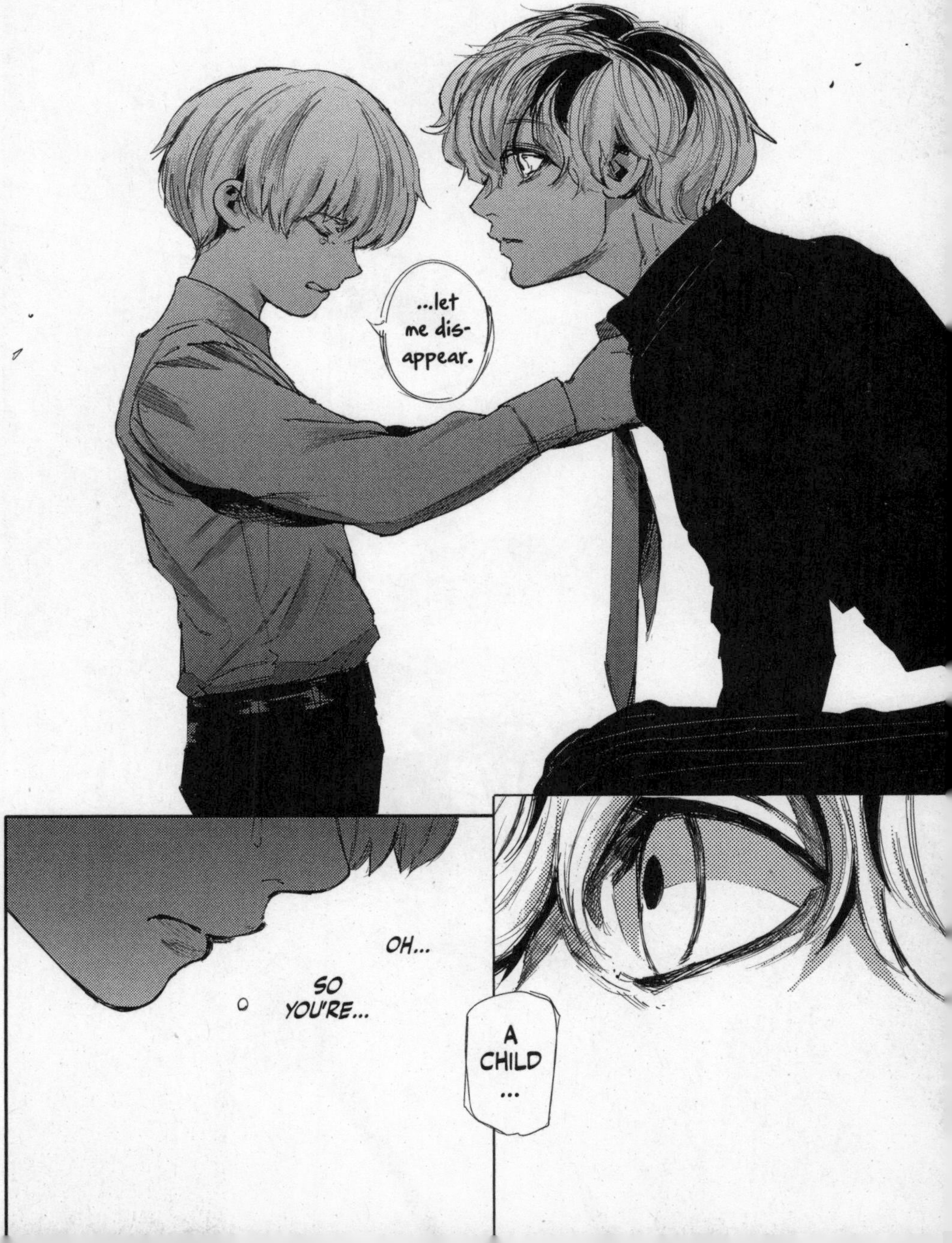
...let me dis-appear.
OH...
SO YOU'RE...
A CHILD ...

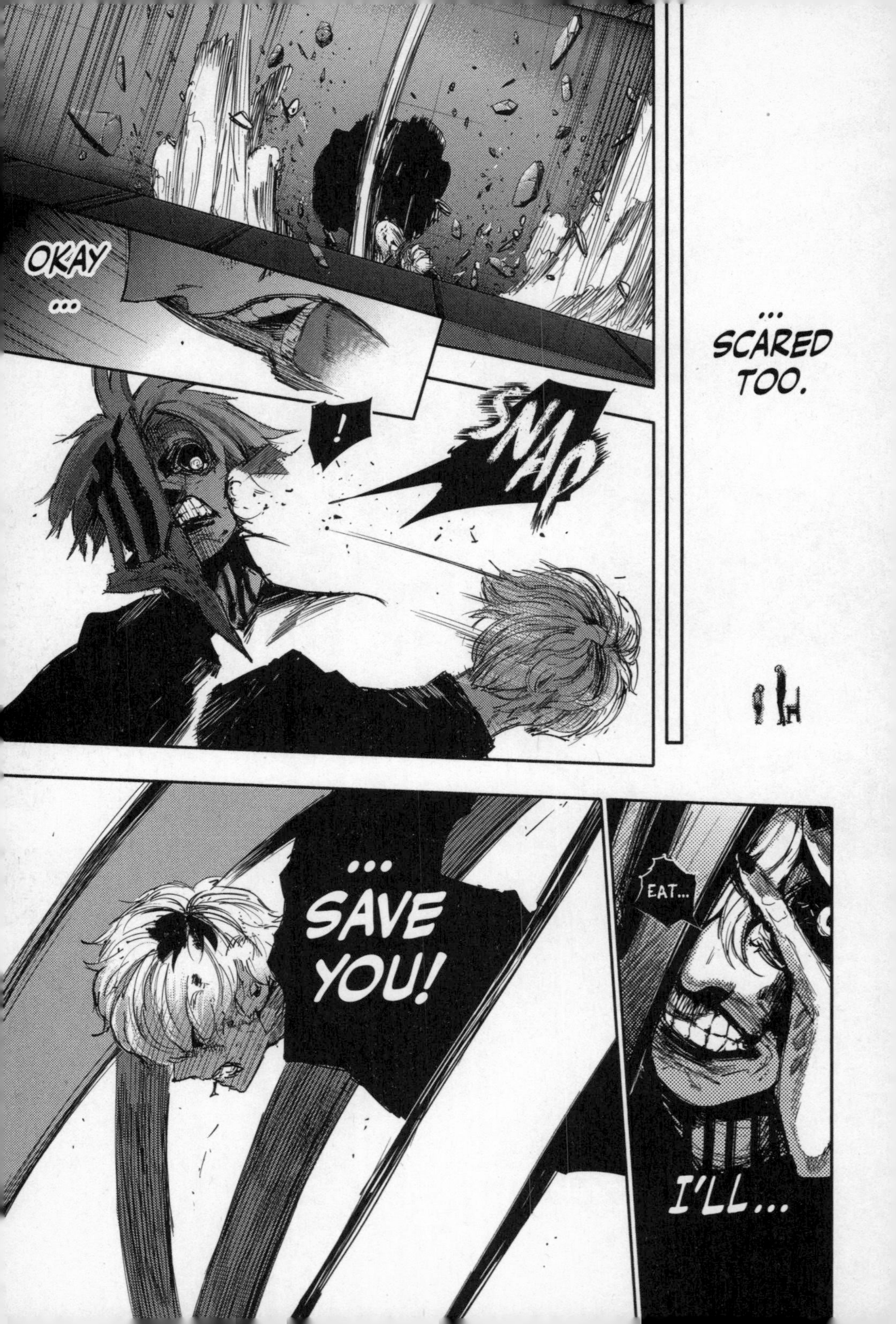
... SCARED TOO.
OKAY ...
!
SNAP
EAT...
I'LL...
... SAVE YOU!

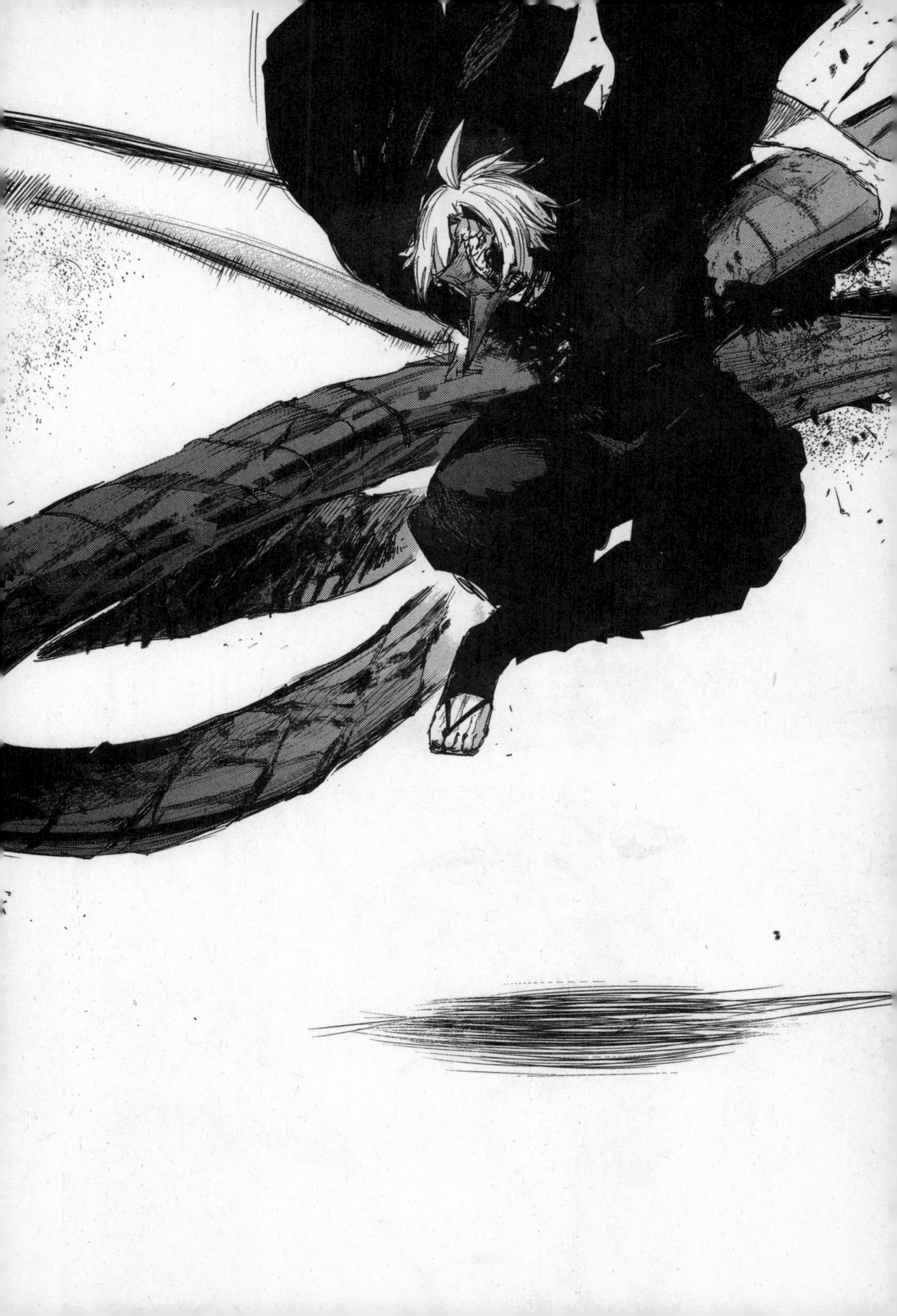

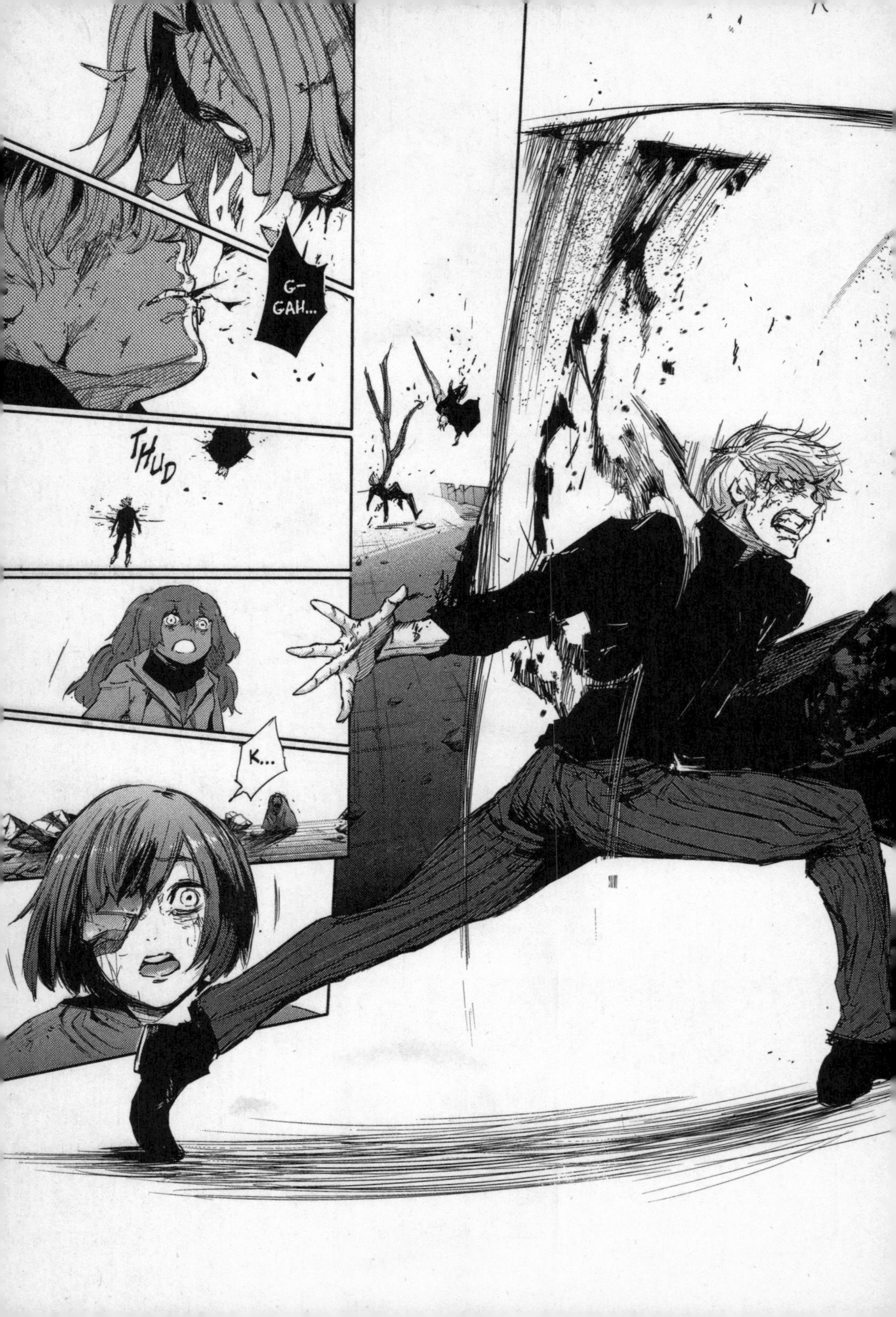
G-GAH...
THUD
K...

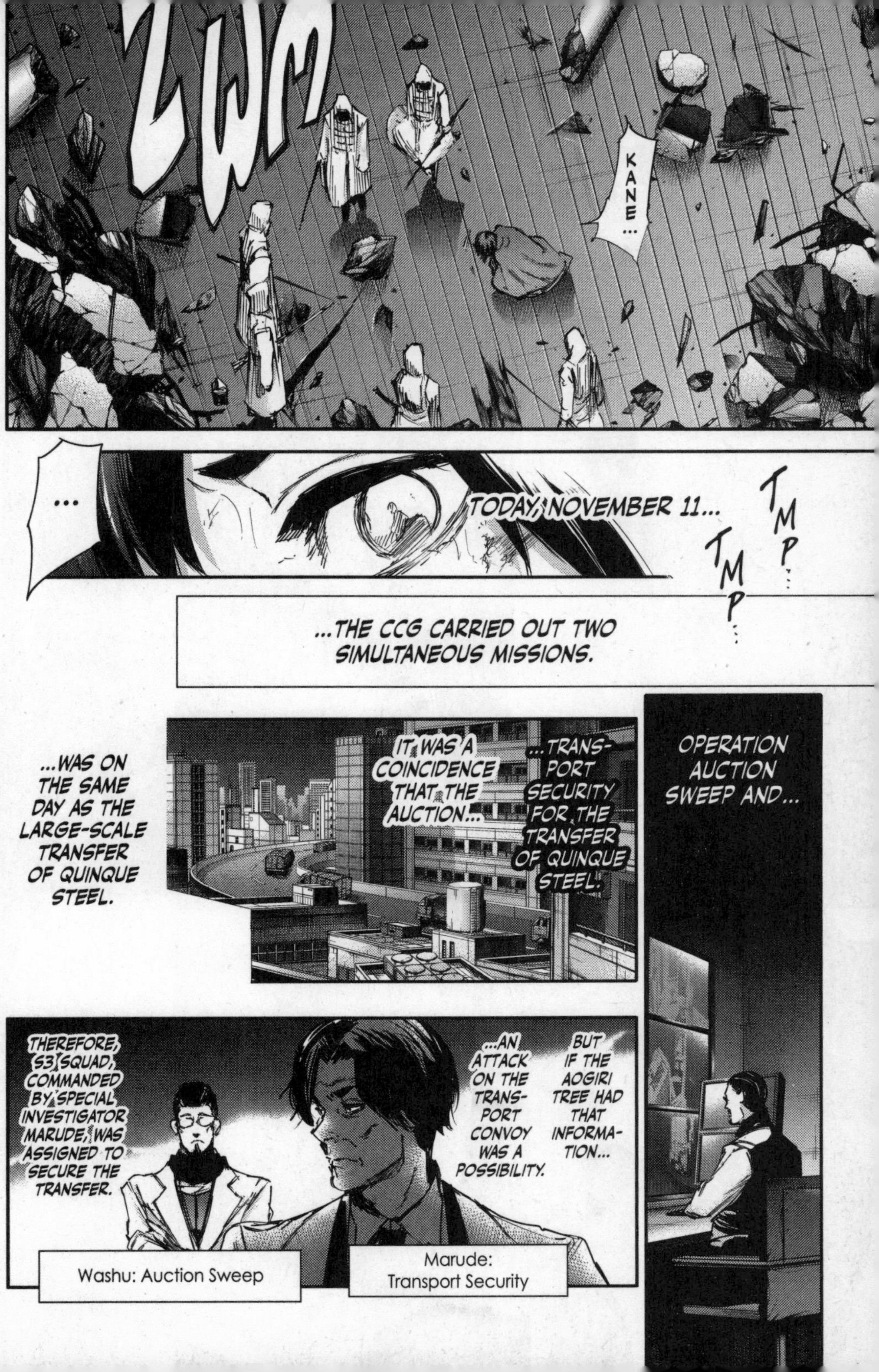
KANE...
TMP TMP...
TMP...
TODAY, NOVEMBER 11...
...
...THE CCG CARRIED OUT TWO SIMULTANEOUS MISSIONS.
OPERATION AUCTION SWEEP AND...
...TRANSPORT SECURITY FOR THE TRANSFER OF QUINQUE STEEL.
IT WAS A COINCIDENCE THAT THE AUCTION...
...WAS ON THE SAME DAY AS THE LARGE-SCALE TRANSFER OF QUINQUE STEEL.
BUT IF THE AOGIRI TREE HAD THAT INFORMATION...
...AN ATTACK ON THE TRANSPORT CONVOY WAS A POSSIBILITY.
THEREFORE, S3 SQUAD, COMMANDED BY SPECIAL INVESTIGATOR MARUDE, WAS ASSIGNED TO SECURE THE TRANSFER.
Marude: Transport Security
Washu: Auction Sweep

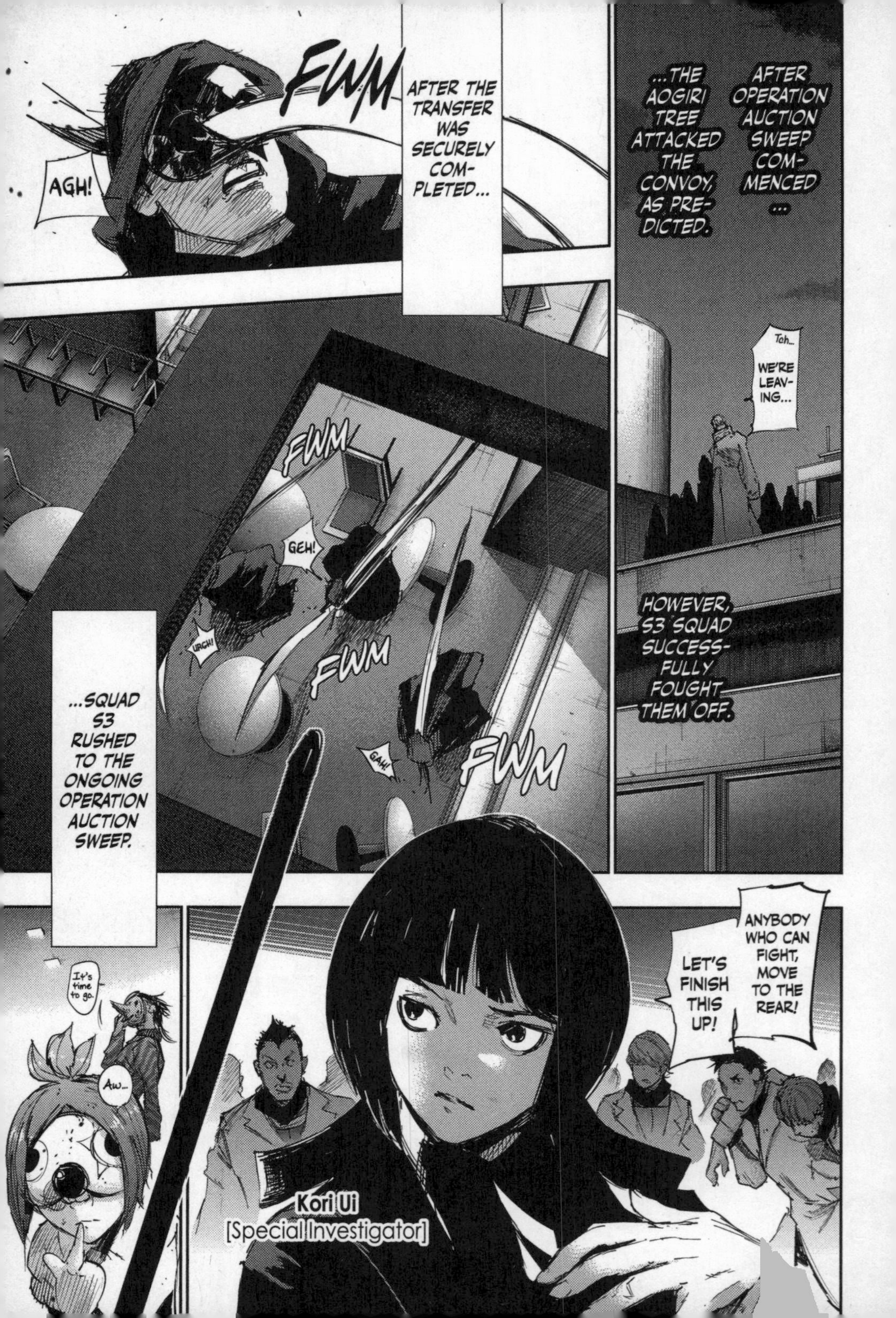
AFTER OPERATION AUCTION SWEEP COMMENCED...
...THE AOGIRI TREE ATTACKED THE CONVOY, AS PREDICTED.
Tch... WE'RE LEAVING...
HOWEVER, S3 SQUAD SUCCESSFULLY FOUGHT THEM OFF.
AFTER THE TRANSFER WAS SECURELY COMPLETED...
FWM
AGH!
FWM
GEH!
URGH!
FWM
FWM
GAH!
...SQUAD S3 RUSHED TO THE ONGOING OPERATION AUCTION SWEEP.
ANYBODY WHO CAN FIGHT, MOVE TO THE REAR!
LET'S FINISH THIS UP!
Kori Ui
[Special Investigator]
It's time to go.
Aw...

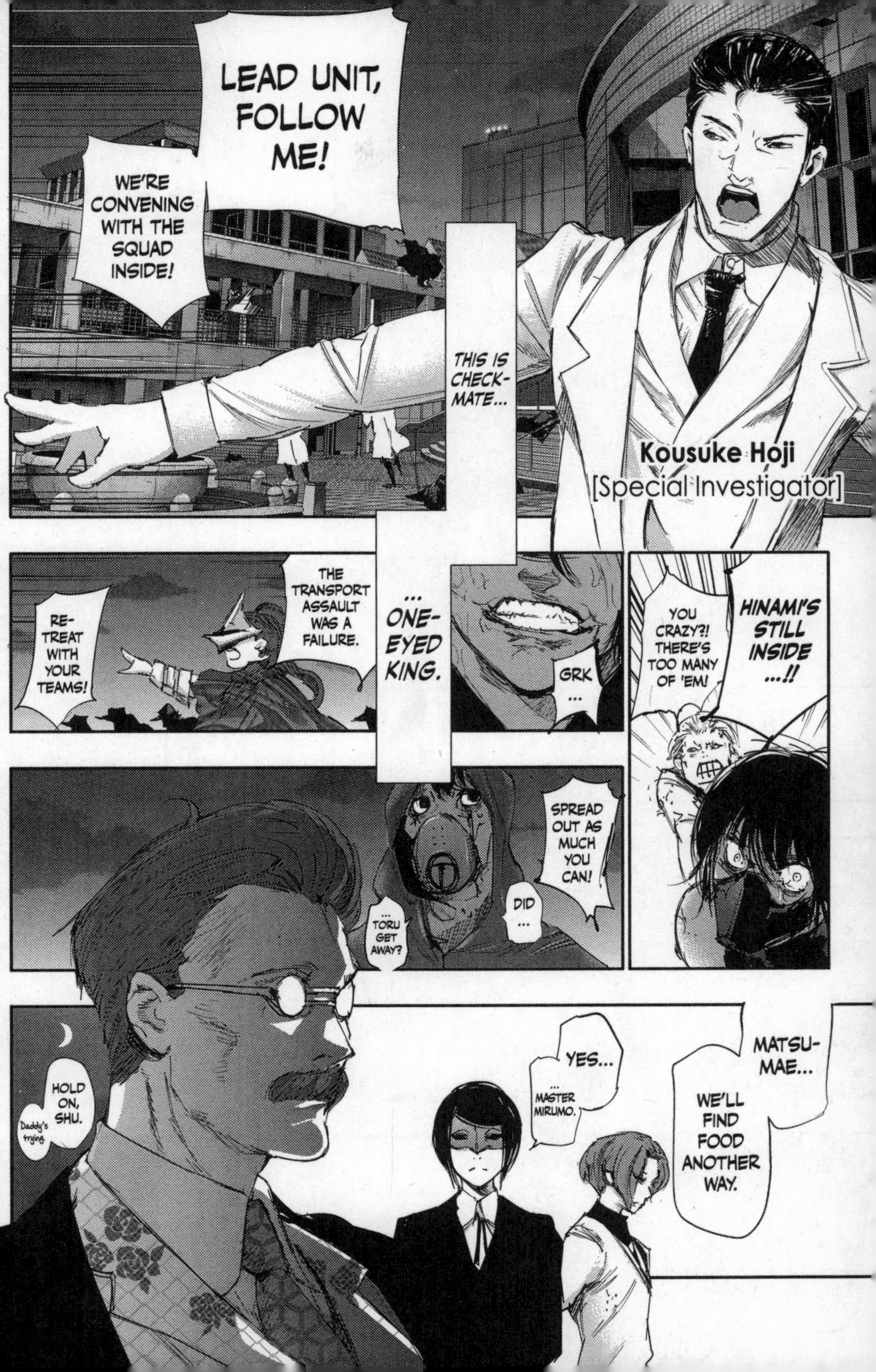
Kousuke Hoji
[Special Investigator]
LEAD UNIT, FOLLOW ME!
WE'RE CONVENING WITH THE SQUAD INSIDE!
THIS IS CHECKMATE...
HINAMI'S STILL INSIDE...!!
YOU CRAZY?! THERE'S TOO MANY OF 'EM!
...ONE-EYED KING.
GRK...
THE TRANSPORT ASSAULT WAS A FAILURE.
RE-TREAT WITH YOUR TEAMS!
SPREAD OUT AS MUCH YOU CAN!
DID...
...TORU GET AWAY?
MATSU-MAE...
WE'LL FIND FOOD ANOTHER WAY.
YES...
...MASTER MIRUMO.
HOLD ON, SHU.
Daddy's trying.

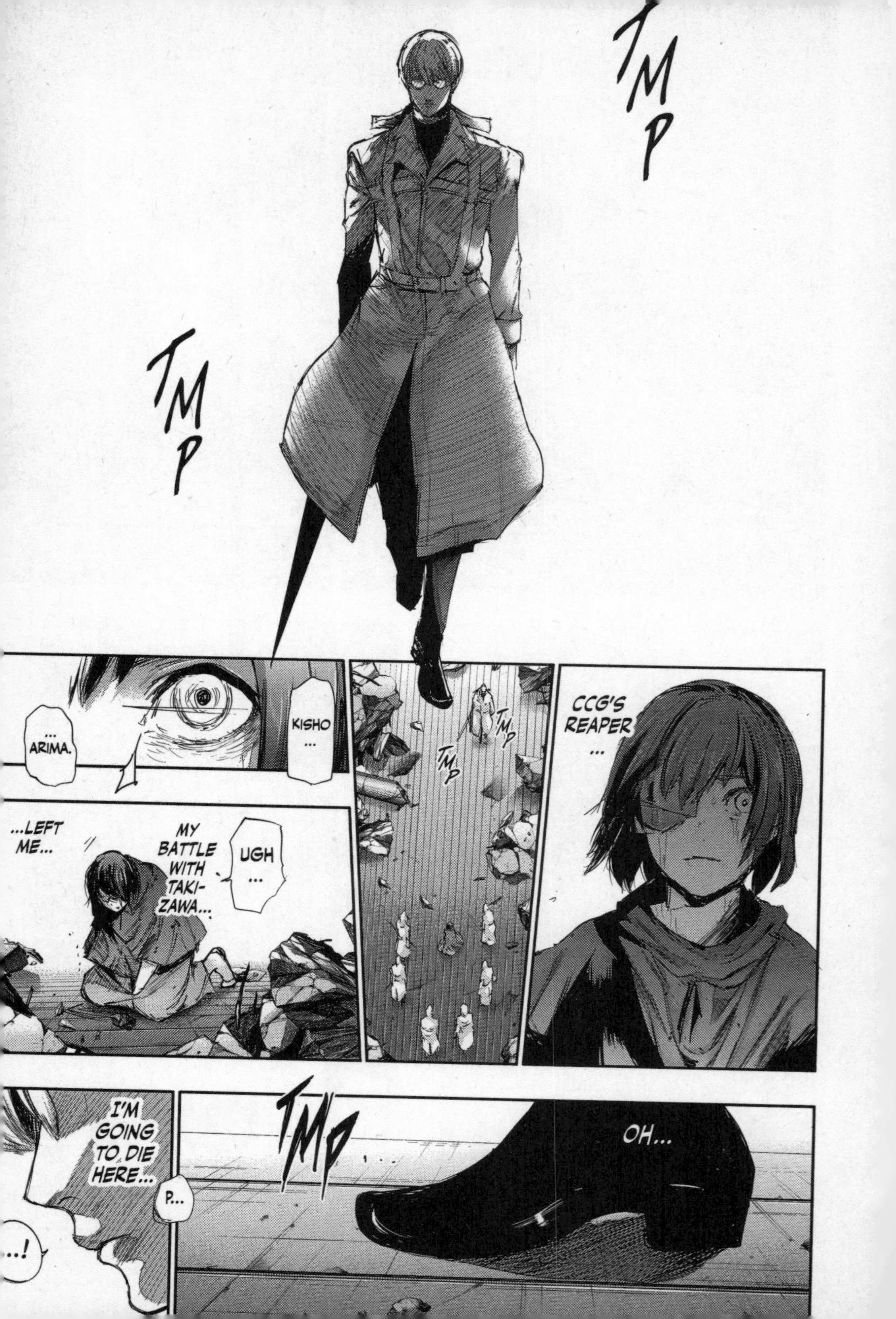
TMP
TMP
CCG'S REAPER ...
TMP
TMP
KISHO ...
... ARIMA.
UGH ...
MY BATTLE WITH TAKI-ZAWA...;
...LEFT ME...
OH...
TMP
P...
I'M GOING TO DIE HERE...
...!

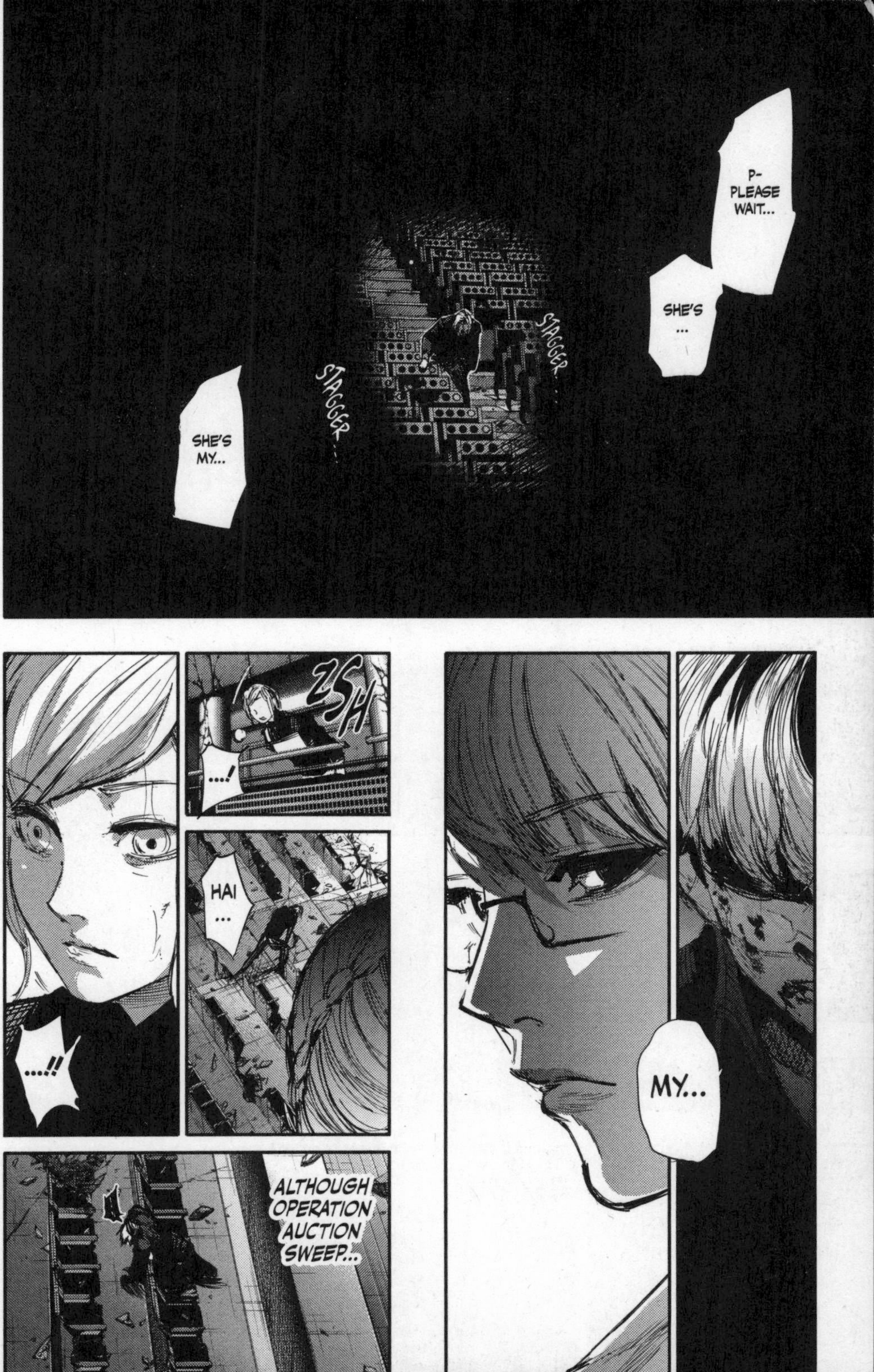
P- PLEASE WAIT...
SHE'S ...
STAGGER...
STAGGER...
SHE'S MY...
MY...
ZSH
...!
HAI ...
...!!
ALTHOUGH OPERATION AUCTION SWEEP...

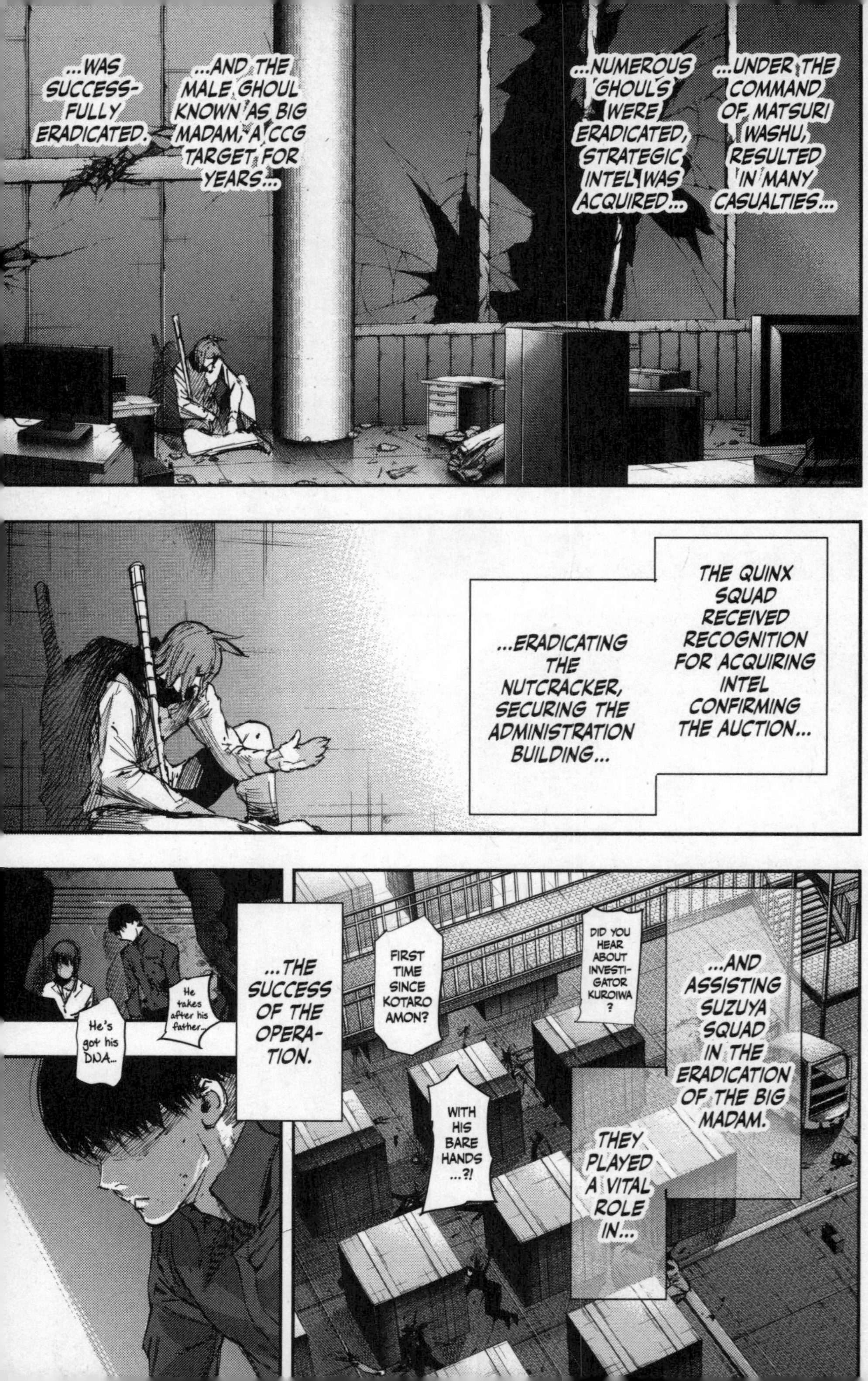
...UNDER THE COMMAND OF MATSURI WASHU, RESULTED IN MANY CASUALTIES...
...NUMEROUS GHOULS WERE ERADICATED, STRATEGIC INTEL WAS ACQUIRED...
...AND THE MALE GHOUL KNOWN AS BIG MADAM, A CCG TARGET FOR YEARS...
...WAS SUCCESSFULLY ERADICATED.
THE QUINX SQUAD RECEIVED RECOGNITION FOR ACQUIRING INTEL CONFIRMING THE AUCTION...
...ERADICATING THE NUTCRACKER, SECURING THE ADMINISTRATION BUILDING...
...AND ASSISTING SUZUYA SQUAD IN THE ERADICATION OF THE BIG MADAM.
THEY PLAYED A VITAL ROLE IN...
DID YOU HEAR ABOUT INVESTIGATOR KUROIWA?
FIRST TIME SINCE KOTARO AMON?
WITH HIS BARE HANDS...?!
...THE SUCCESS OF THE OPERATION.
He takes after his father...
He's got his DNA...

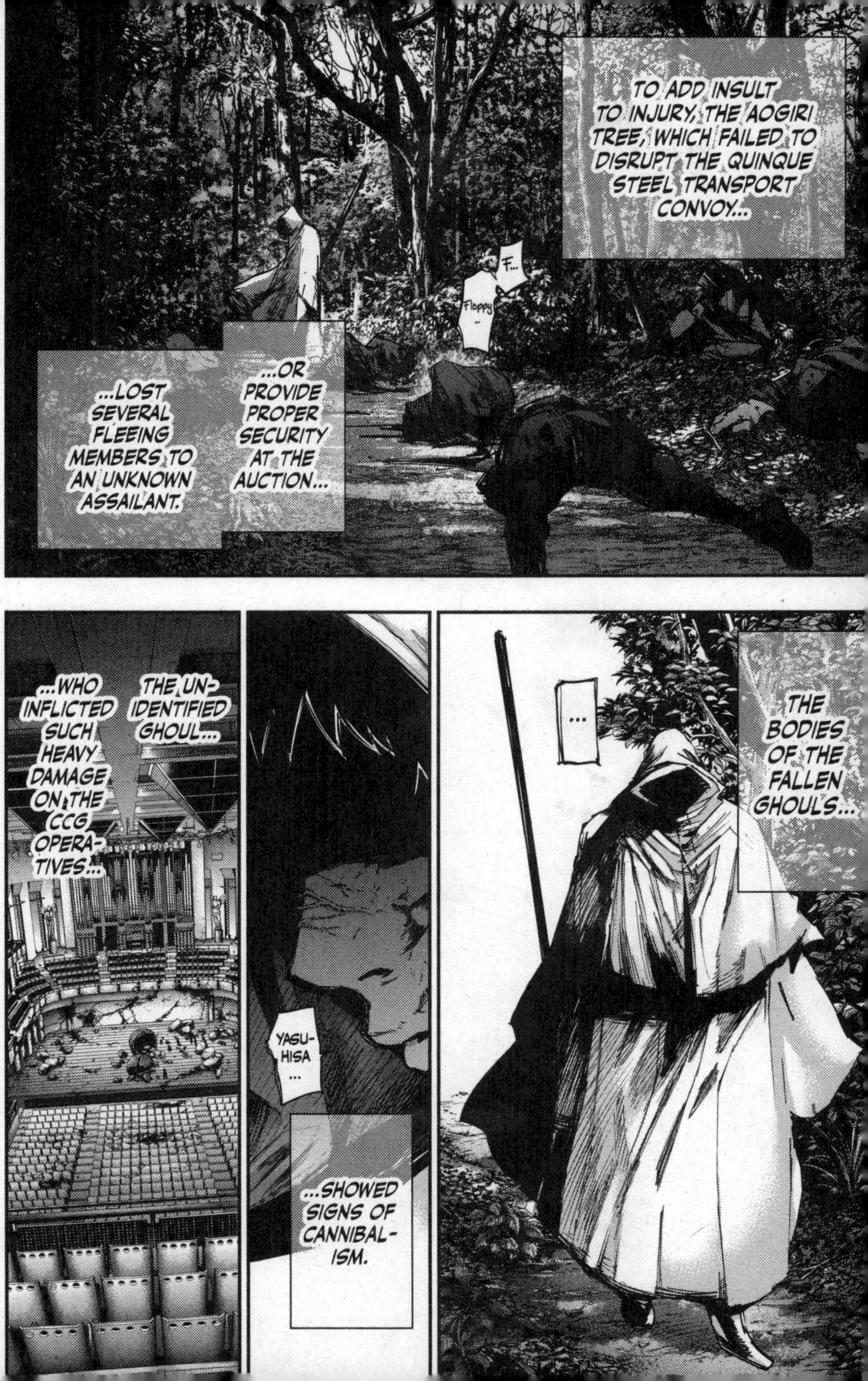
TO ADD INSULT TO INJURY, THE AOGIRI TREE, WHICH FAILED TO DISRUPT THE QUINQUE STEEL TRANSPORT CONVOY...
F...
Floppy...
...OR PROVIDE PROPER SECURITY AT THE AUCTION...
...LOST SEVERAL FLEEING MEMBERS TO AN UNKNOWN ASSAILANT.
THE BODIES OF THE FALLEN GHOULS...
...
YASU-HISA...
...SHOWED SIGNS OF CANNIBAL-ISM.
THE UN-IDENTIFIED GHOUL...
...WHO INFLICTED SUCH HEAVY DAMAGE ON THE CCG OPERA-TIVES...

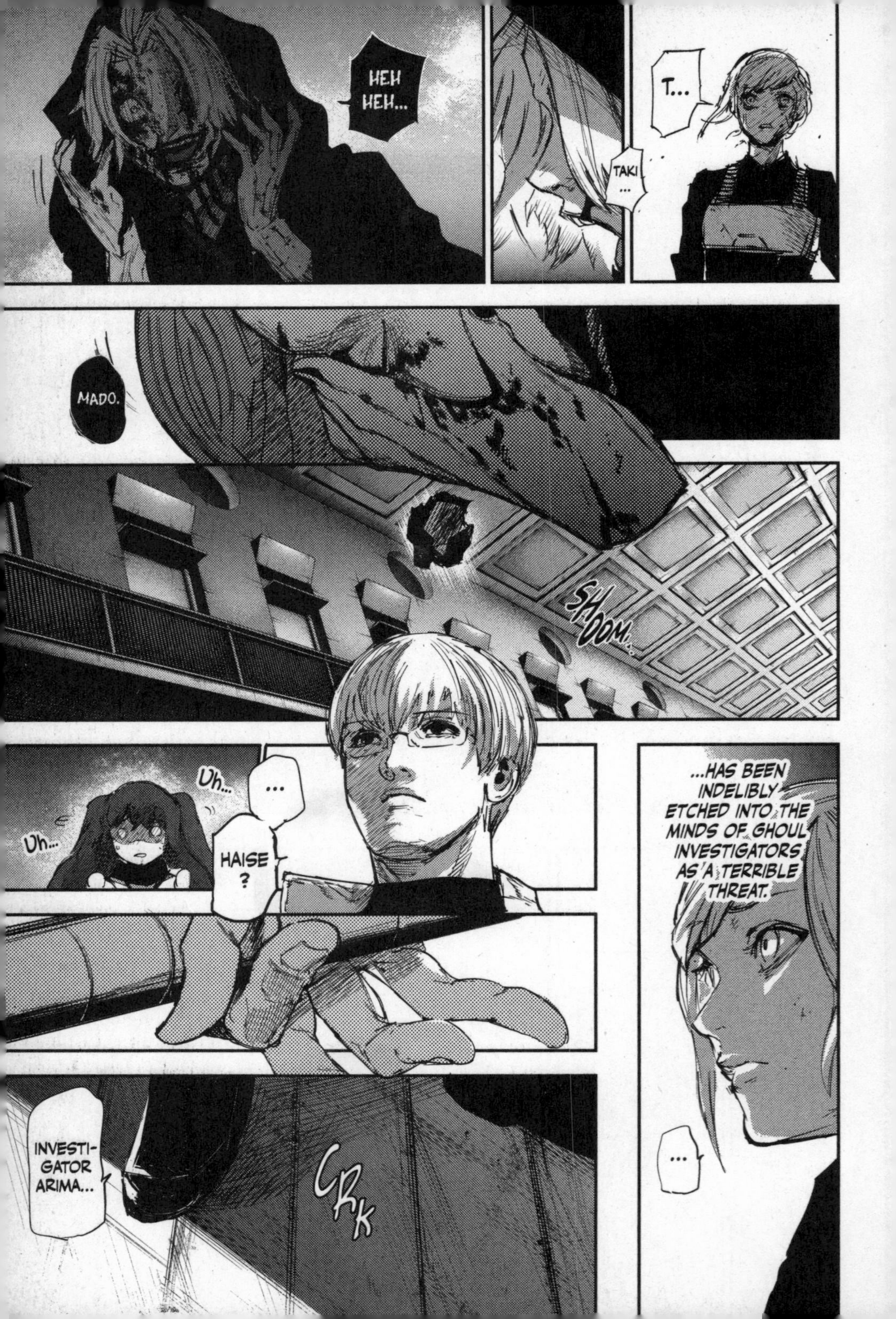
T...
TAKI...
HEH HEH...
MADO.
SHOOOM..
...HAS BEEN INDELIBLY ETCHED INTO THE MINDS OF GHOUL INVESTIGATORS AS A TERRIBLE THREAT.
...
...
HAISE?
Uh...
Uh...
INVESTI-GATOR ARIMA...
CRK

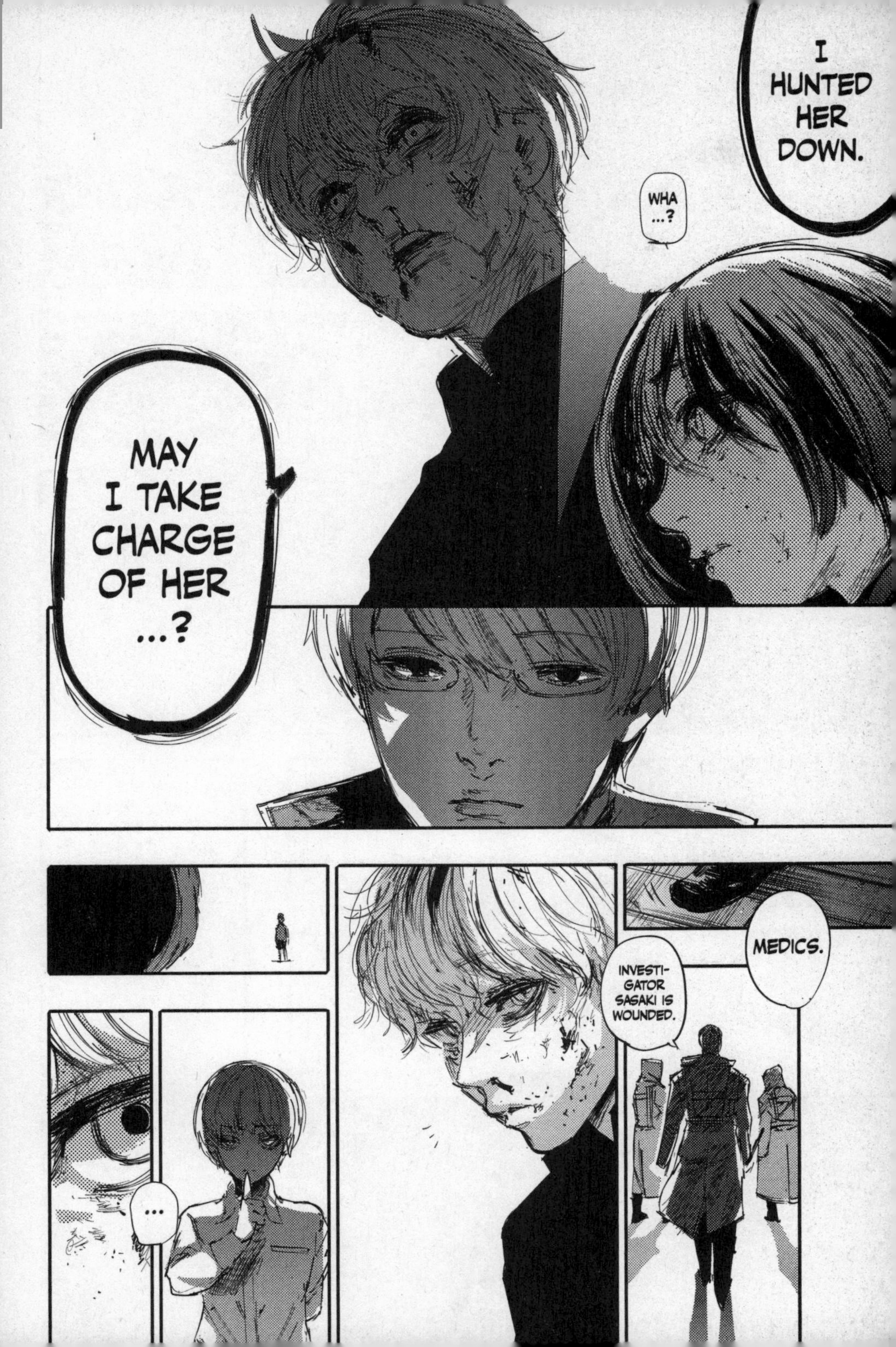
I HUNTED HER DOWN.
WHA ...?
MAY I TAKE CHARGE OF HER ...?
MEDICS.
INVESTIGATOR SASAKI IS WOUNDED.
...

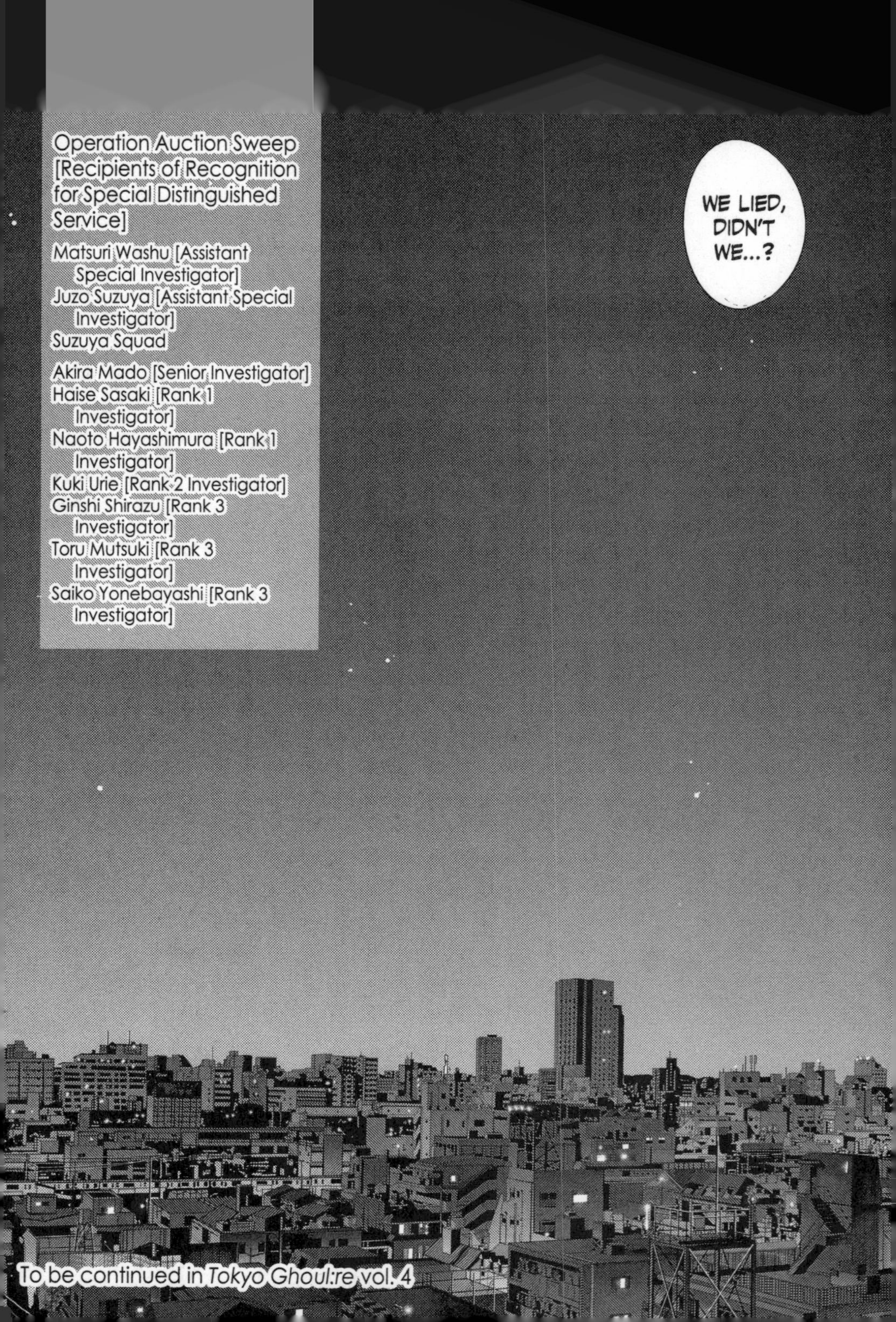
WE LIED, DIDN'T WE...?
Operation Auction Sweep [Recipients of Recognition for Special Distinguished Service]
Matsuri Washu [Assistant Special Investigator]
Juzo Suzuya [Assistant Special Investigator]
Suzuya Squad
Akira Mado [Senior Investigator]
Haise Sasaki [Rank 1 Investigator]
Naoto Hayashimura [Rank 1 Investigator]
Kuki Urie [Rank 2 Investigator]
Ginshi Shirazu [Rank 3 Investigator]
Toru Mutsuki [Rank 3 Investigator]
Saiko Yonebayashi [Rank 3 Investigator]
To be continued in Tokyo Ghoul:re vol. 4

Meanwhile, Madam A
escaped through an air duct.

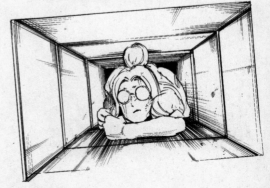

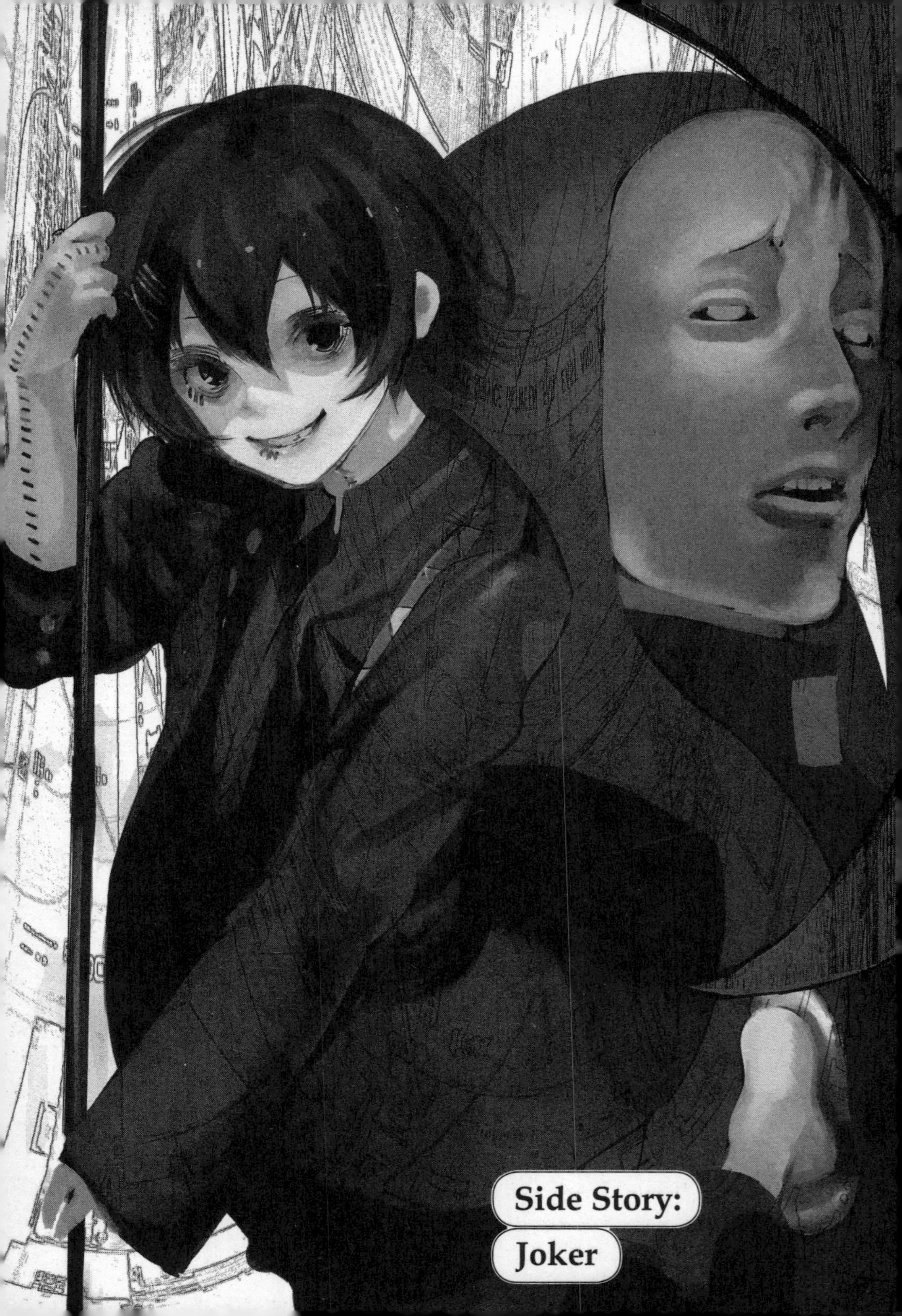

Side Story: Joker

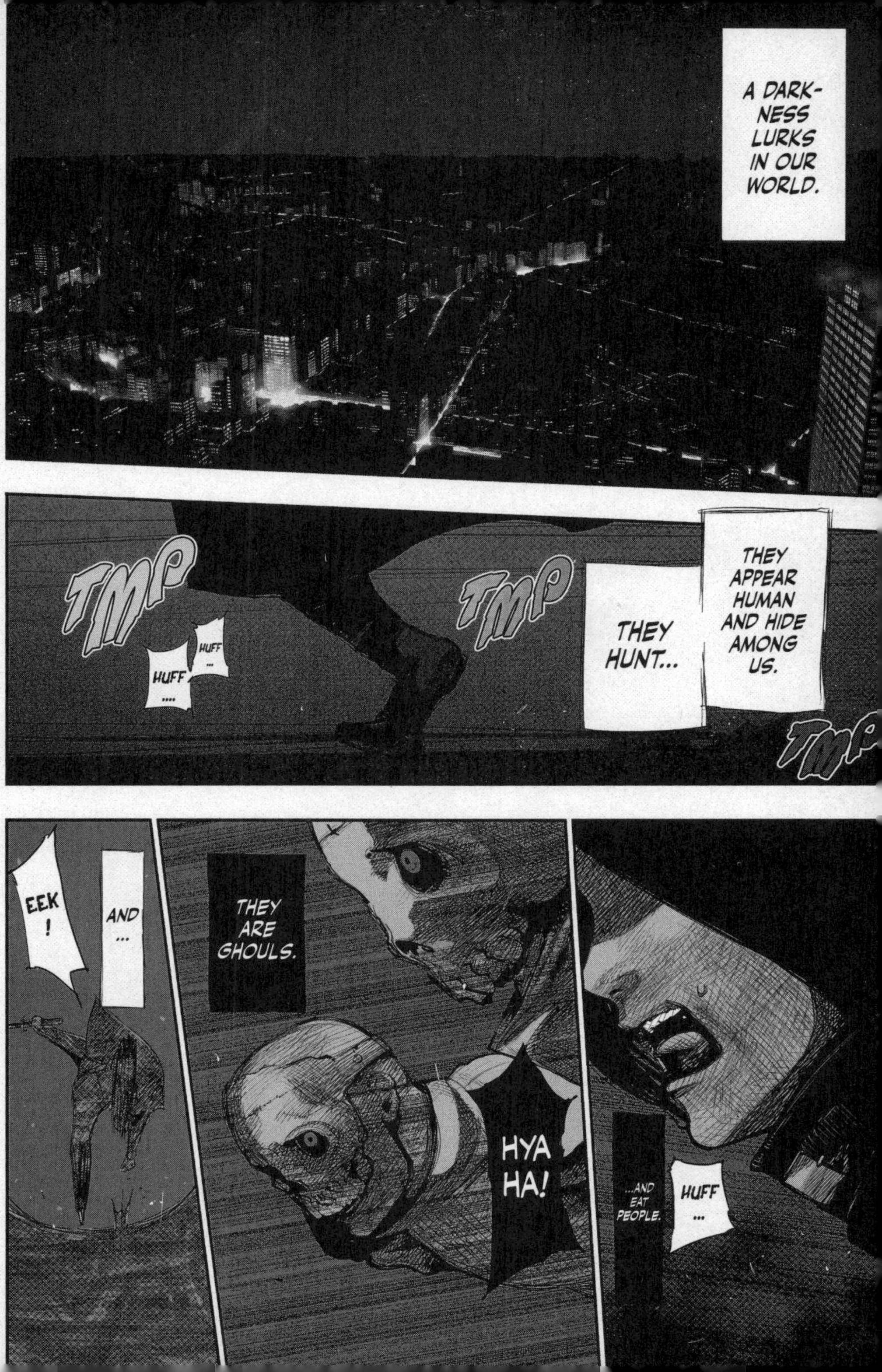
A DARK-NESS LURKS IN OUR WORLD.
TMP
THEY APPEAR HUMAN AND HIDE AMONG US.
THEY HUNT...
TMP
HUFF...
HUFF....
TMP
HUFF...
...AND EAT PEOPLE.
HYA HA!
THEY ARE GHOULS.
AND...
EEK!

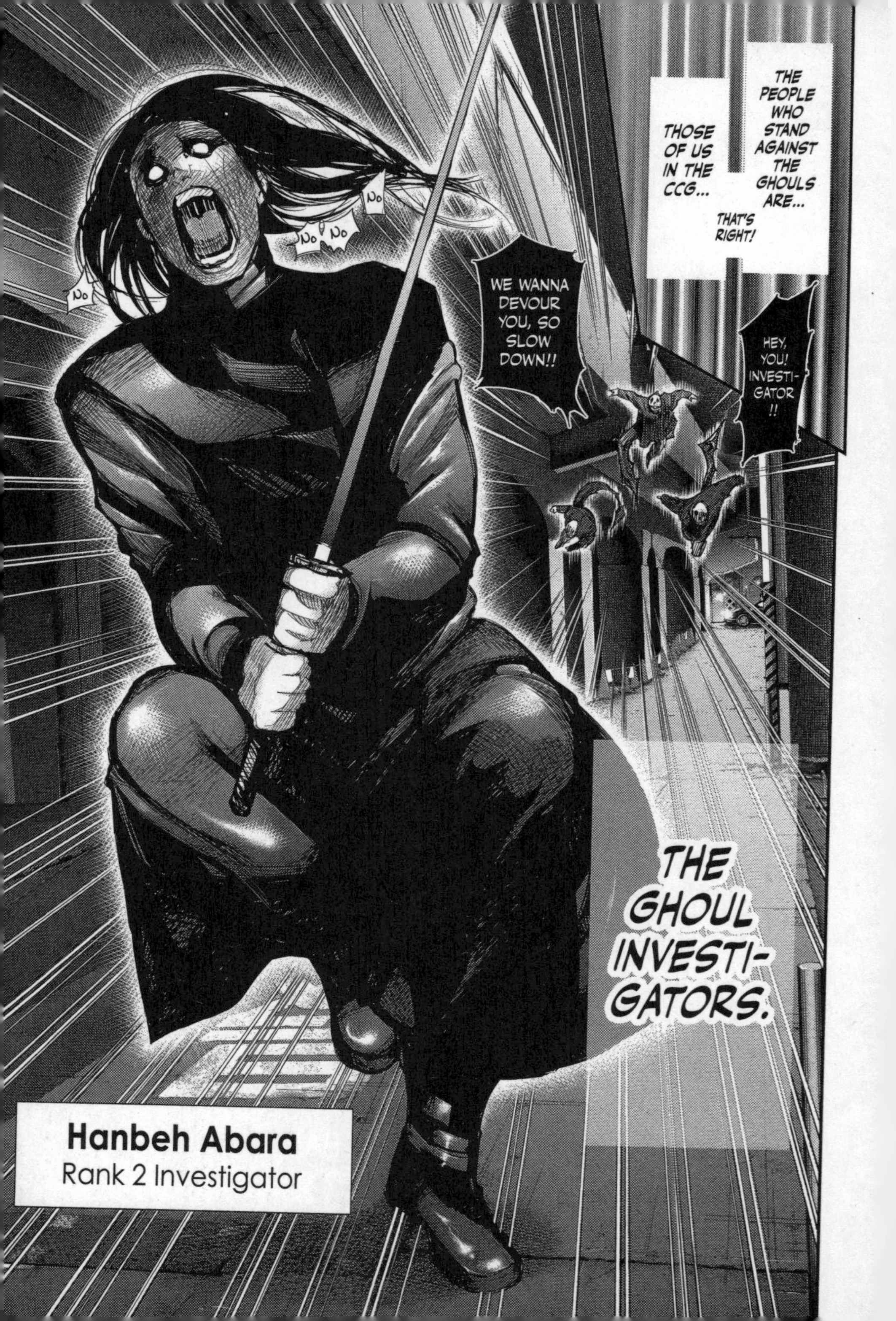
THE PEOPLE WHO STAND AGAINST THE GHOULS ARE...
THOSE OF US IN THE CCG...
THAT'S RIGHT!
HEY, YOU! INVESTI-GATOR!!
WE WANNA DEVOUR YOU, SO SLOW DOWN!!
No
No
No
No
THE GHOUL INVESTI-GATORS.
Hanbeh Abara
Rank 2 Investigator

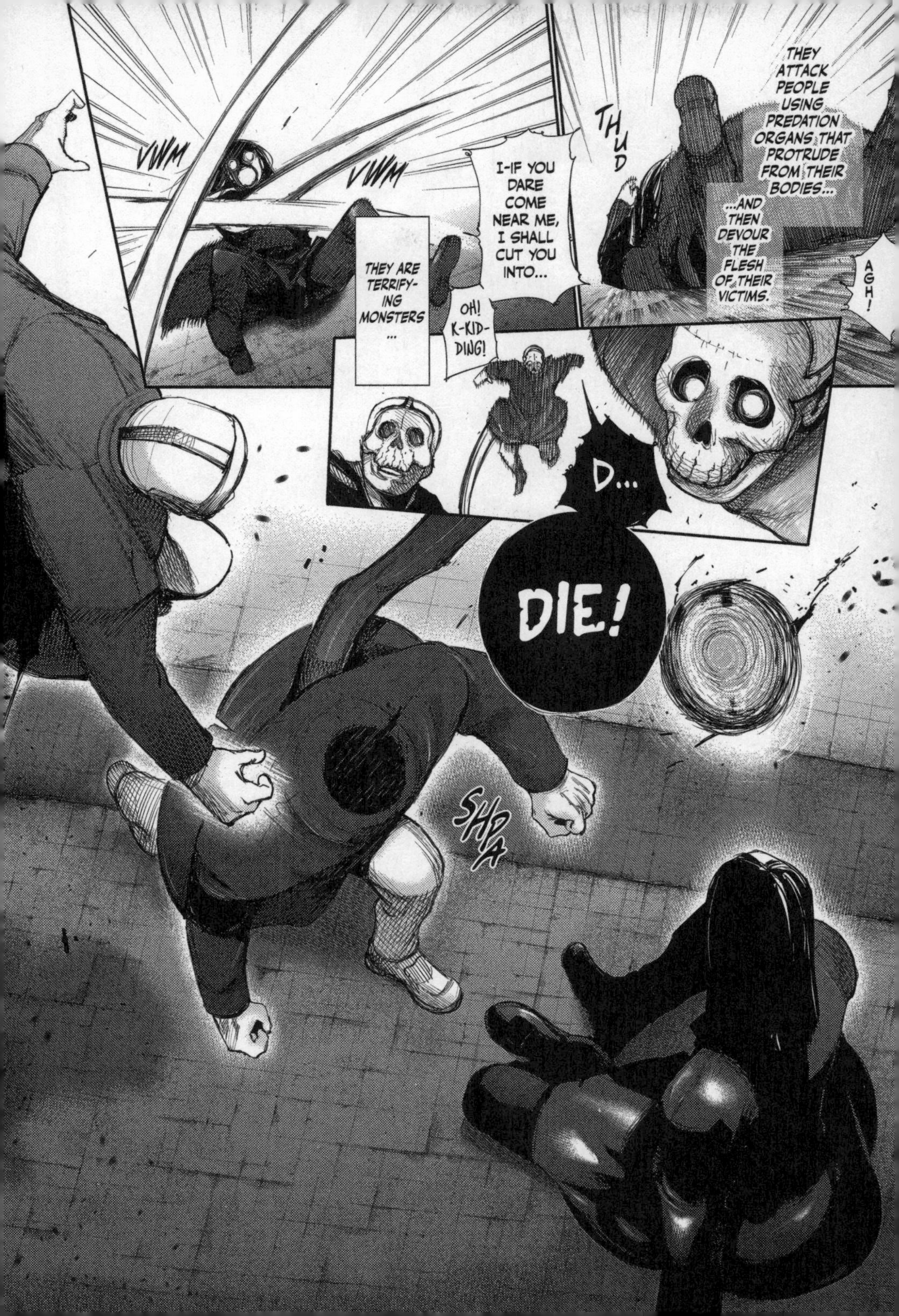
THEY ATTACK PEOPLE USING PREDATION ORGANS THAT PROTRUDE FROM THEIR BODIES...
THUD
...AND THEN DEVOUR THE FLESH OF THEIR VICTIMS.
AGH!
I-IF YOU DARE COME NEAR ME, I SHALL CUT YOU INTO...
VWM
VWM
THEY ARE TERRIFYING MONSTERS...
OH! K-KIDDING!
D...
DIE!
SHPA

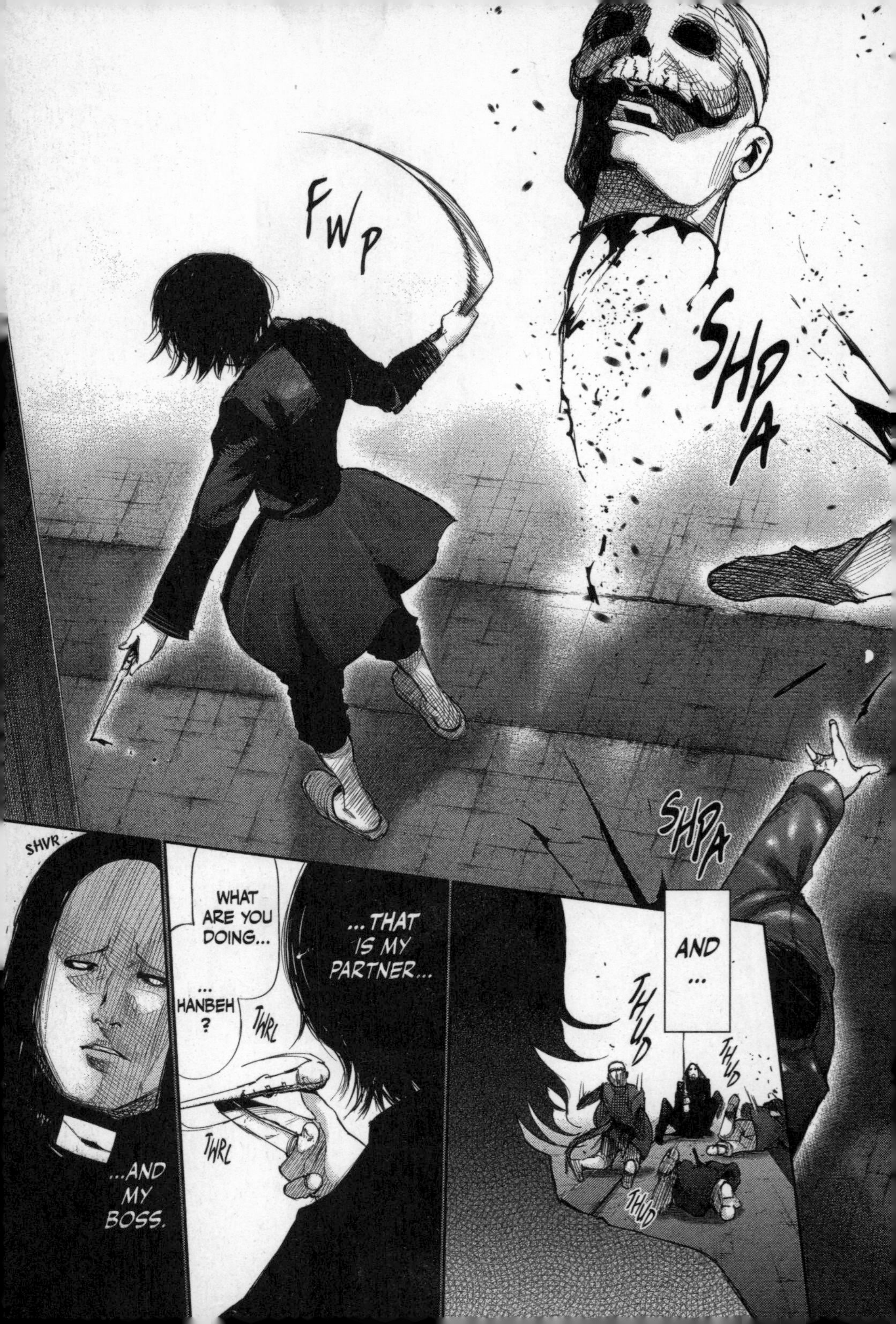

SHPA
FWP
SHPA
AND ...
THUD
THUD
THUD
...THAT IS MY PARTNER...
WHAT ARE YOU DOING...
... HANBEH?
THRL
THRL
SHVR
...AND MY BOSS.

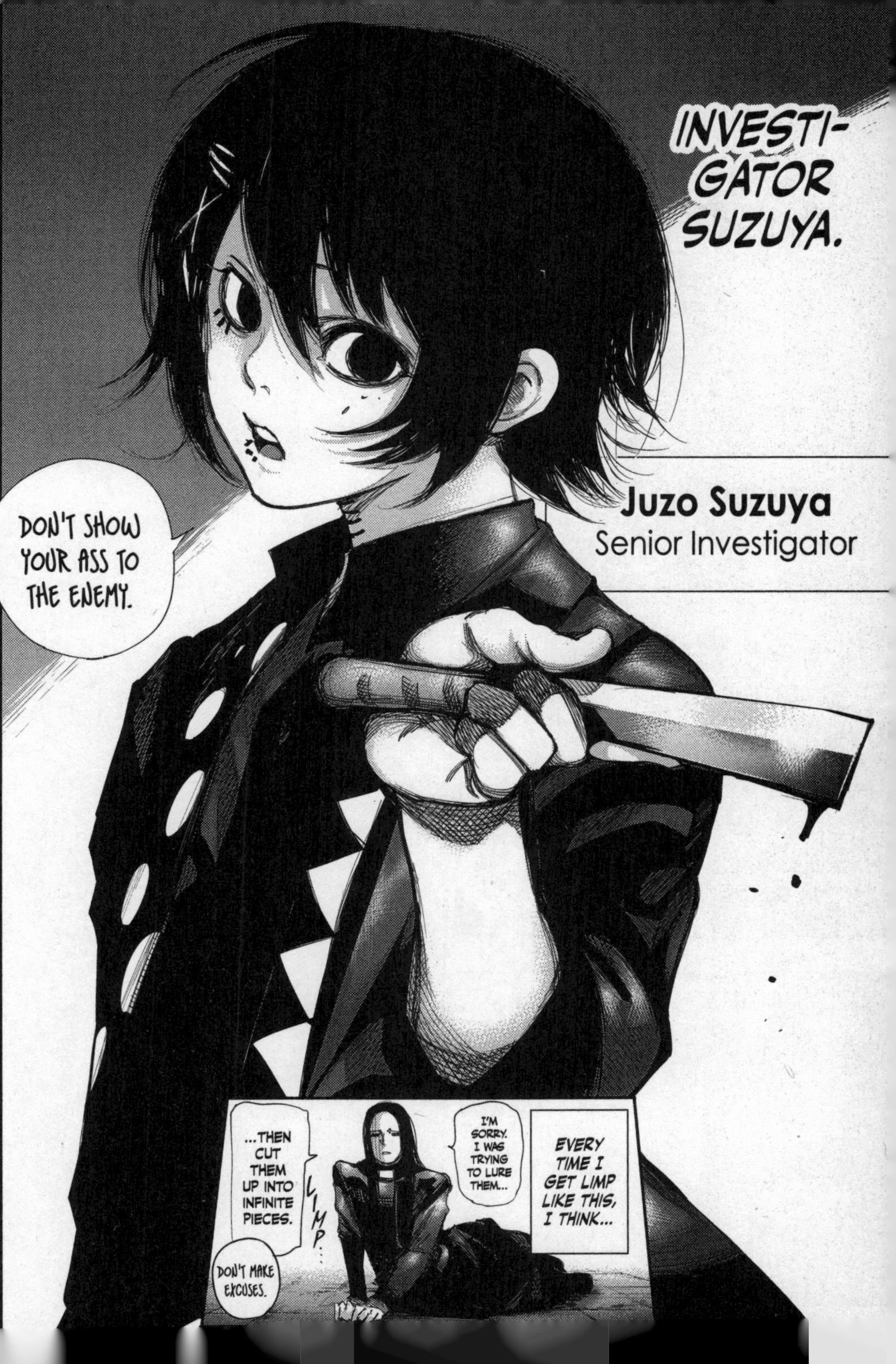
INVESTI-GATOR SUZUYA.
Juzo Suzuya
Senior Investigator
DON'T SHOW YOUR ASS TO THE ENEMY.
EVERY TIME I GET LIMP LIKE THIS, I THINK...
I'M SORRY. I WAS TRYING TO LURE THEM...
LIMP...
...THEN CUT THEM UP INTO INFINITE PIECES.
DON'T MAKE EXCUSES.

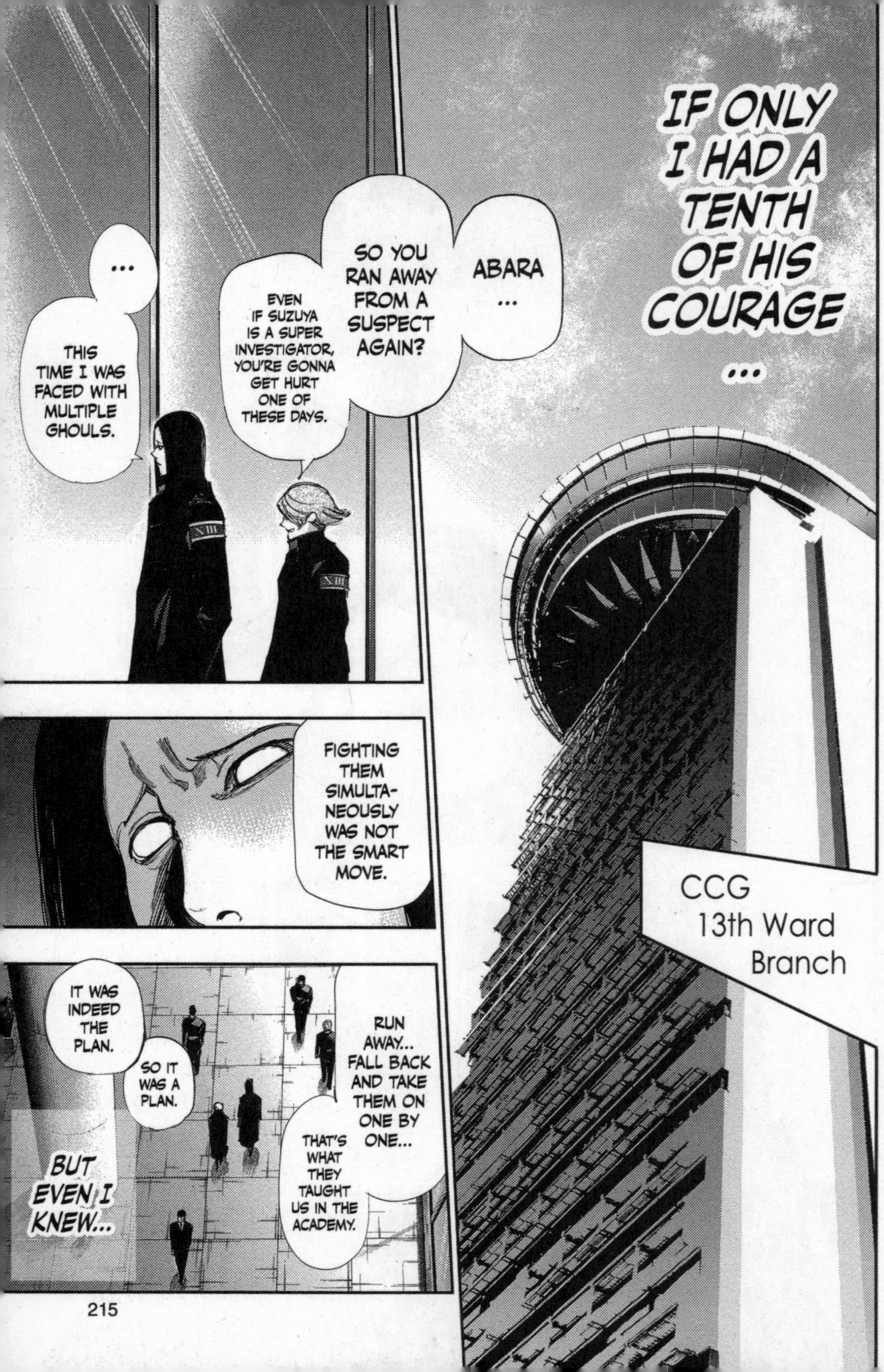
IF ONLY I HAD A TENTH OF HIS COURAGE ...
CCG 13th Ward Branch
ABARA ...
SO YOU RAN AWAY FROM A SUSPECT AGAIN?
EVEN IF SUZUYA IS A SUPER INVESTIGATOR, YOU'RE GONNA GET HURT ONE OF THESE DAYS.
...
THIS TIME I WAS FACED WITH MULTIPLE GHOULS.
FIGHTING THEM SIMULTANEOUSLY WAS NOT THE SMART MOVE.
RUN AWAY... FALL BACK AND TAKE THEM ON ONE BY ONE...
THAT'S WHAT THEY TAUGHT US IN THE ACADEMY.
IT WAS INDEED THE PLAN.
SO IT WAS A PLAN.
BUT EVEN I KNEW...

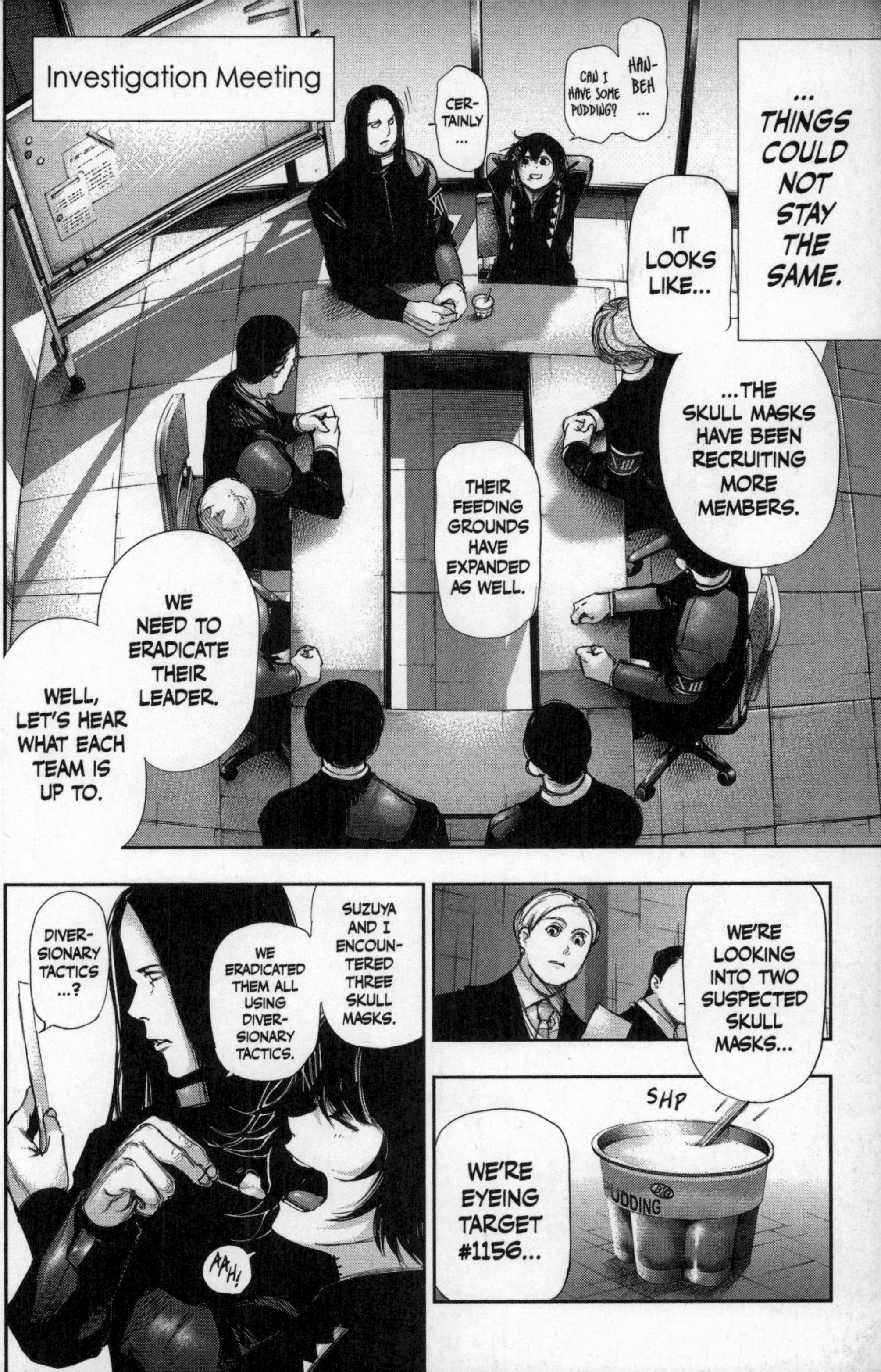

... THINGS COULD NOT STAY THE SAME.
HAN-BEH ...
CAN I HAVE SOME PUDDING?
CER-TAINLY ...
Investigation Meeting
IT LOOKS LIKE...
...THE SKULL MASKS HAVE BEEN RECRUITING MORE MEMBERS.
THEIR FEEDING GROUNDS HAVE EXPANDED AS WELL.
WE NEED TO ERADICATE THEIR LEADER.
WELL, LET'S HEAR WHAT EACH TEAM IS UP TO.
WE'RE LOOKING INTO TWO SUSPECTED SKULL MASKS...
SHP
WE'RE EYEING TARGET #1156...
SUZUYA AND I ENCOUN-TERED THREE SKULL MASKS.
WE ERADICATED THEM ALL USING DIVER-SIONARY TACTICS.
DIVER-SIONARY TACTICS ...?
AAH!

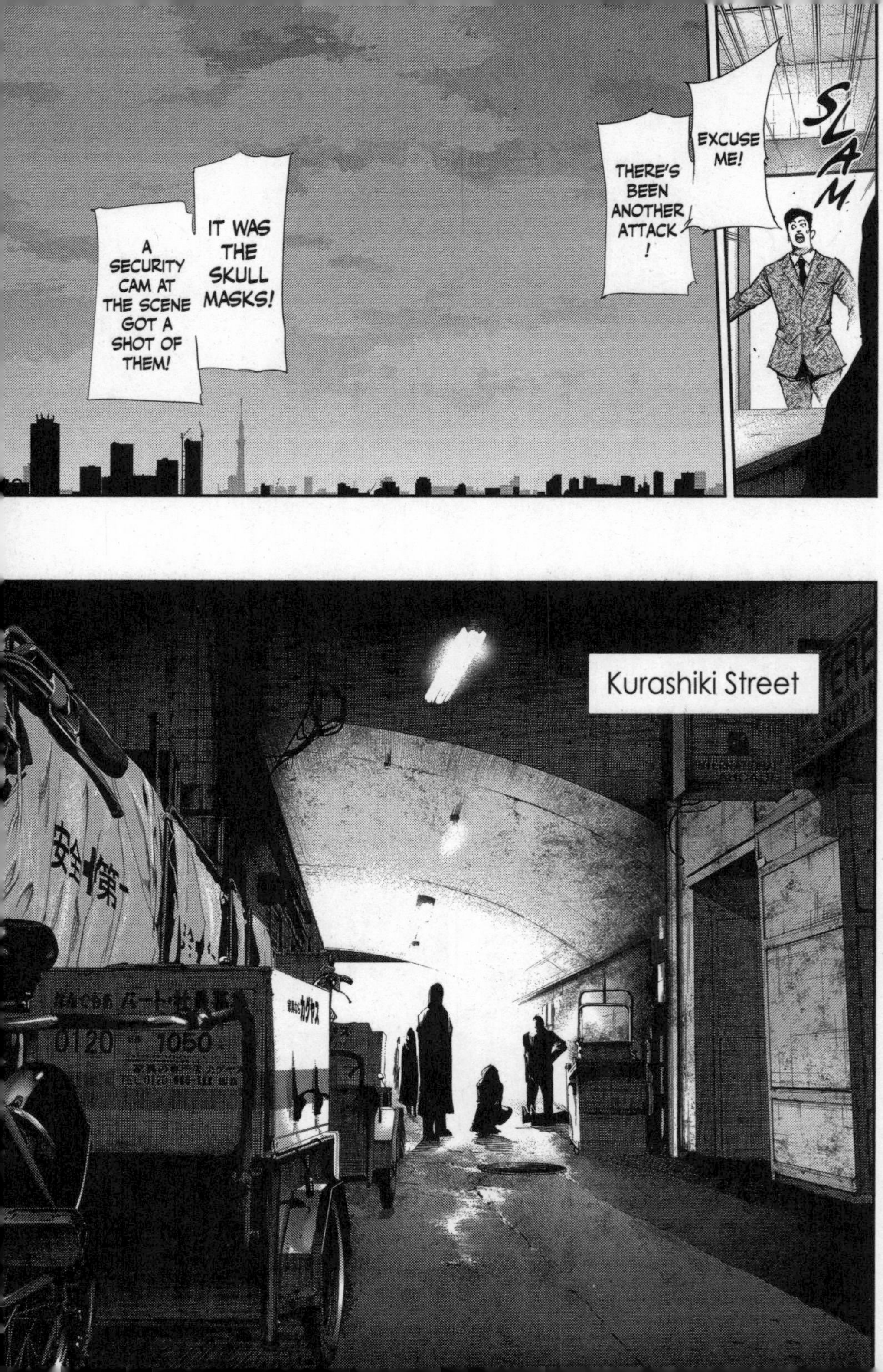
SLAM
EXCUSE ME!
THERE'S BEEN ANOTHER ATTACK!
IT WAS THE SKULL MASKS!
A SECURITY CAM AT THE SCENE GOT A SHOT OF THEM!
Kurashiki Street

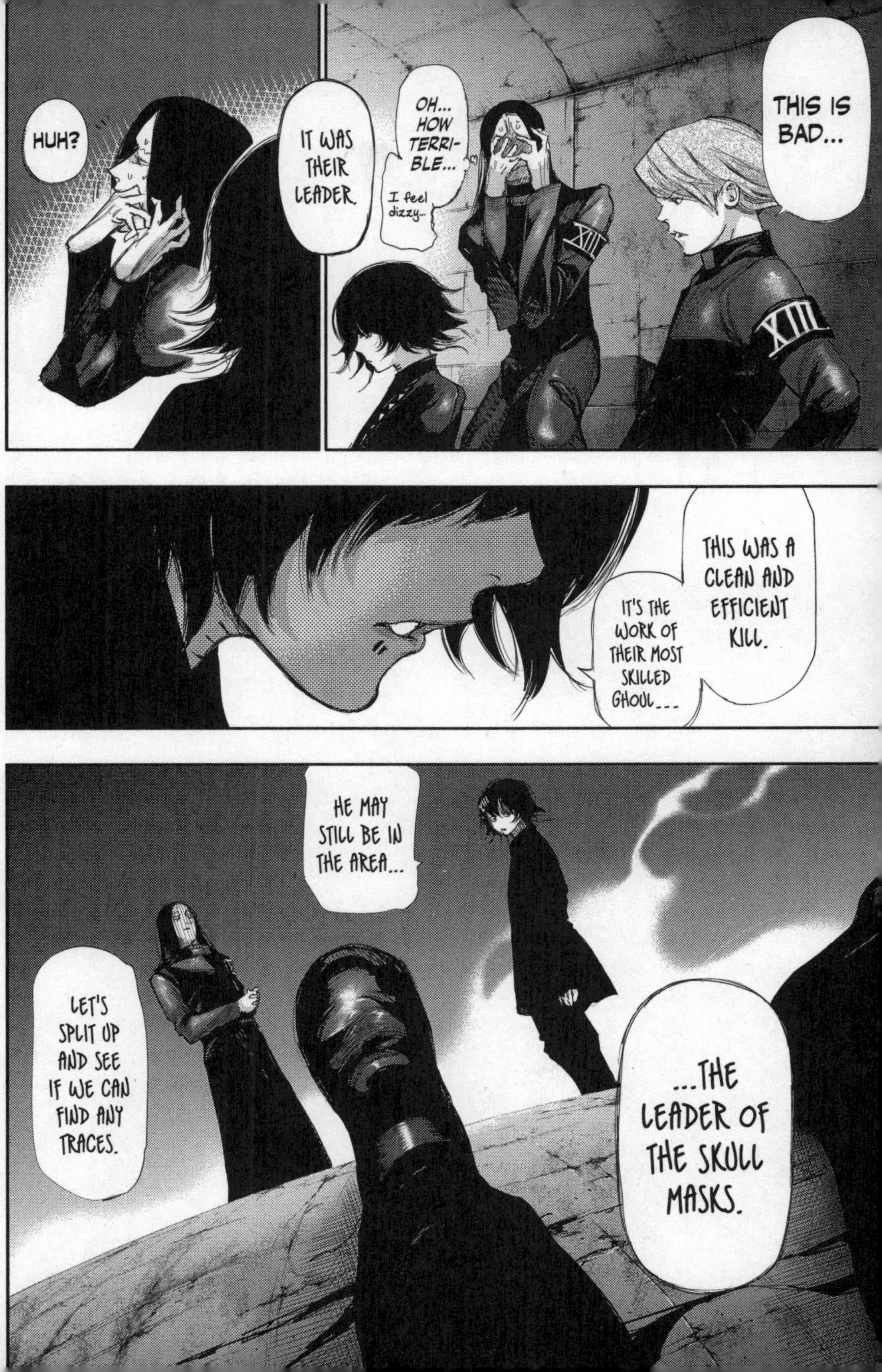
THIS IS BAD...
OH... HOW TERRIBLE...
I feel dizzy...
IT WAS THEIR LEADER.
HUH?
THIS WAS A CLEAN AND EFFICIENT KILL.
IT'S THE WORK OF THEIR MOST SKILLED GHOUL...
...THE LEADER OF THE SKULL MASKS.
HE MAY STILL BE IN THE AREA...
LET'S SPLIT UP AND SEE IF WE CAN FIND ANY TRACES.

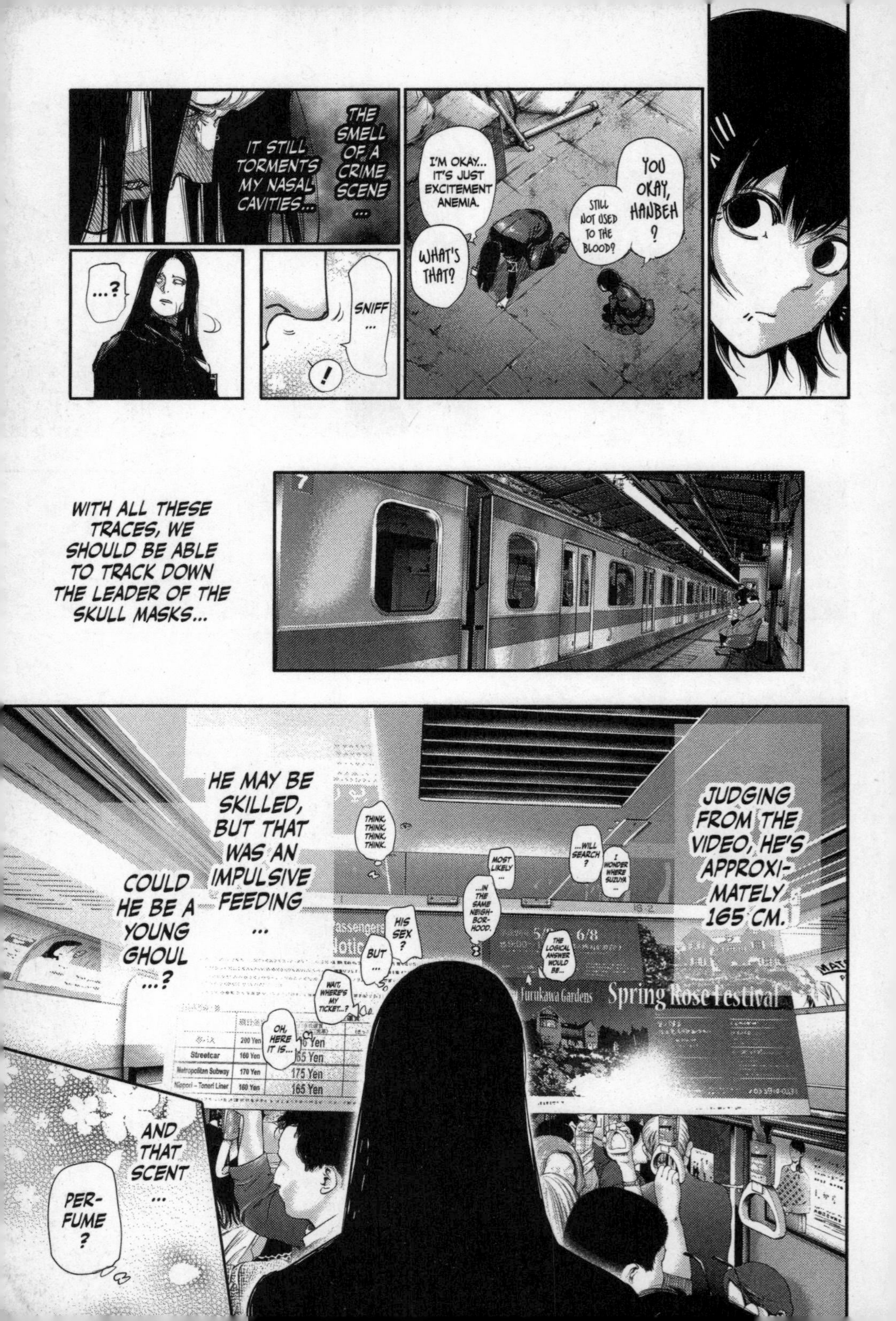
YOU OKAY, HANBEH?
STILL NOT USED TO THE BLOOD?
I'M OKAY... IT'S JUST EXCITEMENT ANEMIA.
WHAT'S THAT?
THE SMELL OF A CRIME SCENE...
IT STILL TORMENTS MY NASAL CAVITIES...
SNIFF...
!
...?
WITH ALL THESE TRACES, WE SHOULD BE ABLE TO TRACK DOWN THE LEADER OF THE SKULL MASKS...
JUDGING FROM THE VIDEO, HE'S APPROXI-MATELY 165 CM.
I WONDER WHERE SUZUYA...
...WILL SEARCH?
MOST LIKELY...
...IN THE SAME NEIGH-BOR-HOOD.
THE LOGICAL ANSWER WOULD BE...
HIS SEX?
BUT...
THINK, THINK, THINK, THINK.
WAIT, WHERE'S MY TICKET...?
OH, HERE IT IS...
Spring Rose Festival
Furukawa Gardens
Streetcar 160 Yen 165 Yen
Metropolitan Subway 170 Yen 175 Yen
Nippori - Toneri Liner 160 Yen 165 Yen
HE MAY BE SKILLED, BUT THAT WAS AN IMPULSIVE FEEDING...
COULD HE BE A YOUNG GHOUL...?
AND THAT SCENT...
PER-FUME?

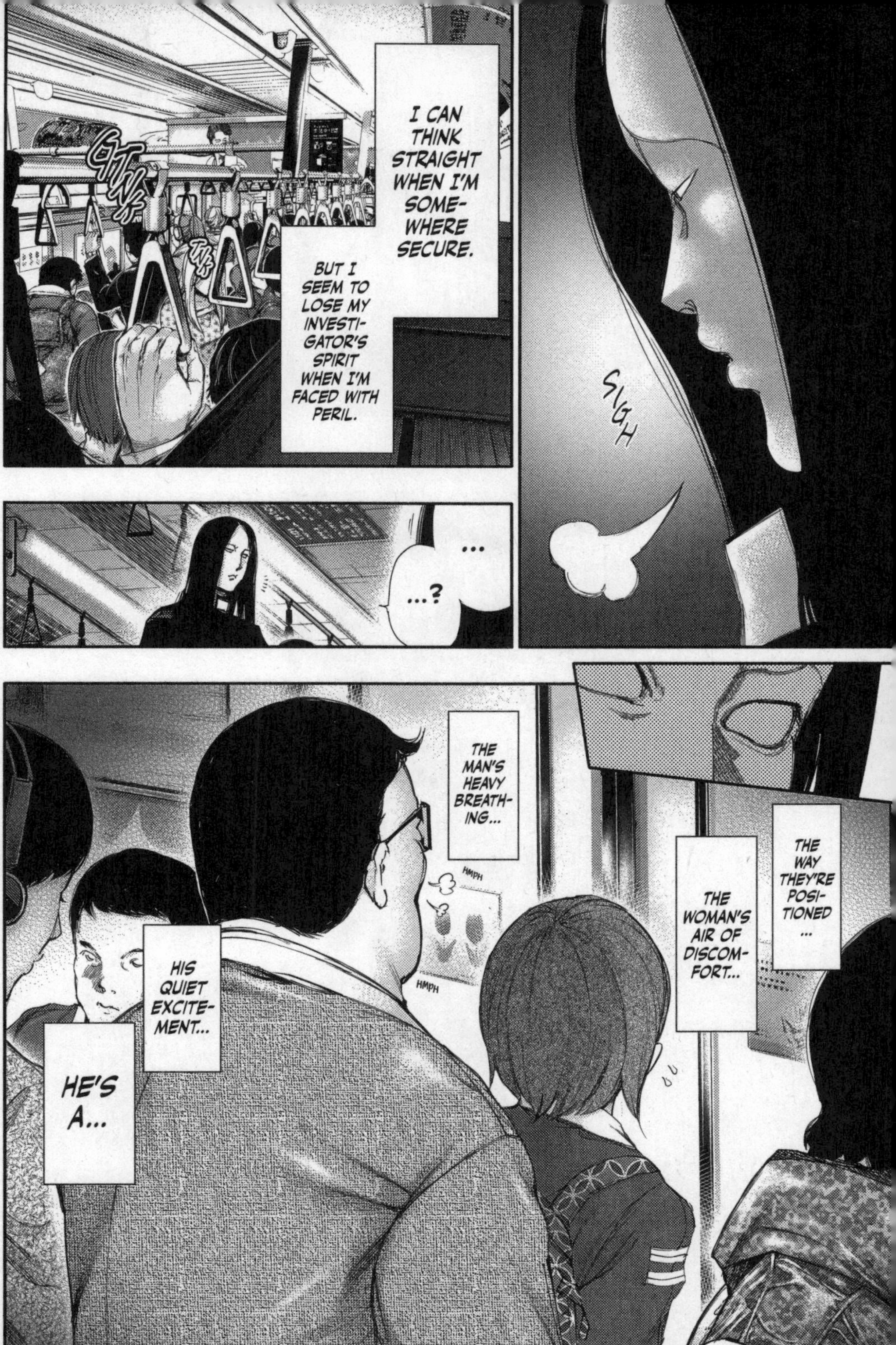
SIGH
I CAN THINK STRAIGHT WHEN I'M SOME-WHERE SECURE.
BUT I SEEM TO LOSE MY INVESTI-GATOR'S SPIRIT WHEN I'M FACED WITH PERIL.
...
...?
THE WAY THEY'RE POSI-TIONED ...
THE WOMAN'S AIR OF DISCOM-FORT...
THE MAN'S HEAVY BREATH-ING...
HMPH
HMPH
HIS QUIET EXCITE-MENT...
HE'S A...

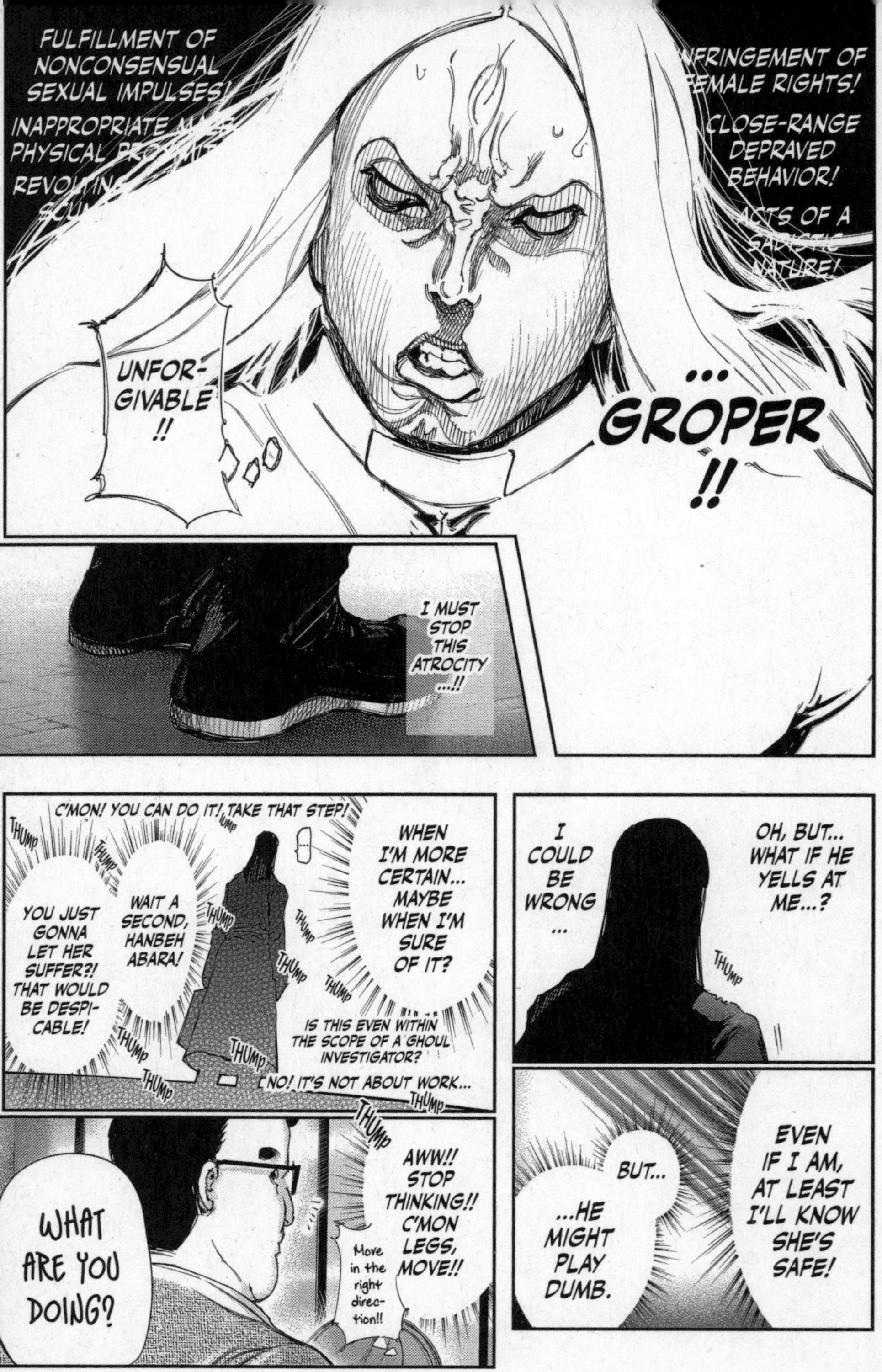

INFRINGEMENT OF FEMALE RIGHTS!
CLOSE-RANGE DEPRAVED BEHAVIOR!
ACTS OF A SADISTIC NATURE!
FULFILLMENT OF NONCONSENSUAL SEXUAL IMPULSES!
INAPPROPRIATE
PHYSICAL
...GROPER!!
UNFORGIVABLE!!
I MUST STOP THIS ATROCITY...!!
OH, BUT... WHAT IF HE YELLS AT ME...?
I COULD BE WRONG...
THUMP
C'MON! YOU CAN DO IT! TAKE THAT STEP!
WHEN I'M MORE CERTAIN... MAYBE WHEN I'M SURE OF IT?
...
WAIT A SECOND, HANBEH ABARA!
YOU JUST GONNA LET HER SUFFER?! THAT WOULD BE DESPICABLE!
IS THIS EVEN WITHIN THE SCOPE OF A GHOUL INVESTIGATOR?
NO! IT'S NOT ABOUT WORK...
THUMP THUMP THUMP
EVEN IF I AM, AT LEAST I'LL KNOW SHE'S SAFE!
BUT...
...HE MIGHT PLAY DUMB.
AWW!! STOP THINKING!! C'MON LEGS, MOVE!!
Move in the right direction!!
WHAT ARE YOU DOING?

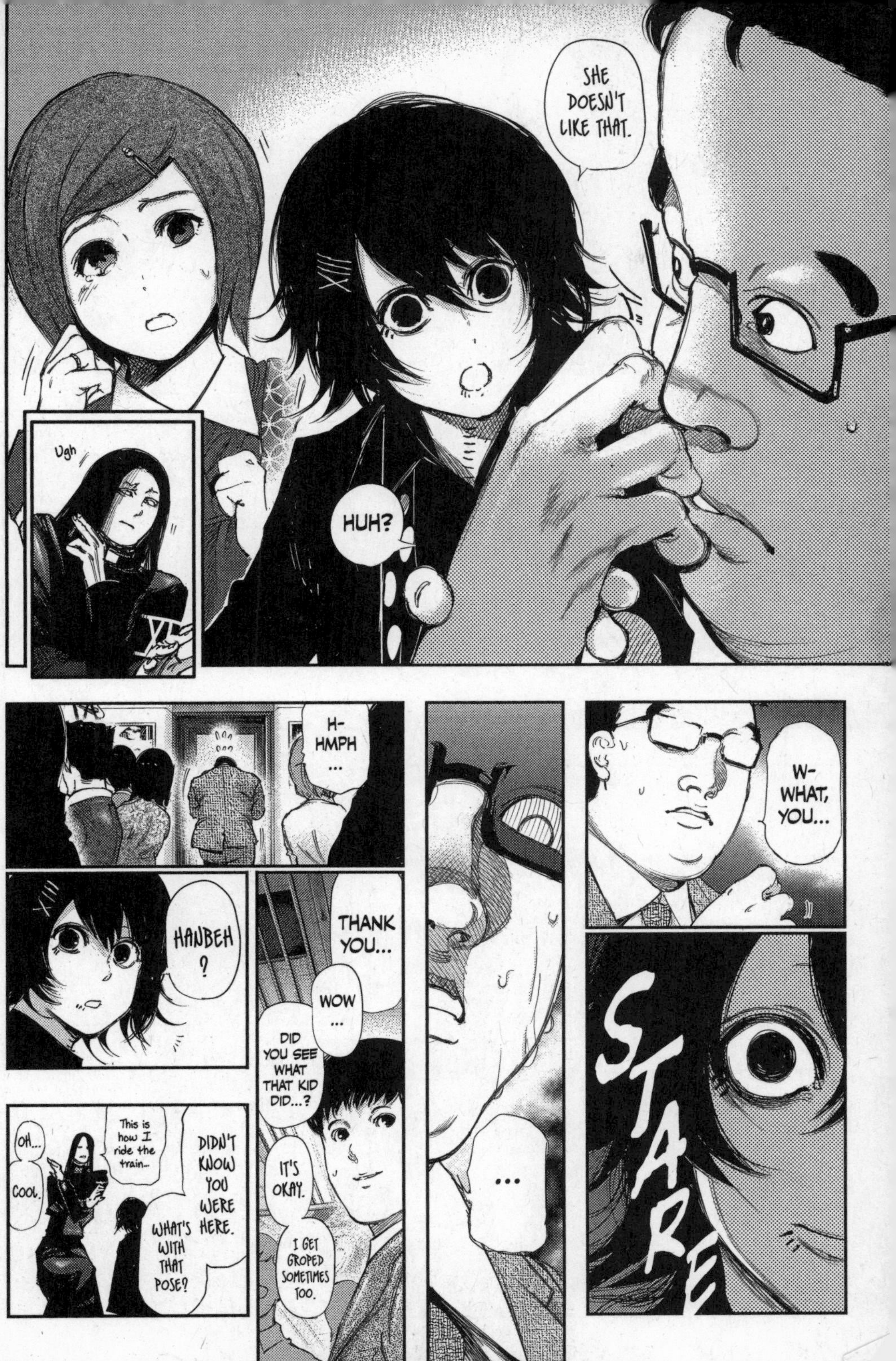
SHE DOESN'T LIKE THAT.
HUH?
Ugh
W-WHAT, YOU...
STARE
...
H-HMPH...
THANK YOU...
WOW...
DID YOU SEE WHAT THAT KID DID...?
IT'S OKAY.
I GET GROPED SOMETIMES TOO.
HANBEH?
DIDN'T KNOW YOU WERE HERE.
WHAT'S WITH THAT POSE?
This is how I ride the train...
OH...
COOL.

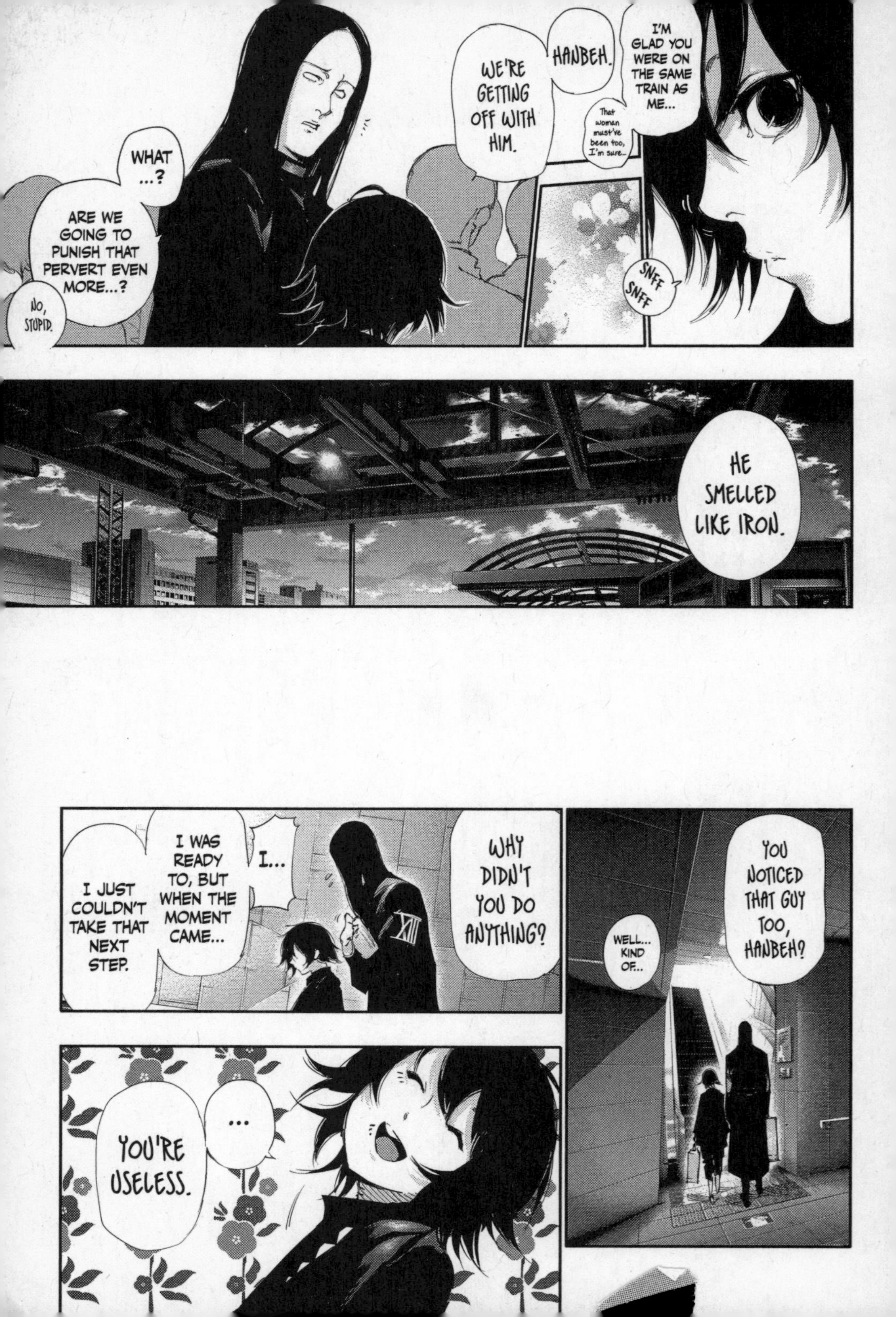
I'M GLAD YOU WERE ON THE SAME TRAIN AS ME...
That woman must've been too, I'm sure...
SNFF SNFF
HANBEH.
WE'RE GETTING OFF WITH HIM.
WHAT ...?
ARE WE GOING TO PUNISH THAT PERVERT EVEN MORE...?
No, stupid.
HE SMELLED LIKE IRON.
YOU NOTICED THAT GUY TOO, HANBEH?
WELL... KIND OF...
WHY DIDN'T YOU DO ANYTHING?
I...
I WAS READY TO, BUT WHEN THE MOMENT CAME...
I JUST COULDN'T TAKE THAT NEXT STEP.
...
YOU'RE USELESS.

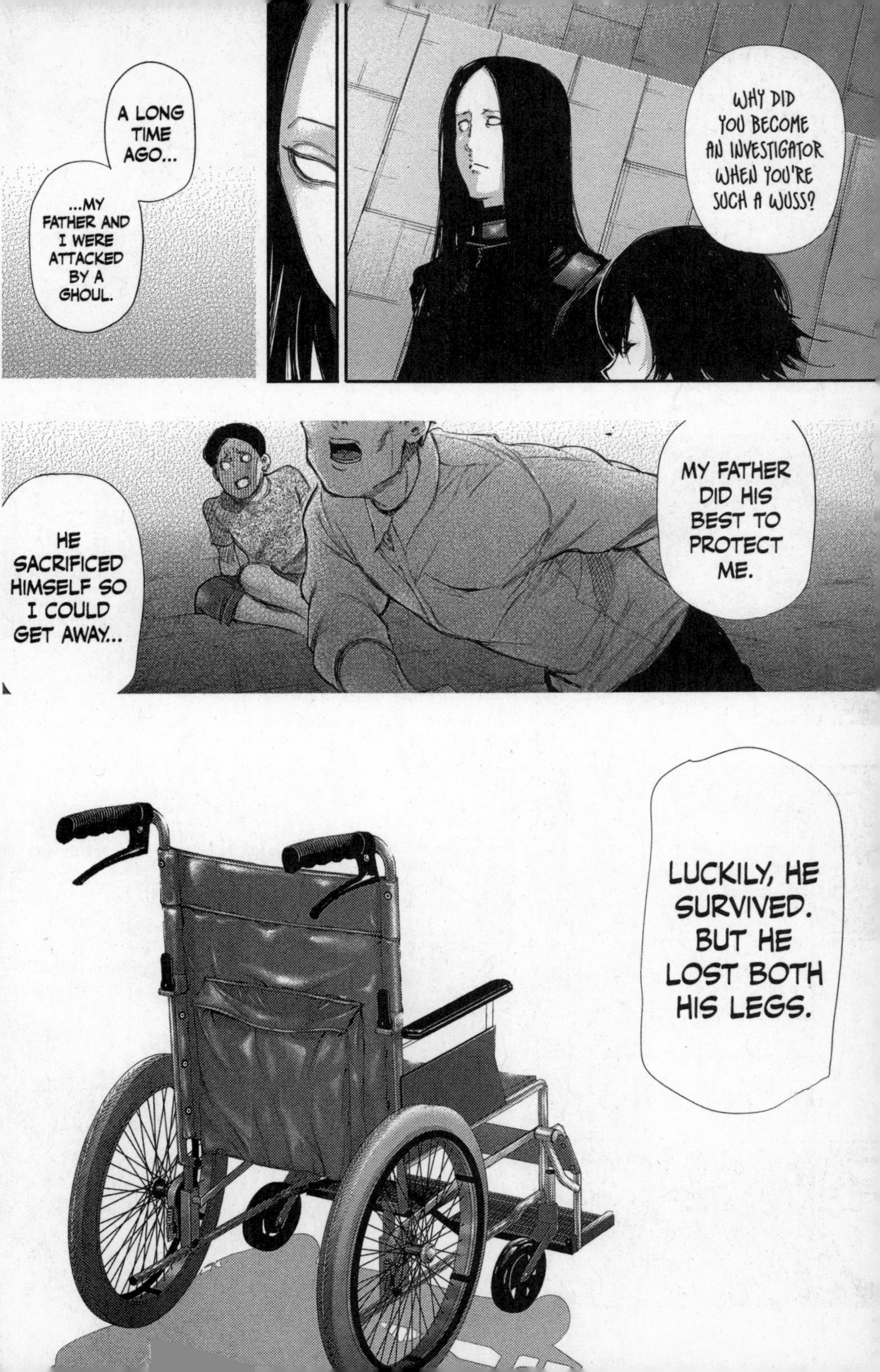
WHY DID YOU BECOME AN INVESTIGATOR WHEN YOU'RE SUCH A WUSS?
A LONG TIME AGO...
...MY FATHER AND I WERE ATTACKED BY A GHOUL.
MY FATHER DID HIS BEST TO PROTECT ME.
HE SACRIFICED HIMSELF SO I COULD GET AWAY...
LUCKILY, HE SURVIVED. BUT HE LOST BOTH HIS LEGS.

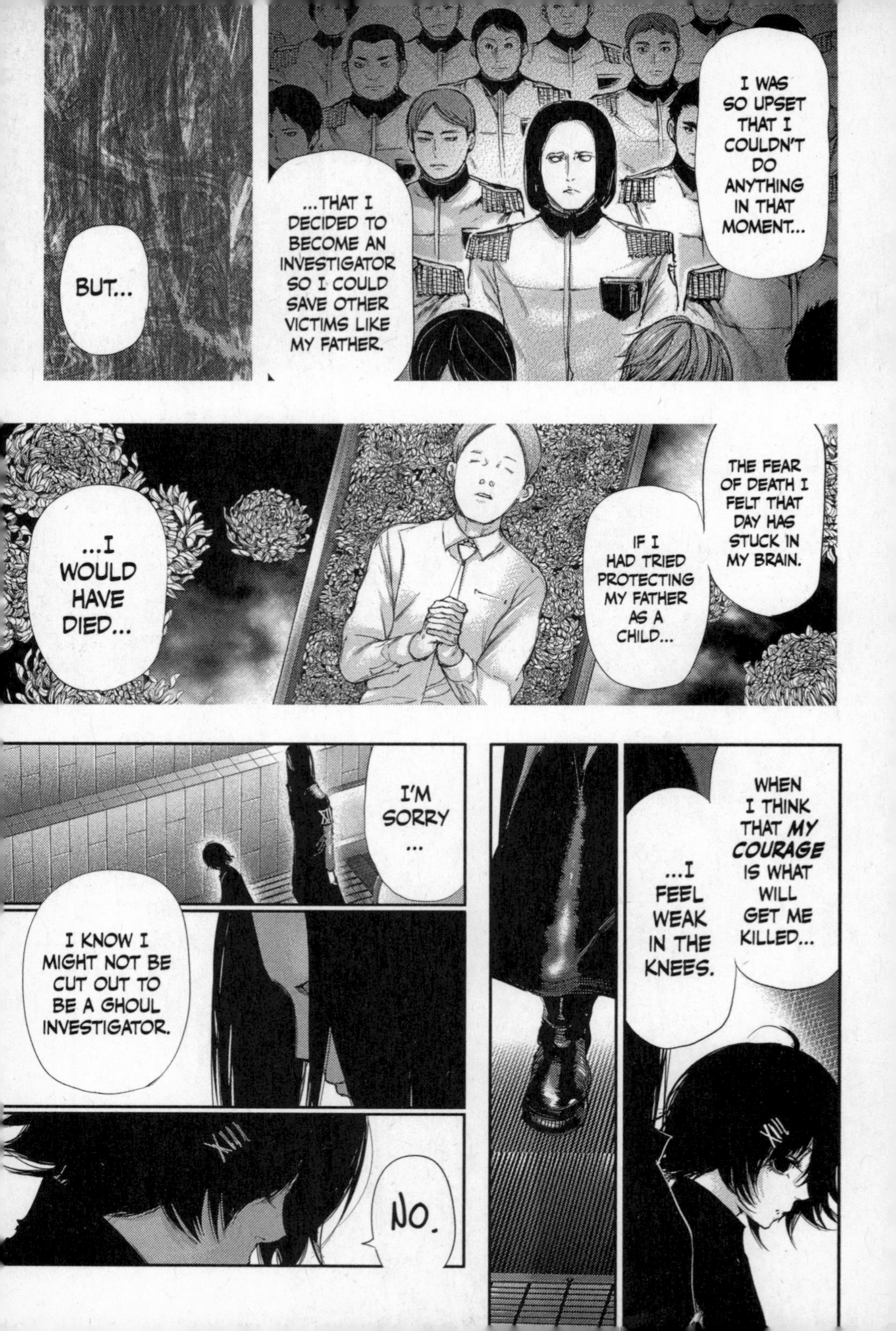
I WAS SO UPSET THAT I COULDN'T DO ANYTHING IN THAT MOMENT...
...THAT I DECIDED TO BECOME AN INVESTIGATOR SO I COULD SAVE OTHER VICTIMS LIKE MY FATHER.
BUT...
THE FEAR OF DEATH I FELT THAT DAY HAS STUCK IN MY BRAIN.
IF I HAD TRIED PROTECTING MY FATHER AS A CHILD...
...I WOULD HAVE DIED...
WHEN I THINK THAT *MY COURAGE* IS WHAT WILL GET ME KILLED...
...I FEEL WEAK IN THE KNEES.
I'M SORRY...
I KNOW I MIGHT NOT BE CUT OUT TO BE A GHOUL INVESTIGATOR.
NO.

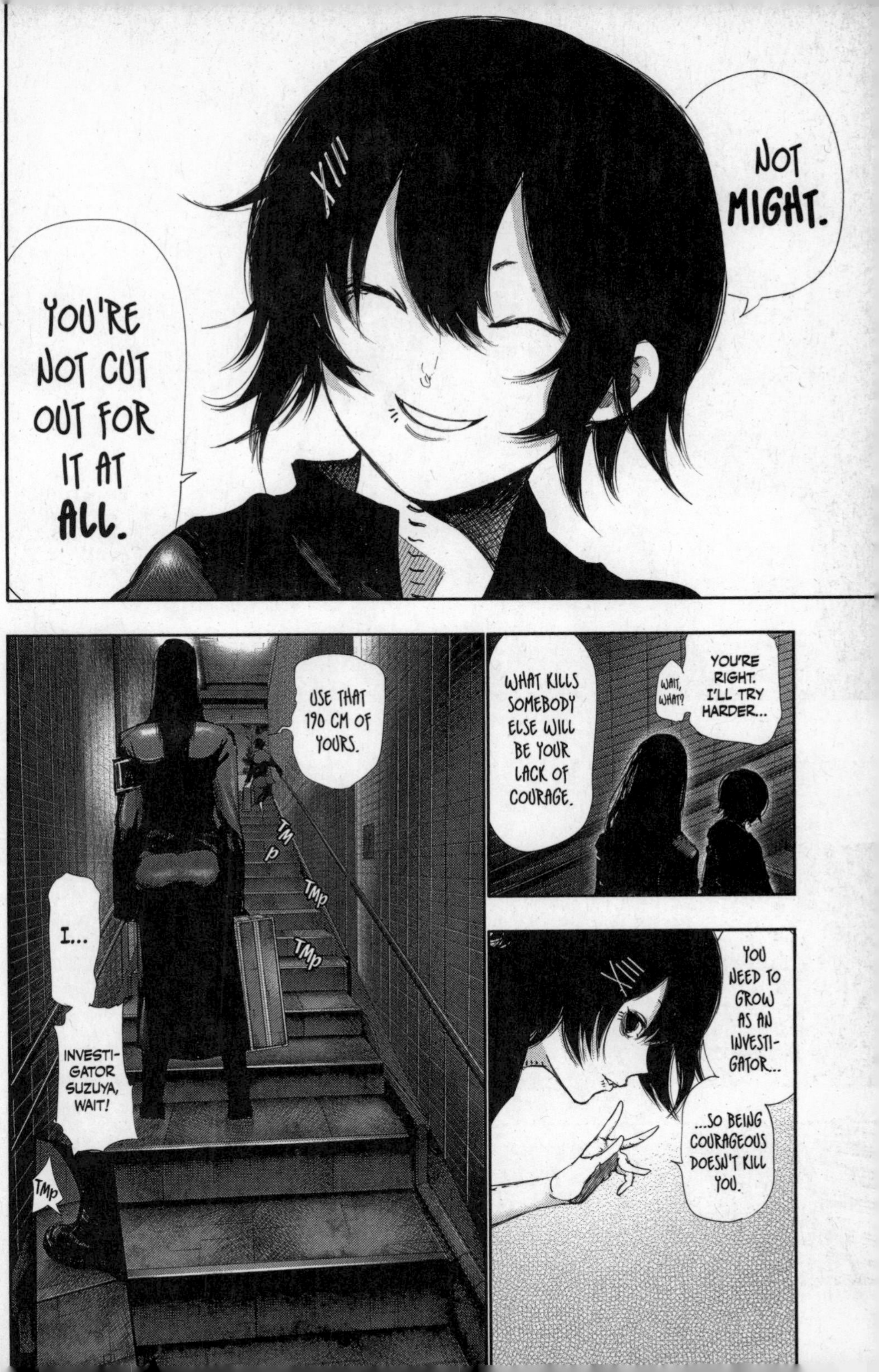
NOT MIGHT.
YOU'RE NOT CUT OUT FOR IT AT ALL.
YOU'RE RIGHT. I'LL TRY HARDER...
WAIT, WHAT?
WHAT KILLS SOMEBODY ELSE WILL BE YOUR LACK OF COURAGE.
YOU NEED TO GROW AS AN INVESTIGATOR...
...SO BEING COURAGEOUS DOESN'T KILL YOU.
USE THAT 190 CM OF YOURS.
TMp
TMp
TMp
I...
INVESTIGATOR SUZUYA, WAIT!
TMp

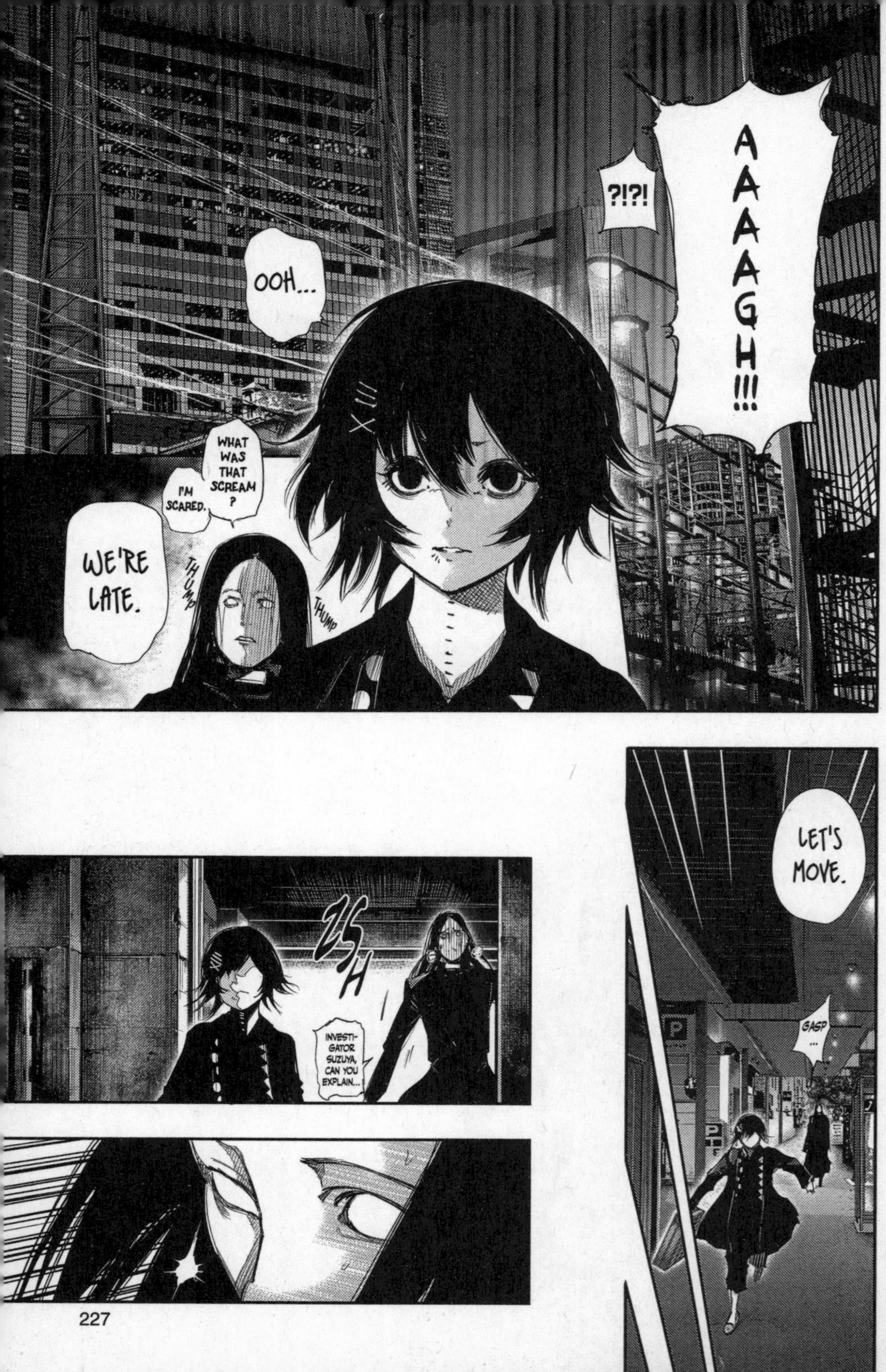
AAAAGH!!!
?!?!
OOH...
WHAT WAS THAT SCREAM?
I'M SCARED.
THUMP
THUMP
WE'RE LATE.
LET'S MOVE.
GASP...
ZSH
INVESTIGATOR SUZUYA, CAN YOU EXPLAIN...

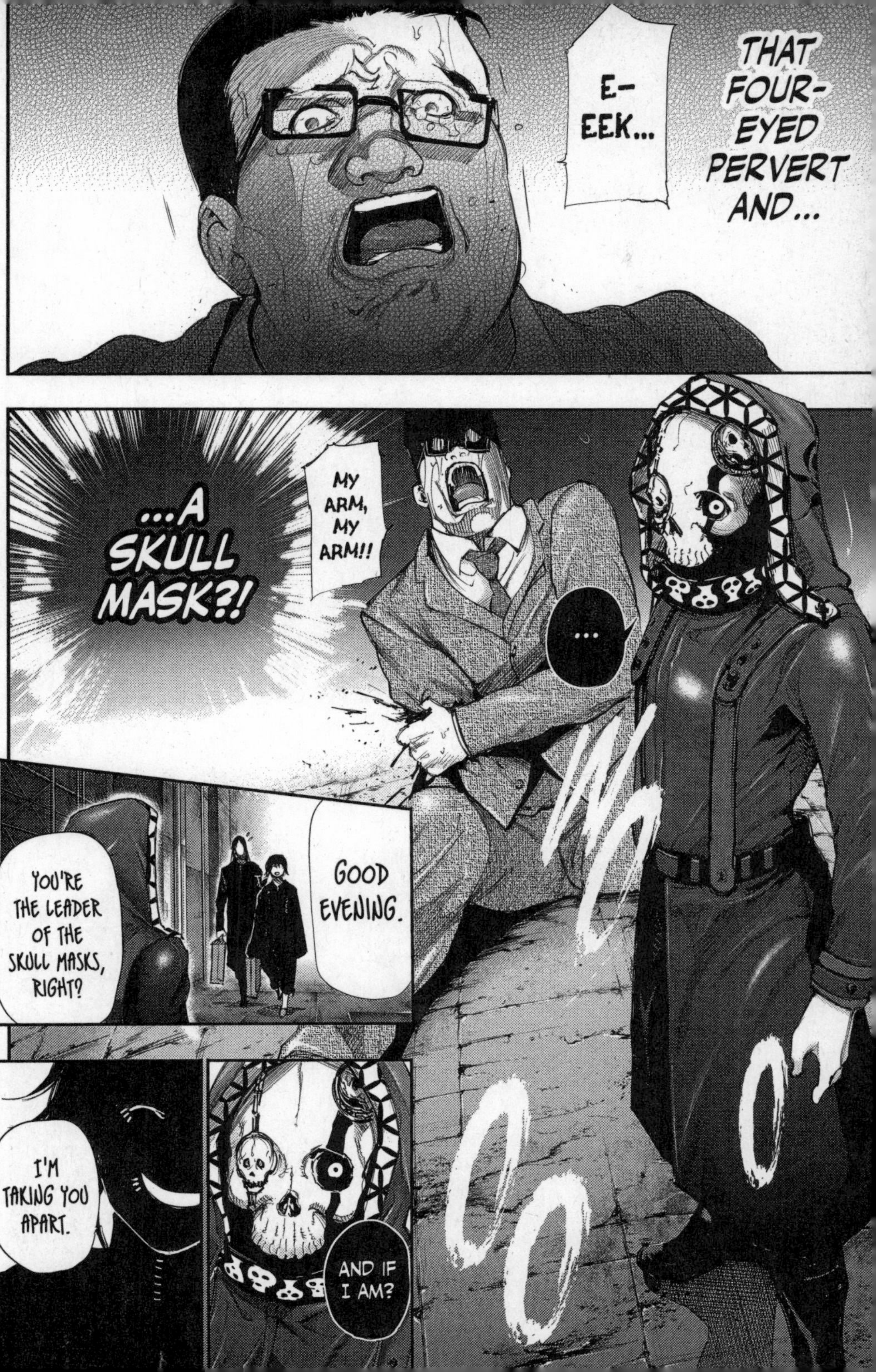
THAT FOUR-EYED PERVERT AND...
E-EEK...
...
MY ARM, MY ARM!!
...A SKULL MASK?!
GOOD EVENING.
YOU'RE THE LEADER OF THE SKULL MASKS, RIGHT?
AND IF I AM?
I'M TAKING YOU APART.

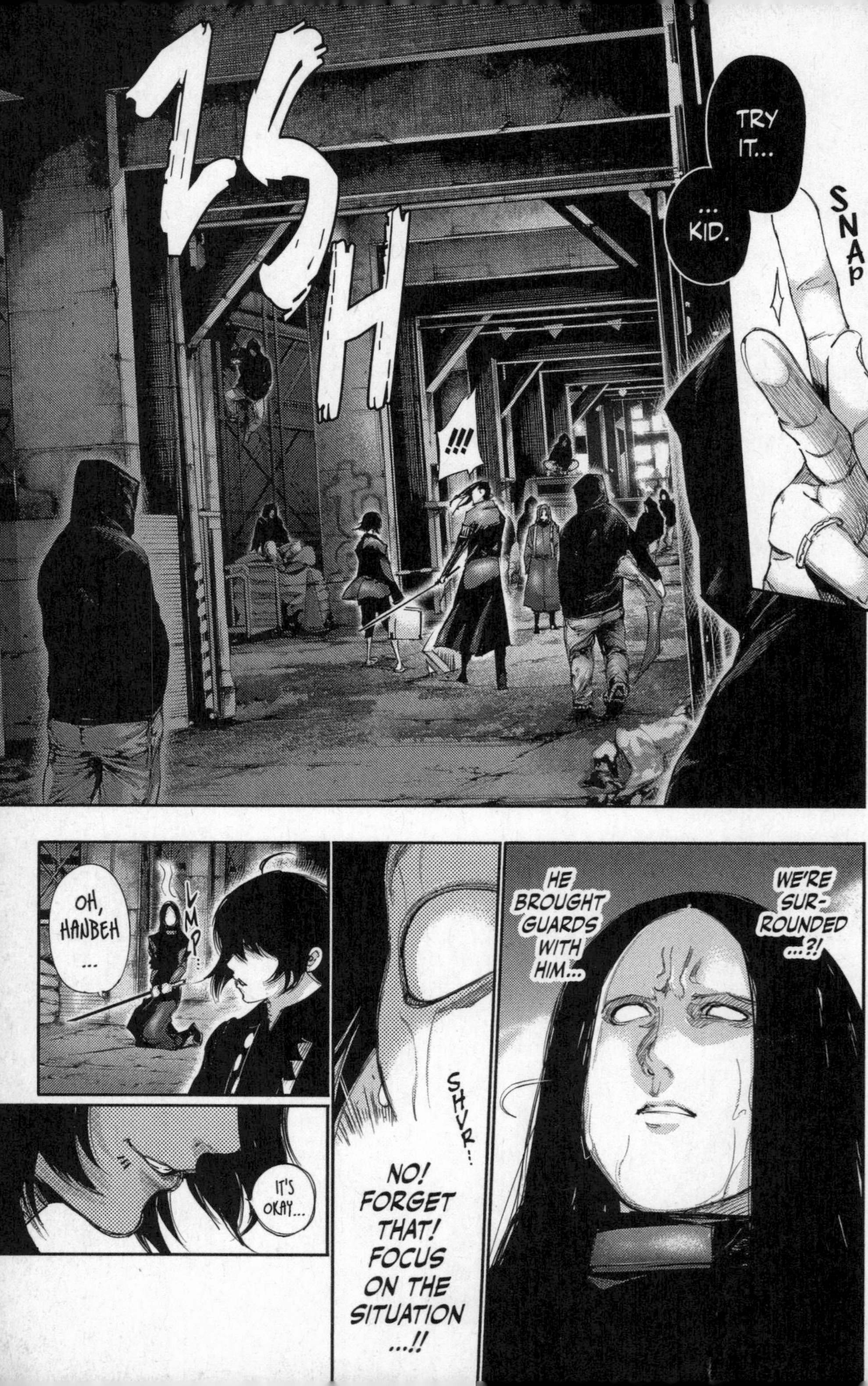
TRY IT...
...KID.
SNAP
ZSH
!!!
WE'RE SUR-ROUNDED ...?!
HE BROUGHT GUARDS WITH HIM...
SHVR..
NO! FORGET THAT! FOCUS ON THE SITUATION ...!!
LMP..
OH, HANBEH ...
IT'S OKAY...

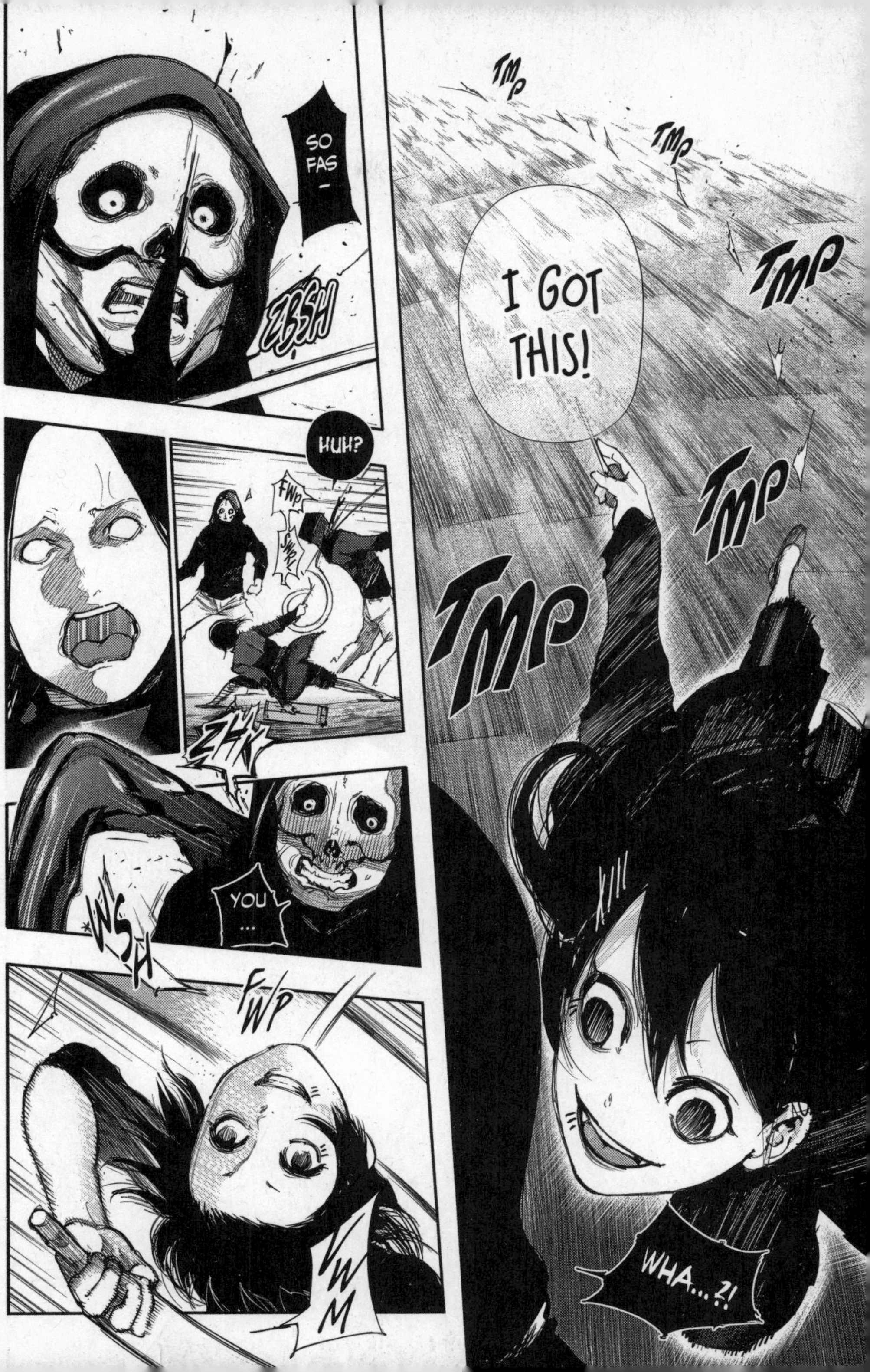
TMP
TMP
TMP
I GOT THIS!
TMP
TMP
WHA...?!
SO FAS –
HUH?
FWP
SWRL
YOU ...
WSH
FWP
VWM

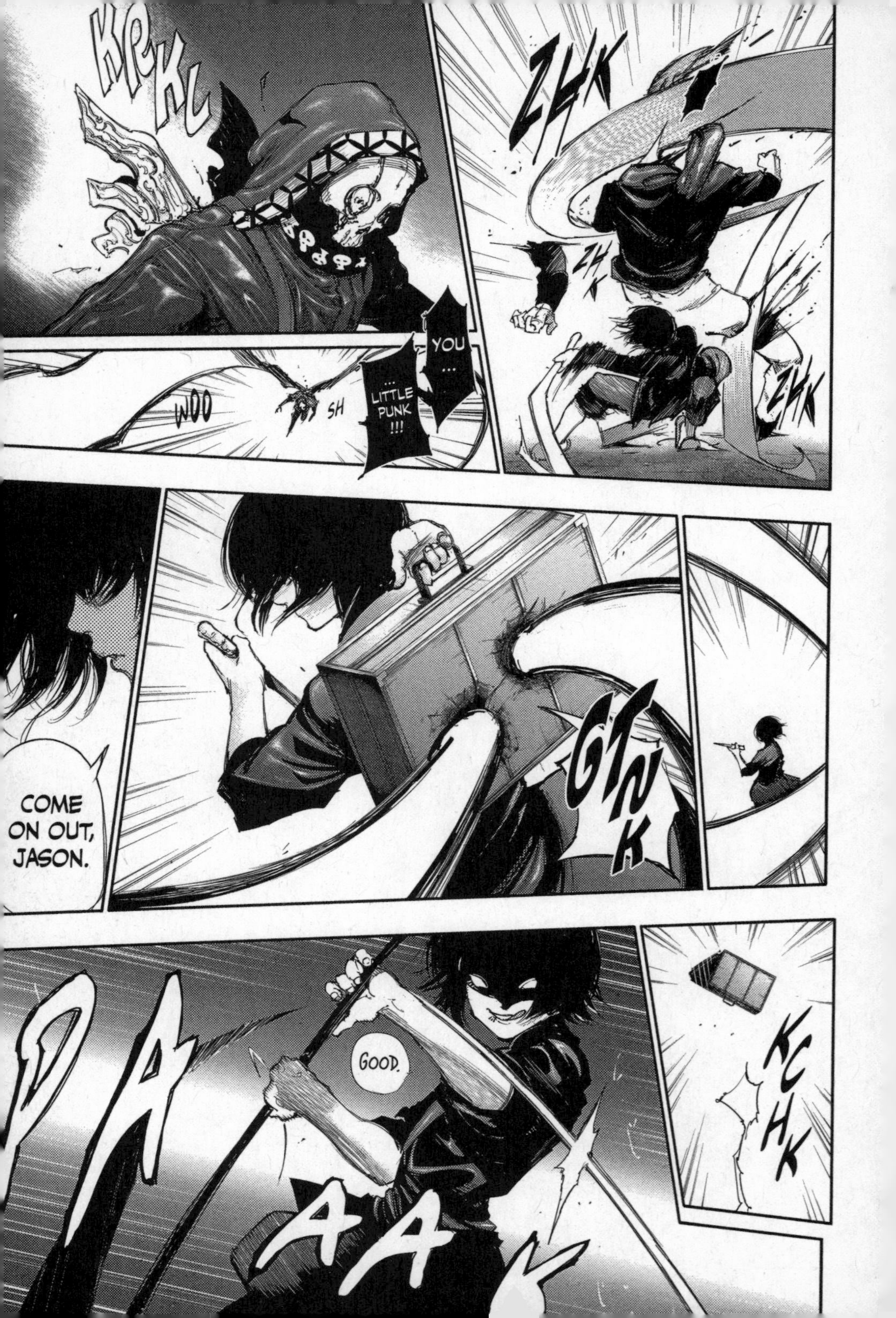
ZKK
ZKK
ZKK
KRKL
WOO
SH
YOU...
...LITTLE PUNK!!!
GTNK
COME ON OUT, JASON.
KCHK
GOOD.
DAAAK

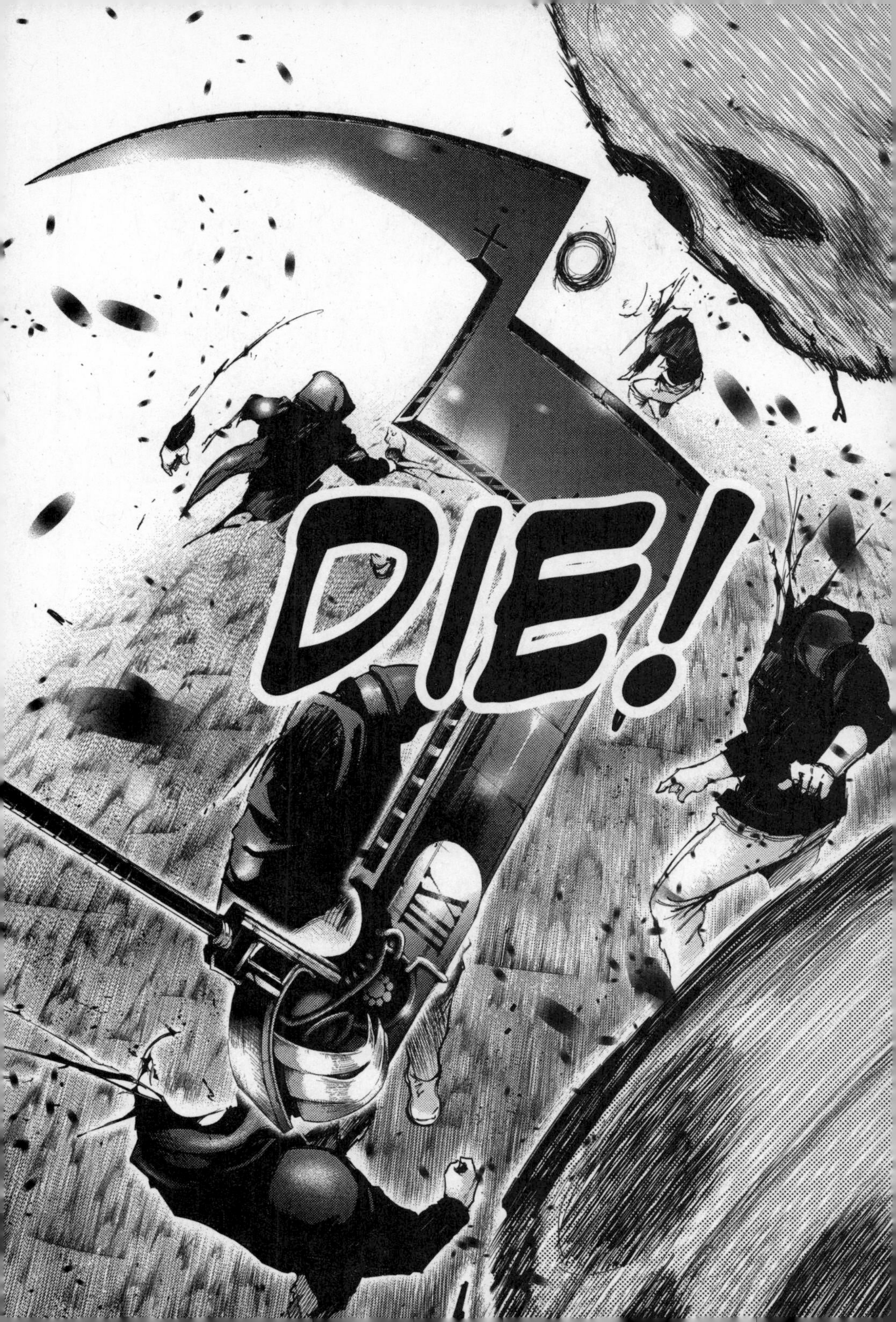
DIE!

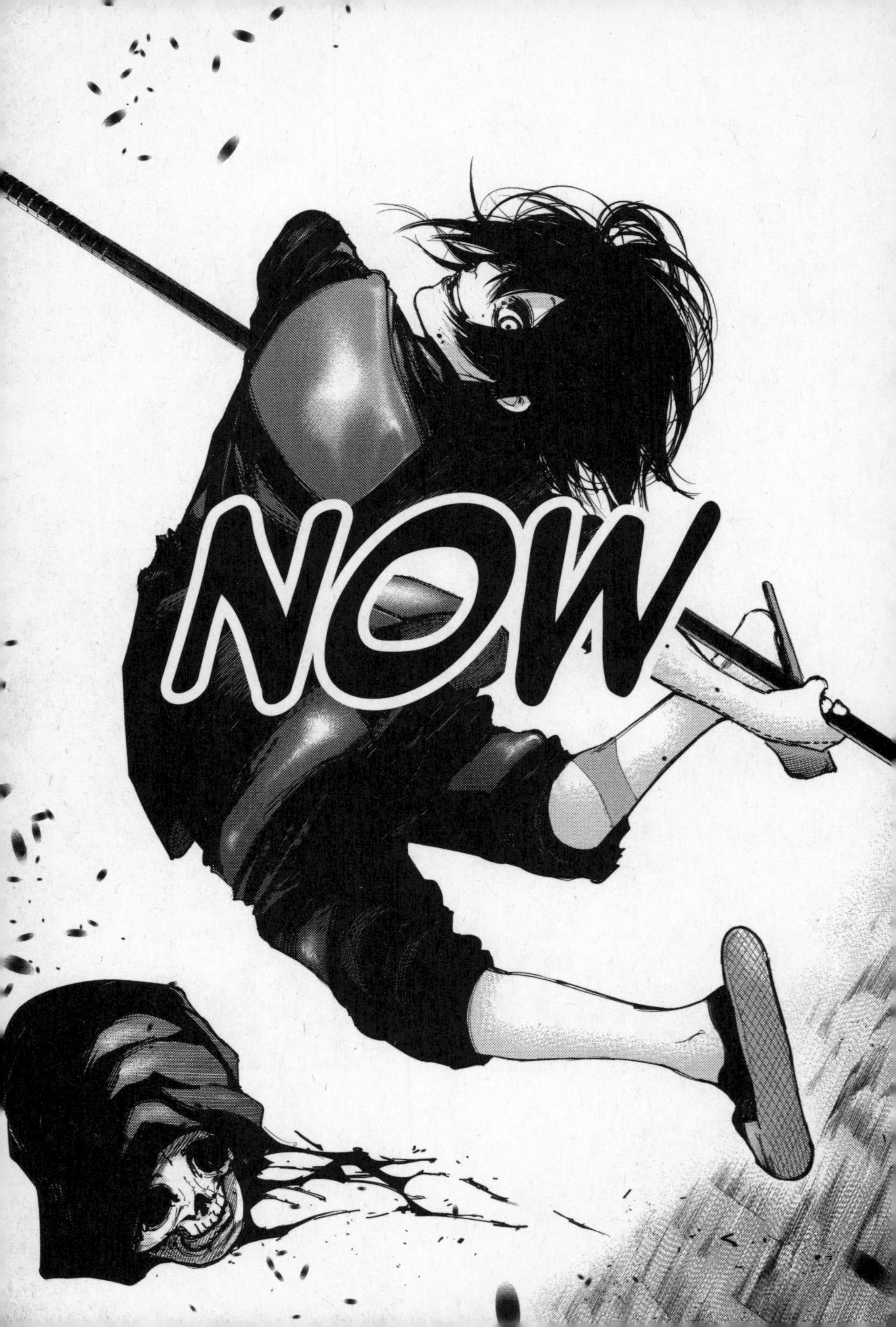
NOW

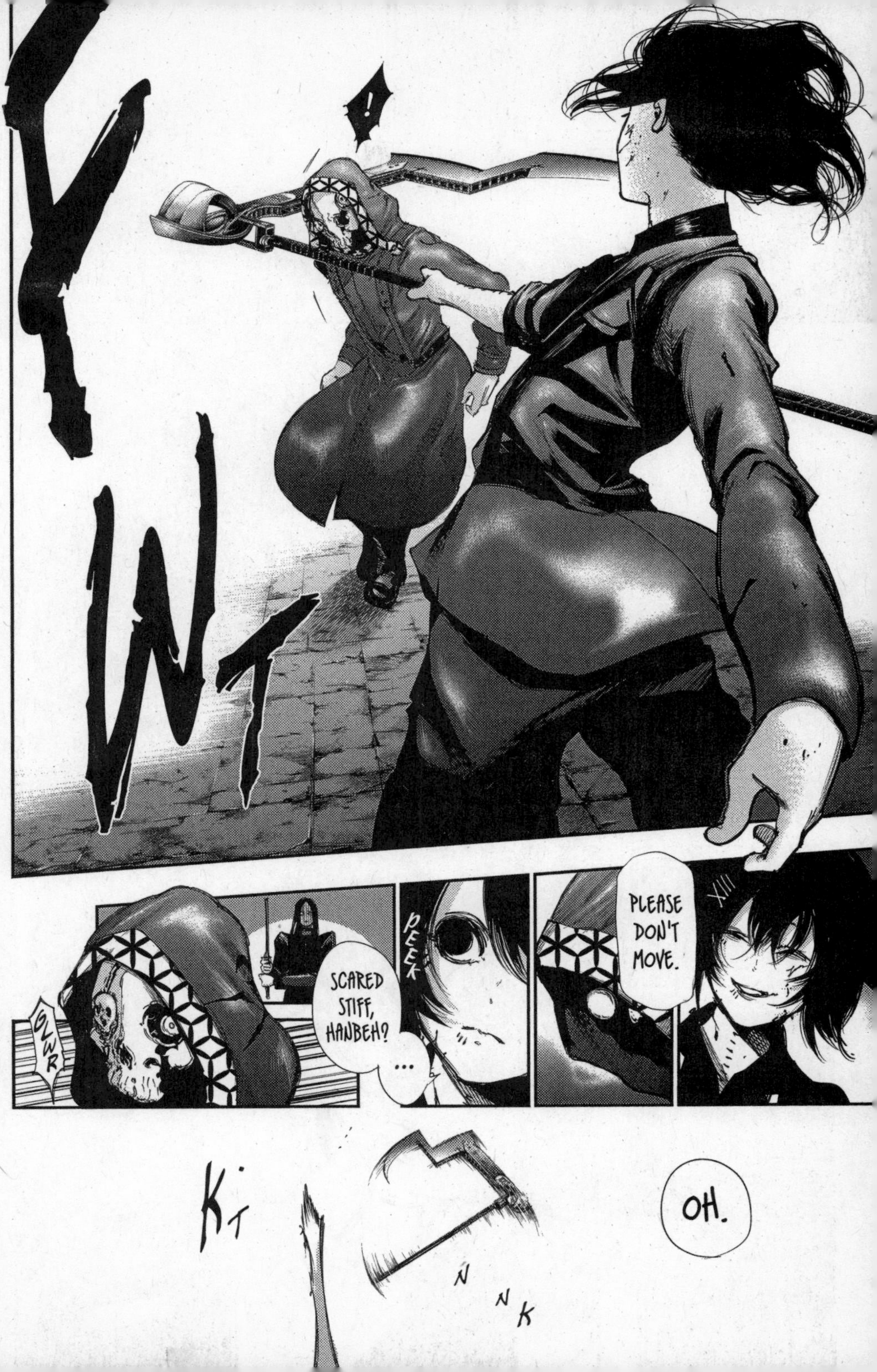
!
PLEASE DON'T MOVE.
PEEK
SCARED STIFF, HANBEH?
...
OH.

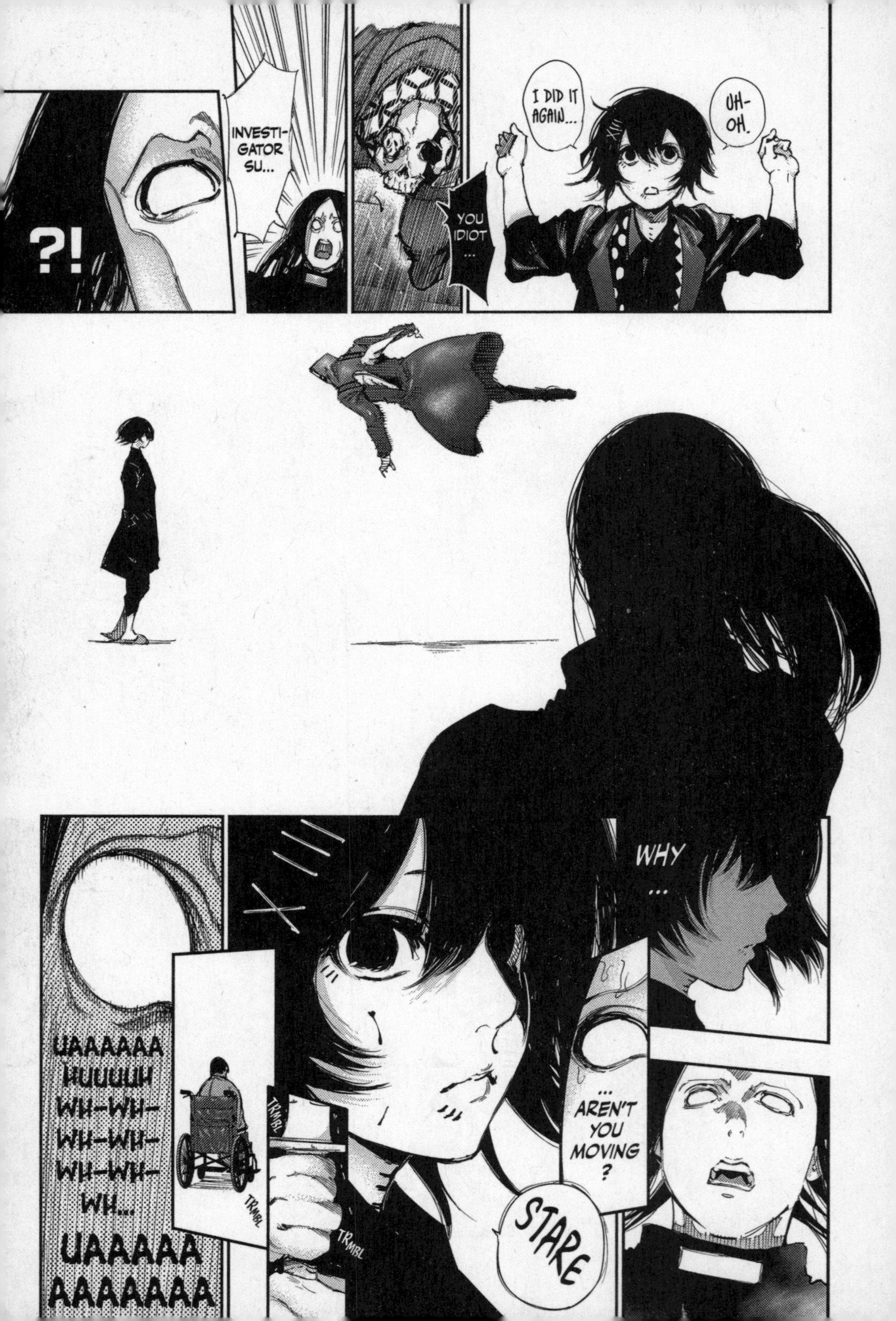
UH-OH.
I DID IT AGAIN...
YOU IDIOT ...
INVESTI-GATOR SU...
?!
WHY ...
... AREN'T YOU MOVING ?
STARE
TRMBL
TRMBL
TRMBL
UAAAAAA HUUUUH WH-WH-WH-WH-WH-WH-WH... UAAAAAA AAAAAAA

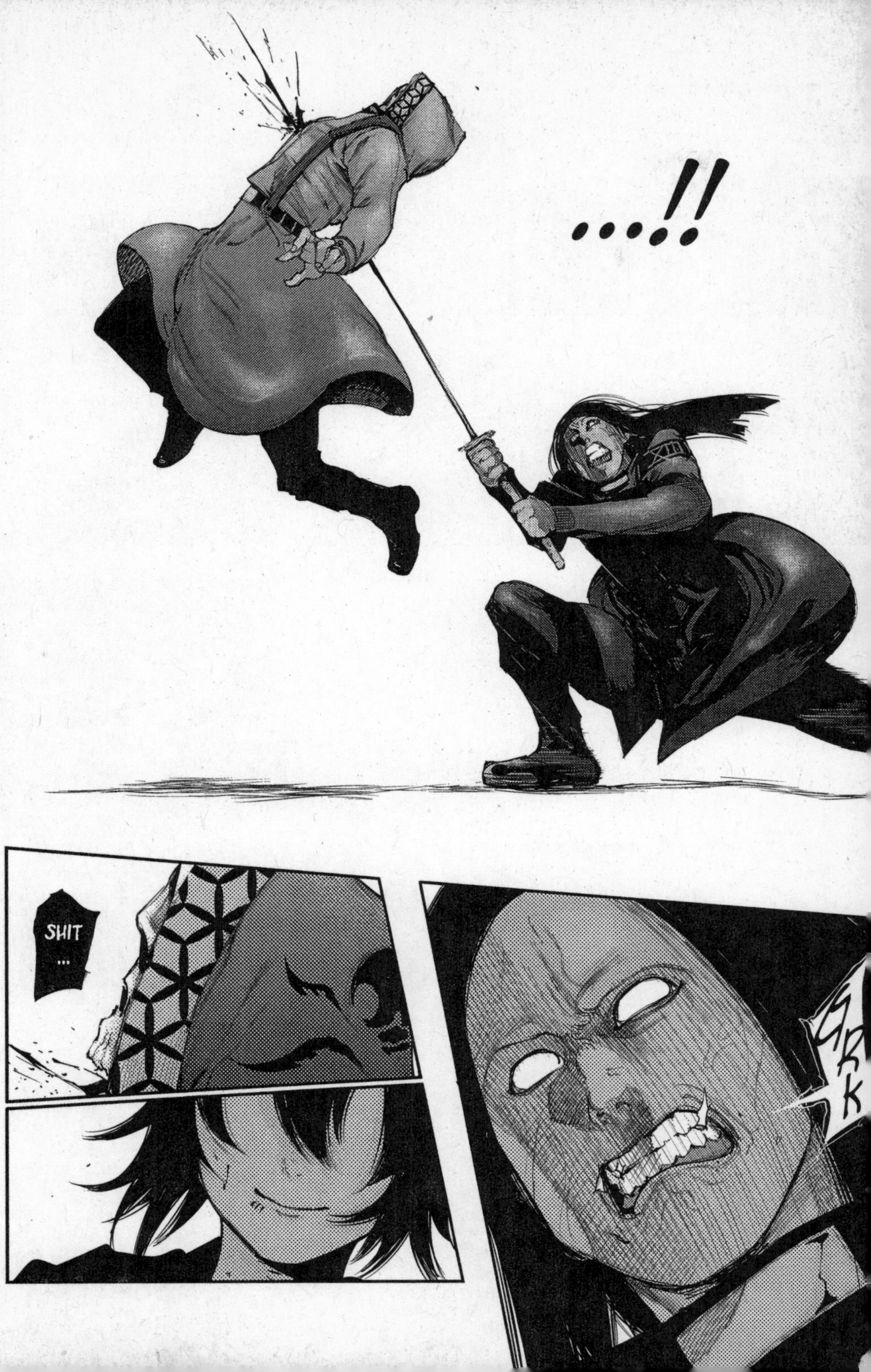
...!!
SRK
SHIT
...

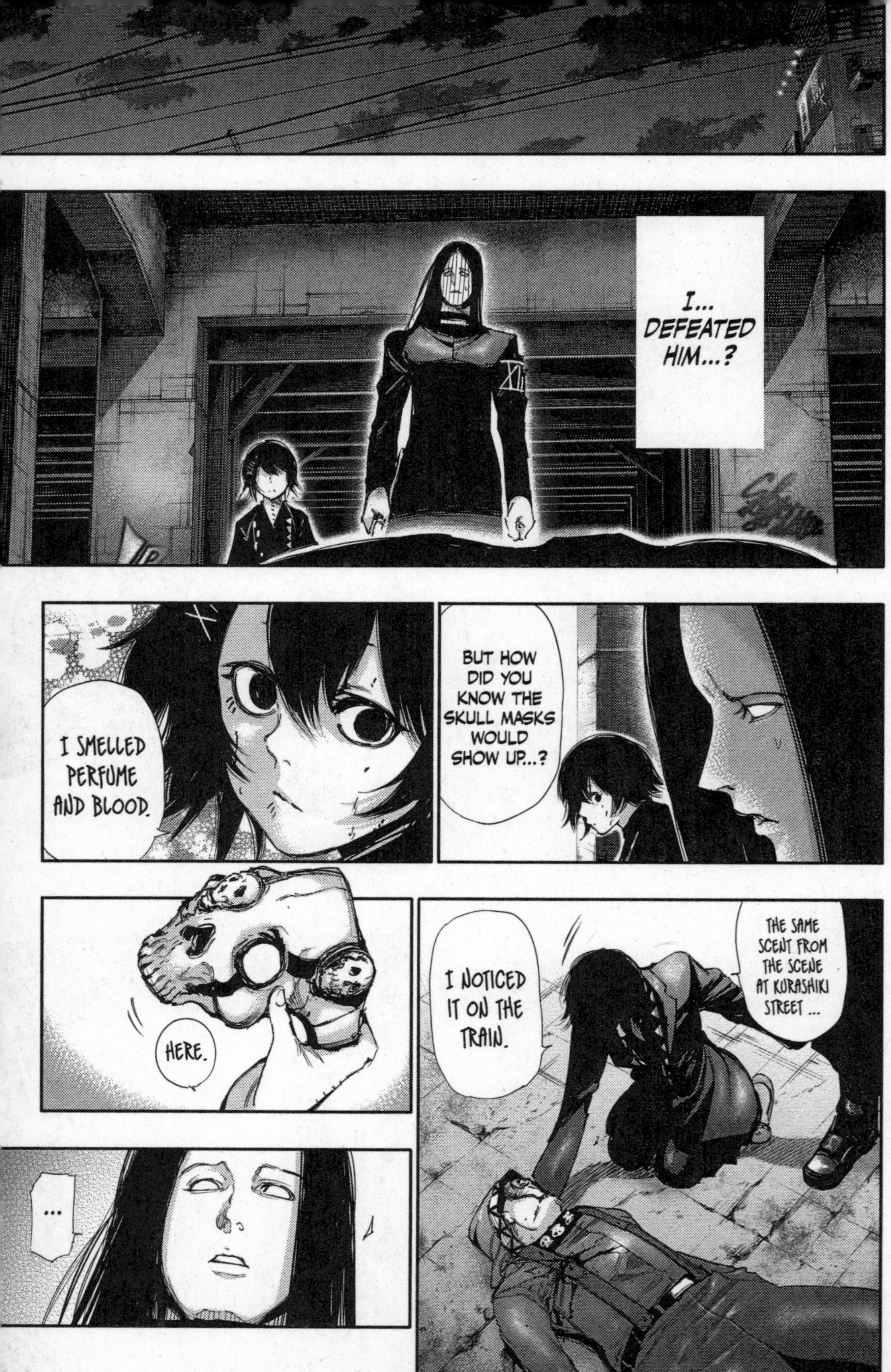
I... DEFEATED HIM...?
BUT HOW DID YOU KNOW THE SKULL MASKS WOULD SHOW UP...?
I SMELLED PERFUME AND BLOOD.
THE SAME SCENT FROM THE SCENE AT KURASHIKI STREET ...
I NOTICED IT ON THE TRAIN.
HERE.
...

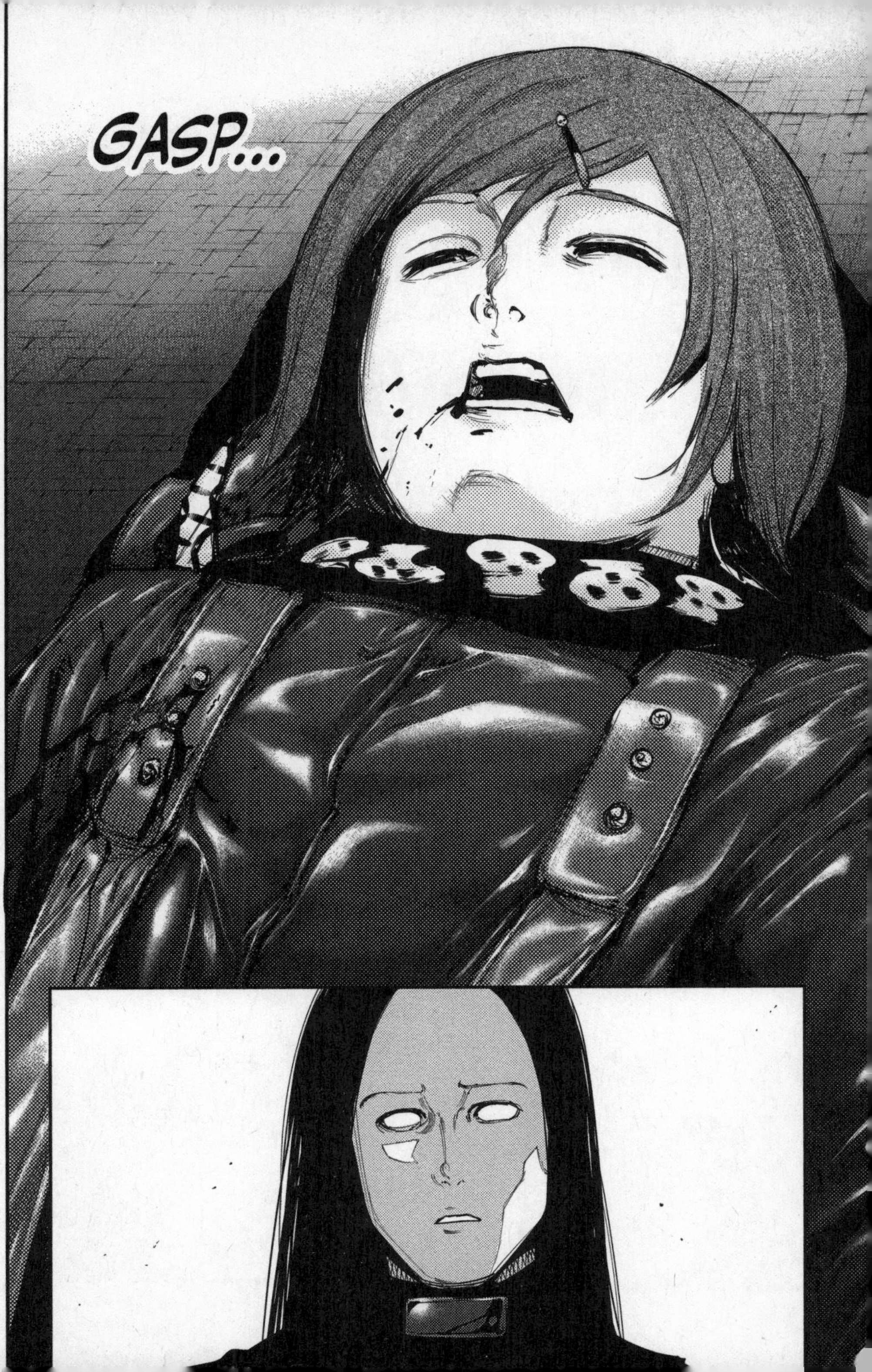
GASP...

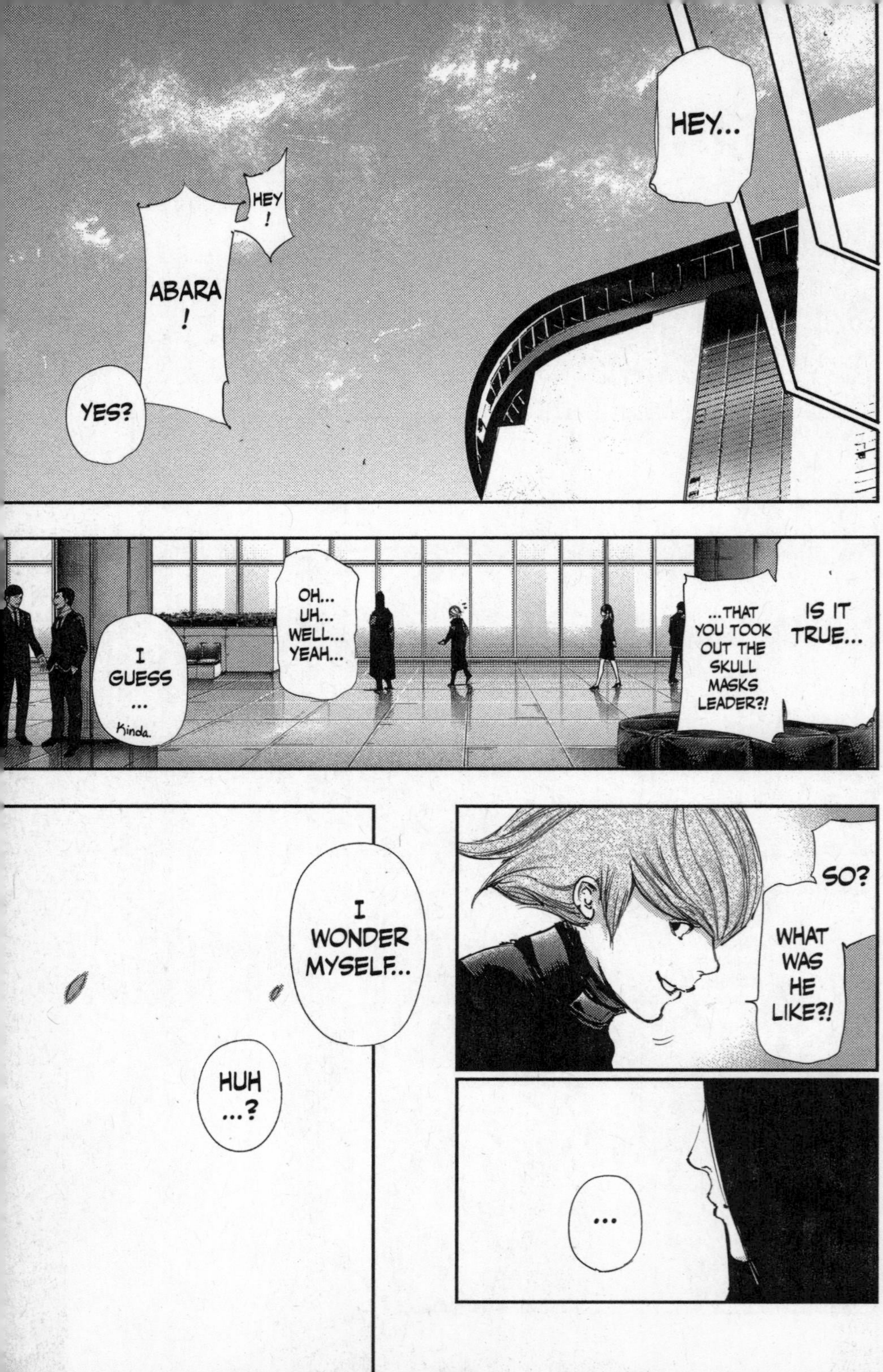
HEY...
HEY!
ABARA!
YES?
IS IT TRUE...
...THAT YOU TOOK OUT THE SKULL MASKS LEADER?!
OH... UH... WELL... YEAH...
I GUESS... Kinda.
SO? WHAT WAS HE LIKE?!
...
I WONDER MYSELF...
HUH...?

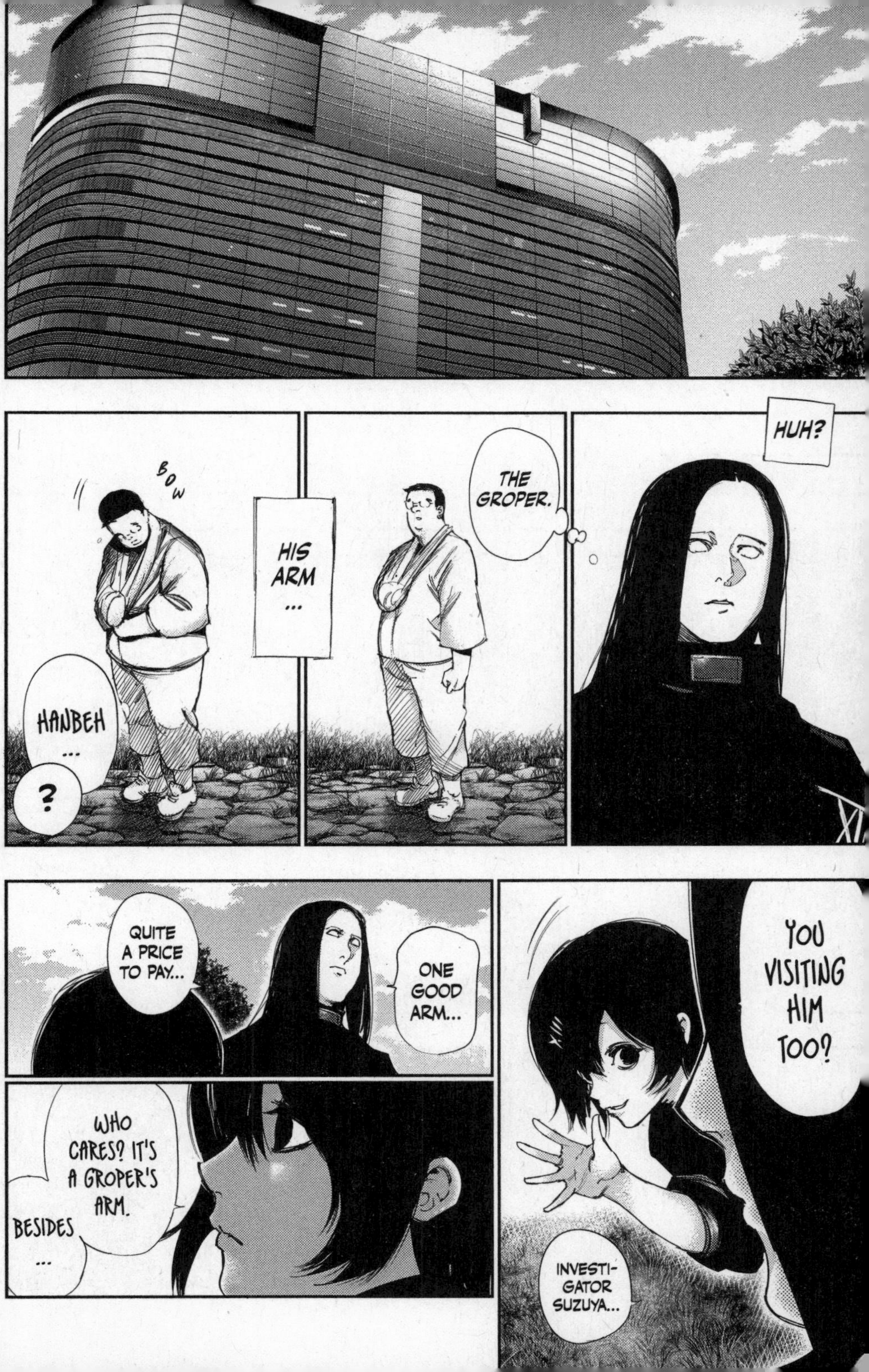
HUH?
THE GROPER.
HIS ARM ...
BOW
HANBEH ...
?
YOU VISITING HIM TOO?
INVESTI-GATOR SUZUYA...
ONE GOOD ARM...
QUITE A PRICE TO PAY...
WHO CARES? IT'S A GROPER'S ARM.
BESIDES ...

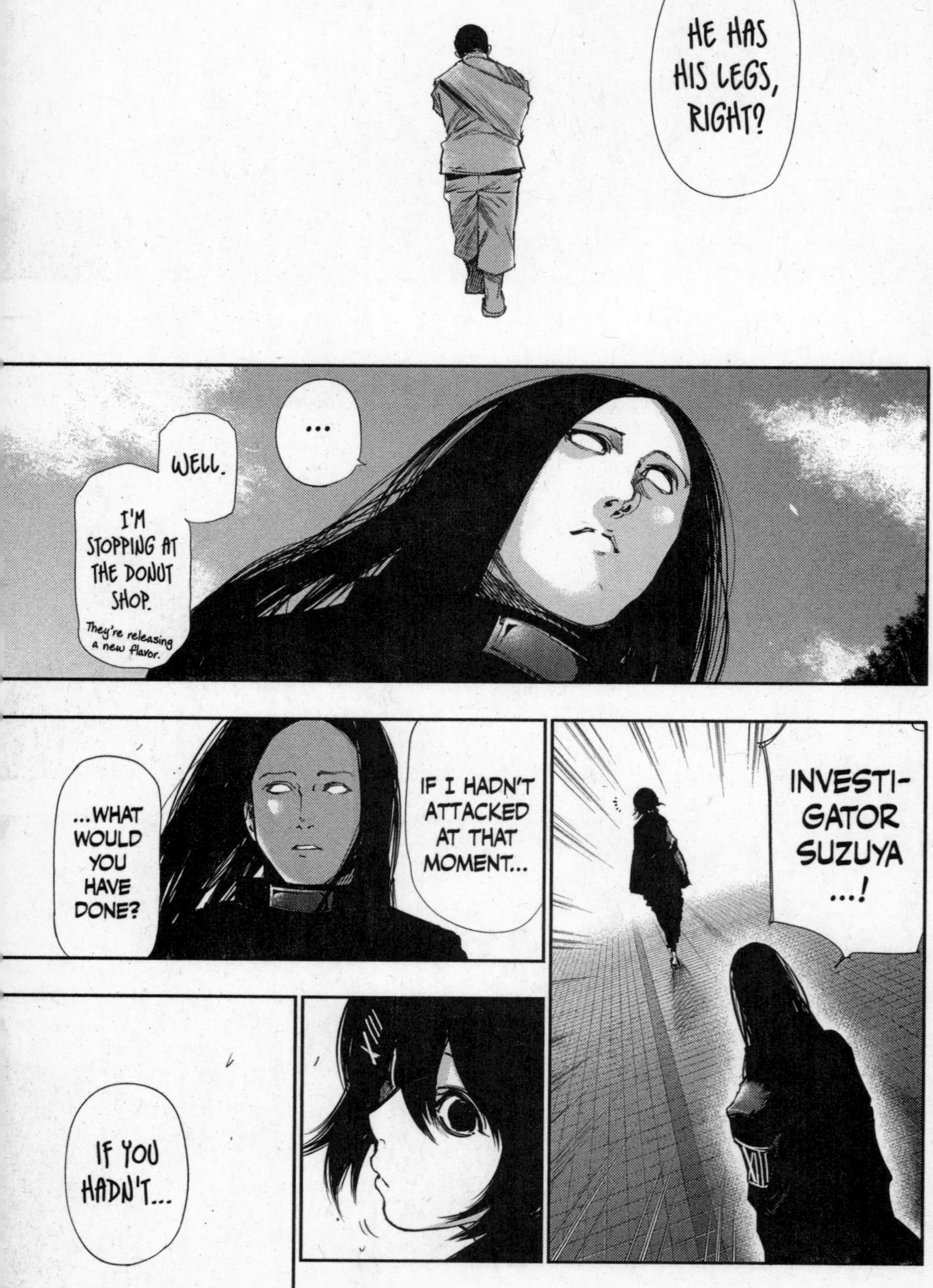
HE HAS HIS LEGS, RIGHT?
...
WELL.
I'M STOPPING AT THE DONUT SHOP.
They're releasing a new flavor.
INVESTI-GATOR SUZUYA ...!
IF I HADN'T ATTACKED AT THAT MOMENT...
...WHAT WOULD YOU HAVE DONE?
IF YOU HADN'T...

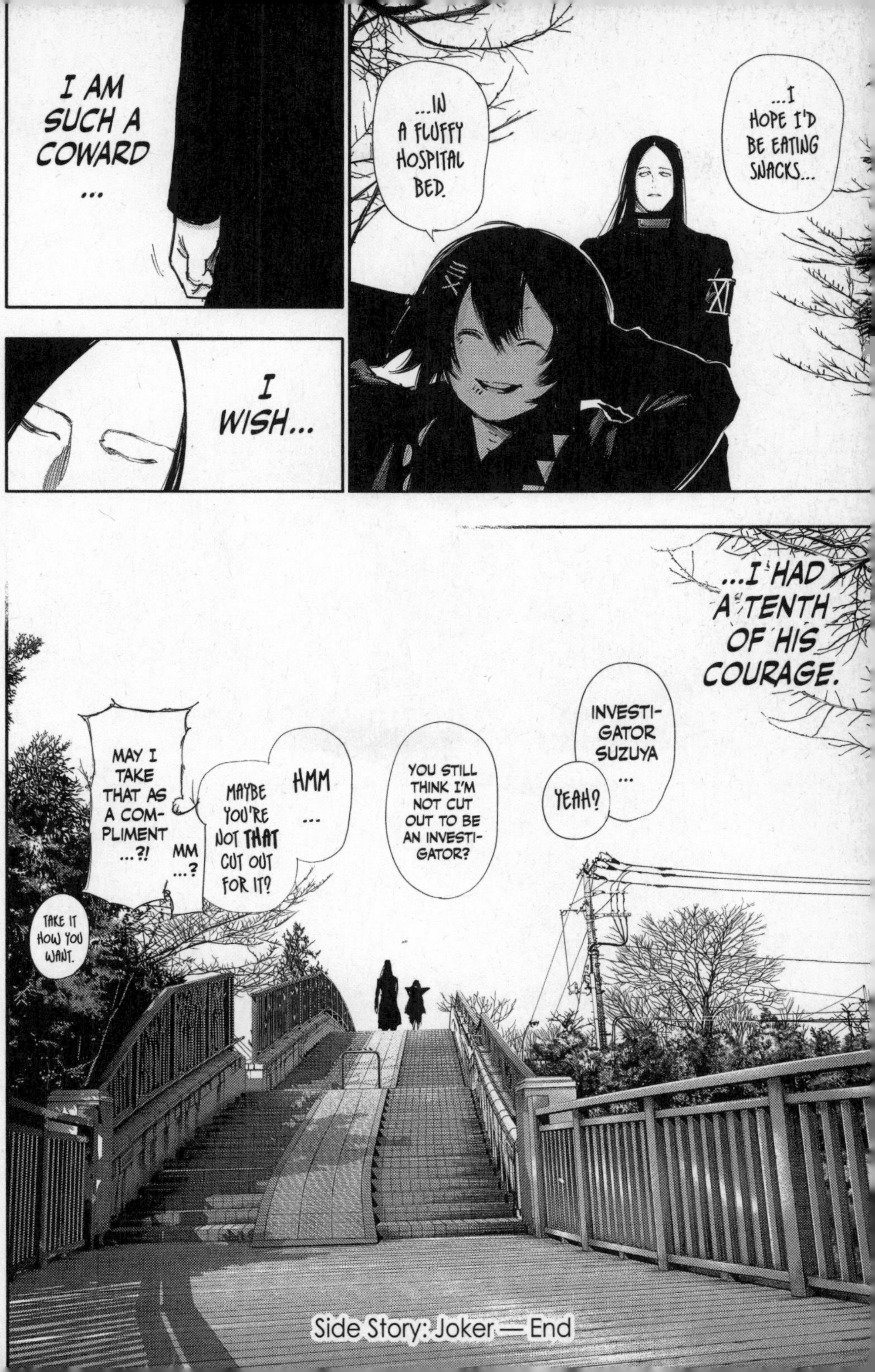
...I HOPE I'D BE EATING SNACKS...
...IN A FLUFFY HOSPITAL BED.
I AM SUCH A COWARD...
I WISH...
...I HAD A TENTH OF HIS COURAGE.
INVESTIGATOR SUZUYA...
YEAH?
YOU STILL THINK I'M NOT CUT OUT TO BE AN INVESTIGATOR?
HMM...
MAYBE YOU'RE NOT THAT CUT OUT FOR IT?
MM...?
MAY I TAKE THAT AS A COMPLIMENT...?!
TAKE IT HOW YOU WANT.
Side Story: Joker — End

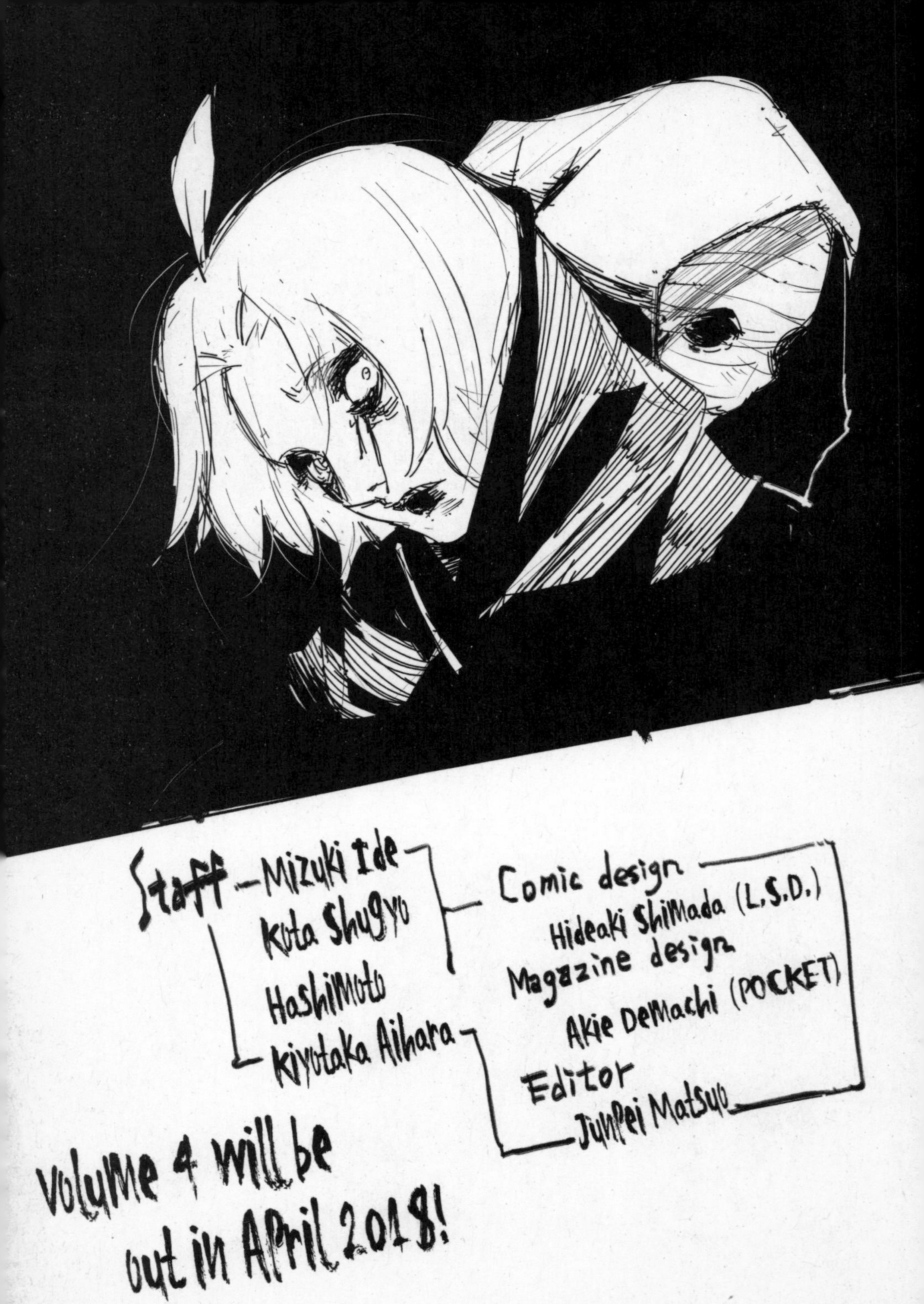

Staff — Mizuki Ide
Kota Shugyo
Hashimoto
Kiyotaka Aihara

Comic design
Hideaki Shimada (L.S.D.)
Magazine design
Akie Demachi (POCKET)
Editor
Junpei Matsuo

Volume 4 will be out in April 2018!

L:re

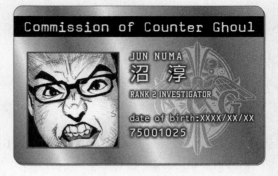

Commission of Counter Ghoul

JUN NUMA
沼 淳
RANK 2 INVESTIGATOR

date of birth:XXXX/XX/XX
75001025

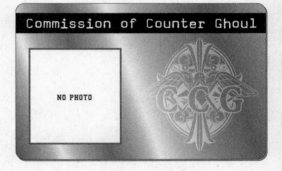

Commission of Counter Ghoul

NO PHOTO

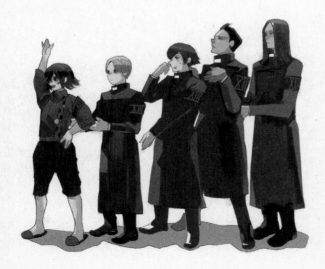

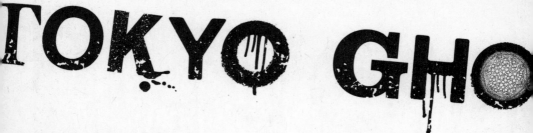

Suzuya Squad

- **Juzo Suzuya** (Squad Leader) Assistant Special Investigator (Class 72)
  鈴屋 什造 (すずや じゅうぞう)   2nd Academy Junior

  - Age: 22 (DOB 6/8) ♂ • Blood type: AB • Height/weight: 160cm/48kg
  - Quinque: Scorpion 1/56 (Bikaku-Rate/B)/13's Jason (Rinkaku-Rate/S+)
  - Honors: Ryukichi Badge, Double White Wing Badge, Gold Osmanthus
    Badge, Superior Squad, etc.
  - Hobbies: Serious games of hide-and-go-seek, throwing Hanbeh

- **Keijin Nakarai** (Deputy Squad Leader) Rank 1 Investigator (Class 73)
  半井 恵仁 (なからい けいじん)   1st Academy Junior

  - Age: 23 (DOB 8/23) ♂ • Blood type: B • Height/weight: 167cm/62kg
  - Quinque: Right (Kokaku-Rate/B+), Left (Kokaku Rate/B+)
  - Honors: Single White Wing Badge, Osmanthus Badge,
    academy salutatorian
  - Hobby: Bird-watching

- **Miyuki Mikage**   Rank 2 Investigator (Class 74)
  御影 三幸 (みかげ みゆき)   4th Academy Junior

  - Age: 22 (DOB 4/12) ♂ • Blood type: B • Height/weight: 184cm/76kg
  - Quinque: Dream and Space (Bikaku-Rate/A+)
  - Honors: Silver Osmanthus Badge
  - Hobbies: Origami, thinking about space, fantasizing

- **Mizuro Tamaki**   Rank 2 Investigator (Class 75)
  環 水郎 (たまき みずろう)   5th Academy Junior

  - Age: 21 (DOB 6/15) ♂ • Blood type: A • Height/weight: 172cm/66kg
  - Quinque: Beef (Bikaku-Rate/A) • Honors: Silver Osmanthus Badge
  - Hobbies: Spending money (clothes, figures, games)

- **Hanbeh Abara**   Rank 2 Investigator (Class 75)
  阿原半兵衛 (あばら はんべえ)   5th Academy Junior

  - Age: 21 (DOB 5/21) ♂ • Blood type: O • Height/weight: 190cm/79kg
  - Quinque: Silver Skull (Ukaku-Rate/A)
  - Honors: Osmanthus Badge, Best Partner Award (self-awarded)
  - Life's work: Personal care of Investigator Suzuya

GHOUL:re

SUI ISHIDA is the author
of the immensely popular
Tokyo Ghoul and several
Tokyo Ghoul one-shots,
including one that won
second place in the *Weekly
Young Jump* 113th Grand
Prix award in 2010. *Tokyo
Ghoul:re* is the sequel to
Tokyo Ghoul.

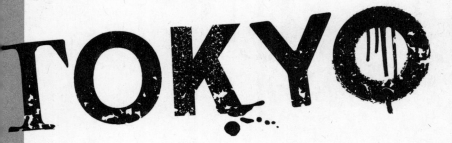

Story and art by
SUI ISHIDA

TOKYO GHOUL:RE © 2014 by Sui Ishida
All rights reserved.
First published in Japan in 2014 by SHUEISHA Inc., Tokyo.
English translation rights arranged by SHUEISHA Inc.

Translation Joe Yamazaki
Touch-Up Art & Lettering Vanessa Satone
Design Shawn Carrico
Editor Pancha Diaz

Printed in the U.S.A.

Published by VIZ Media, LLC
P.O. Box 77010
San Francisco, CA 94107

10 9 8 7 6 5 4 3 2 1
First printing, February 2018

viz.com

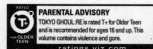
PARENTAL ADVISORY
TOKYO GHOUL:RE is rated T+ for Older Teen
and is recommended for ages 16 and up. This
volume contains violence and gore.
ratings.viz.com

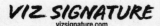
VIZ SIGNATURE
vizsignature.com

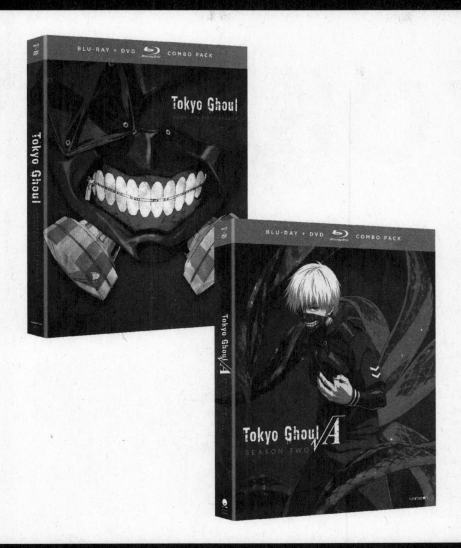

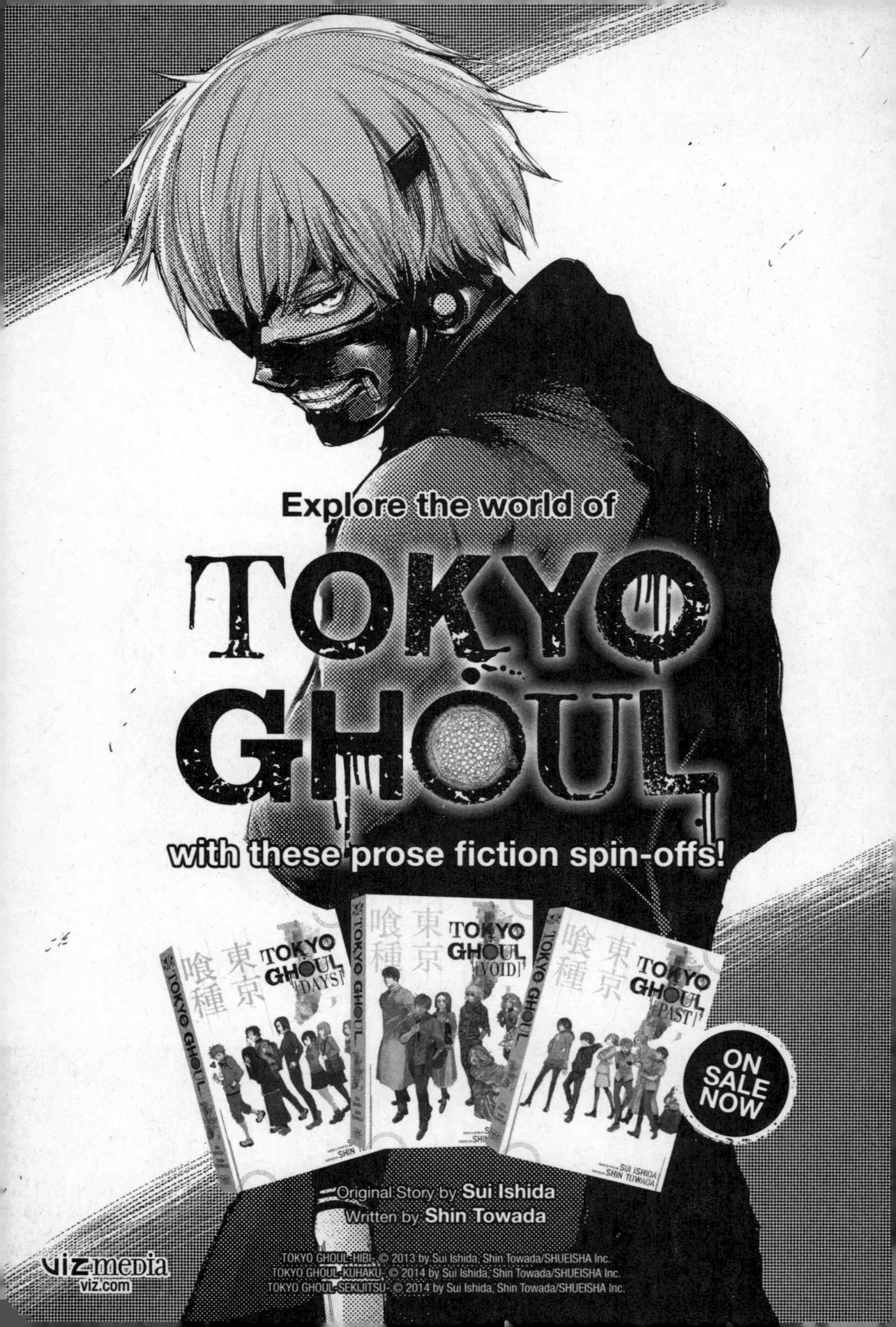
Explore the world of
TOKYO GHOUL
with these prose fiction spin-offs!
東京喰種
TOKYO GHOUL [DAYS]
TOKYO GHOUL [VOID]
TOKYO GHOUL [PAST]
SUI ISHIDA
SHIN TOWADA
ON SALE NOW
Original Story by Sui Ishida
Written by Shin Towada
viz media
viz.com

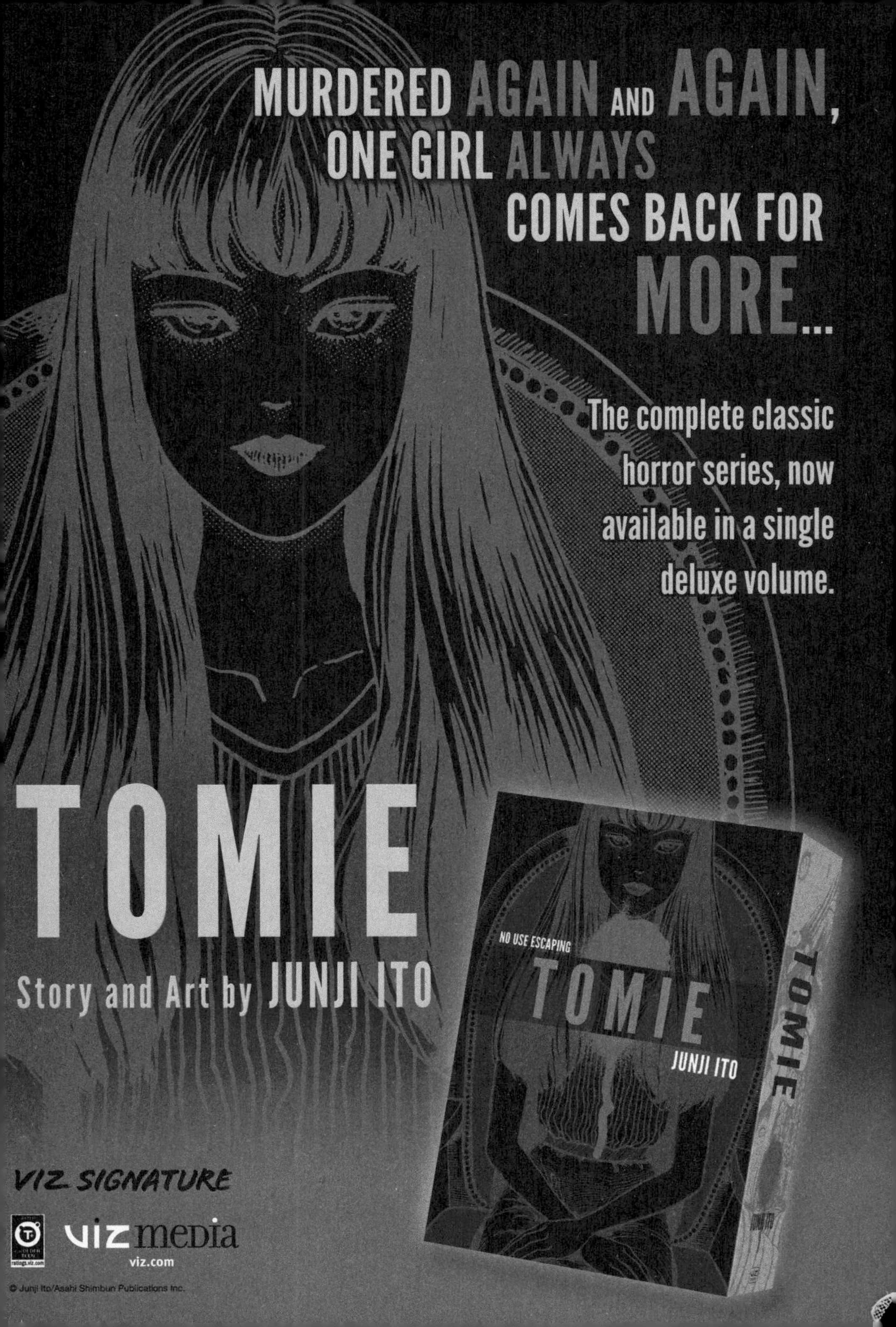

MURDERED AGAIN AND AGAIN,
ONE GIRL ALWAYS
COMES BACK FOR
MORE...
The complete classic horror series, now available in a single deluxe volume.
TOMIE
Story and Art by JUNJI ITO
NO USE ESCAPING
TOMIE
JUNJI ITO
TOMIE
VIZ SIGNATURE
viz media
viz.com
© Junji Ito/Asahi Shimbun Publications Inc.

U Z U M A K I

Story and Art by JUNJI ITO

SPIRALS... THIS TOWN IS CONTAMINATED WITH SPIRALS...

Kurouzu-cho, a small fogbound town on the coast of Japan, is cursed. According to Shuichi Saito, the withdrawn boyfriend of teenager Kirie Goshima, their town is haunted not by a person or being but by a pattern: uzumaki, the spiral, the hypnotic secret shape of the world. It manifests itself in everything from seashells and whirlpools in water to the spiral marks on people's bodies, the insane obsessions of Shuichi's father and the voice from the cochlea in our inner ear. As the madness spreads, the inhabitants of Kurouzu-cho are pulled ever deeper into a whirlpool from which there is no return!

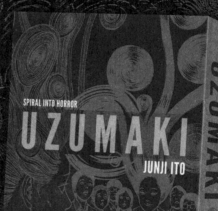

A masterpiece of horror manga, now available in a
DELUXE HARDCOVER EDITION!

TOKYO GHOUL

This is the last page.
TOKYO GHOUL:re reads right to left.